Paul Portner, Klaus von Heusinger and Claudia Maienborn (Eds.)
Semantics – Noun Phrases and Verb Phrases

This volume is part of a larger set of handbooks to Semantics

1   **Semantics: Foundations, History and Methods**
    Klaus von Heusinger, Claudia Maienborn, Paul Portner (eds.)

2   **Semantics: Lexical Structures and Adjectives**
    Claudia Maienborn, Klaus von Heusinger, Paul Portner (eds.)

3   **Semantics: Theories**
    Claudia Maienborn, Klaus von Heusinger, Paul Portner (eds.)

4   **Semantics: Noun Phrases and Verb Phrases**
    Paul Portner, Klaus von Heusinger, Claudia Maienborn (eds.)

5   **Semantics: Sentence and Information Structure**
    Paul Portner, Claudia Maienborn, Klaus von Heusinger (eds.)

6   **Semantics: Interfaces**
    Claudia Maienborn, Klaus von Heusinger, Paul Portner (eds.)

7   **Semantics: Typology, Diachrony and Processing**
    Klaus von Heusinger, Claudia Maienborn, Paul Portner (eds.)

Semantics
Noun Phrases and Verb Phrases

Edited by
Paul Portner
Klaus von Heusinger
Claudia Maienborn

DE GRUYTER
MOUTON

ISBN 978-3-11-058721-0
e-ISBN (PDF) 978-3-11-058944-3
e-ISBN (EPUB) 978-3-11-058730-2

Library of Congress Cataloging-in-Publication Data
Names: Portner, Paul, editor. | Heusinger, Klaus von, editor. | Maienborn,
  Claudia, editor.
Title: Semantics : noun phrases, verb phrases and adjectives / edited by Paul
  Portner, Klaus von Heusinger, Claudia Maienborn.
Description: Berlin ; Boston : De Gruyter, [2019] | Series: Mouton reader |
  Includes bibliographical references and index.
Identifiers: LCCN 2018031262| ISBN 9783110587210 (print) | ISBN 9783110589443
  (e-book (pdf) | ISBN 9783110587302 (e-book (epub)
Subjects: LCSH: Semantics. | Grammar, Comparative and
  general--Grammaticalization.
Classification: LCC P325 .S37996 2019 | DDC 401/.43--dc23 LC record available at
https://lccn.loc.gov/2018031262

Bibliographic information published by the Deutsche Nationalbibliothek
The Deutsche Nationalbibliothek lists this publication in the Deutsche Nationalbibliografie;
detailed bibliographic data are available in the Internet at http://dnb.dnb.de.

© 2019 Walter de Gruyter GmbH, Berlin/Boston
Cover image: /iStock / Getty Images Plus
Typesetting: Integra Software Services Pvt. Ltd.
Printing and binding: CPI books GmbH, Leck

www.degruyter.com

Contents

1. Daniel Büring — **Pronouns** — 1

2. Irene Heim — **Definiteness and indefiniteness** — 33

3. Klaus von Heusinger — **Specificity** — 70

4. Edward Keenan — **Quantifiers** — 112

5. Veneeta Dayal — **Bare noun phrases** — 149

6. Chris Barker — **Possessives and relational nouns** — 177

7. Peter Lasersohn — **Mass nouns and plurals** — 204

8. Gregory Carlson — **Genericity** — 232

9. Hana Filip — **Aspectual class and Aktionsart** — 274

10. Paul Portner — **Perfect and progressive** — 313

11. Paul Portner — **Verbal mood** — 369

12. Jane Grimshaw — **Deverbal nominalization** — 407

	Toshiyuki Ogihara	
13	**Tense** —— 436	

	Valentine Hacquard	
14	**Modality** —— 463	

	Kai von Fintel	
15	**Conditionals** —— 503	

	Eric Swanson	
16	**Propositional attitudes** —— 532	

	Philippe Schlenker	
17	**Indexicality and *De Se* reports** —— 562	

Index —— 619

Daniel Büring
1 Pronouns

1 Pronoun types and basic interpretation —— 1
2 The meaning of definite pronouns —— 6
3 Pronoun binding —— 16
4 Pronominal content —— 22
5 Binding theory —— 27
6 References —— 30

Abstract: We introduce the main types of pronouns in natural language — indefinites, definites, demonstratives, and reciprocals — and summarize current analyses of their semantics. For definite pronouns, we discuss question of whether pronouns are akin to variables or descriptions, in particular so-called pronouns of laziness, paycheck pronouns and E-type pronouns. Pronoun binding is analyzed in detail, including the questions of if and when semantic binding becomes obligatory. For all these issues, different formal implementations, including an explicit semantics for plural pronouns, are provided and discussed. The article closes with a short overview of semantic approaches to Binding Theory.

1 Pronoun types and basic interpretation

The class of pronouns in English includes expressions like *he, she, it, us, they, her, herself, ourselves, each other, here, there, now, someone, somewhere, this, that* and *these*. It is a closed class of mostly one-word expressions in the category DP or PP (perhaps among others), whose semantic content is limited to basic features such as number, gender and person. Most, if not all, languages have expressions of this type, but no definition of the term will be attempted here, and examples will mostly be drawn from English. We can cross-classify pronouns according to their ontological status — e.g. personal (*you, she, this, someone*), temporal (*now, then, sometimes*), or locative (*here, there, somewhere*); in each group we can distinguish definite pronouns (*you, she, this, now, then, here, there* etc.) from indefinite ones (*someone, somewhere* etc.); definites can be demonstrative (*this, that*) or non-demonstrative, the latter in turn deictic (or

---
Daniel Büring, Vienna, Austria

https://doi.org/10.1515/9783110589443-001

indexical: *you, now, here*) or non-deictic (*she, then, there*). Among the definite non-demonstratives (indexical or not), English furthermore distinguishes *reflexive* pronouns (*herself, ourselves*), *non-reflexive* pronouns (*she, her, our*), and *reciprocals* (*each other, one another*).

In what follows we will concentrate on personal pronouns, which have received by far the most attention in the literature; many aspects of the semantics of temporal and locative pronouns will be analogous, but their details will hinge to a large extent on the chosen ontology for temporal and locative expressions in general, which this article will be agnostic about. In this section we will in turn discuss the three major classes indefinite, definite, and demonstrative pronouns; discussion of reciprocals will be found in section 4.3. Section 2 then details the semantics of definite pronouns, followed by a treatment of pronoun binding in section 3. Section 4 is concerned with the semantic content of pronouns (sometimes called 'phi-features'), followed by a short discussion of (the semantic aspects of) binding theory in section 5.

1.1 Indefinite pronouns

Indefinite pronouns come in several *series* like the English *some-, no-* and *any-*series, with each series having exponents for the major ontological categories, such as English *-one/body, -thing, -where, -how* etc. (Haspelmath 1997, especially chapter 3). We won't discuss the peculiarities of the *any-*series here (see article 3 [Semantics: Sentence and Information Structure] (Giannakidou) *Polarity items*); the *some-* and *no-*series seem to have the same denotation as the parallel quantified DPs like *some person, no thing* etc. In a generalized quantifier framework, see for example article 4 [this volume] (Keenan) *Quantifiers*, their interpretation would be along the lines of (1a), and their translation into second-order logic like in (1b):

(1) a. 〚someone〛 = that function from sets of individuals to truth values that maps any set of individuals p to True iff p contains one or more people
    b. someone $\rightsquigarrow \lambda P_{et}.\exists x_e[person'(x) \& P(x)]$

Since indefinite pronouns can be modified by relative clauses as well as adjectives, it seems plausible to analyze them as a determiner *some/no/any* plus NP *body, one, where*, the latter of which can be modified. The Pron+AP order may then be derived by movement of the N to D:

(2) a. nobody I know = [$_{PDP}$ no [$_{NP}$ body [$_{RelCl}$ I know]]]
    b. someone important = [$_{PDP}$ some [$_{NP}$ [$_{AP}$ important] one]]

Numerous arguments in favor of alternative semantic analyses for indefinite DPs have been put forth in the literature, and these apply to indefinite pronouns to varying degrees. Indefinite pronouns occur as antecedents in donkey sentences (cf. section 2.2.2. below), where they appear to display quantificational variabilty, suggesting they should perhaps be analyzed as containing unbound variables:

(3) Mostly, if I call someone, they hang up on me.
     'most people who I call hand up on me'

On the other hand, they part ways with lexical indefinite DPs in generic and adverbial sentences: (4a, b) can be paraphrased roughly as 'few/most people/ men have enough time', but no similar interpretation is available for (4c) (replacing *someone* in (4c) with *one* yields the reading in question; we will not discuss generic pronouns in this article, see Moltmann 2006):

(4) a. People rarely/usually have enough time.
     b. A man rarely/usually has enough time.
     c. Someone rarely/usually has enough time.

Finally, indefinite pronouns seem less prone to wide scope or specific interpretations; (5a) has a reading which is true even if only one specific relative will bequeath a fortune on her, but the same reading seems less available for (5b) with an indefinite, arguing against an analysis of indefinite pronouns in terms of choice functions (Reinhart 1997; Winter 1997):

(5) a. If some relative of hers dies, she'll inherit a fortune.
     b. If someone in her family dies, she'll inherit a fortune.

Since the arguments and analyses here entirely parallel those in the discussion of indefinite DPs in general, I refer the reader to article 2 [this volume] (Heim) *Definiteness and indefiniteness* for more analytical options regarding the semantics of (the determiner part in) indefinite pronouns.

1.2 Demonstrative pronouns

We briefly discuss here the English singular demonstratives *this* and *that* on their individual-denoting use, ignoring plural demonstratives, and putative locative, temporal or propositional demonstratives; also, many languages show an ostensibly demonstrative use of bare definite articles, e.g. German *der, die, das*. Demonstratives display at least two properties that distinguish them from non-demonstrative pronouns: a proximal/distal specification, and a heightened sensitivity to speakers' extralinguistic demonstrations (see article 13 [Semantics: Interfaces] (Diessel) *Deixis and demonstratives*). To a first, crude approximation, *this/that* are most naturally used when accompanied by a pointing gesture; *this* additionally expresses closeness (in some sense) to the speaker, *that* lack thereof:

(6) (pointing at a picture on the wall) This is a Picasso.

As Kaplan (1977) famously points out, demomstratives appear to be *directly referential*: (7) is not true even if there is a Pollock painting hanging opposite the Picasso (note that the definite paraphrase in (7) seems true under these circumstances):

(7) (pointing at a Picasso on the wall) If I were pointing to the opposite wall, this would be a Pollock.
(can't mean '... the picture I would be pointing to would be a Pollock')

This is reflected in (8), where the referent of the demonstrative is fixed with no regard to the world *w* of evaluation, but only to the context of utterance (see article 12 [Semantics: Interfaces] (Zimmermann) *Context dependency*):

(8) $[\![this/that]\!]^{w,g}$ = the unique proximal/distant object the speaker is actually pointing at at the time of utterance
(Or perhaps: intending to demonstrate, cf. Bach 1992 and Kaplan 1989)

Several things are worth noting, though: First, the sensitivity to demonstrations is found equally with second, third, and first person plural non-demomstrative pronouns:

(9) She/they/you/we (pointing at appropriate group) are better at the game than she/they/you/we (pointing at different appropriate group).

Likewise, these appear directly referential in the same way:

(10) (pointing at a picture of Pollock, which is next to a picture of Picasso) If I were pointing at the next picture, he would be a Spaniard.

One might conclude from this that we generally use demonstrative gestures as a clue to discern speakers' (actual) referential intentions, and that the semantics shouldn't distinguish demonstratives in that regard.

Second, demonstratives seem to allow for 'special' uses much like ordinary pronouns (examples from Elbourne 2008):

(11) a. (A new faculty member picks up her first paycheck from her mailbox. Waving it in the air, she says to a colleague:) Do most faculty members deposit this in the Credit Union? (*this* = their paycheck)
b. Every man who owns a donkey beats that and nothing else.

This in turn suggests that the meaning of demonstratives should include some variable that can be locally, linguistically bound, be it in the form of an index pointing to an individual in the assignment, or a situation variable. The semantic literature on simple demonstratives is rather scarce, but the reader is referred to the rich literature on complex demonstratives, among others (Elbourne 2008; King 2001 and Roberts 2002).

1.3 Non-demonstrative definite pronouns

Traditional grammars distinguish between the anaphoric, deictic and bound uses of third person definite pronouns:

(12) a. Every soprano brought her union card.   (bound)
b. Josh met a soprano. He liked her.   (anaphoric)
c. (*scenario: A woman walks in.*)
 She must be a soprano.   (deictic)

A bound pronoun acts like a bound individual variable in quantificational logic; crucially, no contextual information is necessary in order to interpret (12a) or the pronouns therein. This is different in the case of anaphoric and deictic pronouns (12b,c), where we need to know the (linguistic or extralinguistic) context in order to interpret the pronouns.

Anaphoric uses, however, do not always involve more than one sentence: *her* in (13a) is anaphoric to *Joan* within the same sentence. One might think that (13a) involves a bound pronoun, but note that binding of *her* by a true quantificational DP like *every soprano* is impossible in the structurally identical (13b); thus the relation between *Joan* and *her* in (13a) must be anaphoric coreference, not binding:

(13) a. What the doctor told Joan impressed her.
b. What the doctor told every soprano impressed her.
c. Claudia knows her password.

The case in (13c), on the other hand, is less clear, since *her* can be bound by *every soprano* in the structurally parallel (12a); but it could also just corefer with, and hence be anaphoric to, the subject *Claudia* (obviously not an option with *every soprano*, which doesn't refer to begin with). We will return to this issue in section 3.3.

2 The meaning of definite pronouns

2.1 Pronouns as variable-like expressions

2.1.1 Pronouns as variables

The basic semantics of personal pronouns is often likened to that of variables in predicate logic. A straightforward implementation of this idea will assume pronouns to be *indexed* with a natural number, and have their interpretation depend on an *assignment function*, i.e. a sequence of, or a function from numbers to, DP meanings. The interpretation rule (14) (where i is a variable over natural numbers, and g a variable over assignment functions) provides a simple illustration:

(14)   for any assignment function g, $[\![[_{pron} X]_i]\!]^g = g(i)$ ($\approx$ the i-th member of g)

Rule (14) certainly oversimplifies, most clearly in ignoring any lexical content of the pronoun (i.e. gender, person, number), which we will discuss in 4.1., as well as types of pronouns that appear to have meanings more complex than just individuals (see section 2.2.). It can serve, however, to explicate the deictic, anaphoric and bound uses of definite pronouns mentioned in 1.3. more formally.

We will discuss bound pronouns in much detail in section 3. In a nutshell, the binder of a pronoun, for example a quantificational DP like *every soprano* in (12a) (*every soprano brought her union card*), can manipulate the assignment function in much the same way the quantifiers ∃ and ∀ do in quantified logic. The interpretation of a sentence that contains bound pronouns will thus not, as a whole, depend on the assignment, which plays an ancillary role only: $[\![(12a)]\!]^g$ is the same for any g.

This is different for sentences with non-bound, i.e. anaphoric and deictic pronouns. For example, a sentence like *Josh liked her$_i$*, for any assignment g, is true iff Josh liked $g(i)$; which proposition it expresses crucially hinges on g, that is, the assignment here models an essential part of the context. Specifying how this comes about is not part of the semantics of pronouns proper, but we will give some indications in the next subsection (see article 11 [Semantics: Theories] (Kamp & Reyle) *Discourse Representation Theory* and article 12 [Semantics: Theories] (Dekker) *Dynamic semantics*).

All of this of couse presupposes that all three uses of pronouns — bound, anaphoric and deictic — involve the same semantics for the pronoun (here: that of a variable, (14)). A common alternative view is that pronouns are ambiguous between two or more interpretations for pronouns. Most commonly, a distinction is made between bound pronouns, which are usually treated as variables (or their equivalents in variable-free theories), and deictic pronouns, which are treated differently; anaphoric pronouns are then usually grouped with one or the other of those. We will return to some of these issues in section 2.2., see also article 14 [Semantics: Sentence and Information Structure] (Geurts) *Accessibility and anaphora*.

2.1.2 Assignments, discourse, and saliency

Given what was said so far, a pronoun like *her* can refer to any element in the range of the assignment function, depending on its index. If we want the semantics to model the range of available referents for pronouns, we need to include a theory of how assignments are incrementally 'built' in a discourse.

As a first step, assume that assignment functions are partial, and that their domain reflects the anaphoric options in a given context, i.e. which *discourse referents* (DRs), modelled by indices, are available at a given point in the conversation. A pronoun like her_7, if unbound, will thus only be interpretable in a context that has previously introduced the discourse referent 7 (and only if $g(7)$ is female, see again 4.1. below). Discourse referents can be introduced (i.e. indices can be added to the domain of an assignment) in at least two different ways: Linguistically, by the use of full DPs, in particular indefinites, and extralinguistically, by pointing to an object, or simply by virtue of that object becoming salient.

One may wish to go further and model the intuition that, say, *she* can't usually refer to *any* female individual previously introduced, but will refer to the most *salient* one. To do this, the context needs to provide an ordering among the available DRs; since assignments are sequences, a straightforward way of achieving this is to assume that the last element in the assignment is more salient than the one before it, which in turn is more salient than the one before it, etc. Using an indefinite, for example, will serve not only to introduce a new DR, but also to make that DR maximally salient, i.e. put it at the end of the list. Other linguistic devices, say marking a DP as a topic, or referring to an existing DR using a definite description, may yield the same effect, as will pointing to an object etc.

Using assignments in this way allows for a radically different semantics of unbound pronouns, using lexical entries like (15):

(15) ⟦she⟧^{g} = the final (=most salient) female individual in the sequence g

A semantics along these lines allows us to eliminate indices on free pronouns. It will, however, need refinements to model cases of genuinely ambiguous pronouns like *she* in (16):

(16) Norma hates Sally. She criticized her novel.

To allow for either interpretation, one must assume that the first sentence can leave either Norma or Sally as the maximally salient female (to then be referred to by *she*). Furthermore, *her* most naturally picks out that woman *she* doesn't, which would mean that the saliency ordering 'flips' somewhere between *she* and *her*.

Saliency orderings along these lines have been used to model definite DPs. Thus ⟦the dog⟧^{g} denotes the most salient dog under g, ⟦the neighbor's dog⟧^{g} the most salient among the neighbor's dogs etc. (e.g. von Heusinger 1997 and Peregrin & von Heusinger 2004). The view just sketched can thus be straightforwardly adopted to a theory like the one we'll develop in section 2.2. according to which, say, *she* is just a surface rendering of something like *the female person*, picking out, again, the most salient female person under the given assignment.

2.1.3 Pronouns in variable-free semantics

As is well-known, variables and assignment functions are eliminable. Accordingly, it is possible to maintain the general idea that pronouns behave like variables in quantified logic without actually eschewing the formal apparatus of indices and assignments, as is done most prominently in the work of Anna Szabolcsi and Pauline Jacobson (Jacobson 1999, 2000, Szabolcsi 1987, 1992 and 2003). It is important to stress that this question of implementation is independent of the question whether all pronouns should be interpreted uniformly, and in a term-like fashion.

The key ingredient of a variable-free semantics for pronouns is to treat an expression E containing a free DP pronoun semantically parallel to one that is a function from ordinary DP meanings to the type of meaning E would have without any free pronouns in it. This is achieved in two steps. First, the pronoun itself is interpreted as an identity function, for example the identity function on individuals:

(17) ⟦her⟧ = $\lambda x_e.x$ (defined only if x is female)

Note that this follows the characterization just given: The pronoun denotes a function from ordinary DP meanings, type e, to ordinary DP meanings, type e. The second step is a propagation mechanism that allows an expression E containing pronouns to combine with any element it could 'normally' combine with (i.e. if E didn't contain pronouns), while 'bequeathing' its open argument slots onto the resulting expression. For example, *her* in (17) combines with a transitive verb, resulting in a VP meaning like (18):

(18) ⟦likes her⟧ = $\lambda x_e \lambda y_e . y$ likes x (defined only if x is female)

This is a function from DP meanings to 'ordinary' VP meanings, type ⟨e, et⟩, the same as that of a transitive verb (indeed this function is almost the same as ⟦likes⟧). The different distributional properties of, say, a transitive verb and a VP with a free pronoun in it, in particular the fact that the expression in (18) cannot combine with two DPs to form a sentence, is logged in the syntactic category of the expression. In Jacobson system, *likes Mary* and *likes* are of the (standard) categories S\NP and (S\NP)/NP, respectively ('S\NP' is the category of an expression requiring an NP to its left to form an S, i.e. a VP; 'X/NP' that of an expression requiring an NP to its right to form an X; analogously for any two categories X, Y); *likes her*, on the other hand, is of the category (S\NP)^{NP}, i.e. a verb phrase with a free NP pronoun in it (accordingly, the pronoun itself is of category NP^{NP}). Roughly, syntactic combinatorics are 'blind' to superscripts, that is X^Y combines with whatever plain X combines with, while the superscript and the semantic argument position corresponding to it are propagated upwards by function composition.

If an expression contains free, i.e. anaphoric or deictic, pronouns, it will end up being of category X^{NP} or X$^{NP^{NP}}$ etc. In particular, a sentence containing a free pronoun will be of category S^{NP}, and denote a function of type ⟨e, t⟩. This may seem odd at first but is, as Jacobson points out, entirely parallel to the idea that a sentence denotes a function from assignments to truth values.

Bound pronoun uses are modelled by a rule that 'swallows' a superscript category and identifies its semantic argument with an open 'proper' argument position. (19) gives a very simplified version of such a rule, whose application is illustrated in (20) (| ranges over \ and /):

(19) ⟦z⟧ = $\lambda p_{e,\langle e,a\rangle} \lambda x_e . p(x)(x)$; (X|NP)|(X|NP)^{NP}

(20) a. ⟦likes her cat⟧ = $\lambda v_e \lambda y_e . y$ likes v's cat; (S\NP)^{NP}
      b. ⟦z(likes her cat)⟧ = $[\lambda p_{e,\langle e,a\rangle} \lambda x_e . p(x)(x)](\lambda v_e \lambda y_e . y$ likes v's cat)
          (i) = $\lambda x_e . [\lambda v_e \lambda y_e . y$ likes v's cat$](x)(x)$
          (ii) = $\lambda x_e . x$ likes x's cat; S\NP

This must suffice to illustrate the general treatment of pronouns in variable-free semantics. For arguments in favor of a variable treatment and a thorough formal treatment see (Jacobson 1999).

2.1.4 Resumptive pronouns

Gaps corresponding to displaced constituents ('traces') usually receive an interpretation identical to bound pronouns, e.g. as bound variables. The difference between gaps and pronouns, then, is a purely syntactic one (roughly whether there has to be an antecedent, and whether that antecedent can bear its own thematic relation to an element in the clause or not). Given that, the existence of *resumptive* pronouns, i.e. pronouns that occur in the thematic position of a dislocated element (in the position where a trace might be expected) is unproblematic from a semantic point of view.

2.2 Pronouns as descriptions

In this subsection we will contrast the 'pronouns as variables' view outlined in the previous subsection with one that essentially assumes pronouns to have the logical form of definite noun phrases, call that the 'pronouns as descriptions' view. To motivate this view, consider the examples in (21):

(21) a. I know this woman. She ('this/the woman') is a famous soprano.
  b. Bill owns some sheep. Harry vaccinates them ('the sheep (Bill owns)').
  c. This year the president is a Republican, but one fine day, he ('the president') will be a member of the Green party.
  d. Mary, who deposited her paycheck at the ATM, was smarter than any woman who kept it ('her paycheck') in her purse.
  e. Every farmer who owned a donkey had Lucy vaccinate it ('the donkey (he owns)').

(21a,b) involve referential pronouns; while the paraphrase in terms of a definite may be suggestive, there is no obstacle to assuming instead that the pronuns are simply individual variables. This is different in (21c–e). Here, the pronouns aren't referential. Rather, they denote functions: from world/times to the president in/at that world/time; from women to their paychecks; from farmers to the sheep they own. These functions, it seems, are provided by the linguistic context.

And even (21b) is not straightforward on the pronouns-as-variables view, as pointed out in (Evans 1980): Plural pronouns anaphoric to quantificational DPs have a 'maximum interpretation'. For example, (21b) is judged false unless Harry vaccinates *all* of Bill's sheep. This follows if we interpret *them* synonymous with *Bill's/the sheep*. A theory that has *them* denote a (plural) individual variable has to employ additional means to ensure that an utterance of *Bill owns some sheep* triggers the introduction of a discourse referent including all the sheep Bill owns, rather than some sub-group thereof (see e.g. Kamp & Reyle 1993).

2.2.1 Pronouns of laziness and paycheck pronouns

Historically, pronouns that stand for a literal repetition of a full definite DP, e.g. (21a) and (21c)/(22a), are called *pronouns of laziness* (Geach 1962). In case these DPs contain bound pronouns, (21d)/(22b) one often finds the term *paycheck pronouns* (Karttunen 1969); finally pronouns in configurations like (21e), whose content seems 'distilled' from a previous sentence, but that don't have a literal DP antecedent go by the name of 'donkey pronouns' or -- especially for those researchers who eschew the pronouns-as-descriptions view -- *E-type* pronouns (Evans 1977, 1980). We will now develop an implementation of the idea that in all of these cases the pronouns are indeed essentially definite descriptions.

For concreteness, let us model these pronouns as *bona fide* definite DPs of the general form *the NP*. Interpreted at world/time *w, t*, they denote the unique (singular) or maximal (plural) element in the extension of NP at *w, t*. NP consists of a lexical head, e.g. the nouns *woman, sheep, president, paycheck* plus an appropriate number of unpronounced individual variables (one for *paycheck*, zero for the others). This whole complex DP is spelled out as an appropriate pronoun if the content of N is contextually recoverable; thus the pronouns in examples (21c) and (21d) are grammatically represented as in (22):

(22) a. ⟦he ~~the president~~⟧^{g,w,t} = the president at *w, t*
   b. ⟦it ~~the paycheck of v_n~~⟧^{g,w,t} = $g(n)$'s paycheck at *w, t*
      (where v_n will be bound by *any woman* in (21d))

Pronouns of lazyness, including paycheck pronouns, then simply involve N(P)-ellipsis under identity; the definite determiner is spelled out as a pronoun if and only if everything in the NP following it is unpronounced. (Alternatively, we could assume with Postal 1970 and Elbourne 2001 that pronouns *are* definite determiners (with additional feature specifications) followed by ellided NPs.) In the following subsections we will explore to what extent this view can be extended to other uses of pronouns.

2.2.2 Donkey sentences

Extending the pronouns-as-descriptions approach to donkey pronouns runs into several problems, as pointed out famously in Heim (1982), most vexing among them the *uniqueness problem* (cf. Egli 1983): If *he* in (23a) is interpreted as 'the unique man who is in Athens', we wrongly predict (23a) to imply that there is only one man in Athens; likewise, (23b) is predicted to be infelicitous, since its assertion contradicts that there is 'the unique sage plant that (s)he bought':

(23) a. If a man is in Athens, he is not in Rhodes.
 b. Everyone who bought a sage plant here bought eight others along with it.
 c. No father with a teenage son would lend him the car on the weekend.

Similarly, Rooth (1987) points out that (23c) is understood to quantify over all fathers, not just those that have a unique teenage son.

Heim (1982) instead develops an account in keeping with the pronouns-as-variables view, on which these pronouns are bound individual variables in logical forms like (24) (variables corresponding to pronouns underlined for clarity); crucially, adverbial as well as adnominal quantifiers are taken to *unselectively bind n-tuples of variables* (see article 11 [Semantics: Theories] (Kamp & Reyle) *Discourse Representation Theory* and article 12 [Semantics: Theories] (Dekker) *Dynamic semantics* on how such logical formulae are built):

(24) a. for all x, if x is a man in Athens, $\underline{x}$ is not in Rhodes.
 b. for all x, y, if x bought y here and y is a sage plant, x bought eight other sage plants along with $\underline{y}$
 c. there are no x, y such that, if x is a man and y is a teenage son of x, x lends $\underline{y}$ the car on the weekend.

Various researchers have argued that the pronouns-as-descriptions view, too, can be modified to handle such cases. For starters, note that (25), where the pronouns have been replaced by definite DPs, provide intuitively accurate paraphrase for the exemples in (23):

(25) a. If a man is in Athens, that man is not in Rhodes.
 b. Everyone who bought a sage plant here bought eight others along with that sage plant.

c. No father with a teenage son would lend his son the car on the weekend.

This suggests that the problem lies with the assumption that definite DPs strictly require uniqueness of their referent among the elements in ⟦NP⟧. Heim (1990), building on work in Berman (1987), suggests instead that definites in general, and E-type pronouns in particular, refer to the unique element in ⟦NP⟧ in a given *situation* (see article 10 [Semantics: Theories] (Ginzburg) *Situation Semantics* and article 2 [this volume] (Heim) *Definiteness and indefiniteness*). Situations are parts of worlds, but crucially contain fewer things than the world they are part of. Take (23a)/(25a): The conditional is interpreted as a universal quantifier over minimal situations described by the antecedent clause, i.e. situations that contain a man in Athens. Crucially, each such minimal situation contains only one man (else it wouldn't be minimal), and now *the man who is in Athens* can refer to the unique man in Athens *in that situation*, cf. (26a); (26b,c) sketch a parallel treatment for (23b)/(25b) and (23c)/(25c):

(26) a. for every situation *s*, if *s* is a minimal situation containing a man in Athens, then *s* can be extended to a minimal situation *s'* containing the unique man in Athens in *s* not being in Rhodes
b. for every person *y* and minimal situation *s* of *y* buying a sage plant here, there is an extension *s'* of *s* in which *y* buys eight other sage plants along with the unique sage plant he buys in *s*
c. for no man *x* and minimal situation *s* of *x* having a teenage son in *s* is there an extension *s'* of *s* in which *x* lets *x*'s unique son in *s* borrow the car on the weekend

A necessary assumption of this approach, seen in (26b,c), is that DP quantifiers such as *everyone*... or *no man*... quantify over pairs of individuals and situations. Generally, where the unselective binding approach has quantifiers quantify over *n*-tuples of individuals, the situation approach uses pair of individuals and situations. On virtually all ontologies for situation semantics, we can find, for every *n*-tuple of individuals, an appropriate situation that contains only those individuals; on the other hand, for every situation, we can presumably find an appropiate tuple of entities that are unique to it ((23a)/(25a), for example, should more realistically be interpreted as quantfying over occasions of men being in Athens, which can be thought of as temporally limited situations, or pairs of individuals and time intervals). Thus, the two approaches are more similar (conceptually and empirically) than might appear at first, differing essentially only in how they spell out the notion of what Lewis (1975) calls a *case*.

2.2.3 The formal link problem

Expanding on such situation-based approaches, Elbourne (2001, 2005) argues that the descriptive content of E-type pronouns is indeed poorer than hitherto assumed. For example, the pronoun in (21e) would, in a standard E-type approach, be 'the unique donkey he owns in s', where s is a minimal situation of a farmer owning a donkey. But given such a minimal situation, the simpler description 'the unique donkey in s' would identify the same donkey. Assuming poorer descriptions like that allows Elbourne to argue that *all* descriptive pronouns involve simple NP ellipsis, thereby solving a second problem for E-type approaches to donkey pronouns, called the *problem of the formal link* since Kadmon (1987). The problem can be put as follows: What makes, for example, the meaning 'wife of x' available for the E-type pronoun in (27a), but not (27b), given that neither contains an NP-antecedent meaning 'wife of x'?

(27) a. Every man who has a wife should bring her along.
 b. #Every married man should bring her along.

According to Elbourne, the pronoun in (27b) is simply *the wife*, yielding the meaning 'the unique wife in s', where for each man x, s is a minimal situation containing, roughly, x and his wife. Ellipsis of NP (i.e. the use of a pronoun) now can be assumed to require that NP have a syntactic antecedent, as is the case in (27a); consequently, ellipsis of NP is impossible for lack of an NP antecedent $[_{NP}$ *wife]* (the formal link) in (27b). Note that this argument would not go through if (27a) would need to be 'the wife of his', which doesn't have an NP antecedent in (27a) either.

2.2.4 Alternative implementations of the 'pronouns as descriptions' view

It seems controversial at present whether all instances of 'non-standard' pronouns, including donkey-pronouns, should be analyzed as definites, or whether other analytical options such as unselective binding should be used as well. But it appears that some kind of descriptive pronouns will be required to model pronouns of lazyness as in (21c) and especially (21d). This doesn't mean that the very implementation used above has to be used. One may assume, for example, that rather than containing deleted lexical nouns, descriptive pronouns contain a variable over *n*-ary relations (e.g. Heim & Kratzer 1998). For example, instead of *the ~~paycheck~~ v_n* we'd have *the $R_m v_n$*, where R_m is the *m*-th variable over relations, which gets assigned the value 'paycheck' ($\lambda x.\lambda y.y$ is a paycheck of *x*) by the context in question. Assignment functions as part of the context, then, keep track of an inventory of 'nominal relations' that can serve as antecedents to (the N-part inside) descriptive pronouns (see e.g. van Rooy 1997), just as we assumed for individual referents above (including the possibility of ordering them by salience etc.). Going that route, one can also assume that the variable in question is indeed simply a function from e.g. people to (the intension of) their unique paycheck (Cooper 1979); as a limiting case, instead of *he* ~~the president~~ in (21c)/(22a) one then simply has a variable expression he_n that is assigned the function from world/times or situations to the president at that world/time/situation as its value; sample logical forms are given in (28):

(28) a. [$_{DP}$ the [paycheck v_n]]   NP ellipsis
 b. [$_{DP}$ the [$R_m v_n$]]   relational variable
 c. [$_{DP}$ $P_m v_n$]   functional variable

These approaches may be empirically indistinguishable, especially if one spells out the theory of NP ellipsis along the lines of e.g. Merchant (2004), where ellipsis of a constituent *α* is itself licensed by an operator that requires a silent anaphoric argument; that argument in turn must denote the same as *α*. So deletion of, say, *paycheck* is licensed by virtue of an operator whose argument is a silent anaphoric pronoun that denotes the meaning of *paycheck* – effectively R from (28b).

2.2.5 Bound pronouns as descriptions

Given that descriptive pronouns of some sort seem necessary, is it possible, on the other hand, to give up the idea that definite pronouns are variables ever, and use *only* descriptive pronouns? Referential anaphoric pronouns would simply be pronouns of lazyness, cf. (21a), but what about ordinary bound pronouns, as in (29)?

(29) Every girl played her trumpet.

There are two ways to achieve a bound pronoun interpretation here: The first uses the idea, introduced above, that *every girl* quantifies over pairs consisting of a girl and a situation, namely for each girl *x* the minimal situation containing *x*. *Her* in (29) is then interpreted as 'the unique girl in s', cf. (30a). The second takes the pronoun to be something like 'the ID$_n$' or 'the girl ID$_n$', where for any *n*,

$[\![ID_n]\!]^{w,g} =_{def} \lambda x.x = g(n)$ (cf. Elbourne 2005); thus, if n is bound by *every girl*, we get (30b) as the meaning for (29):

(30) a. for every girl x and minimal situation s containg girl x, s can be extended to a situation in which x plays the unique trumpet of the unique girl in s
   b. for every girl x, x played the unique trumpet of the unique y that is (a girl and) identical to x

See Elbourne (2005, 2008) for discussion of these options and critical discussion.

3 Pronoun binding

In this section we discuss a particular implementation of the semantics and syntax of pronoun binding. For concreteness, we adopt the 'pronouns as variables' view, but *mutatis mutandis*, our discussion carries over to variable free treatments, as well as either of the adoptions of the 'pronouns as description' view to bound pronouns sketched in 2.2.5. above.

3.1 Bound v. free pronouns

The clearest examples of bound pronouns are pronouns whose antecedents are non-referring expressions such as *no one, every stork, fewer than two sopranos* etc.:

(31) No soprano forgot her hat.

To achieve binding of *her* (by assumption an individual variable) by *no soprano*, we introduce a binding operator β, defined in (32), closely modelled on the z-operator from section 2.1.3., which binds any free occurrence of pronouns with a given index to the next open argument of a function (see Büring 2005a chapter 3 for more on this rule and its pedigree). A logical form and derivation for (31) is then as in (33):

(32) $[\![\beta_i\, \alpha]\!] =_{def} \lambda x_e. [\![\alpha]\!]^{g[i \to x]}(x)$

(33) a. [[no soprano] [β_2[forgot [her$_2$ hat]]]]
   b. (i) $[\![$forgot her$_2$ hat$]\!]^g = \lambda y_e. y$ forgot $g(2)$'s hat
      (ii) $[\![\beta_2\,$[forgot her$_2$ hat]$]\!]^g = \lambda x_e. [\![$forgot her$_2$ hat$]\!]^{g[2 \to x]}(x)$
      $= \lambda x_e. [\lambda y_e. y$ forgot $g[2 \to x](2)$'s hat$](x)$

$= \lambda x_e.x \text{ forgot } g[2 \to x](2)\text{'s hat}$
$= \lambda x_e.x \text{ forgot } x\text{'s hat}$

3.2 Structural conditions on pronoun binding

Rule (32) above imposes a structural condition on the binder-bindee relation: the bindee must be contained in the sister constituent to the binder; if this isn't the case, β applies vacuously. This corresponds to the syntactic condition that a binder must *c-command* its bindee (α c-commands β if every node that dominates α dominates β, α doesn't dominate β and α isn't the root of the phrase marker).

There are two empirical generalizations we may try to tie to this c-command requirement. First, the *scope generalization*: the putative binder has to be able to take scope over the pronoun position. Take (34): *every man* in (34a) can't scope over *a schnapps* (which would yield as many schnappses for us as there were men who left); unsurprisingly *him* in (34b) can't be bound by *every man* either:

(34) a. Once every man left we drank a schnapps.
     b. Once *every man* left we talked about *him*.

But secondly, there are examples in which the putative binder clearly *can* take scope over the position in question, yet is unable to bind a pronoun therein; (35a) can describe a scenario in which there are as many pictures as there are desks, but (35b) can't mean that each picture showed the owner of the desk it was standing on:

(35) a. A picture was standing on every desk.
        for every desk x, there is a picture y standing on x

   b. A picture of *its* owner was standing on *every desk*.
        not: for every desk x, there is a picture of x's owner on x

It seems, then, that scoping over a pronoun's position is a necessary, but not a sufficient condition for binding that pronoun. In addition, the binder apparently has to sit in the position where it receives it's thematic role. Call this the *a(rgument)-command generalization*; for example, the adjunct DP *every desk* in (35) can scope over the matrix subject (say via a covert movement step to a scope position), but it is unable to bind into the subject from that (non-thematic) position.

Wh-movement patterns analogously: Even within its overt c-command domain a *wh*-expression can only bind pronouns in positions lower than its original thematic position (the so-called *weak cross-over effect*):

(36) a. *Who* did you tell that *he* won?
for which x is it true that you told x that x won?

b. *Who* did *his father* tell that Mary won?
not: for which x is it true that x's father told x that Mary won?

Assuming the generalization to be correct, the c-command requirement on binding imposed by the semantics of β in (32) is too lenient. We need to stipulate in addition that β cannot be adjoined to positions that are created by *wh*-movement or covert scoping movement; it can only apply to lexical predicates (cf. again the z-rule in 2.1.3., as well as Büring 2004 and 2005a, chapter 4).

There are, however, notorious counter-examples to the a-command requirement, such as *binding out of DP* and binding by an object into an adjunct (often collectively called *indirect binding*):

(37) a. *Whose* mother loves *him*?
b. *Every senator*'s portrait was on *his* desk.
c. Somebody from *every city* despises *it/its*
d. We will drink *no wine* before *its* time.

In keeping with the scope generalization, the binders in (37) can take semantic scope over the pronoun positions: in (38) for example, an indefinite in the place of the pronoun in (37b) takes scope below the universal (there are as many glasses of schnapps as there are senators):

(38) Every senator's portrait sat next to a glass of schnapps.

But clearly, *every senator* in (37b) receives its thematic role within the subject DP, from where — according to the a-command generalization — it shouldn't be able to bind the pronoun.

Analyzing these examples then involves two steps: First, let the binders scope over the pronoun position, presumably by whatever scoping mechanisms one employs in (35a). Second, explain why such scoping results in a configuration that allows binding, unlike in (35b). This has been done in at least three different ways in the literature: First, by refining the definition of a position from which binding is possible (the a-command condition) to include derived scope positions of the kind found in (37), but not (35b) (Shan & Barker 2006, Higginbotham 1983, May 1988). Second, by replacing the c-command condition by one that allows the quantificational DPs in (37) to bind from their surface, thematic position (Hornstein 1995). And third, by assuming that there is no binding relation between the quantificational DPs and the pronoun, but rather that the pronoun is an E-type pronoun whose argument is bound by the DP that c-commands the pronoun; (37c) for example, would get be analyzed roughly as (39) (see Büring 2004 for details):

(39) for every city x, some person y from x despises [it ~~the city (y is from)~~]

3.3 Binding v. coreference

In section 1.3. we asked whether the relation between *Claudia* and *her* in (13c), repeated here, is binding, or mere coreference; we can now spell these options out as in (40a,b):

(40) *Claudia* knows *her* password.
    a. Claudia β_2 [knows her$_2$ password]   (binding)
    b. Claudia knows her$_2$ password   (coref.: $g(2)$ = Claudia)

(40a) and (40b) yield the same truth conditions. But in other cases, the two readings can be teased apart, for example by making the antecedent an associated focus (here and henceforth I will write e.g. *her*$_{2=Claudia}$ to abbreviate that 2 is a free index which is assigned the value Claudia by the assignment function):

(41) I only want CLAUdia$_F$ to know her password.
    a. I only want Claudia$_F$ β_2 [to know her$_2$ password]   (binding)
    'Claudia should know her own password, no one else should know theirs.'
    b. I only want Claudia$_F$ to know her$_{2=Claudia}$ password (coreference)
    'Claudia's password should be known to Claudia only.'

If *her* is bound to *Claudia* as in (41a), it will co-vary with the focus alternatives to Claudia, yielding the meaning paraphrased. If pronoun and name merely corefer, as in (41b), the pronoun's referent is constant for all focus alternatives, as indicated in the second paraphrase. Clearly, these two readings are truth-conditionally different. Since both readings are available for sentence (41), we can conclude that both binding and coreference are possible between names (indeed all referring DPs) and pronouns anaphorically related to them.

It has been argued, however, that, *ceteris paribus*, binding is preferred over coreference, or more precisely, that configuration (42a) is preferred over (42b) if the resulting interpretation is the same (see Büring 2005b for a more precise statement and discussion):

(42)   Binding is Preferred:
       (42b) is ungrammatical ('blocked') if (42a) yields the same interpretation.
       a. ... DP'$_i$ β_j ...DP$_j$
       b. ...DP'$_i$ ...DP$_i$

(Note that DP' in (42a,b) may itself be bound by a higher DP", in which case the relation between DP' and DP in (42b) wouldn't be one of coreference, but of 'co-binding'. The claim is that coreference as well as co-binding are 'blocked' wherever binding as in (42a) is possible.)

But how can we know which of two semantically equivalent representations an unambiguous sentence has? At least two phenomena have been argued to be probes into this question: Reinhart (1983), and following her Heim (1993), argue that Binding Condition violations (see section 5. below) occur only with binding, not coreference. For example, (43) is acceptable despite what appears to be a Condition B violation, but only on a reading where *him* corefers with *John* (LF (43a)), rather than being bound by it (Binding Condition B, roughly, prohibits non-reflexive pronouns from being coreferent with a higher coargument, such as the subject in (43)):

(43)   (Not many people voted for John. In fact,) only JOHN voted for him.
       a. only John$_F$ voted for him$_{1=John}$
          'no one but John voted for John'
       b. *only John$_F$ β_1 voted for him$_1$
          'no one but John voted for themselves'

This suggests, the argument goes on, that Binding Condition B ignores the coreferent construal in (43a), but renders ungrammatical the local binding in (43b). But if coreference can 'circumvent' Binding Conditions, how come sentences with two referring DPs ever violate them? Why, that is, is (44) ungrammatical (with 〚him〛 =John), if LF (44b) is not in violation of Binding Condition B (L(ogical) F(orm)s are those syntactic representations that are interpreted by the semantic rules)?

(44) *_John_ voted for _him_.
  a. *John $β_1$ voted for him$_1$
  b. *John voted for him$_{1=John}$

The answer Reinhart and Heim suggests is that (44a), an instance of (42a), binding, blocks, and thereby renders ungrammatical, (44b), an instance of (42b), coreference (since both have identical interpretations). And (44a) in turn is ruled out as a Condition B violation (see Büring 2005b for detailed discussion of this argument).

The second argument for something like (42) comes from the discussion of 'Dahl's puzzle' in Fox (2000, chapter 4). It is based on the premise that sloppy identity in VP-ellipsis requires 'parallelism' in binding. Thus _his_ in the elided VP in (45) can be bound by _Bob_ (yielding the sloppy reading) because the corresponding _his_ in the antecedent is bound by the corresponding subject _John_:

(45) John said his name, and Bob did ~~say his name~~, too.

Dahl's puzzle goes like this: Why can't (46) report the following two statements: John: 'I'll pay for my drinks'; Bill: 'John will pay for my drinks, too'?

(46) John says he will pay for his drinks. Bill does, too.

To get to this reading, we would need the following LF:

(47) John $β_1$ says he$_1$ will pay for his$_1$ drinks.
  Bill $β_3$ does say ~~that he$_{2=John}$ will pay for his$_3$ drinks, too~~

His$_3$ is bound, sloppily as it were, to _Bill_, which, by assumption, requires _his_$_1$ to be bound in structurally parallel fashion by _John_. But that means that _he_$_1$ and _his_$_1$ in the first conjunct are both bound by _John_, an instance of (42b), illegitimately so, since the same interpretation could have been achieved by _he_$_1$ binding _his_$_1$, as in (48), an instance of (42a).

(48) John $β_1$ says he$_1$ $β_2$ will pay for his$_2$ drinks

Since (48) is the only proper LF for the first conjunct in (47), parallelism makes it impossible for _his_ in the second conjunct of (47)/(48) to be directly bound to _Bill_, explaining Dahl's puzzle (cf. Fox 2000, Büring 2005b).

4 Pronominal content

4.1 Semantic features on pronouns

The most common semantic information encoded in pronouns are person, number, and gender or class. Generally, this information does not contribute to the assertive or at-issue content of an utterance: If I point to a boy saying *If she is in your class, she's skipping school right now*, what I am saying is not true — or false, for that matter — but infelicitous. This can be modelled by making features like human, male, singular etc. presuppositions of pronouns:

(49) ⟦she$_i$⟧^{g} = $g(i)$ if $g(i)$ is a singular female, undefined otherwise

An utterance of a sentence containing a free occurrence of *she$_7$*, then, will only be defined if the context provides an assignment function that maps 7 onto a single female individual.

Which values the features person, number and gender/class can take differs from language to language. For example, besides the familiar singular and plural, Boumaa Fijian (Austronesian, Fijii, Dixon 1988) has *dual* pronouns (denoting groups of two) as well as *paucals* (groups of more than two, but not many), cf. Tab. 1.1.

Tab. 1.1: Boumaa Fijian cardinal pronouns (Dixon 1988, 54f)

	SINGULAR	PLURAL	DUAL	PAUCAL
1st exclusive	—	'eimami	'eirau	'eitou
1st inclusive	yau	'eta	'eetaru	'etatou
2nd	i'o	'emunuu	'emudrau	'emudou
3rd	'ea	(i)ra	(i)rau	(i)ratou

Since the number of properties expressed by pronouns cross-linguistically is limited, we can think of them as privative syntactic features as in (50), given with their obvious interpretations:

(50) a. ⟦[SINGULAR]⟧ = $\lambda x_e.x$ is an atomic individual
b. ⟦[FEMININE]⟧ = $\lambda x_e.x$ is female
c. ⟦[1ST]⟧ = $\lambda x_e.x$ is (a group containing) the speaker
d. ⟦[2ND]⟧ = $\lambda x_e.x$ is (a group containing) the addressee

On the 'pronouns as variables' view, the interpretation of a pronoun is now as in (51a); (51b) does the same for a variable-free system; on the 'pronouns as descriptions view', we can simply assume that these features are adjoined to the elided NP as in (52):

(51) Let α be a definite pronoun with index i and features F_1 through F_n, then for all assignments g
   a. $[\![\alpha]\!]^g = g(i)$ if $g(i) \in [\![F_1]\!]... [\![F_n]\!]$, undefined otherwise
   b. $[\![\alpha]\!] = \lambda x.x$, if $x \in [\![F_1]\!] ... [\![F_n]\!]$, undefined otherwise

(52) $[_{DP}$ pron $] = [$ the $[F_1 [... [F_n$ NP $]]]]$

Pronoun types such as the inclusive first person plural (referring to a group containing (at least) speaker and addressee) can be modelled by combining more basic features, e.g. [1st] and [2nd]. Other pronoun types, such as *logophoric pronouns* may require additional refinements of this machinery (see article 17 [this volume] (Schlenker) *Indexicality and de se*).

The inventory of features necessary also depends on theoretical choices. It has, for example, been argued that certain unmarked properties, for example masculine, 3rd, and plural should not be represented by features in their own right, but rather just as the absence of other features, i.e. the pronoun *they* would simply be completely unspecified. The grammar then imposes a requirement that any referent be referred to by an expression that is as semantically specific as possible, leaving third person plural as the default for which there are no features. This might also explain why, for example, such less specified forms can be used to avoid, say, gender specification, as in *no one brought their homework*.

It has been observed, though, that sometimes grammar appears to 'ignore' features even on more specific pronoun forms. For example, (53) has a natural reading on which it entails that other people did their own homeworks (not the speaker's) (Irene Heim, unpubl. notes; discussed e.g. in Rullman 2004):

(53) Even I did my homework.

In other words, (53) asserts that the property denoted by β_i *did my$_i$ homework* applies to individuals that are not the speaker. But if the pronoun *my$_i$* is defined only if $g(i)$ is or includes the speaker, this reading should be impossible. This dilemma could be avoided if we assume that features on bound pronoun aren't interpreted, but simply grammatically inherited from the antecedent (i.e. the pronoun is a *bona fide* unrestricted variable). Of course, since features evidently *are* interpreted on free pronouns (anaphoric as well as deictic), we'd have to say that features are interpreted as indicated above on free pronouns, but can be semantically inert on bound pronouns.

4.2 Plural pronouns

So far we assumed the denotation of a plural pronoun to be the same as that of a plural name like *the Kennedies* or plural definite DP *the boxes*. Concretely, all of these denote plural individuals, or pluralities, for short, which are themselves in the domain of individuals (type e; see article 7 [this volume] (Lasersohn) *Mass nouns and plurals*). The assignment function then has to assign a plurality to the index *i* on a plural pronoun, lest the presupposition encoded by the feature [PLURAL] be violated.

Like singular pronouns, plural pronouns can be referring or bound. Interestingly, looking at bound plural pronouns we find cases in which a plural pronoun can have *split antecedents* (P. Schlenker p.c.; Rullman 2004, Büring 2005a, section 9.3.3):

(54) *Every boy* has asked *some girl* if *they* could go out on a date.

The reading we are interested in here is one were each boy asked some girl: 'Can the two of us go out on a date?' To represent this reading we have to allow for the pronoun *they* to be bound simultaneously by *every boy* and *some girl*. An LF that expresses this reading is given in (55), assuming a rule like (56) to replace (14):

(55) every boy [β_1 has asked some girl β_2 [if they$_{1,2}$ could go on out on a date]]

(56) $[\![\text{they}_{i,j,\ldots n}]\!]^g$ = the smallest group $X \in D_e$ s.t. $g(i), g(j), \ldots g(n)$ are all (possibly improper) parts of X

At an extreme, (56) allows for a pronoun to bear a distinct index for every atomic individual that is part of the pronoun's denotation, but nothing requires this; a plural pronoun can also bear a single index, as before, which is then mapped onto a group of arbitrary cardinality, or any combination of 'singular' and 'plural' indices.

4.3 Reciprocal pronouns

A particular exotic subcase of plural pronouns are *reciprocals*. The truth condition for a simple reciprocal sentence are easily stated:

(57) $[\![A \text{ and } B \text{ R-ed each other}]\!]$ = 1 iff $[\![R]\!]$ ($[\![A]\!]$) ($[\![B]\!]$) and $[\![R]\!]$ ($[\![B]\!]$)($[\![A]\!]$)

But what meaning to assign to *each other* to derive (57)? And how does this recipe generalize to cases of more than two? Starting with the second question, *strong reciprocity* seems an appropriate generalization in cases such as (58) ($\sqsubseteq_A$ stands for 'be an atomic part of'; recall that we treat pluralities as individuals, not sets of individuals):

(58) The suspects knew each other.
 'each suspect knows all the other suspects, and is known by them'
 $\forall x, y \sqsubseteq_A X[x \neq y \rightarrow R(y)(x)]$ (strong reciprocity)

But weaker notions such as *weak reciprocity* and *chaining* seem to be required in other instances:

(59) The contestants killed each other.
 'each killed one of the others, and was killed by one of them'
 $\forall x \sqsubseteq_A X, \exists y, z \sqsubseteq_A X[y, z \neq x \wedge R(y)(x) \wedge R(x)(z)]$ (weak reciprocity)

(60) The children followed each other into the room.
 'each child follows, or is followed by, one of the other children'
 $\forall x \sqsubseteq_A X, \exists y \sqsubseteq_A X[y \neq x \wedge [R(y)(x) \vee R(x)(y)]]$ (chaining)

While these notions of reciprocity become successively weaker, it seems problematic to just find the weakest meaning and assume that to be the meaning of reciprocal sentences. For example, (58) seems intuitively false if among suspects A–D, A knows B, B knows C, C knows D, but no one else knows anyone (a possible chaining scenario); similarly if A and B know each other, as do C and D, and no one else (a weak reciprocity scenario). This leads Dalrymple et al. (1998) to the *Strongest Meaning Hypothesis*: Each reciprocal sentence has to be interpreted using the strongest reciprocal relation applicable in its case. What constitutes the set of applicable relations, though, is unclear. Why, for example, do we judge *These two women gave birth to each other* to be false if said of a mother-daughter pair, although they meet chaining, and biologically, no stronger reciprocal relation could possibly hold between them?

Turning to the first question above, the easiest way to think of the meaning of the reciprocal itself is as a function that maps a relation onto a property of (plural) individuals. This is illustrated (for the case of strong reciprocity) in (61):

(61) ⟦R each other⟧ = $\lambda X_e.\forall x, y \sqsubseteq_A X[x \neq y \rightarrow R(y)(x)]$

However, *each other* does not always apply locally to a relation, as for example if it occurs within a complex DP, (62a), or with a long-distance antecedent as in (62b):

(62) a. They read each other's biographies.
b. Fred and Sarah are convinced that they can beat each other.

(One may think that the antecedent for *each other* in (62b) should be *they* rather than *Fred and Sarah*, but inspection of the truth conditions shows that *they* denotes an atomic individual here, hence cannot antecede *each other*; see Heim, Lasnik & May 1991)

The predicates corresponding to R in (61) in these cases are (63a, b), respectively:

(63) a. λxλy.y read x's bibliography
b. λxλy.y is convinced that y can beat x

But neither of these correspond to a constituent that would likely be the sister of *each other*.

If we instead try to interpret *each other* as a term, we have to give it two indices, which are bound to the plural antecedent (the *range*) and the distributed part of it (the *contrast*), respectively:

(64) $[\![$each other$_{r,c}]\!]^g$ = the biggest plurality X such that X is a part of $g(r)$ and $g(c)$ is not a part of X; defined only if $g(c)$ is a part of $g(r)$

For any assignment g, any two pluralities $X = g(r)$ and $Y = g(c)$, each other$_{r,c}$, if defined, will denote X-Y, i.e. those X that are not part of Y. (65) gives representative LFs for some reciprocal sentences, using a silent *each*, which we call DIST, defined in (66):

(65) a. the suspects β_1 [DIST [β_2 [knew each other$_{1,2}$]]]
b. Fred and Sarah β_1 [DIST[β_2 [are convinced that they$_2$ can beat each other$_{1,2}$]]]

(66) $[\![$DIST$]\!] = \lambda P_{e,t}.\lambda X_e.\forall x \sqsubseteq_A X.P(x)$

If we want to capture weaker reciprocities along these lines, further refinements are required, see e.g. Schwarzschild (1996).

5 Binding theory

As mentioned at the beginning of this article, pronouns come in different varieties such as reflexive and non-reflexive. Usually these morphological classes are subject to *binding conditions*, often jointly referred to as *binding theory*; that is, for each morphological class, the grammar may specify whether its elements have to be be bound, or must not be bound, and if so, within which structural domain. It is important to note that in this more syntactic context, 'binding' and 'bound' are used indiscriminately to mean 'coreferring' or 'semantically bound' (in the sense of sections 2. and 3. above).

The literature both on the finer points of the English system as well as on binding systems crosslinguistically is huge (see Dalrymple 1993, Koster & Reuland 1992, Huang 2000, and Büring 2005a for overviews and references). Most of these proposals use syntactic conditions that filter out certain configuration of indices on pronouns, e.g. the classical 'ABC' of binding in Chomsky (1981), roughly paraphrased in (67) (where 'bound' means 'be coindexed with a c-commanding DP'):

(67) Binding Conditions A–C
 a. A reflexive or reciprocal pronoun ('anaphor') must be bound within the smallest clause containing it.
 b. A non-reflexive pronoun ('pronominal') must not be bound within the smallest clause containing it.
 c. A non-pronominal DP must not be bound at all.

Some languages don't have separate reflexive and non-reflexive pronouns, while many others have more pronoun classes than just these two, and the binding conditions associated with these can be considerably more complex. In particular, one and the same class can have more than one condition (for example that it be free within one domain, but bound within the other), and members of two or more classes can have overlapping distribution.

Apart from purely syntactic approaches to binding theory, which won't be discussed any further here, there are attempts to derive binding conditions semantically. A common idea is that reflexive pronouns are simply functions from transitive relations to intransitives, as in (68):

(68) 〚herself〛 = $\lambda R_{e,et}.\lambda x.R(x)(x)$, defined only if x is female

Without further ado (and in particular without the use of indices), this lexical entry derives that reflexives must be locally 'bound' by the next higher co-argument. By the same token, however, it requires modification in all cases where the antecedent to the reflexive can be any one of its higher coarguments, or not a coargument at all:

(69) a. Gilbert$_1$ told Spencer$_2$ about himself$_{1/2}$.
 b. Fritz lässt mich für sich arbeiten. (German)
 F. lets me for SELF work
 'Fritz has me work for him.' (lit. 'for himself')

The ban on locally bound non-reflexive pronouns can be explained by a preference principle that forces the use of the reflexive wherever possible. Alternatively, Jacobson (2007) proposes that predicates are irreflexivized whenever they combine with a pronoun. The irreflexivizing operation is given in (70):

(70) for any two-place predicate R, IRR(R) $=_{def}$ $\lambda x.\lambda y.R(x)(y)$, defined only if $x \neq y$

By assumption, the syntactic category of pronouns is different from that of regular NPs, e.g. NP[p] instead of NP. For a predicate to syntactically combine with a pronoun, it has to undergo a rule that shifts it from, say, category (S\NP)/NP to (S\NP)/NP[p]; the semantics of that rule in turn applies IRR to the meaning of the predicate. Hence, coreference between the two arguments results in presupposition failure. Note that this result holds regardless of whether the subject actually binds the object or just corefers with it, preempting any need to force binding over coreference in order to enforce binding conditions (as per section 3.3. above).

A different semantic implementation of binding theory is presented in Schlenker (2005) (see also Dekker 1994 for a similar proposal). Schlenker assumes that assignment functions, conceived of as sequences of individuals, are subject to 'Non-Redundancy': An individual can occur at most once in a given sequence. In interpreting a sentence top down, sequences grow longer; in particular, each referring DP adds its referent r to the end of the sequence s (symbolized as $s + r$):

(71) If α is a non-pronominal referential DP, $[\![\alpha\,\beta]\!]^s =_{def} [\![\beta]\!]^{s+[\![\alpha]\!]^s}$
 e.g. $[\![John\,\beta]\!]^s = [\![\beta]\!]^{s+[\![John]\!]^s} = [\![\beta]\!]^{s+John}$

(71), combined with Non-Redundancy yields binding condition C: If α is c-commanded by a coreferential DP, the referent r of DP has been added to the sequence s under which α is interpreted; by (71), α appends r to s, yielding a new sequence s' in which r occurs twice, in violation of non-redundancy.

Pronouns, on the other hand, serve exactly the purpose of retrieving a pre-existing referent from a sequence s. Bound pronouns are given negative indices $-n$, which instruct the interpretation procedure to remove the n-th element counting from the end of the current sequence and appending it to the end of the sequence. This is illustrated for one particular sequence s in (72) (# marks the original position of that element, for reasons that need not concern us yet):

(72) $[\![\text{she}_{-2}\beta]\!]^{Bob+Sally+Sue+Tom} = [\![\beta]\!]^{Bob+Sally+\#+Tom+Sue}$

It follows that negatively indexed pronouns are the only way to get coreference with a c-commanding expressions. It follows, too, that there can be no such thing as a pronoun that is coreferent with, rather than bound by, a c-commanding DP; in other words, the preference for binding over coreference, expressed in (42) above, is derived.

Note that neither (71) nor (72) seem to use the interpretation of the DP (α/ John/she) other than appending its referent to the sequence under which its sister is interpreted. This is so because any n-place predicate R is automatically interpreted relative to the n last elements of the sequence (which, by (71) are the referents of the last n DPs that minimally c-command R), as illustrated in (73) (where for any n-place predicate p, p' stands for the extension of α, i.e. a set of n-tuples):

(73) a. $[\![\text{run}]\!]^{Bob+Sally+Sue+Tom} = 1$ iff run'(Tom)=1
 b. $[\![\text{see}]\!]^{Bob+Sally+Sue+Tom} = 1$ iff see'(Sue, Tom)=1

(74) a. $[\![\text{Steve ran}]\!]^{Bob+Sally} = [\![\text{ran}]\!]^{Bob+Sally+[\![Steve]\!]^{Bob+Sally}}$
 $= [\![\text{ran}]\!]^{Bob+Sally+Steve}$
 $=$ ran'(Steve)
 b. (Steve told Mary that) $[\![\text{he}_{-2} \text{ran}]\!]^{Steve+Mary}$
 $= [\![\text{ran}]\!]^{\#+Mary+Steve} =$ ran' (Steve)

Since, say, two-place predicates take the last two elements of the evaluation sequence as their arguments, and sequences are subject to non-redundancy, it is impossible to express reflexive statements given what we've said so far (note that e.g. *John praised him$_{-1}$* would yield the interpretation praised'(#,John), which by assumption is undefined); we thus have an overly strongly 'generalized' version of binding condition B: no predicate can have two identical arguments. Essentially like in the approaches to reflexives discussed above, then, reflexive pronouns serve to reflexivize a predicate by reducing its arity, sketched in (75):

(75) $[\![\text{John recommended himself}]\!] = [\![\text{recommended himself}]\!]^{John}$
 $=$ SELF(recommended')(John) = recommended'(John)(John)

With these sketchy and exemplary illustrations we end our overview of semantic approaches to binding theory. Note that these approaches to conditions A and B all crucially equate the domain in question with some variant of the coargument domain of a given predicate (as do several more syntactic approaches such as Pollard & Sag 1992 and Reinhart & Reuland 1993). It seems fair to say, then, that the more intricate facts about the reflexive/non-reflexive distribution in less canonical argument positions such as inside DPs, in clause-sharing constructions such as ECM, and as complements to prepositions, in English and cross-linguistically, pose the strongest challenge to a comprehensive development of such semantic approaches.

6 References

Bach, Kent 1992. Intentions and demonstrations. *Analysis* 52, 140–146.
Berman, Stephen R. 1987. Situation-based semantics for adverbs of quantification. In: A. Vainikka (ed.). *University of Massachusetts Occasional Papers, vol. 12*. Amherst, MA: University of Massachusetts, 46–68.
Büring, Daniel 2004. Crossover situations. *Natural Language Semantics* 12, 23–62.
Büring, Daniel 2005a. *Binding Theory*. Cambridge: Cambridge University Press.
Büring, Daniel 2005b. Bound to bind. *Linguistic Inquiry* 36, 259–274.
Chomsky, Noam 1981. *Lectures on Government and Binding*. Dordrecht: Foris.
Cooper, Robin 1979. The interpretation of pronouns. In: F. Heny & H. S. Schnelle (eds.). *Syntax and Semantics 10*. New York: Academic Press, 61–92.
Dalrymple, Mary 1993. *The Syntax of Anaphoric Binding*. Stanford, CA: CSLI Publications.
Dalrymple, Mary, Makoto Kanazawa, Yookyung Kim, Sam Machombo & Stanley Peters 1998. Reciprocal expressions and the concept of reciprocity. *Linguistics & Philosophy* 21, 159–210.
Dekker, Paul 1994. Predicate logic with anaphora (seven inch version). In: L. Santelmann & M. Harvey (eds.). *Proceedings of Semantics and Linguistic Theory (= SALT) IV*. Ithaca, NY: Cornell University, 79–95.
Dixon, Robert M. 1988. *A Grammar of Boumaa Fijian*. Chicago, IL: The University of Chicago Press.
Egli, Urs 1983. The Stoic theory of arguments. In: R. Bäuerle, Ch. Schwarze & A. von Stechow (eds.). *Meaning, Use and the Interpretation of Language*. Berlin: de Gruyter, 79–96.
Elbourne, Paul 2001. E-type anaphora as NP-deletion. *Natural Language Semantics* 9, 241–288.
Elbourne, Paul 2005. *Situations and Individuals*. Cambridge, MA: The MIT Press.
Elbourne, Paul 2008. Demonstratives as individual concepts. *Linguistics & Philosophy* 31, 409–466.
Evans, Gareth 1977. Pronouns, quantifiers, and relative clauses. *The Canadian Journal of Philosophy* 7, 467–536.
Evans, Gareth 1980. Pronouns. *Linguistic Inquiry* 11, 337–362.
Fox, Danny 2000. *Economy and Semantic Interpretation*. Cambridge, MA: The MIT Press.
Geach, Paul 1962. *Reference and Generality*. Ithaka, NY: Cornell University Press.

Haspelmath, Martin 1997. *Indefinite Pronouns*. Oxford: Clarendon Press.
Heim, Irene 1982. *The Semantics of Definite and Indefinite Noun Phrases*. Ph.D. dissertation. University of Massachusetts, Amherst, MA. Reprinted: Ann Arbor, MI: University Microfilms.
Heim, Irene 1990. E-type pronouns and donkey anaphora. *Linguistics & Philosophy* 13, 137–177.
Heim, Irene 1993. *Anaphora and Semantic Interpretation: A Reinterpretation of Reinhart's Approach* (SfS Report 07–93). University of Tübingen. Reprinted in: U. Sauerland & O. Percus (eds.). *The Interpretive Tract* (MIT Working Papers in Linguistics, 25). Cambridge, MA: MIT, 1998, 205–246.
Heim, Irene & Angelika Kratzer 1998. *Semantics in Generative Grammar*. Oxford: Blackwell.
Heim, Irene, Howard Lasnik & Robert May 1991. Reciprocity and plurality. *Linguistic Inquiry* 22, 63–101.
von Heusinger, Klaus 1997. *Salienz und Referenz—Der Epsilonoperator in der Semantik der Nominalphrase und anaphorischer Pronomen*. Berlin: Akademie Verlag.
Higginbotham, James 1983. Logical form, binding, and nominals. *Linguistic Inquiry* 14, 395–420.
Hornstein, Norbert 1995. *Logical Form—From GB to Minimalism*. Oxford: Blackwell.
Huang, Yan 2000. *Anaphora—A Cross-Linguistic Study*. Oxford: Oxford University Press.
Jacobson, Pauline 1999. Towards a variable free semantics. *Linguistics & Philosophy* 22, 117–184.
Jacobson, Pauline 2000. Paycheck pronouns, Bach-Peters sentences, and variable free semantics. *Natural Language Semantics* 8, 77–155.
Jacobson, Pauline 2007. Direct compositionality and variable free semantics: The case of "Principle B" effects. In: C. Barker & P. Jacobson (eds.). *Direct Compositionality*. Oxford: Oxford University Press.
Kadmon, Nirit 1987. *On Unique and Non-unique Reference and Asymmetric Quantification*. Ph.D. dissertation. University of Massachusetts, Amherst, MA.
Kamp, Hans & Uwe Reyle 1993. *From Discourse to Logic*. Dordrecht: Kluwer.
Kaplan, David 1977. Demonstratives. In: J. Almog, J. Perry & H. Wettstein (eds.). *Themes from Kaplan*. Oxford: Oxford University Press, 481–563.
Kaplan, David 1989. Afterthoughts. In: J. Almog, J. Perry & H. Wettstein (eds.). *Themes from Kaplan*. Oxford: Oxford University Press, 565–614.
Karttunen, Lauri 1969. Pronouns and variables. In: R. Binnick et al. (eds.). *Papers from the Fifth Regional Meeting of the Chicago Linguistic Society (= CLS)*. Chicago, IL: Chicago Linguistic Society, 108–116.
King, Jefirey 2001. *Complex Demonstratives: A Quantificational Approach*. Cambridge, MA: The MIT Press.
Koster, Jan & Eric Reuland (eds.) 1992. *Long-Distance Anaphora*. Cambridge: Cambridge University Press.
Lewis, David 1975. Adverbs of quantification. In: E. L. Keenan (ed.). *Formal Semantics of Natural Language*. Cambridge: Cambridge University Press, 3–15.
May, Robert 1988. Bound variable anaphora. In: R. Kempson (ed.). *Mental Representations*. Cambridge: Cambridge University Press, 85–104.
Merchant, Jason 2004. Fragments and ellipsis. *Linguistics & Philosophy* 27, 661–738.
Moltmann, Friederike 2006. Generic one, arbitrary PRO, and the first person. *Natural Language Semantics* 13, 257–281.
Peregrin, Jaroslav & Klaus von Heusinger 2004. Dynamic semantics with choice functions. In: H. Kamp & B. Partee (eds.). *Context Dependence in the Analysis of Linguistic Meaning*. Amsterdam: Elsevier, 309–329.

Pollard, Carl & Ivan Sag 1992. Anaphors in English and the scope of binding theory. *Linguistic Inquiry* 23, 261–303.
Postal, Paul M. 1970. On so-called pronouns in English. In: R. Jacobs & P. Rosenbaum (eds.). *Readings in English Transformational Grammar.* Waltham, MA: Ginn and Company, 56–82.
Reinhart, Tanya 1983. *Anaphora and Semantic Interpretation.* Chicago, IL: The University of Chicago Press.
Reinhart, Tanya 1997. Quantifier scope: How labor is divided between QR and choice functions. *Linguistics & Philosophy* 20, 335–397.
Reinhart, Tanya & Eric Reuland 1993. Reflexivity. *Linguistic Inquiry* 24, 657–720.
Roberts, Craige 2002. Demonstratives as definites. In: K. van Deemter & R. Kibble (eds.). *Information Sharing: Reference and Presupposition in Language Generation and Interpretation.* Stanford, CA: CSLI Publications, 89–196.
Rooth, Mats 1987. Noun phrase interpretation in Montague Grammar, File Change Semantics, and Situation Semantics. In: P. Gärdenfors (ed.). *Generalized Quantifiers: Linguistic and Logical Approaches.* Dordrecht: Reidel, 237–268.
van Rooy, Robert 1997. *Attitudes and Changing Contexts.* Doctoral dissertation. University of Stuttgart.
Rullman, Hotze 2004. First and second person pronouns as bound variables. *Linguistic Inquiry* 35, 159–168.
Schlenker, Philippe 2005. Non-redundancy: Towards a semantic reinterpretation of Binding Theory. *Natural Language Semantics* 13, 1–92.
Schwarzschild, Roger 1996. *Pluralities.* Dordrecht: Kluwer.
Shan, Chung-Chieh & Chris Barker 2006. Explaining crossover and superiority as left-to-right evaluation. *Linguistics & Philosophy* 29, 91–134.
Szabolcsi, Anna 1987. Bound variables in syntax (are there any?). In: J. Groenendijk, M. Stokhof & F. Veltman (eds.). *Proceedings of the 6th Amsterdam Colloquium.* Amsterdam: ILLC, 331–351.
Szabolcsi, Anna 1992. Combinatory grammar and projection from the lexicon. In: I. Sag & A. Szabolcsi (eds.). *Lexical Matters.* Stanford, CA: CSLI Publications, 241–269.
Szabolcsi, Anna 2003. Binding on the fly: Cross-sentential anaphora in variable-free semantics. In: G.-J. Kruijff & R. T. Oehrle (eds.). *Resource Sensitivity in Binding and Anaphora.* Amsterdam: Kluwer, 215–229.
Winter, Yoad 1997. Choice functions and the scopal semantics of indefinites. *Linguistics & Philosophy* 20, 399–467.

Irene Heim
2 Definiteness and indefiniteness

1   What makes definites definite and indefinites indefinite? —— 34
2   Scopal properties of definites and indefinites —— 49
3   References —— 67

Abstract: Our subject matter are the meanings of the definite and indefinite articles, or of the abstract features that these morphemes realize. The main goal of the article is to elucidate and test the best known approach to the definite-indefinite contrast in contemporary formal semantics: a Fregean semantics for definites and an existential (Russellian) semantics of indefinites. This approach posits differences between definites and indefinites along three dimensions: semantic type, uniqueness, and presuppositionality. We review some successful predictions that this familiar picture makes in combination with plausible accounts of various independent semantic and pragmatic mechanisms, such as grammatical number, covert domain restriction, scalar implicature, genericity operators, binding of situation variables, and charitable communication. We will also encounter some reasons to entertain departures from the standard semantics, for example, reasons to loosen the connection of presuppositionality with definiteness, and reasons to distinguish indefinites from the existential quantification that accompanies them.

The study of definiteness begins with the working hypothesis that the definite and indefinite articles in English correspond transparently to two primitive building blocks of linguistic structure with fixed and distinct meanings. As the inquiry proceeds, of course, we are prepared to find a less than perfect match between article morphology and the underlying semantic features that it realizes. But we will start with minimal pairs containing *the* and *a* to get off the ground. In the first section of the article, we will mostly examine semantic and pragmatic contrasts between simple sentences with definites and indefinites. The second section turns to scopal properties of definites and indefinites in complex sentences, with an eye to learning more about their internal semantics from their compositional interactions. The main goal of the article is to explain, motivate, and push the limits of a classical analysis, based on Frege and Russell with conservative extensions. Discussion will touch on guiding

Irene Heim, Cambridge, MA, United States

ideas behind some alternative approaches, but for reasons of space, these cannot be reviewed explicitly. For complementary or competing viewpoints, see especially articles 4 [Semantics: Foundations, History and Methods] (Abbott) *Reference*, 3 [this volume] (von Heusinger) *Specificity*, 5 [this volume] (Dayal) *Bare noun phrases*, 8 [this volume] (Carlson) *Genericity*, and 14 [Semantics: Sentence and Information Structure] (Geurts) *Accessibility and anaphora*.

1 What makes definites definite and indefinites indefinite?

1.1 Russell and Frege

Russell (1905) argued that *the book* and *a book* do not refer to individuals any more than *every book* or *no book*. All such phrases express quantificational statements. Implemented in modern compositional semantics, this means that the definite and indefinite articles, along with quantifiers such as *every* and *no*, denote functions of type <et,<et,t>>.

(1) a. $[\![the]\!] = \lambda P.\ \lambda Q.\ \exists x[\forall y[P(y) \leftrightarrow x = y]\ \&\ Q(x)]$
　　b. $[\![a]\!] = \lambda P.\ \lambda Q.\ \exists x[P(x)\ \&\ Q(x)]$

Simple clauses with definite and indefinite phrases thus have the following truth conditions. (2a) is true if there is exactly one book and this book arrived; it is false otherwise (if there are no books or multiple books or if the unique book there is did not arrive). (2b) is true if there is at least one book that arrived, and false otherwise (if no book arrived).

(2) a. The book arrived.
　　b. A book arrived.

For Russell, the difference between definites and indefinites is a difference in truth conditions. Substituting *the* for *a* leads to a stronger assertion. (2a) entails (2b), but not vice versa. (2a) makes the additional claim that there is only one book.

Frege (1892) and Strawson (1950) argued that what the definite expresses over and above the indefinite is not so much an additional assertion but a presupposition. A speaker who asserts (2a) presupposes there to be a unique book. If there is not, the question of whether he speaks truly or falsely is beside the point.

One can implement this by having *the* denote a partial function (notation from Heim & Kratzer 1998).

(3) ⟦*the*⟧ = λP: ∃x∀y[P(y) ↔ x = y]. λQ. ∃x[P(x) & Q(x)]

Given (3), (2a) is true if there is exactly one book and it arrived, false if there is exactly one book and it didn't arrive, and without truth value otherwise (if there are no or multiple books).

Evidence for the presuppositional status of existence and uniqueness comes from the usual tests for presupposition, particularly their characteristic patterns of projection from embedded contexts (cf. article 14 [Semantics: Interfaces] (Beaver & Geurts) *Presupposition*). To the extent that lexically triggered presuppositions are thought to exist at all, the definite article is uncontroversially a prime candidate. I will assume without discussion that (3) is the more accurate of the two entries for *the* we have seen so far.

(1a), (1b) and (3) all give *a* and *the* the semantic type of a quantificational determiner, as is done wherever determiner phrases (DPs) are treated uniformly as generalized quantifiers. But only for the indefinite and the Russellian definite is this high type required. The Fregean truth conditions can be captured also if definite DPs denote entities of type e. (3) can be replaced by (4), which is more faithful to Frege.

(4) ⟦*the*⟧ = λP: ∃x∀y[P(y) ↔ x = y]. ιx. P(x)

("ιx." abbreviates "the unique x such that".) Fregean definites then differ from indefinites in semantic type as well as in the fact that only they carry presuppositions.

1.2 Extension to plurals and mass nouns

The Russellian and Fregean analyses cover only DPs with singular count nouns. These happen to be the only nouns that cooccur with *a*, but *the* combines with plural and mass nouns too. Consider *the books* or *the ink*. Do these contain a homophonous determiner, or can a uniform entry for *the* work in tandem with suitable treatments of number and the count/mass distinction? The latter is surely preferable. Mass and plural nouns have extensions that are cumulative (closed under sum formation, cf. article 7 [Semantics: Noun Phrases and Verb Phrases] (Lasersohn) *Mass nouns and plurals*). Combined with our semantics for *the* in (4), this leads to inadequate predictions. If there are three books, there exist multiple pluralities of books and (5) comes out truth-value-less.

(5) The books arrived.

To remedy this, Sharvy (1980) proposed to amend the classical semantics for *the* to one which invokes maximality. This can be done by rewriting (4) as (6a).

(6) a. $[\![the]\!] = \lambda P: \exists x \forall y [\text{MAX}(P)(y) \leftrightarrow x = y].\ \iota x.\text{MAX}(P)(x)$
    b. $\text{MAX}(P) := \lambda x.\ P(x)\ \&\ \neg \exists y[P(y)\ \&\ x < y]$

< stands for the proper-part relation between portions of stuff or pluralities. To illustrate, let there be three books, a, b, and c. $[\![books]\!]$, the extension of the pluralized noun, then contains the pluralities a+b, b+c, a+c, a+b+c (and possibly the atoms a, b, c). Given the proper-part relations between these elements, $\text{MAX}([\![books]\!])$ contains only a+b+c. So $\text{MAX}([\![book]\!])$ is a singleton, as required by the presupposition built into (6a), and *the books* denotes a+b+c. In the same situation, $[\![book]\!]$, the singular noun's extension, contains only the atoms a, b, c. None of these is a proper part of another, so $\text{MAX}([\![book]\!]) = [\![book]\!]$ and as a non-singleton fails the presupposition of (6a).

On this treatment, the definite article still introduces presuppositions of existence and uniqueness, but not about the whole extension of the noun but about the set of its maximal elements. In the extension of a singular count noun, every element is a maximal element, hence the semantics of singular count definites is unaffected by the revision. The extensions of plural count nouns and mass nouns, being closed under sums, always have a unique maximal element unless they are empty. So the presuppositions of plural or mass definites boil down to mere existence presuppositions.

Since the indefinite article *a* is limited to count singular nouns in the first place, the issue of generalizing to plural and mass does not present itself in the same way. However, if we are interested in definiteness and indefiniteness, not just in the overt articles, we should look for counterparts of *a book* in the plural and mass domain. Plausibly these are bare plurals and mass nouns.

(7) Books arrived.

Given the semantics for mass and plural nouns we assumed above in conjunction with (6), we might as well redeploy our entry (1b) as an entry for an abstract indefinite determiner, which happens to be realized as phonetically null before mass and plural nouns and as *a(n)* before singular count nouns.

(8) a. $[\![-\text{DEF}]\!] = \lambda P.\ \lambda Q.\ \exists x[P(x)\ \&\ Q(x)]$
    b. $[_D -\text{DEF}] \to a(n)/\ \_\_[_N \text{COUNT SG}],\ [_D -\text{DEF}] \to \emptyset$ elsewhere

This predicts the desired truth conditions for (7): some plurality of books arrived.

But is *a* really just the allomorph of indefiniteness before singular count nouns? Diachronically, *a* is a reduced form of the numeral *one*, and the fact that *one* combines with count singulars and not plurals or mass nouns lends itself to an explanation that is semantic rather than morphological. Perhaps *a* still is a numeral too. In that case, it ought to share the adjectival semantics of *two* etc. and combine with the noun to form another predicate. The morphology of −DEF then is simple: it is null everywhere. But we lose the prediction that an article is obligatory with singular count nouns. A bare noun should be able to express the indefinite meaning just as well.

Our foray into plurals and mass nouns has led to a revised meaning for definiteness (based on maximality) and a loosening of the correspondence between indefiniteness and article morphology. The result can be summed up in the entries in (9), to be accompanied with suitable morphological rules to spell out these abstract features. Even +DEF is not always *the*, if we accept a common analysis of possessive constructions like *John's book*.

(9)   a. ⟦+DEF⟧ = λP: ∃x∀y[MAX(P)(y) ↔ x = y]. ιx.MAX(P)(x)
     b. ⟦−DEF⟧ = λP. λQ. ∃x[P(x) & Q(x)]

We have not strayed far from the classical analysis designed for count singulars. Indefiniteness still expresses existential quantification and indefinite DPs are generalized quantifiers. Definiteness still carries a presupposition of existence and uniqueness, and definite DPs denote entities of type e. Definites still asymmetrically entail their indefinite counterparts.

1.3 Presuppositionality

Our Fregean analysis endows definites with presuppositions, while indefinites have none. This is one of the semantic differences between them. But discussions starting with Strawson's work in the 1950s and taken up by linguists since the 1980s have called the simple correlation between definiteness and presuppositionality into question. Diesing (1992) (building on Milsark 1977) argues that indefinites have both presupposing and non-presupposing readings, disambiguated by their location in syntactic structure. She proposes in a nutshell that indefinites, with the exception of bare plurals and mass nouns, are ambiguous and have a presuppositional reading of the sort exemplified in (10).

(10) ⟦a_{pres}⟧ = λP: ∃x P(x). λQ. ∃x[P(x) & Q(x)]

This coexists with another, non-presupposing, reading which yields the standard interpretation we assumed so far. Many surface occurrences of indefinites are ambiguous, but indefinites that are outside of VP at LF are obligatorily presupposing. This includes subjects of individual-level predicates and scrambled DPs in German. We must look at such disambiguating contexts to detect the presupposing readings. Relevant examples are not easy to construct, since a situation which verifies the presupposing reading always verifies the non-presupposing one as well. The most convincing cases were constructed by von Fintel (1998).

(11) I don't know if he sent us any papers with mistakes in them. But if
  a. ?? a mistake in this paper is serious, it has to be sent back.
  b. there is a serious mistake in this paper, it has to be sent back.

The oddity of (11a) is predicted if *serious*, an individual-level predicate, forces a presupposing reading of its subject. The presupposition, which projects from the *if*-clause, clashes with the speaker's stated agnosticism.

If indefinites can be presupposing or not, the dissociation of presuppositionality from definiteness might be pushed even further. Suppose both indefinites and definites came in two versions, and for both of them, presupposing readings were forced in the same environments.

(12) a. $[\![a_{pres}]\!] = \lambda P: \exists x\, P(x).\, \lambda Q.\, \exists x[P(x) \& Q(x)]$
  $[\![a]\!] = \lambda P.\, \lambda Q.\, \exists x[P(x) \& Q(x)]$

  b. $[\![the_{pres}]\!] = \lambda P: \exists x \forall y[\text{MAX}(P)(y) \leftrightarrow x = y].$
  $\lambda Q.\, \exists x[\forall y[\text{MAX}(P)(y) \leftrightarrow x = y] \& Q(x)]]$
  $[\![the]\!] = \lambda P.\, \lambda Q.\, \exists x[\forall y[\text{MAX}(P)(y) \leftrightarrow x = y] \& Q(x)]]$

This picture has some *prima facie* support from observations by Strawson (1954) about truth-value judgments on examples (13a,b).

(13) a. The king of France is wise.
  b. Our exhibition was visited by the king of France.

There being no king of France, people are more inclined to judge (13b) plainly false while conceding that (13a) is in some sense neither true nor false. This could be a contrast on a par with (11a,b) and attributable to an alternation of the two readings of *the* in (12b). However, von Fintel (2004) argues that truth-value judgments do not correlate so cleanly with presuppositionality and that both sentences in (13) carry presuppositions, despite the difference between speakers' willingness to judge them false.

1.4 Predicative uses and semantic type

On one analysis of predicate nominals, the noun *cat* in (14) is predicated directly of the subject, and copula as well as determiner are semantically vacuous.

(14) Toña is a cat.

I.e., the logical form (LF) of (14) contains no piece with the meaning of *a* in (1b) or −DEF in (9b). On another analysis due to Montague (1973), *be* denotes identity (λx.λy. x = y) and the postcopular indefinite has its standard existential semantics, scoping over the verb like quantificational objects in any transitive sentence. Since $\exists x[C(x) \& x = a]$ is equivalent to $C(a)$, the two analyses capture the same truth conditions.

Given the success of the second analysis, why would one posit two readings for indefinites, one existential and the other predicative? The identity analysis of *be* has some weaknesses, for instance its failure to predict constraints on possible predicate nominals (**John is every student, *There is a cat that Antonia is*). Also, there is a wider range of predicative constructions to consider, involving verbs such as *become* and *remain*, which defy an analysis as relations between individuals. It is widely held therefore that these verbs, and the plain copula as well, select for properties, and that indefinites can supply this type of meaning.

What about definites? These too occur after copulas and the wider range of relevant verbs.

(15) a. Toña is the boss.
      b. Toña became the boss.

If *be* and *become* select properties, how can a definite satisfy this demand? *the* can't just be vacuous, since the meaning is clearly not the same as with *a*. There is an inference of uniqueness, evidently contributed by *the*. If a definite can denote a property, then, it is not just the property expressed by its NP. Partee (1986) posits a covert type-shifting operator that constructs sets from individuals, or (for (15b)) properties from individual concepts.

(16) a. extensional IDENT: $\lambda x_e.\, \lambda y_e.\, x = y$
      b. intensional IDENT: $\lambda x_{\langle s,e \rangle}.\, \lambda t.\, \lambda y_e.\, x(t) = y$

If IDENT is freely generated where needed, it can combine with definites after *be* and *become* and deliver the needed property. There is a danger of overgeneration: if traces of QR and wh-movement can be shifted to properties also, this is no better than Montague's approach.

A more unconventional response (Graff 2001) reanalyzes *the* as a predicate modifier.

(17) a. plain version:
$[\![+\text{DEF}]\!] = \lambda P. \lambda x. \forall y[P(y) \leftrightarrow x = y]$

b. presupposing version:
$[\![+\text{DEF}_{pres}]\!] = \lambda P: \exists z. \forall y[P(y) \leftrightarrow z = y]. \lambda x. P(x)$

With the b-version, (15a,b) get the same interpretation as through type-shifting by IDENT: existence and uniqueness of a boss are presupposed. With the variant in (17a), these are merely asserted. The data bearing on the choice between the two variants are hard to assess. Whichever we adopt, how should we view the relation between the predicative definites that are created by this new entry and the definites in argument positions that we analyzed before? We could posit an ambiguity, analogous to the existential-vacuous ambiguity in indefinites. Or we could say that the new entry is the only meaning for +DEF and both definites and indefinites in argument positions combine with a silent existential quantifier (now no longer associated with indefiniteness). If we were to aim for a Russellian meaning for definites, this would be straightforward: the existential determiner that was our original meaning for *a* combines with (17a) to yield just that meaning. If we aim for a Fregean meaning with presuppositions, things are trickier. Combining the plain existential determiner with (17b) might work if we have the right rule for presupposition projection through existential quantifiers.

1.5 Domain restriction

Definites sometimes refer to entities that are literally the unique existing instances of their restrictors (*the current president of the USA*, *the tallest mountain in Europe*, *my mother*), but more often than not, uniqueness obtains at best in a domain of contextually relevant entities that is narrower than what a speaker assumes to exist. Philosophers call this the problem of "incomplete descriptions". We routinely speak of *feeding the cat* even though we countenance many cats. (I illustrate with singular count nouns, but the problem generalizes to plurals and mass nouns: *feeding the cats* rarely means all the cats in the world.) How do we do justice to this fact? Does it undermine uniqueness-based accounts of definiteness?

The ubiquity of pragmatic domain restriction for natural language quantifiers is well known. Typical felicitous uses of *Every child got a present* or *No child complained* do not make claims about all the children in the world. As Neale (1990) argues, "incompleteness" is not a special property of definites. Suppose any DP can contain a covert predicate which in the semantic computation conjoins with the overt NP. If such a covert restrictor in *the cat* denotes the set of things in our house, then the uniqueness presupposition will be that there is exactly one cat in our house. Or it could denote the set of things we have talked about recently, in which case *the cat* will presuppose that only one cat was recently mentioned. In this way, we capture as a special case the "anaphoric" uses of definites. The covert restrictor may happen to pick out the set of entities mentioned in the previous sentence or some even smaller stretch of previously processed text. Hawkins's (1978) "associative anaphoric" uses are covered as well. The covert restrictor in (18) may pick out the parts of the watch that is responsible for the truth of the first sentence. Among those there is only one battery.

(18) I found a watch under the tent. It was fine except for the battery.

This approach pursues the appealing idea that there is nothing special about *the* compared to other determiners. For all we know, any determiner may be construed with a covert restrictor in addition to its overt one and thus apply to a narrowed set of contextually relevant entities. We may not detect this as easily with some determiners as with others. *the*, *every*, and *no* are not upward monotone, so covert restrictors weaken the presupposition or assertion, giving an otherwise truth-value-less or false claim a chance to be felicitous and true. *the* and *every* also are not symmetrical, so we know for sure that the implicit narrowing is on the restrictor rather than the nuclear scope. Existential determiners, by contrast, are upward monotone and symmetrical. The claim that results from positing a covert restrictor thus always entails the claim without it, and we lack direct evidence for its presence from judgments of truth. Even consulting intuitions about falsity, we can't tell which of the determiner's two arguments is covertly restricted. Although we perceive (19) to make a stronger claim than it would without contextual restriction, the implicit restriction might be in the VP.

(19) An indicator light is broken.

But the evidence is at least consistent with free availability of covert restrictors for all determiners, and so nothing special should have to be said about *the*.

Supplemented by a nimble pragmatic mechanism of inferring covert restrictors from contextual clues, the classical uniqueness/maximality-based semantics for definites becomes virtually indistinguishable from an alternative due to Lewis (1973) and developed further by von Heusinger (1997) and others. On Lewis's "non-monotonic" semantics, *the P* denotes not the unique but the most salient element of *P*. He motivates this proposal with examples like (20).

(20) The pig is grunting, but the pig with floppy ears is not grunting.

On a simple-minded uniqueness-analysis of definites, any possible scenario that supports the presupposition of (20) should guarantee its falsity. Lewis's analysis allows (20) to be true in a universe with multiple pigs, as long as one pig is the most salient at the beginning of the utterance. However, once we acknowledge that each DP can come with its own covert restrictor, examples like (20) are no longer problematic for a uniqueness-based analysis. And as Westerstahl (1984) observed, cases analogous to (20) are also found with determiners other than *the*. Future research may still uncover subtle but systematic differences between covert domain restriction for run-of-the-mill quantifiers and the mechanisms which disambiguate "incomplete" definite descriptions. (See Schlenker 2004 for a promising attempt.) For the time being, it is reasonable to hold out for the null hypothesis that there is no special connection between covert domain restriction and definiteness.

1.6 Definite descriptions and pronouns

The Fregean approach to *the* yields denotations of type e, thus putting definite descriptions in a class with other individual-denoting DPs: complex and simple demonstratives (*that cat*, *this*), personal pronouns (*she*), and proper names. The various members of this class share at least superficial family resemblances in their semantics, pragmatics, and morphology. Expressions like *the Pacific* feel like proper names dressed as definite descriptions, and run-of-mill names also take definite articles in some languages. Definite articles often are etymologically related to demonstrative determiners, as are third person pronouns. Even first and second person pronouns have determiner-like uses, as in *we linguists*, arguably the form that *the linguists* or *those linguists* takes when the speaker is included in its denotation. Postal (1966) treated English pronouns as determiners with elided restrictors and identified third person pronouns and definite articles as allomorphs of each other. In their meaning and use, pronouns, demonstratives, and many definites have in common that they allow anaphoric uses along with deictic ones and that their reference is heavily dependent on context. When the spotlight is on such similarities, classical treatments of pronouns as variables and of names and demonstratives as directly referential look disturbingly dissimilar from the standard semantics for definites. We will not talk here about either names or demonstratives (see e.g. Elbourne 2005, Roberts 2002 for recent attempts at unification with definites). We will limit attention to pronouns and try to get a little clearer on what analogies between definites and pronouns might teach us about definites.

Heim (1982) took the standard analysis of pronouns as variables as the model for an analysis of definites. Definites, like pronouns, carried an index in the syntactic representation. The descriptive content of the NP was treated as adding a presupposition.

(21) $[\![the_i]\!]^g = \lambda P: P(g(i)). g(i)$

This approach predicts that definite descriptions, like pronouns, can be bound variables as well as free. Bound definites do occur, at least in environments where condition C of Binding Theory doesn't interfere.

(22) a. Hemul gave every child a gift that he himself enjoyed more than the child.
b. Every student's advisor makes sure the student's work is cited.

An entry like (21) leaves no need to posit covert restrictors in addition to the overt NP when the latter does not denote a singleton. Context-dependency is already built in with the individual-variable index, and unique satisfaction of the NP is not required. The NP may, of course, happen to be true of exactly one thing. The presupposition contributed by the NP will in many contexts be a crucial clue to the speaker's intentions regarding the variable assignment, and it will be a stronger clue the more informative the NP is. This creates pragmatic pressure in favor of restrictors with smaller extensions; singletons are optimal in this regard, even though there is no semantic presupposition of uniqueness. The analysis of examples like *the tallest mountain in Europe* and *my mother* seems strained in this approach. They are intuitively not context-dependent and the restrictor's uniqueness does all the work. But if presuppositions do play a systematic role as clues to otherwise not manifest contextual parameters, this is not a real objection. A harder problem arises with definites that themselves contain a bound variable (as part of a complex restrictor). Consider the representation and interpretation of the definite *the mouse it caught* in (23).

(23) a. Every cat ate the mouse it caught.
b. $[\![the_1 \text{ mouse } it_2 \text{ caught}]\!]^g = g(1)$ if $g(1)$ is a mouse caught by $g(2)$, undefined otherwise.

Even when *it₂* is bound by *every cat*, the variable *1* is free, and this gives an inadequate prediction of presupposition failure unless every cat caught the same mouse.

This problem may be solvable and worth solving if the definites-as-variables view has genuine advantages over the classical uniqueness-based approach elsewhere. But as we already saw, once we admit covert restrictors of the sort that are needed for quantificational determiners, we have a handle on the context's role in helping fix reference and can also treat anaphoric uses of definites. Even bound-variable uses can be modeled in this way if covert restrictors may be complex and contain bound variables. The covert restrictor on *the child* in (22a) could be of the form *f(x)*, where the variable *x* is bound by the relative pronoun and *f* denotes a function which maps each present to the child who received it. There are questions here about what sorts of complex covert restrictors can be generated and how the function variables in them get their values, but some of this machinery is needed already to capture certain readings of quantificational DPs, as in (24), where the sets of students quantified over vary with the classes.

(24) No class was so bad that
     a. every student flunked.
     b. no student passed.

Furthermore, the study of pronouns has long moved away from the simple view that every pronoun is a free or bound variable (cf. article 1 [this volume] (Büring) *Pronouns*, but see article 14 [Semantics: Sentence and Information Structure] (Geurts) *Accessibility and anaphora* for a dissenting opinion). Paycheck sentences, donkey sentences, and others exhibit what are known as E-Type pronouns: pronouns that are definite descriptions with a covert restrictor (typically containing a bound variable). Exactly which pronouns should receive E-Type analyses is debated, but once at least some do, there already is a unified semantics for (this subset of) pronouns and definites, without any departure from standard uniqueness-based analyses of definites. It is not clear that more of a unification is warranted by the data. A lexical entry for definites-as-variables like (21) then is uncalled for, whether intended as a replacement for or coexisting with the standard entry.

1.7 Competition and pragmatic strengthening

A sentence with a definite entails the corresponding indefinite sentence. The indefinite sentence always is a no less truthful description of a state of affairs that supports the truth of the definite. In practice, however, replacing *the* by *a* often leads to infelicity.

(25) This bowl belongs to
  a. the cat upstairs.
  b. a cat upstairs.

(26) The bicycle was fine after
  a. the seat was replaced.
  b. #a seat was replaced.

(25a,b) are both fine, but if it is already common knowledge that there is a cat, and only one, who lives upstairs, then (25b) is odd and (25a) the only natural choice. In (26), the indefinite b-variant is strange because bicycles have only one seat.

Contrasts like these make it look as if indefinites presuppose the opposite of what definites do, non-uniqueness. If this were the right diagnosis, our entry for −DEF would have to be revised. But a closer look at the data shows otherwise. If (25a) presupposed uniqueness and (25b) non-uniqueness, neither would be appropriate in a conversation where the existence and number of cats upstairs has not yet been established. In fact, (25b) is fine in this case and does not compel the hearer to accommodate that there are multiple cats. The standard non-presupposing entry for *a* makes just the right prediction here. A better way to explain the infelicity judgments, due to Hawkins (1991) and Heim (1991), is to attribute them to implicatures, analogous to the quantity implicatures that cause *some* to be read as *some but not all* and *or* as exclusive. This requires assuming that *a* and *the* form a scale of competing alternatives. The speaker's choice of the logically weaker indefinite triggers an inference that the conditions for the definite are not met, i.e., that he cannot presuppose both existence and uniqueness—be it because he is aware of multiple instances or agnostic about the matter, or because his knowledge on this point is not in the common ground and not accommodable.

The competition between indefinites and definites can interact in complex ways with the pragmatics of domain selection. This creates the superficial impression that indefinites resist anaphoric construals or are governed by a novelty condition. In the minimal pair in (27) (modeled on materials from Maratsos 1976) we understand the definite to pick out the same chair that John sat on, and the indefinite to imply that different chairs were sat on and knocked over.

(27) There were four chairs. John sat down on a chair. Then Mary
  a. knocked the chair over.
  b. knocked a chair over.

According to our current analysis, both the definite and indefinite can be construed with a covert restrictor, which may limit the set of chairs either to the four in the scene or to the single chair involved in the last action described (John sitting down). Only the narrower covert restrictor allows the singular definite to escape presupposition failure, so this is how we interpret (27a). In (27b), with no presuppositions triggered, the narrower covert restrictor, the wider one, or none at all are equally viable choices. But for each choice we must consider the corresponding definite competitor and compute a non-uniqueness implicature. In the case of the narrowest restrictor, this implicature is odd (i.e., there is more than one chair that John just sat down on). Therefore, this choice is discarded and we disambiguate in favor of the wider (or no) covert restrictor.

The competition analysis of the semantics and pragmatics of English indefinites also provides a satisfying answer to a question posed by cross-linguistic variation. Many languages do not have a definite-indefinite distinction but use the same forms to translate an English definite and its indefinite counterpart. Does this mean that DPs in these languages are systematically ambiguous between definite and indefinite meanings? Or do they have some third meaning that is vague between the two? The answer suggested by our analysis of English is that the "ambiguous" DPs in such languages are simply indefinites. They are semantically equivalent to English indefinites, but have a wider range of felicitous uses because they do not compete with definites and therefore do not induce the same implicatures.

1.8 Generic uses, "weak" definites

We have set aside generic uses of definites and indefinites. To be justified in this, we want to be sure that these uses do not contain crucial clues to the real meanings of the articles. Genericity is a huge research area of its own (cf. article 8 [this volume] (Carlson) *Genericity*). Our limited interest here is in assessing whether there is such a thing as a generic reading of an indefinite or definite article, or whether the source of genericity is always in the larger construction to which the definite or indefinite contributes its ordinary meaning.

At least one source of genericity is a silent adverbial-like element at the clause level, in complementary distribution with overt adverbs of quantification like *always* and *usually*. A common approach to this element treats it as a quantifier over situations, GEN, with a near-universal quantificational force that is hard to pin down precisely. Like its overt cousins, GEN may be overtly restricted by an *if* or *when*-clause, but more often than not is restricted covertly, with focus marking in the clause acting as a clue to the intended restrictor and presuppositions playing a role as well. These mechanisms provide for generic readings in many sentences not containing definite or indefinite articles (*John walks to school*). When definite or indefinite DPs happen to be in the scope of GEN, this can lead to the emergence of apparent generic readings for these DPs, expressing generalizations over multiple or arbitrary instances of them.

(28) a. The department chair (always) is appointed by the dean.
b. A blue-eyed bear is (always) intelligent.

Even though the net effect is that these sentences quantify (near-)universally over multiple department chairs and blue-eyed bears, arguably what is really quantified over are situations, and the definites or indefinites are interpreted in their standard Fregean and existential ways, with restrictors whose extensions vary with the situations. E.g., (28a) says that every minimal chair-appointment situation is such that the unique chair in it is appointed by the unique dean in it. (28b) says that every minimal situation which contains a blue-eyed bear extends to a minimal situation in which a blue-eyed bear is intelligent. This line of analysis encourages the hope that generic readings of definites and indefinites are an epiphenomenon. But it faces many challenges, of which I mention only the best-known or most serious.

Consider the distribution of the generic reading of singular (count) definites.

(29) The domestic cat came to Australia in the 18th century.

(29) is an episodic sentence, not about multiple situations in any obvious way, so it cannot be analyzed in terms of GEN. Yet the definite here does not refer to a particular cat. Rather it appears to refer to an abstract individual, the kind or species *felis catus*. If these examples are to involve the regular meaning of the definite article, then it must be combining with a special meaning for the common noun *domestic cat*. Indeed there is separate evidence that common nouns are sometimes reinterpreted as applying to kinds instead of the instances of those kinds they normally apply to.

(30) There are only three great apes.

Hopefully (29) can be unified with cases like (30).

Bare plurals (mass nouns) also have been argued to allow a generic reading that is not reducible to GEN.

(31) Domestic cats evolved from African wildcats.

Again, because the sentence reports a single (if protracted) event, GEN is not applicable. Could the analysis be that some plurality of domestic cats evolved from (some plurality of) African wildcats? But the intended claim is not one that is verified by some subset of the domestic cats in the world (it would be out of place to ask 'which ones are they?'), rather it pertains to all domestic cats. Is the verifying plurality then the maximal plurality of all the cats there are? The existential semantics of indefinites does not disallow this, but we have seen that there normally is a prohibition against using an indefinite when the speaker knows that the maximal individual picked out by a definite would also verify the relevant predicate. In other words, we would expect the speaker's choice of (31) over (32) to give rise to an implicature of non-maximality.

(32) The domestic cats evolved from the African wildcats.

The fact that (31) is fine thus suggests that this is not an existential indefinite. The accepted diagnosis, due to Carlson (1977), is that such uses of bare plurals also refer to kinds (here *felis catus* again), and kinds are what predicates like *evolve* ("kind-level" predicates) select. On this view, at least some bare plurals (and mass nouns) are not actually indefinites at all; they do not contain an existential determiner like our –DEF and thus differ from singular count definites much more fundamentally than merely in number.

(32) raises issues on its own. Why is this not a good paraphrase of (31)? On the received Carlsonian view, the reason is that *evolve* selects for kinds, which are not the same as maximal pluralities. But even if we choose predicates that elsewhere have no difficulty applying to pluralities of ordinary individuals, we still don't get good sentences when the definite plural is not contextually restricted and is intended to pick out the sum of all existing instances of the noun. Unlike (33b), (33a) is not acceptable out of the blue.

(33) a. The cats number over 27 billion.
b. The cats that there are in the world today number over 27 billion.

(33a) requires a discourse context in which a set of cats has been introduced previously. (It may be the set of all cats in existence, but it still must be introduced.) Whatever the reason for this curious restriction on plural definites, it presumably applies to (32) as well, and we may not need an additional ontological distinction between kinds and maximal pluralities.

It is of interest that many languages with a definite-indefinite distinction otherwise similar to English do use definite plurals to express the meaning of (31). This may just mean that there is variation in how languages refer to kinds—some with bare plurals and some with definite plurals. But it may also suggest that kinds and maximal pluralities are the same thing, and it is English that is the odd language out. Unlike e.g. Spanish, it has a special restriction on its definite article, not allowing it to occur with plurals that have no covert restrictor (or relative clause). Instead, +DEF in these environments is spelled out in English as zero. The so-called kind-denoting bare plurals of English then are just unrestricted definites. We have a further dissociation between the abstract determiners +DEF and −DEF and their surface realizations, and the definite-indefinite distinction is systematically neutralized in certain cases in English.

To sum up what this brief excursion into genericity has taught us about the topic of definites and indefinites: First, "generic readings" are a mixed bag, and a good amount of what we find are run-of-the-mill definites and indefinites whose restrictors happen to contain situation variables bound by sentence-level operators. But second, there are at least some English bare plurals which are not plural indefinites, but rather some sort of referring terms—perhaps names of kinds or perhaps plural definite descriptions.

Another set of cases that challenge standard analyses of *the* may or may not belong in this section on genericity.

(34) You should go to the hospital.

(34) can be used to say effectively that you should go to *a* hospital. No specific hospital need be intended as the referent. An addressee who asked "which hospital do you mean?" would have misunderstood. Does this show that uniqueness, even uniqueness relative to covert contextually fixed restrictors, is not part of definiteness after all? Some have thought so (e.g. Ludlow & Segal 1994), but Carlson et al. (2006) argue that this is misguided. They show that, while the phenomenon is too widespread and systematic to classify these constructions simply as idioms, they do have a number of idiom-like properties that make it impossible to generate them in a compositional fashion with an all-purpose meaning for *the*.

2 Scopal properties of definites and indefinites

2.1 Predicted scope interactions with Russellian and Fregean definites

Russell (1905) based much of the case for his analysis on scopal interactions of definite descriptions with other scope-bearing items. His examples included negation, conditionals, and attitude verbs.

(35) a. The king of France is not bald.
　　 b. If Ferdinand is not drowned, then Ferdinand is my only son.
　　 c. George V wished to know whether Scott was the author of Waverley.

In Russell's judgment, (35a) can be read as either true or false (given that France has no king). It is false when read as 'the king of France is non-bald' and true when read as the negation of 'the king of France is bald'. The surface sentence is compatible with two LFs, one in which the subject outscopes negation and one in which negation outscopes the subject.

(36) a. [the king of France] λx. not [x is bald]
　　 b. not [the king of France is bald]

If the definite denoted an individual, (36a) and (36b) would be equivalent, but on Russell's analysis of *the*, they are not: (36a) is false and (36b) is true. (35b), Russell notes, is true if Ferdinand is drowned and the speaker has no other sons. This is correctly predicted on his analysis if the definite description *my only son* scopes within the consequent of a material implication. In the scenario envisaged, both antecedent and consequent come out false. Russell's point about (35a,b) is that sentences containing definites can be true in scenarios in which these definites don't have referents—provided that they have non-maximal scope. (35c), Russell observes, is read as crediting George V with ignorance about a contingent matter, and his analysis captures this meaning by scoping *the author of Waverley* within the embedded clause.

In all three examples (35), the Russellian analysis predicts a truth-conditional difference between an LF where the definite takes minimal scope and an LF where it takes maximal scope. More generally, Russellian definites are not scopally commutative with truth-functional connectives or intensional operators.

This result does not carry over to the Fregean analysis. Under a standard bivalent truth-functional analysis of connectives, the relative scope of negation and material implication with respect to a definite description does not affect truth values. For example, both LFs (36a, b) are truth-value-less when France does not have a king: *not* maps 1 to 0 and 0 to 1, so when φ has no truth value, neither does *not* φ. Fregeans therefore must give a different account of Russell's judgment of ambiguity in (35a), in particular of the true reading (metalinguistic negation, ambiguous connectives in a three-valued logic, local presupposition accommodation—cf. article 14 [Semantics: Interfaces] (Beaver & Geurts) *Presupposition*). The putative narrow-scope definites in conditionals also require a different account in a Fregean theory. I refer to the literature on presupposition projection.

Let us concentrate on the scope of definites with respect to intensional operators, where both Fregeans and Russellian predict truth-conditional effects of structural ambiguity. I will phrase the discussion in terms of the Fregean analysis. Fregean definites denote individuals, but when their NPs express contingent properties, they do so contingently: whether the definite denotes, and what it denotes, depends on the situation of evaluation. This allows the complement clause in Russell's (35c) to express a contingent proposition, provided the definite *the author of Waverley* is interpreted with local scope. If it were scoped over the attitude predicate, we would get a different meaning. It is better to avoid Russell's original example in which the definite is a predicate nominal. Examples like (37) make the point too: we judge these to be ambiguous in a way that is naturally accounted for by allowing either scope relation between the definite and the modal or temporal operator.

(37) a. The man in the purple shirt could have worn a white sweater.
 b. John always argues with the man in the corner.

On one reading of (37a), obtained by scoping the modal widest, we assert the existence of (accessible) worlds in which there is a unique purple-shirted man and he (moreover) wears a white sweater. Another reading, obtained by scoping the definite over the modal, is verified by the accessibility of worlds in which the man who in actual fact wears a purple shirt (instead) wears a white sweater. Similarly, (37b) can mean that John always argues with whoever occupies the corner at the time, or that he always argues with the man who happens to be in the corner right now. This ambiguity is predicted if the definite can scope above or below the adverb *always*. (More precisely, the readings with low scope for the definite presumably carry a presupposition that is filtered through the modal or adverb; e.g., the first reading of (37b) presupposes that every situation in the domain of *always* has a unique man in the corner.)

2.2 "Wide scope" definites

We just saw how certain attested ambiguities can be accounted for by manipulating relative scopes of a definite DP and an intensional operator. But this is not the only way to generate these ambiguities. The apparent scope ambiguity might arise from an ambiguity *within* the definite DP, which might make itself felt even if its scope were fixed below the intensional operator. Such a definite-internal ambiguity could have two possible sources. It could reside in the definite determiner itself, or in the NP that restricts it. Exploring these additional possibilities has led semanticists to entertain three different accounts of the ambiguities we saw in (37), which I will dub the "DP-Scope" account, the "Indexicality" account, and the "Index-Binding" account. I will describe each of them in turn, using example (37b) throughout to exemplify.

I have already sketched the DP-Scope account. It is typically set in a standard intensional semantics, where semantic values are assigned relative to an evaluation index like a world, world-time-pair, or situation, and where a function-denoting expression may apply to the extension or the intension of its argument. Lexical entries for the items in (37b) are in (38). (39) gives the two LFs for the sentence, accompanied by their predicted truth conditions. s_u is the utterance situation.

(38) a. $[\![the\ \alpha]\!]^s = \iota x.\ [\![\alpha]\!]^s(x)$

b. $[\![man\text{-}in\text{-}the\text{-}corner]\!]^s = \lambda x.\ M(x, s)$
   $(M(x, s) := x$ is a man-in-the-corner in $s)$

c. $[\![argue\text{-}with]\!]^s = \lambda x.\ \lambda y.\ A(y, x, s)$
   $(A(y, x, s) := y$ argues with x in $s)$

d. $[\![John]\!]^s = j$

e. $[\![always\ \phi]\!]^s = \forall s' \leq s:\ [\![\phi]\!]^{s'}$

(39) a. always [the mitc λx. John argue-with x]
   $\forall s \leq s_u:\ A(j, \iota x.M(x, s), s)$

b. the mitc λx. always [John argue-with x]
   $\forall s \leq s_u:\ A(j, \iota x.M(x, s_u), s)$

The Indexicality account is embedded in a Kaplanian two-dimensional framework, where semantic values are doubly relativized to two situations, a context and an evaluation point (cf. article 12 [Semantics: Interfaces] (Zimmermann) *Context dependency*). The crucial source of the ambiguity is the coexistence of two homophonous definite articles. Lexical entries, LFs, and interpretations are as follows.

(40) a. $[\![the\ \alpha]\!]^{c,i} = \iota x.\ [\![\alpha]\!]^{c,i}(x)$
   b. $[\![the_{ind}\ \alpha]\!]^{c,i} = \iota x.\ [\![\alpha]\!]^{c,c}(x)$
   c. $[\![man\text{-}in\text{-}the\text{-}corner]\!]^{c,i} = \lambda x.\ M(x, i)$
   d. $[\![argue\text{-}with]\!]^{c,i} = \lambda x.\ \lambda y.\ A(y, x, i)$
   e. $[\![John]\!]^{c,i} = j$
   f. $[\![always\ \phi]\!]^{c,i} = \forall i' \leq i:\ [\![\phi]\!]^{c,i'}$

(41) a. always [the mitc λx. John argue-with x]
∀s ≤ s$_u$: A(j, ιx.M(x, s), s)

b. always [the$_{ind}$ mitc λx. John argue-with x]
∀s ≤ s$_u$: A(j, ιx.M(x, s$_u$), s)

There may or may not be additional LFs in which the definite (with either reading of the determiner) scopes outside of the operator. If so, these get the same meaning as (41b). The crucial point is that two different readings are generated even if the scope of the DP is held constant and narrow. The indexical reading of the determiner provides a separate route to the same interpretation that the DP-Scope account only produces by scoping out the DP.

The Index-Binding account, finally, is at home in an extensional framework, in which the object-language (LF) contains variables for situations and operators that bind them. Semantic values are not relativized to situations either singly or doubly (only to variable assignments).

(42) a. ⟦*the* α⟧ = ιx. ⟦α⟧(x)
b. ⟦*man-in-the-corner*⟧ = λs. λx. M(x, s)
c. ⟦*argue-with*⟧ = λs. λx. λy. A(y, x, s)
d. ⟦*John*⟧ = j
e. ⟦*always* φ⟧ = λs. ∀s' ≤ s: ⟦φ⟧(s')

(43) a. λs. always(s) λs'. [the mitc(s') λx. John argue-with(s') x]
∀s ≤ s$_u$: A(j, ιx.M(x, s), s)
b. λs. always(s) λs'. [the mitc(s) λx. John argue-with(s') x]
∀s ≤ s$_u$: A(j, ιx.M(x, s$_u$), s)

Once again, there may be further LFs with wide scope for the definite, but both desired readings can already be obtained with the definite taking narrow scope. The reason in this case is the freedom we have in choosing situation arguments for the nouns, particularly the noun that restricts the definite article. Assuming that all variables must ultimately be bound in the complete LF, we still have a choice between binding them locally, to the nearest binder they are in the scope of, or non-locally to a more distant binder, such as the operator contributed by the matrix complementizer. The second option yields the reading that the other two accounts attribute either to an indexical reading of *the* or (exclusively) to wide scope.

So far this has been a technical exercise in multiplying alternative routes to the same interpretation. Which is the real route, the one that the grammar of

English actually employs to make (37) and other sentences like these ambiguous? Can we give testable empirical content to this question? Yes, the three mechanisms make different predictions about the distribution of the ambiguity, and we can confront these predictions with linguistic data.

A notable prediction of the Index-Binding account is that the same options for filling in the NP's situation argument should be available when the determiner is something other than *the*, e.g. a quantificational determiner. A number of authors (e.g. Abusch 1994) have noted that this is borne out.

(44) If every semanticist owned a villa in Tuscany (instead), the world would be a boring place.

As Percus (2000) observes, (44) can be about counterfactual states of affairs in which villas are owned by all those who are actually semanticists. This reading is predicted if the situation-argument of *semanticist* is bound non-locally by the matrix complementizer, not locally by the counterfactual modal. The significance of the example is that this reading cannot be obtained by manipulating the scope of the *every*-DP. Matrix scope for this DP produces a meaning that concerns itself with actual semanticists, but not the meaning just described. Rather, the sentence then would say that if even one actual semanticist (any one) were a villa-owner, that would suffice to make the world boring. So the standard intensional semantics which formed the backdrop of the DP-Scope analysis for the ambiguity in (37) cannot account for the relevant reading in (44). What about the Indexicality account? It evidently won't apply if only the definite article has an indexical homonym; but the ambiguity could, of course, be generalized to other determiners, and defining a suitable indexical homonym of *every* is routine.

The existence of cases like (44) shows that grammar must provide at least one of the non-scopal mechanisms which mimic "wide-scope" definites, either Indexicality or Index-Binding. We have ample independent reason to assume that true scope ambiguity does exist and DPs have a certain degree of scopal flexibility in relation to other DPs and to negation, adverbs, modal verbs. In monoclausal configurations like (37), there is evidence for two LFs. But scopal mobility of DPs also is known to obey locality constraints (even if it is not fully known what those are). Under the reasonable working hypothesis that those constraints apply indiscriminately to DPs regardless of internal make-up, we can use evidence about the possible scopes of quantificational DPs to draw conclusions about the possible scopes of definite DPs. This leads us to conclude, for example, that a DP in the antecedent of a conditional cannot take matrix scope: the widest-scope-*every* reading for (44) that we earlier contrasted with its intended reading is not a grammatical reading for this sentence. In light of this fact, examples like (45) constitute further evidence for the existence of a non-scopal mechanism.

(45) If the man in the purple shirt had better taste, he would be wearing something else.

(45) can be about counterfactual situations in which the actual purple-shirted man does not wear a purple shirt. Such a reading could in principle be obtained by scoping the definite out of its clause, but given that *if*-clauses are scope islands, it must have another source.

Which of our two non-scopal mechanisms then is the right one? Both Indexicality and Index Binding predict that apparent wide-scope readings for definites are available beyond the configurations within which DPs are scopally mobile. But their predictions are not the same. We see this in more complex sentences where there is more than one potential "wide-scope" reading outside a scope island.

(46) John thinks he would arrive earlier if he wasn't in the bus he is in.

Suppose John says "I would arrive earlier if I wasn't on the #4," but he is actually on the #3. (46) can describe this scenario. The definite *the bus he is in* then is *de dicto* relative to *thinks*, picking out the bus John is riding in his belief-worlds rather than the one he is riding in fact. At the same time, it is not dependent on the counterfactual modal, or else the *if*-clause would be contradictory. (On the DP-Scope account that we have already ruled out, the reading would be one where the definite takes "intermediate" scope outside the conditional but below the attitude verb.) Such a reading is easily produced in the Index-Binding account, where it gets an LF in which the situation variable of *bus he is in* is free in the counterfactual and bound under *think*. The Indexicality account has trouble. Given that the definite's denotation is not the bus that John takes in the utterance world, *the* cannot be the_{ind}. Because *if*-clauses are scope islands, it also cannot scope out of the counterfactual. Then it can only be a narrowest-scope non-indexical definite, but that would make the *if*-clause contradictory.

Based on this type of evidence, it is widely accepted that something like the Index-Binding account is needed. There is then no motivation left for positing an indexical *the* as well. The readings generated by the Indexicality account are a proper subset of those generated by Index-Binding.

2.3 Indexical definites and the referential-attributive distinction

Notwithstanding the conclusion just reached, the idea that definite descriptions have an indexical reading has a long tradition of support from philosophers and linguists. It is often traced to Donnellan's distinction between "attributive" and "referential" definites, though Donnellan's observations have been interpreted in multiple ways by his commentators. Not everyone agrees that the distinction was supposed to be a semantic one at all, and those who do treat it as such have explicated it in different ways. Let us take a brief detour from our examination of the scopal properties of definites and indefinites and look at Donnellan's famous distinction.

The main empirical contribution of Donnellan (1966) is the observation that an utterance containing a definite description is sometimes heard to make a true claim even when the description fails to denote.

(47) A: This woman's husband is very kind to her.
B: Yes, you are right, but he's actually not her husband.

"Yes" indicates that B judges A's claim true, yet B's continuation makes clear that the proposition he judged true was not the one that a standard (Russellian or Fregean) semantics associates with A's sentence. Donnellan imagines the dialogue taking place as A and B are observing a woman and her male companion at a party. A takes the companion to be the woman's husband, B knows better. Both A and B judge the companion to be kind to the woman, and it is this opinion that B evidently understands to be the content of A's claim.

If we take this data at face value, we are led to a semantics that makes it possible for the definite *this woman's husband* to denote the woman's companion, despite the fact that he is not in the extension of the NP. None of the proposals we have contemplated so far allows this, but here is an entry, from Stalnaker (1970), which does.

$$[\![the_{ref\text{-}stal}\, \alpha]\!]^{c,i} = \iota x\, [\text{the speaker in } c \text{ presupposes } \lambda i'.\, [\![\alpha]\!]^{c,i'}(x)]$$

As Stalnaker puts it, definite descriptions show a "pragmatic ambiguity", and on one of their readings, the "referential" one, they denote the (unique) individual which is presupposed to have the property denoted by the restrictor NP. It is clear how this fits Donnellan's example. If the (covert) definite article in *this woman's husband* is interpreted in this way, the DP will denote not the man who in fact is the husband, but the man whom A presupposes to be the husband. This being the companion, the proposition expressed by A's sentence then is true or false according to whether the companion is kind to the woman. So it can be true even when the presupposition that determines the definite's reference is false.

But should we let data like (47) dictate our semantic analyses so directly? Real-life communicators often exercise charity, treating their interlocutors as having said what they manifestly intended even when they actually said something else. Isn't (47) just an instance of this more general feature of cooperative human interaction? Kripke (1977) argued that it is. As he noted, while B's response to A in (47) is natural, so are various others.

(48) A: This woman's husband is kind to her.
B': No, her husband is in jail for abusing her. That guy is her brother.
B": Her husband? She isn't married. That's her dad.

Do we want to say that hearers who respond like B' and B" do so because they resolved an ambiguity in A's utterance differently than B did? All three responders manifestly understood what A was thinking and trying to convey. As Kripke and Neale (1990) elaborate, we can explicate notions of 'speaker's reference' as distinct from 'semantic reference', or of 'proposition conveyed' as distinct from 'proposition expressed', to describe what happens in dialogues of this kind. We also need a theory of pronominal anaphora that allows the *he* in B's response to pick out someone other than the denotation of its "antecedent". But there is no reason to alter the semantics of definites on account of such data. A commonsensical pragmatic story can be told on the basis of the very semantics of definite descriptions that the standard analysis provides.

Kripke's response to Donnellan convinced subsequent authors that data like (47) do not by themselves suffice to support a semantic ambiguity or departure from standard analyses. However, Stalnaker's explication of Donnellan's referential reading brought another aspect to the forefront. Stalnaker's referential definites differ from their ordinary ("attributive") homonyms not only in that they can refer to something that does not fit the description, but also in that they are indexicals, whose denotation only depends on facts of the utterance situation and does not vary across different points of evaluation. As a result, they do not scopally interact with intensional operators. Whatever scope a Stalnaker-referential definite takes with respect to such an operator, the proposition expressed by the sentence is the same. Stalnaker recognized that this paved the way for a different kind of empirical argument for the ambiguity than the one that Kripke's criticism would later demolish. If definites could be shown to exhibit what looks like widest scope even when they were syntactically embedded in constructions that limit scopal mobility, this could be attributed to their referential readings rather than to actual wide scope. As we saw in the previous section, however, subsequent closer study of the scopal behavior of definites and other DPs ultimately led to a different conclusion. We need a framework in which the situation arguments of NPs restricting determiners can be bound non-locally, across intervening operators that are closer potential binders. Thus in the end no evidence for an additional indexical reading came from data about the interaction of definites and scope-bearing elements.

The indexical reading we contemplated in the previous section was not Stalnaker's, but a version suggested by Kaplan (1977). The Kaplanian version does not fit cases like (47), since even on the indexical reading the definite must pick out the real husband. In this respect, Kaplan implicitly seconded Kripke and acknowledged a discrepancy between speakers' manifest referential intentions and successful reference.

In Kaplan's paper one senses an insistence that widest scope readings of non-indexical (attributive) definites are not the same thing as indexical (referential) readings, so that even when no intensional operators or other scope-bearing elements are involved, the two will come apart. Indeed there is a technical distinction between them in the two-dimensional frameworks advocated by Stalnaker and Kaplan. On the indexical interpretation, *the F is G* expresses different propositions in different utterance contexts, with each of these propositions about a particular individual. On the (widest-scope) non-indexical interpretation, the sentence expresses the same proposition in every utterance context, but this proposition does not concern a fixed individual. But what difference in linguistic behavior, if any, corresponds to this technical difference? Truth-value judgment tasks cannot distinguish the two cases. In making such judgments, speakers contemplate whether a given sentence would be true if the world in which it was uttered had such and such properties. The same imagined world serves as both utterance world and world of evaluation, and therefore the difference between indexical and widest-scope non-indexical meanings is systematically neutralized.

Are there other judgment tasks which do not have this characteristic? We cannot ask informants directly what proposition they think an utterance expresses, but there may be less direct ways of getting at the proposition expressed. Stalnaker suggests that anaphoric *it* and *that* have uses in which they pick out propositions expressed by previous utterances. If so, truth-conditional ambiguities in the sentences containing these anaphors can be traced to indexical/non-indexical ambiguities in their antecedents.

(49) The man in the purple shirt won. I had expected that.

I had expected that can mean either of two things: I had expected that whoever would be wearing purple would win. Or I had expected that this person, who happens to be in purple, would win. The sentence containing the anaphoric *that* seems to exhibit the same *de re-de dicto* ambiguity as the sentence *I had expected that the man in the purple shirt would win*. But whereas for the latter sentence we can easily posit two LFs (by varying the definite's scope or by exercising different options for the world-variable in its restrictor), there is no room for such maneuvers when the object of *expect* is just a simple pronoun. Therefore, Stalnaker argues, the ambiguity can only reside in the antecedent sentence. Depending on whether *the man in the purple shirt* is referential or attributive, the antecedent sentence expresses two different propositions. They have the same truth value in the utterance world, but when plugged in as objects of *expect*, they can lead to different truth-values for the second sentence.

Is there another way to analyze the ambiguity in (49), consistent with the view that definites are unambiguously non-indexical, though their restrictors may contain either locally or distantly bound world variables? There is, but it requires a more complex covert structure in the representation of the supposedly simple anaphoric *that*. *that* might be a kind of paycheck-pronoun. The following example indicates that some such more flexible approach to propositional anaphora is unavoidable.

(50) Every time the most controversial candidate ended up getting the job, people later claimed they had expected that all along (and denied that there had been any controversy).

(50) generalizes over a number of job searches, each with its own most controversial candidate. The definite description thus cannot be referential or scoped outside its clause. The propositional anaphor *that*, however, is interpreted as 'that this person would get the job' and not 'that whoever was most controversial would get the job'. So even if we recognize the existence of a referential reading in addition to attributive readings with various scopes, *that* cannot be analyzed as denoting the same proposition that its antecedent clause expresses.

The upshot of this discussion is that there remains no compelling argument for a referential-attributive ambiguity in definites, at least not for any of the proposed semantic implementations of Donnellan's distinction.

2.4 Narrowest scope indefinites

The classical analysis of indefinites as existential quantifiers predicts scope interaction with negation and other connectives, quantifiers, and intensional operators. The null hypothesis is that their scopal freedom should mirror that of other quantificational DPs, constrained by the same scope island constraints. The facts depart notoriously from this expectation, in two directions. Certain types of indefinites, notably bare plurals, seem limited to narrowest scope. Other types display an ability to take wide scope out of islands. We will look at the first phenomenon in this section and the second one in the next.

Carlson (1977) documents that English bare plurals lack the scopal freedom of other indefinites, such as singular indefinites with *a*, singular and plural DPs with *some*, and DPs with numerals. His data include contrasts like (51) and (52).

(51) a. Miles is looking for a policeman.
    (i) 'there is a policeman that Miles is looking for'
    (ii) 'if Miles' search succeeds, there is a policeman he finds'

   b. Miles is looking for policemen.
    (i) *'there are policemen that Miles is looking for'
    (ii) 'if Miles' search succeeds, there are policemen he finds'

(52) a. ?? A dog is everywhere.
    (i) 'there is a dog that is in every place'
    (ii) *'in every place, there is a dog'

   b. Cats are everywhere.
    (i) *'there are cats that are in every place'
    (ii) 'in every place, there are cats'

Carlson therefore rejects the idea that singular indefinites with *a* and bare plurals share a common abstract indefinite determiner. Instead he proposes that existential quantification with bare plurals has a radically different source, not contributed by a determiner or anywhere within the DP, but by the predicate that takes it as its argument. He proposes that a VP like *be in the room* effectively means 'have manifestations that are in the room'. When this is predicated of an ordinary individual like John, manifestations are something like time-slices, so *John is in the room* means literally that some time-slices of the temporally extended John are in the room. But this VP can also be predicated of more abstract individuals, particularly kinds, in which case we obtain the meaning that some time-slices of some (ordinary) individuals which instantiate the kind are in the room. If *cats* in *cats are in the room* denotes the species *felis catus*, then the sentence will come to mean that there are some time-slices of instances of *felis catus* in the room. Carlson proposes that bare plurals are *always* names of kinds.

This proposal spawned various variants. Most did away with the time-slices and assume that the predicate meanings which have built-in existential quantification are not the only or most basic meanings of those predicates. Modern Neo-Carlsonians also acknowledge a semantic role for the plural morphology (which Carlson disregarded) and assume that the existential quantification ranges over pluralities rather than atoms. Common to the variants, however, and crucial here, is that the locus of existential quantification is in the predicate that the bare plural saturates and not in the bare plural itself. This is what carries the burden of explaining the narrowest-scope restriction observed in (51) and (52). Even if the bare plural itself moved to different scope sites as freely as any quantificational DP, existential quantification would keep its same narrow scope, quantifying effectively over manifestations of the denotation of the bare plural's (lowest) trace. Its scope is semantically inert like a proper name's.

Diesing (1992) recast Carlson's theory somewhat differently, both empirically and theoretically. The core generalization for her is not that existential bare plurals always have the narrowest possible scope, but that their scope is confined to the (smallest) VP which contains them. She also argues that the same is true for *a*-indefinites, once we set aside their presuppositional readings (which have the same scope options as other quantificational DPs). Both claims are rather difficult to test empirically in the areas where they come apart from Carlson's. If Diesing is right, the unity of *a*-indefinites and bare plurals is restored and their difference reduced to the predictable contribution of number—though only as far as their non-presupposing variants are concerned.

There are a couple of systematic exceptions to Carlson's narrowest-scope generalization. One was observed by Partee (1985) and relates to the phenomenon of "dependent plurals". (53) patterns with the singular (51a) and not with (51b) in permitting the ∃ > *look-for* reading, provided that the subject plural distributes over the matrix predicate.

(53) The two boys are looking for policemen.
    ok "for each of the two boys, there is a policeman that he is looking for"

Another exception was seen by Carlson himself and further analyzed by Chierchia (1998) and arises with certain modified bare plurals.

(54) Miles is looking for people who are sitting over there.
    ok "there are people sitting over there that Miles is looking for"

Carlson and Chierchia suggest that modifiers expressing purely extrinsic or non-predictive attributes make an NP express a property which does not correspond to any kind. I.e., not every expressible property corresponds to a kind that is instantiated by all and only the bearers of this property, only that subset of properties which play a role in law-like generalizations. When a bare plural in argument position is formed from an NP which expresses a kind-less property, then it can be construed with a silent existential determiner and be a regular scopally mobile DP. Chierchia posits an economy principle that ensures this option is only a last resort and not available in (51), (52).

In summary, the limited scopal options of certain indefinites, particularly bare plurals, have been attributed to a non-quantificational semantics for them, locating their apparent existential force outside of them in the surrounding structure.

2.5 "Wide scope" indefinites

Fodor & Sag (1982) drew attention to the apparent ability of indefinites to take wide scope in configurations where other quantifiers cannot. They presented minimal pairs like (55).

(55) John overheard the rumor that
 a. every student of mine was called before the dean.
 b. a student of mine was called before the dean.

The complex DP *the rumor that ...* is a scope-island for ordinary quantifiers, and (55a) can only refer to a rumored universal generalization. (55b), by contrast, need not refer to a rumor with existential content. It also can assert that there is a student of mine about whom John overheard the rumor that he was called before the dean. The indefinite seems to scope over the matrix clause.

Fodor and Sag proposed that the apparent wide-scope reading of the indefinite is not due to wide scope but to an indexical ("referential") reading. The proposal is modeled on the Indexicality account of "wide scope" definites that we saw in section 2.2. Fodor and Sag's meanings for the ambiguous indefinite determiner are in (56).

(56) a. $[\![a_{quant}\alpha]\!]^{c,i} = \lambda Q.\ \exists x[[\![\alpha]\!]^{c,i}(x)\ \&\ Q(x)]$
 b. $[\![a_{ref}\alpha]\!]^{c,i}$ is defined only if there is a unique individual that the speaker of c has in mind in c, and this individual is in $[\![\alpha]\!]^{c,c}$;
 where defined, $[\![a_{ref}\alpha]\!]^{c,i}$ = this individual.

(56a), the usual existential meaning, gives rise to quantificational DPs with the same scopal mobility as other quantificational DPs. (56b) creates an individual-denoting

DP whose reference depends only on the context of utterance. Accordingly, the scope of this DP vis-à-vis other elements does not affect truth-conditions. Fodor and Sag argue that the perceived "wide scope" reading of (55b) is due to an LF like (57a), not (57b).

(57) a. John overheard the rumor that
          [a_{ref} student of mine was called ...]
     b. * a_{quant} student of mine λx.
          [John overheard the rumor that x was called ...]

These two LFs do not receive exactly the same interpretation. (57b) expresses a proposition context-independently (namely that there is a student of mine such that John overheard the rumor that he was called before the dean). (57a) expresses different propositions in different contexts and no proposition in some. It carries the presupposition that the speaker has a particular student of hers in mind, and when this presupposition is true, it expresses the proposition that John overheard the rumor that this student was called before the dean. Despite these differences, data from tasks like truth value judgments will not easily discriminate between the two. A speaker prepared to assert the existential proposition expressed by (57b) will typically have a verifying instance in mind. If so, the utterance context supports the presupposition of (57a), and this presupposition together with the assertion of (57a) entails (57b). Arguably, therefore, our judgment that (55b) permits the reading in (57b) is an illusion and the reading we really are witnessing is (57a). (But see Ludlow & Neale 1990.)

Fodor and Sag noted and sought to confirm a prediction of their analysis that set it apart from the competing hypothesis that quantificational indefinites can scope out of islands. If the latter were true, we would see not only apparent widest-scope readings but also readings where the indefinite appears to scope above an island but below another operator. An indexical analysis cannot mimic such "intermediate" readings and thus predicts them to be impossible. Here is an example sentence and its relevant potential reading.

(58) a. Every teacher overheard the rumor that a student of mine was called before the dean.
     b. 'for every teacher x there is a (potentially different) student of mine y such that x overheard the rumor that y has been called before the dean'

Fodor and Sag judged that (58a) could not describe a scenario where each teacher heard a rumor about a different student. More generally, they found no cases where an indefinite took non-maximal scope yet scope out of an island.

Subsequent authors (Farkas 1981 and others), however, soon reached a consensus that such readings exist. For example, (59) can have *his* bound by *every student*, yet need not mean that every student read all the books recommended by *any* of his teachers. Instead it can be true on the grounds that every student had *some* teacher whose recommendations he heeded.

(59) Every student read every book that a teacher of his recommended.

Because of this type of data, Fodor and Sag's indexical analysis was abandoned.

Kratzer (1998) and Schwarzschild (2002) proposed conservative amendments of Fodor & Sag (1982) that extend to the cases of "intermediate scope". I focus on Schwarzschild's version. Like Fodor and Sag, he maintains that apparent wide scope indefinites have local scope despite appearances, but unlike them, he does not posit ambiguity in the indefinite article. Maintaining a classical existential analysis, he instead exploits the ubiquity of covert restrictors. As he observes, when the NP restricting a (quantificational) indefinite article happens to denote a singleton, different scopes for the indefinite systematically collapse in truth-value. Conceivably then, the indefinite *a student of mine* in (55b) scopes within its minimal clause but is covertly restricted by something like 'whom I am thinking of right now' or 'who is called Mary Smith'. Provided that the relevant covert restrictor applies to only one actual student of mine (and is construed *de re*), this has the consequence that the LF says the same thing as it would if the indefinite had matrix scope. Schwarzschild can effectively mimic Fodor and Sag's analysis by positing a covert 'which I now have in mind' wherever they posit referential *a*. But it is more flexible and also can handle apparent intermediate scopes, since covert restrictors can contain bound variables. In (59), for example, the covert restrictor could be 'who is his (the student's) favorite teacher', or whatever else describes a unique but possibly different teacher per student.

This approach raises murky issues about the pragmatics of covert domain restriction and context-dependency more generally. Other cases of context-dependency, such as deictic pronouns or covert restrictors for universals and definites, lead to infelicity unless the hearer can in some sense identify the intended value for the contextual parameter or covert element. There are complicating factors like vagueness and the fact that the relevant values may be intensions rather than extensions, but even allowing for these, the covert restrictors invoked by Schwarzschild seem different. When we hear *He is nice* or *Every student got an A*, we insist on understanding which male is referred to, or whether the universal claim is about just one class or the whole school. We are not content with just letting it be whoever the speaker has in mind or whoever fits some description of unknown content. The attempted reduction of the phenomenon of "wide scope" indefinites to the run-of-the-mill mechanism of covert domain restriction is thus not entirely successful.

Other evidence against Schwarzschild's project could come from examples of a sort discussed by Chierchia (2001) and Schwarz (2001, 2004), which involve apparent intermediate scope below negation.

(60) No boy ate the cookies that a girl from his class had brought.

Schwarz reports a reading for this sentence that is falsified by the existence of any boy-girl pair such that the girl is in the boy's class and he ate the cookies she brought. If this judgment is representative, Schwarzschild's (and Kratzer's) approach is insufficient.

Another influential proposal was the choice-function analysis of Reinhart (1997) and Winter (1997). These authors also agreed with Fodor and Sag that apparent wide-scope or intermediate-scope indefinites did not really have wide or intermediate scope. They proposed that indefinite DPs contain a variable over choice functions which is bound by existential closure somewhere higher in the sentence. One can implement this by introducing the choice function variable through the lexical entry of the indefinite article, and the existential closure operation through a silent morpheme freely generated at the edges of propositional domains in LF.

(61) a. $[\![a_{chfi}\alpha]\!]^g = g(i)([\![\alpha]\!]^g)$
 b. $[\![\exists_{chfi}\phi]\!]^g = 1$ iff $\exists f_{<et,e>} [\forall P \in dom(f): f(P) \in P \ \& \ [\![\phi]\!]^{gi/f} = 1]$

A simple indefinite sentence could have the LF in (62), meaning literally that some way of mapping the set of cats to one of its members yields a value that arrived—a roundabout way of saying that a cat arrived.

(62) $\exists_{chf1}$ [a_{chf1} cat arrived]

The key to capturing wide scope readings is the free distribution of the existential closure operator, which need not be local to the indefinite it binds. As the following possible LF illustrates, the indefinite itself can remain in a low position within the scope of another quantifier, yet appear to have wider scope in virtue of the high position of its binder.

(63) $\exists_{chf1}$ [every boy petted a_{chf1} cat]
 lit.: "some way of mapping the set of cats to one of its members maps it to something which every boy petted"

While (63) does not involve a scope island, the mechanism carries over to examples which do, since there are no locality constraints on variable binding. Non-maximal island-escaping scope also is not a problem, since the ∃ operator can be generated at any level.

The analysis was later amended in light of observations by Kratzer (1998), Chierchia (2001) and others, replacing plain choice functions by so-called skolemized choice functions. But the reasons for and details of this further refinement need not preoccupy us, since Schwarz (2001, 2004) has shown that choice-function analyses do not solve the puzzle of wide-scope indefinites. Schwarz points out a problem of overgeneration which already afflicts the simpler version presented above and only gets worse in the skolemized version. This problem arises with indefinites in the scope of non-upward-monotone quantifiers. Consider (64a) with the potential LF in (64b).

(64) (a) No candidate submitted a paper he had written.
 (b) $\exists_{chf1}$ [no candidate$_2$ [t$_2$ submitted a$_{chf1}$ paper he$_2$ had written]]

(64b) is equivalent to 'no candidate submitted *every* paper he had written', a reading clearly not attested for (64a). The choice-function analysis would have to be constrained so as not to generate LFs like (64b). Schwarz argues that there are no plausible constraints that accomplish this and leave intact the positive results of the approach. If Schwarz is right, we may have to concede what Fodor and Sag and most subsequent authors wanted to avoid: indefinites are existential quantifiers that enjoy a greater degree of scopal mobility than other kinds of quantificational DPs. We may have to look for an appropriately differentiated syntactic theory that will make sense of this, or perhaps admit scoping mechanisms that are not strictly syntactic along the lines of Abusch (1994).

A brief note on indefinites with *a certain* is in order before we wrap up. Although Schwarz concludes that wide-scope indefinites are better handled by real scoping than any of the alternative mechanisms we surveyed, he adds a qualification. This concerns a set of examples which he classifies as "functional indefinites" and which invariably contain the adjective *certain*. As observed by Winter (2001), adding *certain* to an indefinite can bring about readings which are clearly not generated in a classical existential analysis, regardless of what is assumed about scopal freedom. The following minimal pair illustrates.

(65) Every boy who hates
 a. a relative of his
 b. a certain relative of his
  develops a complex.

Holding constant a bound interpretation of the pronoun *his*, (65a) can only mean that every boy who hates any of his relatives develops a complex. This is expected, given that the scope of the indefinite *a relative of his* is roofed by the relative pronoun that binds into it. But (65b) means something different, something like: 'for a certain kinship-relation R, every boy who hates the person he bears R to develops a complex'. This could be true while (65a) is false, e.g., if every boy who hates his mother develops a complex but some boys who hate their father do not. For examples with *a certain*, the approach of Kratzer (1998) and Schwarzschild (2002) makes the right predictions. *certain* appears to restrict the indefinite to a proper subset of the NP it modifies and may well mean something like 'standing in the kinship-relation I have in mind'. But this then needs to be cashed out in the analysis of the word *certain* and is not a matter of *covert* domain restriction or of the indefinite article or –DEFeature. Does the analysis of *certain* have *any* intrinsic connection with the study of indefiniteness? That remains to be seen. But what is not the case is that the meanings of indefinites with *a certain* are also possible readings of plain indefinites without *certain*.

3 References

Abusch, Dorit 1994. The scope of indefinites. *Natural Language Semantics* 2, 83–136.
Carlson, Gregory 1977. *Reference to Kinds in English*. Ph.D. dissertation. University of Massachusetts, Amherst, MA.
Carlson, Gregory, Rachel Sussman, Natalie Klein & Michael Tanenhaus 2006. Weak definite noun phrases. In: C. Davis, A. R. Deal & Y. Zabbal (eds.). *Proceedings of the North Eastern Linguistics Society (= NELS) 36*. Amherst, MA: GLSA, University of Massachusetts, 179–196.
Chierchia, Gennaro 1998. Reference to kinds across languages. *Natural Language Semantics* 6, 339–405.
Chierchia, Gennaro 2001. A puzzle about indefinites. In: C. Cechetto, G. Chierchia & T. Guasti (eds.). *Semantic Interfaces: Reference, Anaphora, and Aspect*. Stanford: CSLI Publications, 51–89.
Diesing, Molly 1992. *Indefinites*. Cambridge, MA: The MIT Press.
Donnellan, Keith 1966. Reference and definite descriptions. *The Philosophical Review* 75, 281–304.
Elbourne, Paul 2005. *Situations and Individuals*. Cambridge, MA: The MIT Press.
Farkas, Donka 1981. Quantifier scope and syntactic islands. In: R. Hendrick, C. Masek & M. Miller (eds.). *Papers form the Regional Meeting of the Chicago Linguistic Society (= CLS) 17*. Chicago, IL: University of Chicago, 59–66.
von Fintel, Kai 1998. *Evidence for Presuppositional Indefinites*. Ms. Cambridge, MA, MIT. http://web.mit.edu/fintel/www/presupp_indef.pdf. December 12, 2010.
von Fintel, Kai 2004. Would you believe it? The king of France is back. In: M. Reimer & A. Bezuidenhout (eds.). *Descriptions and Beyond*. Oxford: Oxford University Press, 315–341.

Fodor, Janet & Ivan Sag 1982. Referential and quantificational indefinites. *Linguistics & Philosophy* 5, 355–398.
Frege, Gottlob 1892. Über Sinn und Bedeutung. *Zeitschrift für Philosophie und philosophische Kritik* 100, 25–50. English translation in: P. Geach & M. Black (eds.). *Translations from the Philosophical Writings of Gottlob Frege*. Oxford: Blackwell, 1980, 56–78.
Graff, Delia 2001. Descriptions as predicates. *Philosophical Studies* 102, 1–42.
Hawkins, John 1978. *Definiteness and Indefiniteness*. London: Croom Helm.
Hawkins, John 1991. On (in)definite articles: Implicatures and (un)grammaticality prediction. *Journal of Linguistics* 27, 405–442.
Heim, Irene 1982. *The Semantics of Definite and Indefinite Noun Phrases*. Ph.D. dissertation. University of Massachusetts, Amherst, MA. Reprinted: Ann Arbor, MI: University Microfilms.
Heim, Irene 1991. Artikel und Definitheit. In: A. von Stechow & D. Wunderlich (eds.). *Semantik—Semantics. Ein internationales Handbuch zur zeitgenössischen Forschung— An International Handbook of Contemporary Research* (HSK 6). Berlin: de Gruyter, 487–535.
Heim, Irene & Angelika Kratzer 1998. *Semantics in Generative Grammar*. Oxford: Blackwell.
von Heusinger, Klaus 1997. *Salienz und Referenz. Der Epsilonoperator in der Semantik der Nominalphrase und anaphorischer Pronomen*. Berlin: Akademie Verlag.
Kaplan, David 1977/1989. Demonstratives. Ms. Los Angeles, CA, University of California. Printed in: J. Almog, J. Perry & H. Wettstein (eds.). *Themes from Kaplan*. Oxford: Oxford University Press, 1989, 408–565.
Kratzer, Angelika 1998. Scope or pseudoscope? Are there wide-scope indefinites? In: S. Rothstein (ed.). *Events and Grammar*. Dordrecht: Kluwer, 163–196.
Kripke, Saul 1977. Speaker's reference and semantic reference. In: P. French, T. Uehling & H. Wettstein (eds.). *Midwest Studies in Philosophy II: Studies in the Philosophy of Language*. Minneapolis, MI: University of Minnesota Press, 255–276.
Lewis, David 1973. *Counterfactuals*. Oxford: Blackwell.
Ludlow, Peter & Stephen Neale 1991. Indefinite descriptions: In defense of Russell. *Linguistics & Philosophy* 14, 171–202.
Ludlow, Peter & Gabriel Segal 2004. On a unitary semantical analysis for definite and indefinite descriptions. In: M. Reimer & A. Bezuidenhout (eds.). *Descriptions and Beyond*. Oxford: Oxford University Press, 420–436.
Maratsos, Michael 1976. *The Use of Definite and Indefinite Reference in Young Children*. Cambridge: Cambridge University Press.
Milsark, Gary 1977. Toward an explanation of certain peculiarities of the existential construction in English. *Linguistic Analysis* 3, 1–29.
Montague, Richard 1973. The proper treatment of quantification in ordinary English. In: J. Hintikka, J. Moravcsik & P. Suppes (eds.). *Approaches to Natural Language*. Dordrecht: Reidel, 221–242.
Neale, Stephen 1990. *Descriptions*. Cambridge, MA: The MIT Press.
Partee, Barbara 1985. *Dependent Plurals are Different from Bare Plurals*. Ms. Amherst, MA, University of Massachusetts. http://people.umass.edu/partee/docs/Dependent_Plurals_Partee.pdf December 12, 2010.
Partee, Barbara 1986. Noun phrase interpretation and type-shifting principles. In: J. Groenendijk, D. de Jongh & M. Stokhof (eds.). *Studies in Discourse Representation Theory and the Theory of Generalized Quantifiers*. Dordrecht: Foris, 115–143.

Percus, Orin 2000. Constraints on some other variables in syntax. *Natural Language Semantics* 8, 173–229.
Postal, Paul 1966. On so-called pronouns in English. In: F. Dinneen (ed.). *Report on the 17th Annual Round-Table Meeting on Linguistics and Language Studies*. Washington, DC: Georgetown University Press, 177–206.
Reinhart, Tanya 1997. Quantifier scope: How labor is divided between QR and choice functions. *Linguistics & Philosophy* 20, 335–397.
Roberts, Craige 2002. Demonstratives as definite noun phrases. In: K. van Deemter & R. Kibble (eds.). *Information Sharing: Reference and Presupposition in Language Generation and Interpretation*. Stanford, CA: CSLI Publications, 89–106.
Russell, Bertrand 1905. On denoting. *Mind* 14, 479–493.
Schlenker, Philippe 2004. Conditionals as definite descriptions. *Research on Language and Computation* 2, 417–462.
Schwarz, Bernhard 2001. Two kinds of long-distance indefinites. In: R. van Rooy & M. Stokhof (eds.). *Proceedings of the 13th Amsterdam Colloquium*. Amsterdam: ICCL, 192–197.
Schwarz, Bernhard 2004. Indefinites in verb phrase ellipsis. *Linguistic Inquiry* 35, 344–353.
Schwarzschild, Roger 2002. Singleton indefinites. *Journal of Semantics* 19, 289–314.
Sharvy, Richard 1980. A more general theory of definite descriptions. *The Philosophical Review* 89, 607–624.
Stalnaker, Robert 1970. Pragmatics. *Synthese* 22, 272–289.
Strawson, Peter 1950. On referring. *Mind* 59, 320–344.
Strawson, Peter 1954. A reply to Mr. Sellars. *Philosophical Review* 63, 216–231.
Westerståhl, Dag 1984. Determiners and context sets. In: J. van Benthem & A. ter Meulen (eds.). *Generalized Quantifiers in Natural Language*. Dordrecht: Foris, 45–71.
Winter, Yoad 1997. Choice functions and the scopal semantics of indefinites. *Linguistics & Philosophy* 20, 399–467.
Winter, Yoad 2001. *Flexibility Principles in Boolean Semantics*. Cambridge, MA: The MIT Press.

Klaus von Heusinger
3 Specificity

1 Introduction —— 70
2 Specificity as a grammatical phenomenon —— 75
3 Opaque contexts —— 78
4 Exceptional scope behavior —— 83
5 Epistemic specificity —— 93
6 Referential anchoring —— 98
7 D-linking, partitivity and presuppositionality —— 102
8 Topicality —— 104
9 Discourse prominence —— 105
10 Summary —— 106
11 References —— 107

Abstract: Specificity is a semantic-pragmatic notion that distinguishes between different uses or interpretations of indefinite noun phrases. Roughly speaking, it corresponds to the referential intentions of the speaker using an indefinite noun phrase. The speaker can intend to refer to a particular entity using an indefinite noun phrase, or not. This very general communicative option is mirrored in the linguistic category of specificity, which has become a central notion in analyses of syntactic as well as semantic phenomena. This article reviews different types of specificity discussed in the research literature: (i) referential specificity, (ii) scopal specificity, (iii) epistemic specificity, (iv) partitive specificity, (v) topical specificity, (vi) noteworthiness as specificity, and (vii) discourse prominence as specificity. It also presents recent approaches to specificity, including choice function approaches. Based on this review, the article argues that there is a core semantic notion of specificity, namely "referential anchoring", which connects the semantic properties of specific indefinites with their discourse properties.

1 Introduction

Specificity is a semantic-pragmatic notion that distinguishes between different uses or interpretations of indefinite noun phrases. It is related to the communicative or pragmatic notion of "referential intention". A speaker uses an indefinite noun

---

Klaus von Heusinger, Cologne, Germany

phrase and intends to refer to a particular referent, the referent "the speaker has in mind". This communicative function of the indefinite affects sentence and discourse semantics in various ways. Specificity was originally introduced to describe the different potential of two types of indefinites to introduce discourse referents. In subsequent work, this contrast was related to the referential properties of indefinites in opaque contexts and to the scopal behavior of indefinites with respect to extensional operators. In the course of time, specificity has been employed to describe further contrasts, such as different epistemic states of the speaker, different grades of familiarity and different levels of discourse prominence. The intuitive contrast between specific and non-specific indefinites was quickly adopted. The new notion of specificity spread throughout the linguistic community, from formal semantics and pragmatics to syntax, as well as to descriptive and functional linguistics, and as a consequence, a large number of different types of specificity has been introduced. There is no agreed set of semantic and pragmatic properties of specific indefinites. Rather, specific indefinites have been characterized in several ways, as for instance, (i) (direct) referential terms, (ii) rigid designators, (iii) always showing wide scope, (iv) signaling the certainty of the speaker about the identity of the referent, (v) licensing discourse anaphora, (vi) being presuppositional, and (vii) signaling discourse prominence. It is controversial which of the mentioned characteristics are essential for a definition of specificity. Research on specificity in the last four decades has not only proven very productive, introducing new theories and tools such as the use of choice functions. It has also deepened our understanding of the semantics and pragmatics of indefinites and of the interpretation of noun phrases in general. Furthermore, research has defined new questions and challenges for the semantics-pragmatics interface as well as the semantics-syntax interface. Yet, questions about the nature of specificity are still open: What are the linguistic phenomena that should count as good instances of specificity contrasts? Is specificity just a general communicative principle or a proper semantic category? If the latter is the case, how can the semantic contrast between a specific and a non-specific indefinite be modelled?

Traditional grammarians did not address the contrast associated with specificity directly. They were certainly aware of different readings of indefinites, such as referent establishing, generic, and predicational readings, as well as subclasses thereof, such as dependent readings and examples that refer to "particular individuals". However, they did not explicitly use or name the concept of specificity. The first wave of investigations on specificity was initiated by Karttunen's (1968, 1969/1976) observation that a certain type of indefinites licenses discourse anaphors in contexts in which other indefinites do not. The contrast was first associated with Quine's (1956, 1960) observation that indefinite noun phrases in opaque contexts show an ambiguity that is similar to the *de re* vs. *de dicto* readings of definite noun phrases, and it was termed "specific" vs. "non-specific" (Baker 1966). Karttunen proposed two alternative analyses: in his first analysis Karttunen (1968) assumed two lexical representations, while Karttunen (1969, 26/1976, 378), Fodor (1970) and the generative semanticists put forth an account in terms of scope. Partee (1970) argued that specificity corresponds more closely to Donnellan's (1966) distinction between referential vs. attributive readings for definites. Specific indefinites directly refer to their referents and the sentence asserts a predicate of this referent, while non-specific indefinites contribute their descriptive content to the assertion. Kripke (1977 based on a talk in 1971), however, maintained that this contrast is pragmatic, as it follows from general communicative principles and does not show truth-conditional effects.

Fodor & Sag (1982) have summarized the discussions on specificity of the first decade in their seminal paper "Referential and Quantificational Indefinites". They propose that noun phrases with the indefinite article are lexically ambiguous between a referential (or specific) interpretation and an existential (or non-specific) interpretation. They argue that specific indefinites differ in their semantic properties from non-specific ones: they allow *de re* readings in opaque contexts, show special scope behavior and make an epistemic contribution. Subsequent theories have focused on particular aspects and claims of Fodor and Sag's investigation, such as the exceptional scope behavior of indefinites (Farkas 1981, Ruys 1992, Abusch 1994, Reinhart 1997, Winter 1997, Kratzer 1998, Chierchia 2001, Schwarz 2001), or the parallelism between contrasts in opaque contexts and epistemic readings in transparent contexts (Farkas 1994, Kamp & Bende-Farkas submitted).

Other research traditions associate specificity with discourse-linking (Pesetsky 1987), partitivity (Enç 1991), presuppositionality (Yeom 1998, Geurts 2010), the contrast between weak and strong quantifiers (Diesing 1992, de Hoop 1995), topicality (Cresti 1995, Portner 2002, Endriss 2009), or discourse properties like topic continuity and referential persistence (Givón 1983), or noteworthiness (MacLaran 1982, Ionin 2006). Specificity has also become an important category underlying syntactic phenomena such as wh-movement and island violations (e.g. Pesetsky 1987, Szabolcsi & Zwarts 1992, Diesing 1992, de Hoop 1995). There is an increasing interest in exploring the crosslinguistic differences in the encodings of specificity, such as articles in Bantu (Givón 1973), St'át'imcets (Lillooet Salish) (Matthewson 1999) and Maori (Chung & Ladusaw 2004), differential object marking in Turkish (Enç 1991) and Spanish (Leonetti 2004), and indefinite pronouns in Russian (Dahl 1970, Ioup 1977, Geist 2008), to name just a few.

The broad variety of data associated with specificity, the different types of specificity, and the multitude of theories of specificity make a comprehensive overview and a straightforward classification of this notion very difficult (but see Karttunen 1968, 1969/1976, Fodor 1970, Abbott 1976, Fodor & Sag 1982, Abusch 1994, Farkas 1994, 2002, Yeom 1998, Ruys 2006, Kamp & Bende-Farkas 2006,

Ionin 2006, Endriss 2009). The various uses of the notion are related in one way or another to the communicative or pragmatic notion of "referential intention", according to which the speaker uses a specific indefinite to refer to an object "s/he has in mind". These uses can roughly be classified into seven types of specificity, illustrated by the following pairs of sentences:

(1) a. Paula believes that Bill talked to *an important politician*.
    (→ there is an important politician)
   b. Paula believes that Bill talked to *an important politician*.
    (but there is no important politician)

(2) a. If *a friend of mine from Texas* had died in the fire, I would have inherited a fortune. (possible reading: there is a friend of mine and if he ...)
   b. If *each friend of mine from Texas* had died in the fire, I would have inherited a fortune. (not possible: for each of my friends, if one of them ...)

(3) a. *A student in Syntax 1* cheated in the exam. I know him: It is Jim Miller.
   b. *A student in Syntax 1* cheated in the exam. But I do not know who it is.

(4) a. 50 students entered the room. I knew *two girls*.
   b. 50 students entered the room. They greeted *two girls* (already in the room).

(5) a. *Some ghosts* live in the pantry; others live in the kitchen.
   b. There are *some ghosts* in this house.

(6) a. He put *a/this 31 cent stamp* on the envelope, and only realized later that it was worth a fortune because it was unperforated.
   b. He put *a/#this 31 cent stamp* on the envelope, so he must want it to go airmail.

(7) a. There was a king and the king had a daughter and he loved his daughter ...
   b. #There was a king and the season was very short and hot ...

The different types of specificity are characterized as follows: (i) specificity in opaque contexts (*referential specificity*) expresses a contrast between a reading that allows existential entailment (1a) and a reading that does not (1b); (ii) *scopal specificity* (often also including type (i)) refers to the ability of certain indefinites to escape scope islands like the conditional in (2a), that a universal quantifier cannot escape (2b); (iii) *epistemic specificity* expresses the contrast between speaker's knowledge (3a) and speaker's ignorance (or indifference) (3b) about the referent of the indefinite; (iv) specificity is sometimes associated with different types of familiarity such as d-linking, partitivity, and presuppositionality: the indefinite is part of an already introduced set, as in (4a), or not, as in (4b); (v) specificity is also related to topicality as in (5a), where the topical element can be understood as a specific expression. There are two further notions of specificity that concern the forward referential potential of indefinites: (vi) *specificity as noteworthiness* assumes that the presentative *this* in (6) signals that the speaker intends to assert a noteworthy property of the referent, as in (6a), while (6b) is reported to be infelicitous since no such property is mentioned. (vii) *specificity as discourse prominence* refers to one aspect of discourse prominence, namely "referential persistence" or "topic shift", i.e. the potential of an indefinite to introduce a referent that will be mentioned again and that may even become a topic in the subsequent discourse as in (7).

There are different ways to group these types of specificity together: Fodor & Sag's (1982) notion of specificity covers the types (i) to (iii), while Farkas (1994) argues that epistemic specificity, scopal specificity, which, in her view, includes referential specificity, and partitive specificity are independent of each other and can cross-classify. Still they show the common effect of reducing the restrictor set of the indefinite, i.e. the set of potential referents is restricted to a few, or possibly to only one element. This concept of "referential stability" (Farkas & von Heusinger 2003) can be extended to various types of specificity and motivate why languages use the same encodings for these types. However, in this survey I maintain the stronger hypothesis that there is a core semantic notion of specificity which is defined in terms of "referential anchoring": the referent of a specific indefinite is functionally dependent on the referent of another expression (von Heusinger 2002). This is a generalization of the original claim by Fodor & Sag (1982) with some crucial modifications (see also Kamp & Bende-Farkas 2011, Onea & Geist 2011). It covers the types (i) to (iii), but also allows establishing links to familiarity oriented or discourse-oriented notions of specificity.

In section 2, I present different types of encodings and typical linguistic contexts for specificity contrasts. These will later function as tests for specific vs. non-specific readings. Section 3 discusses the relation between (referential) specificity in opaque contexts and the relation to *de re* vs. *de dicto* readings of definites. Section 4 presents the crucial observation about the "exceptional" scope behavior of indefinites and the discussion of choice functions as a more adequate representation for indefinites. Section 5 provides a brief overview of epistemic readings of indefinites and their relation to the *referential* vs. *attributive* readings of definites. Section 6 introduces the unifying view of specificity as referential anchoring based on the observations and theoretical discussions made up to this point. Sections 7 and 8 discuss the characterization of specificity in terms of familiarity (d-linking, partitivity, presuppositionality) and topicality, respectively. Section 9 presents intriguing correlations between the sentence semantic properties of specific indefinites and their discourse behavior. Finally, section 10 summarizes the findings and presents some of the many open research questions.

2 Specificity as a grammatical phenomenon

This article primarily focuses on specificity distinctions within indefinite noun phrases. It is generally assumed that indefinite noun phrases in argument positions make two semantic contributions: they express an existential assertion and they introduce a discourse referent (see articles 11 [Semantics: Theories] (Kamp & Reyle) *Discourse Representation Theory* and 2 [this volume] (Heim) *Definiteness and indefiniteness*). Depending on the theory and the type of indefinite, the one or the other aspect is more prominent. Indefinites in English have the form of an indefinite article with a simple or modified noun as in *a book, an interesting book, a book recommended by Professor Schiller*, etc. However, languages provide more lexical items, intonational patterns or syntactic configurations to express indefiniteness in general, or certain aspects of it, see (8a-f) for English:

(8) a. Every student recited a poem of Pindar.
  b. Every student recited this$_{indef}$ poem of Pindar.
  c. Every student recited SOME poem of Pindar.
  d. Every student recited a certain poem of Pindar.
  e. Every student recited at least one poem of Pindar.
  f. Every student recited poems of Pindar.

(8a) is the unmarked form with the indefinite article, the indefinite or presentative *this* in (8b) forces a specific (or referential) reading, the focused *some* in (8c) allows a wide scope reading more easily than the form with the indefinite article in (8a); the specificity marker *a certain* in (8d) forces a wide scope or a functional reading (see section 4), the expression *at least one* in (8d) uncontroversially corresponds to a quantificational reading, while the bare noun in (8f) only allows for a narrow scope reading. Other languages encode specificity contrasts in their article system. For example, Maroccan Arabic has a definite article *l-* and two indefinite articles (in addition to the bare form also expressing indefiniteness): the specific indefinite article *wahed-l*, composed of the numeral 'one' and the definite article (9a), and the non-specific indefinite article *shi* (9b), from Fassi-Fehri (2006, 15).

(9) a. Ja   wahed   l-weld.
       came one   the-boy
       'One (individuated) boy came.'
    b. Ja   shi   weld.
       came some boy
       'Some (non-identified) boy came.'

There is no quantitative or systematic overview of languages with specific articles, but it seems that there is a considerable number of such languages (see e.g. Givón 1973 for Bantu, Matthewson 1999 for in St'át'imcets (Lillooet Salish) and Chung & Ladusaw 2004 for Maori). We also find other morpho-syntactic contrasts expressing specificity: Many languages show a complex system of indefinite pronouns (see Haspelmath 1997 for an overview). Russian, for example, provides different indefinite pronouns composed of wh-words, such as *kakoj*, and additional elements. **Koe**-*kakoj* signals speaker identifiability (10a) and *kakoj*-**to** indicates speaker ignorance, (10b) (Dahl 1970, Geist 2008):

(10) a. **Koe**-*kakoj*   student spisyval na ekzamene.   Ego zovut Ivan Petrov.
        koe-wh   student cheated on exam   he is-called Ivan Petrov
        'A student [known to the speaker] cheated on the exam. His name is Ivan Petrov.'
     b. *Kakoj*-**to** student spisyval na ekzamene. Ja pytajus' vyjasnit', kto eto byl.
        wh-to   student cheated on exam   I try   to find-out who it was
        'A student [not known to the speaker] cheated on the exam. I am trying to figure out who it was.'

Turkish uses accusative case to express specificity of the direct object, as discussed in section 6. There are many more means for marking specificity by lexical items, functional markers or other constructions. In the remainder we will mainly focus on the semantics of unmarked indefinite noun phrases like *a book*, but the analysis can be extended to the class of monotone increasing weak determiners, such as *a, several, some, three*. We will use particular encodings in order to support the one or the other reading.

Fodor & Sag (1982, 358–365; based on Karttunen 1968, Fodor 1970 and others) give a helpful list of linguistic indicators that favor either specific or non-specific readings of indefinites: (i) A main indicator is the content of the noun phrase: the more descriptive content a noun phrase has, the more likely it is to have a specific reading. (ii) Longer restrictive relative clauses represent a good indicator of specificity as well. Non-restrictive relative clauses trigger specific interpretations even more strongly. (iii) Topicalization and left dislocation strongly favor a specific interpretation. (iv) Indefinite or presentative *this* strongly, perhaps uniquely, favors a specific reading (cf. Prince 1981). (v) *There*-insertion is characteristically used for weak quantificational readings, but it also shows an additional discourse function as introducing referents and in this function it allows for referential (specific) indefinites. (vi) Imperatives only allow non specific readings. This set of indicators together with particular determiners or indefinite pronouns constitute reliable diagnostics for most of the relevant cases of specific indefinites (see also article 12 [Semantics: Foundations, History and Methods] (Krifka) *Varieties of semantic evidence*).

Karttunen wrote the two founding papers on specificity, and even though he was not the one to use the term for the first time, he has established it as a linguistic category. The paper *What do referential indices refer to?* from 1968 and the classic paper *Discourse referents* from 1969, which was reprinted in 1976, cover more or less the same phenomena and make the same claims with one important exception: Karttunen (1968) proposes a lexical ambiguity theory of specificity, while Karttunen (1969/1976) suggests a scope analysis. Both papers argue for the introduction of the new concept of *discourse referents*, i.e. referents at an additional semantic-pragmatic discourse level in order to account for the potential of definite and indefinite noun phrases to act as antecedents for intersentential pronouns (see also articles 11 [Semantics: Theories] (Kamp & Reyle) *Discourse Representation Theory* and 38 (Dekker) *Dynamic semantics*). Karttunen makes the following observations: First, definite and indefinite noun phrases behave alike in that they introduce discourse referents in episodic contexts, while quantifiers do not, as (11) shows. Second, definite and indefinite noun phrases differ in the contexts in which they can introduce discourse referents. An indefinite in the scope of an intensional operator like *want* in (12) does not license discourse anaphors (at least in its prominent reading). Still, there is a certain class of indefinite noun phrases that does not follow this restriction, but they have "strikingly different" interpretations (Karttunen 1968, 11) and license discourse anaphora, as in (13). This is exactly the class that is characterized by the specificity indicators listed above.

(11) a. Anna owns the Porsche. It is red.
b. Anna owns a Porsche. It is red.
c. Anna owns every Porsche. *It is red.

(12) a. Chris wants to own the Porsche. It is red.
b. Chris wants to own a Porsche. *It is red.

(13) a. Chris wants to own this$_{indef}$ Porsche. It is red.
  b. Chris wants to own a certain Porsche. It is red.
  c. Chris wants to own a Porsche he saw a day before. It is red.

Anaphoric pronouns play various roles in the investigation of specific indefinites: First, their analysis led to the discovery of specific indefinites, and they are one of the main phenomena that are expected to be better understood, once we have a good theory of specificity. Second, they are often used as a means to disambiguate between a specific and a non-specific reading, as in (3a) or (10a). It must be noted that the anaphor test can only be illustrative, since it is not clear whether the analysis of discourse anaphors is independent of the analysis of specificity. Moreover, specificity is not the only licensor for discourse anaphors—there are many more. Therefore, we cannot directly infer the specificity of an indefinite antecedent from an anaphoric pronoun. This is also the position of Karttunen (1968, 17–18): "the notion of 'discourse referent' as we have used it, is not at all the same as 'the individual the speaker has in mind'." Third, anaphoric pronouns, like *it* in (13), are taken as a strong argument for a referential reading of specific indefinites, assuming that the anaphoric pronoun is of the same referential type as its antecedent, which, however, is not uncontroversial, as already indicated by the last quotation from Karttunen (for further discussion see Partee 1970, Neale 1990, Heim 1991, Dekker 2003 and articles 12 [Semantics: Theories] (Dekker) *Dynamic semantics* and 1 [this volume] (Büring) *Pronouns*).

3 Opaque contexts

According to first investigations of the topic, (referential) specificity was associated with the different readings of the indefinite noun phrases in opaque contexts created by intensional verbs, verbs of propositional attitude, modals, future tense, conditionals, etc. (Quine 1960, Karttunen 1968, 1969/1976, Fodor 1970, Abbott 1976, and more recently Kamp & Bende-Farkas submitted, article 16 [this volume] (Swanson) *Propositional attitudes*). It is argued that indefinites show a contrast that is similar to the *de re* vs. *de dicto* readings of definite noun phrases. Sentence (14) has two prominent readings: In the *de re* reading, the speaker identifies a referent with the definite description *the chairperson of the German Conservatives* and then makes the assertion that Paula has a singular belief about this referent, namely that Bill talked to her. In the *de dicto* reading the sentence asserts that Paula has a belief and that belief has the form of Bill's talking to the chairperson. The *de re* reading allows for the substitution of a referentially identical expression, i.e. if Angela Merkel is the chairperson, we can infer (15) from (14).

(14) Paula believes that Bill talked to the chairperson of the German Conservatives.

(15) Paula believes that Bill talked to Angela Merkel.

Indefinite noun phrases show a very similar contrast in opaque contexts, as in (16). There are two prominent readings, which we will also call *de re* vs. *de dicto* readings. Under the *de re* reading, the speaker refers to a particular referent she has in mind (e.g. Angela Merkel) by using the indefinite noun phrase and then makes the assertion that Paula has the singular belief that Bill talked to her. In the *de dicto* reading, the speaker just makes an assertion that Paula has the general belief that Bill was involved in the activity of talking to an important politician. The *de re* reading allows the two logical inferences of existential entailment (or existential generalization) and substitution of referentially identical expressions. We can infer the existential entailment (17) from the *de re* reading of (16), and together with the identity statement in (18) we can infer (19). The *de dicto* reading does not allow these inferences.

(16) Paula believes that Bill talked to an important politician.

(17) There is an important politician.

(18) an important politician = Angela Merkel

(19) Paula believes that Bill talked to Angela Merkel.

In the philosophical literature the contrast between the *de re* and the *de dicto* reading is often described in the following way: In the *de re* reading the speaker attributes a singular proposition (a proposition about a particular individual, i.e. a thing or a *res*) to the subject of the attitude verb, while in the *de dicto* reading an existential belief is attributed to the subject. The *de re* reading allows for different ways to fix the particular individual. In the default situation both the speaker and the subject of the attitude verb know that individual, but it is also possible that only the speaker or only the subject of the attitude verb knows that individual (see Kamp & Bende-Farkas submitted, n. 1). The latter case still allows for existential entailment and thus licenses discourse anaphora, but it does not correspond to the pretheoretical description of specificity as "the referent the *speaker* has in mind" or of the "referential intention of the *speaker*".

In the following we present three accounts dealing with different readings of indefinites in opaque contexts: (i) the lexical ambiguity theory, (ii) the scope theory, and (iii) the type-shifting theory. The lexical ambiguity approach assumes two indefinite articles in the lexicon, a referential indefinite article and an existential indefinite article, which happen to be homophonous in English (Karttunen 1968, Fodor & Sag 1982, Kratzer 1998, among others), but which may be overtly expressed by different markers in other languages, such as in Maroccan (see above). Actually, it seems that the referential indefinite article of Fodor & Sag (1982) comes very close to the semantics of English indefinite *this* (Prince 1981). Karttunen (1968, 16) represents the specific reading as a constant in predicate logic, as in (21). Fodor & Sag (1982, 387) represent it by a referential operator a_{ref}, which takes a set and picks out the referent the speaker has in mind in the actual world; see (22). They add in footnote 27 that the syntax of this operator corresponds to the epsilon operator of Hilbert & Bernays (1939), although they use a different semantics, namely Kaplan's (1978) semantics of demonstratives. Karttunen (1968, 16) represents the non-specific indefinite article by using Reichenbach's eta operator (originally also from Hilbert & Bernays 1939), as in (23). Like Russell's (1905) iota operator for definite noun phrases, the eta operator has a contextual definition that yields for (23) the two translations (24) and (25), which are in fact the two representations given by the scope theory.

(20) Paula believes that Bill talked to an important politician.

(21) BELIEVE(p, talked_to(b, c)) & important_politician(c)

(22) BELIEVE(p, talked_to(b, a_{ref} x [important_politician(x)]))

(23) BELIEVE(p, talked_to(b, ηx [important_politician(x)]))

(24) ∃x [important_politician(x) & BELIEVE(p, talked_to(b, x))]

(25) BELIEVE(p, ∃x [important_politician(x) & talked_to(b, x)])

The scope theory (McCawley 1968, Karttunen 1969/1976, Fodor 1970) assumes that the indefinite article corresponds to an existential quantifier that binds the variable in the noun phrase and forms a quantificational expression that takes scope with respect to other operators including operators creating opaque contexts. It predicts the two representations (24) and (25), which express a wide scope (*de re*) reading and a narrow scope (*de dicto*) reading, respectively. One problem with this scope theory is that the wide scope representation (24) for the specific reading makes an existential assertion, which is too strong for fictional objects such as witches or dragons. Therefore, Fodor (1970) and Ioup (1977) assume that the quantifier expressing the specificity contrast does not assert (real world) existence, which led Abbott (1976, 2010) to conclude that it quantifies over individual concepts, rather than real world objects. The third theory, the type-shifting approach (Zimmermann 1993, van Geenhoven & McNally 2005) is based on the idea that indefinites like definites can either behave as regular arguments of type *e*, as properties of type <*e,t*>, or as quantifiers of a higher type (see Partee 1987 and article 8 [Semantics: Interfaces] (de Hoop) *Type shifting*). Intensional verbs like *to want, to seek, to hunt, to owe*, etc. (which may occur intensionally with a simple NP object rather than a sentential complement) can take the indefinite in any of its forms. In the property type <*e,t*> the indefinite is semantically incorporated into the predicate and does not introduce a discourse referent; therefore it cannot serve as an antecedent for anaphoric expressions. Although Zimmermann (1993) does not attempt to extend his analysis to complement clauses of the type (20), there are approaches that apply type-shifting rules to derive the two types for the two different readings of indefinites in complement clauses (e.g. Chung & Ladusaw 2004, Chierchia 2005).

The three theories differ in the following way: The type-shifting approach predicts that specificity arises only in opaque contexts. Specific indefinites are indefinites that take scope out of opaque contexts and license discourse anaphora, while non-specific indefinites are predicates that do not license definite anaphoric pronouns. The type-shifting approach explains specificity with the potential of introducing discourse referents. This view, however, is too broad, as other types of indefinites can also license discourse anaphors, as originally noted by Karttunen (see quotation above). The scopal approach correlates specificity with scope and accounts for the *de re* vs. *de dicto* reading by the different scope of the existential quantifier in (24) and (25). The lexical ambiguity approach predicts three logical forms for indefinites in opaque contexts: the *de dicto* reading is illustrated in (25), while (22) and (24) are two representations for *de re* readings. (22) is the *de re* reading where the speaker has a particular individual in mind, while (24) represents the reading where the subject of the attitude verb determines the individual. Fodor & Sag (1982) would only regard (22) as a specific or referential reading, and (24) as a wide scope non-specific or existential reading, since they only relate specific indefinites to the speaker, but not to other attitude holders. The contrast between (22) and (24) is often discussed as being similar to the contrast between referential and attributive readings of definites (Partee 1970 and see section 5 for more discussion).

Indefinites under two operators including opacity show more readings, as illustrated in (26) from Kripke (1977, 259)—similar observations go back to Bach (1968, 107), Karttunen (1969/1976), Fodor (1970).

(26) Hoover charged that the Berrigans plotted to kidnap a high American official.
    a. ....but he said they couldn't decide which one (to kidnap)
    b. ....but he didn't know which one (they plotted to kidnap)
    c. ....guess which one (he charged they plotted to kidnap)
    d. ... but he [i.e. Kissinger] was informed in time.

(27) a. Hoover charged(the Berrigans$_x$ plotted($\exists y$[h-a-o(y) & x kidnap y]))
    b. Hoover charged($\exists y$[h-a-o(y) & the Berrigans$_x$ plotted(x kidnap y)])
    c. $\exists y$[h-a-o(y) & Hoover charged(the Berrigans$_x$ plotted(x kidnap y))]
    d. Hoover charged(the Berrigans$_x$ plotted(x kidnap c])) & h-a-o(c)

Kripke assumes three readings, indicated by the continuations in (26a–c) and represented as (27a–c). There is obviously at least a fourth reading, given in (26d) and represented by (27d), according to which the speaker intended to refer to one particular high American official (according to Kripke this might have been Kissinger). Kripke (1977) claims on the basis of this example that if we understand specificity as a two-way distinction (similar to the referential vs. attributive contrast in definites), the notion of specificity cannot account for the three readings. Instead, he assumes that specificity is a pragmatic notion which follows from general communicative principles. Karttunen (1969, 33/1976, 382) uses similar examples to argue that specificity is not a simple two-way distinction, but "has a relative nature" and is best represented by the scope of the existential quantifier. According to their view of specificity as speaker intended referential expressions, Fodor & Sag (1982) would propose a specific reading (26d) and three non-specific readings (26a–c). For these and other examples, even more complex ones, involving opaque contexts (see Fodor 1970, Ioup 1977), the above theories yield the following options without providing clear criteria to decide between them: (i) The type shifting approach will assign a specific reading to the indefinite if it is interpreted higher than at least one intensional operator. (ii) The scope theory comes in two versions: (iia) According to Karttunen (1969/1976), Fodor (1970) and others, specific indefinites allow for special scope behavior, best represented by the scope of the existential quantifier. This corresponds to the *de re* vs. *de dicto* contrasts. (iib) Kripke (1977), Neale (1990) and others assume that indefinites differ in scope with respect to opaque contexts, explaining the *de re* vs. *de dicto* contrast, but they consider specificity a pragmatic notion orthogonal to this scope behavior. This is the standard position among many philosophers and formal semanticists. (iii) The lexical ambiguity approach predicts a referential reading, which does not interact with scope, and existential readings that show regular scope behavior. The widest scope existential reading shows the same truth conditions as the referential reading. This situation calls for additional criteria to distinguish between specific and non-specific indefinites, such as those provided by languages with particular specificity markers or structural constraints, as discussed in the next section.

4 Exceptional scope behavior

Fodor & Sag (1982) consider three types of specificity: referential specificity as discussed in the last section, scopal specificity discussed in this section, and epistemic specificity presented in section 5. To argue for their lexical ambiguity theory, they relate the specific vs. non-specific contrast to the central issue of the semantics-syntax interface: scope. Scopal specificity is defined as the interpretation of indefinites outside the scope of certain operators—in this section we focus on extensional quantifiers as in (28) (many authors also subsume under scopal specificity the behavior of indefinites in opaque contexts). In the scopal specific or wide-scope reading the indefinite refers to one girl such that five boys are in love with her. In the scopal non-specific, narrow-scope or dependent reading the value of the girl varies with the value of the boys. Here, indefinites show the same scope options as other quantifiers such as the universal quantifier in (29).

(28) Five boys on this street are in love with a girl on this street.

(29) Five boys on this street are in love with every girl on this street.

The ambiguity theory and the scope theory of specificity can both account for these data in languages that allow free Q(antifier) R(aising) and that do not restrict scope to surface order. Fodor & Sag (1982) make a stronger claim: They argue that specific indefinites are able to escape "scope islands", while other quantifiers are not. Scope islands are created by *that*-complements (with lexical heads) as in (30), or by conditionals, as in (31):

(30) a. John overheard the rumor that *each of my students* had been called before the dean.
 b. John overheard the rumor that *a student of mine* had been called before the dean.

(31) a. If *each friend of mine from Texas* had died in the fire, I would have inherited a fortune.
 b. If *a friend of mine from Texas* had died in the fire, I would have inherited a fortune.

(30a) does not have a reading with wide scope for *each of my students*, i.e. there is no reading paraphrasable as: for each of my students, John overheard the rumor that the student had been called before the dean. Yet, the wide-scope reading is easily available for the indefinite *a student of mine* in (30b): There is a student of mine such that John overheard that the student had been called before the dean. The same holds for the conditional: (31a) has only one reading, according to which all of my Texan friends must die before I inherit a fortune. (31b) allows for the wide-scope reading of the indefinite, according to which there is a friend of mine such that if he dies I inherit a fortune. This observation is very stable and can be extended to other scope islands (see Fodor & Sag 1982, Ruys 1992, Szabolcsi 2010). It is called "exceptional wide scope", "long-distance construal", or "non-local scope". Fodor & Sag's (1982) lexical ambiguity theory predicts the exceptional wide-scope reading since the referential reading of the indefinite is scopeless and thus always entails widest scope. They argue that the data force us to accept that either the existential quantifier is not an adequate representation for all indefinites, or that it has a more flexible behavior with respect to scope islands. The latter option has serious consequences for the semantics-syntax interface and for a uniform treatment of all quantifiers. Besides this very general concern, Fodor & Sag (1982) present two further arguments against a scope theory with such flexible restrictions: the lack of intermediate readings and violations of conditions on variable binding in VP-deletion contexts. Ruys (1992) and Winter (1997) add a third observation concerning distributive readings of indefinites. In the following we only focus on the discussion of exceptional wide-scope readings and the prediction of the absence of the intermediate reading. (See Schwarz 2004 for VP-deletion contexts and Ruys 1992, Winter 1997, von Stechow 2000 for distributive readings.)

Fodor & Sag (1982) replace the proper name in (30b) by a universal quantifier in (32a) creating three different scope positions for the indefinite, as represented in (32b–d):

(32) a. Each teacher overheard the rumor that *a student of mine* had been called before the dean.
 b. (a student of mine: y) [(each teacher: x) [x overheard the rumor that [y had been called before the dean]]]
 c. (each teacher: x) [(a student of mine: y) [x overheard the rumor that [y had been called before the dean]]]
 d. (each teacher: x) [x overheard the rumor that [(a student of mine: y) [y had been called before the dean]]]

The lexical ambiguity theory predicts two readings: a referential reading (with apparent widest scope) corresponding to the truth conditions of (32b) and an existential narrow-scope reading (32d). It also predicts the unavailability of the intermediate reading (32c), which would be "for every teacher there is a possibly different student such that the teacher overheard the rumor that this student had been called before the dean". This is because the existential quantifier cannot leave the scope island (assuming regular quantifier properties) and the referential reading always entails truth conditions corresponding to the widest scope reading. Fodor & Sag (1902) report that (32a) has no intermediate reading, which confirms their prediction. However, in reaction to this claim in a preprint, Farkas (1981) provides examples like (33a) that show three different scope readings for the indefinite, paraphrased as (33b–d), including the intermediate-scope reading (33c), which contradicts Fodor and Sag's claim.

(33) a. Every professor rewarded every student who read a book on the semantics-pragmatics interface.
   b. widest scope: a book > every professor > every student
   There is particular book on the s-p-i such that every professor rewarded every student who read that book.
   c. intermediate scope: every professor > a book > every student
   For every professor there is a certain (possibly different) book on the s-p-i, such that the professor rewarded every student who read that book.
   d. narrowest scope: every professor > every student > a book
   Every professor rewarded every student who read a (= any) book on the s-p-i.

Particular readings can be brought out or forced by using certain forms: a very short and uninformative indefinite, as *a book*, tends to trigger the narrowest-scope reading as in (34a); a very informative and descriptively rich indefinite as in (34b) or an indefinite that contains a proper name or a demonstrative expression as in (34c) tends to trigger the widest-scope reading.

Indefinites with pronouns in their descriptive content that are bound by some higher operator are forced to take scope under this operator, as in (34d).

(34) a. Every professor rewarded every student who read a book.
   b. Every professor rewarded every student who read a book on the semantics-pragmatics interface that was discussed recently on the LinguistList.
   c. Every professor rewarded every student who read a book that Prof. Schiller/this professor had recommended.
   d. Every professor rewarded every student who read a book that she had recommended.
   e. Every professor rewarded every student who read a certain book.

f. Every professor rewarded every student who read the first book that she had recommended.
g. Every professor rewarded every student who read SOME book.

Before we discuss the different approaches to the two problems, namely the exceptional wide-scope behavior of indefinites and intermediate readings, we have to distinguish between different kinds of intermediate readings and introduce the appropriate terminology (Schwarz 2001, Endriss 2009). In all intermediate readings (34d–g), the indefinite varies with the value for the universal quantifier *every professor*, but in different ways. In (34d) the intermediate-scope reading goes back to an overtly expressed variable x in the descriptive content *book x has recommended* that is bound by a higher operator, here by *every professor*. The set of books depends on the professors and so the selected book varies with the choice of professors, exhibiting a so-called "apparent intermediate-scope" reading. The specificity marker *a certain* in (34e) triggers a so-called "wide-scope functional" reading that allows for the widest-scope reading, similar to (33b). But it also licenses a reading according to which professors systematically select books. This can be described by a function with widest scope, yet the books vary with the professors yielding "apparent intermediate scope" for the book. If the function is explicitly expressed, as in (34f), we have to use a functional definite noun phrase with apparent intermediate scope. Finally, there is also a "genuine intermediate-scope" reading, as in (34g), often triggered by *some* or even more strongly by accented SOME. Here the indefinite actually takes scope over the universal quantifier *every student*. The difference between this "genuine intermediate" scope reading and the "(wide-scope) functional (apparent) intermediate reading" is that books co-vary unsystematically in the former case and systematically (according to a "method") in the latter case. Functional readings are restricted to nameable and informative functions (see Hintikka 1986, Endriss 2009, 92–101), such as *the first book she has recommended* or *his supervisor*.

We compare four general strategies to account for the exceptional scope behavior and intermediate-scope readings: (i) Under the *long-distance scope shift* approach (dubbed so by Schwarz 2001) fewer restrictions than normal are ascribed on movement to the existential quantifier. The other approaches all assume that the indefinite is not moved but stays in situ. (ii) In the *existentially closed choice function* approach, scope is derived by assuming that the indefinite article introduces a choice function variable that can be bound freely at different scope sites (Winter 1997); (iii) In the *contextually determined choice function* approach the free choice function variable is contextually determined (Kratzer 1998) or existentially bound at the discourse level (Matthewson 1999), and (iv) Under the *singleton indefinite* or *implicit domain restriction* approach the indefinite is enriched by descriptive material until it expresses a singleton and therefore gives the illusion of wide scope, similarly to other domain restriction approaches (Portner 2002, Schwarzschild 2002). Approach (i) stands in the tradition of the scopal theory, while Kratzer's *choice function* approach (iii) is an instantiation of Fodor and Sag's ambiguity theory. The *existentially closed choice function* approach (ii) comes in both variants: Reinhart (1997) assumes lexical ambiguity, whereas Winter (1997) is just a scopal approach with choice functions.

A choice function f is defined as an operation that assigns to any non-empty set one of its elements (It is not defined for empty sets—we ignore this, but see Winter 1997 for a discussion).

(35) f is a choice function: ch(f) iff P(f(P)), where P is nonempty

The indefinite *a book* is represented by $f(book)$, with the choice function variable f that is either existentially bound, as in (36c) (Reinhart 1997, Winter 1997) or free, i.e. is determined by the speaker or some other salient agent in the context, as in (36d) (Kratzer 1998). Note that this choice function must not be available for the hearer. If the hearer knows the referential intentions of the speaker or the method to identify the object, we have to use a definite expression as in (34f) above, rather than an indefinite one.

(36) a. Peter reads a book.
 b. ∃y[book(y) & read(p, y)]
 c. ∃f [ch(f) & read(p, f(book))]
 d. read(p, f(book))
 e. read(p, ε_ix [book(x)])

Given that there are books and a speaker-given choice function, the representations with choice functions have the same truth conditions as the classical representation (36b) with an existential quantifier. Furthermore, the representations are equivalent to the indexed epsilon formula in (36e) (Egli 1991, Egli & von Heusinger 1995), where the epsilon operator (Hilbert & Bernays 1939) forms a term out of a predicate. Its interpretation is a choice function and the index allows binding this choice function by some operator or contextual parameter. The epsilon notion has the advantage of providing a formal representation of the indefinite as a term-creating operator—similar to the iota operator. However, we will use the more common choice function notation.

The widest-scope reading of the indefinite in a scope island (37a) has the representation (37c) for a flexible scope theory. The existential choice function approach is represented in (37d) with the paraphrase: There is a choice function such that every professor rewarded every student who read the book on the semantics-pragmatics interface selected by that choice function. (37e) is the representation with a contextually given choice function. Again, all formulas are equivalent given that there are books and one contextually given choice function.

(37) a. Every professor rewarded every student who read a book on the semantics-pragmatics interface.
　　　b. wide scope: a book on the s-p-i > every professor > every student
　　　　 There is a particular book on the s-p-i, such that every professor rewarded every student who read that book.
　　　c. $\exists y[\text{book-on-s-p-i}(y)\ \&\ \forall x[\text{professor}(x) \rightarrow x$ rewarded every student who read $y]]$
　　　d. $\exists f[\text{ch}(f)\ \&\ \forall x[\text{professor}(x) \rightarrow x$ rewarded every student who read $f(\text{book-on-s-p-i})]]$
　　　e. $\forall x[\text{professor}(x) \rightarrow x$ rewarded every student who read $f(\text{book-on-s-p-i})]$

In the following we focus on the intermediate-scope reading of (38a), as paraphrased in (38b) and the representation (38c) for the flexible scope theory. The existentially closed choice function approach introduces a choice function variable attached to the indefinite *in situ* and binds it by an existential quantifier that has scope between the two universal quantifiers, as in (38d). Since the existential quantifier of choice functions is not subject to island constraints, this configuration is not prohibited.

(38) a. Every professor rewarded every student who read a book on the semantics-pragmatics interface.
　　　b. intermediate scope: every professor > a book on the s-p-i > every student
　　　　 For every professor there is a certain (possibly different) book on the s-p-i, such that the professor rewarded every student who read that book.
　　　c. $\forall x[\text{professor}(x) \rightarrow \exists y[\text{book-on-s-p-i}(y)\ \&\ x$ rewarded every student who read $y]]$
　　　d. $\forall x[\text{professor}(x) \rightarrow \exists f[\text{ch}(f)\ \&\ x$ rewarded every student who read $f(\text{book-on-s-p-i})]]$

The contextually determined choice function approach assumes that the choice function variable is contextually determined, entailing a wide-scope reading (similar to the original Fodor and Sag approach), as in (37e) above. The intermediate reading, however, can be forced by a bound variable in the descriptive content, e.g. *book on the s-p-i she has recommended*. Thus the set of books depends on the professor and the selected element co-varies with the values for professors, as in (38e), yielding an "apparent intermediate" or "pseudoscope" reading (Kratzer 1998).

(38) e. ∀x[professor(x) → [x rewarded every student who read f(book-on-s-p-i x *recommended*)]]

The representation (38e) leads to a new problem: If two professors have recommended the same books, the choice function *f* would select the same book, since the sets are extensionally identical. This is too strong a restriction for the intermediate reading, which intuitively allows for different choices of books depending on professors, even if they recommend the same set of books. Therefore, Kratzer (1998) introduces a "Skolemized" choice function in (38f), i.e. a contextually given Skolem function *g* that takes one individual argument (or parameter) and a set argument and yields one element of the set. Note that the latter representation is equivalent to a representation with an ordinary Skolem-function f_{sk}, as in (38g) given that there are books and speaker-given Skolem functions.

(38) f. ∀x [professor(x) → [x rewarded every student who read g(x)(book on the s-p-i x has recommended)]] with *g* assigning choice functions to professors such that the choice function selects a book on the s-p-i that the professor has recommended
  g. ∀x [professor(x) → [x rewarded every student who read f_{sk}(x)]] with f_{sk} assigning books on the s-p-i to professors such that the professor has recommended it

Schwarzschild (2002) proposes an alternative view on the exceptional scope behavior of indefinites. He applies the domain restriction approach of other quantifiers and shows that enriching the descriptive material of the indefinite leads to truth-conditional effects that are equivalent to Kratzer's approach. The wide-scope reading is entailed by an indefinite that is restricted to a singleton set ('singleton indefinite'), while the intermediate-scope reading is derived by a restriction resulting in a function that depends on the highest quantifier, as in (38h), expressing a functional reading. Even though domain restriction is necessary for other quantifiers, it is not clear whether the restriction to a singleton set is always justified, as examples with partitives show (see Endriss 2009, 136).

(38) h. ∀x [professor(x) → [x rewarded every student who read *a book on the s-p-i x had put on top of her_x reading list*.]

So far all four theories do quite well, although by different means. The flexible scope theory and the existential choice function approach reconstruct the different readings by different scopes of the existential quantifier for the indefinite and the choice function, respectively. The contextual choice function approach and the domain restriction approach both use contextually given information to fix the referent; they allow for "apparent" intermediate-scope readings via wide-scope functions. These two types of analyses correspond to the two types of intermediate scope readings. The first group accounts for "genuine" intermediate-scope readings by existential binding at different levels, while the second group accounts for "functional apparent intermediate scope" by assuming a contextually given function.

Following Schwarz (2001), Chierchia (2001) and Roberts (2007) we can make the following observations: (i) functional indefinites allow for widest scope, but also for apparent intermediate scope; (ii) not all non-narrowest scope indefinites are functional, i.e. there is a difference between genuine intermediate scope and functional apparent intermediate scope; (iii) the difference becomes evident in downward entailing contexts, as discussed below. The specificity marker *a certain* triggers functional readings, while *some* favors non-functional, i.e. genuine scope readings. The literature does not agree whether the indefinite article allows for both readings. Schwarz (2001) maintains that in English it only has a non-functional reading, while Kratzer (1998) opts for both readings following the lexical ambiguity theory of Fodor & Sag (1982). Endriss (2009) argues that the German indefinite article *ein* also allows for both readings. We discuss the two readings with examples involving *a certain* and *some* for clarity: Observation (i) is vindicated by (39a), which shows a functional reading with the *supervisor-of*-function for the indefinite *a certain professor*. In this reading, the value for professor systematically co-varies with the value for student yielding apparent intermediate scope.

(39) a. Every student read every article a certain professor has written, namely his supervisor.
b. Every student read every article some professor has written.

(39b) allows for an intermediate reading, where we can unsystematically assign professors to students. Observation (ii) concerns the difference between the two readings. In a situation where we have three students with supervisors from Stuttgart and two of the students read every article by their supervisors while the third one read every article by a professor from MIT, (39a) becomes false, while (39b) is true. For addressing observation (iii) we consider the downward entailing contexts in (40):

(40) a. No student read every article a certain professor has written, namely his supervisor.
b. No student read every article some professor has written.

A situation where one student read all the papers of a professor from MIT makes (40b) false, while (40a) may be true. The situation where no student read every article by his supervisor (but perhaps every paper by the MIT professor), verifies (40a), but not necessarily (40b). This shows that we have two different intermediate scope readings. There are clearly distinct readings for *a certain* and *some* conforming to the lexical ambiguity theory of Fodor & Sag (1982) with the contextually given functional reading corresponding to the specific reading and the genuine scope reading to the non-specific reading. However, we have to add the following observations: First, it is controversial whether indefinite noun phrases with an indefinite article are ambiguous in the same way. Second, if the contrast also holds for the indefinite article (Kratzer 1998), we still have to modify Fodor & Sag's (1982) original prediction. Specific indefinites show not only a widest-scope "object" reading, but also a widest-scope functional reading, which can in turn depend on further parameters yielding different kinds of "apparent" intermediate scopes. Third, Fodor and Sag were not correct in predicting the lack of the genuine intermediate reading for existential indefinites. There is clear evidence that an existential indefinite can take exceptional scope. This has to be explained by a different mechanism (e.g. Ebert, Endriss & Hinterwimmer 2009 propose that embedded indefinite topics can take genuine intermediate scope). We have learned from the discussion of scopal specificity that the differences in the scope behavior of indefinites are not a very reliable indicator for a specific reading. Before we discuss another aspect of the distinction between specific and non-specific readings in the next section, we have to make some observations with respect to the representation of indefinites as choice functions presented in this section.

Using choice functions allows dissociating the scope of the indefinite from its descriptive content. While the descriptive content stays in situ, the choice function variable can be bound at different places in the sentence representing different scopal properties of the indefinite. Choice functions also capture the intuitive idea that a specific indefinite can be understood as selecting an element out of a set according to a certain method. In a very general sense, choice functions are term-creating operations corresponding to type shifting from a set to an individual, which seems necessary for independent reasons. Furthermore, by representing specific indefinites as choice functions, we can give similar representations for definites and specific indefinites as we can understand the iota operator as a contextually given choice function that is available to speaker and hearer, while a specific indefinite is represented by a hearer-unknown choice function (Egli & von Heusinger 1995, Chierchia 2005, Roberts 2007). On the other hand, choice function approaches are controversial, as the representation of indefinites with choice functions seems to be too flexible: Choice functions do not allow for existential entailments. It is an open issue whether this is a welcome result for fictional objects (see Ruys 2006) or whether this has to be repaired (see Winter 1997). Perhaps specific indefinites presuppose their referent in some way—see section 6 for further discussions. Choice functions are defined for all non-empty sets, but we only use very partial choice functions for representing indefinites, actually only those defined for the relevant set (see Kamp & Bende-Farkas 2006, section 12). Existentially bound choice functions predict wrong readings in downward entailing contexts (see Schwarz 2001, Chierchia 2001 for discussion and additional restrictions on choice function construals). This problem, however, does not arise with contextually bound choice functions (see Kratzer 2003). A final criticism is that once we are forced to use Skolemized choice functions, i.e. functions with one individual argument and a set argument, we may as well take Skolem functions with n-individual arguments and abandon in this way the problematic choice functions (see Hintikka 1986, Steedman 2007, Kamp & Bende-Farkas submitted, Onea & Geist 2011 among others).

There are alternative approaches to the flexible scope behavior of indefinites that are non-configurational, i.e. they assume different mechanisms of interpretation, rather than different representations. Abusch (1994) formulates such an approach in discourse representation theory using Cooper storage for keeping track of the different dependencies. Below, I give a brief sketch of the indexical approach of Farkas (1994, 1997 and more recently Brasoveanu & Farkas 2009) that operates on dependencies between assignment functions (see also Enç 1991). Farkas (1994, 1997) assumes that the semantic content of a sentence consists of the main predication *MP* and a set of arguments constraining conditions. Indefinite noun phrases contribute a discourse referent *x* together with a descriptive content *DC*. The main predication and the descriptive content are interpreted via Kaplan-style evaluation indices with indefinites being free to choose the evaluation index for the descriptive content; it need not be the same as the evaluation index of the main predicate (following an observation by Enç 1986 on the temporal index). Evaluation indices may be free or bound. In the latter case the index must be restricted to a particular value due to local properties. A free index may get any value that is available in the context (or discourse). The indefinite article is unmarked and does not contribute any restrictions, whereas reduced *some*, [*sm*], or indefinite *this* impose particular constraints. This account allows for modeling the different readings of indefinites without assuming lexical ambiguity, a configurational scope theory, or a representation in some way or other. The different scope options of (41a) are derived by different indexations:

(41) a. Every student speaks an Indo-European language.
 b. Narrow scope:
    $(\forall_x (x: student(x))_{G'} (y_{G''} \text{I-E language}(y) \text{ speak}(x,y))_{G''})_g$
 c. Wide scope:
    $(\forall_x (x: student(x))_{G'} (y_g \text{I-E language}(y) \text{ speak}(x,y))_{G''})_g$

In the narrow-scope reading (41b) the value of *y* (standing for the indefinite) is fixed by the local assignment function *G"*, an update of the assignment function *G'*, which is introduced by the universal quantifier. Thus, the value of *y* co-varies with the value of the universal quantifier. In the wide-scope reading (41c), the initial function *g* determines the value of *y*, which is therefore fixed by the context and does not vary with the universal quantifier. This mechanism allows for modeling the intermediate scope of indefinites as well. In a recent modification, Brasoveanu & Farkas (2009) can even store and retrieve quantificational dependencies in order to account for more complex functional readings. The indexical approach can also account for complex examples discussed in the literature where the variable and the descriptive content of an indefinite noun phrase are evaluated according to different indices (i.e. double indexation). The indexical theory is the most flexible theory with respect to the scope of indefinites discussed so far. Therefore it needs additional restrictions to express certain scope preferences and to prohibit overgeneration of the mechanism. It raises the question of what has to be represented in the logical form and what should rather be integrated into the interpretation process.

Summarizing the discussion of specificity and exceptional scope behavior of indefinites, we have seen on the one hand that Fodor & Sag's (1982) claim that only specific indefinites show exceptional scope behavior is not correct, since other indefinites can take exceptional scope by independent mechanisms, as well, and on the other hand, we have seen that there are two different kinds of intermediate exceptional scope readings: the functional or systematic co-variation and the genuine scope or unsystematic co-variation reading. If this contrast corresponds to the specific vs. non-specific contrast, and we have good reasons to assume this, we can conclude that scope is not a sufficient means to account for specificity. This brings us back to the original intuition about the relation between the pragmatic concept of referential intention and the linguistic category of specificity, which will be investigated in more detail in the next section.

5 Epistemic specificity

From the very first discussion, specificity has been closely related to the "referential intentions" of the speaker, paraphrased as "the speaker has a particular individual in mind" (Karttunen 1968, 20). Farkas (1994) uses the term "epistemic specificity" to describe the contrasts that we find in contexts without any other operator and that are caused just by the option of a referential intention, as illustrated in (42) from Karttunen (1968, 14). It is interesting to note that we do not find this example in Karttunen (1969/1976), where he defends a scope theory of specificity.

(42) a. I talked with a logician.
　　　b. I talked with Rudolf.
　　　c. I talked with a famous philosopher.
　　　d. I talked with the author of Meaning and Necessity.
　　　e. ..., and not with a linguist.
　　　f. ..., therefore I now understand the first and second syllogism.

The paraphrases in (42b–d) are possible if the speaker has talked to Rudolf Carnap, a famous philosopher and the author of Meaning and Necessity, and the speaker has this referent in mind. Thus (42a) in its specific reading is an answer to the question "Who did you talk with this morning?". Karttunen (1968, 14) adds: "The speaker has a certain referent in his mind; and, in his knowledge, there also are some properties associated with that particular individual. Any of these properties could presumably be used to describe the individual." The non-specific reading of the indefinite is an answer to "What *kind* of person did you talk with this morning?" This reading is favored by the continuations in (42e–f) and the contrastive accent on *logician*. In the classical example from Fodor & Sag (1982, 355, their (1)), the indefinite is in subject (and topic) position in (43).

(43) a. A student in syntax 1 cheated on the final exam. It was the guy who sits in the very back.
　　　b. A student in syntax 1 cheated on the final exam. I wonder which student it was.
　　　c. A student that Betty used to know in Arkansas cheated on the exam.
　　　d. A friend of mine cheated on the exam.
　　　e. Someone cheated on the exam.

In the specific interpretation (43a) the speaker "has a referent in mind" and makes an assertion about this referent. In the non-specific reading (43b), the speaker just makes an assertion that the set of students in the syntax class who cheated on the final exam is not empty. The reading can be disambiguated by the usual means listed in section 2: the specific meaning is triggered by adding more descriptive material as in (43c–d), and the non-specific one by the uninformative *someone* in (43e). In the following, we focus on the relation between specificity and the contrast between referential and attributive readings for definites. In a next step we discuss different ways to represent the two concepts "the speaker has the referent in mind", and "the speaker can uniquely identify the referent". This discussion brings us to the problem of how to represent speaker-given, but discourse-new and hearer-new information. This question is addressed by briefly reporting on the discourse-oriented account of epistemic specificity by Kamp & Bende-Farkas (submitted).

The contrast between epistemic specific readings and epistemic non-specific readings is often paralleled by Donnellan's (1966) contrast between a referential reading and an attributive reading of definites as in (44) (see Partee 1970 for discussion).

(44) a. The man who lives in Apt. 3 is insane.
 b. The man who lives in Apt. 3 is Smith and, Smith is insane.
 c. Whoever lives in Apt. 3 is insane.

In the referential reading of (44a), paraphrased as (44b), the speaker identifies an individual by the definite description and then asserts about this individual that he or she is insane. In the attributive reading, as in the paraphrase (44c), the speaker asserts that *whoever lives in Apt. 3* is insane. Donnellan (1966) maintains that (44a) has two different semantic forms corresponding to the two paraphrases. (44b) is a singular proposition and (44c) a general proposition; they also differ in truth conditions (e.g. if there is no man living in Apt. 3). Stalnaker (1970) and Kaplan (1978) follow Donnellan's position and provide semantic representations for referential definite noun phrases. Kripke (1977), however, argues that the sentence only has the attributive (or Russellian) reading (44c) (its "semantic reference"), but the speaker can have a certain referential intention ("speaker's reference") as in (44b). Thus the difference between the referential and the attributive reading is located in the pragmatics of using expressions. Neale (1990), Heim (1991) and article 2 [this volume] (Heim) *Definiteness and indefiniteness* give overviews of the controversial discussion of the semantic or pragmatic status of this distinction. They conclude that it is a pragmatic distinction. Ludlow & Neale (1991) discuss the contrast for indefinites and also conclude that the specific vs. non-specific contrast is not part of the semantics (in the sense of truth conditions), but pragmatically motivated. The difference between referential definites and specific indefinites is that for the former, the hearer must also be able to identify the intended referent, while for specific indefinites the intended referent must be unfamiliar for the hearer (Dekker 2004, 369); nevertheless s/he has to establish a permanent representation for that referent. Thus, Stalnaker (1998, 16) holds that the difference between specific and non-specific indefinites is crucial for discourse structure: "The account I am sketching suggests that this difference matters, not to the interpretation of the indefinite expression itself, but only to the evaluation of subsequent statements made with pronouns anaphoric to the indefinite expression." Another aspect is noted by Kamp & Bende-Farkas (submitted) based on Hintikka (1967) and Kaplan (1978), who argue that the difference in (44) becomes truth-conditionally relevant once we use the definite NP in (44a) as the complement of an attitude verb like *want*, as in (45), or the indefinite NP in (42a) as the complement of *believe*, as in (46).

(45) John wants to murder the man who lives in Apt. 3.

(46) John believes that Lauri talked with a logician.

Both sentences have two readings: In the *de re* reading, either the speaker or the attitude holder can identify the referent and the sentence asserts a relation between the subject, the referent and a property. In the *de dicto* reading the sentence expresses a relation between the subject and a property. This perspective connects epistemic specificity with referential specificity as discussed in section 3, rather than with scopal specificity.

The concept of "the referent the speaker has in mind" has been modeled in different ways. Fodor & Sag (1982) propose a referential interpretation of the indefinite, similar to indexical expressions—it appears that they take indefinite *this* as the prototypical specific indefinite. The discussion of the specificity marker *a certain* in English shows that some modifications of Fodor & Sag's original concept are necessary. First, it is not always the speaker who is "responsible" for the referent, but some other salient agent in the context, or the subject of the sentence. For the latter case, see example (47) from Higginbotham (1987), where one can felicitously use *a certain* even in a situation in which only George can identify the student in (47b).

(47) a. George (to Lisa): I met a certain student from Austin today.
　　　b. Lisa: George said that he met a (certain) student from Austin today.

The second modification is that the use of *a certain* need not trigger wide scope for the indefinite, as illustrated in (48) from Hintikka (1986) and already discussed in the last section.

(48) a. Every true Englishman adores a certain woman.
　　　b. namely the Queen
　　　c. $\forall y\ [y$ is a true Englishman $\rightarrow y$ adores $a_{ref}(woman)]$

d. namely his mother
e. ∀y [y is a true Englishman → y adores $f(y)$] and f is a function from Englishmen into their mothers

Besides the reading with wide scope for *a certain woman* as forced by (48b) and represented in (48c), the sentence has also a reading in which the indefinite takes narrow scope due to a functional wide-scope reading, which is represented by the Skolem function *f* in (48e). For a discussion of natural functions and the alternative between choice functions and Skolem functions see section 5. There are different ways to characterize the "vague" function of "having in mind". Yeom (1998) assumes that the speaker can identify the referent of the indefinite by acquaintance and he proposes the function of "having cognitive contact to". This function is transitive, i.e. it is sufficient that the speaker has access to someone who has cognitive contact to the referent. Other approaches use an "identifying property" or an "identifying idea" for restricting the domain of the indefinite to a singleton (Portner 2002, Schwarzschild 2002, Breheny 2003, Umbach 2004). The functional approach as well as the domain restriction allow for different scopal behavior, as illustrated in the previous section.

A final question concerns the distinction between speaker representation, hearer representation and discourse representation or common ground. Approaches to epistemic specificity assume that the speaker has particular knowledge of the referent or of the methods to identify the referent. It is crucial that this knowledge is not in the common ground. If it were also available to the hearer, the speaker would have used a definite expression. The additional knowledge about the referent can be modeled in restrictions on the belief states or worlds of the relevant agents (e.g. Farkas 1994, Alonso-Ovalle & Menéndez-Benito 2010). An epistemic specific indefinite receives a rigid representation in the speaker's knowledge state, which must then be negotiated into the common ground. One way to model this negotiation is to assume some kind of presupposition accommodation (e.g. Yeom 1998, Geurts 2010, see section 8). Kamp & Bende-Farkas (submitted) extend the epistemic view from a speaker perspective to a hearer perspective. They distinguish between a *specific use* of an indefinite by the speaker and a *specific interpretation* by the hearer. The speaker signals by means of a linguistic form associated with specificity (such as *a certain*) that the hearer should create a stable representation for the indefinite introduced. Under this account, specific indefinites behave more like hearer-new proper names, which force the hearer to establish a stable representation for the subsequent discourse. The account also hints at the discourse function of specific indefinites discussed as "referential persistence" or "topic continuity" (Givón 1983) in section 9.

6 Referential anchoring

Different contrasts associated with different kinds of specificity can be best unified by the following generalization: In its prototypical use, the concept of specificity is associated with the communicative notion of referential intention. However, specificity also covers relations between discourse entities, which can only be said to have "referential intentions" of the involved discourse items in a very abstract way. Rather, it seems that specificity in this sense is a grammaticalized means to structure the relations among discourse items: A specific indefinite is *referentially anchored* to a salient discourse participant or another discourse referent, i.e. "the referent of the specific expression is linked by a contextually salient function to the referent of another expression" (von Heusinger 2002, 45). Under this account, the context has to provide two parameters: the anchoring function and the anchor itself. The speaker has to be able to specify the anchoring function, which must be unfamiliar to the hearer in the same way as the intended referent must be unfamiliar. Still the hearer has to represent the fact that there is an anchoring function. The anchor, however, must be familar to both speaker and hearer, which allows speaker and hearer to share the scopal properties of the indefinite. This concept of specificity is a refinement of Fodor & Sag's (1982) original account in terms of referential (Kaplan-style) expressions. Below we first discuss the modifications and then give a brief overview of different versions of referential anchoring proposed in the literature.

Karttunen (1968) represents specific indefinites as individual constants, similar to proper names, while Fodor & Sag (1982, 388) give an indexical interpretation of specific indefinites, analogously to the use of demonstratives, but with the unfamiliarity condition for indefinites. They model specific indefinites with a contextual index c_{IR} for *intended referent*. Other representations of specific indefinites in the same tradition include the descriptive content as well, as in (49b), while (49a) provides the existential interpretation of the indefinite (from Heim 1991, 518, cf. also article 2 [this volume] (Heim) *Definiteness and indefiniteness*).

(49) a. $[\![a_{quant} N]\!] = \lambda Q.\ \exists x.\ [N(x)\ \&\ Q(x)]$
 b. $[\![a_{ref} N]\!]$ is defined only if there is a unique individual that the speaker of the sentence has in mind, and this individual is N

In the approach presented here, the uniqueness condition in the definition (49b) is captured by a function from the anchor to the referent: *f(anchor) = referent*, different versions of which we discuss below. The first modification concerns potential anchors. It has been observed that besides the speaker other attitude holders can also be anchors for the specific indefinite. In one reading of (50), Paula has a referential intention and therefore the sentence asserts that Paula has a singular belief about that referent, which entails the existence of an important politician, as discussed in section 3.

(50) Paula believes that Bill talked to an important politician.

It is often assumed that the anchor must be an attitude holder, who can have referential intentions. This is not always the case, as illustrated by examples in which the anchor is a variable bound by a quantifier, as in (51) and (52). Both examples have readings where the specific indefinite systematically co-varies with its anchor (or binder), giving rise to the apparent intermediate reading discussed in section 4.

(51) Every husband had forgotten a certain date—his wife's birthday.

(52) Every professor rewarded every student who read a book on the semantics-pragmatics interface.

For these cases, we have to make an additional modification concerning the content of the function from anchor to referent. It is not enough to say that the professor has a certain book in mind, but we need systematic co-variation between professors and books, as shown in section 4. Thus the anchoring function does not concern the "referential intention" of the professor or the husband (or what he has in mind, which would be somewhat contradictory) but the assignment between husbands and dates or professors and books. These functions must be natural and informative (see the discussion above). (53) and (54) demonstrate that even though the function must have certain properties and must be contextually given, the exact definition of the function may be unknown even to the speaker. It is a controversial issue whether the speaker should in principle be able to recover the content of the function or not. Yeom (1998) for example argues that there must be a causal chain from the speaker to the agent who is responsible for the content of the function.

(53) The teacher gave every child a certain task to work on during the afternoon.

(54) Each reporter was assigned to a certain politician by the editor of the paper.

We can summarize the characterization of referential anchoring as follows: In the prototypical case the anchoring function takes the speaker as its argument, and its value is the referent of the specific indefinite. However, besides the speaker, other arguments may occupy this position. The content of the function can vary from "x has y in mind" to "there is a natural and informative function from x to y". With these two modifications in place the concept becomes more flexible than Fodor and Sag's account, as it also covers functional apparent intermediate-scope readings. We present three different approaches that spell out referential anchoring by means of (i) anchoring relations in DRT, (ii) Skolemized choice functions and (iii) Skolem functions.

Kamp & Bende-Farkas (2006, based on a manuscript from 2001) use anchored representations in DRT. They distinguish between external anchors, i.e. functions that relate a discourse referent to an object in the world (like proper names to their bearers) and internal anchors, i.e. functions that relate the representation to other discourse referents. These two kinds of anchors allow them to model their distinction between the specific *use* of an indefinite by the speaker and the specific *interpretation* by the hearer. The speaker's specific use is represented by an external anchor to the object that is the intended referent of the indefinite, while the internal anchor is used in the hearer's representation between a representation of the speaker and the discourse referent for the specific indefinite. Speaker and hearer must negotiate the reference and align their representations. However, what is important here is that the internal anchor of the hearer is similar to the referential anchors discussed above.

Von Heusinger (2002 based on earlier work) cashes out the idea of referential anchoring in terms of parameterized or Skolemized choice functions, better known from Kratzer (1998) or Chierchia (2001, 2005). The idea is that the indefinite article can translate into the complex pronominal element f_x with x being a parameter that might be bound by some context agent or some quantifier phrase that has wider scope than the indefinite. The function f applied to the anchor yields a choice function that is applied to the set denoted by the descriptive content of the indefinite yielding the referent, as in (55) adapted from Roberts (2007).

(55) Referential anchoring with parameterized choice functions
 i. complex pronominal element f_x
 ii. x parameter (= anchor), the argument of f, binding is pragmatically given
  a) might be bound by some context agent (speaker etc.)
  b) might be bound by a wider scope QP to yield intermediate scope
 iii. f(x): a choice function that takes a set denoted by DC [descriptive content; KvH] as its argument and yields an element of that set

Onea & Geist (2011) have developed a different implementation of the original idea. They assume a classical account of indefinites as existential quantifiers with additional pragmatic enrichment operations. One such operation is domain restriction (Schwarzschild 2002), another one is referential anchoring. They convincingly argue that domain restriction and referential anchoring have different contextual triggers and semantic effects, as domain restriction enriches the descriptive content of the indefinite and reduces the associated set, while referential anchoring directly identifies one element of the set. They start with the classical semantics of an indefinite as given in (49a), repeated as (56i). They achieve domain restriction with the relation $R(x,y)$, i.e. via relational restriction of the descriptive content, as in (ii). Finally, they allow for referentially anchoring $m(c) = x$, which guarantees the singleton set condition. The anchoring function m and the anchor c are free variables and must get values from the context.

(56) referential anchoring as pragmatic enrichment (Onea & Geist 2011)
  i. lexical semantics: $\lambda Q.\ \exists x.\ [N(x)\ \&\ Q(x)]$
  ii. domain restriction $\lambda Q.\ \exists x.\ [N(x)\ \&\ Q(x)\ \&\ R(x,y)]$
  iii. referential anchoring $\lambda Q.\ \exists x.\ [N(x)\ \&\ Q(x)\ \&\ R(x,y)\ \&\ m(c) = x]$

All three approaches represent specific indefinites by a function that makes the referent of the indefinite unique with respect to the anchor (the speaker, some other agent or a quantifier phrase). The approaches differ on some other issues that are independent of the idea of referential anchoring, such as the question of lexical ambiguity of the indefinite article and the representation of the anchor as a parameterized choice function or as a Skolem function (see Chierchia 2005 and Onea & Geist 2011 for discussion).

Even though there is no agreement about the representation of the indefinite article in English, other encodings seem to need a common semantics for different kinds of specificity, as illustrated by differential object marking in Turkish (Enç 1991, von Heusinger & Kornfilt 2005): in this language all definite direct objects and specific indefinite direct objects are case-marked, while non-specific indefinites lack case. The case marker-*I* (representing the allophones *-i, -ı, -u, -ü*) signals referential specificity in (57b), scopal specificity in (58b) and epistemic specificity in (59b). Kornfilt (p.c.) notes that (58b) may also have a narrow-scope reading, which must be licensed by an additional condition, such as a defined relation or some kind of d-linking.

(57) a. Bir öğrenci arı-yor-um   Bul-a-mı-yor-um
     a   student   look+for-Pr.Prog.-1.sg find-Neg.Abil-Neg.-Pr.Prog.-1.sg
     'I am looking for a student. I can't find him/one.'
   b. Bir öğrenci *-yi* arı-yor-um   Bul-a-mı-yor-um
     a   student-*Acc* look+for-Prog.-1.sg find-Neg.Abil-Neg.-Pr.Prog.-1.sg
     'I am looking for a student. I can't find him/*one.'

(58) a. Her öğrenci   bir kitap   oku-du.
       every student   a book   read-Past-(3.sg)
       'Every student read a book.' (different ones)
    b. Her öğrenci   bir kitab-ı   oku-du.
       every student a   book-Acc read-Past-(3.sg)
       'Every student read a book.' (the same one/ones)

(59) a. (Ben)   *bir* kitap   oku-du-m.
       I   *a* book   read-Past-1.sg
       'I read *a* book.'
    b. (Ben)   *bir* kitab-ı   oku-du-m.
       I   *a* book-*Acc*   read-Past-1.sg
       'I read *a certain* book.'

In summary, the concept of referential anchoring provides a consistent account of specificity. It links the pragmatic concept of referential intention to a semantic representation with an anchoring function and an anchor. The anchor must be familiar to speaker and hearer, while the content of the function must not be familiar to the hearer (and is generally familiar to the speaker). Still, the hearer has to establish a permanent representation for the specific indefinite, based on the assumption of the existence of such an anchoring function. This account is related to the other concepts of specificity, including familiarity-based or discourse-based concepts, discussed in the next sections.

7 D-linking, partitivity and presuppositionality

Partitive specificity has been related to other types of specificity since Enç (1991), who discusses direct object marking in Turkish. However, it is clearly independent of scopal and epistemic specificity (Abbott 1995, Farkas 1994, van Geenhoven 1998). We still discuss the properties of partitive indefinites and the relation of partitive specificity to other types of specificity, since partitive indefinites show interesting properties quite similar to specific indefinites. Indefinites generally introduce new discourse referents together with a description. Partitive indefinites pick out one referent from a discourse-familiar group. Obviously, such indefinites presuppose existence and behave like strong quantifiers. Pesetsky (1987, 107) introduces the term d(iscourse) linking for the different presuppositions of *which* as opposed to *who*: "Roughly, *which*-phrases are *discourse-linked (d-linked)*, whereas *who* and *what* are normally not d-linked." Since wh-phrases can be understood as a kind of indefinite noun phrase, this contrast between d-linked and not-d-linked wh-phrases was transferred to indefinites. Enç (1991) claims that differential object marking in Turkish (i.e. the Acc-case suffix −*I*) expresses specificity and that specificity can be reduced to partitivity, as in (60).

(60) a. Oda-m-a   birkaç çocuk gir-di.
       room-1.sg.-Dat several child enter-Past
       'Several children entered my room.' (Enç 1991, ex. 16)
    b. İki   kız-ı   tanı-yor-du-m.
       two girl-*Acc* know-Prog.-Past-1.sg
       'I knew two girls.' (Enç 1991, ex. 17)

The first sentence introduces a set of children, and the accusative case in the second sentence indicates that the two girls are part of that set. Thus the expression *two girls* presupposes existence. Enç takes this observation as a strong indicator that such an expression is specific and proposes that specificity can be derived from partitivity, or more exactly from familiarity of the superset involved.

Diesing (1992) and de Hoop (1995) take partitivity as an instance of Milsark's (1974) contrast between a weak (cardinal, non-specific) and a strong (presuppositional, quantificational, specific) interpretation. In (61a) the indefinite *some ghosts* receives a weak interpretation, whereas in (61b) it gets a strong or partitive interpretation, i.e. it presupposes that there are other groups of ghosts.

(61) a. There are *some ghosts* in this house.
    b. *Some ghosts* live in the pantry; others live in the kitchen.

Diesing (1992) and de Hoop (1995) also discuss this contrast with respect to syntactic phenomena such as *there*-constructions and scrambling. Alternative approaches link specificity to presuppositionality (Yeom 1998, van Geenhoven 1998, Krifka 2001, Geurts 2010). However, it has often been shown that partitive indefinites can have both a specific and a non-specific reading, as in (62) and (63) from Farkas (1994). The partitive *one of Steve's sisters* receives a scopally non-specific reading in (62), and an epistemic non-specific reading in (63).

(62) John wants to marry one of Steve's sisters. (He doesn't care which)

(63) One of Steve's sisters cheated on the exam. (We have to find out which)

Closer inspection of the Turkish data confirms this observation. The explicit partitive with accusative case in (64) has an (epistemic) specific reading whereas the non-case-marked explicit partitive in (65) only allows for a non-specific reading (see von Heusinger & Kornfilt 2005, 32).

(64) Ali   büro-ya   çocuk-lar-dan   iki   kız-ı   al-acak
     Ali.   office-Dat   child-pl.-Abl   two   girl-Acc   take-Fut
     'Ali will hire, for the office, two (specific, particular) girls of the children.'

(65) Ali   büro-ya   çocuk-lar-dan   iki   kız   al-acak
     Ali.   office-Dat   child-pl.-Abl   two   girl   take-Fut
     'Ali will hire, for the office, two girls of the children.'

In sum, partitive indefinites are not specific indefinites, although both show a kind of discourse anchoring. Partitives are discourse anchored by their superset, which is given, while specific indefinites are discourse anchored by the referential intention of the speaker (or some other agent). In both cases the indefinites are presuppositional and the descriptive content is restricted (as in the case of domain restriction).

8 Topicality

Topicality has also been closely related to specificity. Languages that show differential object marking depending on specificity, like Turkish, obligatorily mark the direct object if it is topicalized by means of left-dislocation (Kornfilt 1997, 190–192). Portner & Yabushita (2001) assume that the restrictor set of the indefinite is topical, either explicitly as in the case of partitives, or implicitly via other information. Portner & Yabushita (2001) argue on the basis of Japanese and Portner (2002) on Chinese data that a topical and very narrow restrictor set triggers specificity effects. This perspective on specificity is very similar to Schwarzschild's domain restriction approach (see section 5) and it is based on a discourse topic view. A different approach assumes that the whole indefinite is topical in the sense of a sentence or "aboutness" topic (see Cresti 1995, Endriss 2009 and article 11 [Semantics: Sentence and Information Structure] (Roberts) *Topics*). The intuitive idea is that the speaker introduces the topic by a separate speech act. Thus, the topic is identified independently of the assertion in the sentence, giving rise to typical specificity contrasts. Endriss (2009) and Ebert, Endriss & Hinterwimmer (2009) model intermediate scope readings by assuming nested topic-comment structures. In this way they account for the difference in readings between (66) and (67).

(66) Every student will leave the party if some lecturer shows up.

(67) Every student announced that she will leave the party if some lecturer shows up.

Both examples show a wide-scope reading (i.e. they will leave if Prof. Schiller shows up), and a functional wide-scope reading (i.e. they will leave if their supervisor shows up), but only (67) shows a genuine intermediate reading (i.e. Ann will leave if Prof. Schiller shows up, Mary will leave if Prof. Wagner shows up, etc.). Ebert, Endriss & Hinterwimmer (2009) explain the possibility of intermediate scope in (67) by assuming nested topic-comment structures triggered by the verb *announce*. This approach nicely models the possibility of genuine intermediate scope and thus complements the view of specificity as referential anchoring developed above. It seems that one cannot reduce specificity to topicality since in section 5 we discussed different kinds of "intermediate" epistemic specific readings without a nested topic-comment structure. Thus topicalization is different from specificity, even though some of the effects are very similar.

9 Discourse prominence

Indefinites introduce new items or referents into a discourse. Referentially anchored indefinites are specific indefinites that have special referential and pragmatic properties: They have wide scope or functional wide scope, and they are anchored to some other discourse item. These properties seem to correlate with discourse prominence. Discourse prominence itself is a vague concept, but I present three aspects that are related to specificity: (i) "noteworthiness", (ii) "referential persistence" and (iii) "topic continuity". English has an indefinite use of the proximal demonstrative *this* that introduces an indefinite that does not interact with other operators, much like a deictically used demonstrative. The use of indefinite *this* is licensed if it introduces a discourse referent that becomes the theme of the subsequent discourse (Prince 1981) or that is "noteworthy", i.e. has an unexpected and interesting property (McLaran 1982, Ionin 2006), as illustrated by the contrast below (Maclaren 1982, 88).

(68) a. He put √a/#this 31 cent stamp on the envelope, so he must want it to go airmail.
  b. He put √a/√this 31 cent stamp on the envelope, and only realized later that it was worth a fortune because it was unperforated.

Both sentences introduce a discourse referent, and there is no other operator and no referential vs. attributive contrast. Nothing prevents either indefinite from introducing a discourse referent, Still, there is an important difference: the indefinite marked by *this* is in (68b) introduces a significant topic for the subsequent discourse. Indefinite *this* signals particular, interesting, new information, while unmarked indefinites signal that they introduce a discourse referent with more or less important properties. Different concepts of discourse prominence include Givón's (1983) notions of "referential persistence" and "topic continuity": Referential persistence is the property of being frequently picked up in the subsequent discourse, and topic continuity is the property of becoming or remaining the topic of the discourse. There are different quantitative measures for these kinds of prominence, including the number of anaphoric links, the distance to the first anaphoric link and the probability of becoming the topic of the discourse. Specific indefinites show a much higher degree of referential persistence and topic continuity than non-specific indefinites. (see Givón 1983 for an overview, Chiriacescu & von Heusinger 2010 for a study on specific indefinite direct objects in Romanian).

The relation between the semantic concept of specificity as referential anchoring, the pragmatic concept of specificity as referential intention and the different types of discourse prominence are not well-understood. A pragmatic account may go like this: The use of a specific indefinite forces the hearer to establish a permanent discourse referent. By Gricean maxims, the speaker would only force the hearer to do that if s/he intends to say more about that referent. Givón (1983) argues that it is the other way around. Diachronic data show that special markers for indefinites are first introduced to mark their discourse prominence, then the speaker's intention, and finally such a marker may acquire semantic properties such as specificity or referentiality (see Stark 2002 for a study on the diachronic development of specificity markers in Italian). This brings us back to the first observations concerning specificity namely to the "strikingly different" interpretations of indefinites with respect to licensing discourse referents (Karttunen 1968, 11), and to Stalnaker's (1998) remark on the discourse function of specific indefinites, quoted in section 5.

10 Summary

The semantic-pragmatic category "specificity", which is motivated by the communicative principle of referential intentions, is used for different contrasts associated with the interpretation of indefinites. The contrasts include different interpretations of indefinites in opaque contexts, exceptional scope behavior, epistemic contrasts, partitive contrasts, topical vs. non-topical readings and different grades of discourse prominence. I have argued that there is a core notion of specificity underlying the intuitive concept, namely referential anchoring. The referent of a specific indefinite is functionally dependent on some discourse participant or on another expression in the sentence. The anchor must be familiar to speaker and hearer, while the content of the anchoring function must be unfamiliar to the hearer (to distinguish specific indefinites from definites). Still, the hearer has to accommodate the fact that there is a function and must establish a permanent representation for the specific indefinite. I have shown that this approach is quite flexible and can account for various particular constraints associated with special specificity markers. However, it cannot explain all phenomena associated with different types of specificity, which might get different kinds of explanations (such as genuine intermediate scope indefinites via embedded topics). I discussed the similarities between specific indefinites and partitive indefinites as well as topic indefinites and showed that they are independent notions, but with similar effects. Finally, I compared the semantic properties of specific indefinites with their discourse pragmatic functions, which opens up a new domain of research, namely the interaction of semantic and pragmatic properties of nominal expressions with discourse properties.

The present version of this paper developed over a long period of time, during which I had the opportunity to discuss earlier versions with many colleagues. I am especially indebted for very detailed and helpful comments on earlier versions to Barbara Abbott, Gennaro Chierchia, Sofiana Chiriacescu, Cornelia Ebert, Donka Farkas, Ljudmila Geist, Jeanette Gundel, Irene Heim, Stefan Hinterwimmer, Tania Ionin, Elsi Kaiser, Hans Kamp and Edgar Onea. The views presented in this article most probably do not correspond to the views of any of the people mentioned above. Needless to say that all remaining errors are mine. I gratefully acknowledge the support for this research by the German Science Foundation (SFB 732 Incremental Specification in Context) and by the Fritz Thyssen Foundation and the VolkswagenStiftung (opus magnum).

11 References

Abbott, Barbara 1976. *A Study of Referential Opacity*. Ph.D. dissertation. University of California, Berkeley, CA.
Abbott, Barbara 1995. Some remarks on specificity. *Linguistic Inquiry* 26, 341–346.
Abbott, Barbara 2010. *Reference*. Oxford: Oxford University Press.
Abusch, Dorit 1994. The scope of indefinites. *Natural Language Semantics* 2, 83–135.
Aloni, Maria 2001. *Quantification under Conceptual Cover* (ILLC Dissertation Series 2001-1). Amsterdam: ILLC, University of Amsterdam.
Alonso-Ovalle, Luis & Paula Menéndez-Benito 2010. Modal indefinites. *Natural Language Semantics* 18, 1–31.

Bach, Emmon 1968. Nouns and noun phrases. In: E. Bach & R. T. Harms (eds.). *Universals in Language*. New York: Holt, Rinehart & Winston, 90–122.

Baker, C. Leroy 1966. *Definiteness and Indefiniteness in English*. MA thesis. University of Illinois, Urbana, IL.

Brasoveanu, Adrian & Donka Farkas 2009. Exceptional scope as discourse reference to quantificational dependencies. In: P. Bosch, D. Gabelaia & J. Lang (eds.). *Logic, Language, and Computation*. Berlin: Springer, 165–179.

Breheny, Richard 2003. Exceptional-scope indefinites and domain restriction. In: M. Weisgerber (ed.). *Proceedings of Sinn und Bedeutung (= SuB) 7* (Arbeitspapiere des Fachbereichs Sprachwissenschaft 114). Konstanz: University of Konstanz, 38–52.

Chierchia, Gennaro 2001. A puzzle about indefinites. In: C. Checchetto, G. Chierchia & M.-T. Guasti (eds.). *Semantic Interfaces: Reference, Anaphora and Aspect*. Stanford, CA: CSLI Publications, 51–89.

Chierchia, Gennaro 2005. Definites, locality, and intentional identity. In: G.N. Carlson & F. J. Pelletier (ed.). *Reference and Quantification. The Partee Effect*. Stanford, CA: CSLI Publications, 143–178.

Chiriacescu, Sofiana & Klaus von Heusinger 2010. Discourse prominence and pe-marking in Romanian. *The International Review of Pragmatics* 2, 298–322.

Chung, Sandra & William A. Ladusaw 2004. *Restriction and Saturation*. Cambridge, MA: The MIT Press.

Cresti, Diana 1995. *Indefinite Topics*. Ph.D. dissertation. MIT, Cambridge, MA.

Dahl, Östen 1970. Some notes on indefinites. *Language* 46, 33–41.

Dekker, Paul 2004. The pragmatic dimension of indefinites. *Research on Language and Computation* 2, 365–399.

Diesing, Molly 1992. *Indefinites*. Cambridge, MA: The MIT Press.

Donnellan, Keith 1966. Reference and definite descriptions. *Philosophical Review* 75, 281–304.

Ebert, Christian, Cornelia Endriss & Stefan Hinterwimmer 2009. Embedding topic-comment structures results in intermediate scope readings. In: *Proceedings of the North Eastern Linguistic Society (=NELS) 38*. Amherst, MA: GLSA, University of Massachusetts, 246–258.

Egli, Urs 1991. (In)definite Nominalphrase und Typentheorie. In: U. Egli & K. von Heusinger (eds.). *Zwei Aufsätze zur definiten Kennzeichnung* (Arbeitspapiere des Fachbereichs Sprachwissenschaft 27). Konstanz: University of Konstanz, 1–28.

Egli, Urs & Klaus von Heusinger 1995. The epsilon operator and E-type pronouns. In: U. Egli et al. (eds.). *Lexical Knowledge in the Organization of Language*. Amsterdam: Benjamins, 121–141.

Enç, Mürvet 1986. Towards a referential analysis of temporal expressions. *Linguistics & Philosophy* 9, 405–426.

Enç, Mürvet 1991. The semantics of specificity. *Linguistic Inquiry* 22, 1–25.

Endriss, Cornelia 2009. *Quantificational Topics. A Scopal Treatment of Exceptional Wide Scope Phenomena*. Dordrecht: Springer.

Farkas, Donka 1981. Quantifier scope and syntactic islands. In: R. Hendrik et al. (eds.). *Papers from the Regional Meeting of the Chicago Linguistic Society (=CLS) 17*. Chicago, IL: Chicago Linguistic Society, 59–66.

Farkas, Donka 1994. Specificity and scope. In: L. Nash & G. Tsoulas (eds.). *Actes du Premier Colloque Langues & Grammaire*. Paris: University of Paris VIII, 119–137.

Farkas, Donka 1997. Evaluation indices and scope. In: A. Szabolcsi (ed.). *Ways of Scope Taking*. Dordrecht: Kluwer, 183–215.

Farkas, Donka 2002. Specificity distinction. *Journal of Semantics* 19, 213–243.
Farkas, Donka & Klaus von Heusinger 2003. *Stability of Reference and Object Marking in Romanian*. Ms. Stuttgart, University of Stuttgart.
Fassi-Fehri, Abdelkader 2006. *Determination Parameters in the Semitic Diglossia*. Ms. Rabat, University of Rabat.
Fodor, Janet 1970. *The Linguistic Description of Opaque Contexts*. Ph.D. dissertation. MIT, Cambridge, MA. Reprinted: Bloomington, IN: Indiana University Linguistics Club, 1976.
Fodor, Janet & Ivan Sag 1982. Referential and quantificational indefinites. *Linguistics & Philosophy* 5, 355–398.
van Geenhoven, Veerle 1998. *Semantic Incorporation and Indefinite Descriptions. Semantic and Syntactic Aspects of Noun Incorporation in West Greenlandic*. Stanford, CA: CSLI Publications.
van Geenhoven, Veerle & Louise McNally 2005. On the property analysis on opaque complements. *Lingua* 115, 885–914.
Geist, Ljudmila 2008. Specificity as referential anchoring: Evidence from Russian. In: A. Grønn (ed.). *Proceedings of Sinn und Bedeutung (= SuB) 12*. Oslo: ILOS 2008, 151–164.
Geist, Ljudmila & Edgar Onea 2010. Epistemic Determiners and Referential Anchoring. Paper presented at the *Workshop on Epistemic Indefinites*, June 10–12, University of Göttingen.
Geurts, Bart 2010. Specific indefinites, presupposition, and scope. In: R. Bäuerle, U. Reyle & T.E. Zimmermann (eds.). *Presupposition and Discourse*. Bingley: Emerald, 125–158.
Givón, Talmy 1973. Opacity and reference in language: An inquiry into the role of modalities. In: J.P. Kimball (ed.). *Syntax and Semantics, vol. 2*. New York: Seminar Press, 95–122.
Givón, Talmy (ed.) 1983. *Topic Continuity in Discourse. A Quantitative Cross-Language Study*. Amsterdam: Benjamins.
Haspelmath, Martin 1997. *Indefinite Pronouns*. Oxford: Clarendon Press.
Heim, Irene 1982. *The Semantics of Definite and Indefinite Noun Phrases*. Ph.D. dissertation. University of Massachusetts, Amherst, MA. Reprinted: Ann Arbor, MI: University Microfilms.
Heim, Irene 1991. Artikel und Definitheit. In: A. von Stechow & D. Wunderlich (eds.). *Semantik. Ein internationales Handbuch der zeitgenössischen Forschung* (HSK 6). Berlin: de Gruyter, 487–535.
von Heusinger, Klaus 2002. Specificity and definiteness in sentence and discourse structure. *Journal of Semantics* 19, 245–274.
von Heusinger, Klaus & Jaklin Kornfilt 2005. The case of the direct object in Turkish: Semantics, syntax and morphology. *Turcic Languages* 9, 3–44.
Higginbotham, James 1987. Indefinites and predication. In: E. Reuland & A. ter Meulen (eds.). *The Representation of (In)definiteness*. Cambridge, MA: The MIT Press, 43–70.
Hilbert, David & Paul Bernays 1939. *Grundlagen der Mathematik*. Vol. II. 2nd edn. Berlin: Springer.
Hintikka, Jaakko 1967. Individuals, possible worlds, and epistemic logic. *Noûs* 1, 33–62.
Hintikka, Jaakko 1986. The semantics of 'a certain'. *Linguistic Inquiry* 17, 331–336.
de Hoop, Helen 1995. On the characterization of the weak-strong disctinction. In: E. Bach et al. (eds.). *Quantification in Natural Language*. Dordrecht: Kluwer, 421–450.
Ionin, Tania 2006. This is definitely specific: Specificity and definiteness in article systems. *Natural Language Semantics* 14, 175–234.
Ioup, Georgette 1977. Specificity and the interpretation of quantifiers. *Linguistics & Philosophy* 1, 233–245.

Kamp, Hans & Ágnes Bende-Farkas 2006. *Specific Indefinites: Anchors and Functional Readings*. Ms. Stuttgart, University of Stuttgart.
Kamp, Hans & Ágnes Bende-Farkas submitted. Epistemic specificity from a communication-theoretical perspective. *Journal of Semantics*.
Kaplan, David 1978. Dthat. In: P. Cole (ed.). *Syntax and Semantics 9: Pragmatics*. New York: Academic Press, 241–244.
Karttunen, Lauri 1968. *What Do Referential Indices Refer To?* Santa Monica, CA: RAND Corporation. http://www.rand.org/pubs/papers/2008/P3854.pdf. December 9, 2010.
Karttunen, Lauri 1969/1976. Discourse referents. In: *Proceedings of the 1969 Conference on Computational Linguistics*. Sång-Säby, Sweden, 1–38. Reprinted in: J. McCawley (ed.). *Syntax and Semantics 7: Notes from the Linguistic Underground*. New York: Academic Press, 1976, 363–385.
Kornfilt, Jaklin 1997. *Turkish*. London: Routledge.
Kratzer, Angelika 1998. Scope or pseudoscope? Are there wide-scope indefinites? In: S. Rothstein (ed.). *Events and Grammar*. Dordrecht: Kluwer, 163–196.
Kratzer, Angelika 2003. *A Note on Choice Functions in Context*. Ms. Amherst, MA, University of Massachusetts. December 2003.
Krifka, Manfred 2001. Non-novel indefinites in adverbial quantification. In: C. Condoravdi & G. Renardel. *Logical Perspectives on Language and Information*. Stanford, CA: CSLI Publications, 1–40.
Kripke, Saul 1977. Speaker's reference and semantic reference. *Midwest Studies in Philosophy* 2, 255–276.
Leonetti, Manuel 2004. Specificity and object marking: The case of Spanish and Catalan. *Journal of Linguistics* 3, 75–114.
Ludlow, Peter & Stephen Neale 1991. Indefinite descriptions: In defense of Russell. *Linguistics & Philosophy* 14, 171–202.
Maclaren, Rose 1982. *The Semantics and Pragmatics of the English Demonstratives*. Ph.D. dissertation. Cornell University, Ithaca, NY.
Matthewson, Lisa 1999. On the interpretation of wide-scope indefinites. *Natural Language Semantics* 7, 79–134.
McCawley, James 1968. The role of semantics in a grammar. In: E. Bach & R. T. Harms (eds.). *Universals in Linguistic Theory*. New York: Holt, Rinehart & Winston, 124–169.
Milsark, Gary 1974. *Existential Sentences in English*. Ph.D. dissertation. MIT, Cambridge, MA.
Neale, Stephen 1990. *Descriptions*. Cambridge, MA: The MIT Press.
Onea, Edgar & Ljudmila Geist 2011. Indefinite determiners and referential anchoring, *International Review of Pragmatics* 3.
Partee, Barbara 1970. Opacity, coreference, and pronouns. *Synthese* 21, 359–385.
Partee, Barbara 1987. Noun phrase interpretation and type-shifting principles. In: J. Groenendijk, D. de Jongh & M. Stokhof (eds.). *Studies in Discourse Representation Theory and the Theory of Generalizd Quantifiers*. Dordrecht: Foris, 115–144.
Pesetsky, David 1987. Wh-in situ. Movement of unselective binding. In: E. Reuland & A. ter Meulen (eds.). *The Representation of (In)definiteness*. Cambridge, MA: The MIT Press, 98–129.
Portner, Paul 2002. Topicality and (non-)specificity in mandarin. *Journal of Semantics* 19, 275–287.
Portner, Paul & Katsuhiko Yabushita 2001. Specific indefinites and the information structure theory of topic. *Journal of Semantics* 18, 271–297.

Prince, Ellen 1981. On the inferencing of indefinite-this NPs. In: A. Joshi, B. Webber & I. Sag (eds.). *Elements of Discourse Understanding*. Cambridge: Cambridge University Press, 231–250.

Quine, Willard van Orman 1956. Quantifiers and propositional attitudes. *Journal of Philosophy* 53, 177–187. Reprinted in: L. Linsky (ed.). *Reference and Modality*. Oxford: Oxford University Press, 1971, 101–111.

Quine, Willard van Orman 1960. *Word and Object*. Cambridge, MA: The MIT Press.

Reinhart, Tanya 1997. Quantifier scope: How labor is divided between QR and choice functions. *Linguistics & Philosophy* 20, 335–397.

Roberts, Craige 2007. Specificity and Incomplete Descriptions. Handout. University of Massachusetts, Amherst, MA. March 27, 2007.

Russell, Bertrand 1905. On denoting. *Mind* 14, 479–493.

Ruys, Eduard 1992. *The Scope of Indefinites*. Doctoral dissertation. Utrecht University, Utrecht.

Ruys, Eduard 2006. Unexpected wide scope phenomena. In: M. Everaert & H. van Riemsdijk (eds.). *The Blackwell Companion to Syntax, vol. 5*. Oxford: Blackwell, 175–228.

Schwarz, Bernhard 2001. Two kinds of long distance indefinites. In: R. van Rooy & M. Stokhof (eds.). *Proceedings of the 13th Amsterdam Colloquium*. Amsterdam: ILLC, 192–197.

Schwarz, Bernhard 2004. Indefinites in verb ellipsis. *Linguistic Inquiry* 35, 244–253.

Schwarzschild, Roger 2002. Singleton indefinites. *Journal of Semantics* 19, 289–314.

Stalnaker, Robert 1970. Pragmatics. *Synthese* 22, 272–289.

Stalnaker, Robert 1998. On the representation of context. *Journal of Logic, Language, and Information* 7, 3–19.

Stark, Elisabeth 2002. Indefinites and specificity in Old Italian texts. *Journal of Semantics* 19, 315–332.

von Stechow, Arnim 2000. Some remarks on choice functions and LF-movements. In: K. von Heusinger & U. Egli (eds.). *Reference and Anaphoric Relations*. Dordrecht: Kluwer, 193–228.

Steedman, Mark 2007. *Surface-Compositional Scope-Alternation Without Existential Quantifiers*. Ms. Edinburgh, University of Edinburgh. Draft 5.2, Sept 2007, http://www.iccs.informatics.ed.ac.uk/~steedman/papers.html. December 9, 2010.

Szabolcsi, Anna 2010. *Quantification*. Oxford: Oxford University Press.

Szabolcsi, Anna & Frans Zwarts 1992. Weak islands and an algebraic semantics for scope-taking. *Natural Language Semantics* 1, 235–284.

Umbach, Carla 2004. Cataphoric indefinites. In: C. Meier & M. Weisgerber (eds.). *Proceedings of Sinn und Bedeutung (= SuB) 8* (Arbeitspapiere des Fachbereichs Sprachwissenschaft 177). Konstanz: University of Konstanz, 301–316.

Winter, Yoad 1997. Choice functions and the scopal semantics of indefinites. *Linguistics & Philosophy* 20, 399–467.

Yeom, Jae-Il 1998. *A Presuppositional Analysis of Specific Indefinites: Common Grounds as Structured Information States*. New York: Garland.

Zimmermann, Thomas E. 1993. On the proper treatment of opacity in certain verbs. *Natural Language Semantics* 1, 149–179.

Edward Keenan
4 Quantifiers

1 Introduction —— 112
2 Scope of the present study —— 113
3 Determiner Quantifiers —— 114
4 Extending the logical type of determiners —— 131
5 Adverbial Quantifiers —— 137
6 Concluding remarks —— 143
7 References —— 143

Abstract: The presentation distinguishes broadly between Determiner (D-) Quantification and Adverbial (A-) Quantification, with the former being much better studied and understood than the latter. We present D-quantification first and use it to study novel types of quantification such as polyadic quantification and mass term quantification. Then we extend the concepts developed to A-quantification.

We characterize semantically over 20 types of Determiner quantification in natural language, focusing on questions of logical expressive power—what we can say and what constraints there are on what we can say. We do not focus on the formalization of syntactic representations, though we do show that there are quantifiers denotable by syntactically complex Determiners that are not denotable by syntactically simple Determiners. We do this within the broad framework of Generalized Quantifier Theory. In terms of the semantic categories of analysis developed we offer several non-obvious semantic generalizations which hold for well studied languages and which we think may hold more generally. In two cases we explicitly suggest that the properties are language universal.

1 Introduction

Quantifiers expressible in natural language have played an important role in linguistic theory since the early days of generative grammar when sentence pairs like *Everyone in this room speaks two languages* and *Two languages are spoken by everyone in this room* were argued to exhibit different quantifier scope relations, whence transformations such as Passive were not meaning preserving. See Katz & Postal (1964). Later generative grammar would include a level of LF, May

---

Edward Keenan, Los Angeles, CA, United States

(1985), on which scopal and binding properties of operators such as quantifiers, negation and relative and interrogative pronouns could be represented, cf. article 1 [Semantics: Sentence and Information Structure] (Szabolcsi) *Scope and binding*. And beginning in the 1980s the semantic study of quantifiers, their denotations and logical types—not their syntactic representations—came to the fore (Barwise & Cooper 1981, Keenan & Moss 1984, Keenan & Stavi 1986). This enabled us to raise, and answer, many substantive questions concerning the logical expressive power of natural languages: Can natural language semantics be given in first order logic? Just what sort of quantifiers are denotable in natural language? Are there universal constraints on denotable quantifiers? This article focuses on these semantic issues.

2 Scope of the present study

We discuss *D(eterminer)-Quantifiers*, as in (1a), and *A(dverbial)-Quantifiers*, as in (1b).

(1) a. *All / Most / Some / No* birds can fly
 b. John *always / usually / often / occasionally / rarely / never* works on Sunday

D-quantifiers are the better studied of the two, but this may be just because they are more accessible to the linguists doing the studying. Also they are semantically simpler, mainly involving relations between arbitrary sets rather than ontologically more complex notions such as events. A-quantifiers, attested in all languages investigated, seem syntactically less uniform than D-quantifiers but at least as rich semantically, justifying the term *quantifier* in both cases. Both types now have some documentation in areally and genetically distinct languages: Bach et al. (1995), Matthewson (2001, 2008).

We begin with D-quantifiers. We are generous regarding what we count as a quantifier, but lack the space to consider the many phenomena which interact with quantification in revealing ways: Passive cf. article 7 [Semantics: Interfaces] (Wunderlich) *Operations on argument structure* (*The box was opened* (*by someone*) vs *John is respected* (*by* most *relevant people*)); Modal Adverbs cf. article 14 [this volume] (Hacquard) *Modality* (*necessarily / must = in* all *relevant worlds, possibly / can = in* some *relevant worlds*), Pronominal binding cf. article 1 [Semantics: Sentence and Information Structure] (Szabolcsi) *Scope and binding*: *Most farmers who own a donkey beat it*. Useful overviews are Westerståhl (1989, 1995), Keenan (1996a), van der Does & van Eijck (1996a), Keenan & Westerståhl (1997), and Peters & Westerståhl (2006). Some important collections of articles are: van Benthem &

ter Meulen (1985), Reuland & ter Meulen (1987), Gärdenfors (1987), Lappin (1988), Kanazawa & Piñón (1994), van der Does & van Eijck (1996b), Szabolcsi (1997) and, from a mathematical perspective, Krynicki, Mostowski & Szczerba (1995).

3 Determiner Quantifiers

The sentences in (1a) have the form [DP+P_1], where the DP (*Determiner Phrase*) is *all birds*, *some birds*, etc. and the P_1 (*one place predicate*) is the Verb Phrase *can fly*. In such contexts this P_1 is sometimes called the *nuclear scope*. It denotes a *property* of objects, extensionally a subset of a domain E of (possibly abstract) objects under discussion. The DP in (1a) has the form [Determiner+NP], for Determiner = *all*, *most*, etc. and NP = *birds*. The NP denotes a property, called the *restriction* of the Determiner. Interpreting sentences as true T, or false F, in a situation, we interpret DPs as functions, called *generalized quantifiers*, which map properties into {T,F}. They are said to be of type (1). Determiners denote functions mapping properties to generalized quantifiers and are of type (1,1). This type notation, due to Lindström (1966), is usual in Generalized Quantifier Theory. Type (1) is the same as ((e,t),t) and type (1,1) as (((e,t),(e,t)),t) in more usual linguistic parlance.

3.1 DPs

We begin with DPs generally. They include not only [Determiner+NP]s but also proper names: *John, Mary*; boolean compounds: *Either Mary or some teacher, neither John nor Mary*; possessives: *every child's doctor*, and partitives: *two of the boys*. The generalization concerns *monotonicity*, a property of diverse expressions, including DPs and Determiners. Properties possess a natural partial order relation, subset, ⊆. (p ⊆ q means that every object in p is also in q). So, noting denotations in upper case, MALE(DOG) ⊆ DOG, meaning the set of male dogs is a subset of the set of dogs. {T,F} also has a natural partial order, the *implication order*, noted ⇒ and read as "if...then...". For X,Y truth values, X ⇒ Y means "If X = T then Y = T". A *partially ordered set* is one on which is defined a partial order relation, generically noted ≤. Below we define monotonicity properties (writing *iff* for *if and only if*).

Def 1   For F a function from a partially ordered set A to a partially ordered set A',
       a. F is *increasing* (↑) iff for all x,y in A, if x ≤ y then F(x) ≤' F(y)
       b. F is *decreasing* (↓) iff for all x,y in A, if x ≤ y then F(y) ≤' F(x)
       c. An expression d is ↑(↓) iff d always denotes an ↑ (↓) function.

So a generalized quantifier F is ↑ iff for all properties p,q if p ⊆ q then F(p) ⇒ F(q); that is, if all p's are q's and F holds of p then F holds of q. Proper names are ↑: if all poets daydream and Ann is a poet then Ann daydreams. Similarly *every student, some student, more than six nurses here*, and *most nurses* are all ↑. Whether [$_{DP}$Determiner+NP] is ↑ is decided by the Determiner, not the NP. If *most nurses* is ↑ then so is *most doctors*. And the generalizations in (2) hold:

(2) a. Conjunctions and disjunctions of increasing DPs are increasing
   b. Possessives [X's NP] are increasing if X is
   c. Partitives [d of the NPs] are increasing if [d+NPs] is (for d any Determiner)

(2a) tells us that *either Mary or some teacher* is increasing (and it is: if all poets daydream and either Mary or some teacher is a poet then either Mary or some teacher daydreams). From (2b) *every student's doctor* is ↑ since *every student* is. And from (2c) *most of the students* is ↑ since *most students* is. In contrast *no nurse* is decreasing (↓): If all poets daydream and no nurse daydreams then no nurse is a poet. Similarly ↓ are: *neither John nor Mary, fewer than six nurses, at most five nurses*, and *less than half the nurses*. And the generalizations in (3) hold:

(3) a. Conjunctions and disjunctions of decreasing DPs are decreasing
   b. Possessives [X's NP] are decreasing if X is
   c. Partitives [d of the NPs] are decreasing if d+NPs is decreasing
   d. Negations of increasing DPs (not always well formed) are decreasing

From (3a), *fewer than ten students and almost no teachers* is ↓. From (3b), *no student's nurse* is ↓ since *no student* is. From (3c), *at most six of the students* is ↓ since *at most six students* is. And from (3d) *not more than four students* is ↓ since *more than four students* is ↑.

We note that while monotonicity properties of DPs are decided by the choice of Determiner, whether a DP satisfies the semantic selection requirements of a predicate is decided by the NP: since *All lamps giggle* is bizarre so is *Most lamps giggle, Some lamps giggled*, etc., as lamps are not the kind of thing that can giggle.

A more classical linguistic generalization concerning ↓ DPs is Gen 1. *NPI's* (*negative polarity items*) are expressions like *ever* and *any* whose presence requires being in the scope of a "negative" element. Decreasing (but not increasing) subjects constitute such elements.

(4) a. John has*n't* *ever* been to Pinsk   *John has *ever* been to Pinsk
   b. Mary did*n't* see *any* birds on the walk   *Mary saw *any* birds on the walk

(5) a. *No pupil* here knows *any* Dutch *Some pupil here knows any Dutch
    b. *No pupil's doctor* has *ever* smoked *Some pupil's doctor has ever smoked

Gen 1 (Ladusaw 1983, Fauconnier 1978)

A subject DP X licenses negative polarity items in the predicate iff X is decreasing

Negation is a decreasing map from properties to properties: WALK FAST ⊆ WALK so NOT WALK ⊆ NOT WALK FAST. Everyone who is walking fast is walking, so everyone who isn't walking isn't walking fast. (Sentence-level NOT is still ↓: X ⇒ Y implies NOT Y ⇒ NOT X). See Ladusaw (1996) and article 3 [Semantics: Sentence and Information Structure] (Giannakidou) *Polarity items*. Some ↓DPs are derived from "*n*-words": neither *boy*, neither *John* nor *Mary*, none *of the boys*. But others have no *n*-word: *Less than half the students here have* ever *been to Pinsk, at most two of the children saw any birds on the walk*. So the generalization uniting NPI licensors is more semantic (they are decreasing) than morphological (derived from *n*-words).

Determiners themselves can be classified as ↑, ↓, or neither on their (first) argument. For example *no* is ↓ on its argument: NO(A)(B) implies NO(X)(B) whenever X ⊆ A. So if no boys are crying then no big boys are crying. Note that NO is also ↓ on its second argument, which just means that NO(A) is ↓: NO(A)(B) implies NO(A)(Y) if Y ⊆ B. *No boys are crying* entails *No boys are crying loudly*. Similarly SOME is ↑ on both arguments. ALL is ↓ on its first argument (and ↑ on its second). So *All poets daydream* entails *All female poets daydream*. And the NPI *ever* is acceptable in *All poets who have* ever *been to Pinsk love it*.

Many DPs are *non-monotonic*—neither increasing nor decreasing: *exactly five boys, between five and ten students, most of the students but not more than two of the teachers, every student but John, more students than teachers*. So Gen 2 (Keenan 1996a) is non-trivial.

Gen 2 a. Syntactically simple DPs are monotonic, almost always increasing.
       b. Syntactically simple Determiners build monotonic DPs, usually increasing.

3.2 Determiners

All As are Bs is true iff each object in A is also in B. Formally, the denotation ALL of *all* is that type (1,1) function which maps a property A to the generalized quantifier ALL(A), that type (1) function which maps a property B to T if and only if A ⊆ B. (6) provides some further Determiner denotations drawn from subclasses to be discussed shortly. |A| is the *cardinality* (number of elements) of A. A∩B, read

"A intersect B", is the set of objects that lie in both A and B; A—B, "A minus B", is the set of those in A not in B, and A∪B, "A union B", is the set of objects in at least one of A, B (perhaps both). ∅ is the empty set and "b ∈ A" means "b is in A".

(6) a. SOME(A)(B) = T iff A∩B ≠ ∅ i.e. $\exists x(x \in A$ and $x \in B)$
    b. NO(A)(B) = T iff A∩B = ∅
    c. (ALL BUT TEN)(A)(B) = T iff |A−B| = 10
    d. MOST(A)(B) = T iff |A∩B| > |A|/2
    e. (MORE THAN SEVEN OUT OF TEN)(A)(B) = T iff |A∩B| > (7/10)·|A|
    f. NEITHER(A)(B) = T iff |A| = 2 and A∩B = ∅
    g. (THE SIX)(A)(B) = T iff |A| = 6 and A ⊆ B

Traditionally *all* and *some* are treated as variable binding operators. But quantification and variable binding are different operations, so it is semantically enlightening to separate them. We use the lambda operator, λ, to bind variables and continue to treat quantifiers set theoretically. The non-trivial binding in (7b) is effected by λ in (7c), and quantification is treated as above (writing → for *if-then*). Note that for φ a sentence, λx. φ denotes a property—the set of objects b such that φ is true when x is set to denote b.

(7) a. All poets admire themselves
    b. ∀x(Poet(x) → Admire(x,x))   "For all x, if x is a poet then x admires x"
    c. (ALL POET)(λx.ADMIRE(x,x))

We consider now several semantically defined subclasses of Determiners. The interest of the classification is twofold. First, it helps us understand what kinds of quantifiers are expressible in natural language, much as classifying verbs into *stative* vs *non-stative*, and among non-statives, telic vs atelic, among telic, achievements vs accomplishments, etc. See van Valin (2006). What distinguishes Determiner classification from Verb classification is that Determiners often have a "mathematical" character (defined shortly), so many of our subclasses are defined in mathematical terms. Second, we can formulate and prove often non-obvious properties of Determiner denotations once we know just which functions they are.

3.3 Three natural classes of determiners

Cardinal Determiners denote type (1,1) functions D whose value at properties A, B just depends on how many objects have both A and B. We define this notion as an invariance condition:

Def 2   D is *cardinal* iff for all subsets A,B,X,Y of the domain E, if |A∩B| = |X∩Y| then D(A)(B) = D(X)(Y)

EXACTLY TEN is cardinal since (EXACTLY TEN)(A)(B) and (EXACTLY TEN)(X)(Y) are the same truth value if the number of As that are Bs is the same as the number of Xs that are Ys.

Here are some further examples: *some, no, a / an, several, a few, more / less / fewer than ten, ((almost) twice) that many, how many?, exactly / at most / at least ten, between five and ten, not more than five, infinitely many, approximately / about / nearly / almost / over / fifty, just finitely many, hardly any, practically no.*

So Cardinal Determiners include the existential quantifier *some*. They also include some vague Determiners like *about 25*: if the number of socks in my drawer is the same as the number of birds on my clothesline then *About 25 socks are in my drawer* and *About 25 birds are on my clothesline* have the same truth value, regardless of whether 21 counts as about 25. Anaphoric Determiners such as *that many* in *Ninety students applied but not that many were admitted* are also cardinal, as are the technical Determiners *just finitely many* and *infinitely many*. Also, *How many?. How many As are Bs?* and *How many Xs are Ys?* have the same true answers when |A∩B| = |X∩Y|. Definition 2 just requires that DAB = DXY without specifying what DAB is.

On the other hand many "mathematical" Determiners fail to be cardinal. Two such classes, defined below, are the universal (co-cardinal) ones, such as *all, all but two, all but finitely many*, and the proportionality ones, like *most, seven out of ten, less than one...in ten*, as in *Seven out of ten sailors smoke Players* and *About one person in ten is left-handed.* We define:

Def 3   A function D of type (1,1) is *co-cardinal* iff DAB = DXY whenever |A−B| = |X−Y|.

ALL is co-cardinal since ALL As are Bs if and only if |A−B| = 0, that is, there is no A which fails to be a B. The italicized Determiners in (8) are also co-cardinal:

(8)   a. *All but (at most) two* students will get scholarships this year
      b. *All but finitely many* natural numbers are less than ten

Finally, *proportionality Determiners* predicate of the proportion of As that are Bs. They are defined below and illustrated in (9) and (10). They build on numerals and admit many of the same kinds of modification as Cardinal Determiners.

Def 4   D of type (1,1) is *proportional* iff DAB = DXY when |A∩B|/|A| = |X∩Y|/|X|

(9) a. *Most* poets daydream
    b. *Seven out of ten* Americans are magnesium deficient
    c. *Thirty per cent of* American teenagers are overweight
    d. *Not one* student *in ten* knows the answer to that question

(10) *more than / less than half of, about / nearly / approximately / thirty percent of (the), at least / at most / exactly / two thirds of (the), all but a tenth, a majority / minority of (the), What percentage / fraction of (the)?, only one... in ten, every second*

3.4 The Boolean Structure of DPs and Determiners

Boolean compounds of expressions are ones built with *and, or, not*, and *neither... nor....* DPs form boolean compounds productively, as do Determiners themselves, illustrated in (11a) and (12a) respectively. They have the same denotations as (11b) and (12b) respectively.

(11) a. Most men and all women like Keats
     b. Most men like Keats and all women like Keats

(12) a. Most but not all women like Keats
     b. Most women but not all women like Keats

Note that both DP denotations and Determiner denotations are functions taking properties as arguments. They both satisfy (13a,b,c) with *and* denoting ∧, *or* ∨ and *not* ¬:

(13) a. $(F \wedge G)(A) = F(A) \wedge G(A)$
     b. $(F \vee G)(A) = F(A) \vee G(A)$
     c. $(\neg F)(A) = \neg(F(A))$

Thus the set of possible DP denotations over a domain E has a boolean structure, as does the set of possible Determiner denotations. This structure is used in establishing the expressive power result in Theorem 1, Keenan & Moss (1984). Keenan & Stavi (1986).

Theorem 1 Over a finite domain E, for each function F from properties into {T,F} there is an English DP (possibly quite complex) which can be interpreted as F.

Theorem 1 is less obvious than it appears. No natural language has lexical DPs which can be freely interpreted in the set in which DPs in general denote. The denotations of syntactically complex Determiners are constrained by compositionality to be a function of the denotations of the expressions that compose it. And the only productive syntactically simple DPs in English are proper nouns, which only denote increasing functions. So they can't denote the functions denoted by *fewer than ten boys*, *exactly ten boys*, etc. The proof of Theorem 1 shows that English can form sufficiently many complex DPs such that each of any finite set of individuals can be denoted. Other generalized quantifiers then are shown to be denotable by boolean compounds of individual denoting ones. Indeed this last point also cuts deep. Linguists and (Western) philosophers—see the introductory paragraphs of Strawson (1959), tend to take individual denoting DPs, such as proper nouns or definite descriptions, as representative of DPs in general. But from a purely semantic perspective this is misguided. Given a domain E of cardinality n, the set of properties over E has cardinality 2^n and the generalized quantifiers then has cardinality 2^{2^n}. But those which are individuals just number n, one for each entity in E. So in a model with just 4 entities there are 4 individuals, but $2^4 = 16$ properties, and $2^{16} = 65,536$ generalized quantifiers. So individuals are scarce among possible DP denotations. Theorem 2 (Keenan & Stavi 1986) then is surprising, and actually provides a basis for treating individual denoting DPs as fundamental.

Theorem 2   Each generalized quantifier over a domain E is a boolean function of individuals.

(For the record: for each b ∈ E, the *individual generated by* b, I_b, is that generalized quantifier mapping each subset A of E to T iff b ∈ A).

A third, seemingly technical boolean property of our three classes of Determiners is given by:

Theorem 3   Boolean functions of cardinal (co-cardinal, proportional) quantifiers are themselves cardinal (co-cardinal, proportional). That is, using (13) we have that (F∧G), (F∨G) and ¬F are cardinal (co-cardinal, proportional) if F and G are.

Thus *at least two and not more than ten* (students will get scholarships) is provably cardinal because *at least two* and *more than ten* are. The fact that the cardinal (co-cardinal, proportional) quantifiers of type (1,1) respect the boolean operations supports that each is a mathematically natural class (a boooolean subalgebra of the full set of type (1,1) functions).

Aside from all being closed under the boolean operations, the three classes of Determiners considered so far share at least four other properties: they form *partitives*, are *conservative, universe independent*, and they have a "mathematical character".

3.5 Partitives: [$_{DP}$Determiner of DP$_{def.pl}$]

Definite (plural) DPs are defined later. They include DPs such as *the / these / John's (n) cats*, for n ≥ 2. All three classes of Determiners considered so far form partitives:

(14) a. [not more than two / about five] of [the ten cats / these cats / John's ten cats]
 b. [all / all but two] of John's children
 c. [most / between ten and twenty per cent / a third] of those students

3.6 Conservativity

This is a formal way of stating the "domain setting" property of the first argument (the *restriction*) of a Determiner. In *Most cats are grey* the role of *cat* is to limit the set of objects we are quantifying over. We only have to evaluate the predicate *is grey* relative to those objects.

Def 5 D of type (1,1) is *conservative* iff for all A, B, B' D(A)(B) = D(A)(B')
  if A∩B = A∩B'

All the Determiners we have considered so far are conservative. Indeed conservativity is a reasonable candidate for a semantic universal of Determiner denotations. To test whether some D is conservative note that the conservativity of D is equivalent to: D(A)(B) = D(A)(A∩B), all properties A,B. So to verify the conservativity of a determiner det (possibly quite complex) verify that (15a,b) are true in the same situations:

(15) a. det cats are grey
 b. det cats are both cats and are grey

For example, substituting *most of John's* for *det* above we judge that *Most of John's cats are grey* and *Most of John's cats are cats and are grey* are true or false together. The predicate of the second sentence just repeats information already in the restriction, so it is redundant (which is why conservativity holds). But this apparent triviality of conservativity is misleading:

Theorem 4 For $|E| = n$, there are 2^{4^n} functions of type (1,1), only 2^{3^n} of which are conservative.

So in a model with $|E| = 2$, there are $2^{16} = 65,536$ functions of type (1,1), only $2^9 = 512$ of which are conservative. The Equi-cardinality quantifier D given by: $DAB = T$ iff $|A| = |B|$ is not conservative. Let $b \in E$. Then $D(\emptyset)(\{b\}) = F$ but $D(\emptyset)(\emptyset \cap \{b\}) = D(\emptyset)(\emptyset) = T$.

Gen 3 Natural language Determiners always denote conservative functions.

An historical note: early works on generalized quantifiers in natural language all noted Gen 3 in varying terms: Barwise & Cooper (1981), Higginbotham & May (1981), and Keenan (1981) who introduced the term *conservativity*. Keenan & Stavi (1986) showed for an arbitrary conservative function D (over finite E), how to construct a Determiner which could be interpreted as D. So no stronger constraint on Determiner denotations can hold. But are in fact all Determiners conservative? *Only* is a widely cited candidate counterexample.

(16) ONLY(A)(B) = T iff $B \subseteq A$

Only women like that joke claims that everyone who likes that joke is a woman (but not all women need like that joke). ONLY as defined in (16) is not conservative: ONLY(A)(A∩B) is always T, but ONLY(A)(B) may be F. But the syntactic status of *only* as a Determiner can be challenged. *Only* forms X's from X's, for various categories X. *only sang* is a VP in *He only sang, he didn't also dance*; *only in the woodshed* is a PP in *He smokes only in the woodshed*, and *only John* is a DP in *Only John came to the party*. On this pattern we might treat *women* as an indefinite plural DP in *Women like that joke*, with *only* modifying that DP. Another option is to say that *only* interfaces with semantic interpretation in an unusual way. Since ONLY(A)(B) = ALL(B)(A), we can say that what is unusual about *only* is just that it is conservative on its second argument (Herburger 1994). We leave this issue open.

3.7 Domain independence

This property was first noted in van Benthem (1984) under the rubric *Extensions*. It is another, very good, candidate for a semantic universal. For Determiners d with just one denotation d_E over a given domain E, we define:

Def 6 d is *domain independent* iff for all E,E', all A,B $\subseteq$ E,E', $d_E AB = d_{E'} AB$.

This property is prominent in data base theory (Abiteboul et al. 1995). To define a Determiner which is not domain independent, imagine *blik*, defined by: $blik_E(A)(B) = T$ iff $|E-A| = 5$, all E. In a 5 element domain with CAT = ∅ *Blik cats are black* is true. But it is false in any six element domain. So *blik* is not domain independent. And we suggest as a semantic universal:

Gen 4   Natural language Determiners are domain independent.

As defined, domain independence and conservativity are independent properties. *Blik* above is conservative, since $blik_E(A)(B) = blik_E(A)(A \cap B)$, all E, but not domain independent. The Equicardinality function defined earlier is domain independent but not conservative. Ben-Shalom (2003) derives them both from a single property. Keenan & Westerståhl (1997) generalize domain independence (slightly).

3.8 On "mathematical character"

Just what does it mean to say that an expression has a "mathematical character"? Can we tell whether a Determiner is "mathematical" just by looking at its denotations in all models? In fact we can, and this enables us to see that not all English Determiners are mathematical. The defining property is *invariance* under the permutations of the domain E. A *permutation* of a set E is a one to one function from E onto E. Given a permutation π of E and $A \subseteq E$, $\pi A =_{def} \{\pi(a) | a \in A\}$, the set derived by replacing each $a \in A$ with $\pi(a)$.

Def 7   A type (1,1) function D over a domain E is *permutation invariant* iff for all permutations π of E and all subsets A,B of E, $D(A)(B) = D(\pi A)(\pi B)$.

If D is (permutation) invariant we can replace A and B in DAB with πA and πB preserving truth value. So we want to know then just when a set A' is a πA for some permutation π. The answer is simple, and accounts for our intuitions linking cardinality to permutation invariance: if E is finite then A' is a πA for some π iff $|A'| = |A|$. So any two sets of the same cardinality can be identified by a permutation. If E is infinite we need the additional condition that $|\neg A'| = |\neg A|$. So for E the set of natural numbers no permutation can map the set of even numbers to the set of numbers greater than 8. The two sets have the same cardinality but their complements don't, the one being infinite the other finite. Theorem 5 shows the classes of Determiners so far considered are mathematical in character. Gen 5 proves one linguistic correlate of permutation invariance.

Theorem 5 Cardinal, Co-Cardinal, and Proportional functions of type (1,1) are permutation invariant.

Gen 5 Syntactically simple Determiners are either permutation invariant (*all, no, most, ten, ...*) or deictic / anaphoric (*this, my, her, ...*).

So the denotations of lexical Determiners are either determined by the context of utterance—deictic / anaphoric, or are drawn from the restricted class of permutation invariant functions.

3.9 (Co-)Intersective determiners

The Cardinal and Co-Cardinal Determiners share some deeper linguistic properties, to the exclusion of the Proportionality Determiners. To see these we generalize the notions of (co-)cardinal, illustrating some non-invariant Determiners in the process.

A cardinal function D of type (1,1) decides whether to map a pair A,B of properties to T by checking a property of a single set, namely A∩B. The property it checks is just the cardinality of that set. Let us generalize the cardinal functions to ones that depend just on A∩B but are allowed to check any property they like. Call these functions *intersective*. Similarly the *co-intersective* functions just check any property of A−B, not just its cardinality. Formally,

Def 8 a. A function D of type (1,1) is *intersective* iff DAB = DXY whenever A∩B = X∩Y
b. A function D of type (1,1) is *co-intersective* iff DAB = DXY whenever A−B = X−Y

All Cardinal (Co-Cardinal) functions are intersective (co-intersective). But are there Determiners denoting intersective (co-intersective) non-(co-)cardinal functions? In fact there are some reasonable candidates. Treating *no...but John* as a Determiner (von Fintel 1993) in (17a), interpreted as in (17a'), yields the correct semantic results. And NO...BUT JOHN is intersective and not cardinal. (17a) is false if only Bill came to the lecture even though {Bill} and {John} have the same cardinality. Similarly *every...but John* interpreted in (17b') is co-intersective and not co-cardinal.

(17) a. *No* student *but John* came to the lecture
 a'. (NO...BUT JOHN)(A)(B) = T iff A∩B = {John}

    b. *Every* student *but John* came to the lecture
    b'. (EVERY...BUT JOHN)(A)(B) = T iff A−B = {John}

Similarly if we interpret the conjuncts in (18a) as the composition of a cardinal Determiner with the intersective adjective the resulting functions are intersective but not cardinal.

(18) a. At least ten male but just two female pupils complained
      a'. (((AT LEAST TEN)∘MALE) ∧ ((JUST TWO)∘FEMALE)))(PUPIL)
      (COMPLAIN)

Analogously *every male but not every female* is co-intersective but not co-cardinal. A further case which only concerns intersective Determiners are one place comparatives such as *as many male as female*. Interpreted as type (1,1) functions they are provably intersective but not cardinal. And a last example is interrogative *Which?* Clearly (19a) asks the addressee to perform (19b).

(19) a. Which students passed?
      b. Identify the members of STUDENT∩PASS

We note that in English the class of intersective Determiners has a greater structural diversity of elements than the co-intersective class, a point that arises again below. We now characterize the (Co-)Cardinal functions in terms of independently needed properties.

Theorem 6 (Keenan & Stavi 1986) For E finite and F of type (1,1),
    a. F is cardinal iff F is intersective and permutation invariant.
    b. F is co-cardinal iff F is co-intersective and permutation invariant.

Note that Theorem (6a) characterizes cardinality in terms of set theoretic intersection and matching, as a permutation just matches one for one elements of E with elements of E, leaving out nothing. So we need not take number as a cognitive primitive.

Now we turn to a deeper similarity between the intersective and co-intersective functions, using the "if-then" arrow, A → B, to abbreviate ¬A ∪ B:

Theorem 7 For D a function of type (1,1) over a domain E,
    a. if D is intersective then for all A,B D(A)(B) = D(E)(A∩B)   and
    b. if D is co-intersective then for all A,B D(A)(B) = D(E)(A → B).

Using intersective SOME, Theorem 7a says that *some cats are grey* is logically equivalent to *some individuals are both cats and grey*, which is how we read $\exists x(\text{cat}(x) \& \text{grey}(x))$. The variable x ranges over the whole domain E of the model. In Theorem 7b, with D = ALL, we have that *all cats are grey* iff *all entities are such that if they are cats then they are grey*, that is, $\forall x(\text{cat}(x) \rightarrow \text{grey}(x))$. These paraphrases we learn in beginning logic courses when translating English into first order logic. Theorem 7 says that for D (co-)intersective we can eliminate the first argument, the restriction, in favor of quantifying over the whole universe E, and compensate by an appropriate boolean compound of A and B in the predicate argument (the nuclear scope). So restricting the domain of quantification is not essential in these cases. We define this notion formally and then state the theorem that eliminating the sortal restriction on the quantifier is limited to (co-)intersective ones. It fails for proportionality Determiners that are not intersective or co-intersective. We use *boolean set function* to mean ones defined in terms of $\cap$, $\cup$, and $\neg$.

Def 9 A type (1,1) function D over a domain E is *sortally reducible* iff there is a two place boolean set function h such that for all A,B $D(A)(B) = D(E)(h(A,B))$.

All intersective D are sortally reducible, the reducing function h is just $\cap$: $DAB = D(E)(A \cap B)$. And co-intersective D reduce by $\rightarrow$: $D(A)(B) = D(E)(A \rightarrow B)$. Surprisingly this exhausts the cases:

Theorem 8 (Keenan 1993) For all E, a conservative type (1,1) function D over E is sortally reducible iff D is intersective or D is co-intersective.

Theorem 8 tells us for example that *Most cats are grey* has no paraphrase of the form "For most x (...cat(x)...grey(x)...)" where x ranges over individuals and (... cat(x)...grey(x)...) is a boolean compound—built from *and, or, not, neither...nor...* in any way we like. Note that *Most cats are grey* is not logically paraphrased by $\text{Most}_x(\text{cat}(x) \rightarrow \text{grey}(x))$. The former is false in a 100 element model of which just ten are cats, only two of which are grey. But the latter is true in that model since $\text{cat}(x) \rightarrow \text{grey}(x)$ is true of 92 of the 100 objects in the model. A further, surprising, expressive power result from (Keenan 1993) is:

Theorem 9 The set of intersective (co-intersective) functions of type (1,1) is booleanly isomorphic to the set of generalized quantifiers. In each case the map $D \mapsto D(E)$ is an isomorphism.

So the isomorphism maps SOME to SOME(ENTITY), ALL to ALL(ENTITY), etc. Theorem 9 is surprising as there are 2^{4^n} functions of type (1,1) and only 2^{2^n} ones of type (1). So being (co-)intersective is a very strong condition: in a model with $|E| = 2$, there are $2^{16} = 65{,}536$ functions of type (1,1), just $2^4 = 16$ of which are intersective (and 16 of which are co-intersective, with two functions in both sets). And since isomorphic structures make the same sentences true (a general theorem in model theory) the set of intersective functions of type (1,1) has the same expressive power as the set of generalized quantifiers, the type (1) functions. The comparable claim holds for the set of co-intersective functions. But the full set of 2^{3^n} conservative functions greatly increases expressive power, though there is still a sense in which the intersective + co-intersective functions are basic. Namely, they *generate* the full set of conservative functions under the boolean operations. For example *some but not all* denotes (SOME ∧ ¬ALL), which is neither intersective nor co-intersective, but is conservative. And Keenan (1993) shows:

Theorem 10   The conservative functions over a finite E are just those constructable from the intersective + the co-intersective ones using the boolean operations ∧, ∨, and ¬ in (13).

We emphasize that Theorem 10 applies to functions, not expressions. *Exactly five* denotes the same function as *at least five and not more than five* but is not syntactically derived from it.

Lastly here, despite the strong commonality among intersective and co-intersective quantifiers, there is one context in English which distinguishes them. DPs built from intersective Determiners occur naturally in *Existential There* contexts in English, ones built from co-intersectve ones do not. Francez (2009) notes that Hebrew does not share this restriction.

(20) a. Aren't there more than two women in your class?
b. How many women were there at the lecture?
c. Is there no one but John in the building?
d. Just which students were there at the party anyway?
e. *Weren't there all / all but five students at the lecture?

3.10 Non-extensional determiners

All the Determiners d considered so far are *extensional*, meaning that if NP and NP' denote the same set then [d+NP] and [d+NP'] denote the same generalized quantifier. The seemingly cardinal Determiners in (21) fail to be extensional.

(21) *too many / few, surprisingly / fairly / (in)sufficiently many, (not) enough, ?many, ?few*

Enough lawyers but not enough doctors attended the meeting may be true even if the doctors and the lawyers in the model happen to be the same individuals—say it's a meeting of the Medical Association whose bylaws require 500 doctors for a quorum and one lawyer to take notes. Only 250 doctor-lawyers show up. In the same situation *More than n doctors attended* and *More than n lawyers attended* have the same truth value regardless of n. So *more than n* is extensional, *(not) enough* is not. We limit ourselves here to extensional Determiners.

3.11 First order determiners

These are ones definable by a sentence in a first order language. More formally:

Def 10   A Determiner d is *first order* iff there is a first order formula ϕ whose only non-logical constants are two one place predicate symbols, say P, Q, such that in an arbitrary model M, [[d+P] + Q] is interpreted as True in M iff ϕ is interpreted as True in M.

A *first order sentence* is one constructable from n-place predicate symbols P_n (the non-logical constants), boolean connectives *and*, *or*, *not*,... and the quantifiers $\exists x$ and $\forall x$, all individual variables x. We allow = as a logical constant. For example, *at least two* is first order definable since *At least two Ps are Qs* is true iff $\exists x \exists y (x \neq y$ & Px & Py & Qx & Qy) is true, and this is a first order sentence. On the other hand *just finitely many* and *all but finitely many* are not first order definable. And more important linguistically, proportionality Determiners such as *less than half, more than seven out of ten*, etc. which are not also intersective (*some, no*) or co-intersective (*all, not all*) are not in general first order definable, in fact not definable even if we limit ourselves to finite models—so their undefinability does not depend on some technical property of large cardinals. For proofs and extensive discussion see Peters & Westerståhl (2006: IV).

These observations resolve earlier discussion in the generative literature concerning whether the expressive power of natural languages lies within first order or not: it does not. The interest in this issue stems from the fact that first order languages have many nice logical properties. For example the set of logically true sentences in a first order language can be syntactically characterized, as can the entailment relation between sentences. But once outside first order we lose most of these nice properties (Lindström 1969).

3.12 Definite determiners and DPs

Building on Barwise & Cooper (1981) we call a DP *definite* if it holds of just the supersets of some non-empty set A (perhaps relative to some presuppositions). Then proper nouns are definite as they denote Montagovian individuals I_j, $j \in E$, which map sets B to **T** iff $\{j\} \subseteq B$. A Determiner d is *definite* if the DPs [d+NP] it builds are definite. Some definite Determiners are *the (n)*, *John's (n)*, and demonstratives: *this / that, these / those (n)*. THE TWO CATS holds of of a property A if CAT $\subseteq$ A, provided |CAT| = 2; otherwise it is not true. The cardinality requirement on the restriction is presupposed. *Aren't the two cats black?* questions only their color, not their number. *The two cats aren't black* only denies that they are black, not that they number two. We note that *the two* is first order definable but is not sortally reducible. So these two notions are completely independent: *some* and *all* are first order and sortally reducible, *infinitely many* is reducible but not first order, and *more than half* is neither.

Definiteness is ubiquitous in linguistics, often held to be a property of subjects (Kinyarwanda, Tagalog) and often triggering differential case marking on objects (Hebrew), cf article 2 [this volume] (Heim) *Definiteness and indefiniteness* and article 3 [this volume] (von Heusinger) *Specificity*. It shows up in plural partitives which select definite (plural) DPs, as in *two of the / John's / these cats* and excludes many non-definite DPs: **two of most / no / all but six cats*. But Peters & Westerståhl (2006: 243) point out that possessives, even with non-definite possessors, may occur here: *two of most students' relatives* (*attended the ceremony*). And Winter (2000) citing Ladusaw (1982) notes "specific" indefinites in partitives, as in *That book belongs to one of three people*. Winter uses a constrained choice function analysis to choose among the three people, the constraints building on other general properties of Determiners, such as conservativity.

The definite Determiners are not closed under the boolean operations. For example the complement of THE TWO is not definite. Nor is the negation of *the two* well formed in isolation: **Not the two boys cried* (compare *Not more than two boys cried*).

3.13 Possessor determiners

These have the form X's in *X's cat(s)* and are most thoroughly studied in Peters & Westerståhl (2006: Ch 7). They note that *'s* imposes few constraints on the choice of DP *X* it combines with. We might expect the definiteness of *X's* to be inherited from the definiteness of the DP *X* (as monotonicity properties are). So *John's* would be definite since *John* is. But they point out cases where *John's friends* may just mean some of his friends; and certainly *John broke his leg* does not entail that John was one legged. So they treat posssessor Determiners as invoking a parameter valued in context for the precise sort of quantification over the possessed object(s). The possession relation itself is also a parameter—just about any relation salient in context can be the relevant one, not just "owning" or "part-whole". And finally Peters and Westerståhl build in *narrowing* from Barker (1995). So in *most peoples' children* we only quantify over people with children, not people in general. They discuss interactions of possessor Determiners with partitivity (*some / all / not more than two of John's cats*) and definiteness, to which we refer the reader for lack of space here.

Concerning properties of Determiners previously discussed we note: (1) DPs built from possessor Determiners inherit their monotonicity from that of the possessor DP. (2) Possessor Determiner's are straightforwardly conservative: *Every student's bicycle is red* is logically equivalent to *Every student's bicycle is a bicycle that is red*. (3) In general possessor Determiners are not permutation invariant, as their denotation can vary with that of the possessor and the choice of possession relation. For similar reasons they are not first order definable, intersective, co-intersective or proportional. But they do form boolean compounds (22a, b), comparatives, (23a, b), and interrogatives, (24a, b).

(22) a. Either John's or Mary's bicycle was stolen
b. Neither every student's nor every teacher's car was vandalized

(23) a. (Not) More of John's than of Mary's friends attended the wedding
b. How many more of John's than of Mary's friends attended?

(24) a. Whose car was vandalized?
b. Which teacher's students did the best on the exam?

Lastly, treating prenominal possessors as Determiners in English accounts for **this John's friend*, but cross linguistically this complementary distribution often fails, the pattern in *this friend of John('s)* being common: *cet ami de ma soeur* (French: 'this friend of my sister'), *ein Freund von mir* (German: 'a friend of mine'), *kol ha-haverim shel Dan* (Hebrew: 'all the-friends of Dan'), *ity tranon-dRabe ity* (Malagasy: 'this house of Rabe this').

3.14 Exception determiners

Some of these determiners have already been mentioned: *no...but John* in *No student but John passed the exam*. More complex examples using *except* instead of *but* are (25a,b).

(25) a. *No* students *except foreigners* need visas
   b. ...*most* dishwashers *except very low-end models* have a water saving feature

These are taken from Peters & Westerståhl (2006: Ch 8) who discuss this construction extensively, building on von Fintel (1993), Moltmann (1995) and Garcia-Alvarez (2003).

4 Extending the logical type of determiners

4.1 Determiners for mass nouns

Combined with plural count nouns, percentage and fraction expressions denote proportionality functions as indicated earlier. But they treat singular count nouns as "mass":

(26) a. About 20% / Over a third of the house will have to be repainted
   b. Most / (Not) more than three quarters of the façade was destroyed
   c. (Less than) Half (of) the cake was eaten by the time we arrived.

English has a few quantifiers—*(not) (very) much, How much?*, (a) *little*, which select for mass terms. They correspond to the count terms *(not) (very) many, How many?*, and *(a) few*, (27b,c).

(27) a. Much (of the) flour was spilled / (A) little (of the) flour was spilled
   b. *Much / *A little buildings were destroyed
   c. Many / (A) few buildings were destroyed
   d. Much / (A) little *(of the) building was destroyed

Some (co-)intersective Determiners combine with singular count nouns with no mass interpretation: (*more than / all but*) *one, which?, each, every*. But (*some / most / a lot*) *of*, and (*not*) *all (of)* allow both in construction with partitive *of*:

(28) a. All / Most of the house was repainted / All / Most of the houses were repainted
   b. Some / A lot of the barn was destroyed / Some / A lot of the barns were destroyed

Impressionistically it is common that the same Determiners combine with count and mass nouns: French *beaucoup de sel* 'much salt' and *beaucoup de livres* 'many books'. Spanish *mucha fruta* 'much fruit' and *muchas casas* 'many houses'. Hebrew *harbeh zman* 'much time' and *harbeh anashim* 'many people'. In Malagasy *Be vola* 'much money' and *Be zanaka* 'many children'. Note too the count vs mass use of *large* in *a* large *number of cans* and *a* large *amount of salt*.

At time of writing we are just discovering cross language patterns in this domain. One well documented construction is *noun classifiers* (Gil 2005, Greenberg 1978). They enable mass nouns to combine with cardinal numerals: *ten* ears *of corn*, *two* sticks *of gum*, *one* sheet *of paper*, *a* bar *of soap*, **two gums*, **ten soaps*, etc. Often, as in English, the classifier is itself a Noun. Languages which use classifiers extensively include Burmese, Vietnamese and Japanese. Additionally we convert mass terms to count ones with container expressions—*a* box *of candy*, *two* glasses *of milk*, and measure phrases: *forty* liters *of gas*, *five* tons *of fertilizer*.

Measure phrases provide a key to understanding mass term quantification. Higginbotham (1994) presents the core idea, building on ontological work in Gillon (1992), Pelletier & Schubert (1989a), Lønning (1987) and the foundational Link (1983). Like count nouns which take their denotations in a boolean lattice (the set of subsets of a domain E), so too mass terms denote in a boolean lattice. The underlying partial order is a "part of" relation, not the subset relation as in the count domain. Its exact nature and properties are a matter of on-going research. See Lønning (1997). But given such a domain, we quantify over masses using *measures*, denoted by nominals like *meter*, *square foot*, *liter*, even *cup*. A measure μ maps a boolean lattice into the non-negative real numbers in such a way that its value at the least upper bound of (finitely many) disjoint elements is the sum of its values at the elements. Then quantification on mass terms is done as for count terms using the values of the mass terms under appropriate measures. (For permutation invariant quantifiers we require measures that map x and π(x) to the same value, π a permutation). Thus *Most of the beer was drunk* is true iff the value an appropriate volume measure assigns to THE DRUNK BEER is greater than half the value it assigns to THE BEER. Much remains to be refined and generalized, but we do now have a conceptual framework for representing mass quantification cf. article 7 [this volume] (Lasersohn) *Mass nouns and plurals* and article 3 [Semantics: Typology, Diachrony and Processing] (Doetjes) *Count/mass distinctions*.

4.2 Non-subject DPs

In *Ann praised every student*, the DP *every student* combines with a P_2 to form a P_1 *praised every student*. We know just what set that P_1 denotes. It is the set of individuals which stand in the PRAISE relation to each student. We can represent this just by extending the domains of type (1) functions to include binary relations. They will map them to unary relations (properties) and their value at a binary relation is determined by the values they assign to unary relations. In general, for A a set and R a binary relation, (EVERY(A))(R) = {b∈E|(EVERY(A)(bR) = T}, where bR is just the set of objects that b stands in the relation R to. More generally we let type (1) functions take n+1-ary relations as arguments, mapping them to n-ary ones, all n (See Nam 2005). So the type (1) functions are ones that reduce arity by 1. For simplicity we illustrate them with binary (1+1-ary) relations, not arbitrary n+1-ary ones. So the *in situ* interpretation of (29a) is given by (29b). It is the object narrow scope reading. The object wide scope reading is (29c).

(29) a. Some teacher praised every student
 b. SOME(TEACHER)((EVERY(STUDENT))(PRAISE)
    = T iff TEACHER ∩ {b|(EVERY(STUDENT))(bPRAISE)} ≠ ∅
 c. EVERY(STUDENT)(λx.(SOME(TEACHER))(PRAISE x))

And the intersection in (29b) is non-empty iff for some teacher b, (EVERY(STUDENT)) holds of the set of things b praised, the object narrow scope reading of (29a). (29c) asserts that for each student b, some teacher praised b, the object wide scope reading of (29a). (29c) can be true if different teachers praised different students even though no one teacher praised them all. In general transitive sentences in English virtually always have the *in situ* interpretation. Furthermore often the object wide scope reading is less available or not available at all. For example, *No teacher praised every student* only has the object narrow scope reading. It is not used to assert that every student has the property that no teacher praised him. Similarly *Some teacher praised no student* only has the object narrow scope reading. See Liu (1996), Szabolcsi & Zwarts (1997) and article 1 [Semantics: Sentence and Information Structure] (Szabolcsi) *Scope and binding*. Equally Takahashi (2006) notes that comparative cardinal Dets, as in *Every student read* more than six *poems*, do not scope over the subject. And there are several cases in which subjects but not objects scope over fronted interrogatives (May 1985, Beghelli 1997). *Which book did every student read?* is scopally ambiguous, but *Which student read every book?* is not. Note that on the representations given in (29b,c), the greater complexity of the object wide scope reading correlates with its lesser availability.

Quantified DPs in independent sentences are usually scope independent: *Every student came to the party and some teacher spoke there* does not have a reading on which the choice of teacher varies with the choice of student. And occasionally co-argument DPs may have independent ("branching") readings. See Liu (1996), Westerståhl (1987) and Sher (1997):

(30) a. I told many of the men three of the stories   (Jackendoff 1972)
= There's a set of many men and a set of three stories
such that I told each of the men each of those stories.
b. A majority of the students read those two stories   (Liu 1996)
c. Quite a few boys in my class and most girls in your
class have all dated each other   (Barwise 1979)

4.3 Two place (polyadic) determiners

Two place Determiners have been studied in Keenan & Moss (1985), Keenan (1987), Beghelli (1994) and Zuber (2007, 2009). We note a few of their properties. First, the expression they build with two NPs has the basic distribution of a DP. It is subject in (31a); object in *I know more men than women*; object of a Preposition in *He has argued with more men than women* and possessor in *More men than women's bikes were stolen*. Such DPs may occupy several argument positions of the same predicate: *More students than teachers attended as many demonstrations as concerts*. Such DPs raise to object and passivize to subject: *More men than women were believed to have objected*. Second, nominal modifiers apply simultaneously to both NPs: *More men than women at the party signed the petition* naturally means *More men at the party than women at the party signed...* supporting that neither NP is subordinate to the other. Third, such DPs host across the board extraction: *a senator who$_i$ we interviewed more friends of t$_i$ than enemies of t$_i$*. Lastly, the P$_1$ imposes selectional restrictions on both NPs: #*Fewer men than chairs laughed at that joke* entails that at least one chair laughed.

These Determiners are interpreted in type ((1,1),1), where the brackets indicate that the first two properties form the argument of the Determiner. In (31) the truth of [Det(NP,NP') + P$_1$] just depends on the cardinality of the intersection of the P$_1$ property with each of the NP properties, so these Determiners are *cardinal* and hence also *intersective*.

(31) a. *More / Fewer* men *than* women signed the petition
b. *The same number of* students *as* teachers attended the lecture
c. *More than twice / n times / at least / exactly / almost as many* men *as* women attended
d. *Half again / not as many* students as teachers attended

Like their unary counterparts, two place intersective Determiners build DPs which occur naturally in Existential-There contexts:

(32) a. Weren't there *more* men *than* women at the lecture?
   b. *How many more* men *than* women are there in your class?
   c. There were *the same number of* students *as* teachers at the concert

Comparative Determiners also combine with one NP and two P_1s, italicized in (33):

(33) a. More/Fewer students *came early* than *left late*
   b. Half again / not as many students *came early* as *left late*
   c. The same (number of) students *came early* as *left late*

So here they are interpreted in type (1,(1,1)) and build type (1) functions logically equivalent to their *symmetric* variants (below), first noted in Zuber (2009):

(34) a. More students than teachers are Buddhists
   b. More Buddhists are students than teachers

To define symmetric variants we define a function *sym* mapping each pair (σ,τ) of finite sequences of non-negative integers to (τ,σ). Then for F a quantifier of type (σ,τ), F_{sym} is that quantifier of type (τ,σ) given by: $F_{sym}(X,Y) = F(Y,X)$. So if MT is that map of type ((1,1),1) in (34a) then MT_{sym} is that map of type (1,(1,1)) in (34b) sending each pair $(Y,(X_1,X_2))$ to $MT((X_1, X_2) Y)$, We should stress however that these two types are logically quite distinct—there are many more conservative functions of type ((1,1),1) than of type (1,(1,1)) for example.

Proportionality Determiners also occur as two place Determiners:

(35) a. *A greater percentage of* men *than* women were drafted
   b. *Proportionately more* students *than* teachers attended the rally
   c. *The same proportion / percentage of students as* teachers came to the party

It is natural to query whether comparatives in the diverse formats above increase logical expressive power. In fact they do. Beghelli (1994) shows that (MORE A THAN B) cannot be paraphrased by any boolean compound of F(A) and G(B), for any F,G of type (1,1). Keenan & Moss (1985) treat *every ... and...* in (36a) as of type ((1,1),1). If we just interpret *and* at the property level the result is (36b). But the preferred reading of is (36c), which we obtain if (EVERY...AND...) maps a pair (A,B) of sets to EVERY(A) ∧ EVERY(B).

(36) a. Every man and woman jumped overboard
   b. Everyone who was both a man and a woman jumped overboard
   c. Every man and every woman jumped overboard

Theorem 11   Basic two place cardinal Determiners such as *more...than...* are not first order.

A sufficient reason is that we can define many one place proportional Determiners in terms of cardinal two place ones: MOST(A)(B) = MORE(A∩B)THAN(A−B)(E). That is, *Most As are Bs* iff *More As that are Bs than As that aren't Bs exist*. More generally: 1/n OF THE (A)(B) = n TIMES AS MANY (A∩B) AS (A−B)(E). So if the two place cardinal Determiners are first order then so are these proportionality Determiners, but they aren't. By the same reasoning the use of cardinal comparatives in type ((1,1),(1,1)) as in *More students drank beer than teachers drank wine* are also not first order.

4.4 Type 2 quantifiers

These are ones that map binary relations to truth values (more generally n+2-ary relations to n-ary ones). Of course the composition of two type 1 functions yields a type 2 one: NO(DOG) composes with EVERY(CAT) to form the type (2) (NO(DOG)∘EVERY(CAT)), which maps the binary relation CHASE to (NO DOG) ((EVERY CAT)CHASE), the interpretation of *No dog chased every cat*. Such an analysis is unmotivated as the same interpretation derives from treating the relevant DPs as of type (1) as we have done. But in (37) the subject-object pairs of DPs are non-Fregean quantifiers of type (2)—provably (Keenan 1992, 1996b) there are no pairs F,G of type (1) quantifiers such that D = F∘G; that is, for all binary R, D(R) = F(G(R)).

(37)   a. *Different* people like *different* things
   b. *All the students* answered *the same questions* on the exam
   c. *John and Bill* support *rival political parties*
   d. John criticized Bill but *no one else* criticized *anyone else*
   e. Joe doesn't know Sue but *everyone else* knows *everyone else*   (Moltmann 1996)
   f. *Which students* read *which plays*?
   g. *Three teaching assistants* graded *114 papers between them* (See Scha 1981)

All the Sentences in (37) are ones whose truth (or answerhood) conditions can be described by conditions on the pairs of individuals in the binary relation. Such type (2) Determiners are conservative. For example, in (37a) we can restrict the first argument of LIKE to PEOPLE and the second to THING. A second sort of type (2) expression is given by gapping (Nam 2005):

(38) a. The teacher showed [[every girl two plays] and [every boy three novels]]
     b. John-i Mary-lul, (kuliko) Harry-ka Sue-lul salanghanta   (Korean)
        John-nom Mary-acc (and) Harry-nom Sue-acc loves
        John loves Mary and Harry Sue

In (39) by contrast the italicized DPs denote groups and the predicates express properties of the groups not expressible as relations between their members.

(39) a. *The teachers at our university* outnumber *the students*
     b. *The billiard balls* formed a triangle near the end of the table
     c. *All (of) the pupils* held hands and circled the fountain
     d. I saw *two men* carrying *three suitcases* between them   (adapted from Gil 1995)

Such *collective* predication resembles mass predication (Link 1983): *The children huddled in small groups in the courtyard*, *The rainwater collected in small pools in the courtyard*. In (39a,b,c) the choice of predicate forces the collective construal of the DP; in (39d) it is the adverb *between them* which is forcing. Replacing it with *apiece* (or *each*) forces a *distributive* reading: each of the two men was carrying three suitcases. In English plural DPs usually allow both collective and distributive construals. Gil (1995) supports cross linguistically that distributively interpreted universal quantifiers are more restricted in their distribution. *Bare plurals* (Carlson 1977; also article 5 [this volume] (Dayal) *Bare noun phrases* and article 7 [this volume] (Lasersohn) *Mass nouns and plurals*) are another case in which the predicate forces variation in the interpretation of its argument. The *stage level* predicate in *Firemen are available* forces an existential interpretation of firemen, whereas the *individual level* predicate in *Firemen are intelligent* forces a generic reading, firemen in general.

5 Adverbial Quantifiers

A-Quantification is associated with the predicate in diverse ways. One, cardinal quantifiers may be the predicate, as in Asurini (Tupi-Guarani, Brazil; Vieira 1995), Straights Salish, (40a) from Jelinek 1995, and Malagasy (Austronesian, Madagascar; Keenan 2008), (40b).

(40) a. čəsə + ∅   cə   qʷəqʷel'
        two + 3abs Determiner+spoke
        The ones who spoke were two

b. Roa ny mpikabary
two Determiner -er+act+speech
The speech-makers are/were two

Intensional cardinals such as *many* and *few* also occur as predicates, but universal Determiners do not (**The boys are all*) in these two languages. Two, Evans (1995) notes in Australian languages cases where quantificational force is expressed by preverbs, co-verbs, or just verbal affixes.

(41) barrik-djarrk-dulubom   gunj   (Mayali; Gunwinggu, Australian)
      3pl+past-all-shoot+past.perf kangaroo
      They all shot the kangaroo **They shot all the kangaroos*

The affix *-djarrk-* implies "acting together" and so quantifies only the Agent. In contrast Evans cites (42) from Straights Salish where the predicate level universal is not argument fixed:

(42) mək^w + ɬ   w'   na-t   tsə   sčenx^w
      all + 1pl linker   eat-trans   det   be.fish
      We ate all the fish / We all ate the fish / We ate the fish up completely

Similarly Bittner (1995) cites a verbal affix universal quantifier in Greenlandic Eskimo:

(43) Nukappiaraq balloni-si-gaannga-mi   minuttit qulit naatinnagit
      boy+abs   balloon-get-when.iter-3sProx, minutes ten   within
      qaartuur-tuaan-nangajap-p-a-a
      break-always-almost-ind-3-3
      When a boy gets a balloon, he almost always breaks it within ten minutes

Three, as in (1b) repeated as (44a), A-quantification can be expressed with independent adverbs or PPs: Lewis (1975), Heim (1982), de Swart (1996a, b). Also cf article 14 [Semantics: Lexical Structures and Adjectives] (Maienborn & Schäfer) *Adverbs and adverbials*.

(44) a. John *always / usually / often / occasionally / rarely / never* trains in the park
      b. John took his driver's exam *twice / (more than) three times*
      c. Mary brushes her teeth *every day / twice a day / daily*

There is a striking semantic correspondence between the adverbial quantifiers above and the D-Determiners presented earlier. *Always* corresponds to *all*, *never* to *no*, *twice* to *two*, *usually* to *most*, *occasionally* / *sometimes* to *some*, and *often* and *rarely* to *many* and *few*. Similarly Bittner (1995) lists pairs of A- and D- quantifiers (translating *always, mostly, often, sometimes*) in Greenlandic Eskimo formed from the same root but differing in adverbial vs nominal morphology. And Evans (1995) lists pairs of semantically similar D- and A- quantifiers in Mayali (Australia).

In general what we quantify over in the D-cases is given by the NP the Determiner combines with. But in A-quantification there is often no such clear constituent, and precisely what we are quantifying over is less clear. One influential approach to A-quantification is *unselective binding* (Lewis 1975). Examples that illustrate A-quantifiers best and which seem empirically most adequate are ones lacking independent D-quantifiers. (45) is from Peters &Westerståhl (2006):

(45) a. Men are usually taller than women
 b. $MOST_2(\{<x,y>|x \in MAN \& y \in WOMAN\}, \{<x,y>|xTALLERy\})$
 c. = T iff $|(MAN \times WOMAN) \cap TALLER|/|(MAN \times WOMAN)| > 1/2$

On this interpretation (45a) is true iff more than half the man-woman pairs are such that the first is taller than the second—the intuitively correct truth conditions. So $MOST_2$ takes a pair of binary relations MAN×WOMAN and TALLER as arguments, as it does in simpler cases like *Most colleagues are friends*. Its semantics is that of MOST (in the sense of *more than half*), but now the sets it intersects and compares cardinalities of are sets of ordered pairs. In general for D any of our type (1,1) functions, D_k, the *k-resumption* of D, is that function like D except that its arguments are k-ary relations. Resumption is one way A-quantifiers are characterized in terms of D-quantifiers. Thus it is immediate how to interpret the sentences differing from (45a) by replacing *usually* with *always, occasionally,* and *never*.

To what extent is resumptive quantification adequate characterize A-quantifiers? We can't give a definite answer to this question, as we lack a clear circumscription of the expressive power of A-quantifiers. But there is one more type of case that has been treated as unselective binding. Namely, biclausal constructions built from *when* / *if* clauses and generic or indefinite DPs (constructed with the indefinite article *a* / *an*). See Kratzer (1995).

(46) a. (Always) when a linguist buys a book he reads its bibliography first
 b. $ALL_2(R,S)$, where
  $R = \{<x,y>|x \in LINGUIST, y \in BOOK \text{ and } xBUYy\}$ and
  $S = \{<x,y>|x \text{ READ } y\text{'s BIBLIOGRAPHY FIRST}\})$
 c. = T iff $R \subseteq S$

ALL$_2$ is just ALL with binary not unary relation arguments. (46c) says that (46a) is true iff for all linguists x, all books y, if x buys y then x reads y's bibliography first, which seems right. *Always* can be replaced by *Sometimes*, *Never*, and *Not always*, interpreted by SOME$_2$, NO$_2$, and ¬ALL$_2$ with the intuitively correct truth conditions. However further extensions in which A- and D-quantification interact have not been successful. A much studied example is Geach's (1962) "donkey" sentence, as in (47a) with *it* anaphoric to *donkey*. Kamp (1981) and Heim (1982) among others have tried to interpret it with resumptive quantification as in (47b).

(47) a. Every farmer who owns a donkey beats it
 b. ALL$_2$({<x,y>|x ∈ FARMER, y ∈ DONKEY and xOWNy}, {<x,y>|xBEATy})

This yields the "strong" interpretation on which every farmer who owns a donkey beats every donkey he owns. Several linguists either accept this interpretation or at least feel that it is the closest clear statement of the truth conditions of (47a). But most choices of initial quantifier do not yield correct resumptive interpretations.

(48) a. At least two farmers who own a donkey beat it.
 b. Most farmers who own a donkey beat it.

Kanazawa (1994) notes that the resumptive reading of (48a) would, incorrectly, make it true in a model in which there are just two farmers, one owns one donkey and doesn't beat it, the other owns two and beats them both. Rooth (1987) notes the comparable problem for (47b) in which say all but one of ten farmers owns just one donkey and beats it, but the last farmer owns 100 donkeys and doesn't beat any of them. This problem is called the *proportion* problem, a misnomer since, per Kanazawa, it arises with non-proportional Dets like *at least two* as well. Indeed Peters and Westerståhl attribute to van der Does (1996) the claim that only *all*, *some* and their complements don't lead to a proportion problem. In addition Chierchia (1992) cites cases in which Sentences like (48a) get a "weak" or "existential" reading, not a universal one.

(49) a. Everyone who has a credit card will pay his bill with it (Cooper 1979)
 b. Everyone who has a dime will put it in the meter (Pelletier & Schubert 1989b)

Evans (1977), Cooper (1979) and, in a different way, Heim (1990) try to handle the "dangling" *it* in donkey sentences with E-type pronouns, in effect replacing *it* by a full DP such as *the donkey he owns*, where *he* refers back to *farmer*. But the results are less than satisfactory when some farmers own more than one donkey. For our purposes these proposals do not so much invoke new quantifiers as establish the scope of familiar ones. Later proposals by Groenendijk & Stokhoff (1991), Chierchia (1992), Kanazawa (1994) himself and de Swart (1996b) have invoked dynamic logic (cf. article 12 [Semantics: Theories] (Dekker) *Dynamic semantics*), where natural language expressions are represented in a logical language and variables not in the syntactic scope (the c-command domain) of a variable binding operator can nonetheless be bound by it, cf. article 11 [Semantics: Theories] (Kamp & Reyle) *Discourse Representation Theory* and 12 [Semantics: Theories] (Dekker) *Dynamic semantics*.

In the cases so far considered the domain of the resumptive quantifier is not denoted in a systematic way. In (45a) the two NPs *man* and *woman* are part of independent DP constituents, yet the domain of the quantifier is the cross product of their denotations. In (46a) it was the subordinate *when* clause in which we abstracted twice to form a binary relation denoting expression. Now returning to our initial example (44a), repeated as (50a), we don't find naturally constructable binary relations of the relevant sorts. Rather, following de Swart (1996a), it seems that we are comparing the "times" John trains with the times he trains in the park.

(50) a. John always / usually / ... trains in the park
 b. ALL ({t|John trains at t},{t|John trains in the park at t})

So the sentences in (50a) compare the set of times John trains with the set of times he trains in the park. ALWAYS says that the first set is included in the second; NEVER says they are disjoint; SOMETIMES says they are not; USUALLY says that the set of times he trains in the park number more than half of the number of times that he trains, etc. So here A-quantification is handled as D-quantification over times. This approach is not unnatural given A-quantifiers which overtly mention *times*—as *sometimes*, *five times*, *most of the time*, *from time to time*. Moreover it enables us to test whether the properties we adduced for D-quantifiers extend to their corresponding A-ones. And several do, as de Swart (1966a) shows.

The cases in (50a) are trivially Conservative. For any A-quantifier Q, Q(TRAIN) (TRAIN IN THE PARK) = Q(TRAIN)(TRAIN ∩ TRAIN IN THE PARK). They are also Domain Independent: if more times are added to the model but the two arguments of an A-Quantifier are unchanged then the value Q assigns them is unchanged. Further some A-Quantifiers are intersective: SOMETIMES, NEVER; some are co-intersective: ALWAYS, WITH JUST TWO EXCEPTIONS, (51a); and some properly proportional, (51b): USUALLY, MORE THAN TWO THIRDS OF THE TIME. As with D-quantifiers the notion of proportion is clearest when the arguments are finite and non-empty.

(51) a. With two exceptions, John has always voted for a Democrat for President
 b. More than two thirds of the time when John prayed for rain it rained

De Swart (1996a) also handles some temporal clauses with *before* and *after* which are not mere place holders for quantificational domains in the way that *when* and *if* clauses seem to be.

(52) a. Paul *always* takes a shower just before he goes to bed
b. Paul *never* exercises immediately after he has had dinner

(52a) says that the times just before Paul goes to bed are all among those when he takes a shower. (52b) says that the times immediately after he has had dinner are disjoint from the times he exercises. *Usually, always, sometimes* and *never* are interpretable by their corresponding D-Determiners. Using *when* as an argument slot definer we see that the A-quantifiers above have the monotonicity properties of their D-counterparts. Like *all*, *always* is ↑ on its second argument, ↓ on its first, so the inferences in (53) are valid and NPI's are licensed in the first argument but not the second, (54).

(53) Always when John travels he reads a book
⇒ Always when John travels he reads something
⇒ Always when John travels by train he reads a book

(54) a. Always when *anyone* travels he reads a book
b. *Always when John travels he reads *any* book

Lewis (1975) cautioned against a "times" approach noting that donkey sentences refer to a state, not an event, and sentences like *A quadratic equation usually has two different solutions* are not time dependent at all. This is true, though it leaves unexplained why we naturally use temporal metaphors in mathematical discourse, as when we say that a set of sentences is semantically consistent if they can be *simultaneously* true. Lewis himself notes that Russell & Whitehead (1910–1913) use *always* and *sometimes* to explain their (now standard) universal and existential quantifiers: $(x).\varphi x$ means φx *always*, $(\exists x).\varphi x$ means φx *sometimes*. It is not problematic to interpret sentences as functions taking "abstract times" as arguments, with truly "timeless" sentences denoting constant functions, as with vacuous quantification generally. Artstein (2005), building on Pratt & Francez (2001), treats *before* and *after* phrases (*after the meeting, before John left*) as temporal generalized quantifiers—they map properties of time intervals to {T,F}, cf article 13 [this volume] (Ogihara) *Tense* and article 17 [this volume] (Schlenker) *Indexicality and de se*.

6 Concluding remarks

Quantification remains an area of very active research. Since the first version of this article was submitted at least 12 new articles and two books have appeared on quantification. Some concern psycholinguistic properties of quantifiers or the inferences they license: (Politzer 2007, Szabolcsi 2007, Hackl 2009, Chemla 2009). We have not been able to discuss this area at all, though it is fair to say that *Experimental Semantics* has now taken root as a subfield of semantics. Other areas we have not been able to cover here concern quantifier modification: (Beaver & Condoravdi 2007, Yabushita 2007), computational complexity classes of quantifiers (Szymanik 2007, 2009), quantification in comparative clauses (Krasikova 2007, and the earlier foundational Schwarzschild & Wilkinson 2002), various types of functional and polyadic quantification (Burnett 2009, Winter 2004, de Swart & Sag 2002), and the semantic interaction of Determiners and predicates (Hallman 2009). D-quantification over count domains remains the best understood type of quantification in natural language. Our knowledge of it has grown enormously since 1980. And it proves helpful in understanding mass and A-quantification, both areas currently being researched and in which many empirical and conceptual issues remain unexplored, even unformulated.

7 References

Abiteboul, Serge, Richard Hull & Victor Vianu 1995. *Foundations of Databases*. Reading, MA: Addison-Wesley.
Artstein, Ron 2005. Quantificational arguments in temporal adjunct clauses. *Linguistics & Philosophy* 28, 541–597.
Bach, Emmon et al. (eds.) 1995. *Quantification in Natural Languages*. Dordrecht: Kluwer.
Barker, Chris 1995. *Possessive Descriptions*. Stanford, CA: CSLI Publications.
Barwise, Jon 1979. On branching quantifiers in English. *Journal of Philosophical Logic* 8, 47–80.
Barwise, Jon & Robin Cooper 1981. Generalized quantifiers and natural language. *Linguistics & Philosophy* 4, 159–219.
Beaver, David & Cleo Condoravdi 2007. On the logic of verbal modification. In: M. Aloni, P. Dekker & F. Roelofsen (eds.). *Proceedings of the 16th Amsterdam Colloquium*. Amsterdam: ILLC, 3–11.
Beghelli, Filippo 1994. Structured quantifiers. In: M. Kanazawa & C. Piñón (eds.). *Dynamics, Polarity, and Quantification*. Stanford, CA: CSLI Publications, 119–145.
Beghelli, Filippo 1997. The syntax of distributivity and pair-list readings. In: A. Szabolcsi (ed.). *Ways of Scope Taking*. Dordrecht: Kluwer, 349–409.

Ben-Shalom, Dorit 2003. One connection to standard invariance conditions on modal formulas and generalized quantifiers. *Journal of Logic, Language and Information* 12, 47–52.

van Benthem, Johan 1984. Questions about quantifiers. *Journal of Symbolic Logic* 49, 443–466.

van Benthem, Johan & Alice ter Meulen (eds.) 1985. *Generalized Quantifiers in Natural Language*. Dordrecht: Foris.

Bittner, Maria 1995. Quantification in Eskimo: A challenge for compositional semantics. In: E. Bach et al. (eds.). *Quantification in Natural Languages*. Dordrecht: Kluwer, 59–81.

Burnett, Heather 2009. *Formal Approaches to Semantic Microvariation: Adverbial Quantifiers in European and Québec French*. MA thesis. University of California, Los Angeles, CA.

Carlson, Greg 1977. A unified analysis of the English bare plural. *Linguistics & Philosophy* 1, 413–457.

Chierchia, Gennaro 1992. Anaphora and dynamic binding. *Linguistics & Philosophy* 15, 111–183.

Chemla, Emmanuel 2009. Presuppositions of quantified sentences: Experimental data. *Natural Language Semantics* 17, 299–340.

Cooper, Robin 1979. The interpretation of pronouns. In: F. Heny & H. Schnelle (eds.). *Syntax and Semantics 10*. New York: Academic Press, 61–92.

van der Does, Jaap 1996. Quantification and nominal anaphora. In: K. von Heusinger & U. Egli (eds.). *Proceedings of the Konstanz Workshop "Reference and Anaphoric Relations"*. Konstanz: University of Konstanz, 27–56.

van der Does, Jaap & Jan van Eijck 1996a. Basic quantifier theory. In: J. van der Does & J. van Eijck (eds.). *Quantifiers, Logic and Language*. Stanford, CA: CSLI Publications, 1–47.

van der Does, Jaap & Jan van Eijck (eds.) 1996b. *Quantifiers, Logic and Language*. Stanford, CA: CSLI Publications.

Evans, Gareth 1977. Pronouns, quantifiers, and relative clauses. *Canadian Journal of Philosophy* 7, 467–536.

Evans, Nick 1995. A-Quantifiers and scope in Mayali. In: E. Bach et al. (eds.). *Quantification in Natural Languages*. Dordrecht: Kluwer, 207–271.

Fauconnier, Gilles 1978. Implication reversal in a natural language. In: F. Guenthner & S. Schmidt (eds.). *Formal Semantics and Pragmatics of Natural Language*. Dordrecht: Reidel, 289–301.

von Fintel, Kai 1993. Exceptive constructions. *Natural Language Semantics* 1, 123–148.

Francez, Itamar 2009. Existentials, predication and modification. *Linguistics & Philosophy* 32, 1–50.

Garcia-Alvarez, Ivan 2003. Quantifiers in exceptive NPs. In: G. Garding & M. Tsujimura (eds.). *Proceedings of the West Coast Conference on Formal Linguistics (= WCCFL) 22*. Somerville, MA: Cascadilla Press, 207–216.

Gärdenfors, Peter (ed.) 1987. *Generalized Quantifiers: Linguistic and Logical Approaches*. Dordrecht: Reidel.

Geach, Peter 1962. *Reference and Generality*. Ithaca, NY: Cornell University Press.

Gil, David 1995. Universal quantifiers and distributivity. In: E. Bach et al. (eds.). *Quantification in Natural Languages*. Dordrecht: Kluwer, 487–540.

Gil, David 2005. Numeral classifiers. In: M. Haspelmath et al. (eds.). *The World Atlas of Language Structures*. Oxford: Oxford University Press, 226–230.

Gillon, Brendon 1992. Toward a common semantics for English count and mass nouns. *Linguistics & Philosophy* 15, 597–640.

Greenberg, Joseph 1978. Generalizations about numeral systems. In: J. Greenberg, C. Ferguson & E. Moravcsik (eds.). *Universals of Human Language 3*: *Word Structure*. Stanford, CA: Stanford University Press, 249–95.

Groenendijk, Jeroen & Martin Stokhof 1991. Dynamic predicate logic. *Linguistics & Philosophy* 14, 39–100.

Hackl, Martin 2009. On the grammar and processing of proportional quantifiers: *most* versus *more than half*. *Natural Language Semantics* 17, 63–98.

Hallman, Peter 2009. Proportions in time: Interactions of quantification and aspect. *Natural Language Semantics* 17, 29–61.

Heim, Irene 1982. *The Semantics of Definite and Indefinite Noun Phrases*. Ph.D. dissertation. University of Massachusetts, Amherst, MA. Reprinted: Ann Arbor, MI: University Microfilms.

Heim, Irene 1990. E-type pronouns and donkey anaphora. *Linguistics & Philosophy* 13, 137–177.

Herburger, Elena 1994. Focus and NP quantification. In: E. Duncan, D. Farkas & P. Spaelti (eds.). *Proceedings of the West Coast Conference on Formal Linguistics (= WCCFL) 12*. Stanford, CA: CSLI Publications, 517–533.

Higginbotham, James 1994. Mass and count quantifiers. *Linguistics & Philosophy* 17, 447–480.

Higginbotham, James & Robert May 1981. Questions, quantifiers and crossing. *The Linguistic Review* 1, 41–79.

Jackendoff, Ray 1972. *Semantic Interpretation and Generative Grammar*. Cambridge, MA: The MIT Press.

Jelinek, Eloise 1995. Quantification in Straits Salish. In: E. Bach et al. (eds.). *Quantification in Natural Languages*. Dordrecht: Kluwer, 487–540.

Kamp, Hans 1981. A theory of truth and semantic representation. In: J. Groenendijk, T. Jansen & M. Stokhof (eds.). *Formal Methods in the Study of Language, vol. 1*. Amsterdam: Mathematical Centre, 277–322.

Kanazawa, Makoto 1994. Weak vs. strong readings of donkey sentences and monotonicity inferences in a dynamic setting. *Linguistics & Philosophy* 17, 109–159.

Kanazawa, Makoto & Christopher J. Piñón (eds.) 1994. *Dynamics, Polarity, and Quantification*. Stanford, CA: CSLI Publications.

Katz, Jerrold & Paul Postal 1964. *An Integrated Theory of Linguistic Descriptions*. Cambridge, MA: The MIT Press.

Keenan, Edward L. 1981. A Boolean approach to semantics. In: J. Groenendijk, T. Janssen & M. Stokhof (eds). *Formal Methods in the Study of Language, vol. 2*. Amsterdam: Mathematical Centre, 343–379.

Keenan, Edward L. 1987. Multiply-headed NPs. *Linguistic Inquiry* 18, 481–490.

Keenan, Edward L. 1992. Beyond the Frege boundary. *Linguistics & Philosophy* 15, 199–221.

Keenan, Edward L. 1993. Natural languages, sortal reducibility and generalized quantifiers. *Journal of Symbolic Logic* 58, 314–325.

Keenan, Edward L. 1996a. The semantics of determiners. In: S. Lappin (ed.). *The Handbook of Contemporary Semantic Theory*. Oxford: Blackwell, 41–65.

Keenan, Edward L. 1996b. Further beyond the Frege boundary. In: J. van der Does & J. van Eijck (eds.). *Quantifiers, Logic and Language*. Stanford, CA: CSLI Publications, 179–203.

Keenan, Edward L. 2008. Quantification in Malagasy. In: L. Matthewson (ed.). *Quantification: A Cross-Linguistic Perspective*. Bingley: Emerald, 319–352.

Keenan, Edward L. & Lawrence Moss 1984. Generalized quantifiers and the expressive power of natural languages. In: J. van Benthem & Alice ter Meulen (eds.). *Generalized Quantifiers in Natural Language*. Dordrecht: Foris, 73–124.

Keenan, Edward L. & Jonathan Stavi 1986. A semantic characterization of natural language determiners. *Linguistics & Philosophy* 9, 253–326.

Keenan, Edward L. & Dag Westerståhl 1997. Generalized quantifiers in linguistics and logic. In: J. van Benthem & A. ter Meulen (eds.). *Handbook of Logic and Language*. Amsterdam: Elsevier, 837–893.

Krasikova, Sveta 2007. Quantification in *than*-clauses. In: M. Aloni, P. Dekker & F. Roelofsen (eds.). *Proceedings of the 16th Amsterdam Colloquium*. Amsterdam: ILLC, 133–138.

Kratzer, Angelika 1995. Stage-level and individual-level predicates. In: G. Carlson & F. J. Pelletier (eds.). *The Generic Book*. Chicago, IL: The University of Chicago Press, 125–175.

Krynicki, Michal, Marcin Mostowski & Leslaw W. Szczerba (eds.) 1995. *Quantifiers, Logics, Models and Computation 1*. Dordrecht: Kluwer.

Ladusaw, William 1982. Semantic constraints on the English partitive construction. In: D. Flickinger, M. Macken & N. Wiegand (eds.). *Proceedings of the West Coast Conference on Formal Linguistics (= WCCFL) 1*. Stanford, CA: Stanford Linguistics Association, 232– 242.

Ladusaw, William 1983. Logical form and conditions on grammaticality. *Linguistics & Philosophy* 6, 389–422.

Ladusaw, William 1996. Negation and polarity items. In: S. Lappin (ed.). *Contemporary Semantic Theory*. Oxford: Blackwell, 321–343.

Lappin, Shalom 1988. The syntax and semantics of NPs. *Linguistics* 26, 903–909.

Lewis, David 1975. Adverbs of quantification. In: E. Keenan (ed.). *Formal Semantics for Natural Language*. Cambridge: Cambridge University Press, 3–15.

Lindström, Per 1966. First order predicate logic with generalized quantifiers. *Theoria* 32, 186–195.

Lindström, Per 1969. On extensions of elementary logic. *Theoria* 35, 1–11.

Link, Godehard 1983. The logical analysis of plurals and mass terms: A lattice-theoretical approach. In: R. Bäuerle, Ch. Schwarze & A. von Stechow (eds.). *Meaning, Use and Interpretation of Language*. Berlin: de Gruyter, 302–323.

Liu, Feng-Hsi 1996. Branching quantification and scope independence. In: J. van der Does & J. van Eijck (eds.). *Quantifiers, Logic and Language*. Stanford, CA: CSLI Publications, 255–269.

Lønning, Jan 1987. Mass terms and quantification. *Linguistics & Philosophy* 10, 1–52.

Lønning, Jan 1997. Plurals and collectivity. In: J. van Benthem & A. ter Meulen (eds.). *Handbook of Logic and Language*. Amsterdam: Elsevier, 1009–1054.

Matthewson, Lisa 2001. Quantification and the nature of cross-linguistic variation. *Natural Language Semantics* 9, 145–189.

Matthewson, Lisa (ed.) 2008. *Quantification: A Cross-Linguistic Perspective*. Bingley: Emerald.

May, Robert 1985. *Logical Form: Its Structure and Derivation*. Cambridge, MA: The MIT Press.

Moltmann, Friederike 1995. Exception sentences and polyadic quantification. *Linguistics & Philosophy* 18, 223–280.

Moltmann, Friederike 1996. Resumptive quantifiers in exception sentences. In: M. Kanazawa, C. Piñón & H. de Swart (eds.).*Quantifiers, Deduction, and Context*. Stanford, CA: CSLI Publications, 139–171.

Nam, Seungho 2005. N-ary quantifiers and the expressive power of DP-compositions. *Research on Language and Computation* 3, 411–428.

Pelletier, Francis J. & Lenhart K. Schubert 1989a. Mass expressions. In: D. Gabbay & F. Guenthner (eds.). *Handbook of Philosophical Logic IV*. Dordrecht: Reidel, 327–407.
Pelletier, Francis J. & Lenhart K. Schubert 1989b. Generically speaking. In: G. Chierchia, B. Partee & R. Turner (eds.). *Properties, Types and Meaning 2*. Dordrecht: Kluwer, 193–268.
Peters, Stanley & Dag Westerståhl 2006. *Quantifiers in Language and Logic*. Oxford: Oxford University Press.
Politzer, Guy 2007. The psychological reality of classical quantifier entailment properties. *Journal of Semantics* 24, 331–343.
Pratt, Ian & Nissim Francez 2001. Temporal prepositions and temporal generalized quantifiers. *Linguistics & Philosophy* 24, 187–222.
Reuland, Eric J. & Alice ter Meulen 1987. *The Representation of (In)definiteness*. Cambridge, MA: The MIT Press.
Rooth, Mats 1987. Noun phrase interpretation in Montague Grammar, File Change Semantics, and Situation Semantics. In: P. Gärdenfors (ed.). *Generalized Quantifiers: Linguistic and Logical Approaches*. Dordrecht: Reidel, 237–268.
Russell, Bertrand & Alfred North Whitehead 1910–1913. *Principia Mathematica*. Cambridge: Cambridge University Press.
Scha, Remko 1981. Distributive, collective and cumulative quantification. In: J. Groenendijk, T. Janssen & M. Stokhof (eds.). *Formal Methods in the Study of Language 2*. Amsterdam: Mathematical Centre, 483–512.
Schwarzschild, Roger & Karina Wilkinson 2002. Quantifiers in comparatives: A semantics of degree based on intervals. *Natural Language Semantics* 10, 1–41.
Sher, Gila 1997. Partially-ordered (branching) generalized quantifiers: A general definition. *Journal of Philosophical Logic* 26, 1–43.
Strawson, Peter F. 1959. *Individuals: An Essay in Descriptive Metaphysics*. London: Methuen.
de Swart, Henriëtte 1996a. Quantification over time. In: J. van der Does & J. van Eijck (eds.). *Quantifiers, Logic, and Language*. Stanford, CA: CSLI Publications, 311–337.
de Swart, Henriëtte 1996b. (In)definites and genericity. In: M. Kanazawa, C. Piñón & H. de Swart (eds.). *Quantifiers, Deduction, and Context*. Stanford, CA: CSLI Publications, 171–195.
de Swart, Henriëtte & Ivan Sag 2002. Negation and negative concord in Romance. In: *Linguistics & Philosophy* 25, 373–417.
Szabolcsi, Anna (ed.) 1997. *Ways of Scope Taking*. Dordrecht: Kluwer.
Szabolcsi, Anna 2007. Do negative polarity items facilitate the processing of decreasing inferences? In: M. Aloni, P. Dekker & F. Roelofsen (eds.). *Proceedings of the 16th Amsterdam Colloquium*. Amsterdam: ILLC, 11–16.
Szabolcsi, Anna & Frans Zwarts 1997. Weak islands and an algebraic semantics for scope taking. In: A. Szabolcsi (ed.). *Ways of Scope Taking*. Dordrecht: Kluwer, 217–263.
Szymanik, Jakub 2007. Strong meaning hypothesis from a computational perspective. In: M. Aloni, P. Dekker & F. Roelofsen (eds.). *Proceedings of the 16th Amsterdam Colloquium*. Amsterdam: ILLC, 211–216.
Szymanik, Jakub 2009. *Quantifiers in Time and Space*. Doctoral dissertation. University of Amsterdam.
Takahashi, Shoichi 2006. More than two quantifiers. *Natural Language Semantics* 14, 57–101.
van Valin, Robert 2006. Some universals of verb semantics. In: R. Mairal & J. Gil (eds.). *Linguistic Universals*. Cambridge: Cambridge University Press, 155–178.
Vieira, Marcia D. 1995. The expression of quantificational notions in Asurini do Trocara. In: E. Bach et al. (eds.). *Quantification in Natural Languages*. Dordrecht: Kluwer, 701–721.

Westerståhl, Dag 1987. Branching generalized quantifiers and natural language. In: P. Gärdenfors (ed.). *Generalized Quantifiers: Linguistic and Logical Approaches*. Dordrecht: Reidel, 269–299.

Westerståhl, Dag 1989. Quantifiers in formal and natural languages. In: D. Gabbay & F. Guenthner (eds.). *Handbook of Philosophical Logic IV*. Dordrecht: Reidel, 1–133.

Westerståhl, Dag 1995. Quantifiers in natural language: A survey of some recent work. In: M. Krynicki & M. Mostowski (eds.). *Quantifiers: Logic, Models and Computation 1*. Dordrecht: Kluwer, 359–408.

Winter, Yoad 2000. What makes choice natural? In: K. von Heusinger & U. Egli (eds.). *Reference and Anaphoric Relations*. Dordrecht: Kluwer, 229–247.

Winter, Yoad 2004. Functional quantification. *Research on Language and Computation* 2, 331–363.

Yabushita, Katsuhiko 2007. Partition semantics of *at least* & *at most*. In: M. Aloni, P. Dekker & F. Roelofsen (eds.). *Proceedings of the 16th Amsterdam Colloquium*. Amsterdam: ILLC, 247–252.

Zuber, Richard 2007. Symmetric and contrapositional quantifiers. *Journal of Logic, Language and Information* 16, 1–13.

Zuber, Richard 2009. A semantic constraint on binary determiners. *Linguistics & Philosophy* 32, 95–114.

Veneeta Dayal
5 Bare noun phrases

1   Introduction —— 149
2   Empirical landscape —— 150
3   Theories of variation: syntactic parameterization —— 154
4   Theories of variation: semantic parameterization —— 157
5   Theories of variation: number, definiteness and lexicalization —— 164
6   Challenges for theories of variation —— 169
7   Conclusion —— 173
8   References —— 174

Abstract: The distribution and interpretation of bare NPs varies across languages. This article surveys the range of these possibilities and the theoretical accounts that deal with it. Bare NPs are canonically associated with reference to kinds and the semantic operations involved in kind formation are central to the discussion. Differences between singular and plural terms with respect to kind formation, the relationship between kind formation and the semantics of definite and indefinite NPs, the correlation between lexical exponents of a semantic operation and its availability as a covert type shift, and the syntactic location of semantic operations are among the issues explored in these accounts. The study of bare NPs thus overlaps with the study of genericity, number marking and (in)definiteness. The primary focus here is on recent research which addresses the issue of cross-linguistic variation in semantics. Current challenges for theories of variation are also discussed.

1 Introduction

The study of bare NPs spans thirty years of semantic research and can be divided almost evenly into two phases. The first focused on the proper analysis of English bare plurals, with particular emphasis on the role of reference to kinds and the principles of quantification at play in statements with such NPs. The second took insights from the study of bare plurals beyond English to other languages. While questions regarding denotation and quantification remained important, this second phase was marked by a concern with cross-linguistic issues. Three questions emerged as particularly significant in this enterprise: Is variation in the

Veneeta Dayal, New Brunswick, NJ, United States

https://doi.org/10.1515/9783110589443-005

mapping between form and meaning predictable? What is the impact of number morphology on bare NPs/kind terms? Is there a correlation between determiners in a language and available readings for bare NPs? This survey focuses on the second phase of the investigation. It fleshes out the empirical landscape that current work on the topic assumes, discusses three approaches to cross-linguistic variation that have been proposed, and identifies the research questions that remain open. For the first phase of the investigation the reader is referred to Krifka et al. (1995), Carlson (1991, 1999), Delfitto (2006) and article 8 [this volume] (Carlson) *Genericity*.

2 Empirical landscape

English bare plurals, the focus of Carlson's (1977) influential work, are a natural starting point for any survey of the topic, being the most familiar and best-understood case of bare NPs. They have three primary readings: kind, generic and existential. English typically does not allow bare singular arguments, setting aside exceptions like *man is mortal* etc. Bare mass nouns, which trigger singular verb agreement, align with bare plurals in terms of available readings (see also article 7 [this volume] (Lasersohn) *Mass nouns and plurals*).

(1) a. *Dinosaurs* are extinct.
    b. *Dogs* bark.
    c. *Dogs* are barking.

An intuitively natural way of grouping these sentences might be to classify (1a) and (1b) together as statements applying to a whole class or species, separating them out from (1c), which describes properties of some members of the class at a particular point in time. Although (1a) and (1b) are both general statements, they are crucially different. While it is possible to relate the statements in (1b) to corresponding statements in which the predication applies to a particular individual, it is not possible to do so with the statement in (1a): *Fido barks* vs. **Fido is extinct*.

We also know that bare plurals cannot be used deictically or anaphorically. A definite is needed for that:

(2) a. **(The) dogs*, namely Fido and Rover, are barking.
    b. Some $dogs_i$ are barking. **(The) $dogs_i$* must be hungry.

This suggests an inverse correlation between the presence of overt determiners and meanings of bare NPs but two points are worth noting in this connection. One, definite NPs and bare plurals are not truly in complementary distribution. There are contexts in which one can be substituted for the other with no shift in meaning (Condoravdi 1992):

(3) There was a ghost on campus. *(The) students* were aware of the danger.

Two, if the generalization about the relation between overt determiners and bare plurals is to hold, there must be some distinction between the existential/generic readings of bare plurals and such readings of indefinite NPs. The difference in existential readings was established early on by Carlson (1977):

(4) a. Miles didn't see/is looking for *policemen/a policeman/some policemen.*
     b. #*A building/#Some buildings/Buildings* will burn in Berlin and in Frankfurt.

The bare plural in (4a) can only take narrow scope, while the indefinites, singular and plural, can take wide or narrow scope. The readings of bare plurals are not, however, a subset of the readings of indefinites. (4b) with either indefinite cannot have the plausible reading in which different buildings burn in the two cities. With a bare plural, it readily allows for this differentiated scope reading.

Generic readings of bare plurals and singular indefinites can also be separated. Generic indefinites seem to be restricted to statements in which definitional rather than accidental properties are at issue, though what counts as definitional is open to contextual manipulation. The contrast in (5) is discussed in Krifka et al. (1995), cases like (6) by Greenberg (1998) and Cohen (1999). The unacceptability judgments indicated are for generic readings only:

(5) a. *Madrigals* are polyphonic/popular.
     b. *A madrigal* is polyphonic/#popular.
     c. *A basketball player* is popular.

(6) a. *Italian restaurants* are closed today.
     b. #An *Italian restaurant* is closed today.

The rough generalization, then, is that bare plurals are a distinct kind of NP, characterized by their ability to serve as arguments of kind-level predicates, by their propensity for narrowest scope, and by their more liberal distribution in generic statements.

This empirical picture has been extended in a number of directions. A minimal but significant modification comes from a consideration of Romance languages, which like English generally disallow bare singular arguments. They differ from English, however, on plurals and mass nouns. French does not allow such arguments to be bare while Italian and Spanish allow them only in well-governed positions. The following from Chierchia (1998) shows a subject-object asymmetry in Italian:

(7) a. *Bambini* sono venuti da noi.
 'Kids came by.'
 b. Ho preso *biscotti* con il mio latte.
 '(I) had cookies with my milk.'

Furthermore, these bare plurals arguably do not have kind or generic readings:

(8) *Leo odia *gatti*.
 'Leo hates cats.'

It bears emphasizing though that Romance bare plurals, like English bare plurals, cannot refer deictically or anaphorically and are unable to have wide scope readings.

Another extension of the empirical landscape is prompted by languages like Chinese which do not mark number in the nominal system. Bare NPs in Chinese display the full range of readings associated with English bare plurals (Yang 2001). In addition, they are able to refer deictically and anaphorically, in keeping with the fact that Chinese has no definite determiner. They are also thought to have indefinite readings, again in keeping with the absence of indefinite determiners, but this generalization is subject to two caveats. In subject position, there is a tendency, not an absolute requirement, that the bare NP have definite rather than indefinite readings. And, in positions where an indefinite reading is available, the bare NP only has narrow scope. That is, in spite of the absence of indefinite determiners, the scopal properties of Chinese bare NPs are like those of English bare plurals, not English indefinite NPs.

Finally, there are languages that fall in between Chinese and English. Hindi and Russian, for example, display morphological number like English but like Chinese do not have articles. Interestingly, these languages freely allow bare singular arguments as well as bare plurals and both display kind and generic readings. However, bare singulars are not trivial variants of bare plurals. In the Hindi example below the same child is assumed to be playing everywhere, an implausible reading. Its plural counterpart, however, would readily allow for a plausible reading (Dayal 2004):

(9) #caaro taraf *bacca* khel rahaa thaa
    four ways child play PROG PAST
    'The (same) child was playing everywhere.'

The bare singular in (9) may appear to behave like a wide scope indefinite but standard diagnostics, such as those in (4), show that they resist wide scope readings just like bare plurals. The bare singular picks out an entity in the domain that uniquely satisfies the descriptive content of the NP. While this may be similar to a wide scope indefinite, it is not identical to it (see also articles 2 [this volume] (Heim) *Definiteness and indefiniteness* and 3 [this volume] (von Heusinger) *Specificity*). Such languages thus reveal the importance of number morphology as well as the presence/absence of determiners in identifying interpretive possibilities for bare NPs.

Turning to theoretical issues, two broad approaches to the semantics of English bare plurals can be taken as the current baseline. Both follow Carlson (1977) in including kinds in the ontology. Both also agree with him that the quantificational force of bare plurals is external to the NP. They hold that quantification in bare plurals is sensitive to the same factors that Lewis (1975), Kamp (1981) and Heim (1982) identified for indefinites: schematically, $[Q_{unselective}]$ *[Restrictor]* $\exists$*[Nuclear Scope]*. They differ, however, in whether bare plurals must always refer to kinds. According to the so-called ambiguity approach (Wilkinson 1991, Gerstner-Link & Krifka 1993, Kratzer 1995 and Diesing 1992), they refer to kinds when the predication is kind level but are property denoting otherwise. The neo-Carlsonian approach (Carlson 1989, Chierchia 1998 and Dayal 2004) holds that object level predication also takes kinds as arguments but accesses their instantiation sets. The difference between the ambiguity approach (10b, 11b) and the neo-Carlsonian approach (10c, 11c) is illustrated below, where superscript k indicates reference to kinds, R the realization relation between kinds and their instances, and s the world/situation index:

(10) a. Dogs bark.
     b. Gen x,s [dogs(x,s)] [bark(x,s)]
     c. Gen x,s [R(x, dogs$_s^k$)] [bark(x,s)]

(11) a. Dogs are barking.
     b. $\exists$x,s [dogs(x,s) & are-barking(x,s)]
     c. $\exists$x,s [R(x, dogs$_s^k$) & are-barking(x,s)]

The two approaches yield essentially the same truth conditions for the core cases but the neo-Carlsonian view, which formally distinguishes between bare plurals and indefinites, may have an advantage over the alternative, given that the two types of NPs do not display identical behavior.

Formal semantic analyses of individual languages contributed to and were, in turn, influenced by the possibility of cross-linguistic variation in the semantics of natural language (see article 2 [Semantics: Typology, Diachrony and Processing] (Bach & Chao) *Semantic types across languages*). In the domain of bare NPs and genericity, the notion of parameterization within a set of universally available options emerged as the leading idea in this research agenda. We will see the results of this shift in perspective as we turn to theories that deal with the distribution and interpretation of bare NPs across languages.

3 Theories of variation: syntactic parameterization

Longobardi (1994, 2000, 2001) analyzes the variation between Germanic and Romance languages as instantiating different settings of a parameter. He follows Stowell (1991) and Szabolcsi (1994) in taking reference to individuals to be tied exclusively to the D(eterminer) node and proposes that this can be established by means of chain formation via movement of a nominal expression to D: $[_{DP} N_i [_{NP} t_i]]$ or by means of CHAIN formation via coindexing of a nominal with an expletive in D: $[_{DP} D_{i\,expl} [_{NP} N_i]]$. Languages differ in the level at which the link with D must be established. Romance languages instantiate the strong D setting of the parameter and force chain/CHAIN formation overtly. Germanic languages instantiate the weak D setting and do not require overt association. A general economy constraint that takes overt chain/CHAIN formation to be a last resort effectively works to make this association invisible in weak D languages.

Longobardi adduces strong support for his claim from Italian, where an adjective precedes a proper name only in the presence of a definite determiner:

(12) *l' antica Roma / Roma antica / *antica Roma*
      the ancient Rome Rome ancient ancient Rome

D being the locus for marking arguments and proper names being quintessentially argument-like, the paradigm is readily derived from the strong D parameter:

(13) a. $[_{DP} [_{D} la_i [_{AP} antica [_{NP} Roma_i]]]]$
      b. $[_{DP} [_{D} Roma_i [_{AP} antica [_{NP} t_i]]]]$
      c. *$[_{DP} [_{D} e [_{AP} antica [_{NP} Roma]]]]$

In (13a) *Roma* forms a CHAIN with a semantically vacuous element in D. (13b) has internal movement of *Roma* from N to D. (13c) is ungrammatical because the link with D is unrealized. A covert operator in D cannot bind a name which is inherently referential. Grammaticality judgments about word order thus provide compelling evidence for the dependence between a syntactic node D and the semantics of proper nouns.

The extension of this account to common nouns is less clear-cut. Since common nouns are not inherently referential, they cannot form a chain by N to D movement. They can, however, form a CHAIN with an expletive or enter into an operator-variable relation with a covert ∃ in D. This yields the following:

(14) *i grandi cani / grandi cani / *cani grandi*
      the big dogs big dogs dogs big

(15) a. [$_{DP}$ i$_{i\text{-}<e>}$ [$_{AP}$ grandi [$_{NP}$ (cani$_{<e,t>}$)$_i$]]]
     b. *[$_{DP}$ [SHIFT(cani$_{i\text{-}<e,t>}$)$_{<e>}$] [$_{AP}$ grandi [$_{NP}$ t$_i$]]]
     c. [$_{DP}$ ∃$_{<<e,t>, <<e,t>, t>>}$ [$_{AP}$ grandi [$_{NP}$ cani$_{<e,t>}$]]$_{<e,t>}$]

Note though that an expletive, by hypothesis, cannot effect semantic change and a covert type shift from <e,t> to <e> has to be assumed in order for the CHAIN in (15a) to be well formed. One might ask, then, what blocks N to D movement of the kind shown in (15b), since the situation is now essentially parallel to the proper name case seen in (13b). A possible answer to this could be that CHAIN formation with an expletive in D is precisely the trigger needed to activate the requisite type shift, appealing perhaps to the principle of last resort as an underlying motivating factor (see also article 8 [Semantics: Interfaces] (de Hoop) *Type shifting*).

The option in (15c) is consistent with Longobardi's view that Italian bare plurals are not kind terms. It also derives the restricted syntactic distribution of bare plurals by requiring the null operator to be licensed through government, as in Contreras (1986). And it provides an explanation for unexpected restrictions on generic readings. Syntactic licensing prevents the bare plural from occurring above VP (Diesing 1992), effectively ruling out generic readings. When syntactic conditions such as focus or modification allow bare plurals to occur above VP, generic readings become available (Longobardi 2000). Why focus or modification has this effect is not explored. I note in passing an unclarity about the role of the operator inside bare plurals. A quantificational determiner fits in with the idea of an operator in D but is at odds with the view of indefinites as predicates bound by external operators. This technical detail can be fixed by melding Diesing's Mapping Hypothesis with a quantificational view of indefinites, as in Chierchia (1995), for example.

Turning to languages like English, the weak D parameter delays linking of N with D. English proper names therefore cannot occur with an expletive nor can they precede adjectives. Similarly, English common nouns do not form an overt chain/CHAIN, allowing bare plurals to occur in the order adjective-noun:

(16) a. *the ancient Rome / *Rome ancient / ancient Rome
 b. *the big dogs / *dogs big / big dogs

(17) a. [$_{DP}$ e [$_{NP}$ Rome$_{<e>}$/Dogs$_{<e,t>}$]]
 b. [$_{DP}$ Rome$_{<e>}$/ [SHIFT(Dogs$_{<e,t>}$)$_{<e>}$] [$_{NP}$ t$_i$]]

English is postulated to have an empty D in overt syntax (17a). N to D movement takes place at LF, with covert type shift yielding kind reference for bare plurals (17b). This implies that kind formation is not dependent on the presence of an overt element in D, a dependence that we suggested could be used to rule out N to D movement of Italian bare plurals.

Longobardi's postulation of an empty D in English forces further comparisons with Italian bare plurals. He suggests that the licensing of empty Ds occurs at LF in English but at S-structure in Italian, taking structures with common nouns to have the same semantics as indefinites. As mentioned above, he takes indefinites inside VP to map into the nuclear scope and yield existential readings while taking indefinites outside VP to map into the restrictor and yield generic readings. Since licensing works differently in the two languages and Italian bare plurals are necessarily VP-internal, they only have existential readings. English bare plurals, on the other hand, because they are not syntactically restricted, can be mapped into either domain, resulting in existential as well as generic readings.

The case of English bare plurals in subject positions with existential readings, however, remains problematic for Longobardi. The presence of an empty D in the subject position of episodic sentences is needed to ensure existential interpretation, but N to D movement has to take place in order to make it possible for bare plurals to appear in the ungoverned subject position. To deal with this, Longobardi proposes that existential interpretation is read off prior to LF movement but licensing is checked after LF movement in English.

Turning to singular terms, Longobardi takes the Italian definite singular to be in a CHAIN: [il$_{expl}$ [dodo$_{<e>}$]], as in Vergnaud & Zubizarreta (1992):

(18) *Il dodo* è estinto.
 'The dodo is extinct.'

The evaluation of this proposal depends on the analysis of the bare singular as a kind term. It is generally thought that the type-shift used to derive plural kind terms is not defined for singular terms. If, however, bare singulars are taken to be inherently kind denoting, it should be possible for them to form CHAINS with expletives. The problem is that this makes the wrong prediction for English. Just as English bare plurals correspond to Italian definite plural kind terms, English bare singulars should correspond to Italian definite singular kind terms. But we know that the two languages converge in ruling out bare singulars. The alternative is to take the singular common noun to denote predicates of taxonomic kinds, bound by *iota* (see section 5). Under this view, the definite determiner has semantic content, denoting a function from sets to entities: $[il_{<<e,t>,e>} [dodo_{<e,t>}]]$. This delivers the correct result for both languages, but undercuts the notion of the definite determiner as an expletive.

To conclude, Longobardi's parametric approach gives a compelling account of the association of proper names with D in terms of chain/CHAIN formation and a very plausible account of the structural restrictions on Italian bare plurals. The notion of an expletive determiner in the case of common nouns, the conditions under which type-shifting operations are invoked, and the cross-linguistic variation between kind and existential readings, however, raise questions. Nevertheless, Longobardi's work which tied interpretation to fixed positions in the structure was extremely influential in propelling research in this domain.

4 Theories of variation: semantic parameterization

I now turn to another influential theory, proposed by Chierchia (1998). I first discuss its essential features, reserving modifications and criticisms prompted by further investigations for later sections.

4.1 Germanic vs. Romance

Chierchia (1998) starts at the other end of the spectrum from Longobardi, taking languages to vary on the syntactic level at which reference to individuals is located. Four principles and three semantic operations derive the range of paradigms considered by him:

(19) a. *The Nominal Mapping Parameter (NMP):* N ⇒ [+/− pred, +/− arg]
Languages without Mass-Count Distinction
  i. [− pred, + arg] every lexical noun is mass: Chinese
Languages with Mass-Count Distinction
  ii. [+pred, +arg] bare arguments are allowed. with articles: Germanic
                                                without articles: Slavic
  iii. [+pred, −arg] bare arguments disallowed. with $\delta_{\text{null-det}}$: Italian
                                                without $\delta_{\text{null-det}}$: French
b. *Avoid Structure:* Apply SHIFT at the earliest level.
c. *Blocking Principle (BP):*
For any type shifting operation π and any X: *π(X) if there is a determiner D such that for any set X in its domain, D(X) = π(X).
d. *Ranking:* ∩ > {ι, ∃}

(20) a. *Nom* (∩): $\lambda P_{\langle s, \langle e,t \rangle \rangle}$ λs ιx [P_s (x)]
b. *Pred* (∪): $\lambda k_{\langle s,e \rangle}$ λx [x ≤ k_s]
c. *Derived Kind Predication (DKP):* If P applies to ordinary individuals and k denotes a kind, P(k) = ∃x [∪k(x) ⋀ P(x)]

To elaborate, according to *NMP* NPs in some languages can denote type <e>, in others not. Economy requires that a language in which an NP may denote an individual should shift covertly from type <e,t> to <e> without projecting a DP structure. The *BP* requires lexical determiners to be used over covert type-shifts. The availability of the three basic type shifts are regulated by ranking and *BP*. *Nom* is the kind forming operator that takes a property and returns the corresponding kind, conceptualized as a function from indices to the maximal entity that realizes the kind at that index. *Pred* takes the extension of the kind at an index, the maximal entity k_s, and returns the set of singular and plural entities that are its individual parts, yielding the instantiations of the kind at that index. Finally, *DKP* provides sort adjustment when an object level predicate combines with a kind level argument. Most importantly, *DKP* builds in local existential binding and delivers the narrow scope behavior that Carlson had shown to be integral to kind terms.

Chierchia treats English as a [+pred, +arg] language. Bare plurals are NPs of predicative type <e,t>, which shift via the kind forming operator to type <e>, consistent with the [+arg] setting of the parameter and economy of structure. The rest follows under a neo-Carlsonian approach to kinds where bare plurals uniformly denote kinds but the mapping to the quantificational structure, determined on independent grounds, is roughly as in the case of indefinites. With object level predicates, the inverse operation *pred* comes into play, yielding quantification over instances of the kind.

Chierchia also treats Italian bare plurals as kind terms. Italian being a [+pred, −arg] language, the bare plural projects a DP structure, with a null D encoding *nom*. The observed subject-object asymmetry follows from the licensing requirement on null elements, as in Longobardi. The absence of generic readings derives from the theory of mapping in Chierchia (1995). Details aside, the cross-linguistic difference in generic readings rests on the absence of D in English and the licensing requirement for null Ds in Italian.

Examples like (21) form the basis of the claim that Italian bare plurals denote kinds:

(21) *Insegnanti davvero dediti* nella scuola di oggi sono quasi estinti
    teachers really devoted in schools of today are nearly extinct
    'Really devoted teachers are nearly extinct in today's schools.'

The propensity of Italian bare plurals for narrow scope, a property that is entailed by an analysis in terms of kind reference, is the motivation behind this claim. Nevertheless, it has been challenged by Longobardi as well as Zamparelli (2002), though the data in (21) is not easily accommodated by their view of Italian bare plurals as non kind denoting indefinites. Note, once again, the presence of modification in examples suggesting kind reference.

Chierchia's analysis of Italian bare plurals has an interesting consequence for his analysis of Italian definite plurals. *BP* dictates that null determiners or covert operations not duplicate the meaning of lexical operators. This is substantiated by the fact that in languages with definite determiners, bare plurals cannot be used deictically/anaphorically while in languages without such determiners, they can. But if the Italian bare plural is indeed a kind term, *BP* incorrectly predicts that the Italian definite plural cannot also be a kind term. Chierchia appeals to a formal difference between *nom* for the bare plural (22a) and an equivalent derivation involving the intensionalising of *iota* for the plural definite (22b) to handle this problem:

(22) a. extinct ($^{\cap}$dinosaurs)
    b. extinct ($\lambda s\ \iota[\text{dinosaurs}_s]$)

This does not fully account for cross-linguistic differences. If it is possible to abstract over the world variable in a definite in Italian, there is no reason why it should not be possible to do so in English, but we know that English definite plurals are not kind terms. Chierchia is aware of this and appeals to *Avoid Structure*, claiming that economy forces the simplest possible structure to be used for a given meaning. Since English allows NPs to denote kinds, that is preferred over DPs with a definite for the purpose. Note that this explanation rests on the premise that the two options given in (22) are in competition in English. In proposing that the Italian bare plural is a kind term, on the other hand, Chierchia argues that kind formation is not subject to *BP* precisely because they are not in competition. Thus there seems to be some conceptual unclarity about the relation between these two equivalent ways of deriving kind readings.

Turning to singular terms, Chierchia draws on the idea that the uniqueness imposed by number morphology on kind formation clashes with the notion of kinds and rules out bare singular kind terms (Dayal 1992). Languages that are like English or Italian in having the singular-plural distinction but unlike them in not having articles, then, need to be accounted for. As noted, such languages have bare singulars in addition to bare plurals. Chierchia analyzes them as [+arg, +pred] languages like English. However, because they do not have a lexical definite determiner, *BP* does not block *iota* from functioning as a covert type shift and bare nominals are able to have deictic and anaphoric readings. Furthermore, because they do not have indefinite determiners, he suggests, indefinite readings are also allowed. Finally, bare plurals are able to denote kinds via the application of *nom* but not bare singulars. We will discuss arguments against the specifics of this account in section 5.1. Here we continue to examine *NMP*, looking at languages with a different setting of the parameter than Germanic ([+pred, +arg]) or Romance ([+pred, −arg]), namely those with [−pred] specification.

4.2 Chinese

The discussion so far has revolved around count nouns, which denote predicates that shift covertly to argument type in [+arg, +pred] languages and via a lexical or null D in [−arg, +pred] languages. We now turn to mass nouns which require us to step back and place Chierchia's cross-linguistic claims within his view of the count-mass distinction. This also allows us to separate those predictions that derive from his account of the mass-count distinction independently of *NMP* from those that rely crucially on the [+arg, −pred] setting of the parameter.

Contrary to the view of mass nouns as mereological sums, Chierchia takes mass nouns to have the same atomic structure as count nouns, noting that an individual chair or table would be identified as atomic parts of the denotation of mass nouns like *furniture*. Similarly, the denotation of mass nouns like *water* also includes atoms, even though those atomic entities may not be ordinarily identifiable. The real difference, he claims, is that count nouns denote a set of atomic entities, with plural entities entering the denotation as a result of pluralization, whereas mass nouns come out of the lexicon with both atomic and plural entities in their denotations (see also Krifka 1991, Landman 1996, Chierchia 2010 and article 7 [this volume] (Lasersohn) *Mass nouns and plurals*):

(23) a. $PL(F) = \lambda x\, [\neg F(x)\, \&\, \forall y\, [y \leq x\, \&\, AT(y) \rightarrow F(y)]]$
b. If *dog* (a count noun) = {f, b, s}, then *dogs* = {{f, b, s}, {f,b}, {f,s}, {b,s}}
c. If *furniture* = {{t, c, s}, {t, s}, {t, c}, {c, s}, t, c, s}, then *furnitures* = ∅

(23a) defines the semantic contribution of the plural morpheme as an operation that takes a set of atomic entities and returns the set of pluralities generated by that set, minus the atoms. (23b) illustrates the denotation of singular and plural count terms. If Fido, Barky and Spotty are the dogs in the context, the singular term will be true of them while the plural term would be true of the groups they belong to but not of them. (23c) illustrates the denotation of mass nouns. If an individual table, chair and sofa are all the items of furniture in the world, the mass noun will denote them as well as the four groups they are part of.

Chierchia claims that the absence of pluralization on mass nouns and the inability of numerals to combine directly with them follows from this distinction. Mass nouns do not show a singular-plural contrast: *tables* vs. *furnitures, because PL applied to a mass noun would denote the empty set. Since all the pluralities were already in the original set, they would all be removed. (Note that even if PL did not exclude members of the original set, one could argue that pluralization would be ruled out because it would be vacuous: *PL(furniture) = furniture*.) Furthermore, mass nouns do not lend themselves to direct counting by numerals because counting requires a salient level of individuation. In the case of count nouns, this is the level of atoms. In the case of mass nouns, no distinguished level is available since the singular-plural distinction is neutralized in the basic meaning of the noun. A measure phrase serves to individuate an appropriate level for counting: **three furniture(s)* vs. *three items of furniture*. Every language is expected to have some mass nouns for extra-grammatical reasons (there are substances whose atomic elements are not perceptible) and these properties will hold of them. Parameterization is not at play. Semantic parameterization is brought into the picture to account for languages in which no nouns manifest visible plural morphology or the ability to combine directly with numerals. It is worth emphasizing that Chierchia does not take languages which only have the first property to fall in the same class (see also section 6, Chierchia 2009 and article 3 [Semantics: Typology, Diachrony and Processing] (Doetjes) *Count/mass distinctions*).

Chinese is sometimes thought to have a plural morpheme -*men* Li (1999). Yang (1998), however, shows that this morpheme yields definite plural readings and is not a bona-fide plural marker (see also Kurafuji 2004 for Japanese). It cannot occur in *there-* insertion contexts or as a predicate nominal, for example. Thus it seems reasonable to treat Chinese as a language lacking morphological plurality. Chierchia takes such languages to be [+arg, −pred], with NPs that are obligatorily individual denoting. He further takes the following properties to be characteristic of such languages: (a) generalized bare arguments, (b) the extension of all nouns as mass, (c) no pluralization and (d) a generalized classifier system. Properties (b)–(d) cluster together, as already discussed. It is (a), the absence of determiners, where the semantic parameter plays a crucial role.

Chierchia takes mass nouns to always denote individuals, specifically kinds. But we know that kinds can be shifted to properties by *pred* (20b). Thus the following schematic possibilities are available in principle (although Chierchia's system does not have expletive determiners, I include the option here for completeness):

(24) a. $[_{DP} \, D_{expl} \, [_{NP} \, N_{<e>}]]$
 b. $[_{DP} \, D_{<<e,t>,e>} \, [_{NP} \, pred(N_{<e>})_{<e,t>}]]$
 c. $[_{NP} \, N_{<e>}]$

In a [+arg, −pred] language like Chinese, (24b) is not an option since NPs cannot denote properties, by hypothesis. And economy of structure rules out an expletive (24a). Thus the only viable option is (24c). The fact that classifier languages with definite determiners are not attested is explained in a surprisingly simple way. Now consider mass nouns in [−arg, +pred] languages. Here the only option is (24b), precisely the situation attested in languages like Italian. The distribution and interpretation of mass terms mirrors the distribution and interpretation of plural count nouns in requiring a definite determiner. Finally, consider [+arg, +pred] languages like English. Here (24b) is allowed and we indeed see the definite determiner with mass nouns in anaphoric and deictic contexts. We also see (24c) with kind denoting bare mass nouns, (24a) being ruled out by economy. One question that arises for such languages is why the extension of the kind (the maximal entity that is the sum of the instantiations of the kind at a given index) cannot be used to deliver the interpretive functions of *iota* without added structure, the unattested definite readings for bare nominals. By and large, however, the patterns of distribution and interpretation across languages are captured by the interaction of the *NMP* with economy of structure.

Finally, although Chierchia seems committed to the view that count nouns start out as properties while mass nouns start out as kinds, not much seems to ride on it. The same predictions about the form of mass nouns would obtain in his system if they were to denote properties:

(25) a. $[_{DP} D_{expletive} [_{NP} \text{nom}(N_{<e,t>})_{<e>}]]$
b. $[_{DP} D_{<<e,t>, e>} [_{NP} N_{<e,t>}]]$
c. $[_{NP} \text{nom}(N_{<e,t>})_{<e>}]$

In [+arg, −pred] languages like Chinese, NPs would be forced to denote individuals, shifting from properties to individuals covertly via *nom* (or *iota*), as in (25a) or (25c), with economy ruling out (25a). This would yield determiner-less languages. The obligatory presence of the determiner in [−arg, +pred] languages with mass nouns would follow exactly as in the case of count nouns. (25a) and (25c) would be ruled out by the [−arg] setting. And the selective occurrence of the determiner in [+arg, +pred] languages would follow the explanation for the same pattern in count nouns. Reference to kinds would be derived most economically in (25c), while (25b) would be needed to host the anaphoric/deictic definite determiner.

Although the choice between properties and kinds is not crucial for predicting distribution and interpretation, it does have different implications for Chierchia's overall picture of variation. If mass nouns are basically kind denoting and the language prevents NPs from shifting to properties, determiners would have to be functions from expressions of type <e>. They would have to include the shift to properties via *pred*: $\lambda x^k \iota[\text{pred}(x)]$. Though Chierchia does not propose this, it is in keeping with his view of numerals and classifiers, which builds on the idea that Chinese nouns are kind terms (Krifka 1995). (Another possibility for deriving deictic and anaphoric readings of bare nominals is to take the extension of the kind at the relevant index. This would be the simplest and most economical solution but not one that Chierchia entertains.) This move is obviously not required if mass nouns are properties that *iota* can apply to directly. Determiners can continue to be functions from properties, albeit with the intervention of measure phrases/classifiers for purposes of individuation, as required. A question worth speculating on is whether languages that distinguish count and mass but do not have determiners could be [+arg, −pred] languages. This would align Russian and Hindi with Chinese rather than English but without a deeper investigation, no claims can be hazarded.

I have tried to separate three aspects Chierchia's theory, the claim that mass nouns have an atomic structure like count nouns but are lexically plural, the claim that mass nouns are necessarily kinds, and the claim that parameter setting predicts the presence or absence of determiners. These distinctions will be useful to keep in mind when we discuss languages that have been claimed as problematic for *NMP* in section 6. In section 5, however, we will consider some modifications to the theory that are not specifically related to this parameter. To sum up, Chierchia's is the first substantive proposal addressing issues of syntax as well as semantics, and the most articulated theory of variation in the mapping from nominal structure to interpretation. For this reason it has had a tremendous impact on research in this area.

5 Theories of variation: number, definiteness and lexicalization

In this section I summarize my own work, which highlights the role of number in kind formation and explicates the relation between definite determiners and kind formation.

5.1 Modifications of the neo-Carlsonian approach

A key observation about languages with number marking but no determiners is that bare plurals in such languages behave more or less like English bare plurals, but bare singulars are substantively different. This observation for Hindi prompted Dayal (1992) to propose that the semantics of singular morphology clashes with the conceptual notion of a kind (see also Chierchia 1998), ruling out *nom* as a potential type shift for bare singulars. The implications of this position were further explored in Dayal (2004).

Bare singulars and bare plurals in Hindi and Russian allow for kind as well as anaphoric/deictic readings. Their existential reading, however, is distinct from that of regular indefinites in two respects. They cannot take wide scope over negation or other operators. They also cannot refer non-maximally. So, bare NPs cannot be used in translating (26b) or (26c) to refer to a subset of the children mentioned in (26a):

(26) a. There were several children in the park.
 b. A child was sitting on the bench and another was standing near him.
 c. Some children were sitting on the bench, and others were standing nearby.

Even though there are no definite or indefinite determiners in these languages, only readings associated with definites are available to bare NPs. This shows that the availability of covert type shifts is constrained, as proposed by Chierchia (1998), but that the correct ranking is $\{\cap, \iota\} > \exists \text{ not } \cap > \{\iota, \exists\}$.

The second set of issues raised by these languages bears on the connection between singular number and kind reference. Though bare singulars are kind terms, they are not a trivial variant of bare plurals. The awkwardness of the Hindi example (9) (cf. *child is playing everywhere*) is interesting because the only locus of difference between it and its acceptable plural counterpart is in the number specification in the bare NP. Neither of the approaches discussed in section 2 uses number in a way that can explain this difference. The neo-Carlsonian approach yields a representation like (27a), which is incorrect for the singular term. The ambiguity approach yields representations like (27b)-(27c), depending on where existential closure applies. (27b) is incorrect for the singular case, (27c) for the plural:

(27) a. ∀x [place(x) → ∃y [ᵘⁿkid/kids(y) ∧ play-in-x(y)]]
 b. ∃x [place(x) → ∃y [kid/kids(y) ∧ play-in-x(y)]]
 c. ∃y [kid/kids(y) ∧ ∀x [place(x) → play-in-x(y)]]

Dayal resolves this impasse by differentiating between singular and plural kind terms in the way they relate to their instantiations. An analogy can be drawn with ordinary sum individuals *the players* whose atomic parts are available for predication, and collective nouns or groups like *the team* which are closed in this respect: *The players live in different cities* vs. **the team lives in different cities* (Barker 1992, Schwarzschild 1996). *Nom* applies only to plural nouns and yields a kind term that allows semantic access to its instantiations, analogously to sums. A singular kind term restricts such access and is analogous to collective nouns.

Similarly telling contrasts between singular and plural kind terms are also evident in English:

(28) a. *Airports* are busy places / *The airport* is a busy place.
 b. Due to the weather, *airports* are closed today/ *the airport* is closed today.

While both the singular and plural in (28a) work equally well as generic statements, only the plural in (28b) can be about airports in general. The singular refers to the salient airport in the context. Since English kind terms differ in definiteness and number, evidence from languages that do not have determiners underscores the importance of number in differentiating plural and singular kind formation.

Taking *nom* to be undefined for singular terms, then, begs the question of how to characterize singular kind formation. Dayal argues that in these cases, the common noun has a taxonomic reading and denotes a set of taxonomic kinds, here indicated by superscripted *tk*. It can then combine with any determiner and yield the relevant reading:

(29) a. *Every dinosaur*^{tk} is extinct.
b. *The dinosaurs*^{tk} are extinct.
c. *The dinosaur*^{tk} is extinct.

The presupposition that *every* range over a plural domain or that *the* denote a maximal plural individual can be satisfied in (29a) and (29b) if the quantificational domain is the set of sub-kinds of dinosaurs. The uniqueness requirement of *the* with a singular noun in (29c) can be satisfied if the quantificational domain is the set of sub-kinds of mammals. In other words, singular kind formation is argued to require an adjustment in our view of common noun denotations, not of type-shift operations. Depending on whether the language does or does not have definite determiners, *iota* will be either overt or covert, and singular kind formation will result in definite or bare singular kind terms.

Although the evidence that bare NPs are not true indefinites in languages like Hindi (and Russian) is strong, there remains a residue of cases for which the most natural translation into English uses an indefinite:

(30) lagtaa hai   kamre meN *cuhaa* hai
     seems be-PR room in   mouse   be-PR
     'There seems to be a mouse in the room.'

The explanation rests on the view that covert and overt type shifts agree on semantic operations but not on presuppositions. English *the* encodes the same operation that Hindi bare NPs use to shift to type <e> covertly, namely *iota*. Thus both versions entail maximality/uniqueness. In addition, *the* has a familiarity requirement that Hindi bare NPs do not. This non-familiar maximal reading can be confused with a bona fide existential reading of the Hindi bare singular but is distinct (see also article 12 [Semantics: Theories] (Dekker) *Dynamic semantics*, article 2 [this volume] (Heim) *Definiteness and indefiniteness* and article 3 [this volume] (von Heusinger) *Specificity*).

The claim about the unavailability of the ∃ type shift also applies to languages without determiners or number and is consistent with the account of Chinese in Yang (2001), for example. The claims with regard to singular kind formation obviously do not extend to such languages. All nouns are expected to undergo plural kind formation via *nom*.

5.2 Cross-linguistic patterns

Dayal (2004) also deals with cross-linguistic generalizations about the correlation between kind terms and their syntactic form. A prediction made by her account of singular kinds, for example, is that deictic/anaphoric nouns and singular kind terms will agree in lexicalization. In a given language they will either both be bare or both definite, depending on whether *iota* is lexicalized or not. This prediction seems to be borne out across a wide range of languages.

Another cross-linguistic pattern addressed is the absence of dedicated kind determiners in natural language. Plural kind terms are either bare (English, Hindi, Chinese), or definite (Italian, Spanish). The rather simple explanation for this robust generalization is that *nom* is the intensional counterpart of *iota* (cf. (22)) and languages do not lexically mark extensional/intensional distinctions. This way of looking at *nom*, however, opens up an interesting alternative way of looking at the Romance definite plural kind term.

Recall that Longobardi treated the definite determiner in Italian kind terms as expletives and Chierchia argued that their semantics was similar, but not identical, to *nom*. Dayal claims that the Romance definite determiner, in fact, lexically encodes *nom* (see also Zamparelli 2002). One advantage of this approach is that it does not predict complete identity of meaning between bare plural kind terms and definite plural kind terms, given that only lexical items are taken to be triggers for presuppositions. In the Italian (31), the kind term does not have the existential reading that the corresponding English bare plural would have:

(31) *I cani* stanno abbaiando
 the dogs are barking
 '(Some) dogs are barking.'—*unavailable*

This is because the definite retains a weak presupposition of existence, which prevents it from occurring in contexts where existence is asserted. Bare plurals (if syntactically licensed) or bare partitives must be used in such cases (see Dobrovie-Sorin & Laca 1996, Chierchia 1997, Dobrovie-Sorin 2004, and Robinson 2005).

We have discussed definites at length in an article on bare NPs because variation in kind terms across languages ranges between bare NPs and definites. Even within this range of possibilities there are unexpected restrictions that call for an explanation. If a given language uses bare nominals for deictic/anaphoric readings, then it also uses them as plural kind terms. If a language uses definites as plural kind terms it also uses them for deictic/anaphoric readings. Had the correlation between form and meaning been arbitrary, we would expect there to be languages where bare plurals could refer deictically/anaphorically (as in Hindi or Chinese) and definite plurals could refer to kinds (as in Italian or Spanish) but such languages are not attested.

Dayal takes these patterns to follow from a universal principle of lexicalization in which *iota* (which is canonically used for deictic and anaphoric reference) and *nom* (which is canonically used for generic reference) are mapped along a scale of diminishing identifiability: *iota* > *nom*. Languages lexicalize at distinct points on this scale, proceeding from *iota* to *nom*. Languages without determiners use the extreme left as the cut-off for lexicalization, with both *iota* and *nom* functioning as covert type-shifts. The cut-off point for mixed languages is in the middle, with *iota* lexicalized and *nom* a covert type-shift. Obligatory determiner languages have their cut-off at the extreme right, encoding both *iota* and *nom* lexically. For a language to have a lexical determiner for plural kind formation, its cut-off point would have to be at the extreme right. This would mean that *iota* could not be covert. That is, the unattested language type would be one where lexicalization would not conform to the proposed direction of lexicalization.

Dayal notes that although definite descriptions are readily used for identity oriented modes of reference, they also have attributive uses, in the sense of Donnellan (1966) (see article 4 [Semantics: Foundations, History and Methods] (Abbott) *Reference*). This leads to the kind of overlap observed in (3): *There was a ghost on campus. (The) students were afraid.* The presupposition of *iota* can be satisfied because the existence of students on a campus is readily accommodated. And *nom* allows for existential quantification over instances of students in the situation without identifying any particular group of students. The semantic requirements of the two overlap, leading to a situation where either the bare plural or the definite can be used. Summing up, *nom* cannot be used referentially and *iota* cannot be used to assert existence but this allows for an overlap in the use of definites and bare plurals in mixed languages.

Dayal (2004), then, stresses the importance of number morphology in kind formation, establishes that bare NPs in languages without determiners are not true indefinites, and accounts for cross-linguistic variation between bare and definite NPs without appealing to the notion of expletive determiners. The problem of non-kind denoting bare NPs in Romance, and the tendency of classifier languages to be determiner-less are not addressed. As such, the issue of whether languages are subject to Chierchia's semantic parameterization is left unexplored.

6 Challenges for theories of variation

Having presented the essential aspects of current theories of variation, I now turn to some questions that remain open, using data from Brazilian Portuguese as illustrative.

6.1 Brazilian Portuguese

Chierchia's *NMP* was enormously successful in provoking interest in the meaning and form of NPs. It prompted, almost immediately, papers on Brazilian Portuguese by Munn & Schmitt (1999, 2005), followed by Müller (2001, 2002) and more recently Dobrovie-Sorin & Pires de Oliveira (2008). Like other Romance languages, Brazilian Portuguese has definite singular and plural kind terms. It differs from them in admitting bare singulars as well as bare plurals, both of which are acceptable in generic contexts. Both allow for existential readings in episodic contexts, and take narrow scope with respect to other operators.

Bare singulars, however, have some unexpected properties. Though morphologically singular, they are number neutral in interpretation:

(32) Chegou *crianca*
 arrived child
 'A child/children arrived.'

There is also some disagreement about their status as kind terms. Müller argues that they are not, since they cannot serve as arguments of kind-level predicates like *invent*. Munn & Schmitt and Dobrovie-Sorin & Pires de Oliveira, on the other hand, take them to be kind denoting. Finally, unlike other Romance languages, Brazilian Portuguese does allow bare plural subjects. However, bare singulars are not always acceptable subjects of episodic statements. (32) has a singular in post-verbal position, but its pre-verbal subject counterpart is only good in the plural.

Munn and Schmitt claim that Brazilian Portuguese shows *NMP* to be either incorrect or irrelevant. The possibility of bare NPs as subjects shows, they argue, that there cannot be a null determiner in need of licensing, ruling out a [−arg, +pred] setting. The presence of definite plural kind terms, according to them, shows a [+arg, +pred] setting to be ruled out. The presence of determiners and the absence of a generalized classifier system makes a [+arg, −pred] setting unavailable. Similar criticisms against the parameter have been leveled on the basis of data from Creole languages (see the articles in Baptista & Guéron 2007). I will not try here to determine the extent to which Brazilian Portuguese is or is not a problem for Cheirchia's approach (but see section 5, Chierchia 2009 and article 3 [Semantics: Typology, Diachrony and Processing] (Doetjes) *Count/mass distinctions*). Instead, I will use the data to comment on three phenomena that are of general relevance to theories of variation and, I believe, worth keeping in mind while investigating bare nominals in specific languages: optionality, number neutrality, scope.

6.2 Optionality

Brazilian Portuguese calls into question the empirical basis of the *Blocking Principle* but before one can account for the facts, some care is needed in establishing the nature of the optionality at issue. Independent diagnostics are needed for *nom*, *iota* and ∃, the three operations relevant to cross-linguistic investigations into the semantics of bare NPs. For *nom*, we can take as definitive the ability to serve as arguments of true kind predicates like *be extinct, be endangered* or *evolve*, or any predicate that can apply to a species but not to its individual instantiations. This test, dating back to Carlson (1977), has held up to scrutiny.

For *iota* we can use the test from Löbner (1985), which distinguishes a true definite from its close-kin demonstrative determiner, which all languages seem to have. The hallmark of a true definite determiner is the maximality/uniqueness this test turns on:

(33) a. #*The dogs* are sleeping and *the dogs* are not.
  b. *Those dogs* are sleeping and *those dogs* are not.

The ∃ operator is identifiable by its scopal properties, discussed earlier. In addition, it must have the ability to function generically (Chierchia 1998). Substituting *a/an* with *some* in (34) results in the loss of this reading. These two tests together establish that only the former encodes ∃:

(34) *A dog* barks if it is hungry.

This diagnostic establishes that the numeral *one* in languages without determiners does not lexicalize ∃. In Hindi, for example, it does not have generic indefinite readings, at least in the basic cases, nor a neutral narrow scope reading (Dayal 2004):

(35) jaun-ne ek kitaab nahiiN khariidii.
  John-ERG one book not bought

'John didn't buy a particular book/even one book.'
'John didn't buy any book.' – *unavailable*

Turning back to Brazilian Portuguese we must first ask what the bare NPs are optional variants of. It turns out that they can never be used deictically or anaphorically, so they clearly do not encode *iota*. Since they do not allow for wide scope readings, they do not encode ∃. Optionality, clearly, is limited to generic/kind readings, suggesting that the overlap may be on *nom*.

Optionality between generic bare plurals and definite plurals was noted previously by Krifka et al. (1995) for dialects of German. Dayal (2004) pointed out that optionality does not hold across the board in those dialects. Bare NPs cannot be used to refer deictically or anaphorically. The suggestion is that such optionality calls for a distinction between canonical and non-canonical meanings. *Iota*, as the canonical meaning of the definite determiner, in any language, delivers the effect of the *Blocking Principle* via the lexicalization principle. This leaves open the possibility of covert type shifts for non-canonical meanings of the definite determiner. Under this perspective, German has the same cut-off point as English, lexicalizing *iota* and effectively blocking it as a covert type shift but it differs from English in partially lexicalizing *nom*, allowing for optionality. It also differs from Romance where the lexicalization of *nom* is firmly entrenched, effectively blocking both *iota* and *nom* as covert type shifts.

This approach still rules out a number of logically possible language types. Languages in which a lexical determiner would be needed for plural kind terms but not for deictic/anaphoric readings of plurals are ruled out. A definite determiner in any language is expected to encode the basic semantic operation *iota* as its canonical meaning.

While optionality certainly poses a challenge for theories of variation, it does not appear to pose an insurmountable problem for them. The general point here is that independent diagnostics must be used to determine the operations involved in a given case before the implications for particular theories can be fully evaluated.

6.3 Number neutrality

Brazilian Portuguese bare singulars appear to be morphologically singular but semantically plural. This has been considered a problem for Chierchia's theory, on the view that it exemplifies a language without number marking but no classifiers. Whether this is so, however, depends on what underlies the mismatch between morphology and interpretation.

One obvious solution is to treat the bare singular as having a null plural morpheme. Or one might take the bare NP to denote a set of atoms, with a null determiner bringing in plurality. These ways of conceptualizing the mismatch between form and meaning are in keeping with various analyses that have been proposed (see Chierchia 2009). The challenge is in accounting for differences between bare singulars and plurals in a principled way. Munn and Schmitt note that bare singulars are ruled out from the preverbal subject position of episodic statements, but not bare plurals, surprising if they are simply a variant of bare plurals.

Another option considered by Munn and Schmitt is to treat bare singulars as mass nouns. They reject this, pointing to the contrast in (36). (36b) can be translated using a bare singular, showing that the bare singular could not be a mass noun:

(36) a. *Gold weighs two grams.
b. Children weigh 20 kilos at this age.

Yet another possibility is to treat the plurality of bare singulars in terms of pseudo-incorporation (Farkas & de Swart 2003, Dayal 2011). In Hindi, for example, Dayal argues that the number neutral interpretation of bare singulars is restricted to non case-marked direct objects and is dependent on aspectual specification on the verb. In other words, the noun itself denotes in the atomic domain but properties of the incorporation context produce the effect of plurality. This has been explored though not fully endorsed for Brazilian Portuguese by Traveira da Cruz (2008). If it turns out that their plurality is an epiphenomenon, Brazilian Portuguese bare singulars would have very different implications for theories of variation than they have so far been thought to have.

6.4 Scope

Scope was used crucially by Carlson to distinguish between bare plurals and indefinites. Chierchia's *Derived Kind Predication* rule in (20c) captures Carlson's insight that a kind term can be a direct argument of the verb because, like any name, it is of type *e*. The existential quantification over its instances is due to a sort-adjustment operation whose effect is necessarily local. A true quantifier involving the type shift ∃ can, and in some cases must, take wide scope.

Chierchia (1998) points out that *DKP*, in combination with the notion of ranked type-shifts, accounts for another observation of Carlson, namely that non kind denoting bare plurals have the scopal properties of indefinites (see also Van Geenhoven 1999 and Zucchi & White 2001):

(37) a. *Parts of this machine are widespread.
   b. John didn't see parts of this machine.

Since *nom* is undefined in this case and *iota* lexically blocked, the bare NP shifts by ∃ and takes wide or narrow scope. Dayal's (2004) adjustment of the ranking accounts for an interesting cross-linguistic difference. Even non kind denoting bare NPs in Hindi lack scopal flexibility. This is because there is no definite determiner in Hindi and *iota* is always available as a type shift. The lower ranked ∃ type shift never comes into play.

Brazilian Portuguese bare NPs, singular and plural, obligatorily take narrow scope, not surprising if they are in fact kind terms. If they are not, and if they are not incorporated, however, their inability to take wide scope calls for an explanation. Independently of Brazilian Portuguese, however, the problem holds for Italian bare plurals that also have this propensity for narrow scope though they are not considered kind terms by every one.

The issue of obligatory narrow scope for non kind denoting, non incorporated NPs is an important one and needs to be settled before we can say that the semantics of bare NPs has been truly understood. The only conclusion that we can draw at this point is that the diagnostic of narrowest scope identifies not only kind denoting and incorporated NPs, but also concept denoting NPs, in the sense of Krifka (1995). This, however, begs the question of the relation between concepts and kinds, something that remains to be clearly articulated in the literature on generics.

In this section I used Brazilian Portuguese to illustrate questions that I believe remain open for theories of variation. I restricted myself to a single language, assuming that a focused discussion of issues in one language will be relevant to other languages with similar properties (cf. article 13 [Semantics: Foundations, History and Methods] (Matthewson) *Methods in cross-linguistic semantics* and article 2 [Semantics: Typology, Diachrony and Processing] (Bach & Chao) *Semantic types across languages*).

7 Conclusion

Cross-linguistic work in the semantics of bare NPs is a dynamic area of research that has produced many substantive results. It has allowed researchers to separate out the contributions of different aspects of the morpho-syntax of the noun phrase from its semantics, and expanded our understanding of bare NPs beyond English bare plurals, the initial starting point of research in the area. More generally, it has provided new insights into the way semantics interfaces with syntax.

As knowledge of different languages and language types continues to grow, theories are faced with new challenges. A theory measures up to these challenges if it can be modified and adjusted to account for new and unexpected facts without losing predictive power. The requirement of empirical adequacy thus continues to push theoretical investigations, forcing us to ask deeper questions of languages we are familiar with, as of languages we encounter for the first time.

8 References

Baptista, Marlyse & Jacqueline Guéron (eds.) 2007. *Noun Phrases in Creole Languages. A Multi-Faceted Approach*. Amsterdam: Benjamins.

Barker, Chris 1992. Group terms in English: Representing groups as atoms. *Journal of Semantics* 9, 69–93.

Carlson, Gregory 1977. *Reference to Kinds in English*. Ph.D. dissertation. University of Massachusetts, Amherst, MA.

Carlson, Gregory 1989. The semantic composition of English generic sentences. In: G. Chierchia, B. Partee & R. Turner (eds.). *Properties, Types and Meaning*. Dordrecht: Kluwer, 167–192.

Carlson, Gregory 1991. Natural kinds and common nouns. In: A. von Stechow & D. Wunderlich (eds.). *Semantik—Semantics. Ein internationales Handbuch der zeitgenössischen Forschung—An International Handbook of Contemporary Research* (HSK 6). Berlin: de Gruyter, 370–398.

Carlson, Gregory 1999. No lack of determination. *GLOT International* 4.3, 3–8.

Chierchia, Gennaro 1995. *The Dynamics of Meaning*. Chicago, IL: The University of Chicago Press.

Chierchia, Gennaro 1997. Partitives, reference to kinds and semantic variation. In: A. Lawson (ed.). *Proceedings of Semantics and Linguistic Theory (= SALT) VII*. Ithaca, NY: Cornell University, 73–98.

Chierchia, Gennaro 1998. Reference to kinds across languages. *Natural Language Semantics* 6, 339–405.

Chierchia, Gennaro 2010 . *Mass Nouns and Vagueness*. Synthese 174, 99–149.

Cohen, Ariel 1999. *Think Generic: The Meaning and Use of Generic Sentences*. Stanford, CA: CSLI Publications.

Condoravdi, Cleo 1992. Strong and weak novelty and familiarity. In: C. Barker & D. Dowty (eds.). *Proceedings of Semantics and Linguistic Theory (= SALT) II*. Columbus, OH: Ohio State University, 17–37.

Contreras, Heles 1986. Spanish bare NPs and the ECP. In: I. Bordelois, H. Contreras & K. Zagona (eds.). *Generative Studies in Spanish Syntax*. Dordrecht: Foris, 25–49.

Dayal, Veneeta 1992. The singular-plural distinction in Hindi generics. In: C. Barker & D. Dowty (eds.). *Proceedings of Semantics and Linguistic Theory (=SALT) II*. Columbus, OH: Ohio State University, 39–58.

Dayal, Veneeta 2004. Number marking and (in)definiteness in kind terms. *Linguistics & Philosophy* 27, 393–450.

Dayal, Veneeta 2011. Hindi pseudo-incorporation. *Natural Language and Linguistic Theory* 29, 123–167.
Delfitto, Denis. 2006. Bare plurals. In: M. Everaert & H. van Riemsdijk (eds.). *The Blackwell Companion to Syntax*. Oxford: Blackwell, 214–259.
Diesing, Molly 1992. *Indefinites*. Cambridge, MA: The MIT Press.
Dobrovie-Sorin, Carmen 2004. Genericity, plural indefinites and (in)direct binding. In: F. Corblin & H. de Swart (eds). *A Handbook of French Semantics*. Stanford, CA: CSLI Publications, 55–71.
Dobrovie-Sorin, Carmen & Roberta Pires de Oliveiria 2008. Reference to kinds in Brazilian Portuguese: Definite singulars vs. bare singulars. In: A. Grønn (ed.). *Proceedings of Sinn und Bedeutung (=SuB)12*. Oslo: ILOS, 107–121.
Dobrovie-Sorin, Carmen & Brenda Laca 1996. *Generic Bare NPs*. Ms. Strasbourg/Paris, University of Strasbourg/University of Paris.
Donnellan, Keith 1966. Reference and definite descriptions. *Philosophical Review* 75, 281–304.
Farkas, Donka & Henriëtte de Swart 2003. *The Semantics of Incorporation: From Argument Structure to Discourse Transparency*. Stanford, CA: CSLI Publications.
van Geenhoven, Veerle 1999. Pro properties, contra generalized kinds. In: B. Jackson & T. Matthews (eds.). *Proceedings of Semantics and Linguistic Theory (=SALT) X*. Ithaca, NY: Cornell University, 221–238.
Gerstner-Link, Claudia & Manfred Krifka. 1993. Genericity. In: J. Jacobs et al. (eds.). *Syntax: Ein internationales Handbuch zeitgenössischer Forschung—An International Handbook of Contemporary Research* (HSK 9.1) Berlin: de Gruyter, 966–978.
Greenberg, Yael 1998. Temporally restricted generics. In: D. Strolovitch & A. Lawson (eds.). *Proceedings of Semantics and Linguistic Theory (= SALT) VIII*. Ithaca, NY: Cornell University, 17–37.
Heim, Irene 1982. *The Semantics of Definite and Indefinite. Noun Phrases*. Ph.D. dissertation. University of Massachusetts, Amherst, MA. Reprinted: Ann Arbor, MI: University Microfilms.
Kamp, Hans 1981. A theory of truth and discourse representation. In: J. Groenendijk, T. Janssen & M. Stokhof (eds.). *Formal Methods in the Study of Language*. Amsterdam: Mathematical Centre, 277–322.
Kratzer, Angelika 1995. Stage-level and individual-level predicates. In: G. Carlson & F. Pelletier (eds.). *The Generic Book*. Chicago, IL: The University of Chicago Press, 125–175.
Krifka, Manfred 1991. Massennomina. In: A. von Stechow & D. Wunderlich (eds.). *Semantik—Semantics. Ein internationales Handbuch der zeitgenössischen Forschung—An International Handbuch of Contemporary Research* (HSK 6). Berlin: de Gruyter, 370–398.
Krifka, Manfred 1995. Common nouns: A contrastive analysis of English and Chinese. In: G. Carlson & F. Pelletier (eds.). *The Generic Book*. Chicago, IL: The University of Chicago Press, 398–411.
Krifka, Manfred, Francis Pelletier, Gregory Carlson, Alice ter Meulen, Godehard Link & Gennaro Chierchia 1995. Genericity: An introduction. In: G. Carlson & F. Pelletier (eds.). *The Generic Book*. Chicago, IL: The University of Chicago Press, 1–124.
Kurafuji, Takeo 2004. Plural morphemes, definiteness, and the notion of semantic parameter. *Language and Linguistics* 5, 211–242.
Landman, Fred 1996. Plurality. In: S. Lappin (ed.). *The Handbook of Contemporary Semantic Theory*. Oxford: Blackwell, 425–457.

Lewis, David 1975. Adverbs of quantification. In: E. Keenan (ed.). *Formal Semantics of Natural Languages*. Cambridge: Cambridge University Press, 3–15.

Li, Yen-Hui Audrey. 1999. Plurality in a classifier language. *Journal of East Asian Linguistics* 8, 75–99.

Löbner, Sebastian 1985. Definites. *Journal of Semantics* 4, 279–326.

Longobardi, Giuseppe 1994. Reference and proper names. *Linguistic Inquiry* 25, 609–665.

Longobardi, Giuseppe 2000. Postverbal subjects and the mapping hypothesis. *Linguistic Inquiry* 31, 691–702.

Longobardi, Giuseppe 2001. How comparative is semantics? A unified parametric theory of bare nouns and proper names. *Natural Language Semantics* 9, 335–369.

Müller, Ana 2001. Genericity and the denotation of common nouns in Brazilian Portuguese. *Proceedings of Semantics of Under-Represented Languages* 25. Amherst, MA: GLSA, University of Massachusetts, 72–80.

Müller, Ana 2002. The semantics of generic quantification in Brazilian Portuguese. *Probus* 14, 279–298,

Munn, Alan & Cristina Schmitt 1999. Against the nominal mapping parameter: Bare nouns in Brazilian Portuguese. In: P. Tamanji, H. Masako & N. Hall (eds.). *Proceedings of the North Eastern Linguistic Society (=NELS) 29*. Amherst, MA: GLSA, University of Massachusetts, 339–353.

Munn, Alan & Cristina Schmitt 2005. Indefinites and number. *Lingua* 115, 821–855.

Robinson, Heather 2005. *Unexpected (In)definiteness: Romance Plural Determiners in Generic Contexts*. Ph.D. dissertation. Rutgers University, New Brunswick, NJ.

Schwarzschild, Roger 1996. *Pluralities*. Dordrecht: Kluwer.

Stowell, Tim 1991. Determiners in NP and DP. In: K. Leffel & D. Bouchard (eds.). *Views on Phrase Structure: Papers Presented at a Conference Held at the University of Flordia, Gainsville, in March 1989*. Dordrecht: Kluwer, 37–56.

Szablocsi, Anna 1994. The noun phrase. In: F. Kiefer & K. Kiss (eds.). *The Syntactic Structure of Hungarian*. San Diego, CA: Academic Press, 179–274.

Taveira da Cruz, Ronald 2008. *O Singular nu e a (Pseudo) Incorporação no PB*. Doctoral dissertation. University of Santa Catarina, Florianópolis.

Vergnaud, Jean-Roger & Zubizarreta, Maria-Luisa 1992. The definite determiner and the inalienable constructions in French and in English. *Linguistic Inquiry* 23, 595–652.

Wilkinson, Karina 1991. *Studies in the Semantics of Generic NPs*. Ph.D. dissertation. University of Massachusetts, Amherst, MA.

Yang, Rong 1998. Chinese bare nouns as kind-denoting terms. In: R. Artstein & M. Hiller (eds.). *RuLing Papers 1* (Working Papers from Rudgers University). New Brunswick, NJ: Rutgers University, 247–288.

Yang, Rong 2001. *Common Nouns, Classifiers, and Quantification in Chinese*. Ph.D. dissertation, Rutgers University, New Brunswick, NJ.

Zamparelli, Roberto 2002. Definite and bare kind-denoting noun phrases. In: C. Beyssade et al. (eds.). *Romance Languages and Linguistic Theory 2000: Selected Papers from "Going Romance"*. Amsterdam: Benjamins, 305–342.

Zucchi, Sandro & Michael White 2001. Twigs, sequences and temporal sequences of predicates. *Linguistics & Philosophy* 24, 223–270.

Chris Barker
6 Possessives and relational nouns

1   Preliminaries —— 177
2   Compositionality, type-shifting, and the lexical versus pragmatic distinction —— 181
3   Predicative uses —— 187
4   Definiteness —— 188
5   Possessive compounds —— 192
6   Scope, binding, and quantificational narrowing —— 193
7   Thematic roles —— 195
8   Bare possessives —— 197
9   Double genitives —— 197
10 Plurals and dependent plurals —— 198
11 Some related topics —— 199
12 References —— 200

Abstract: This article concentrates on nominal possessives (John's friend) rather than on verbal possessives (John has a friend). In John's friend, John is the POSSESSOR, and friend describes the entity possessed (the POSSESSEE). Nominal possessives constitute a major construction type in the languages of the world. In contrast with a sortal noun (e.g., person), friend is a (two-place) RELATIONAL NOUN: a person counts as a friend only in virtue of standing in a particular relationship with another individual. Relational nouns are an important element in the study of possessives because the content of a possessive typically, perhaps characteristically, depends on the content of a relational nominal. Possessives provide particularly compelling support for type shifting as a general principle of syntactic and semantic composition. Possessives also inform debates involving definiteness, binding, and a wide variety of other semantic phenomena.

1 Preliminaries

This article will concentrate mainly on English. Although the majority of the semantic work on possessives also concentrates on English, this limitation does not do justice either to the richness of possessives in other languages, or to the richness of the literature.

Chris Barker, New York, United States

https://doi.org/10.1515/9783110589443-006

1.1 Main possessive constructions

English has two main possessive constructions:

(1) John's brother   PRENOMINAL POSSESSIVE
(2) the brother of John   POSTNOMINAL POSSESSIVE

(Other possessive constructions will be introduced below.) The prenominal possessive is often called the Saxon genitive for historical reasons. In the prenominal possessive, the possessive morpheme *'s* is an edge clitic (Miller 1991), since it attaches to the final word at the rightmost edge of a full DP ([*the man*]*'s hat*, [*every man*]*'s hat*, [*the Queen of England*]*'s hat*, [*the person I was just talking to*]*'s hat*, etc.). Because a possessive is itself a DP, possessives can be nested arbitrarily deep (*John's friend's mother's ... lawyer's brother*).

Although English once had a robust case system (a vestige remains in the possessive forms of pronouns, *his*, *hers*, etc.), English no longer has a true genitive case. Nevertheless, English possessive constructions are often called genitives, and I will sometimes refer to them this way. Other constructions mentioned or discussed below include the construct state in Semitic (*beyt ha-more* 'the teacher's house', section 4.3); possessive compounds (*the men's room* 'bathroom', section 5); quantificational possessives (*most planets' rings*, section 6); bare possessives (*John's* 'John's house', section 8); double-genitives (*a friend of John's*, section 9; possessive dependent plurals (*these women's husbands*, section 10); and nominalizations (*the Roman's destruction of the city*, section 11).

Among the constructions that will not be discussed, unfortunately, are verbal possessives (*John has a son*). In addition, it should be noted that in many languages the syntax and semantics of possessives and partitives are intricately and intimately related to a degree that goes far beyond that of the English possessive and partitives constructions discussed below in section 9.

1.2 Relational nouns

The denotation of *male*, for instance, can be modeled as a simple set of individuals. Then Bill is male just in case $b \in [\![male]\!]$. The noun *brother*, in contrast, denotes a relation between individuals, that is, a set of pairs of individuals. Then Bill will be a brother of John just in case $\langle b, j \rangle \in [\![brother]\!]$. Strictly speaking, sortal properties such as the denotation of *male* are (one-place) relations, but it will be useful to use the terms 'sortal' and 'property' exclusively for one-place relations, and 'relation' for two-place relations. Only some nouns are properly relational.

As pointed out by, e.g., Löbner (1985: 292), many pairs of nouns that apply to the same set of objects nevertheless contrast minimally with respect to the sortal/relational distinction:

(3)   SORTAL   RELATIONAL
      a. a day (*of someone)   a birthday of someone
      b. a person (*of someone)   a child of someone
      c. an animal (*of someone) a pet of someone

Each day is somebody's birthday, and each birthday is a day. Likewise, every person is someone's child, and each child is a person. However, a day counts as a birthday only in virtue of standing in a certain relationship to a person. Note that only the relational nouns are able to take a postnominal genitive *of* phrase.

Sortal nouns stand to relational nouns as one-argument verbs stand to two-argument ones. Conceptually, dining, eating, and devouring all entail the existence of an object that gets consumed; yet even assuming the statements in (4) describe the same event, the presence of an overt direct object can be prohibited, optional, or required, depending on the specific lexical item involved:

(4)   INTRANSITIVE   TRANSITIVE
      a. We dined.   *We dined the pizza.
      b. We ate.   We ate the pizza.
      c. *We devoured.   We devoured the pizza.

It is often said that nominal arguments are always optional, and to a first approximation this is true. However, nouns display the full paradigm of optionality illustrated above for their verbal counterparts:

(5)   INTRANSITIVE TRANSITIVE
      a. the stranger   *the stranger of John
      b. the enemy   the enemy of John
      c. *the sake   the sake of John

At the conceptual level, qualifying as a stranger, an enemy, or someone's sake requires the existence of some object that stands in a certain relation to the described object. After all, someone who is a stranger to John may be well known to me, likewise for an enemy; and doing something for John's sake very different than doing it for my sake. This is as much to say that *stranger*, *enemy*, and *sake* are intrinsically relational. Nevertheless, despite the fact that a possessor argument is conceptually obligatory for all three predicates, it is not possible to express the possessor relatum for *stranger* overtly, either by means of a genitive *of* phrase or by a prenominal possessive (**John's stranger*). In contrast, overt expression of the possessor argument is optional for *enemy*, and, as implicitly noted by Quine (e.g., Quine 1960: 236), obligatory for *sake*. Following Partee (1997), we can adopt the verbal terminology and say that *stranger* is obligatorily intransitive, *enemy* is optionally transitive, and *sake* is obligatorily transitive.

1.3 Bindability of the implicit possessor

Partee (1989) notes that the implicit argument of an intransitive relational noun can sometimes be bound by a quantifier, as in *Every soldier faced an enemy*, which has the paraphrase 'Every soldier x is such that x faced x's enemy'. This provides evidence that the suppressed relational argument remains grammatically present, perhaps in the form of a variable. Curiously, as Partee notes, this sort of bound reading is not always possible: compare *Every soldier wrote a mother*, which does not have a paraphrase that entails that each soldier x wrote to x's mother.

1.4 Derived versus underived relational nominals

Derived nominals can have elaborate argument structures inherited from their verbal source, e.g., *the purchase of the property by the woman for a pittance*. For whatever reason, non-derived nouns appear to have a strict upper limit of two on the number of overtly expressible participants. That is, sortal nouns have one participant (*person*, *stick*), relational nouns have two participants (*mother*, *leg*), but there are no non-derived relational nouns that have three participants. To appreciate what such a noun could be like, consider *grandmother*. Two people x and z stand in the grandmother relation just in case there is some y such that x is the mother of y and y is the parent of z. Conceptually, then, *grandmother* is a three-place relation. However, as far as I know there is no language in which all three of the participants can be overtly specified: **Ann is the grandmother of John by Mary*. Klaus von Heusinger (personal communication) suggests that *Switzerland's border with France* might consitute a counter example.

1.5 Inalienability

The most common relational concepts lexicalized in the world's languages include family relations (*mother*, *uncle*, *cousin*); body parts (*hand*, *head*, *finger*);

and intrinsic aspects of entities such as *color, speed, weight, shape, temperature*. In some languages prepositions are frozen possessives (*at the river* is expressed literally as 'the river's place'). Many languages grammatically distinguish between alienable and inalienable possession, where the inalienable nouns express a set of inherently relational concepts. In some languages, alienable possessee nouns receive a special morphological marking; in some languages, inalienable possessives are constructed differently, often by juxtaposition of possessor and possessee rather than with an overt possessive linking particle (Chappell & McGregor 1996). In English, to the extent that only relational nouns can participate in the postnominal genitive possessive construction (*the brother of Mary*, **the cloud of Mary*), English makes a syntactic distinction between alienable (*cloud, squirrel*) and inalienable (*brother, speed*) nouns.

In languages that morphosyntactically mark such distinctions, a two-way contrast is by far the most common (alienable versus inalienable), though some languages make morphosyntactic distinctions among four or more classes of possessed nouns.

2 Compositionality, type-shifting, and the lexical versus pragmatic distinction

Prenominal and postnominal possessives can be very close to paraphrases of each other, as seen in (1) and (2) (*John's friend* versus *the friend of John*). However, we shall see that the prenominal possessive systematically has a wider range of interpretations.

The meaning of a possessive involves three main elements: two individuals (the possessor and the possessee), and a relation between them, which I will call the POSSESSION RELATION. For instance, in *John's sister*, the possessor is John, the possessee is some woman, and the possession relation holding between John and the woman is the sibling relation (or, if you like, the female-sibling-of relation). In this case, the possession relation is identical to the relation denoted by the head noun *sister*. I will call this a LEXICAL interpretation, since the possessive relation is identical to the content of some lexical item.

If the head noun is not relational, a lexical interpretation is obviously not possible. In *John's cloud*, the noun *cloud* is not a relational concept, and the relationship between John and the cloud must come from some source other than the lexical meaning of the noun. Perhaps it is a cloud John is watching, or a cloud that he is painting, or a cloud that is saliently associated with John for some other reason. I will (perhaps somewhat presumptuously) call this a PRAGMATIC interpretation, since the content of the possessive relation must come from the pragmatic context.

There are three related puzzles for compositionality, all of which remain unsettled. First, are there two distinct constructions, or is the lexical interpretation just a particularly salient way of resolving the pragmatic relation? Second, if there are two distinct meanings, where does the ambiguity reside? In the possessive morpheme? In the meaning of the nominal? Third, in the pragmatic use, where does the possession relation come from, and how exactly does it combine compositionally with the other elements of the DP?

In many treatments, pragmatic possession relations are introduced via a context controlled variable, much in the same way that a pronoun that is not grammatically bound receives its value from context. (Note that here, context supplies a relation rather than an individual.) If the interpretation of pragmatic possessives does involve a free relational variable whose value is supplied by context, then possessives are unusual in the typology of variables in failing to be capable of being quantificationally bound. For instance, as Stanley (2000) points out, there is no bound interpretation of *Whenever John has something to do with a cat, he expects it to behave like Mary's cat*. If there were, this sentence would entail that whenever John kicks a cat, he expects it to behave like the cat that Mary kicked, and whenever John looks at a cat, he expects it to behave like the cat that Mary looked at, and so on.

As mentioned above in section 1.5, the postnominal genitive possessive strongly prefers lexical interpretations (Barker 1995, Partee 1997). Thus *John's sister* (with a relational head noun) can be paraphrased as *the sister of John*, but *John's cloud* (which has a sortal head noun) cannot be described as ??*the cloud of John*. This makes the postnominal construction a diagnostic for relational nouns. We can analyze the genitive *of* phrase as semantically inert (an identity function), a purely syntactic marker signalling that the object of the preposition is an argument of the relational head nominal. On this analysis, the possession relation for a postnominal possessive is simply the denotation of the relational head noun.

See also articles 6 [Semantics: Foundations, History and Methods] (Pagin & Westerståhl) *Compositionality*, 10 [Semantics: Lexical Structures and Adjectives] (de Swart) *Mismatches and coercion*, and 8 [Semantics: Interfaces] (de Hoop) *Type shifting*.

2.1 Possession relations for sortal possessees: the π type-shifter

The problem, then, is what to do with the non-relational case: there must be some way to take a non-relational nominal and turn it into a relational nominal, perhaps by means of a type-shifting operator such as π = λPλxλy.P(y) ∧ R(x,y), where R is a free (pragmatically controlled) variable standing for the possession relation. Then ⟦John's cloud⟧ = π (⟦cloud⟧)(j) = λy.cloud(y) ∧ R(j,y), the set of clouds that stand in the R relation to John. (This renders the meaning of the possessive as a property; see sections 3 and 4 on predicative uses and definiteness.)

There is another way of thinking about the composition on which the possessor phrase is in charge. This approach follows, e.g., Abney (1987) in conceiving of the possessive as a determiner phrase (rather than as a noun phrase), with the possessor phrase in the role of the determiner (i.e., the head of the phrase). This gives the possessive clitic (or some silent functional element associated with the prenominal construction) some semantic work to do. For instance, for the relational interpretation we might assign the possessive clitic the denotation λxλPλy.P(y) ∧ R(x,y).

But then we would need an additional denotation for the possessive clitic to allow for lexical possessives, perhaps λxλRλy.R(x,y), so that on a lexical interpretation we would have ⟦John's brother⟧ = λy.brother(j,y).

Note that p, which enabled a sortal noun to shift to a (pragmatically-controlled) relation, is a type-shifter in the sense of Partee (1987): a silent operator that adjusts the syntactic category and the semantic type of an expression in order to allow composition to proceed. It turns out that possessives and relational nouns are a type-shifting playground, with many different opportunities for positing type-shifters. I will mention a few of the type shifters that have been argued to be motivated by possessive interpretations, without trying here to find a principled way of choosing which set of shifters best covers the empirical ground.

2.2 The detransitivization type-shifter *Ex*

Most compositional treatments posit a detransitivizing type-shifter that turns a relational nominal into a non-relational one, perhaps Ex = λRλx.∃yR(x,y). Such a type-shifter aims to capture the systematic relationship between relational uses (*John's relative*) and uses without an overt possessor (*the relative*, which means 'the person x such that there is a y such that x is the relative of y').

But the detransitivizing shifter is far more useful than merely allowing relational nouns to appear without an explicit possessor. Although possessives containing a relational head noun usually receive a relational interpretation, they can also receive a pragmatic interpretation on which the possession relation does not coincide with the lexical relation. On this sort of interpretation, *John's brother* would refer to some male person who has a sibling, and who is related to John through some kind of circumstantial association. Perhaps two journalists have been assigned to profile each of the sons of some famous person; then we can refer to one of the profile targets *John's brother*, the brother of someone that John is assigned to profile. Given the detransitivizing shifter, we can arrive at the observed interpretation by detransitivizing *brother*, and then shifting it back to (a different, pragmatically controlled) relation: π ($Ex(\llbracket brother \rrbracket)$) = $\lambda x \lambda y. \exists z brother(z,y) \wedge R(x,y)$.

In fact, in the presence of a detransitivizing type-shifter, it is at least technically feasible to give a unitary denotation to the possessive clitic in the following way: assume that every nominal denotes a sortal property. If the head noun is relational, this requires shifting it using the detransitivizing shifter *Ex*. Then the only way to arrive at a possessive interpretation is by applying π, which introduces a pragmatically-controlled relational variable. The strong tendency to give prenominal possessives a relational interpretation simply reflects a strong tendency to resolve the pragmatically-controlled relation in favor of the most salient relation around, namely, the relation denoted by the head noun.

One problem with positing a detransitivizing shifter is that although almost every relational noun can be used without an overt possessor, there are some that cannot. For instance, as noted above in section 1.2, **the sake* is ungrammatical, and only a lexical reading is possible for *her sake*. Apparently, *Ex* must not have *sake* in its domain.

2.3 The *favorite* type-shifter

Not all shifting operators are silent. As noted by Barker (1995: 68), Partee (1997), Partee & Borschev (1998, 2000), and Vikner & Jensen (2002), *favorite* is capable of turning a sortal into a relational concept. That is, *favorite cloud* denotes a relation between an individual and a cloud, namely, the likes-best relation. As evidence that the phrase *favorite cloud* is relational, note that it can either take a postnominal genitive *of* phrase (*the favorite cloud of most painters*, *the favorite food of Queen Amy*) in addition to a prenominal possessive (*Most painters' favorite cloud*, *Queen Amy's favorite food*).

Contrary to theories in which type-shifting is always obligatorily motivated only by syntactic or semantic mismatch, the interpretations that motivate type-shifting analyses of possessives combine in intricate ways that strongly suggests (something close to) free optional application. For instance, it is possible to start with a relational noun, detransitivize, then re-transitivize with *favorite*: an actress can express a preference for one of the three daughter roles in *King Lear* by saying *Regan is my favorite daughter* (the speaker's favorite among the set of women who are daughters of some unspecified person). Similarly, it is possible for a nominal with *favorite* to undergo detransitivization (*Macaroni and Cheese—Always a Favorite Recipe*). With a relational nominal (*Cornelia—always a favorite daughter*), we arguably have detransitivized not only *daughter*, but also *favorite daughter* (*Ex(favorite(Ex(daughter)))*).

As noted by Partee & Borschev (2000), it is particularly difficult to force a detransitivized interpretation of *favorite* in the presence of an overt possessor. Nevertheless, if a group of printers is each typesetting one favorite recipe, *John's favorite recipe* can refer to the favorite recipe that John is responsible for typesetting.

2.4 Qualia type-shifters and the control type-shifter

Where do pragmatic possession relations come from? Vikner and Jensen (e.g., 2002) give a partial answer that involves articulating π into a set of type-shifters. They begin from an assumption that even the prenominal possessive uniformly takes a relational nominal. If the head noun is intrinsically relational (e.g., *brother*), that relation can serve as the possession relation directly. If the head noun is not intrinsically relational (e.g., *poem*), the meaning must shift to a relational meaning in a manner partially constrained by lexical information associated with the noun. Following Pustejovsky (1995), Vikner and Jensen suppose that the lexical entries of nouns provide certain regular relational information called QUALIA, and that when non-relational nouns shift to relational meanings, they naturally favor resolving the possession relation in favor of their qualia. Thus *John's poem* can be the poem John read (shifting with the TELIC quale), or the poem John wrote (shifting with the AGENTIVE quale). The CONSTITUTIVE quale is especially important in their system, and governs the relational meaning of nouns referring to parts (e.g., *edge*, *leg*, etc.).

Vikner and Jensen provide the following map of possessive meanings, often discussed in the literature:

Partee & Borschev, Barker	Possession Relation	Vikner & Jensen
lexical	inherent	lexical
	part-whole	
pragmatic	agentive	
	control	
	[others]	pragmatic

Fig. 6.1: Vikner and Jensen's map of possessive meanings

Note that Vikner and Jensen add a special shifter that does not correspond to any of Pustejovsky's qualia called CONTROL. Control here encompasses at least ownership (*John's house*, i.e., legal control) and also physical control (*John's stick*, the stick that John is holding). Thus control is similar to the non-technical meaning of the word 'possess'. Unlike inherent, part-whole, and agentive relations, the control relation is not assumed to vary from one noun to another. The justification for counting control as lexical is that it is supposed to be always available, independently of the pragmatic context.

The distinction between control relations and extemporaneous pragmatic relations is subtle but grammatically genuine, both in English and cross-linguistically. To mention just two instances, Storto (2000, 2004) observes that if John and Bill are attacked by wild dogs in the street, we can say *John's dogs were rabid*, where *John's dogs* expresses a pragmatic relation between John and the dogs that attacked him. John certainly does not stand in a control relation with respect to the dogs in question. But if we use the double genitive *the dogs of John's* (see section 9), we can only be referring to dogs that John owns or otherwise controls. Similarly, Heller (2002) reports that the Construct State in Hebrew can express control relations, but not (non-control) pragmatically-supplied relations.

2.5 The *former* type-shifter

The adjective *former* throws a monkey wrench into some theories of possession relation composition. As noted by Partee (1997), Larson (1998), Partee & Borschev (1998), and Larson & Cho (2003), modified relational nouns as in *old friend* or *my former mansion* can be ambiguous: *old friend* can either describe an aged friend, or else a long-time friend; *my former mansion* can mean either 'the building I own that used to be a mansion' or else 'the mansion that I formerly owned'. In other words, the no-longer entailment of *former* can target either the non-relational properties by virtue of which an object qualifies as a mansion, or else it can target the relation itself. Since *former* combines with the following noun before combining with the possessor phrase (*my [former mansion]*), in order for *former* to modify the possession relation, the possession relation (in this case, control) must already be present in the nominal *mansion*. This suggest that it is not (always) the possessor that shifts a property to a possessive meaning, since this would be too late (compositionally speaking) for *former* to modify the possession relation. (An as yet unexplored possibility is that *former* might lift to take the possessor as an argument, analogously to the way that a quantificational DP in object position can take scope over its transitive verb.)

According to Larson and Cho, the ambiguity of *former* possessives supports a particular theory of the syntactic structure of nominals on which the two interpretations of *former* correspond to the size of the syntactic constituent modified by *former*. Partee and Borschev give a type-shifting analysis which depends on two assumptions: that *former* is polysemous between a version that combines with properties (*former¹ house¹*) and a shifted version (*former²*) that combines directly with relations (*former² wife²*). If a sortal noun shifts to a relation (*former² (π house¹)*), we get the relation-in-the-past interpretation.

Note that it is difficult to get a relation-modifying interpretation when the possession relation is a non-control pragmatic relation. That is, *my former cloud* cannot refer to the cloud that I used to be watching. Following Partee and Borschev's logic, this suggests that non-control pragmatic readings may be introduced only by the possessor phrase, rather than internal to the possessee nominal. In addition, for some reason relation-modifying *former* is incompatible with restrictive modifiers (so in *my former Filipina wife*, *Filipina* must be appositive).

2.6. Summary of section 2

In sum, the variety and flexibility of possessive interpretations argue strongly for a corresponding variety of both overt (*favorite*) and covert (*Ex*, π) typeshifting elements. These typeshifters apply with a high, but incomplete, degree of optionality and freedom.

3 Predicative uses

In many contexts, use of a possessive whose possessor is definite requires reference to a unique object (for singular possessives) or to the maximal set of described objects (for plural possessives). For instance, if I tell you that my children are smart, I normally convey the thought that all of my children are smart. Uniqueness for singulars and maximality for plurals is one of the hallmarks of the definite determiner, so this association of possessives with maximality supports the conclusion that possessives are inherently definite.

However, as discussed by Mandelbaum (1994: chapter 4), Partee (1997), Partee & Borschev (1998, 2000), and especially by Partee & Borschev (2001), and others, in many contexts possessives can be used with non-unique or non-maximal reference. One major class of examples are the so-called weak definite possessives (*That's the leg of a llama*), which are discussed below in section 4. But in some circumstances prenominal possessives can also be used non-maximally. Possessives in the predicate position of a predicative copular sentence in particular do not require maximality. If I tell you that "Those [pointing left] are Harold's tools", I can continue "...and *those* [pointing right] are Harold's tools too". Similarly, saying *John is my friend* differs from saying *John is my only friend* precisely in failing to entail that I have no other friends. Likewise, describing someone as *my good friend Peter* does not entail I have only one good friend.

Non-maximal uses of possessives seem to be strongly correlated with predicative uses. If we put the possessive in subject position, maximality implications return. Thus if I say *Harold's tools are over there*, I must be talking about all of Harold's tools (at least, all of Harold's tools that are going to be relevant for present conversational purposes). These predicative uses are peculiar to possessives. In contrast, definite descriptions do not lose their uniqueness/maximality implications in predicative position: *John is the tall friend* or *Those are the tools* both require that the definite descriptions refer to the maximal set of objects that satisfy their descriptive content.

Because predicative uses correlate with specific syntactic environments, it is tempting to try to analyze the failure of maximality as something that is added to the basic meaning of the possessive in specific syntactic contexts. The difficulty with this idea is that it is far from clear how to do it. If the basic meaning of a possessive is individual-denoting (or the principal ultrafilter generated by an individual), there is no way to shift that individual into a suitable property without recovering the relational noun involved, which violates the part of the principle of non-compositionality that prohibits taking apart a meaning once it has already been built. (If you favor a structured-meaning approach for propositions, however, it might be possible to have a structured-referent approach for possessives, but as far as I know, this has not been proposed.) The obvious alternative would be to assume that the basic meaning of possessives is predicational, and that uniqueness/maximality implications are what is added. If so, then despite the fact that contexts with unique/maximal interpretations are far more common (and do not seem to form a natural class), it is the predicative uses that allow the true nature of possessive meaning to shine through. According to Partee and Borschev (1998, 2000, 2001), predicative interpretations can only involve a control interpretation (see section 2.3).

4 Definiteness

Definiteness is a morphosyntactic category. (See article 2 [this volume] (Heim) *Definiteness and indefiniteness*.) At least those DPs determined by *the* are definite, and at least those DPs determined by *a* are indefinite. Prenominal possessives are often believed to be uniformly definite, but such claims usually are based on semantic considerations. One of the few reasonably reliable syntactic correlates of definiteness is the ability to appear in the existential *there* construction.

Definite DPs can appear in pivot position only with degraded grammaticality (or else a special list interpretation):

(6) a. There is [a tall man] in the garden.
    b. *There is [the tall man] in the garden.

As mentioned, prenominal possessives are often assumed to be uniformly definite. A more accurate alternative generalization, usually attributed to Jackendoff (but hard to find in published work) is that a prenominal possessive can appear in the existential *there* construction if and only if its possessor phrase can:

(7) a. There is [a tall man]'s lawyer in the garden.
    b. *There is [the tall man]'s lawyer in the garden.

Apparently, a prenominal possessive inherits its definiteness status from its possessor phrase.

The key semantic properties that correlate with definiteness are familiarity (Heim 1982) and uniqueness (Russell 1905). If a DP carries a familiarity presupposition (as many definite DPs do, especially pronouns), it can be used only in a discourse that contains a salient, previously established ('familiar') discourse referent corresponding to the referent of the DP.

(8) a. She sat, then [a senator's daughter] asked me a question.
    b. She sat, then [the senator's daughter] asked me a question.

In (8a), *a senator's daughter* must refer to a person different than the referent of *she*, that is, it must be a novel (i.e., non-familiar) use, just as a use of *a senator* in the same position would necessarily be novel. But in (8b), *the senator's daughter* (when deaccented) can refer to the referent of *she*, just as *the senator* can. Thus it is not quite correct (contra Barker 1995, 2000) to say that a possessive inherits its familiarity/novelty status from its possessor phrase. Although a possessive with an indefinite possessor (as in (8a)) appears to have a novelty requirement just like its possessor (i.e., *a senator's daughter* must refer to a novel discourse participant), possessives with definite possessor phrases (as in (8b)) can refer either to a familiar discourse participant, or else can perfectly felicitously serve as a novel description, i.e., provide the first mention of a new discourse participant: in (8b), *the senator's daughter* can very well be the first mention of the described person in the discourse.

It turns out that definite possessives share this familiarity/novelty neutrality with definite descriptions in general. Gundel, Hedberg & Zacharski (1993) reject familiarity as a requirement on definite descriptions. Rather, they propose that definite descriptions must describe an entity that is uniquely identifiable in the discourse context based on the content of the description alone. And, as Birner & Ward (1994) observe, it is perfectly possible to use a definite description as a first mention: *Go into the next room and bring me the bag of chips lying on the bed* is fine even if the bag of chips is not familiar, as long as there is just one (salient) bag of chips on the bed. Once we understand that definite descriptions have a uniqueness requirement but not a familiarity requirement, we can recognize that possessives also inherit their novelty/uniqueness properties from their possessor: a possessive with an indefinite possessor must be novel, just like its possessor, and a possessive with a definite possessor must describe a unique object in the discourse situation, whether that object is discourse-familiar or not.

4.1 Possession relations as functions

In a highly influential paper, Löbner (1985) proposes that the definite determiner "indicates that the head noun is taken to be a functional concept". Since Löbner explicitly assumes that prenominal possessives are definite in the relevant sense, it follows that prenominal possessives can only be used if it is possible to construe the possession relation as functional.

(9) He put his hand on her knee.

This counterexample, due to Christophersen (1939), naturally describes one hand out of two placed on one knee out of two. According to Löbner, such examples involve abstract configurations in which the relevant participants have exactly one hand and exactly one knee. But in addition to this counterexample, predicative uses (discussed above in section 3) and possessive weak definites (discussed immediately below) stand as systematic counterexamples to Löbner's proposal, at least in its strongest form. However, there may be possessive constructions in other languages for which the possession relation must indeed be functional; see section 4.3.

4.2 Possessive weak definites

There are well-known (though still imperfectly understood) exceptions to the generalization that definite descriptions must uniquely identify a referent (Abbott 2004, Carlson et al. 2006). They are fairly sporadic, and in particular, not robust in the face of compositional modification. That is, if you say *Let's take the elevator*, any elevator in the bank of elevators will do. But if you say *Let's take the big elevator*, there had better be at most one (salient) big elevator. There is, however, a class of systematic exceptions noticed by Poesio (1994), which I will call possessive weak definites:

(10) a. I hope the cafe is located on [the corner of a busy intersection].
      b. Then Superman smashed into [the side of a Marlboro-emblazoned truck].

These are definite descriptions. After all, they are headed by the definite determiner. Yet there is no uniqueness implication (let alone a familiarity implication): in (10a), there is no way to tell which of the four corners of the intersection the speaker has in mind. Likewise, in (10b), the relevant side of the truck need not be familiar, nor need it be uniquely identified by the descriptive content.

Woisetschlaeger (1983) observed that possessive weak definites can appear in the existential *there* construction.

(11) There was [the wedding picture of a young black couple] among his papers.

(12) And there was [the picture of a boy I had known slightly in high school].

Woisetschlaeger maintains that these uses are necessarily generic, and therefore still definite. He argues that in (11), wedding pictures of couples are a natural kind. However, it is implausible in (12) that pictures of boys the speaker had known slightly in high school is a natural kind.

Barker (2004) notes that because possessive weak definites are postnominal possessives, these weak definites only occur in the presence of a relational head noun (*corner*, *side*, *picture*). He suggests that there is still uniqueness, just not uniqueness of reference. Rather, what is unique is the contrastive selection of one relation over another: the *corner* of a busy intersection, not the middle; the *side* of a truck, not the top; the *picture* of a couple, not their wedding certificate.

4.3 Construct State: (in)definiteness spread

Semitic languages typically have two possessive constructions called the Construct State and the Free State, which we can view (only very roughly) as homologous with the prenominal Saxon possessive and the postnominal prepositional possessive in English. The following examples are from Hebrew:

(13) a. beyt   ha-more   CONSTRUCT STATE
         house   the-teacher
         'the teacher's house'

b. ha   bayit   šel   ha-more   FREE STATE
      the   house   of   the-teacher
      'the house of the teacher'

In the Construct State, a bare head noun undergoes certain morphophonemic changes (here, *beyt* instead of *bayit*). The Construct State as a whole is usually said to inherit the definiteness of the possessor. The mechanism by which this occurs is often called Definiteness Spread (analogously, Indefiniteness Spread). According to Dobrovie-Sorin (2000b, 2004) and to Heller (2002), (in)definiteness spread is a consequence of the functional nature of the relation expressed by the Construct State. Following Löbner (1985), they assume that the construct state can only express functional relations, either naturally, as a result of the lexical meaning of the possessee nominal (e.g., Hebrew *roš* 'head') or by coercion.

4.4. Summary of section 4

In English, prenominal possessives inherit morphosyntactic definiteness from their possessor. If the possessor phrase is indefinite, the possessive must refer to a novel entity (just as the possessor phrase must). If the possessor phrase is definite, the possessive must describe a uniquely identifiable object (just as the possessor phrase must). Postnominal possessives are definite or not depending on the head article. However, for poorly understood reasons, possessive weak definites (*the corner of a busy intersection*), unlike normal definite descriptions, do not have any uniqueness implications.

Chung (2008) argues that possessives do not automatically inherit (in)definiteness from their possessors in Maori and Chamorro. Similarly, Alexiadou (2005) surveys a number of languages, and concludes that there is considerable variation cross-linguistically in the relationship between the definiteness of a possessive and the definitness of its parts. Haspelmath (1999) considers article/possessive complementarity from a cross-linguistic perspective, concluding that definiteness plays an important role.

5 Possessive compounds

Possessives can sometimes be syntactically ambiguous: *the men's rooms* can either refer to some rooms possessed by some salient group of men ([*the men*]*'s rooms*), or it can refer to some salient group of bathrooms (*the* [*men's rooms*]). In the latter case, *men's rooms* forms a possessive noun-noun compound (Taylor 1996: chapter 11). Possessive compounds are moderately productive. Like other noun-noun compounds, established possessive compounds often take on idiomatic meanings (for instance, *men's room* has an idiomatic meaning on which it means 'bathroom'). When novel, like other noun-noun compounds, they require context to make their intended meaning recoverable, and they must describe some class of objects that are "nameworthy" (Downing 1977) given current conversational purposes.

According to Barker (1995) and Taylor (1996), possessive compounds do not tolerate phrasal components. This means that adding adjectival modifiers or other phrase-level elements to either half of the compound disrupts possessive compounds. Thus [*the tall men*]'*s clean rooms* can only have a structure on which *the tall men* is a constituent, and there is no idiomatic interpretation involving bathrooms. Munn (1995) and Strauss (2004) argue that this conclusion is mistaken, and the relevant constructions can be phrasal.

Possessive compounds reveal a deep similarity between noun-noun compounds on the one hand, and phrasal possessives on the other hand. The connection is that both construction types can express pragmatically-controlled relations over pairs of individuals. Typical (non-possessive) noun-noun compounds (*dog house, rail road, pumpkin bus*) all require there to be some specific type of relation between the objects described by the first noun and the objects described by the second noun (lives-in, made-of, goes-to). By inserting a possessive morpheme, possessive noun-noun compounds merely make the need to recover a pragmatically-supplied relation overt. As a result, the compositionality issues related to understanding where pragmatically-controlled possession relations come from are intimately connected with those relating to compounds (e.g., Kamp & Partee 1995).

6 Scope, binding, and quantificational narrowing

Like other DPs inside of DPs, possessor phrases can take inverse scope (see article 1 [Semantics: Sentence and Information Structure] (Szabolcsi) *Scope and binding*).

(14) a. One person from every city hates it.
      b. One sibling of every celebrity resents her fame.
      c. Every celebrity's siblings resent her fame.

(14a) is a standard (non-possessive) case of inverse linking involving a locative preposition. The point of interest is that the quantificational DP *every city* takes wide scope over the DP that contains it (namely, *one person from___*). Furthermore, the embedded quantifier *every city* can also bind the pronoun *it*, despite the fact that the quantifier does not c-command the pronoun. The second and third examples illustrate analogous behavior for a postnominal possessive and a prenominal possessive.

On the standard Quantifier Raising approach to scope-taking (Heim & Kratzer 1998, Büring 2004), quantificational DPs are generally prohibited from raising out of their container DP. In the case of (non-possessive) prepositional modifiers, as in (14a), the preposition can arguably project clausal structure that could provide a suitable adjunction site within the DP for the quantifier to raise to (Heim & Kratzer 1998: section 8.5). This strategy is not available for prenominal possessives; thus Heim & Kratzer (1998: 231) and Büring (2004: 32) provide a type-shifting rule to deal with (14c).

The ability to bind a pronoun without c-commanding it is a separate problem from inverse scope. Ruys (2000: 517) offers the following generalization: if A can bind B, and A contains C, and C can take scope over B, then C can bind B. Thus in (14c), A is the subject DP *every celebrity's siblings*, and B is *her*. The subject can certainly bind a pronoun in the verb phrase. Since the subject contains *every celebrity*, and since *every celebrity* can take scope over the pronoun (through whatever mechanism allows inverse scope), Ruy's generalization explicitly permits the embedded quantificational DP to bind the pronoun. In other approaches to scope-taking (e.g., Barker & Shan 2008), both inverse scope and binding without c-command fall out without any type-shifters specific to inverse scope, and without any stipulated generalization such as Ruy's.

6.1 Narrowing

Barker (1995: 139) observes that quantificational possessors automatically restrict quantification to only those elements that stand in the relevant possession relation with some possessee.

(15) Most planets' rings are made of ice.

Only planets that have rings are relevant for the truth of (15). This sentence can be true in a solar system in which two of the three planets that have rings have rings made of ice, even if only three planets out of eight even have rings in the first place. (If you're tempted to read *planets' rings* as a compound, insert an adjective: *most round planets' rings*.) It is as if the sentence had been [*Most planets that have rings*]' *rings are made of ice*. Barker named this phenomenon NARROWING.

It is possible that narrowing is a kind of accommodation (Lewis 1979): the listener pragmatically enriches the descriptive content of the possessor in recognition of the apparent intentions of the speaker ("Apparently", reasons the listener of (15), "the speaker intended to talk only about those planets that have rings"). If so, narrowing is a particularly automatic and exceptionless type of accommodation. Furthermore, narrowing is associated specifically with possessives:

(16) Most planets have rings made of ice.

Unlike (15), the truth of (16) does seem to be sensitive to the status of planets that don't have rings, despite the fact that the relation denoted by *have* is similar to the possession relation involved in (15). Presumably whatever makes narrowing automatic in (15) but not in (16) is specific to the syntax and semantics of the possessive construction in (15). Peters & Westerståhl (2006: chapter 7) provide an account on which narrowing is built into the truth conditions of the possessive construction.

7 Thematic roles

It is commonplace (notably Chomsky 1970, Szabolcsi 1983, Abney 1987) to observe that there are rough correspondences between the syntax and the semantics of sentences on the one hand and of DPs on the other. This is seen particularly clearly in derived nominals: compare *The Romans destroyed the city*, in which *the Romans* is the subject, versus *the Romans' destruction of the city*, in which *the Romans* is the possessor.

The argument structure of derived nominals depends closely on the verbs they are derived from, though with many syntactic wrinkles. Similarly, the thematic roles of derived nominals reflect those of the verbs they are derived from (though perhaps not always; see Barker 1998a). Underived relational nouns, however, do not lend themselves to categorization in terms of verbal thematic roles. Instead, Barker & Dowty (1993) suggest that the nominal system has its own thematic role system more appropriate for the job of describing entities (rather than events). Instead of thematic roles that categorize participants in terms of their place in the causal chain (Agent, Instrument, Patient, etc.), nominal roles categorize participants in terms of their mereological properties, where a possessor is the Whole and the possessee is the Part: *the country's coastline, the table's leg, the beginning of the story*.

The part/whole opposition must be somewhat abstractly extended to conceive of properties as metaphorical parts of the objects that possess them (*speed, color, taste, age*). According to Moltmann (2004), the referent of, e.g., *the redness of the apple* is a trope, and quite literally a part of the apple: the part of the apple that instantiates the *red* universal, with concrete existence independent from all of the other properties of the apple. See also article 3 [Semantics: Lexical Structures and Adjectives] (Davis) *Thematic roles*.

7.1 Non-invertibility of relational nouns

Evidence in support of the part/whole proto-role theory comes from the non-invertibility of relational nouns. In the verbal domain, thematic roles correlate strongly with grammatical relations. For instance, the subject participant is typically at least as high on the causal chain of events as the direct object participant, so that we have *John killed Mary*, or *The printer printed the paper*, but never the reverse. That is, there is no (morphologically simple) verb *blick such that *The paper blicked the printer* means "the paper was printed on by the printer".

Just so, relational nouns that express a part/whole relationship invariably assign the possessor participant to the whole, and the possessee to the part: in *the coastline of Chile*, Chile is the whole and the coastline is the part, and indeed Chile is the possessor and the coastline is the possessee. Likewise, for relational nouns expressing the relationship between an entity and one of its qualities or properties, the entity will be expressed as the possessor, and the property as the possessee, e.g., *the speed of the car*, *the shape of the apple*.

There is, of course, a prominent class of relational nouns for which the part/whole opposition is not relevant, namely, family terms (*brother*, *cousin*, etc.). As a result, argument linking is unconstrained, and the prediction is that these lexical items are invertible: there may be pairs of relational nouns that express perfect or near perfect inverses of each other. Thus we have inverse pairs such as *parent/child* and near-inverses such as *uncle/nephew*, which differ only in which element of the relation is entailed to be male (the older member or the younger).

Langacker (1992) also aims to explain the limited invertibility of possessive constructions. He suggests that this pattern derives from the conceptual function of possessives, which is to guide the attention of the listener to a specific described entity by moving from the possessor, a familiar anchor (the "landmark") by means of the possession relation to the target referent (the "trajector"). (See article 1 [Semantics: Theories] (Talmy) *Cognitive Semantics*.) In this way, the possessive allows the listener to arrive at mental contact with the intended entity. The part/whole asymmetry follows: it is natural to direct attention to a specific body part by first referring to the whole in which the part finds itself, so we have *the dog's tail*, moving our attention from the dog to the named part; but it is unnatural to have identified a subpart without yet having identified the whole that contains it. That is why we would be unlikely to describe Rex as *that tail's dog*, and so we never have relational nouns that lexicalize a part/whole relationship where the possessor is the part. (We do have *the tail's owner* or *the tail's possessor*, which can be used in those rare circumstances in which we do need to move from identification of the part to identification of the whole, but these do not constitute counterexamples, since they do not express relationships that are entailed to be part/whole relationships: *the stick's owner* does need not refer to an object of which the stick is a part.)

8 Bare possessives

In some situations, the NP possessee constituent of a possessive can be elided to form a bare possessive (*John's, the man's*). Comparatives often license bare possessives ([speaking of dogs] *John's is bigger than Mary's*). In a neutral context, bare possessives often refer to homes (*Let's go to John's*). English has special morphological forms for bare possessives formed from personal pronouns (e.g., *mine, yours, ours*). Partee (1997) and several papers of Partee and Borschev (especially Partee & Borschev 2001) discuss bare possessives.

9 Double genitives

Double genitives are so-called because they appear to contain both the genitive *of* and a possessive clitic:

(17) a. a friend of John
 b. a friend of John's

The DP in (17a) is a plain postnominal possessive, and (17b) is a double genitive.

Barker (1998b), following work of Jackendoff (e.g., 1968), argues that the double genitive is a kind of partitive construction, and not a true genitive at all. As noted by Jackendoff, standard partitives and double genitives both exhibit an anti-uniqueness effect:

(18) a. the one of John's books *(that I like the best)
 b. the book of John's *(that I like the best)
 c. the friend of John's children (that I like the best)

Like the standard partitive construction in (18a), the double genitive in (18b) is only compatible with the definite determiner if there is a relative clause (or some other form of restrictive modification) that renders the partitive or the double genitive unique. In contrast, the normal postnominal genitive *of* in (18c) can co-occur with the definite determiner whether or not there is further modification.

If the *of* in the double genitive is not the possessive *of*, this also explains why it is compatible with sortal head nouns (e.g., *a stick of Bush's/*Bush*); why it can co-occur with a prenominal possessive (*my favorite book of Mary's/*Mary*); and why it can express pragmatically-controlled possession relations: *a picture of John's* can be a picture that John owns, one that he holds in his hands, etc., but *a picture of John* can only describe a picture that depicts John.

Barker concludes that the *of* in (18b), like the *of* in (18a), is the partitive *of*, not the possessive *of*. Then *a friend of John's* is analyzed as *a friend of$_{part}$ John's (friends)*, roughly paraphrasable as 'one friend out of the set of John's friends'. The anti-uniqueness effect is explained in standard partitives and in double genitives by assuming that partitivity is always proper partitivity, that is, that *of$_{part}$ DP* must denote a property whose extension contains more than one entity. The proper partitivity hypothesis has been challenged by Ionin, Matushansky & Ruys (2006). Zamparelli (1998) and Storto (2000, 2004) also discuss in depth the semantics of double-genitives, in English and in Italian.

10 Plurals and dependent plurals

Possessives sometimes resist an interpretation that distributes possession across a set of possessors.

(19) a. The cream is now part of many men's grooming routine.
     b. ?This parking lot contains many men's car.

In (19a), the men in question need not have identical grooming routines. That is, the possession relation relating each man to his grooming routine distributes over the set of men. In (19b), however, for some reason, a reading on which each relevant man possesses a different car is difficult or impossible.

Perhaps relatedly, Zweig (2007) points out that possessives in some languages, including English, can have dependent plural readings.

(20) a. This bike has wheels.
     b. These unicycles have big wheels.

The plural on *wheels* entails that the bike in (20a) has more than one wheel. But (20b) has an interpretation on which each unicycle has only one wheel, though there must still be more than one wheel in the overall situation. On this interpretation, the plural *big wheels* depends on the plural *These unicycles*.

(21) a. This woman's husbands are annoying.
　　b. These women's husbands are annoying.

Similarly, the plural on *husbands* in (21a) guarantees that the woman in question must have more than one husband. But in the possessive in (21b), although there must be more than one husband in the overall situation, there need not be more than one husband per woman. Thus the plural *husbands* depends (in the relevant sense) on the plural *these women*.

11 Some related topics

In this article, I have concentrated on nominal constructions. Naturally, there are several ways in which possessive constructions and possessive meanings can interact with verbal argument structure. There is a rich literature on nominalizations (*the Roman's destruction of the city*) and gerunds (*John's singing in the shower*), notably including Chomsky (1970) and Grimshaw (1990).

There is likewise a rich literature on the syntax of sentences in which the main verb can have a possessive meaning. That is, many possession relations can be expressed using the verb *have*: *John's friend* ~ *John has a friend*; *John's cloud* ~ *John has a cloud*, though not all: *John's sake* ↛ **John has a sake*; *the pub's vicinity* ↛ **the pub has a vicinity*.

Possessors play an active role in the syntax of many languages. Many languages have possessive constructions in which the possessor appears as a direct argument of the verb. Sometimes known as possessor raising or possessor ascension (e.g., Aissen 1990), these constructions are also known as external possession constructions (Payne & Barshi 1999). Some flavor of these constructions can be perceived by comparing English *John touched Mary's arm* versus *John touched Mary on the arm*. Szabolcsi (1983) is an influential theory of a type of possessor movement in Hungarian. Possessives play an important role in Keenan & Stavi's (1986) classic study on the class of quantifiers expressible by natural language DPs. See article 4 [this volume] (Keenan) *Quantifiers*. Partee and Borschev have a series of papers discussing the semantics of the Genitive of Negation in Slavic, with particular attention to Russian. With certain verbs, arguments that show nominative or accusative case in affirmative contexts can appear in genitive case in the presence of negation. On their analysis, the Genitive of Negation involves denying the existence of some entity with respect to a specific location.

Some bibliographic notes: Partee (1997), an important and highly influential analysis of the possessive, first circulated in manuscript form around 1983 (though my attempts to get hold of a copy in 1990 were not successful). My 1991 dissertation, published in 1995, provides a general introduction to nominal possessives and relational nouns. Taylor (1996) and Heine (1997) are book-length treatments in the Cognitive Grammar tradition. There is a literature in French, discussed in Dobrovie-Sorin (2000a) with special attention to the contributions of Milner. Peters & Westerstål (2006: chapter 7) covers much of the same ground as this article from a different point of view, and Coene & d'Hulst (2003) and Kim, Lander & Partee (2004) contain a number of studies discussing the syntax and semantics of possessives. Some works specific to possessives are available at semanticsarchive.net/links.html, *notably bibliographies and other resources compiled by Yury Lander and by Barbara Partee.*

12 References

Abbott, Barbara 2004. Definiteness and indefiniteness. In: L. R. Horn & G. Ward (eds.). *Handbook of Pragmatics*. Oxford: Blackwell, 22–149.

Abney, Steven 1987. *The English Noun Phrase in its Sentential Aspect*. Ph.D. dissertation. MIT, Cambridge, MA.

Aissen, Judith 1990. Possessor ascension in Tzotzil. In: L. Martin (ed.). *Papers in Mayan Linguistics*. Columbia, MO: Lucas Brothers Publishers, 89–108.

Alexiadou, Artemis 2005. Possessors and (in)definiteness. *Lingua* 11, 787–819.

Barker, Chris 1995. *Possessive Descriptions*. Stanford, CA: CSLI Publications.

Barker, Chris 1998a. Episodic -ee in English: A thematic role constraint on new word formation. *Language* 74, 695–727.

Barker, Chris 1998b. Partitives, double genitives, and anti-uniqueness. *Natural Language and Linguistic Theory* 16, 679–717.

Barker, Chris 2000. Definite possessives and discourse novelty. *Theoretical Linguistics* 26, 211–227.

Barker, Chris 2004. Possessive weak definites. In: J. Kim, Y. Lander & B. H. Partee (eds.). *Possessives and Beyond: Semantics and Syntax*. Amherst, MA: University of Massachusetts, 89–113.

Barker, Chris & David Dowty 1993. Non-verbal thematic proto-roles. In: A. Schafer (ed.). *Proceedings of the North Eastern Linguistic Society 23*. Amherst, MA: GLSA, University of Massachusetts, 49–62.

Barker, Chris & Chung-chieh Shan 2008. Donkey anaphora is in-scope binding. *Semantics and Pragmatics* 1, 1–40.

Birner, Betty & Gregory Ward 1994. Uniqueness, familiarity, and the definite article in English. In: S. Gahl et al. (eds.). *Proceedings of the Annual Meeting of the Berkeley Linguistics Society 20*. Berkeley, CA: University of California, 93–102.

Büring, Daniel 2004. Crossover situations. *Natural Language Semantics* 12, 23–62.

Carlson, Gregory, Rachel Sussman, N. Klein & Michael Tanenhaus 2006. Weak definite NP's. In: C. Davis, A. R. Deal & Y. Zabbal (eds.). *Proceedings of the North Eastern Linguistic Society 36*. Amherst, MA: GLSA, University of Massachusetts, 179–196.
Chappell, Hillary & William McGregor (eds.) 1996. *The Grammar of Inalienability. A Typological Perspective on Body Part Terms and the Part-Whole Relation*. Berlin: Mouton de Gruyter.
Chomsky, Noam 1970. Remarks on nominalizations. In: R. A. Jacobs & P. S. Rosenbaum (eds.). *Readings in English Transformational Grammar*. Waltham, MA: Blaisdell, 184–221.
Christophersen, Paul 1939. *The Articles*. Copenhagen: Munksgaard.
Chung, Sandra 2008. Possessors and definiteness effects in two Austronesian languages. In: L. Matthewson (ed.). *Quantification: A Cross-linguistic Perspective*. Bingley: Emerald, 179–224.
Coene, Martine & Yves d'Hulst (eds.) 2003. *From NP to DP, vol. 2: The Expression of Possession in Noun Phrases*. Amsterdam: Benjamins.
Dobrovie-Sorin, Carmen 2000a. De la syntaxe à l'interprétation, de Milner (1982) à Milner (1955): le génitif. In: J.-M. Marandin (ed.). *Cahier Jean-Claude Milner*. Paris: Verdier, 55–98.
Dobrovie-Sorin, Carmen 2000b. (In)definiteness spread: From Romanian genitives to Hebrew Construct State nominals. In: V. Motapanyane (ed.). *Comparative Studies in Romanian Syntax*. Amsterdam: Elsevier, 177–226.
Dobrovie-Sorin, Carmen 2004. Genitives and determiners. In: J. Kim, Y. Lander & B. H. Partee (eds.). *Possessives and Beyond: Semantics and Syntax*. Amherst, MA: University of Massachusetts, 115–132.
Downing, Pamela 1977. On the creation and use of English compound nouns. *Language* 53, 810–842.
Grimshaw, Jane 1990. *Argument Structure*. Cambridge, MA: The MIT Press.
Gundel, Jeanette, Nancy Hedberg & Ron Zacharski 1993. Cognitive status and the form of referring expressions. *Language* 69, 274–307.
Haspelmath, Martin 1999. Explaining article-possessor complementarity: Economic motivation in noun phrase syntax. *Language* 75, 227–243.
Heim, Irene 1982. *The Semantics of Definite and Indefinite Noun Phrases*. Ph.D. dissertation. University of Massachusetts, Amherst, MA. Reprinted: Ann Arbor, MI: University Microfilms.
Heim, Irene & Angelika Kratzer 1998. *Semantics in Generative Grammar*. Oxford: Blackwell.
Heine, Bernd 1997. *Possession: Cognitive Sources, Forces, and Grammaticalization*. Cambridge: Cambridge University Press.
Heller, Daphna 2002. Possession as a lexical relation: Evidence from the Hebrew Construct State. In: L. Mikkelsen & C. Potts (eds.). *Proceedings of the 21st West Coast Conference on Formal Linguistics*. Somerville, MA: Cascadilla Press, 127–140.
Ionin, Tania, Ora Matushansky, & E. G. Ruys 2006. Parts of speech: Toward a unified semantics for partitives. In: Ch. Davis, A. R. Deal & Y. Zabbal (eds.). *Proceedings of the North Eastern Linguistics Society 36*. Amherst, MA: GLSA, University of Massachusetts, 357–370.
Jackendoff, Ray 1968. Possessives in English. In: S. Anderson, R. Jackendoff & S. J. Keyser (eds). *Studies in Transformational Grammar and Related Topics*. Waltham, MA: Brandeis University Press, 25–51.
Kamp, Hans & Barbara H. Partee 1995. Prototype theory and compositionality. *Cognition* 57, 129–191.

Keenan, Edward L. & Jonathan Stavi 1986. A semantic characterization of natural language determiners. *Linguistics & Philosophy* 9, 253–326.
Kim, Ji-Yung, Yury A. Lander & Barbara H. Partee (eds.) 2004. *Possessives and Beyond: Semantics and Syntax*. Amherst, MA: University of Massachusets.
Langacker, Ronald 1992. The symbolic nature of cognitive grammar: The meaning of *of* and of *of*-periphrasis. In: M. Putz (ed.). *Thirty Years of Linguistics Evolution: Studies in Honour of René Dirven on the Occasion of His Sixtieth Birthday*. Amsterdam: Benjamins, 483–502.
Larson, Richard 1998. Events and modification in nominals. In: D. Strolovitch & A. Lawson (eds.). *Proceedings from Semantics and Linguistic Theory 8*. Ithaca, NY: Cornell University, 145–68.
Larson, Richard & Sungeun Cho 2003. Temporal adjectives and the structure of possessive DPs. *Natural Language Semantics* 11, 217–247.
Lewis, David 1979. Scorekeeping in a language game. In: R. Bäuerle, U. Egli, & A. von Stechow (eds.). *Semantics from Different Points of View*. Berlin: Springer, 172–187.
Löbner, Sebastian 1985. Definites. *Journal of Semantics* 4, 279–326.
Mandelbaum, Deborah 1994. *Syntactic Conditions on Saturation*. Ph.D. dissertation. City University of New York, New York.
Miller, Philippe 1991. *Clitics and Constituents in Phrase Structure Grammar*. Doctoral dissertation. University of Utrecht.
Moltmann, Friederike 2004. Properties and kinds of tropes: New linguistic facts and old philosophical insights. *Mind* 123, 1–41.
Munn, Alan 1995. The possessor that stayed close to home. In: V. Samian & J. Schaeffer (eds.). *Proceedings of the Western Conference on Linguistics 24*, 181–195.
Partee, Barbara H. 1987. Noun phrase interpretation and type-shifting principles. In: J. Groenendijk, D. de Jongh & M. Stokhof (eds.). *Studies in Discourse Representation Theory and the Theory of Generalized Quantifiers*. Dordrecht: Foris, 115–143.
Partee, Barbara H. 1989. Binding implicit variables in quantified contexts. In: C. Wiltshire, R. Graczyk & B. Music (eds.). *Papers from the Regional Meeting of the Chicago Linguistic Society 25*. Chicago, IL: Chicago Linguistic Society, 342–365.
Partee, Barbara H. 1997. Genitives—A case study. Appendix to Theo M.V. Janssen, 'Compositionality'. In: J. van Benthem & A. ter Meulen (eds.). *Handbook of Logic and Linguistics*. Amsterdam: Elsevier, 464–470.
Partee, Barbara H. & Vladimir Borschev 1998. Integrating lexical and formal semantics: Genitives, relational nouns, and type-shifting. In: R. Cooper & T. Gamkrelidze (eds.). *Proceedings of the Second Tbilisi Symposium on Language, Logic, and Computation*. Tbilisi: Center on Language, Logic, Speech, Tbilisi State University, 229–241.
Partee, Barbara H. & Vladimir Borschev 2000. Possessives, favorite, and coercion. In: A. Riehl & R. Daly (eds.). *Proceedings of ESCOL99*. Ithaca, NY: Cornell University, 173–190.
Partee, Barbara H. & Vladimir Borschev 2001. Some puzzles of predicate possessives. In: I. Kenesei & R. M. Harnish (eds). *Perspectives on Semantics, Pragmatics and Discourse. A Festschrift for Ferenc Kiefer*. Amsterdam: Benjamins, 91–117.
Payne, Doris & Immanuel Barshi (eds.) 1999. *External Possession*. Amsterdam: Benjamins.
Peters, Stanley & Dag Westerståhl 2006. *Quantifiers in Language and Logic*. Oxford: Oxford University Press.
Poesio, Massimo 1994. Weak definites. In: M. Harvey & L. Santelmann (eds.). *Proceedings of Semantics and Linguistic Theory IV*. Ithaca, NY: Cornell University, 282–299.
Pustejovsky, James 1995. *The Generative Lexicon*. Cambridge, MA: The MIT Press.

Quine, Willard van Orman 1960. *Word and Object*. Cambridge, MA: The MIT Press.
Russell, Bertrand 1905. On denoting. *Mind* 14, 479–493.
Ruys, E. G. 2000. Weak Crossover as a scope phenomenon. *Linguistic Inquiry* 31, 513–539.
Stanley, Jason 2000. Context and logical form. *Linguistics & Philosophy* 23, 391–434.
Storto, Gianluca 2000. Double genitives aren't (quite) partitives. In: A. Okrent & J. Boyle (eds). *Papers from the Regional Meeting of the Chicago Linguistic Society 36, vol. 1.* Chicago, IL: Chicago Linguistic Society, 501–516.
Storto, Gianluca 2004. Possessives in context. In: J. Kim, Y. A. Lander & B. H. Partee (eds.). *Possessives and Beyond: Semantics and Syntax*. Amherst, MA: University of Massachusetts, 59–86.
Strauss, Uri 2004. Individual-denoting and property-denoting possessives. In: J. Kim, Y. A. Lander & B. H. Partee (eds.). *Possessives and Beyond: Semantics and Syntax*. Amherst, MA: University of Massachusetts, 183–198.
Szabolcsi, Anna 1983. The possessor that ran away from home. *The Linguistic Review* 3, 89–102.
Taylor, John R. 1996. *Possessives in English*. Oxford: Clarendon Press.
Vikner, Carl & Per Anker Jensen 2002. A semantic analysis of the English genitive: Interaction of lexical and formal semantics. *Studia Linguistica* 56, 191–226.
Woisetschlaeger, Erich 1983. On the question of definiteness in 'an old man's book'. *Linguistic Inquiry* 14, 137–154.
Zamparelli, Roberto 1998. A theory of kinds, partitives, and OF/Z possessives. In: A. Alexiadou & C. Wilder (eds.). *Possessors, Predicates and Movement in the Determiner Phrase*. Amsterdam: Benjamins, 259–301.
Zweig, Eytan 2007. *Dependent Plurals and Plural Meaning*. Ph.D. dissertation. New York University, New York.

Peter Lasersohn
7 Mass nouns and plurals

1   Introduction —— 204
2   Issues in the denotation of mass and plural NPs —— 209
3   Issues in the denotation of mass and plural DPs —— 214
4   Collective and distributive readings —— 224
5   References —— 228

Abstract: Mass and plural expressions exhibit interesting similarities in distribution and interpretation, including cumulative reference, the ability to appear bare, and a parallel alternation between existential and generic readings. They also exhibit important differences in agreement, determiner choice, and in the types of quantification available. Major approaches to plural denotation make conflicting claims whether plurality involves reference to collective objects such as sets or mereological sums, or instead requires simultaneous saturation of an argument place by multiple individuals. Theories of mass denotation differ as to whether the count/mass distinction is a difference in discrete vs. continuous denotation, reference to objects vs. the material they are composed of, or reference to mereological sums vs. classes of individuals. Bare plurals and mass nouns sometimes denote "kinds"; there is disagreement whether they also have an indefinite reading. Several kinds of plural and mass quantification can be distinguished, depending on determiner choice, predicate modification, and the use of a classifier or measure phrase. Plural quantifiers may interact to give a "cumulative" reading, in which the quantifiers are scopally independent. Sentences containing plurals sometimes exhibit an ambiguity between collective and distributive readings; the number of readings and mechanisms for producing them is in dispute.

1 Introduction

Many—perhaps all—languages draw a distinction between *mass* nouns, prototypical examples of which denote homogeneous substances such as water or gold, and *count* nouns, prototypically denoting discrete, bounded objects such as people or chairs. Likewise, many languages distinguish between *singular* nouns,

---

Peter Lasersohn, Urbana, IL, United States

https://doi.org/10.1515/9783110589443-007

which refer to single objects, and *plural* nouns, which refer to multiple objects collectively. (Some languages distinguish additional categories such as *dual* or *paucal*.) In this article, we survey a variety of issues related to the count/mass and singular/plural distinctions.

1.1 Parallels between plural and mass expressions

We discuss mass and plural nouns together because they show interesting similarities. Both exhibit *cumulative reference* (Quine 1960: 91); licensing inferences like those in (1):

(1) a. A is water and B is water; therefore A and B together are water
    b. A are apples and B are apples; therefore A and B together are apples

Singular count nouns do not license the same kind of inference; (2) is invalid:

(2) A is an apple and B is an apple; therefore A and B together are an apple

Singular count nouns instead exhibit *divided reference*; as Quine puts it, "To learn 'apple' it is not sufficient to learn how much of what goes on counts as apple; we must learn how much counts as *an* apple, and how much as another."

In addition, mass and plural nouns may appear (in English) with no overt determiner, while a determiner is normally required for singular count nouns:

(3) I see water/horses/*horse

To the extent that *I see horse* is acceptable, it involves either a conversion of *horse* from a count noun into a mass noun, or a special "telegraphic" style of speech in which determiners are omitted generally.

Determinerless (or "bare") mass and plural noun phrases also show a parallel alternation in interpretation, depending on the predicate with which they combine (cf. article 5 [this volume] (Dayal) *Bare noun phrases*). If the predicate is *stage-level* (Carlson 1977a,b), the noun phrase is understood as existentially quantified; (4a,b) are roughly equivalent to *Some water leaked into the floor* and *Some raccoons were stealing my corn*:

(4) a. Water leaked into the floor
    b. Raccoons were stealing my corn

If the predicate is *individual-level*, the sentence is understood as drawing a generalization about objects of the kind picked out by the mass or plural noun:

(5) a. Water is wet
    b. Raccoons are sneaky

If the predicate is *kind-level*, the mass or plural noun is understood as referring to a "kind" of object, and the predicate is applied to this kind collectively, as a whole:

(6) a. Water is common
    b. Raccoons are extinct

Parallels such as these have led many semanticists to treat plural and mass expressions together as "non-singular," or even to identify mass nouns with lexical plurals (Chierchia 1998a,b). But a completely unified analysis would seem to be impossible, because mass nouns also show obvious differences from overtly plural nouns, notably in their inability to combine directly with numerals and their selection by other determiners:

(7) a. two horses/*water
    b. many horses/*water
    c. much *horses/water
    d. few horses/*water
    e. little *horses/water

1.2 Issues in what is meant by *mass* and *plural*

The use of the term *mass* in its technical sense in semantics appears to originate with Jespersen (1913, 1924). *Count* is considerably more recent than *mass*; the earliest occurrence I know of is in the anonymous (1952) *Structural Notes and Corpus*; the term was popularized by Gleason (1955). However, earlier authors did employ comparable terms such as *thing-words* (Jespersen 1913), *bounded nouns* (Bloomfield 1933), or *individual nouns* (Whorf 1941). Jespersen characterized "mass-words" as "words which represent 'uncountables', i.e., which do not call up the idea of any definite thing, having a certain shape or precise limits" (1913: 114), in contrast to thing-words, which represent countable objects. He went on to note various syntactic differences between mass-words and thing-words; but reference to countable or uncountable objects seems to have been the defining distinction.

Jespersen was careful to note that the mass-word/thing-word distinction cross-cuts the distinction between "material" and "immaterial" words, and cited this feature of his terminology as providing an advantage over Sweet's (1892) earlier classification into "class nouns" and "material nouns." Abstract nouns such as *progress*, *admiration*, or *safety* were categorized as mass-words.

Bloomfield (1933: 205) partially continued Jespersen's terminology, but distinguished "mass nouns" from "abstract nouns," placing both under a more general heading of "unbounded nouns," in opposition to "bounded nouns." Many authors have continued Bloomfield's narrower use of the term *mass*, so that abstract nouns are excluded.

A related issue is whether to include words such as *furniture* and *footwear* as mass. These pattern syntactically with ordinary mass nouns, combining with *much* rather than *many*, failing to combine directly with numerals, etc.; but they hardly fit Jespersen's characterization as not calling up the idea of a "definite thing, having a certain shape and precise limits." An observation due to Roger Schwarzschild is that these nouns admit modification with "stubbornly distributive" predicates of shape and size, unlike prototypical mass nouns:

(8) a. This furniture is small
    b. *This water is small

The use of the term *mass* was imported from linguistics into philosophy by Quine (1960), and although Quine was careful to stress that the distinction between count and mass terms was not in the "stuff" they denote, but only in whether they show cumulative or divided reference, much of the subsequent philosophical literature has construed *mass* so narrowly as to include only those words which serve as names for physical substances, and not nouns like *furniture* or *admiration*. But many authors use *mass* in a broader sense and distinguish substance nouns as a special subclass. This variation in what is meant by *mass* leads some writers to eschew the term entirely, preferring *non-count* as more clearly including a broader set of examples (Payne & Huddleston 2002, Laycock 2006).

Another point of variation is in whether *mass* should be understood to include some morphologically plural examples. Jespersen argued that a wide range of plural nouns were actually mass, including examples such as *victuals*, *brains* (as in *blow out somebody's brains*), *dregs*, *proceeds*, *blues*, *creeps*, and others. These impose plural agreement on the verb, but combine with *much* rather than *many*:

(9) a. In this kind of work, brains are less important than guts
    b. It doesn't take much brains to figure this out

Here again Bloomfield (1933) introduced a shift in terminology, stipulating that mass nouns "have no plural," without discussing Jespersen's examples; the idea that mass nouns are always singular has been part of conventional wisdom ever since. Plural mass nouns have been periodically rediscovered (McCawley 1975, Gillon 1992), and are treated in detail in Ojeda (2005).

Another complication is that a single form may sometimes be used as a mass noun, and sometimes as a count noun. *Beer* is ordinarily mass, but may be used as a count noun to refer to individual servings of beer or kinds of beer; many other mass nouns show a similar alternation. Conversely, a count noun may also be used as a mass noun if one imagines the objects it denotes being put through a "universal grinder" (Pelletier 1975); after putting a steak (count) through the grinder, "there is steak all over the floor" (mass).

There is much less variation in what semanticists mean by *plural* than there is with *mass*, but even here there are some complications. Plurality is associated with a variety of morphosyntactic generalizations, which do not always coincide. A common observation is that in some dialects of English, morphologically singular but semantically collective nouns such as *committee* and *government* may impose plural agreement on verbs and pronouns, as in (10):

(10) The government are failing to achieve their goals

These nouns do not combine with plural quantifiers or appear bare, however:

(11) *Many/*Five/*∅ government are failing to achieve their goals

Such nouns should be distinguished from lexical plurals, such as *police* or *cattle*, which do appear bare and combine with some plural quantifiers:

(12) a. Cattle are slaughtered for their meat
      b. This city has too many police

For many speakers, these nouns resist combining with numerals:

(13) ?Five police came walking down the road

Yet they are clearly plural rather than mass – so an inability to combine with numerals should not be taken as the defining characteristic of mass nouns. The main patterns discussed so far may be summarized in Tab. 7.1.

Tab. 7.1: Summary of patterns distinguishing subclasses of singular, plural and mass nouns

	ordinary singulars *cup*	collective singulars *government*	lexical plurals *police*	ordinary plurals *cups*	heterogeneous mass nouns *furniture*	homogeneous mass nouns *water*	plural mass nouns *dues*
agreement	sg	sg/pl	pl	pl	sg	sg	pl
many vs. *much*	*	*	many	many	much	much	much
numerals	*	*	?	✓	*	*	*
bare	*	*	✓	✓	✓	✓	✓
cumulative reference	no	no	yes	yes	yes	yes	yes
combine with "stubbornly distributive" predicates	✓	✓	✓	✓	✓	*	*

2 Issues in the denotation of mass and plural NPs

By an "NP" we here mean a phrase consisting of a common noun, possibly with complements or modifiers, but excluding any determiner; e.g. *water, horse, books written by Mark Twain*, but not *that water, a horse*, or *all books written by Mark Twain*. We turn to phrases including the determiner in section 3. For the sake of discussion, we assume for most of this section that NPs are predicates, and hold or fail to hold of groups and/or individuals; we turn to the idea that NPs may sometimes serve as something like the name of a kind in section 3.1.

2.1 Approaches to plural denotation

Most analyses assume that plural predicates (including nouns) hold true of collective objects of some sort, which I will call "groups." (Readers are cautioned that *group* has a more specific technical sense in some work, especially that derived from Link 1984, Landman 1989a,b, 2000.) Thus, a plural noun such as *horses* will hold true of groups of horses just as a singular noun like *horse* holds true of individual horses.

The issue then arises of what a "group" is. One option is to identify groups with *sets*. However, some authors object to this identification on the grounds that sets are abstract mathematical objects, while the denotata of plural nouns may be concrete (Burge 1977, Link 1983, 1984). As Link (1984: 247) puts it, "If my kids turn the living room into a mess I find it hard to believe that a set has been at work, and my reaction to it is not likely to be that of a singleton set…" However, Black (1971) has argued that regarding the referents of plural terms as sets actually clarifies, rather than distorts, the notion of a set; and in any case not everyone shares the intuition that sets of concrete objects are themselves abstract (Cresswell 1985, Landman 1989a).

If groups are not identified with sets, they are usually taken to be concrete particulars of some sort – often called "plural individuals," though this is quite a departure from the meaning of the word *individual* in ordinary, non-technical usage. The group of John and Mary would be identified with a complex, spatially scattered individual with John and Mary as parts; or, as it is usually termed, the *sum* of John and Mary, which we may notate 'j+m'.

Typically it is assumed that the sum operation is associative, so that a+(b+c)=(a+b)+c. Summing differs in this respect from set-theoretic pairing, since {a,{b,c}}≠{{a,b},c} when a, b and c are distinct. This allows us a way of distinguishing the two approaches completely independently from issues of abstractness and concreteness. This difference will play a role in the analysis of distributivity (section 4). Another line of analysis denies that plural predicates hold true of groups at all. Reference to groups is avoided by locating the plurality in the denotation relation itself, rather than in the denoted object. This idea was pioneered by Boolos (1984, 1985a,b) and developed in more detail by Schein (1993) and subsequent literature; a related analysis of mass nouns is given in Nicolas (2008).

To illustrate, consider a revision to the standard notion of *satisfaction*. In the usual semantics for a language with variables, interpretation is relative to a function assigning exactly one value to each variable. In a system with plural variables, rather than assigning each plural variable exactly one group as its value, we relativize interpretation to relations rather than functions, so that an assignment may match a given variable with more than one value. Then a formula containing a plural variable can be satisfied by an assignment which gives multiple values $a_1,...,a_n,...$ to this variable, without being satisfied by assignments which give the set of all these values $\{a_1,...,a_n,...\}$ as the (sole) value for the same variable. The plurality is located in the assignment relation itself, rather than in the assigned value. Predication in general can be treated as satisfaction; adopting this technique in effect allows an argument place to be saturated simultaneously by more than one individual, rather than by the group containing those individuals. The primary advantage of such a technique is that it allows an analysis of phrases like *the sets which do not contain themselves* which does not give rise to Russell's paradox; see the references above for details.

Whether one analyzes plural NPs as satisfied by sets, or sums, or simultaneously by multiple individuals, certain more purely descriptive, theory-neutral issues must be addressed. In what follows I will continue to phrase these issues in terms of the "groups" denoted by a plural NP, but essentially the same questions arise in any approach; readers who prefer a groups-free approach are invited to rephrase the discussion accordingly.

Prominent among these issues is the question of how the denotation of a plural noun relates to the denotation of the corresponding singular. A natural assumption to make is that the plural noun holds true of all and only the groups of objects of which the corresponding singular noun holds true; so that *horses*, e.g., will hold true of all and only the groups whose members are individual horses. Note that this directly predicts that plural nouns will have cumulative reference, on the plausible assumption that for any groups A and B, there is a group whose members include all and only the members of A and the members of B.

However, if we take seriously the idea that a group must contain more than one member, this idea runs into immediate problems with examples using the determiner *no* (Schwarzschild 1996: 5). A sentence of the form *No A B* is true iff there is nothing of which both *A* and *B* are true. E.g. (14) is true only if there is nothing of which *horses* and *in the corral* both hold true.

(14) No horses are in the corral

But suppose there is only one horse. Then there are no groups containing more than one horse, so by our assumption that plural nouns hold only of groups, *horses* does not hold true of anything. This renders (14) automatically true, even if the one horse is in the corral – the wrong result.

This problem is easily solved if we allow plural NPs to hold of individuals and not just groups. In particular, a plural NP should hold of all the same individuals as the corresponding singular, as well as all groups of such individuals. Then if there is only one horse, the plural noun *horses* will hold true of it and (14) is correctly predicted to be false if the horse is in the corral.

Chierchia (1998b) defends the idea that plural nouns hold only of groups by assigning a more complex denotation to *no*: Rather than taking $no(A,B)$ as true iff A and B do not overlap, he takes it as true iff $\pi(A)$ and B do not overlap, where $\pi(A)$ is the set of all subsets and members of the union of all groups in A (and singletons of members of A). But in the case just described, the plural noun denotation A is empty, so this more complex procedure gains us nothing; incorrect truth conditions are still assigned. See Sauerland, Anderson & Yatsushiro (2005) for additional considerations.

2.2 Approaches to mass denotation

A mass noun like *water* is frequently assumed to hold true of all and only the individual portions of water – with no assumption that an individual "portion" must be physically separated in any way. Thus, *water* will hold of the water in the top half of my glass, as well as the water in the bottom half, the water in the top three quarters and the water occupying the glass as a whole. Nor need portions be physically contiguous; the water in two separate glasses may be considered together as a portion of water, of which the noun *water* holds true. Assuming that for any two portions A and B, there is a portion A+B consisting of them, we may stipulate that mass nouns are cumulative, holding of A+B whenever they hold of A and of B.

Since plurals also show the cumulative reference property, this will not distinguish mass nouns from plurals, or explain the differences between them, such as the ability of plurals but not mass nouns to combine with numerals. We will consider four major strategies for explaining the differences between mass and plural count NPs in semantic terms.

One strategy is to assume that mass nouns, but not plurals, show *distributive reference*, also sometimes known as *divisive reference* (not to be confused with Quine's *divided reference*) or *Cheng's condition* (after Cheng 1973): If a mass noun holds of A, and B is a part of A, then the mass noun holds of B as well. Some versions of this approach go further and require that mass nouns be *non-atomic*; i.e., that for each A of which the mass noun holds, there is some B which is a proper part of A, of which the mass noun also holds. This implies that mass noun denotations have no minimal parts; one may divide them without limit. If a noun's denotation is cumulative, distributive and non-atomic, we may call it *continuous*. Much of the attraction of analyzing mass nouns as denoting continuously is that it offers an explanation why mass nouns do not combine with numerals: One may divide their denotations in any arbitrary fashion into any number of parts, so there is no basis for counting.

Unfortunately, a condition requiring continuous denotation does not achieve even initial plausibility in the case of complex mass NPs like *water covering the floor*, since some water could easily cover the floor without all its parts covering the floor. Yet such complex mass NPs fail combine with numerals and other count determiners, just as simple mass nouns do.

Moreover, it is quite debatable whether even lexical mass noun denotations are really non-atomic; the individual hydrogen and oxygen atoms constituting an H_2O molecule would not seem to be water. (It should be cautioned that the issue here is not whether they would be water if separated from each other and released as gas, but whether they are water when still part of the H_2O molecule –

perhaps a trickier issue.) One may claim that even if mass noun denotations are not actually continuous, the language portrays them as if they were (Bunt 1985); but this would seem to imply that much of our ordinary talk using mass nouns is literally false, a consequence many semanticists would want to avoid.

A different approach to semantically distinguishing count and mass nouns is to regard the mass nouns as holding of portions of material, while count nouns hold of more abstract objects constituted of that material (Link 1983). This way of drawing the distinction allows an easy solution to the "gold ring" paradox: It may be that a ring is gold and the ring is new, but the gold is old. If we distinguish between the ring and the gold which constitutes it, there is nothing to prevent one from being new and the other old.

The philosophical merits of claiming that objects like rings are distinct from the portions of material of which they are constituted may be debated. But in addition, the proposal makes sense only under the very narrowest construal of the term *mass noun*, in which it refers only to those nouns which function as names of physical substances. Even though *chair* is a count noun and *furniture* is, by most definitions, a mass noun, one hesitates to say that chairs are constituted of furniture in the way that rings are constituted of gold, or that a chair can be new while the furniture it is constituted of may be old.

A third approach to the semantics of the mass-count distinction, advanced especially by Chierchia (1998a, 1998b), is to claim that mass nouns are essentially just lexical plurals, so that the part/whole relation on the denotata of mass nouns coincides with the subgroup relation on the denotata of plurals. Under Chierchia's approach, a mass noun like *change* is (nearly) identical in denotation to the plural noun *coins*; the mass noun *footwear* is (nearly) identical in denotation to *shoes*, etc.

An analysis which drew no distinction at all between mass nouns and lexical plurals would face several problems: First, there are clear examples of lexical plurals which are not mass, such as *police* and *cattle*. Second, mass nouns and plurals combine with different classes of determiners, and may not give equivalent truth conditions even when they do combine with the same determiner. *Most change is copper* may be understood as claiming that the copper coins exceed the other coins in some measure such as weight or volume, while *Most coins are copper* requires specifically that the total number of copper coins exceeds the number of other coins. Chierchia's proposal addresses challenges like these by allowing that mass nouns are not completely indistinguishable in denotation from plurals: plural nouns hold only of groups and never of individuals, while mass nouns may hold of both. But as pointed out in section 2.1 above, claiming that plural nouns cannot hold of individuals makes the semantics of determiners like *no* problematic; until a solution to this problem is offered, this strategy for representing the mass-count distinction must be regarded as questionable.

A fourth approach to the semantics of mass NPs treats them not as predicates at all, but as singular terms denoting sums. *Water* is not treated as a predicate holding true of all individual portions of water, but instead as something like a name, denoting the sum of all such portions. The inability of mass NPs to combine with numerals can then be explained in the same way as the inability of proper names to combine with numerals: it makes no sense to count a single object, as opposed to a set. The analogy to proper names must not be pushed too far, since proper names normally do not combine with quantifiers, while mass NPs do, including some quantifiers dedicated just to this purpose. But as stressed by Roeper (1983), Lønning (1987), Higginbotham (1994), this approach can explain a number of otherwise puzzling facts about mass quantification, if we assume that the domain of possible mass NP denotations forms a Boolean algebra; see section 3.2 below.

To summarize, each of these strategies for identifying a semantic difference between mass and count NPs faces significant challenges: There are direct counterexamples to the claim that mass NPs denote continuously. Only a subset of mass NPs denote substances. Treating mass NPs as holding of groups and individuals, but plurals only of groups, seems incompatible with the semantics of *no*. And treating mass NPs as names of sums requires an explanation why mass NPs but not names combine with quantifiers.

3 Issues in the denotation of mass and plural DPs

By a "DP" we mean a phrase consisting of an overt or covert determiner, together with an NP, e.g. *that water, a horse*, or *all books written by Mark Twain*. Phrases of this category may serve directly as arguments to a verb or other predicate. In some analyses, NPs may also sometimes serve directly as arguments to predicates, so we include discussion of the semantics of NPs in such analyses here as well.

We consider in turn bare plurals and mass nouns, plural and mass DPs with overt quantificational determiners, and definite and conjoined DPs.

3.1 Bare plurals and mass nouns

As already mentioned in section 1.1, plural and mass nouns are distinguished from singular count nouns in English by their ability to appear bare, and show a parallel alternation in interpretation among existential, generalizing and kind-level readings, depending on the type of predicate with which they combine (see (4) to (6) above).

The starting point for most modern literature on this pattern is Carlson (1977a,b), which argued that bare plurals and mass nouns are interpreted unambiguously as something like proper names of kinds. In this analysis, the existential interpretation exhibited in examples like *Raccoons were stealing my corn* is not due to the internal semantics of the bare NP, but is built into the meaning of the predicate with which it combines: We relate each kind to the "stages" which realize it via a relation R, then represent *steal*, e.g., as $\lambda x \lambda y \exists z[R(y,z) \& steal(z,x)]$. This predicate can then apply to the kind "raccoons" collectively, to yield truth conditions to the effect that there is at least one realization of this kind that was stealing my corn.

Likewise, individual-level predicates like *are sneaky* are analyzed as containing a hidden generic operator G, allowing them to take kinds as arguments while generalizing about the individuals realizing those kinds. *Raccoons are sneaky* may be represented as G(*sneaky*)(r), where G(P)(k) means that instantiations of kind k generally have property P. (Carlson 1989 replaces G with a similar operator taking scope over entire sentences.) Kind-level readings like those in *Raccoons are extinct* result from direct application of the predicate to its argument, with no hidden quantification.

A major argument for this approach is that it correctly predicts that the existential quantifier associated with bare plurals and mass nouns always takes the narrowest possible scope. Thus (15a) has only the reading which allows everyone to have read different books about caterpillars, while (15b) is ambiguous, and admits a reading which requires everyone to have read the same book about caterpillars – an unexpected difference if the bare plural *caterpillars* expressed existential quantification as part of its internal semantics:

(15) a. Everyone read books about caterpillars
     b. Everyone read a book about caterpillars

A second argument comes from the fact that kind-level, individual-level and stage-level predicates can be conjoined to take a single bare plural or mass argument:

(16) Raccoons are widespread, sneaky and have been stealing my corn

If bare plurals were ambiguous between existential, generalizing and collective readings, examples like this would seem to impose conflicting requirements on how to interpret the bare plural subject; but if bare plurals are unambiguously kind-denoting, such examples are expected. The coordinate VP is straightforwardly analyzed as in (17):

(17) $\lambda x[widespread(x) \& G(sneaky)(x) \& \exists y[R(x,y) \& stealing\text{-}my\text{-}corn(y)]]$

A popular alternative analysis, developed in Wilkinson (1991), Krifka & Gerstner-Link (1993) and Diesing (1992), claims that bare plurals and mass nouns are interpreted as plural indefinites when they combine with stage- or individual-level predicates. Indefinites are interpreted as contributing free variables to the semantic representation, with no quantificational force as part of their internal semantics, as in Discourse Representation Theory (Kamp 1981) or File Change Semantics (Heim 1982). The variable contributed by an indefinite may be bound by a quantifier in the surrounding context, such as the adverb *usually* in (18a), to yield truth conditions represented as in (18b):

(18) a. Bears usually have blue eyes
      b. *usually* x (*bear*(x), x has blue eyes)

Or, the variable may be bound by a general operation of existential closure, as in *Raccoons were stealing my corn*. To obtain a generic reading in examples like *Raccoons are sneaky*, it is assumed that the variable is bound by a "generic operator" analogous to an adverb of quantification:

(19) GEN x (*raccoon*(x), x is sneaky)

In Diesing's version of this proposal, it is claimed that existential closure takes place at the level of VP; bare plural or mass subjects of stage-level predicates are VP-internal, hence existentially bound. Subjects of individual-level predicates are VP-external, hence available for binding by the generic operator or other quantifiers. On the assumption that quantificational determiners must scope higher than the existential closure operation on VP, this correctly predicts that the existential quantification associated with bare plurals in examples like (15a) always takes narrow scope.

This approach has an advantage over Carlson's in that it predicts that bare plurals are available for binding by adverbs of quantification, as in (18); such sentences require extra stipulation if bare plurals are unambiguously kind-denoting. But Carlson's analysis has an advantage in predicting the conjoinability of kind-level with stage-level and individual-level predicates, as in (16); if bare plurals combining with stage- and individual-level predicates are indefinite rather than kind-denoting, extra stipulation must be given for these examples.

A syntactic issue regarding bare plurals and mass nouns is whether they are DPs with an implicit determiner, or simply NPs serving directly as arguments to the verb, with no determiner at all, implicit or explicit. If the latter, it may be necessary to allow that NPs may serve as something like names of kinds. This would force a revision to much of our discussion in section 2, where it was assumed that NPs were predicates.

Chierchia (1998a,b) suggests that this is a point of parametric variation among languages: In languages like Chinese or Japanese, NPs are unambiguously kind-denoting, so that all NPs may appear bare. To combine such NPs with a determiner requires application of a predicate-forming operation, whose output, Chierchia suggests, is mass; this predicts that in such languages, NPs cannot be combined directly with numerals, but require classifiers. In contrast, NPs in languages like French are unambiguously predicates and never function as names of kinds; the prediction is that French NPs may not appear without a determiner. Languages like English allow NPs to function both as predicates and as names of kinds, according to whether they are count or mass. Mass nouns may thus appear bare, while (singular) count nouns may not. Plural marking on a count noun serves to form the name of a kind from a predicate, allowing plurals to appear bare as well. See articles 3 [Semantics: Typology, Diachrony and Processing] (Doetjes) *Count/mass distinctions*, 5 [this volume] (Dayal) *Bare noun phrases*, and 8 [this volume] (Carlson) *Genericity* for more discussion.

3.2 Quantified plurals and mass nouns

Plural DPs with quantificational determiners such as *many*, *few*, *most*, etc. differ from singular DPs in allowing quantification over groups. But there appear to be several different kinds of quantification over groups involved, and trying to give a unified account of all of them is a challenge.

First, many plural quantifiers allow a reading which involves existential quantification over groups of a size given by the determiner. With certain quantifiers, this reading is most natural when the determiner heads a partitive construction as in (20a).

(20) a. Most/Many/All of the students gathered in the hallway
 b. ?Most/?Many/?All students gathered in the hallway

(20a) may be paraphrased as "A group consisting of most/many/all of the students gathered in the hallway." Similar readings are available for non-partitive constructions, but at least with some determiners, many speakers find these slightly degraded in comparison to partitives as in (20b). Other determiners allow this reading naturally even in non-partitives:

(21) Fifty/The students gathered in the hallway

Existential quantification over groups of the size given by the determiner gives the wrong results for determiners like *few*, *exactly fifty* and other non-monotone-increasing quantifiers. Sentence (22a) does not mean that at least one group consisting of few students gathered in the hallway, but rather that the total number of students who gathered in the hallway is few; (22b) does not mean that at least one group of exactly fifty students gathered in the hallway, but rather that the total number of students that gathered in the hallway was exactly fifty:

(22) a. Few of the students gathered in the hallway
     b. Exactly fifty students gathered in the hallway

To obtain correct results in examples like these, the determiner should be analyzed as placing a cardinality restriction on the maximal group satisfying both the NP and the predicate, so that *exactly fifty*, e.g., denotes $\lambda X \lambda Y [|\cup(X \cap Y)| = 50]$, where X and Y range over sets of groups.

An interesting observation due to Dowty (1986), made originally with respect to *all* but equally applicable to many other plural determiners, is that they do not combine naturally with predicates expressing pure cardinality:

(23) ??Most/??Many/??All of the students are numerous

Dowty suggests that although predicates like *gather* hold only of groups and not individuals, they have "distributive subentailments" concerning the individual members of those groups. If a group gathers in the hall, individual members of the group must come into the hall and remain there long enough that they are all present at a common time. In contrast, a predicate like *be numerous* carries no non-trivial entailments about the individual members of the groups of which it holds. The determiners in examples like (20a) serve to indicate that the subentailments of the predicate hold of some quantity or proportion of individual members of the group; thus *All of the students gathered in the hallway* requires that each individual student come into the hallway. Because *be numerous* does not carry any distributive subentailments for the determiner to operate on, the sentences in (23) are anomalous.

A different kind of quantification over groups is noted by Link (1987). (24) seems to involve universal quantification over groups of competing companies:

(24) All competing companies have common interests

In this sort of example, the correct results may be obtained straightforwardly by assigning the determiner its usual semantics in Generalized Quantifier Theory and letting plural NPs and VPs denote sets containing groups. We let a group be in the denotation of *competing companies* iff its members are companies in competition with each other, and a group be in the denotation of *have common interests* iff its members have common interests with each other; the determiner *every* indicates that the former set is a subset of the latter.

However, it should be noted that this kind of reading is generally only available when the NP contains a modifier such as *competing* which forces the NP to hold only of groups. Indeed, if neither the NP nor the VP forces a collective reading, most quantifiers, even if morphologically plural, are most naturally interpreted as quantifying simply over individuals:

(25) Most/Few students wrote a good paper

The sentences in (25) mean that a majority/minority of individual students wrote a good paper.

The definite determiner allows a collective reading even without such modification, as do numerals:

(26) The/Three students wrote a good paper

One natural interpretation of the sentences in (26) is that the students collaborated in writing a good paper.

As noted by Scha (1981), if more than one plural quantifier is present in a clause, a reading is available involving "cumulative quantification" (not to be confused with the "cumulative reference" property discussed in section 1, above). (27) has a reading which claims that the total number of Dutch firms that have an American computer is 600 and the total number of American computers owned by a Dutch firm is 5000:

(27) 600 Dutch firms have 5000 American computers

Roberts (1987: 148ff), following unpublished work by Partee, suggests that the cumulative reading is just a special case of an ordinary collective reading in which the predicate takes two groups as arguments, so that (27) means simply a group consisting of 600 Dutch firms stands in the "have" relation to a group of 5000 American computers. But as van der Does (1993: 545) and Schein (1993: 167) point out, this approach does not extend easily to sentences containing monotone decreasing determiners. The correct truth conditions for (28) are not obtained if we interpret the quantifiers according to their standard semantics and assign them scope in the usual way:

(28) Fewer than 600 firms own fewer than 5000 computers

Scha's analysis of this sort of example requires an unusual syntactic analysis in which the two determiners combine to form a "compound numerical": in (27), *600* and *5000* combine to form an expression denoting $\lambda R[|proj_1(R)|=600$ & $|proj_2(R)|=5000]$, where $proj_n$ maps a relation onto the projection of its nth argument place. The two NPs also combine to form a "compound noun," denoting the Cartesian product of the denotations of the NPs which combine: DF×AC. The compound numerical combines with the compound noun to form a complex DP or "noun phrase sequence" denoting $\lambda R[\ |\ proj_1(\{<x,y>\in DF \times AC\ |R(x,y)\})|=600$ & $|proj_2(\{<x,y>\in DF \times AC|R(x,y)\})|=5000]$. This may then combine with the 2-place predicate *own* to give the desired truth conditions. Many semanticists have viewed this proposal as non-compositional, and a variety of subsequent proposals have been made to interpret such sentences while retaining a more intuitive constituency.

One family of analysis uses special mechanisms to pass information up the tree which would be lost in ordinary semantic composition: Van der Does (1992) employs product types to allow access to NP denotations above the level of the DP. Landman (2000) proposes a complex system in which multiple semantic representations are derived in parallel, then combined to form the asserted content of the sentence as a whole; a related analysis is developed in Krifka (1999a). A different family of solutions appeals to branching quantification (Westerståhl 1987, Sher 1990). Schein (1993) uses to a neo-Davidsonian theory of thematic relations: each argument of the verb corresponds to a separate clause in logical form, over which the corresponding quantifier may take scope; the subject and object quantifiers thus remain scopally independent of one another. The choice among these analyses is a major unresolved issue in the semantics of plurality.

Quantified mass DPs generally fall into two patterns: In the first, a bare mass DP combines with a measure phrase or classifier to form a complex count NP, which may then combine with an ordinary count determiner, as in *two liters of water*, *every loaf of bread*, etc. In the second, the mass NP combines directly with a determiner without a measure phrase or classifier, in which case a mass determiner is required: *much water, all bread.*

Measure expressions such as *liter* or *loaf* are most often analyzed in terms of *measure functions*, i.e., functions from individuals to real numbers. As stressed by Lønning (1987), Krifka (1989), Schwarzschild (2002), this kind of quantification requires *additive* measure functions, so that whenever x and y do not overlap, $f(x+y) = f(x)+f(y)$. (Hence **fifty degrees Celsius of water*.)

Where LITER is the function mapping portions of material onto their volume in liters and R relates kinds to their realizations as in section 3.1 above, we may analyze the measure word *liter* as denoting λkλnλx[R(k,x) & LITER(x) = n]. *Two liters of water* will therefore denote λx[R(water,x) & LITER(x) = 2], the set of individuals realizing the kind "water" and measuring two liters. Note that the numeral *two* is not analyzed as a quantificational determiner, but as something more like a proper name denoting the number 2, and serving as an argument of *liter*.

Alternatively, we might treat *liter* as denoting λkλx[R(k,x) & LITER(x) = 1], so that *liters of water* simply denotes the set of 1-liter volumes of water. (This option must probably be available anyway, for examples like *every liter of water*.) We might then allow this to combine with the ordinary determiner *two*; but since every 2-liter volume of water contains many more than two 1-liter volumes of water, this will not give the right results unless we adopt a non-overlap condition, perhaps as part of the pragmatic background.

This use of measure functions is extended to noun classifiers of the kind exemplified in Chinese, Japanese and other East Asian languages in Krifka (1995). Sometimes it is claimed that in these languages, all nouns are mass, since they all must combine with classifiers before they may combine with numerals (Chierchia 1998a,b; Krifka 1999b). However, even in classifier languages, some sort of mass/count distinction is often detectable (Hundius & Kölver 1983, Cheng & Sybesma 1999).

Direct quantification of a mass NP, with no measure phrase or classifier, is possible in English using quantifiers such as *much, little, most*, etc. As noted by Roeper (1983), Lønning (1987), Higginbotham (1994) and others, we do not obtain correct results by treating mass NPs as predicates holding of individual portions of "stuff" as in section 2.2 above, and treating these quantifiers as binding variables ranging over these portions. (29) does not mean that for every x, if x is a portion of phosphorus, then either x is red or x is black, since (29) may be true in the case where some portions are only partly red and partly black.

(29) All phosphorus is either red or black

A related observation, first made by Bunt (1979), is that direct mass quantification normally requires not only the NP, but also the scope of the DP to show cumulative and distributive reference:

(30) Most water is wet/*heavy

Exceptions to this generalization have been noted and discussed by Higginbotham (1994), but these may be regarded as special cases.

Assuming such a restriction, we define a sum operation on the extensions of cumulative, distributive predicates: let σxP(x) denote the sum of all those objects x of which P holds true, providing P refers cumulatively and distributively; undefined otherwise. We apply this sum operation to both the NP and the verbal predicate before combining them with the mass determiner; this treats the determiner as a relation between sums.

Assuming a Boolean part-whole structure on portions, we may now reconstruct the theory of quantification in this Boolean algebra, rather than the power set algebra of the universe of discourse (Roeper 1983, Lønning 1987, Higginbotham 1994). E.g. *all* may be analyzed as holding between two portions x and y iff x is a material part of y, so that *All water is wet* is true iff the sum of all water is a part of the sum of all wet material; *most* may be treated as holding between x and y iff $\mu(x \wedge y) > 1/2\,\mu(x)$, where μ is some pragmatically salient measure function and $\wedge$ is the Boolean meet operation.

3.3 Plural and mass definites and conjunction

A related use of sum operations may be made in the analysis of plural and mass definite DPs and in the analysis of conjoined DPs. An obvious limitation of Russell's (1905) theory of definite descriptions in terms of unique existential quantification is that it does not apply to plural or mass definites: *The horses are in the corral* does not mean that there is exactly one horse; *The coffee is in the room* does not mean that there is exactly one portion of coffee. Yet the fact that the same word *the* is used both with singular count NPs and with mass and plural NPs seems no accident; one would hope for a unified semantics.

An idea suggested by Sharvy (1980) and popularized in the linguistics literature by Link (1983), is to replace the Russellian representation of 'The A is/are B' in (31a) with the representation in (31b), where '≤' indicates the part-whole relation:

(31) a. $\exists x[A(x)\ \&\ \forall y[A(y) \rightarrow x=y]\ \&\ B(x)]$
     b. $\exists x[A(x)\ \&\ \forall y[A(y) \rightarrow y \leq x]\ \&\ B(x)]$

Now *The coffee is in the room* will be true iff there is a maximal portion of coffee, of which all other portions are part, which is in the room. Assuming that the maximal group of horses has its smaller subgroups and members as parts, *The horses are in the corral* will require this maximal group of horses to be in the corral. But on the assumption that no king of France contains another as part, *The king of France is bald* will require the existence of a unique king of France: the Russellian truth conditions fall out as a special case.

The maximality condition imposed in this analysis has the effect that the definite description picks out the sum of the extension of the NP, on the assumption that the NP refers cumulatively. (The sum operation here should not require that the NP have distributive reference, unlike that used at the end of section 3.2.) If one prefers a presuppositional analysis, the definite determiner may be treated as directly expressing the sum operation, so that 'The A is/are B' is represented as in (32):

(32) $B(\sigma x(A(x))$

Then *the A* will be undefined when A is not cumulative, e.g. if it is a singular count noun with more than one element in its extension; the formula is therefore not assigned a truth value, which we consider to be presupposition failure. See article 2 [this volume] (Heim) *Definiteness and indefiniteness* for more discussion.

A related idea is frequently invoked in analysis of conjoined DPs, as in (33):

(33) John and Mary are a happy couple

The conjunction in this sort of example cannot be reduced in any obvious way to sentential conjunction; (33) does not mean "John is a happy couple and Mary is a happy couple." Instead, most analyses treat the coordinate subject *John and Mary* as referring to the group of John and Mary, and let the predicate *are a happy couple* apply to this group collectively.

Perhaps the simplest way to obtain this result is to treat *and* as ambiguous, between the ordinary truth-functional *and* (or some generalization of it across a type hierarchy) and a "group-forming" *and* which maps any two individuals to the group consisting of them. This idea dates to ancient times and is represented in the modern literature by Partee & Rooth (1983) and many others; see Lasersohn (1995) for a historical overview.

A number of complications arise in such an analysis. First, group-forming readings of conjunction are not limited to proper names and other individual-denoting DPs, but also occur with indefinites and other quantificational DPs:

(34) a. A man and a woman own this house
      b. Every student and every professor met to discuss their plans

Hoeksema (1983, 1988) discusses ways to adapt a group-forming conjunction operation into Generalized Quantifier Theory and Discourse Representation Theory to deal with such examples.

Another complication is that group-forming *and* must sometimes be done "in the argument places" of NPs or other predicates, as in (35):

(35) This man and woman are in love

This can be accomplished by a suitable type-theoretical generalization of the group-forming conjunction operation (Lasersohn 1995, Heycock & Zamparelli 2005).

But perhaps the most unsatisfying feature of an analysis which claims that conjunction is ambiguous between truth-functional and group-forming *and* is the claim that *and* is ambiguous at all. The putative ambiguity is too systematic and too common cross-linguistically to be accidental; an analysis should at least make clear what these readings have in common which leads them naturally to be expressed by the same lexical item, and ideally should unify their semantics completely.

Lasersohn (1992, 1995) argues that examples like (36) require that the conjunction be analyzed in terms of a group-forming operation on events, hence that verbal and sentential conjunction in general can be assimilated to group-forming conjunction:

(36) This refrigerator runs alternately too hot and too cold

Winter (2001) argues for an assimilation in the opposite direction, noting that if one treats proper names as generalized quantifiers in type <<e,t>,t> and allows them to conjoin using the cross-categorial generalization of ordinary truth-functional conjunction in the style of Partee & Rooth (1983), then *John and Mary* denotes the set of sets containing John as a member and Mary as a member; the group of John and Mary is recoverable from this set through a simple type-shifting operation. Conjunction itself is therefore treated as unambiguous; the collective reading is obtained by applying this type-shifting operation to the ordinary conjunction of *John* and *Mary*.

4 Collective and distributive readings

An important observation about sentences containing plural or conjoined DPs is that they may be understood either *collectively*, as in (37a) and (38a), or *distributively*, as in (37b) and (38b):

(37) a. Our problems are numerous
 b. The children are asleep
(38) a. John and Mary are a happy couple
 b. John and Mary are asleep

Sentence (37a) means that our problems, taken together as a group, are numerous – no individual problem is numerous – and (38a) means that John and Mary together form a happy couple, not that they each do. In contrast, (37b) entails that the individual children are asleep, not that the group is somehow asleep independently of its members being asleep, and (38b) is interpreted in the same way. The availability of these collective and distributive interpretations depends in large part on the predicate. Certain predicates, such as *be asleep*, cannot hold of a group without holding of its individual members; others, such as *be numerous*, cannot sensibly apply to an individual.

A third class of predicates may apply both to groups (without necessarily applying to their members) and to individuals: *draw a picture*. Sentences containing this third class of predicates may be understood either collectively or distributively; (39) can mean either that each child drew a picture, or that the children collaborated in drawing a picture together:

(39) The children drew a picture

In examples with conjoined plural subjects, a distributive interpretation is possible even with predicates which do not sensibly apply to individuals:

(40) The students and the professors met to discuss the issue

(40) may be understood as meaning either that the students met to discuss the issue, and so did the professors; or that the students met with the professors to discuss the issue.

Examples like (40) suggest that distributive interpretations do not necessarily involve application of a predicate to individuals as opposed to groups; but rather, application to the members of the group denoted by the DP, whether these members are themselves groups or individuals. Returning to an issue raised in section 2.1 above, this supports the idea that group-formation is not associative, since an associative operation does not permit the representation of higher-order groups: Where a and b are the students and c and d are the professors, $((a+b)+(c+d)) = (a+b+c+d)$ if $+$ is associative.

The idea that group-formation is associative has been defended in the face of such examples by Schwarzschild (1992, 1996), who argues that the denotations of plural DPs may be analyzed as always having a "flat" structure if interpretation is relativized to a pragmatically established cover of the group denoted by the DP, following Gillon (1987). (A *cover* of a set S is a set of subsets of S whose union equals S.) In this analysis, a predicate applies to each cell in a pragmatically salient cover of the group denoted by its plural argument. Shoes conventionally come in pairs, so we interpret (41) relative to a cover which divides the set of shoes into matching pairs, yielding a reading that each pair of shoes costs $50, rather than each individual shoe or the group of shoes as a whole:

(41) The shoes cost $50

Describing the group whose members are the individual students and the individual professors using a coordinate DP like *the students and the professors* makes salient a cover of this group which divides it into the group of the students and the group of the professors, so that (40) may be interpreted as meaning that the students met and so did the professors.

It should be noticed that even though a covers-based analysis allows the use of an associative group-formation operation for the denotations of plural DPs, covers themselves have a non-associative structure: {{a}, {b,c}} and {{a, b}, {c}} are both covers of {a, b, c}, but must be distinguished from one another. The need for some technique for representing non-associative groupings seems beyond dispute.

A covers-based analysis generates non-existent readings in some cases (Lasersohn 1989). If John, Mary and Bill are the teaching assistants and earned exactly $7000 each last year, (37) is false, even though each cell in the cover {{John, Mary}, {John, Bill}} earned exactly $14,000:

(42) The teaching assistants earned exactly $14,000 last year

Whether distributive interpretations make reference to covers, or simply involve applying a predicate to each member of the group denoted by its plural argument, the issue arises whether the collective/distributive alternation represents authentic ambiguity, or rather a single reading which is general enough to cover both possibilities. Lasersohn (1995) argues for an ambiguity, based on examples like (43):

(43)   a. John and Mary earned exactly $10,000
       b. John and Mary earned exactly $5000

Suppose John and Mary each earned exactly $5000; then both (43a) and (43b) are true. This is easy to explain if there is an ambiguity, since then (43a) might be true relative to one reading, while (43b) is true relative to the other. But if there is no ambiguity, we face the paradox that there are two distinct amounts, both of which are *the* exact amount which John and Mary earned .

As Roberts (1987) points out, an ambiguity is also helpful in explaining patterns of anaphora. Sentence (44a) may be true in any of three types of situation: ones in which John and Mary collectively lifted a piano, ones in which they each lifted the same piano, and ones in which they each lifted a potentially different piano. But only the first two cases may the sentence be continued as in (44b), where *it* is anaphoric to *a piano*:

(44) a. John and Mary lifted a piano
    b. It was heavy

If the three types of situation in which the sentence is true correspond to formally distinct meanings of the sentence, one can attribute the difference in anaphoric potential to differences in meaning. But if the sentence is assigned just one very general reading, true in any of these three situation types, it is difficult to see how rules governing the distribution of discourse anaphors could be coherently stated. Gillon (1987) provides additional arguments for an ambiguity.

Given that an authentic ambiguity exists, the issue arises where in the sentence it is located. Early analyses often took for granted that DPs were ambiguous between collective and distributive readings, but many analyses now attribute the ambiguity to the predicate. A standard argument for this approach (e.g. Dowty 1986) comes from examples like (45):

(45) John and Mary met in a bar and had a beer

The natural interpretation is that John and Mary met collectively in the bar, but each had a separate beer; if we locate the collective/distributive alternation in the subject DP, this example would seem to impose conflicting requirements on the interpretation of *John and Mary*. But the correct interpretation may be obtained by locating it in the predicates: under its distributive reading, *had a beer* holds of a group iff each of its members had a beer; this predicate may be sensibly conjoined with *met in a bar* to yield a complex predicate applying to the group of John and Mary.

Frequently, distributive readings are attributed to a hidden operator attached to the predicate, following Link (1991) and Roberts (1987); predicates may be ambiguous because this operator may be present or absent. Notated '^{D}', this operator may be defined as in (41), where 'yΠx' means that y is a member of group x:

(46) $^D P = \lambda x \forall y [y \Pi x \rightarrow P(y)]$

See Schwarzschild (1996) for an analogous operator making reference to covers. Lasersohn (1998a) generalizes a similar operator type-theoretically to account for distributivity in non-subject argument places.

A collective reading may be forced by modifying a predicate with an adverbial expression such as *together* or *as a group*. As pointed out by Lasersohn (1990, 1995, 1998b), this presents a problem for analyses in which the extensions of distributive predicates are not distinguishable in principle from the extensions of collective predicates. If John and Mary lifted the piano distributively but not collectively, (47) is false; if they each lifted the piano individually and also lifted it collectively, (47) is true. But in either case, the extension of *lifted the piano* would seem to be the set containing John, Mary and the group of John and Mary – and if the extensions are identical, there is no way for *together* to operate on them differently to provide distinct truth values in the two cases:

(47) John and Mary lifted the piano together

Lasersohn suggests that collective and distributive readings may be extensionally distinguished using a hidden event argument, as in Davidson (1967). An event of John and Mary lifting the piano distributively will be composed of smaller events of John lifting the piano and Mary lifting the piano; an event of John and Mary collectively lifting the piano will not. This allows a definition of *together* as $\lambda P \lambda g \lambda e [P(g)(e) \ \& \ \sim \exists e' \exists x [e' \leq e \ \& \ x \neq g \ \& \ P(x)(e')]]$. For alternative analyses, see Schwarzschild (1994), Moltmann (1997, 2004).

5 References

Anonymous 1952. *Structural Notes and Corpus*. Washington, DC: American Council of Learned Societies.
Black, Max 1971. The elusiveness of sets. *Review of Metaphysics* 24, 614–636.
Bloomfield, Leonard 1933. *Language*. New York: Holt, Rinehart & Winston.
Boolos, George 1984. To be is to be the value of a variable (or to be some values of some variables). *Journal of Philosophy* 81, 430–449.
Boolos, George 1985a. Nominalist Platonism. *Philosophical Review* 94, 327–344.
Boolos, George 1985b. Reading the "Begriffsschrift". *Mind* 94, 331–344.
Bunt, Harry C. 1979. Ensembles and the formal semantic properties of mass terms. In: F. J. Pelletier (ed.). *Mass Terms: Some Philosophical Problems*. Dordrecht: Reidel, 249–277.
Bunt, Harry C. 1985. *Mass Terms and Model-Theoretic Semantics*. Cambridge: Cambridge University Press.
Burge, Tyler 1977. A theory of aggregates. *Noûs* 11, 97–117.
Carlson, Greg 1977a. *Reference to Kinds in English*. Ph.D. dissertation, University of Massachusetts, Amherst, MA.
Carlson, Greg 1977b. A unified analysis of the English bare plural. *Linguistics & Philosophy* 1, 413–457.
Carlson, Greg 1989. On the semantic composition of English generic sentences. In: G. Chierchia, B. Partee & R. Turner (eds.). *Properties, Types and Meaning, vol. II: Semantic Issues*. Dordrecht: Kluwer, 167–192.
Cheng, Chung-Ying 1973. Comments on Moravcsik's paper. In: J. Hintikka, J. Moravcsik & P. Suppes (eds.). *Approaches to Natural Language*. Dordrecht: Reidel, 215–220.
Cheng, Lisa Lai-Shen & Rint Sybesma 1999. Bare nouns and not-so-bare nouns and the structure of NP. *Linguistic Inquiry* 30, 509–542.

Chierchia, Gennaro 1998a. Reference to kinds across languages. *Natural Language Semantics* 6, 339–405.
Chierchia, Gennaro 1998b. Plurality of mass nouns and the notion of "semantic parameter". In: S. Rothstein (ed.). *Events and Grammar*. Dordrecht: Kluwer, 53–103.
Cresswell, Max 1985. Review of F. Landman & F. Veltman (eds.). *Varieties of Formal Semantics* (Dordrecht, 1984). *Linguistics* 23, 626–634.
Davidson, Donald 1967. The logical form of action sentences. In: N. Resher (ed.). *The Logic of Decision and Action*. Pittsburgh, PA: University of Pittsburgh Press, 81–95.
Diesing, Molly 1992. *Indefinites*. Cambridge, MA: The MIT Press.
van der Does, Jaap 1992. *Applied Quantifier Logics: Collectives, Naked Infinitives*. Ph.D. dissertation. University of Amsterdam.
van der Does, Jaap 1993. Sums and quantifiers. *Linguistics & Philosophy* 16, 509–550.
Dowty, David 1986. Collective predicates, distributive predicates, and *all*. In: F. Marshall (ed.). *Proceedings of the Third Eastern States Conference in Linguistics* (= ESCOL '86). Columbus, OH: Ohio State University, 97–115.
Gillon, Brendan 1987. The readings of plural noun phrases in English. *Linguistics & Philosophy* 10, 199–219.
Gillon, Brendan 1992. Toward a common semantics for English count and mass nouns. *Linguistics & Philosophy* 15, 597–639.
Gleason, Henry Allen 1955. *An Introduction to Descriptive Linguistics*. New York: Holt, Rinehart & Winston.
Heim, Irene 1982. *The Semantics of Definite and Indefinite Noun Phrases*. Ph.D. dissertation. University of Massachusetts, Amherst, MA. Reprinted: Ann Arbor, MI: University Microfilms.
Heycock, Caroline & Roberto Zamparelli 2005. Friends and colleagues: Plurality, coordination, and the structure of DP. *Natural Language Semantics* 13, 201–270.
Higginbotham, James 1994. Mass and count quantifiers. *Linguistics & Philosophy* 17, 447–480.
Hoeksema, Jack 1983. Plurality and conjunction. In: A. ter Meulen (ed.). *Studies in Modeltheoretic Semantics*. Dordrecht: Foris, 63–84.
Hoeksema, Jack 1988. The semantics of non-Boolean 'and'. *Journal of Semantics* 6, 19–40.
Hundius, Harald & Ulrike Kölver 1983. Syntax and semantics of numeral classifiers in Thai. *Studies in Language* 7, 165–214.
Jespersen, Otto 1913. *A Modern English Grammar on Historical Principles, Part II: Syntax (1st vol.)*. London: Allen & Unwin.
Jespersen, Otto 1924. *The Philosophy of Grammar*. New York: W.W. Norton & Co.
Kamp, Hans 1981. A theory of truth and semantic representation. In: J. Groenendijk, T. Janssen & M. Stokhof (eds.). *Formal Methods in the Study of Language*. Amsterdam: Mathematical Centre, 277–322.
Krifka, Manfred 1989. Nominal reference, temporal constitution, and quantification in event semantics. In: R. Bartsch, J. van Benthem & P. van Emde Boas (eds.). *Semantics and Contextual Expression*. Dordrecht: Foris, 75–115.
Krifka, Manfred 1995. Common nouns: A contrastive analysis of Chinese and English. In: G. Carlson & F. Pelletier (eds.). *The Generic Book*. Chicago, IL: The University of Chicago Press, 398–411.
Krifka, Manfred 1999a. At least some determiners aren't determiners. In: K. Turner (ed.). *The Semantics/Pragmatics Interface from Different Points of View*. Amsterdam: Elsevier, 257–291.

Krifka, Manfred 1999b. Mass expressions. In: K. Brown & J. Miller (eds.). *Concise Encyclopedia of Grammatical Categories*. Amsterdam: Elsevier, 221–223.

Krifka, Manfred & Claudia Gerstner-Link 1993. Genericity. In: J. Jacobs et al. (eds.). *Syntax: Ein internationales Handbuch zeitgenössischer Forschung—An International Handbook of Contemporary Research* (HSK 9.1) Berlin: de Gruyter, 966–978.

Landman, Fred 1989a. Groups I. *Linguistics & Philosophy* 12, 559–605.

Landman, Fred 1989b. Groups II. *Linguistics & Philosophy* 12, 723–744.

Landman, Fred 2000. *Events and Plurality*. Dordrecht: Kluwer.

Lasersohn, Peter 1989. On the readings of plural noun phrases. *Linguistic Inquiry* 20, 130–134.

Lasersohn, Peter 1990. Group action and spatio-temporal proximity. *Linguistics & Philosophy* 13, 179–206.

Lasersohn, Peter 1992. Generalized conjunction and temporal modification. *Linguistics & Philosophy* 13, 381–410.

Lasersohn, Peter 1995. *Plurality, Conjunction and Events*. Dordrecht: Kluwer.

Lasersohn, Peter 1998a. Generalized distributivity operators. *Linguistics & Philosophy* 21, 83–93.

Lasersohn, Peter 1998b. Events in the semantics of collectivizing adverbials. In: S. Rothstein (ed.). *Events and Grammar*. Dordrecht: Kluwer, 273–292.

Laycock, Henry 2006. *Words without Objects: Semantics, Ontology, and Logic for Non-Singularity*. Oxford: Clarendon Press.

Link, Godehard 1983. The logical analysis of plural and mass terms: A lattice-theoretical approach. In: R. Bäuerle, Ch. Schwarze & A. von Stechow (eds.). *Meaning, Use and Interpretation of Language*. Berlin: de Gruyter, 302–323.

Link, Godehard 1984. Hydras. In: F. Landman & F. Veltman (eds.). *Varieties of Formal Semantics*. Dordrecht: Foris, 245–257.

Link, Godehard 1987. Generalized quantifiers and plurals. In: P. Gärdenfors (ed.). *Generalized Quantifiers: Linguistic and Logical Approaches*. Dordrecht: Reidel, 151–180.

Link, Godehard 1991. Plural. In: A. von Stechow & D. Wunderlich (eds.). *Semantik—Semantics. Ein internationales Handbuch der zeitgenössischen Forschung—An International Handbook of Contemporary Research* (HSK 6). Berlin: de Gruyter, 418–440.

Lønning, Jan Tore 1987. Mass terms and quantification. *Linguistics & Philosophy* 10, 1–52.

McCawley, James 1975. Lexicography and the count-mass distinction. In: *Proceedings of the Annual Meeting of the Berkeley Linguistics Society (=BLS) 1*. Berkeley, CA: Berkeley Linguistics Society, 314–321.

Moltmann, Friederike 1997. *Parts and Wholes in Semantics*. Oxford: Oxford University Press.

Moltmann, Friederike 2004. The semantics of *together*. *Natural Language Semantics* 12, 289–318.

Nicolas, David 2008. Mass nouns and plural logic. *Linguistics & Philosophy* 31, 211–244.

Ojeda, Almerindo 2005. The paradox of mass plurals. In: S. S. Mufwene, E. J. Francis & R. S. Wheeler (eds.). *Polymorphous Linguistics: Jim McCawley's Legacy*. Cambridge, MA: The MIT Press, 389–410.

Partee, Barbara & Mats Rooth 1983. Generalized conjunction and type ambiguity. In: R. Bäuerle, Ch. Schwarze & A. von Stechow (eds.). *Meaning, Use and Interpretation of Language*. Berlin: de Gruyter, 361–383.

Payne, John & Rodney Huddleston 2002. Nouns and noun phrases. In: R. Huddleston & G. Pullum (eds.). *The Cambridge Grammar of the English Language*. Cambridge: Cambridge University Press, 323–523.

Pelletier, Francis Jeffry 1975. Non-singular reference: Some preliminaries. *Philosophia* 5, 451–465.
Quine, Willard van Orman 1960. *Word and Object*. Cambridge, MA: The MIT Press.
Roberts, Craige 1987. *Modal Subordination and Pronominal Anaphora in Discourse*. Ph.D. dissertation. University of Massachusetts, Amherst, MA.
Roeper, Peter 1983. Semantics for mass terms with quantifiers. *Noûs* 17, 251–265.
Russell, Bertrand 1905. On denoting. *Mind* 14, 479–493.
Sauerland, Uli, Jan Andersen & Kazuko Yatsushiro 2005. The plural is semantically unmarked. In: S. Kepser & M. Reis (eds.). *Linguistic Evidence: Empirical, Theoretical and Computational Perspectives*. Berlin: Mouton de Gruyter, 413–434.
Scha, Remko 1981. Distributive, collective and cumulative quantification. In: J. Groenendijk, T. Janssen & M. Stokhof (eds.). *Formal Methods in the Study of Language 2*. Amsterdam: Mathematical Centre, 483–512.
Schein, Barry 1993. *Plurals and Events*. Cambridge, MA: The MIT Press.
Schwarzschild, Roger 1992. Types of plural individuals. *Linguistics & Philosophy* 15, 641–675.
Schwarzschild, Roger 1994. Plurals, presuppositions and the sources of distributivity. *Natural Language Semantics* 2, 201–248.
Schwarzschild, Roger 1996. *Pluralities*. Dordrecht: Kluwer.
Schwarzschild, Roger 2002. The grammar of measurement. In: B. Jackson (ed.). *Proceedings of Semantics and Linguistic Theory (= SALT) XII*. Ithaca, NY: Cornell University, 225–245.
Sharvy, Richard 1980. A more general theory of definite descriptions. *Philosophical Review* 89, 607–624.
Sher, Gila 1990. Ways of branching quantifiers. *Linguistics & Philosophy* 13, 393–422.
Sweet, Henry 1892. *A New English Grammar, Logical and Historical*. Oxford: Clarendon Press.
Westerståhl, Dag 1987. Branching generalized quantifiers and natural language. In: P. Gärdenfors (ed.). *Generalized Quantifiers: Linguistic and Logical Approaches*. Dordrecht: Kluwer, 269–298.
Whorf, Benjamin Lee 1941. The relation of habitual thought and behavior to language. In: L. Spier (ed.). *Language, Culture and Personality: Essays in Memory of Edward Sapir*. Menasha, WI: Sapir Memorial Publication Fund, 75–93.
Wilkinson, Karina 1991. *Studies in the Semantics of Generic Noun Phrases*. Ph.D. dissertation. University of Massachusetts, Amherst, MA.
Winter, Yoad 2001. *Flexibility Principles in Boolean Semantics: The Interpretation of Coordination, Plurality, and Scope in Natural Language*. Cambridge, MA: The MIT Press.

Gregory Carlson
8 Genericity

1. Preliminaries —— 232
2. Sentential genericity —— 234
3. Generic reference —— 247
4. Rationale for generic reference —— 251
5. What types of English DP's can have generic interpretations? —— 254
6. Generic quantification —— 258
7. What types of DP's can express generic reference across languages? —— 259
8. Indefinite singulars —— 264
9. If there are genera, what are they? —— 266
10. References —— 269

Abstract: Generic and habitual sentences are how natural language expresses regularities, laws, generalizations, habits, dispositions, etc. One example would be "Bears eat honey." They are opposed in concept to episodic sentences, whose truth conditions concern whether or not an event of a given type occurs or fails to occur in a world of evaluation, whether as singular events or quantified over. An example would be "Some bears are eating some honey". Generic sentences often include as a part a generic noun phrase such as "bears" whose denotation is argued to be a kind of thing, rather than being some quantification over individuals. This article reviews the recent conclusions and points of contention in both how noun phrases are represented in a semantics, and how the semantics of full sentences is to be represented.

1 Preliminaries

Genericity is a phenomenon whereby generalizations are expressed by sentences that typically abstract over events, situations, etc. So if one says

(1) Bears eat honey.

one is saying something to the effect that there is a strong tendency for this type of situation – one where a bear or some bears are eating some honey – to recur, without direct reference to any particular such situation. Opposed to genericity

---

Gregory Carlson, Rochester, NY, United States

https://doi.org/10.1515/9783110589443-008

are sentences that talk directly about the particular situations themselves as in (2) below:

(2) This morning, a bear ate some honey.

Such *episodic* examples (to use a term originally suggested by Gennaro Chierchia) talk non-generically about what occurred, and not about generalizing over such occurrences.

There is another side to genericity as well. In uttering a sentence like (1), there is the intuition that one is doing something more than generalizing over situations; one is also somehow generalizing over bears as well, discussing them "as a class", without reference to any particular bears, unlike the example found in (2). It is common to understand examples such as (1) as discussing some distinctive characteristic that is attributed to "all" bears. Krifka (in collaboration with C. Gerstner) (1987) distinguishes these two faces of genericity terminologically, referring to the generalization over situations, events, etc., that have to do with sentence semantics ("IP" semantics) as *I-genericity*. The reference to things "as a class", without discussion of particular individuals, is *D-genericity* (involving the semantics of generic DP's), a property of noun phrase meanings, and not entire sentences. While these two sides of the phenomenon of genericity often cooccur, they are separable not only in this intuitive way, but also empirically, since each may occur without the other.

We can distinguish these different faces of genericity by examining a few examples. There are versions of a sentence like (1) where all of the noun phrases in the sentence (henceforth, DP's for "determiner phrases") almost certainly refer to individuals of an ordinary sort. So, in an example like (3), the DP's refer to specific individuals (John, his office, and Elm Street), yet the sentence expresses a generalization:

(3) John drives to his office via Elm Street.

Such examples would commonly be described at talking about a habit or propensity of John's. While such sentences may only have individuals referred to in its noun phrases, they are unlike similar examples such as (2) in that they still report something more general. Examples like (3) are often called "habitual" sentences in the descriptive literature (though their semantic range is much wider than discussion of habits alone), and the term "generic" is then sometimes reserved for examples such as (1), in which a D-generic expression also appears, typically as sentence subject. In this work, however, habituality is going to be considered a type of genericity, so that (3) is also a "generic' sentence.

The difference between examples (1) and (3) is that (1) contains as its subject a bare plural DP, which expresses a general term "bears" (as well as the general term "honey" in the direct object position), which is over and above the genericity originating from the sentence itself. Thus, we have on the one hand what the sentence contributes – something like the habituality as in (3) – and what the general noun phrases introduce in addition to the dimension of (3), both occurring in (1).

This contribution of D-genericity alone can be witnessed by placing general terms in the context of episodic examples (such as (2)), in which the generalizing character of the sentence as a whole is absent. Consider an example of a sentence exhibiting the "avant-garde" reading of generic DP's (Krifka et al. 1995):

(4) a. *The potato* was first cultivated in South America.
    b. *Potatoes* were first cultivated in South America.

These examples are about potatoes in general, and not about any particular potato or potatoes. The implicit comparison drawn by the adverb "first" is when potatoes – again, not any particular potatoes – were cultivated at another time, and makes the assertion that of all those instances of potato-cultivation, the initial instance in South America occurred earlier than all others. It is not that similar examples cannot be about particular individuals. We easily say things like "Einstein first visited Princeton in 1953" about particulars, but example (4) is not about particulars on the only sensible reading of the examples. The particular type of example in (4) is not some isolated instance; many other types of sentences might have been employed to illustrate the same point about the independence of D-genericity.

Research on genericity has for the most part dealt with both sentence-meaning (I-generic) and noun phrase meaning (D-generic) more or less side by side. We will, however, continue make a somewhat artificial division between the two and discuss them separately. We will first discuss the sentence semantics required for I-genericity, and then return to the semantics of generic non phrases (D-genericity) a little later on.

2 Sentential genericity

2.1 Bases for generalization in the semantics

The central problem of generic sentences as currently framed by research is understanding the relationship between an underlying set of instances or particulars, and the overall generalization expressed by the sentence. So, for instance, in (1) the underlying instances might be some bears eating some honey, and the overarching generalization would be what is expressed by the sentence, perhaps some propensity bears have. In (3) it is, perhaps, instances of John driving to work via Elm St., and the generalization is something about the habit of John's the sentence expresses.

Since the early semantic work of Lawler (1973), determining the truth conditions of the whole sentence based upon something about the occurrence of the instances has persisted as the framing of the problem, much in the same way as the problem of induction is framed. The central representational claim is that the type of instances from which a generic generalization is derived forms a component of the interpretation of the sentence itself. By this, I intend that a generic/habitual such as "John wears a hat" is based upon instances of hat wearings by John, and that the sentence structure contains parts whose denotation is hat-wearing events by John, which forms the *base* for the generalization. Events (using the term in its general sense, i.e. to include processes, states, accomplishments, etc.) serve as the base for all habitual sentences.

However, in a sentence such as "Horses have manes," the base for the generalization is not such an event, but rather an instance of a given, particular horse being in the state of having a mane; for "Giraffes are tall" it is an instance of a giraffe being tall, etc. In these cases, the statement about the individual (having a mane, being tall, etc.) does not readily appear to be a habitual generalization based upon an event instance.

In many instances of generic sentences, there is a double generalization involved. Take an example like "Lions eat meat." This is at once a generalization about lions, based upon instances of individual lions being meat-eaters, and also, a habitual generalization over individual lions, with the base being events of eating meat by an individual lion. The claim seems to be that lions, in the first generalization, are individuals that, in the second generalization, engage "habitually" in events of eating meat. Whether there are "direct" generalizations between non-individual subjects such as "lions" and habitual events that dispense with the intermediate generalization based on individual properties remains unclear. Carlson (1979) suggests some possible instances, but we set aside such cases for the present, as most generics with a habitual base appear to be double generalizations.

We can see the effects of this generalization structure, which includes as a part the base for the generalization within the compositional semantics of the sentences. This can perhaps be most clearly seen in sentences involving anaphora. Consider example (5):

(5) Bob's cat Fred eats his evening snack and *then* sharpens his claws.

Suppose this is a habit Fred the Cat has that has persisted for years, say. Clearly, the meaning of the sentence takes as its base particular event-pairs, one is an eating by Fred, and the other an ensuing sharpening of claws. It is the pair that forms the base for the generalization. *Then* makes anaphoric reference to a particular instance of eating, and situates a particular event of claw-sharpening after it. So then the base of the generalization is a pair of events e_1, e_2 such that $e_1 < e_2$. Were the episodic event structure not within the compositional semantics of the sentence, such a straightforward analysis of *then* in this sentence would not be possible. The claim is, however, that it is operating in exactly the same way it does in (6).

(6) Fred ate his evening snack and then sharpened his claws.

At the level of individual properties being generalized over, such cases as (7) are commonly found:

(7) Mammals tend to *their own* young.

The base of the generalization to mammals here is a property of tending to an individual's young (x tends to x's own young). There needs to be an anaphoric connection drawn between an instance in the subject position of the base, and the pronoun, an individual mammal. Again, if there were no substructure encoding the base for the generalization in the semantics, the interpretation of "their" would be unclear. However, on the analysis suggested it is interpreted as it would be in a nongeneric.

This generalization structure from events or individual instances can easily accommodate cases of event modification. For instance, in (8):

(8) In cooking, Sam tastes the soup *just once*.

If we assume that this has no generalization structure in its semantics, it is hard to make sense of what 'just once' is modifying. After all, one might reason, we are discussing here something like a habit of Sam's, something which by its very nature recurs repeatedly, so there are many tastings, not just one. However, given a generalization structure within the semantics of the sentence, this becomes a relatively straightforward case of event modification within the episodic base of the generalization, so we get the intended sense that there is just one tasting per soup-making event.

This generalization structure also can give rise to scoping effects, depending upon what we take the base to be. Take an example such as (9):

(9) Sam took out Sarah and then took out Mindy.

Understood as a past generalization (the past tense in English usually allows a very salient episodic reading in addition), the sentence can be understood in two ways. One is the more plausible interpretation that Sam dated Sarah for a time, and, after he took her out on dates no more, took Mindy out on dates. Here, there are two generalizations attributed to Sam, and the temporal order of when the generalizations held is indicated by "then". There is, however, another reading, where on a given evening, Sam's habit was to, say, take out Sarah, and then having taken her home, go get Mindy and take her out on that same evening. We might schematically represent the situation in this way:

> Reading 1: Sam (Gen: take out S) & then (Gen: take out M)
> Reading 2: Sam (Gen: take out S & then take out M)

On the level of generalizations from individual properties, we find similar effects. Consider (10):

(10) Stoves use just one type of fuel.

This can be construed as saying there are different types of stoves, each using a single fuel (wood, coal, gas, etc); or it can be understood as saying, contrary to reality, that there is just one type of fuel that stoves use (e.g. wood but not coal, gas, etc). It depends on whether the quantifier 'one' is within the scope of the generalization (in which case, a given stove uses just one type, but fuel type can vary from stove to stove), or outside the generalization (there is just one type, x, such that stoves use x). A somewhat more complex example of scoping is suggested by Schubert & Pelletier (1987):

(11) Storks have a favorite nesting area.

Allowing for the fact that 'favorite' requires implicit indexing, this could either be a generalization about a given individual stork's favorite area (in which case, there are many such areas), or about the fact that there is a favorite nesting area for storks in general, outside the generalization, and hence the reading that there is only one such area (with "favorite" implicitly indexed to one thing, the kind storks).

A generalization structure of this sort also allows for a natural account of "modal subordination" type phenomena (Roberts 1989). Roberts examines sentences in which overt modals appear, which allow for subsequent pronominal reference to intensional entities. An example is (12):

(12) A thief <u>might</u> break into the house. *He* <u>would</u> steal the silverware. (Cf: #He is/was wearing a hat.)

The presence of the modal permits the subsequent sentence to be interpreted as modally subordinate to the first proposition, allowing for such reference in intension. Absence of modals (without supplanting them with other intensional operators) results in a lack of anaphoric reference by subsequent pronouns. Schubert (1999) and Carlson & Spejewski (1997) argue that modal subordination structure appear with generalizations as well.

(13) On weekends, John catches fish. He eats *them* fried in butter. (#We are eating *them* now).

We now examine in a little more detail questions about how a given generic sentence is composed, and then consider the difficult question of what the semantics of the result of that composition is supposed to be. We will then turn to the question of generic reference, where we focus on the character of generic noun phrases themselves.

2.2 The generic operator

Kuroda (1972) discusses two types of sentences that he calls "categorical judgments" and "*thetic* judgments" (see also Sasse 1987). The difference between the two is that categorical judgments involve a two-part structure, similar to a topic/focus kind of arrangement: of *that* one says *this*. Thetic judgments have only a single part structure (*this holds*). While the aims of Kuroda's work do not directly include a comprehensive semantics for generic sentences, in retrospect an asymmetry reveals itself. Most, nearly all, instances of generic and habitual sentences would naturally be analyzed as categorical judgments; nearly all natural instances of thetic judgments are episodic sentences, though categorical judgment analysis applies commonly to them as well.

The same general idea--that generics have a two-part structure--emerges in the Krifka et al. (1995) framework that has provided a setting for much work on genericity to date. The task in analyzing the semantics of a generic is to provide a means of identifying two distinct pieces of the interpretation, and then relating them to one another "appropriately" (a matter we turn to in the next section). In the simplest cases, it is fairly clear that the two parts are the subject, and the predicate:

(14) a. Birds fly.
    b. John smokes.
    c. Ravens are black.

In Carlson (1977a and elsewhere), this subject-predicate form led to an analysis whereby there was a "generic operator" posited that had the effect of mapping episodic predicates (in the analysis, "stage-level predicates") to their habitual counterparts. So the habitual sentence (14b), setting aside tenses and intensions, would have the form

Gn(smoke)(j)

while the nongeneric counterpart (again, setting aside tense and intensions) would be the expected

smoke(j)

This analysis makes the implicit claim that habituals and generics are more complex semantically than their episodic counterparts.

However, it is very clear that, even just examining English, the subject-predicate form, while perhaps the most common, is by no means privileged. Consider a case from Carlson (1988), due to Barbara Partee:

(15) A computer computes the daily weather forecast.

Typically, a generic sentence with an indefinite singular subject says something vaguely "definitional" about the subject (Cohen 2001; Greenberg 2003).

(16) A triangle has three sides.

(15) however is not a generalization about computers. It is instead a generalization about the daily weather forecast (that it is created by a computer model), despite the noun phrase appearing in direct object position of the sentence, and not the subject. Further, what the generalization is about need not be an argument noun phrase at all. Consider the 'when' clause in (17):

(17) When a crack appears in a ceiling, a handyman should fill it in.

This is not a generalization about cracks, ceilings, or handymen, but about times or situations where a crack appears, roughly, the contents of the 'when' clause.

In the past couple of decades, it has been common to account for genericity by positing a covert generic operator which takes sentential scope and has the logical form of an adverb of quantification, akin to "usually, generally, often" etc, as was originally argued for in Farkas & Sugioka (1983). The analysis presented in Krifka et al. (1995), due in main to Krifka (1987), posits an operator GEN that, like a quantificational adverb, takes two arguments (a restrictor, and a matrix or nuclear scope), whose contents is largely determined by the two parts of the sentence identified. The nuclear scope is the portion that functions as the base for the generalization. In the rendering, the analysis is situated within a version of the theory of indefinites derived from DRT and related work (Kamp 1981, Heim 1982) which included unselective binding, and a general theory of tripartite operators that encompassed a range of quantificational or quantification-like operators (e.g. determiners, frequency adverbs, modals, focus operators, etc.; Partee 1992, 1995).

In the simplest cases, the representation of restrictor and matrix (or base) is fairly straightforward. (16) above, with a subject-predicate structure, comes out as:

GEN(triangle x; x has three sides)

GEN is to be understood provisionally as something like a universal that allows exceptions; it binds free variables within its scope unselectively. One might paraphrase this formula as saying that *generally*, if something is a triangle, it has three sides. Taking some technical liberties, (15) would be perhaps represented thus:

GEN(daily weather forecast x; ∃y computer y & y compute x)

In some instances, portions of the contents of the restrictor need to be drawn from context. Consider the simple case of "Daffy flies", where Daffy is a duck. This is, as you recall, a generalization over events, or situations. But this does not mean anything like "Daffy is generally flying", so one needs to narrow down the set of situations considered to achieve anything like universality-with-exceptions. Let us use the symbol "F" to pick out those situations in which it is appropriate/expected of Daffy (d) that he'll be flying, and add that information to the restrictor. We arrive at a representation that stands a decent chance of being an adequate analysis.

GEN(s is a d-situation & F(s); d flies in s)

There is ample precedent for this extra contents attributed to the restrictor coming from context. To mention just one instance, the domain of interpretation for quantifiers is just one such example (e.g. saying "Everyone is in the elevator" in a given situation clearly restricts the interpretation to a smallish number of all people). See also von Fintel (1994) for discussion of contextual restriction on frequency adverbs in particular.

One issue that arises almost immediately is the status of "individual-level" predicates that are not based upon generalizations over events (or event-like instances). Intuitively, the same type of considerations that go into classifying "Birds fly" as a generic also apply equally well to sentences such as the following:

(18) a. Ravens are black.
b. Houses are expensive.
c. Bears are mammals.

On the one hand, such examples could easily be represented by:

GEN(Raven(x); Black(x))

The question this gives rise to is why such sentences need to have a GEN operator in them to combine subject and predicate. In the theoretical setting of the Krifka et al. (1995) formulation, one would have also expected an existential reading for these, which simply does not occur – examples like those in (18) are unambiguous. It appears that matters of topicality and information structure more generally must be taken into account. One line of research that offered promise is Diesing's (1992) "Mapping Hypothesis," which applies to generics as a special case and offers insight into how such a division might take place. Diesing argues that there are two positions subject noun phrases can appear in, one being internal to the predicate of the sentence ("VP-internal"), and the other being in a higher position, outside the sentence predicate. The higher position is the one reserved for generic subjects, and the lower one for weakly-interpreted noun phrases. Jäger (2001) makes use of this difference in positions in assessing the distinction between individual-level and stage-level predicates. He concludes that topicality is actually the feature associated with the upper subject position, and that individual-level predicates require their subjects to be topics. Chierchia (1995) offers a slightly different approach in which he argues that individual level predicates such as those in (18) have as a part of their lexical meanings a GEN operator which binds, within the lexical semantics, situation or event-type variables. In any event, it is common to posit a generic operator for examples such as (18) as well as for event-based instances like (15), and it is the perspective we will take in much of what follows.

That a GEN operator would appear with individual-level predicate examples such as (18) is by no means the only alternative out there. For example, Dayal

(2004) presents a framework in which the attribution of predicates like "be black" or "be a mammal" to bare plural and other kind-denoting expressions takes place via type-shifting of the predicate, which has correlated semantic effects.

One feature of the framework, as well as the Krifka et al. (1995) analysis, is that more than one element from the sentence may be "extracted" to form a part of the restrictor. Krifka (1987) considers examples that have been observed to be ambiguous between an "existential" and "universal" reading (Lawler 1973; Dahl 1975). The following sentence is intuitively ambiguous:

(19) John drinks beer.

On the one hand, the sentence can be understood as saying that John has a beer-drinking habit; on the other, it can be understood to intend a willingness of John to drink beer on a given occasion (it might be said in considering, for instance, what to offer for beverages when John drops over). Krifka offers two potential analyses for (19) positing a single unambiguous GEN operator that derives the two readings by varying the contents of the restrictor and matrix.

The GEN analysis is both rich and complex, interacting with the context, information structure, and subtleties of the syntax in a variety of ways. While the details of various analyses that have employed the GEN operator may be called into question, it is currently a reasonably secure claim that there is *some* kind of operator akin to GEN in generic sentences; this holds despite the fact that the GEN operator does not have a direct and fully consistent morphological/phonetic realization in English or any languages that have been studied extensively to date (though many languages do have "habitual" markers, and other correlated phenomena, see Filip & Carlson 1997). The primary area of contention has to do with what a generic sentence means, and we now turn to considering that question.

2.3 The meaning of a generic

In considering the semantics of generics, it is important to bear in mind the distinction between quantification and (generic) generalization. Perhaps it is best to begin with an example, a variant of an example from Dahl (1975) intended to illustrate much the same point.

(20) All of John's friends are leftists.

The sentence has two readings. On one reading, perhaps the more prominent, if a, b, and c are all the friends John has, then the sentence is true just in case a, b, and c are leftists, and false in case one or more of them is not. Let's call this the quantificational reading. There is another reading besides, as Dahl notes. This is the one that would be used to speak about how John chooses his friends – he likes to make friends with leftists. This entails the quantificational reading, but is a stronger statement that goes beyond the present circumstances, placing a constraint on what it takes to be a friend of John's. Without putting too fine a point on it, we're generalizing about John's friends, bringing into play not only real but potential friends. We'll call this the generalization reading. Note that the generalization reading (in this instance) does involve quantification, but it involves something more, namely, the generalizing on top of the quantification. The basic structure of the quantificational reading is, I will take it, characterized by generalized quantifier theory (Barwise & Cooper 1981; Keenan & Stavi 1986, among others). It is a very specific type of relation between sets. Its most prominent feature is that it is extensional. No truth conditions specified in generalized quantifier theory depend on anything other than the relevant two sets.

Generalizing, however, is intensional in character, since it "goes beyond" the sample in the extension. This is what makes it so difficult to evaluate the truth or falsity of a generic generalization; it's because the truth or falsity lies beyond the reach of the present circumstance one has access to. This makes generics different from accidental generalizations. Cohen (1999) asks us to imagine that, by some quirk, all Supreme Court justices of the United States to date who have been assigned social security numbers, have had even social security numbers. While it is true that "All supreme court justices have even SSN's", it seems intuitively false to claim that "Supreme court justices have even SSN's," since the latter suggests, contrary to supposition, that it is no accident. If one were, somehow, to discover that there was a way of assigning such numbers that systematically resulted in this assignment of even numbers (that, say, all federal employees are given even numbers), then our intuitions would change, as the generalization would "go beyond" the present sample.

In examples of sentences with bare plural subjects, the "quantificational" reading, consistent with accidental arrangements, is missing, leaving only the generalization reading.

(21) Socialists are leftists.

The reason the quantificational reading is missing is simply, many believe, that there is no quantifier in the sentence at all, so in such cases we are directly observing the effects of generalization without additional quantification. However, it should be pointed out that some English quantifiers favor a generalization reading. For instance, "all" with a simple noun following favors a generalization environment, whereas 'every' is more neutral.

(22) a. ?All men are here. vs. All men are mortal.
      b. Every man is here. vs. Every man is mortal.

So certain quantifier expressions and generalization may be closely associated—this seems particularly so in the case of frequency adverbs functioning quantificationally.

(23) John's friends are always leftists.

The meaning of (23) corresponds to just the generalization reading of (20).

The initial instinct in analyzing examples like (24) is to treat them as generalizations involving universal quantification (this is stock in trade in introductory symbolic logic books, especially). While more sophisticated treatments may salvage a role for universal quantification, the straightforward truth conditions of an example like (24) are simply misrepresented by such quantification.

(24) Birds fly. $\neq \forall x\, (Bx \rightarrow Fx)$

The basic problem is that generics tolerate exceptions (and at times seemingly lots of them). If elephants are huge, then an occasional small elephant does not challenge the generalization about their size. However, treating exceptions as indicative of a weaker quantificational treatment will simply not work in any simple way. Most summaries of work on generics provide an overview of the challenges any theory faces which pins genericity on finding some adequate substitute for the universal quantifier, including Carlson (1977a,b), Schubert & Pelletier (1987), Krifka et al. (1995), Cohen (1999, 2002), Greenberg (2003). Delfitto (2002, ch. 4) provides extensive arguments from a syntax/semantics interface point of view that a quantificational analysis is going to be inadequate. One particular technical issue any proposed generic quantifier faces (whether as a nominal determiner or as a frequency adverbial) is that, unlike other quantifiers, it is not *conservative* (Barwise & Cooper 1981); see Cohen (1999, 53–54) for one exposition.

To sum up the arguments, no matter what quantifier one selects, counterexamples are easy to generate. For instance, if one considers that "more than half" is criterial, then (25), which is plausibly considered true, would be false, and (26) normally considered false, would be true.

(25) Mammals give live birth. (The males, the young, and some females do not.)

(26) Sea turtles die at a young age. (Most are eaten by predators upon hatching.)

This has turned researchers towards analyzing generics in terms of intensional notions, rather than quantificational terms. Psychological notions such as prototypes would appear to hold some promise since, if modeled in a formal semantics they would have the appropriate intensionality. However, it is not presently clear how to integrate these insights into a fully combinatorial semantics, nor does the approach seem to offer a ready path towards the understanding of habitual sentences. One notion discussed in ter Meulen (1986) takes generics to be constraints on situations, that is, determinants of what the contents of any given situation might be. Barwise & Seligman (1994) develop an approach based upon notions about how information is transmitted ("channel theory") to provide an account of natural regularities. Another notion, inherited from computer science, is that of a *default* (Reiter 1980), and suggestions that generics be analyzed in this way go back at least to Platteau (1980). Intuitively, a default is what occurs if nothing special happens instead (the default then becomes the "normal" or "expected" case). Analyzing a system of such defaults and applying it to reasoning results in a non-monotonic logic. In such a system, the intensionality is indirectly represented by the inheritance being defined among categories in a system, with the categories understood as intensional objects like properties (i.e. not defined by their extensions). Such systems are known and have been explored for treating generics (see Asher & Morreau 1995, Pelletier & Asher 1997 for overviews). However, since the systems are developed for reasoning purposes, direct development in theories of formal semantics has been limited. An intrinsic limitation on their applicability is that their truth-conditions are unclear. If one wishes to say that redness is the default color of cardinals, for instance, one need to deal with the fact that one can as easily build a reasoning system employing that notion as selecting not-red (or, the brownish cast of the female cardinals) as the default. More needs to be said regarding how to derive the defaults in a compositional, truth-conditional semantics.

Probability (as opposed to frequency) is an intrinsically intensional idea that has been explored extensively in the work of Cohen (1999). The idea here is that probabilities are derived from the frequencies observed in the world. They are generated from a prior division of the sentence into two components as just discussed. In a sentence "A's are B" for instance, the probability of an A being a B is generated, with a condition imposed upon them of "homogeneity". This analysis is a combination of an intensional notion, an alternatives structure, and a pragmatic condition. The probability condition will, among other things, prevent attributing accidental generalizations generically, and provides the basis for considering the sentence true. The pragmatic condition is present to deal with examples that seem not obviously true despite having a probability of occurrence higher than 50% (which, on his view, is sufficient). Consider the following:

(27) Buildings are less than five stories tall.

This seems a strange claim to make, but upon reflection one will agree that the majority of buildings in the world are less than five stories in height. Cohen's homogeneity condition states, however, that in partitioning the set in "salient" ways must result in the same probability occurring throughout. So, partitioning buildings by the function they serve is, let us assume, a salient partition. We quickly see that buildings serving as single-family houses have close to a 100% chance of being less than five stories tall, whereas office buildings would have a considerably smaller probability of being less than five stories tall. On the other hand, if we state "Buildings have roofs", we find the probability (hovering just short of 100%, one might guess) pretty much the same for houses and office buildings. One of the difficult issues for this analysis is articulating exactly what constitutes a salient partition, when it may be applied, as well as determining the appropriate criterial value of the probability (see Leslie 2007, 2008 for some critical discussion).

Another intensional notion with significant intuitive appeal, and promise, is that of normality. The notion that one can say "Dogs have four legs" depends, in some way, on the idea that it is normal for dogs to have four legs. Note that the intuitive notion of normality extends to generalizing over events as well (as when one talks about Aunt Sally's behavior, and what is normal for her, and what is not). One may think of analyzing in terms of normality as the outgrowth of a quantificational analysis employing a universal quantifier that derives its intensionality from extending the domain of objects quantified over to possible objects, as well as the real (or rather, the subset of the real) ones that are normal. Simply quantifying over all objects of the appropriate type in all worlds will of course not do, since we do not wish to consider worlds too unlike our own, where dogs fly and fish talk, for instance. The notion of "normal worlds" was introduced in Delgrande (1987) as a means of restricting the intensional entities encompassed by the quantification. However, Pelletier and Asher find the approach problematic in its truth conditions; further, the simple, unanalyzed worlds accessibility structure proposed there is argued in Eckardt (1999) to find itself in difficulty with examples that introduce both normal objects, and normal behaviors (as in dogs biting postmen). The approach is elaborated and considerably refined within a compositional semantics in Eckardt (1999). Nickel (2008) also takes up a normality approach in a slightly different way, arguing that there are different ways of being normal for a given class. This allows for generic predication to hold of a smallish portion of a class, and still be considered a true generic.

Normality has an intuitive appeal. However, it must be emphasized that for natural language semantics, at any rate, normality is actually contingent upon what happens to be. If baseball players get paid nine hundred times what top teachers receive, or if some celebrity bathes daily in a tub of lime Jell-o, it's normal for them to be so compensated or for him to do so, because it happens to be. Normality also gets stretched and tested by the fact that it is normal for some percentage of a class to be abnormal (e.g. among humans schizophrenia is considered not normal, but it is normal for a smallish percentage of a population to be schizophrenic). Finally, in trying to articulate the accessibility relation to other worlds, there is potential for circularity to be achieved. If what we do in extending the domain of quantification to other worlds is to select those that are "close enough" or "much like" our own, might the cashing out of that structure end up essentially selecting worlds in which (most of) the generics that hold in our own world, hold in theirs as well?

One theme that has emerged in work on genericity is to doubt that it is a single, unified phenomenon. It is clear that notionally, generics can be put to use describing a wide variety of phenomena, to include habits, dispositions, rules of games, cultural mores, functions, and more. It is usually assumed, and I believe quite correctly, that the notional categories do not determine true semantic distinctions. And, this is largely supported by facts about natural language forms across languages (see, for example, Filip & Carlson 1997), that the forms provide no hint of a cleavage into a rich set of notional domains. It is often implicitly assumed that there is a single semantics that is put to use in a variety of ways. However, this uniformity has been put into some doubt by a number of researchers. Bittner (2008) has argued on the basis of data from Kaalillut (Greenlandic), and Boneh & Doron (2008), on the basis of modern Hebrew, that this semantic domain should be (at least) bifurcated. In Eckardt's terms, there seems to be some kind of distinction between "normal-generic" and "ideal-generic" sentences, the former much more statistically-driven in conception, the latter more directive, relatively immune to statistical observation. If one asserts that "Turtles live 100 years or so" to be true, the masses of turtles that do not live to that age count for little if we are talking about the "ideal" turtle; normal-turtles do not live so long. Pondering a distinction along these lines will form a part of the continuing discussion on the semantics of generic sentences.

3 Generic reference

The term *generic reference* is used in a variety of ways in the linguistics and philosophy literature. Its root notional use is to provide a description of the meanings of nominals in a sentence which do not appear to make any reference, definite or indefinite, to particular individuals of that sort. So, for instance, in the compound noun "car-door", the term "car" is occasionally said to refer generically to cars since, from an intuitive point of view, no individual cars seem to be talked about in using that word in the context of the compound. Or, the nominal element typically understood as an object, that appears incorporated into verbs in languages that exhibit the structure is commonly talked about as referring "generically". Again, it does not appear that the construction's meaning requires any sort of reference to particular individuals.

More commonly, the term is used to talk about generic noun phrases, typically found in generic or habitual sentences, which likewise do not appear to make reference to particular individuals of the sort. Thus, in sentences like (1) the subject noun phrase is often said to refer generically.

However, as is common in discussion of purely notional terms, intuitions can only take one so far. In example (1), it does not appear that any particular honey is "under discussion" either, so does that mean that the NP "honey" refers "generically"? It may, or may not. The underlying descriptive intuitions would appear to include indefinite descriptions within the scope of other operators, such as negation (28), or even nonspecific indefinites, as in (29).

(28)　The professor did not wear *a tie* to class last Thursday.

(29)　*Some thief* took my computer!

One example among others that Quirk et al. (1985, 281) use to illustrate "the generic use of the indefinite article" has an indefinite appearing in an intensional context:

(30)　The best way to learn *a language* is to live among its speakers.

Whether there is something "generic" about the noun phrase above and beyond its non-generic use appearing in an intensionalized context is a difficult issue to resolve by direct appeal to intuition.

This is all by way of introduction to the issue we are going to focus on: the theoretical question of whether there is something one can properly call "generic reference" in a semantic theory of natural language. Our primary focus will be on the types of noun phrases exhibited in the subject noun phrases in (1), since if such instances do not refer generically then it is likely nothing does. We return to consideration of remaining constructions only after an examination of the core constructions.

Let us first present a working definition of "generic reference". In the abstract, this is a reasonably straightforward thing to do within the confines of a truth-conditional approach to semantics. First, we take the phenomenon of "reference" to be that of semantic value; the reference of a phrase is just that object which determines the phrase's contribution to the calculation of the truth or falsity of a sentence containing that phrase. So, for instance, if at the appropriate parameters the predicate "is smart" is some set of individuals S, and the phrase "Laura's sister" refers to a certain individual a, then the semantic value of the whole sentence "Laura's sister is smart" will depend upon the contribution the individual a makes to the whole. If, as is often assumed, a sentence of the form "NP is Adj" is true iff the reference of the NP is a member of the set denoted by the adjective, then the sentence's truth depends just on whether $a \in S$. If we take some object that the NP does not intuitively refer to, say, the individual l (let's assume this is Laura), then the truth value of the whole does not depend on whether $l \in S$, which is why we say that a, and not l, is the reference of the NP "Laura's sister". While a great deal more could be, and needs to be added, we deal with qualifications and questions as they arise.

The second part is also fairly straightforward, and that is, what makes a reference "generic"? The obvious answer would be that a reference is generic just in case the semantic value of a phrase in a sentence is an object that is, well, generic. Assuming that ordinary individuals, such as Laura and her sister, are not generic objects, then generics must not make reference to such things, but to some other things. For reasons we will go into later, groups or collections of individuals (let us call these "pluralities") are not appropriate candidates for such objects. From an intuitive standpoint, for an object X to be generic it must be related to particular individuals y by something like the "y is an instance of X/y an exemplar of X" relation. Its reference with regard to the exemplars needs to be in some sense "unbounded," in that it is also intended to include not only existent but also potential instances. This would appear to work for the core instances we examine, such as (1). After all, I can point to an animal nearby and say "This (pointing at a certain object) is an exemplar of/is an instance of a bear". It would also seem to be an intuitive condition that if y is an exemplar of the generic object X, then the phrase used to refer to X must also be truly predicated of y (so, for instance, if a is an exemplar of a smart person, then a must be a smart person and not, say, enjoy surfing but may, or may not, be smart). This then will be our working definition of "generic reference".

There are two matters that need to be dealt before turning to the semantic issues. One is that of quantification. We are going to assume a traditional view for now that a quantified noun phrase has no reference of its own (though on a generalized quantifier treatment it may denote (the intension of) a set of properties). However, it still is germane to the question of generic reference. We will assume the analysis of unrestricted quantification as found in first-order predicate logic.

A quantified formula consists of an open formula containing one or more instances of variables, and operators that bind those variables. The truth-conditions (in the simplest instances) consist of a) a set of truth-value calculations for each individual in the domain when assigned as a value of the bound variable, and b) a condition associated with the binder which designates certain sets of results as "True" and others as "False". For instance, if the domain is the odd numbers between one and ten and x is bound, then the open formula [x<7] will be a set of evaluations [1<7]...[9<7] (coming out T, T,..., F, F), which is a false pattern of results if the binder is $\forall x$, true if it's $\exists x$. In first-order predicate logic it is typically assumed that the values assigned to variables are just "ordinary" individuals. However, if the domain includes generic objects, then the possibility is raised that variable values may be assigned from that domain as well. Thus, we might ask, alongside whether there is reference to generic objects, also whether there is quantification over generic objects as well.

In simply posing the question as to whether there is generic reference, one appears to be presuming a positive answer to the question of whether there are genera that can be referred to in the first place. Being a type of universal, their existence is bound up with the longstanding question of the existence and standing of universals in general. There are many candidates for that role that have been proposed, such as Plato's forms, Aristotle's secondary substances, Locke's "real essences," the quidditas of the medievals, sorts, properties, natural kinds, and so forth. Nominalists have in general been inclined to treat genera as abstractions, or as predicates applying to individuals. This is a common practice in advising students how to represent things in logical notation. For instance, Stebbing (1930, 149) advises that, "'The whale is a mammal' expresses a universal proposition and in this usage 'The whale' is not a definite description." This point also gets expressly argued for (and against). Bacon (1974) weighs in on a controversy between Leśniewski and Twardowski regarding whether the sentence

(31) The lion is a mammal.

is best analyzed as meaning the same thing as "All lions are mammals", i.e. as a universal proposition, or whether "The lion" can be understood as a "representative object." The title of Bacon's (1974) article, "The untenability of genera", makes clear where he comes down on the issue (see also Bacon 1973, for a similar conclusion). On the other hand, Putnam (1975) in his often-cited article regarding the liquids water and XYZ, is perhaps best understood as relying upon the idea that there are natural kinds that can serve as the reference of indexicals and certain names. We will have a bit more to say about natural kinds below.

Having recognized the underlying metaphysical controversy, however, we are going to move on. In part, it is clearly outside the scope of this article, it is much too complex an issue, and there is no chance whatsoever of resolution here. More importantly, it is not clear that there be a resolution in order to construct a theory of semantics. Bach's (1981, 1986) idea that there may be a "natural language metaphysics" looms as one possibility that deserves consideration; the possibility that abstractions have reified interpretations is another; or that natural language semantics proper is a matter of creating "spontaneous fiction" (Kamp & Reyle 1993). So if semantics is about the relation between natural language forms and "the world", the structure of "the world" would seem to have *some* bearing on matters. But exactly what bearing it might have is, at this point, a matter without a clear consensus.

4 Rationale for generic reference

The beginning motivation for countenancing something like generic reference is found in those instances where a quantificational analysis would appear to be implausible. Moore (1942), for instance, notes that Russell's theory of descriptions will not get the sentence "The whale is a mammal" correct in its generic sense (only possibly in the sense of referring to some particular animal in the context). He further notes such examples as, "The lion is the king of beasts," "The triangle is a figure to which Euclid devoted a great deal of attention," or "The right hand is apt to be better developed than the left." In such instances, these do not seem to be even universal propositions, not to say misanalyzed in the Theory of Descriptions. It does not seem plausible to say of each individual lion that that lion is the king of beasts, that Euclid paid particular attention to each individual triangle, or that a given right hand is "apt to be" more highly developed than the left (in a given instance, it either is, or isn't). And this sets aside any issues arising from consideration of phrases like "the left hand" or "the king of beasts".

It is not too difficult to find additional such examples, where any calculation based on the use of bound individual variables will lead to an implausible analysis. Consider the following:

(32) a. The lion is a type of mammal.
 b. The helicopter is a kind of flying machine.
 c. The praying mantis is a species of insect.

Predicates prefixed by such words as "kind", "sort," "type," "species", are systematically constructible for nearly any predicate nominal. Clearly, to say of this particular lion that it is "a type of mammal", or that this particular helicopter is itself "a kind of flying machine" is either patently implausible, or at least not at all what is intended in saying such things.

A plausible reanalysis suggests itself, provided that one is willing to absorb the cost of positing genera as objects to which reference is possible. The extent to which one is unwilling to bear such costs will mostly determine the extent to which the analysis is objectionable. Consider first the analysis of an ordinary predicate nominal, as in (33).

(33) The house is a bungalow.

This is said with respect to a certain house in context (e.g. the one across the street). Its analysis, to a first approximation, is straightforward:

> The phrase "the house" denotes/refers to a given individual house h
>
> The phrase "is a bungalow" is a predicate B denoting/referring to the set of individual things that are bungalows.
>
> The sentence (33) is true iff h is an element of B.

This analysis assumes that the subject noun phrase, a definite description, denotes a given object, and that the predicate denotes a set of objects. Truth and falsity are defined by set membership. Using genera, we can apply this straightforwardly to an example such as (32a):

> The phrase "The lion" denotes/refers to a generic object l
>
> The phrase "is a type of mammal" is a predicate M' denoting/referring to the set of generic things that are types of mammals.
>
> The sentence (32a) is true iff l is an element of M'

We might do exactly the same thing with equative sentences, where the copula is plausibly analyzed as identity. We assume, again somewhat simplistically, that a sentence like (34) should be analyzed thus:

(34) The house (across the street) is the Smith residence.

> The phrase "the house" denotes a given thing h
>
> The phrase "the Smith residence" denotes a given thing h'
>
> (34) is true iff h=h'

And once again a parallel analysis for a sentence like (33) is straightforwardly available:

(35) The lion is the king of beasts.

> The phrase "the lion" denotes a given (generic) thing l
>
> The phrase "the king of beasts" denotes a given (generic) thing l'
>
> (35) is true iff l=l'

Considered as an argument, this does not establish the necessity of countenancing genera; but any analysis that preserves such parallelism is surely worth considering further, since no additional, different-looking rules of semantic interpretation for copular structures or for definite descriptions would need to be constructed. So, for instance, we are no longer in a position of saying that some definite descriptions refer to objects, whereas others do not but are instead understood as expressions of universal quantification.

Krifka et al. (1995) and Carlson (1977a) point out that there are further predicate types beyond predicate nominals that likewise do not appear readily amendable to a quantificational analysis. These "kind-level" predicates include adjectives of distribution such as "widespread," "common," or "rare". Such properties are not readily predicated of individuals, nor are they readily predicated of groups or pluralities of individuals:

(36) a. The grizzly bear is common/widespread/rare.
b. ??My neighbor's pet bear is common/widespread/rare.
c. ??Those bears are common/widespread/rare.

Other predicates which select for generic referents include "be extinct", "come in" (as in "Dogs come in a wide variety of shapes and sizes"), "be indigenous to," the object of the verb "invent" (cf. the object of "discover"), or, as observed by Schubert & Pelletier (1987), both the subject and object of "evolve from":

(37) a. Monkeys evolved from lemurs.
b. ??Jackie's monkey evolved from this lemur.

A wider class of predicates which do not seem to select for generic reference can nonetheless be identified, where the intended reading relies upon the referent being understood as generic, rather than as specific. Consider, for instance, the following sentence with the adjective "popular":

(38) In the months following the release of the movie "Jaws," *sharks* became highly popular among school-age children.

(38) is not making the claim that there was one particular shark, or even any particular group of sharks, of which it might be said that it is popular. It is easily understood as describing a situation where sharks as a species, or a type of thing, are popular without there being any increase in the "popularity" of any singular shark at all.

Similarly, it appears one can *fear* bears, or ghosts, without fearing any particular ones, one can *discuss* insects or bacteria without discussing any particular ones, or one can *worship* bears or eagles, again without singling out any particular ones, or even any particular groups of such things.

All these examples, and many more, also have individual readings alongside the generic ones. For example, the sentence "Jacob worships bears" does have a reading which is roughly equivalent to saying that Jacob has a propensity where, if he encounters a bear x, he will worship x. However, there is above and beyond this a reading where the object of Jacob's attention is never any particular bear at all. (In Spanish, the two readings are formally distinguished from one another, Laca 1990.) For example, in the case of fearing ghosts, this is the plausible reading given normal assumptions about the existence of ghosts. This latter, generic reading of the noun phrase is the one that is a promising candidate for generic reference.

5 What types of English DP's can have generic interpretations?

Thus far, the use of particular noun phrases in the English examples has been aimed at creating a means of identifying when one has a generic reading for a given DP. The two types of English DP's used thus far have been the bare plural construction ("bears", etc.), and the definite singular construction ("the lion"), which is also systematically ambiguous between a generic and an individual reading (e.g. discussing a certain lion that is nearby).

As mentioned in the introduction, the indefinite singular is generally considered to have a truly generic reading. It often results in paraphrase for the other generics:

(39) a. *The lion* is ferocious.
    b. *Lions* are ferocious.
    c. *A lion* is ferocious.

However, the indefinite singular does not combine well with distributional predicates:

(40) A grizzly bear is ??common/??widespread/?rare.

And results are somewhat mixed with other predicates which select for generic readings:

(41) a. ??A grizzly bear evolved from a cave bear.
 b. ??Charles Babbage invented a computer (cf: the computer)
 c. ?A grizzly bear is indigenous to North America.
 d. ??A dodo is extinct.

Further, they generally do not have the generic reading in instances of predicates that can combine with individual-denoting or generically-denoting arguments. "John fears a ghost", for many speakers, has a generic reading only marginally at best.

On the other hand, indefinite singulars do set well in the copular constructions with kind-type predicates:

(42) a. A lion is a type of mammal.
 b. A helicopter is a kind of flying machine.
 c. (?) A praying mantis is a species of insect.

Intuitively then indefinite singulars have a generic reading alongside their more common individual reading. However, the evidence discussed so far does not clearly support the view that this generic reading is kind-referring. We are going to need to return to this issue of indefinite singulars as generics further below.

The other type of noun phrase that gives rise to intuitions of genericity is the "free choice" sense of 'any', as in:

(43) Any lion is ferocious.

This does not, however, combine with any of the generic-selecting predicates or result in generic readings in the other instances mentioned above. Further, it does not allow for apparent external quantification, as the other generics do:

(44) A lion/The lion/Lions/??Any lion is(are) usually ferocious.

In one form or another, the free-choice 'any' does appear to have inherent quantification over individuals as a part of its meaning.

Mass (or non-count) expressions, of English appear to pattern much like the determinerless bare plurals, and display the relevant patterning of the generically-referring count expressions:

(45) *Water/gold/mud* is common/widespread/rare.

(46) *Gold/iron* is a kind of metal.

The syntactic twist with mass and abstract terms is that they do not take a definite singular form—"the gold," "the water", etc. have only nongeneric reference (cf. German). So, while alongside "lions" there is the generic "the lion", there is no "*the water" alongside "water". However, the determinerless form functions the same as the definite singular does for count terms. Those few contexts that select just for the definite singular but discomfit the bare plural, such as the object of "invent", allow the determinerless mass expression there with ease.

(47) a. Babbage invented *the computer/?computers*.
　　　b. The Italians invented *ice cream*.

Yet the determinerless mass expressions also parallel the semantics of the bare plural as well. They can, for example, occur with collective predicates which seem not to go with the definite singular generic at all easily, but with the bare plural form quite well.

(48) a. *Monarch butterflies/??The monarch butterfly* collect(s) each autumn for migration south.
　　　b. *Algae* collects near river deltas due to the outflow of chemical fertilizers in the river water.

In addition, as traditional grammars of English unexceptionally note, there is one distinguished count term that appears in the singular without article, namely 'man', in the generic sense referring to people or mankind in general and not just to mature human males.

There is one other type of construction that plays a role here, albeit a marginal one. This is the use of Latinate generic terms naming species, phyla, orders, etc., such as the following:

(49) a. *Acer rubrum* (=the red maple tree) grows 40 to 60 feet tall.
　　　b. *Ursus Malayanus* (=the sun bear) is native to southeast Asia.

These names are a consciously-produced scientific addition to any language that cares to try and add them, so it is a little difficult to assess their significance within the bounds of a discussion of the semantics of a language. For English, at any rate, the semantics of these stilted scientific names would appear to be most similar to that of the definite singular ("the sun bear", "the red maple", etc.), and possibly identical. Their significance could perhaps best be assessed within the context of a theory of naming, a matter beyond the scope of the present article.

There are also a couple of variants worthy of note. There is a use of distal demonstrative DP's that expresses some sort of affective attitude by the speaker towards things. This usage may appear with proper names of people, for example:

(50) *That Howard* is such a comedian!

The affect may be positive, as in this instance, or it may be negative in others. However, this is also applicable to generic terms. The following is from Bowdle & Ward (1995):

(51) *Those spotted owls* are constantly being talked about by environmentalists.

This means that spotted owls (in general) have the environmentalists riled, and the demonstrative adds affect (in this case, it could be positive or negative, depending on who is speaking).

In English, plural count nouns with the definite article are not typically understood generically. Thus, examples such as the following are a little strange if intended generically:

(52) a. ??The lions are ferocious/widespread/indigenous to the eastern hemisphere
b. ??The maple trees are related to roses.

However, when it comes to referencing people, the definite plural is much better as a generic, and in fact the definite singular, while interpretable and grammatical, sounds slightly demeaning, or is to be used in a jocular sense. Thus one normally talks about "the ancient Greeks" instead of "the ancient Greek", or "the Russians" in place of "the Russian". The bare plurals, "ancient Greeks", and "Russians," for instance, are perfectly normal as generics as well.

It is fairly well-known that there exist restrictions on the use of the definite singulars as well. Krifka et al. (1995) characterize the limitation to "well-established" kinds of things, but the nature of this restriction remains poorly understood and an open question (see Carlson 2009 for one attempt to understand the matter). Also unclear is the extent to which these restrictions in English are shared more widely by other languages.

An interim summary. The Latinate names aside, genericity in English is a feature of bare plurals and mass terms (i.e. determinerless DP's), definite singulars (on one reading) and definite plurals (on one reading) in some more limited instances, and perhaps indefinite singulars.

6 Generic quantification

However, complex expressions can also be systematically built up using expressions such as "kind", "type", "sort", etc., which have the hallmarks of a generic semantics as well:

(53) a. This kind of salamander (e.g. pointing at a given animal) is indigenous to Central Europe.
b. The largest type of mammal lives in the ocean.

One also finds such expressions in quantified DP's as well:

(54) a. Not every kind of fish has tail fins.
b. One species of snake eats only bird eggs.
c. Most breeds of dogs respond well to firm, consistent training.

Further, as the reader has doubtless already noted, the prefixed "sort/kind of" can easily be dropped, and one still find a reading quantifying over or referring to a kind of thing. This is the "taxonomic" reading. For instance:

(55) a. *Two birds* are common in Antarctica.
b. *Few minerals* are rare.

So then a sentence such as:

(56) *Several mammals* eat primarily nuts and berries.

is ambiguous between individuals, and types. This is a systematic ambiguity that is most often noted in discussions of mass terms. If one takes a mass term and uses it in a count sense, one prominent reading is a "kind" reading:

(57) *One liquid* (namely, water) is found nearly everywhere on earth.

The most straightforward analysis would seem to be one where the common noun, whether mass or count, which presumably has a "more basic" reading where it applies to individuals or perhaps particular quantities, can also be used then as a predicate that applies to sets of kinds of things of that sort, which then may be quantified over by existing mechanisms. So while, in a context, "Every man (in the context)" quantifies over individuals Tom, Dick, and Harry, in another instance an expression like "Every tree (in the context)" quantifies over apple trees, peach trees, and cherry trees. If one posits a variable in the representations that takes on values, Tom would be the value of an assignment in the one instance, and apple trees (*malus domestica*) a value in the other. It appears that this process might be one that also allows for kinds of kinds to be values, though we omit discussion here. One apparent fact this points up is that it is difficult to find nouns which only designate sets of kinds, and not individuals. Pelletier & Schubert (1989) bring up the case of the term "halogen", a chemistry term which seems best used as a classification of kinds of gases, but does not do well used to talk about individual quantities ("??Some halogen escaped into the air during the experiment"), or the word "element" used in the same scientific sense (?"The element fell into the waste basket"), though here again we may be dealing with the uneasy case of consciously-produced scientific classificatory terms as in the case of the Latinate names.

7 What types of DP's can express generic reference across languages?

Thus far, the sorts of noun phrases that may express genericity has been limited to the cases of determinerless expressions (bare plurals and mass terms) and definite singulars and some plurals. If we think of the bare plural in English as a type of indefinite (possibly with a null determiner), and include the indefinite singular, we find that the phenomenon of genericity is limited to expressions of definiteness and indefiniteness. The question is whether this represents a general pattern throughout the world's languages. A number of authors have examined a variety of languages, some examining a wide range of languages (Gerstner-Link 1998), and others a more limited range of languages but in great theoretical depth (Chierchia 1998, Dayal 2004, Krifka 2004, Behrens 2005). From these studies, and a wider range of descriptions which do not necessarily focus on genericity, it is possible to draw some conclusions. One thing that is perhaps a little surprising is that there has yet to be uncovered an instance of a language which clearly has a specifically generic article or quantifier. Perhaps the closest are languages with classifiers, which have a "general" classifier roughly equivalent to the word "kind", also present for taxonomic readings (Gerstner-Link 1998). However, it appears that nominal genericity does not make use of specific morphological devices. Linguists have had some time to examine this claim, and thus far not a single serious contender has been put forward. So if there is specifically nominal genericity overtly marked, it is certainly not at all common. This is quite different from the case of I-genericity or "habituality", where specifically habitual markers, typically a part of the verbal complex, can be found with some ease, even if not especially common (Dahl 1985, 1995). This suggests, albeit only generally, that the referential and quantificational resources of natural language that are adequate for the discussion of individuals and their groups or quantities, is also adequate for the discussion of genera, and that genera require no special devices to enhance that machinery.

Discussion of the particulars of generic reference has tended to focus on the status of the bare plural construction. This is in part because the bare plural appears to play the role of a generic on the one hand (e.g. as in (1)), and a sort of plural indefinite on the other (58).

(58) *Policemen* arrived at the scene with *sirens* howling and *lights* flashing.

These two meanings – generic reference and plural indefiniteness – seem, intuitively, distant from one another. The formulation of Carlson (1977a,b) sought to close the gap between the two, treating the bare plural in (almost) all instances as the name of a *kind*, and deriving the usage in (58) from the interaction of the semantics of the bare plural with the semantic context it appears in; chiefly, if the context required reference to particulars, as in (58), then one got the effect of existential quantification over instance of the kind named by the bare plural.

The analysis relied upon motivating the needs for a "generic" operator that expresses I-genericity or "habituality". In the Carlson (1977a) formulation this takes the form of a predicate operator which maps predicates that are "stage-level" to ones that may apply directly to individuals (thus "individual-level" predicates), and can subsequently be "raised" to apply to kinds ("kind-level" predicates). Nothing but a programmatic semantics is suggested for it. However, it is the ingredient that introduces I-genericity into the semantics of the sentence.

Compelling subsequent work reconstrued this analysis within the context of the "theory of indefiniteness", a line of work initiated by the discourse-oriented work of Kamp (1981) and Heim (1982). The primary feature of this approach is that the contribution of an indefinite (as well as a definite) expression was a property, and a variable construed in Kamp (1981) as a "discourse marker" or in Heim (1982) as affecting a "file" of discourse markers. So, for instance, the contribution of the DP "a man" would be effectively *man*(x) with conditions concerning what values x may take. The primary effect of interest is that a variable is thus introduced into the structure of the semantic interpretation via the semantics of the indefinite DP itself, and that this variable then can be bound by other operators (though if not bound by other operators, a default existential closure operation binds the free variable).

Put in spare form, a sentence like (59a) below might be represented as (59b).

(59) a. A cat is walking.
  b. ∃ [*cat*(x) & *walk*(x)]
  c. ∃x [*cat*(x) & *walk*(x)]

The unselective existential binds all free variables within its scope, and so (59b) is equivalent to (59c).

However, the default existential is not the only available binder, as other elements of the sentence may also play that role as well. Consider a generic-seeming sentence with a frequency adverb "often" in it:

(60) Cats *often* have sharp claws.

(60) appears to mean about the same thing as (61):

(61) Many cats have sharp claws.

This result can be derived if we treat 'often' as an instance of A-quantification (Bach et al. 1995, Lewis 1975) and as an unselective binder as well. The spare form of (60) would then be something like (62a), which again ends up equivalent to (62b), treating the meaning of 'often' as represented by *Many*.

(62) a. *Many* [*cat*(x) & *have-sharp-claws*(x)]
  b. *Many*(x) [*cat*(x) & *have-sharp-claws*(x)]

The treatment of (63) is parallel, provided the generic operator GEN is, as presented in Krifka et al. (1995), a tripartite operator that binds variables within its scope.

(63) A cat has sharp claws.

This contains a "generic" indefinite singular. The GEN operator remains, in English and many other languages, morphologically unexpressed. Assuming this, the representation of (63) then becomes:

(64)   GEN [*cat*(x); *have-sharp-claws*(x)]

with the GEN operator binding the free variable and providing the relation between the two parts of the formula in its scope (in this instance, roughly an "if...then..." structure, e.g. "If something is a cat it normally has sharp claws").

On the analysis sketched in (64) then, the indefinite singular (e.g. "a cat") is not generically referring at all. Rather the meaning of the sentence arises from the binding of the variable introduced by the indefinite NP by (mostly) independently-motivated operators already in the sentence. If one can do this with the singular indefinites, one can do the same with the bare plurals provided one takes the (plausible) step of assuming they are also indefinites. Unlike the indefinite singulars, however, one assumes that the plural forms may also range over sums of individuals of that sort, perhaps in addition to the individuals. So, a sentence like "cats have sharp claws" will, aside from the range of the variable being restricted to singular individual cats in (64), be otherwise identical to it:

(65)   GEN [*cats*(x); *have-sharp-claws* (x)]

The upshot is that given an already well-developed theory of indefinites, with some seemingly minor adjustments such as including a GEN operator, generic sentences with indefinite singulars and bare plurals very much seem to fall right out. This basic idea was developed considerably by Wilkinson (1991), Diesing (1992), Kratzer (1995), and Krifka (1987), among others. One of the chief strengths of the analysis is that it quite successfully predicts the interpretations of various generic readings of the same sentence according to its focal structure.

This approach has a number of consequences. For one, while it gives a uniform treatment of existentially-quantified and generic indefinites in terms of the contribution of the meaning of the noun phrase to the whole, the initial cost is to assume that bare plurals are also kind-denoting when combined with the "kind-level" predicates exemplified above in (32), (36) and (37), as these do not appear easily represented as a quantification over individuals. This leaves lingering the question then of why, if a generic reference analysis is required there, it is not carried through more generally. Since this is an argument from parsimony, its force is unclear, as a whole set of additional theoretical assumptions come along with the compared analyses.

This line of analysis seems to suggest that genericity is associated with indefiniteness. However, cross-linguistic evidence suggests otherwise. A number of articles discussing this issue include de Swart (1993), Dobrovie-Sorin & Laca (1997) and Cohen & Erteschik-Shir (1999). Gerstner-Link's (1998) survey, which keyed into the parameters of definiteness and number, yields in fact very few languages of the forty examined which allow for a "generic" reading of the indefinite article, as appears to be found in English. In general, it was the determinerless forms, and even more frequently the definite forms that had genericity associated with them. No clear cases are cited where clearly indefinite forms are associated with generic reference to the exclusion of definites.

Gerstner-Link (1998) points out that the type of definiteness is also of interest. In general, definites appear to have two (possibly non-distinct) uses: an anaphoric use to refer to something that has just been mentioned, for example, as in "John bought a car. *The car* was expensive." Or, it can refer to something known to be unique or familiar from background information, such as the earth or the sun. Some dialects of German, as well as Frisian, use two different forms of the definite article to distinguish these uses. Only one of them may be used generically, which is the form used also to refer to unique or contextually familiar things like the sun or the earth. In the Amern dialect of German, the non-anaphoric form is 'der' and the anaphoric form 'dä'. Only the former may be used to refer generically.

(66) Der/ *dä Fuchs stiehlt Hühner.
      'The fox steals hens/ Foxes steal hens'

Not all languages, however, have articles, and those languages which lack articles altogether always use the bare forms to express genericity (e.g. Chinese, Russian). I will not discuss any details at this point as they are substantially covered in article 5 [this volume] (Dayal) *Bare noun phrases*. Such languages are discussed at length in Chierchia's landmark (1998) article. Chierchia raises the issue of whether nominal forms in different languages can have different type properties, aiming at an analysis that makes significant use of type-shifting devices to arrive at the appropriate interpretations and to make predictions about which determiners will be used, and why; in particular Chierchia presents an account of why bare singulars in languages with a singular/plural distinction are not used generically, and why it is the definite article that so often appears, even with singular forms in such languages. Chierchia's analysis has been ably evaluated by others. In Krifka (2004), a somewhat different set of assumptions are introduced concerning bare plurals, and he concludes they are neither kind-referring nor indefinites, but instead designate properties. Dayal (2004) takes matters a step further in the discussion of whether indefiniteness is a feature of genericity. Languages that do not make use of articles appear to have both definite and indefinite interpretations available for the determinerless forms. The interpretation is mostly sensitive to the context of usage, but such matters as local construction demands, and especially sentence position may limit the choices. As a rough generalization, the earlier in a sentence a bare nominal appears, the more likely it is to be interpreted as a definite – or as a generic. This is expressly noted in Cheng & Sybesma (1999) with regard to Mandarin and Cantonese both; the fact that preverbal bare plurals in Romance are unacceptable (or require extra material to be acceptable as generics), while postverbal bare plurals are natural but only interpreted indefinitely has been pointed out by e.g. Contreras (1986), Torrego (1989), and Longobardi (1994). Dayal argues in fact that a detailed examination of languages such as Russian and Mandarin which have no articles shows an affinity between the definite reading and the generic, to the exclusion of the indefinite interpretations. This is consonant with the kind-referring analysis of Carlson (1977a,b), in which it was argued that bare plurals are names of kinds of things, and names are normally taken as a species of definiteness. (See section 1.8 of article 2 [this volume] (Heim) *Definiteness and indefiniteness* for some further discussion).

8 Indefinite singulars

Carlson (1977a,b) also attempted an analysis of the indefinite singular in terms of kind-reference as well. Essentially, the analysis treated the indefinite singular as a set of properties of the kind, less those that were not also properties of individual instances of the kind (this eliminated "widespread, common", etc. from the property set). However, it would appear that a kind-referring analysis of the indefinite singular is perhaps not correct, and that something akin to the GEN-binding analysis might be more to the point. Gerstner-Link (1998) and Cohen (2001) point to the fact that indefinite singular generics do not appear to make very good topics, and topicality is a sign of reference. This was noted by Reinhart (1981), using example such as the following:

(67) a. She said about sharks that they will never attack unless they are very hungry.
  b. She said about a shark that it will never attack unless it is very hungry.

While (67a) with the bare plural has a sensible generic reading, (67b) with the indefinite singular is difficult to read as a generic, and seems to have only a specific existential reading. The relevance of topic and focus structure on the interpretation of generics in general is fairly clear. It has been known among semanticists for some time that Japanese topic-marking (-wa) is a feature of Japenese generics (see Brockett 1991 for extended discussion). Krifka (2004) makes a similar point about the sensitivity of generic reference to the information structure of a sentence. Jäger (2001) discusses the role of topicality in the (putative) stage-level/individual-level contrast; Kiss (1998), Longobardi (1994) and Erteschik-Shir (1997) note that focus structure of a sentence can affect the interpretation of bare plurals.

Two more recent analyses of the indefinite singular, by Cohen (2001) and Greenberg (2003), key in on the idea that (English) indefinite singulars have a special "flavor" to them that distinguishes them from the definite generic and the bare plural forms. Cohen notes that they often have a 'normative' type of reading. Following Burton-Roberts (1977), he notes that of the following sentences, only the second has a reading of "moral necessity".

(68) a. Gentlemen open doors for ladies.
     b. A gentleman opens doors for ladies.

Cohen characterizes this property in terms of Carlson's (1995) distinction between "rules and regulations" and "inductive" readings of generics, with indefinite singulars having only the former reading because such sentences do not require topics – they function as topics themselves in their entirety. In support of this view, Cohen cites the example from French with the partitive *des* construction (unusually) in subject position:

(69) a. Des agents de police ne se comportent pas ainsi dans une situation d'alarme.
       'INDEF-PL police officers do not behave like that in an emergency situation.'

   b. Les agents de police ne se comportent pas ainsi dans une situation d'alarme.
      'DEF-PL police officers do not behave like that in an emergency situation.'

(69a) can only be understood as a normative statement, and not as a description of typical police officer behavior, unlike (69b). So while there is no generic reference, one still gets the effect of a generic sentence.

Greenberg's treatment is more extended and has a slightly different emphasis, but like the Cohen analysis it takes as its main interest the distinction between indefinite singular generics, and those with bare plurals or definite singulars (again, in English). Her lead examples concern a distinction between "accidental" and "principled" generalizations. For example, the pair in (70) seem pretty much synonymous, while the pair in (71) has only the (71a) version seeming at all natural.

(70) a. Carpenters in Amherst earn very little.
b. A carpenter in Amherst earns very little.

(71) a. Carpenters in Amherst gives all their sons names ending with 'a' or 'g'.
b. ??A carpenter in Amherst gives all his sons names ending in 'a' or 'g'.

One can imagine (71a) being a slightly strange generalization to arrive at, but if one were to arrive at it, (71b) would not be its expression. Similarly, one might observe the following as a generalization:

(72) Uncles like marshmallows.

But to put this banal generalization in the indefinite singular would likewise seem very strange:

(73) ??An uncle likes marshmallows.

Greenberg makes the case that indefinite singulars have an "in virtue-of" reading and presents a formalization of the contents and presuppositions of indefinite singular generics which model that lead intuition: That what is wrong with examples like (71b) and (73) is that one is reluctant to say that a carpenter in Amherst give his sons such names *by virtue of being a carpenter in Amherst*, or that uncles like marshmallows *by virtue of being an uncle*. The bare plural alternatives are acceptable because they have no such presuppositions associated with them. In the end, Greenberg's analysis, like Cohen's, does not rely upon making the indefinite singular a generically referring term. For Greenberg, it contributes a property (being an uncle, or being a carpenter from Amherst), and the originality of the analysis lies in the way the property relates to its predicate.

9 If there are genera, what are they?

If the mechanisms of quantification and reference that are available to the discussion of individuals and their groups, are also automatically transferable to the task of referring to and quantifying over genera, it would seem a rather odd situation if genera were something completely alien to the world of individuals and their sums. It cannot of course be ruled out. Carlson (1977a,b) suggests that genera, like individuals, are entities of the model, and are of the same type as individuals. In particular the inherent intensionality of individuation is stressed, relating it to the intensionality of kinds.

One point of view, discussed in this volume (cf. article 2 [this volume] (Heim) *Definiteness and indefiniteness* 1.8.), is that kinds are the maximal sum individuals of the individuals of that kind in a world. Assuming, in line with work by Link (1983), Landman (1989), and others that a singular count noun has as its extension a set of (atomic) individuals, we can define a pluralization operator * that takes a singular noun and returns the meaning of its plural form. This is defined by taking all the (plural) sums of the atomic individuals in the singular denotation and generating the set of all such sums. So if BEAR is a noun denoting the set of individual bears, then *BEAR will denote the set of all sums of (two or more) bears. Among these sums will be a largest (the supremum). We can define a maximality operator ι that takes the denotation of a plural noun and picks out that largest sum; so ι(*BEAR) will then be the sum of all individual bears.

If this is the meaning of a plural noun, e.g. 'polar bears', then ι(*POLAR BEAR) will be the sum of all the world's polar bears. Ojeda (1991, 1993) refers to such a sum as a 'kind'. Now suppose we take the world as it is to be the way it always has been with respect to bears, especially that polar bears are the only white bears in the universe. Then ι(*WHITE BEAR) = ι(*POLAR BEAR). If this sum is the kind, then the two kinds are identical. However, one's (slippery) intuitions seem to be that white bears and polar bears are not the same kind of thing. And if we confine ourselves to extensional predication, anything we say about white bears will be what we can say about polar bears. If I am attacked by one, I'm attacked by the other. The two also share individual-level properties. If one swims, the other swims; if one hunts seals, the other does too. The two also share those kind-level predicates of distribution: if one is widespread or rare, the other is too. In short, one can get a lot of mileage out of taking such a sum to be the kind.

But they are clearly not the same in terms of modalized properties, such as found in contrafactuals. Clearly, if polar bears were no longer white, they would no longer be white bears, and they could still be polar bears. But it's far from clear that if white bears were no longer white, they would no longer be white bears, but could still be white bears. It would also seem a necessary truth that white bears are white, but a contingent truth that polar bears are white. White bears do not seem to be a species of bear, whereas polar bears do seem to be such a species. If polar bears evolved from ancestor X, do we say that white bears did as well? But clearly, polar bears did. It becomes something of a matter of terminology as to whether one treats a sum individual in a world as a 'kind', or whether the 'individual concept' that picks it out the sum individual in this particular world and all others is 'the kind'.

There is also another distinction between polar bears and white bears. The English definite singular generic sounds natural with one, but not the other:

(74) a. The polar bear is slowly disappearing.
b. ??The white bear is slowly disappearing. (cf: "White bears are...")

This is the phenomenon mentioned above of reference to "well-established" kinds. It is tempting in this instance to think that perhaps the definite singular is limited to *natural kinds*, as polar bears, and not white bears, would seem to be the natural kind. It is quite clear that if there is kind reference, it is not confined to reference to 'natural kinds' as commonly understood in the philosophical literature. Natural kinds are assumed to be those underlying structural capacities, such as atomic structure or genetic endowment, that create the distinctions of the world. The term 'natural' here does not rule out such things as 'plastic' or 'polio vaccine' as such terms, even if they do not occur in nature. Kripke's (1980) examples of natural kind terms include 'water', 'gold', 'cat', 'tiger', 'whale', 'heat', 'hot', 'loud', 'red', and 'pain'. But typically excluded are artifactual or social kind terms like 'money', 'pencil', 'tennis match', 'hammer', 'marriage', etc. (Braun 2006). Discovery of natural kinds is the product of scientific investigation. For example, one might think, for instance, that trees form a natural kind, but this turns out not to be so.

Language, however, is indiscriminate in its applications, even in the definite singular. There are no *linguistic* distinctions that will discriminate natural kinds from others kinds (often called 'nominal kinds'). We can easily speak of "the modern wedding ceremony", "the ball-point pen", "the symphony", "the wine bottle", and so forth with great ease. The bare plural form is even more widely applicable, it would appear, also allowing us to speak of, beyond white bears, wounded white bears, people with suntans, groggy students, unsalted stone-ground wheat crackers, and so on. In general, it appears that (nearly) any nominal meaning can be made to refer to a 'kind', which obviously takes us far beyond the range of natural kinds alone. Chierchia's (1984) original idea, inspired by Cocchiarella's work, that bare plural noun phrases make reference to the nominalization of the property expressed by the nominal, and the nominalization's denotation is to be found in the domain of entities, would seem to be an excellent program for representing the nature of kinds (if one takes these entities to play the role of "individual concepts" as mentioned above).

Not absolutely every nominally expressed property may be turned into a kind. Carlson (1977a) notes that such examples as found in (75) cannot function as kinds, by the criteria given there:

(75) a. parts to this (particular) machine
 b. people in the next room
 c. books that John lost yesterday.

Intuitively, such expressions have a finite, limited extension that does not generalize beyond that limited extension. Precisely understanding what this intuition ammounts to is not a simple matter, particularly when we observe that such examples as "polar bears" also have a finite, though not especially small, extension as well. ι(*PART TO THIS MACHINE) would seem to be just as definable as ι(*POLAR BEAR), yet it appears the two need to be distinguished. Chierchia (1998) proposes an elegant partial solution to the problem, suggesting that it is not possible to nominalize such phrases (which then invokes a type-shifting operation of another sort that results in existential quantification).

10 References

Asher, Nicholas & Michael Morreau 1995. What some generic sentences mean. In: G. Carlson & F. J. Pelletier (eds.). *The Generic Book*. Chicago, IL: The University of Chicago Press, 300–339.
Bach, Emmon 1981. On time, tense and aspect: An essay in English metaphysics. In: P. Cole (ed.). *Radical Pragmatics*. New York: Academic Press, 63–81.
Bach, Emmon 1986. Natural language metaphysics. In: R. Barcan Marcus, G. J. W. Dorn & P. Weingartner (eds.). *Logic, Methodology, and Philosophy of Science. Vol. VII*. Amsterdam: Elsevier, 573–595.
Bach, Emmon, Eloise Jelinek, Angelina Kratzer, and Barbara H. Partee (eds.) 1995. *Quantification in Natural Languages*. Dordrecht: Kluwer.
Bacon, John 1973. Do generic descriptions denote? *Mind* 82, 331–347.
Bacon, John 1974. The untenability of genera. *Logique et Analyse* 17, 197–208.
Barwise, Jon & Robin Cooper 1981. Generalized quantifiers and natural language. *Linguistics & Philosophy* 4, 159–219.
Barwise, Jon & Jerry Seligman 1994. The rights and wrongs of natural regularity. *Logic and Language* 8, 331–364.
Behrens, Leila 2005. Genericity from a cross-linguistic perspective. *Linguistics* 43, 275–344.
Bittner, Maria 2008. Aspectual universals of temporal anaphora. In: S. Rothstein (ed.). *Theoretical and Crosslinguistic Approaches to the Semantics of Aspect*. Amsterdam: Benjamins, 349–385.
Boneh, Nora & Edit Doron 2008. Habituality and habitual aspect. In: S. Rothstein (ed.). *Theoretical and Crosslinguistic Approaches to the Semantics of Aspect*. Amsterdam: Benjamins, 321–347.
Bowdle, Brian & Gregory Ward 1995. Generic demonstratives. In: J. Ahlers et al. (eds.). *Proceedings of the Twenty-First Annual Meeting of the Berkeley Linguistics Society*. Berkeley, CA: Berkeley Linguistics Society, 32–43.

Braun, David 2006. Names and natural kind terms. In: E. Lepore & B. Smith (eds.). *Handbook of Philosophy of Language*. Oxford: Oxford University Press, 490–515.

Brockett, Chris 1991. *Wa-Marking in Japanese and the Syntax and Semantics of Generic Sentences*. Ph. D. dissertation. Cornell University, Ithaca, NY.

Burton-Roberts, Noel 1977. Generic sentences and analyticity. *Studies in Language* 1, 155–196.

Carlson, Gregory 1977a. *Reference to Kinds in English*. Ph. D. dissertation. University of Massachusetts, Amherst, MA.

Carlson, Gregory 1977b. A unified analysis of the English bare plural. *Linguistics & Philosophy* 1, 413–457.

Carlson, Gregory 1979. Generics and atemporal when. *Linguistics & Philosophy* 3, 49–98.

Carlson, Gregory 1988. The semantic composition of English generic sentences. In: G. Chierchia, B. Partee & R. Turner (eds.). *Property Theory, Type Theory, and Semantics*. Dordrecht: Reidel, 167–192.

Carlson, Gregory 1995. Truth-conditions of generic sentences: Two contrasting views. In: G. Carlson & F. J. Pelletier (eds.). *The Generic Book*. Chicago, IL: The University of Chicago Press, 224–237.

Carlson, Gregory 2009. Generics and concepts. In: F. J. Pelletier (ed.). *Kinds, Things and Stuff*. Oxford: Oxford University Press, 16–35.

Carlson, Gregory & Francis J. Pelletier (eds.) 1995. *The Generic Book*. Chicago, IL: The University of Chicago Press.

Carlson, Gregory & Beverly Spejewski 1997. Generic passages. *Natural Language Semantics* 5, 101–165.

Cheng, Lisa & Rint Sybesma 1999. Bare and not-so-bare nouns and the structure of NP. *Linguistic Inquiry* 30, 509–542.

Chierchia, Gennaro 1984. *Topics in the Syntax and Semantics of Infinitives and Gerunds*. Ph.D. dissertation. University of Massachusetts, Amherst, MA.

Chierchia, Gennaro 1995. *The Dynamics of Meaning*. Chicago, IL: The University of Chicago Press.

Chierchia, Gennaro 1998. Reference to kinds across languages. *Natural Language Semantics* 6, 339–405.

Cohen, Ariel 1999. *Think Generic!* Stanford, CA: CSLI Publications.

Cohen, Ariel 2001. On the generic use of indefinite singulars. *Journal of Semantics* 18, 183–209.

Cohen, Ariel 2002. Genericity. *Linguistische Berichte* 10, 59–89.

Cohen, Ariel & Nomi Erteschik-Shir 1999. Are bare plurals indefinite? In: F. Corblin, C. Dobrovie-Sorin & J. Marandin (eds.). *Empirical Issues in Formal Syntax and Semantics. Selected papers from the Colloque de Syntaxe et de Sémantique de Paris (CSSP'97)*. The Hague: Thesus, 99–109.

Contreras, Heles 1986. Spanish bare NP's and the ECP. In: I. Bordelois, H. Contreras & K. Zagona (eds.). *Generative Studies in Spanish Syntax*. Dordrecht: Foris, 25–49.

Dahl, Östen 1975. On generics. In: E. Keenan (ed.). *Formal Semantics of Natural Language*. Cambridge: Cambridge University Press, 99–111.

Dahl, Östen 1985. *Tense and Aspect Systems*. Oxford: Blackwell.

Dahl, Östen 1995. The marking of the episodic/generic distinction in tense/aspect systems. In: G. Carlson & F. J. Pelletier (eds.). *The Generic Book*. Chicago, IL: The University of Chicago Press, 412–425.

Dayal, Veneeta 2004. Number marking and (in)definiteness in kind terms. *Linguistics & Philosophy* 27, 393–450.

Delfitto, Denis 2002. *Genericity in Language*. Allessandria: Edizioni dell'Orso.
Delgrande, James P. 1987. A first-order conditional logic for prototypical properties. *Artificial Intelligence* 33, 105–130.
Diesing, Molly 1992. *Indefinites*. Cambridge, MA: The MIT Press.
Dobrovie-Sorin, Carmen & Brenda Laca 1997. On the definiteness of generic bare NP's. Paper presented at the Institute for Advanced Studies, The Hebrew University, Jerusalem.
Eckardt, Regine 1999. Normal objects, normal worlds, and the meaning of generic sentences. *Journal of Semantics* 16, 237–278.
Erteschik-Shir, Nomi 1997. *The Dynamics of Focus Structure*. Cambridge: Cambridge University Press.
Farkas, Donka & Yoko Sugioka 1983. Restrictive if/when clauses. *Linguistics & Philosophy* 6, 225–258.
Filip, Hana & Gregory Carlson 1997. Sui generis genericity. In: A. Dimitriadis et al. (eds.). *Proceedings of the 21st Annual Penn Linguistics Colloquium* (Penn Working Papers in Linguistics 4). Philadelphia, PA: Penn Linguistics Club, 91–110.
von Fintel, Kai 1994. *Restrictions on Quantifier Domains*. Ph.D. dissertation. University of Massachusetts, Amherst, MA.
Gerstner-Link, Claudia 1998. *A Typological Approach to Generics*. Ms. München, University of München.
Greenberg, Yael 2003. *Manifestations of Genericity*. London: Routledge.
Heim, Irene 1982. *The Semantics of Definite and Indefinite Noun Phrases*. Ph.D. dissertation. University of Massachusetts, Amherst, MA. Reprinted: Ann Arbor, MI: University Microfilms.
Jäger, Gerhard 2001. Topic-comment structure and the contrast between stage-level and individual-level predicates. *Journal of Semantics* 18, 83–126.
Kamp, Hans 1981. A theory of truth and semantic representation. In: J. Groenendijk, T. Janssen & M. Stokhof (eds.). *Formal Methods in the Study of Language*. Amsterdam: Mathematical Centre, 277–322.
Kamp, Hans & Uwe Reyle 1993. *From Discourse to Logic*. Dordrecht: Kluwer.
Keenan, Edward L. & Jonathan Stavi 1986. The semantic characterization of natural language determiners. *Linguistics & Philosophy* 9, 253–326.
Kiss, Katalin 1998. On generic and existential bare plurals and the classification of predicates. In: S. Rothstein (ed.). *Events and Grammar*. Dordrecht: Kluwer, 145–162.
Kratzer, Angelika 1995. Stage-level and individual-level predicates. In: G. Carlson & F. J. Pelletier (eds.). *The Generic Book*. Chicago, IL: The University of Chicago Press, 125–174.
Krifka, Manfred 1987. *An Outline of Generics* (SNS-Bericht 87–23). Tübingen: University of Tübingen. (Partly in collaboration with Claudia Gerstner).
Krifka, Manfred 2004. Bare NPs: Kind-referring, indefinites, both, or neither? In: O. Bonami & P. Cabredo Hofherr (eds.). *Empirical Issues in Formal Syntax and Semantics 5*. Paris: University of Paris/Sorbonne Press, 111–132.
Krifka, Manfred, F. Jeffry Pelletier, Gregory Carlson, Alice ter Meulen, Gennaro Chierchia, & Godehard Link 1995. Genericity: An introduction. In: G. Carlson & F. J. Pelletier (eds.). *The Generic Book*. Chicago, IL: The University of Chicago Press, 1–124.
Kripke, Saul 1980. *Naming and Necessity*. Cambridge, MA: Harvard University Press.
Kuroda, Sige-Yuki 1972. The categorical and the thetic judgment. *Foundations of Language* 9, 153–185.
Laca, Brenda 1990. Generic objects: Some more pieces of the puzzle. *Lingua* 81, 25–46.

Landman, Fred 1989. Groups I. *Linguistics & Philosophy* 12, 559–605.
Lawler, John 1973. *Studies in English Generics*. Ph.D. dissertation. University of Michigan, Ann Arbor, MI. Reprinted: Ann Arbor, MI: University Microfilms.
Leslie, Sarah-Jane 2007. *Generics. Cognition, and Comprehension*. Ph.D. dissertation. Princeton University, Princeton, NY.
Leslie, Sarah-Jane 2008. Generics: Cognition and acquisition. *Philosophical Review* 117, 1–47.
Lewis, David 1975. Adverbs of quantification. In: E. Keenan (ed.). *Formal Semantics of Natural Languages*. Cambridge: Cambridge University Press, 3–15.
Link, Godehard 1983. The logical analysis of plurals and mass terms: A lattice-theoretical approach. In: R. Bäuerle, Ch. Schwarze & A. von Stechow (eds.). *Meaning, Use and the Interpretation of Language*. Berlin: de Gruyter, 303–323.
Longobardi, Giuseppe 1994. Reference and proper names: A theory of N-movement in syntax and logical form. *Linguistic Inquiry* 25, 609–669.
ter Meulen, Alice 1986. Generic information, conditional contexts and constraints. In: E. Traugott et al. (eds.). *On Conditionals*. Cambridge: Cambridge University Press, 123–146.
Moore, George Edward 1942. Russell's "Theory of Descriptions". In: P. A. Schilpp (ed.). *The Philosophy of G. E. Moore*. Evanston, IL: Northwestern University Press, 177–225.
Nickel, Bernhard 2008. Generics and the ways of normality. *Linguistics & Philosophy* 31, 629–648.
Ojeda, Almerindo 1991. Definite descriptions and definite generics. *Linguistics & Philosophy* 14, 367–397.
Ojeda, Almerindo 1993. *Linguistic Individuals*. Stanford, CA: CSLI Publications.
Partee, Barbara 1992. Topic, focus and quantification. In: A. Wyner & S. Moore (eds.). *Proceedings of Semantics and Linguistic Theory (=SALT) I*. Ithaca, NY: Cornell University, 159–187.
Partee, Barbara 1995. Quantificational structures and compositionality. In: E. Bach et al. (eds.). *Quantification in Natural Languages*. Dordrecht: Kluwer, 541–601.
Pelletier, F. Jeffry & Nicholas Asher 1997. Generics and defaults. In: J. van Benthem & A. ter Meulen (eds.). *Handbook of Logic and Language*. Cambridge, MA: The MIT Press, 1125–1179.
Platteau, Frank 1980. Definite and indefinite generics. In: J. van der Auwera (ed.). *The Semantics of Determiners*. London: Croom Helm, 112–123.
Putnam, Hilary 1975. The meaning of 'meaning'. In: K. Gunderson (ed.). *Language, Mind, and Knowledge*. Minneapolis, MN: University of Minnesota Press, 131–193.
Quirk, Randolph, Sidney Greenbaum, Geoffrey Leech & Jan Svartvik 1985. *Comprehensive Grammar of the English Language*. London: Longmans.
Reinhart, Tanya 1981. Pragmatics and linguistics: An analysis of sentence topics. *Philosophica* 27, 53–94.
Reiter, Raymond 1980. A logic for default reasoning. *Artificial Intelligence* 13, 81–132.
Roberts, Craige 1989. Modal subordination and pronominal anaphora in discourse. *Linguistics & Philosophy* 12, 683–721.
Sasse, Hans-Jürgen 1987. The thetic/categorical distinction revisited. *Linguistics* 25, 511–580.
Schubert, Lenhart 1999. Dynamic skolemization. In: H. Bunt & R. Muskens (eds.). *Computing Meaning, vol. 1*. Dordrecht: Kluwer, 219–253.
Schubert, Lenhart & F. Jeffry Pelletier 1987. Problems in the representation of the logical form of generics, plurals, and mass nouns. In: E. LePore (ed.). *New Directions in Semantics*. London: Academic Press, 385–451.

Stebbing, Susan 1930. *A Modern Introduction to Logic*. London: Methuen.
de Swart, Henriëtte 1993. Definite and indefinite generics. In: P. Dekker & M. Stokhof (eds.). *Proceedings of the 9th Amsterdam Colloquium*. Amsterdam: ILLC, 625–644.
Torrego, Esther 1989. Unergative-unaccusative alternations in Spanish. In: I. Laka & A. Mahajan (eds.). *Functional Heads and Clause Structure* (MIT Working Papers in Linguistics 10). Cambridge, MA: MIT, 253–269.
Wilkinson, Karina 1991. *Studies in the Semantics of Generic Noun Phrases*. Ph. D. dissertation. University of Massachusetts, Amherst, MA.

Hana Filip
9 Aspectual class and Aktionsart

1. Overview: Main research traditions and terminology —— 274
2. Origins of the Aristotelian tradition —— 278
3. Tense logic —— 284
4. Dowty's aspect calculus —— 287
5. Event semantics —— 294
6. Current trends —— 301
7. References —— 306

Abstract: This contribution provides an overview of the main categories of aspectual class and Aktionsart, and a review of the development of typologies from Aristotle to the present day. Key theories of aspectual classes in linguistics and philosophy are discussed, and their contribution to our understanding of how verb meaning, compositional processes and pragmatic principles of interpretation determine the aspectual class of particular sentences. Meaning components that motivate the assignment of simple verbs and complex predicates to aspectual classes also play a role in other areas of semantic and pragmatic research, namely in the thematic role theory, for example, and intersect with the grammar of measurement and scalar semantics.

1 Overview: Main research traditions and terminology

The grammar of natural languages systematically distinguishes between two kinds of description of states of affairs: those that necessarily involve some end or limit (e.g., *leave, find, die*) and those that do not (e.g., *walk, see, know*). This essential distinction is taken to originate in Aristotle's dichotomy KINÊSIS ('motion', also 'change') vs. ENERGEIA (translated as 'actuality', 'actualization', also 'activity') (*Metaphysics*, Θ6, 1048b, 18–36). While KINÊSEIS (plural form) are always for the sake of some external end, ENERGEIAI (plural form) have ends that are 'actualized' as soon as they begin. In contemporary linguistics, this distinction is best known

---

Hana Filip, Düsseldorf, Germany

https://doi.org/10.1515/9783110589443-009

as the TELIC vs. ATELIC distinction, coined by Garey (1957), based on the Greek word *télos* 'goal' or 'purpose'. Telic predicates express "an action tending towards a goal" (Garey 1957: 106), while atelic predicates describe situations that "are realized as soon as they begin" (Garey 1957: 106). Despite the implication of agentivity inherent in the term 'telic', Garey illustrates his telic class with the non-agentive verb *se noyer* 'to drown', which means that his distinction is compatible with subsequent agentivity-neutral Aristotelian classifications (e g , Bennett & Partee 1972; Comrie 1976; Mourelatos 1978; Bach 1981).

The semantic (and ontological) nature of this basic distinction and its encoding in natural languages are at the core of the studies in ASPECTUAL CLASS and AKTIONSART (German, lit.: 'manner of action', also used in its plural form AKTIONSARTEN 'manners of action'). These two terms reflect the historical division of the field into two main strands. The English-language term ASPECTUAL CLASS is used co-extensively with the term 'Aristotelian class' (see Dowty 1979: 52). What 'Aristotelian' here means is shaped by the works of Oxford philosophers of language and mind, Ryle (1949) and Kenny (1963), in particular, with Ryle in turn inspiring Vendler (1957) whose impact on linguistics has been by far the most profound. The early theory formation in linguistics in the late 1960s and in the 1970s was carried by logicians and formal semanticists who laid the methodological foundations within tense logic (cf. article 13 [this volume] (Ogihara) *Tense*), Montague Semantics and Generative Semantics (Bennett & Partee 1972; Dowty 1979; Montague 1968, 1973; Scott 1970; Taylor 1977). In the 1980s, the domain of aspectual classes was established as an important area of research and also received a new impetus with the advent of event semantics (Bach 1981, 1986) (cf. article 8 [Semantics: Theories] (Maienborn) *Event semantics*), and its ties to the semantics of mass terms and plurals (Link 1983, 1987) (cf. article 7 [this volume] (Lasersohn) *Mass nouns and plurals*). Much of the work in the Aristotelian tradition was originally motivated by the goal of formulating explanatory hypotheses for the existence of aspectual classes and understanding the nature of compositional processes needed in the derivation of aspectual classes at the level of VPs and sentences (Krifka 1986; Verkuyl 1971). This in turn stimulated new insights into the syntax-semantics interface (cf. article 6 [Semantics: Interfaces] (von Stechow) *Syntax and semantics*), lexical semantics of verbs as well as the theory of THEMATIC ROLES and ARGUMENT SELECTION (Dowty 1987, 1991) (cf. article 3 [Semantics: Lexical Structures and Adjectives] (Davis) *Thematic roles*). The most recent developments concern the crosslinguistic variation in the encoding of aspectual classes, implications for the status of aspectual classes as (possible) semantic universals (cf. article 2 [Semantics: Typology, Diachrony and Processing] (Bach & Chao) *Semantic types across languages*) and their consequences for theories of language acquisition (cf. article 11 [Semantics: Typology, Diachrony and Processing] (Slabakova) *Meaning in second language acquisition*).

The German-language term AKTIONSART(EN) has its roots in the (Proto-)Indo-European (e.g., Sanskrit, Greek, (Old Church) Slavic, Romance, Germanic) and Semitic studies in the continental philology of the late 19th and early 20th century. The term AKTIONSART(EN) was coined by Agrell (1908) to cover the lexicalization of various 'manners of action' (e.g., terminative, resultative, delimitative, perdurative, iterative, semelfactive, attenuative, augmentative) by means of overt derivational word-formation devices, and set apart from grammatical ASPECT, as instantiated, for instance, in Slavic languages by its two main formal categories, PERFECTIVE and IMPERFECTIVE (identified earlier by Miklosich 1868–1874). The theoretical elaboration of the Aktionsart vs. grammatical aspect distinction was the focus of much of the traditional European descriptive and structuralist research during the first half of the 20th century. The relevant discussions mainly regarded form-oriented issues: namely, the differentiation of morphemes dedicated to the encoding of Aktionsart, as opposed to grammatical aspect, in complex verb forms in Indo-European languages. A large part of debates hinged on what exactly 'grammatical' is supposed to mean, and many settled on 'expressed by INFLECTIONAL morphology', i.e., morphology relevant to syntax (e.g., Anderson 1982) (cf. article 2 [Semantics: Interfaces] (Kiparsky & Tonhauser) *Semantics of inflection*). This led to the search for the requisite invariant meanings of the perfective and imperfective morphology (for overviews see Comrie 1976; Forsyth 1970), while the markedness theory (Isačenko 1962; Jakobson 1936 and reference therein) introduced theoretical constraints into the relevant discussions, which have since then shaped approaches to grammatical aspect. On one dominant view, mainly formulated in Slavic linguistics, the perfective is the marked category in the privative opposition to the unmarked imperfective, and often characterized in terms of some boundary (*predel'nost'* in Russian) with respect to which described situations are viewed as having reached their end, or can be viewed in their totality (*celostnost' dejstvija* 'totality of an event' in Russian). This idea became widespread in contemporary aspect studies largely due to Comrie's (1976) characterization: "perfectivity indicates the view of a situation as a single whole (...), while the imperfective pays essential attention to the internal structure of the situation" (Comrie 1976: 16); generally, the grammatical aspect distinguishes "different ways of viewing the internal temporal constituency of a situation" (Comrie 1976: 16). This characterization is aptly highlighted in Smith's (1991) term VIEWPOINT ASPECT for grammatical aspect, which is set apart from SITUATION ASPECT, meant to be coextensive with 'aspectual class' in Dowty's (1979) sense. One of the most influential formalizations of the 'viewpoint' semantic characterization of grammatical aspect is given by Klein (1994), who ties Reichenbach's (1947) theory of tense with work in formal semantics: the progressive/imperfective aspect is characterized as 'topic time (i.e., Reichenbach's 'reference time') within event time' (i.e., looking at event from within), and perfective aspect as 'event time within topic time' (i.e., looking at event as a completed whole). The widespread use and intuitive appeal of the 'viewpoint' based characterizations may also stem from the etymological origins of the term 'aspect'. This term is a loan translation of the Slavic term VID, etymologically cognate with 'view' and 'vision', and related to the Latin word *aspectus* translated as 'view', '(the act of) seeing, looking at'. As a linguistic term, *vid* was first used in the early 17th century work on Old Church Slavic by Smotritsky (1619) (see Binnick 1991: 135–214 for a terminological overview).

Starting in the early 1970s, there have been gradually increasing efforts to integrate insights from the two until then largely separate research traditions in which the terms ASPECTUAL CLASS and AKTIONSART originated. In the 1970s, in the European generative grammar frameworks (e.g., Platzack 1979; Verkuyl 1972), the association of the notion of 'Aktionsart(en)' with lexical semantics led to loosening of its dependence on overt derivational morphology and its merging with aspectual classes in the Aristotelian sense of Dowty (1979). In this sense, 'Aktionsart(en)' made entrance into American linguistics in the mid 1980s (Hinrichs 1985). In the late 1960s and the early 1970s, philosophers, logicians and formal semanticists who studied the progressive vs. non-progressive contrast in English (cf. article 10 [this volume] (Portner) *Perfect and progressive*) in dependence on the Aristotelian classes became increasingly aware of the studies devoted to grammatical aspect in the continental philology of the 19th and early 20th century, and in later descriptive and structuralist traditions. The terms 'perfective' and 'imperfective' became standard in contemporary linguistics in the 1970s (Mourelatos 1978: 195, n. 10), mainly through the wide-spread reception of Comrie (1976) and Dowty (1977, 1979). These developments raised difficult questions about the relation between the perfective and imperfective GRAMMATICAL ASPECT, or 'aspectual form' (Dowty 1979: 52), and aspectual classes, which also came to be known as LEXICAL ASPECT, and often used not only with reference to expressions at the lexical V level, but also misleadingly at the levels of VPs and sentences. On one proposal, the function of the perfective/imperfective morphology is to encode aspectual classes (Mourelatos 1978: 194–195), which is taken to justify a single, possibly universal, semantic/conceptual dimension in terms of which phenomena belonging to both the grammatical aspect and aspectual/Aristotelian classes are analyzed. On another widespread view, aspectual classes are to be clearly distinguished from the grammatical aspect, formally and also semantically, as each is taken to require distinct analytical tools (cf. Dahl 1985; Depraetere 1995; Dowty 1977, 1979; Filip 1993; Klein 1994; Smith 1991, among others). While both positions are advocated by different strands of aspect theories, there has been a steadily growing awareness of differences between the semantic system of aspectual classes, on the one hand, and grammatical aspect systems, on the other hand, which preclude straightforward one-to-one mappings between them; the systematic relations between these two systems vary from language to language depending on how grammatical aspect is realized in a given language, if it is an overt grammatical category or possibly treated as a covert one.

2 Origins of the Aristotelian tradition

2.1 Ryle, Kenny and Vendler

Ryle (1949) coined the term ACHIEVEMENTS for end-oriented actions (Ryle 1949: 149) and contrasted them with ACTIVITIES lacking any end, goal or result over and above that which consists in their performance (Ryle 1949: 150). The criterion of agentivity distinguishes ACHIEVEMENTS involving some result preceded by an intentional 'subservient task activity' (*score a goal, prove the theorem, win a race*) from 'purely lucky achievements' like *notice* that are not agentive: **My mother carefully noticed the spot* (Ryle 1949: 151). Kenny (1963) introduces a clear distinction between ACTIVITIES and STATES, and sets them apart from PERFORMANCES that are specified by their ends: "[a]ny performance is describable in the form: 'bringing it about that *p*'" (Kenny 1963: 178). "[E]very performance must be ultimately the bringing about of a state or of an activity" (Kenny 1963: 178) in order to prevent an infinite regress. Kenny motivated his three classes with diagnostic tests which now belong to the standard toolkit for detecting aspectually relevant meaning components (cf. Dowty 1979: 55ff; Parsons 1990: 34–39). For example, activity and performance predicates freely occur in the progressive, but not all state predicates can. In the simple present tense, activities (*John smokes*) and performances (*Mary bakes cakes faster than Jane*) have a habitual interpretation, while states do not (*John loves cigars*). Performance predicates prohibit the conclusion of "x has ɸ-ed" from "x is ɸ-ing", but activity predicates often allow it.

Vendler (1957) defines four classes that are intended to capture "the most common time schemata implied by the use of English verbs" (Vendler 1957: 144):

(1) STATES: *desire, want, love, hate, dominate*;
ACTIVITIES: *run, walk, swim, push (a cart)*;
ACHIEVEMENTS: *recognize, reach, find, win (the race), start/stop/resume, be born/die*;
ACCOMPLISHMENTS: *run a mile, paint a picture, grow up, recover from illness*.

Both accomplishments and activities involve *periods of time*, but only accomplishments also require that they be unique and definite (Vendler 1967: 149). Both states and achievements involve *time instants*, but only achievements "occur at a single moment" (Vendler 1967: 147), while states hold at *any* instant during the interval at which they are true (Vendler 1967: 149). The idea that *only* activities and accomplishments 'go on in time' is taken to motivate their compatibility with the 'continuous tense', i.e., the progressive, a property not shared by states and achievements. Hence, Vendler uses the progressive test to group activities and accomplishments into one basic class and states with achievements into another. Activities are distinguished from accomplishments due to their differential behavior with temporal adverbials. As (2) shows, only accomplishment predicates freely combine with *in NP* modifiers like *in an hour*. (The interpretation of *in NP* that is relevant for this test measures the extent of events described by accomplishment predicates, the irrelevant interpretation concerns the measure of time until their onset from 'now' or some other reference point, see also Vendler 1957: 147.) In contrast, only activity predicates can be freely modified with *for NP* temporal adverbials.

(2)

	in an hour	for an hour	
a. John ran a mile in an hour	√	*	ACCOMPLISHMENT
b. John reached the summit	*	*	ACHIEVEMENT
c. John ran	*	√	ACTIVITY
d. John knew the answer	*	?	STATE

Although the progressive and *in/for* tests are widely used, caution must be taken in their application. Vendler's achievements, just like his accomplishments, can appear in the progressive: *he is winning the race/dying/reaching the top/leaving* (Dowty 1977; Mourelatos 1978: 193). This effectively undermines Vendler's key diagnostic test for the separation between achievements and accomplishments, which is one of the most criticized weaknesses of his proposal. In addition, most states can be used in the progressive in the appropriate context, albeit often with special interpretations: *I'm really loving the play, I'm understanding you but I'm not believing you* (Bach 1981: 77), *I am understanding more about quantum mechanics as each day goes by* (Comrie 1976: 36; also Zucchi 1999, among others). There are also states that pattern with activities, rather than with achievements, in so far as they are compatible with *for NP* temporal adverbials: *Locals believed for years that a mysterious monster lurked in the lake.*

In connection with the temporal adverbial *in/for* test, Vendler introduced one of the most important criterial properties into aspect studies: namely, the semantic property of homogeneity. Only activities like "running and its kind go on in time in a homogeneous way; any part of the process is of the same nature as the whole"

(Vendler 1957: 146). If John ran *for an hour*, then, at any time during that hour it was true that John ran. In contrast, accomplishments are not homogeneous. If John wrote a letter *in an hour*, then it is not true that he wrote a letter at any time during that hour. This in turn follows from the characterizing property of accomplishments: namely, they "proceed toward a terminus which is logically necessary to their being what they are" (Vendler 1957: 146), and which implies that they consist of ordered parts, none of which includes this terminus, apart from the very last one.

2.2 Areas of research in linguistics

It is not entirely clear whether the Aristotelian categories that Ryle, Kenny and Vendler envisioned are of linguistic or ontological nature, which raises the following basic questions: Are these categories inherent in descriptions, in predicates of natural languages? Or, are they properties of states of affairs in the domain, inherent in 'nonlinguistic things in the world' (Parsons 1990: 20)? (cf. article 12 [Semantics: Typology, Diachrony and Processing] (Kelter & Kaup) *Conceptual knowledge, categorization and meaning*.) Some believe they are true ontological categories (Bach 1986; Parsons 1990: 34). Others question this view (Gill 1993) or even reject it (Filip 1993; Krifka 1986; Partee 2000), and one of the reasons for this may be illustrated with the following example. Seeing Ben eat ice cream, we have a choice among a number of possibilities to describe this situation, including *Ben ate ice cream* (activity/atelic) and *Ben ate a bowl of ice cream* (accomplishment/telic). There is nothing in the nature of the world itself that would force us to use one description and not the other. It is predicates that offer us different choices in the description of the world's phenomena and that impose categorization schemas on the world. Aristotelian classes then concern predicates of natural languages, and consequently, it only makes sense to speak of 'accomplishment predicates' or 'telic predicates', for instance, but not of 'accomplishment events' or 'telic events' (Krifka 1998: 207).

Although Vendler's (1957) classification has enjoyed the most widespread use, its four-fold division as well as the program of motivating it in terms of "the most common time schemata implied by the use of English verbs" (Vendler 1957: 144) have been subjected to much criticism and revisions. First, Vendler's own examples clearly indicate that his classes do not just concern the meaning of individual verb lexemes or surface verbs. Second, the grounding of Vendler's classes – or any Aristotelian classes for that matter – is not to be seen in purely temporal properties of moments and intervals of time, but is at least partly if not entirely based on properties that are not of temporal nature. Turning to the first point, all agree with Dowty (1979) that Vendler's (1957) attempt "to classify surface verbs once and for all" (Dowty

1979: 62) into Aristotelian classes is "somewhat misguided" (ibid.). The reason for this has to do with the observation that verbs manifest a considerable variability in their assignment to aspectual classes in dependence on their context of use, and hence the aspectual class of basic (underived) verbs does not always (fully) determine the aspectual class of their projections. Consequently, the domain of Vendler's classification in natural languages extends from basic verbs to at least VPs, and according to some, following Verkuyl (1972) and Dowty (1972, 1979), it also extends to sentences, since they take the (external) subject (argument) to be one among the determining factors of aspectual classes. Dowty (1979: 185) goes even further in extending the empirical scope of Aristotelian categorization by concluding that it "is not a categorization of verbs, it is not a categorization of sentences, but rather of the propositions conveyed by utterances, given particular background assumptions by speaker and/or hearer about the nature of the situations under discussion". This insight has only gradually been gaining prominence, and although it is now generally accepted across a wide spectrum of theoretical frameworks (Bennett & Partee 1972; Depraetere 2007; Filip 1993; Jackendoff 1996; Kratzer 2004; Krifka 1986, 1992; Langacker 1990; Levin & Rappaport Hovav 2005; Partee 1999, among others), the integration of the relevant pragmatic and cognitive principles of interpretation into full-fledged theoretical frameworks remains one of the outstanding problems.

At the same time, Dowty's conclusion, also independently later recognized by many others, raised doubts whether Aristotelian categories constitute generalizations over classes of predicates that ought to be a part of the grammar of natural languages. Two main arguments can be provided in defense of their grammatical status. First, they are grammatically significant due to the way in which they interact with the syntactic and morphological structure in natural languages (Dowty 1979: 185; Carlson 1981). Second, when a given verb, a verb phrase or a sentence changes its aspectual class in dependence on context, this change follows systematic patterns. For instance, epistemic verbs like *know* or *understand* predictably shift from their dominant state sense to an achievement 'insight' sense in the context of time-point adverbials like *suddenly* or *once*: *And then suddenly I knew!* (Vendler 1957: 153), *Once Lisa understood (grasped) what Henry's intentions were, she lost all interest in him* (Mourelatos 1978: 196). To take another example, virtually any activity verb can have an accomplishment sense in an appropriate linguistic context, possibly in interaction with extra-linguistic knowledge. One triggering context is the temporal *in NP* adverbial, as in *Today John swam* [i.e., a certain distance] *in an hour* (Dowty 1979: 61), another is the embedding under a phasal verb, as in *Today John finished/ stopped/started swimming early* (Dowty 1979: 61). Verbs derived from gradable adjectives ('degree achievements' in the sense of Dowty 1979) predictably alternate between the activity and accomplishment interpretation in dependence on temporal adverbials: *The soup cooled for/in 10 minutes.* It is precisely the task of a theory of aspectual classes to formulate correct and testable predictions about such patterns. The strategy is to derive aspectual classes in a systematic way from the meaning of verbs in interaction with the properties of temporal modifiers, phasal verbs, verbal affixes, adverbs of quantification (cf. article 14 [Semantics: Lexical Structures and Adjectives] (Maienborn & Schäfer) *Adverbs and adverbials*), tense operators (e.g., present tense), grammatical aspect operators (e.g., progressive) as well as quantificational and referential properties of nominal arguments (cf. article 4 [this volume] (Keenan) *Quantifiers*, article 5 [this volume] (Dayal) *Bare noun phrases*, article 7 [this volume] (Lasersohn) *Mass nouns and plurals*). The main theoretical focus of recent and contemporary aspectual studies is on the compositional processes implicated in the observed patterns, and we have a number of competing proposals to analyze data that are of non-compositional nature, including underspecification (cf. article 9 [Semantics: Lexical Structures and Adjectives] (Egg) *Semantic underspecification*), ambiguity (cf. article 8 [Semantics: Lexical Structures and Adjectives] (Kennedy) *Ambiguity and vagueness*), general lexical rules, aspect shift and coercion (see e.g., de Swart 1998) (cf. article 10 [Semantics: Lexical Structures and Adjectives] (de Swart) *Mismatches and coercion*), null morphology, and constructional approaches (cf. article 9 [Semantics: Interfaces] (Kay & Michaelis) *Constructional meaning*).

As semanticists today agree, it is the meaning components lexicalized in verbs that constitute a large part of the explanation for the way in which aspectual properties of VPs and sentences are derived from their parts. They motivate Vendler's (1957) rudimentary time schemata associated with surface verbs, and later more explicit characterizations by means of temporal meaning postulates, as in Taylor (1977). This idea, which originated in the works of Verkuyl (1972) and Dowty (1972, 1977, 1979), raises two main questions that are still discussed today: (1) What exactly are the aspectually relevant meaning components, how are they related to each other and how do they uniquely determine the relevant Aristotelian classes and no other? (2) How are aspectually relevant meaning components lexicalized in verbs related to their other meaning components and how do they interact with the syntactic, morphological and semantic structure of sentences in natural languages? Answers to such questions reveal the basic need for clarifying the empirical basis for a well-motivated theory of Aristotelian classes. What is still needed are *reliable* criteria that would allow us to provide systematic answers to the above questions. It is not always entirely clear what exactly the diagnostic criteria used by various researchers test for in linguistic expressions, and since the most common linguistic tests were developed based on English data (Dowty 1979: 55ff), not all the tests are transferable across natural languages, due to language-specific properties, and those that seem to be require some clarification whether they in fact access the same aspectually relevant properties in different languages (Sasse 2002). Moreover, the diagnostic tests commonly used in English

(Dowty 1979: 55ff) do not converge on coherent categories, such as Vendler's, but identify overlapping clusters which merely distinguish subsets of such categories (Dowty 1979: 60; Parsons 1989) or supersets.

The second main point regards the temporal grounding of Vendler's classes, and generally any aspectual classes of the Aristotelian type. In accordance with Vendler's (1957) explicit statements, they are commonly identified with 'temporal aspect' (L. Carlson 1981), the 'temporal constitution of verbal predicates' (Krifka 1992), or the 'temporal contours' introduced by verbs (Levin & Rappaport Hovav 2005), which would seem to suggest that their purely temporal grounding is taken for granted. Indeed, much of the research on aspectual classes was conducted within tense logic (introduced by Prior 1957, 1967) (cf. article 13 [this volume] (Ogihara) *Tense*), and related modal logic (cf. article 14 [this volume] (Hacquard) *Modality*), starting in the late 1960s until the early 1980s (Section 3). However, Vendler (1957: 149) himself, despite his emphasis on temporal criteria, cautions that the time element is insufficient observing that non-temporal factors like the presence or absence of an object argument, speaker's intention (Vendler 1957: 143) and agentivity (Vendler 1957: 149), for example, also play a role. Since Dowty's decompositional analysis (Section 4) and the advent of event semantics in the 1980s (Section 5) (cf. article 12 [Semantics: Theories] (Maienborn) *Event semantics*), non-temporal criteria have been gaining prominence among aspectually relevant meaning components lexicalized in verbs. In this connection, we see the rise of mereologically-based properties (Bach 1981, 1986), which are defined based on the part-whole structure of space-occupying objects, as originally proposed by Taylor (1977). Starting in the 1990's, aspectually relevant meaning components have been derived from the concepts used to structure space and from scalar semantics (Section 6). The inclusion of such non-temporally grounded properties into the inventory of aspectually relevant properties raises questions about the purely temporal grounding of Aristotelian categories in general, namely, to what extent they are emergent properties arising from the interaction of more basic properties that are not of purely temporal nature (see also Dowty 1979). This also led to refinements of empirical tests grounding aspectual classes and to classifications of verb meanings that cannot be neatly aligned with Vendler's four-way schema.

Despite mounting evidence to the contrary, many scholars still take Vendler's classification as a linguistic fact, or at least a convenient point of reference, routinely crediting Dowty (1979) for introducing Vendler's classes into linguistics and providing arguments in their support. What is often failed to be recognized or fully appreciated is that Dowty (1979) does not just provide a decompositional analysis of Vendler's classes, but instead proposes an alternative classification (Dowty 1979, Chapter 3.8; see below Section 4), and others have followed suit since then. Dowty's revised classification comes close to Mourelatos' (1978) tripartite agentivity-neutral classification into STATES, PROCESSES (Dowty's 'indefinite change of state' predicates) and EVENTS (Dowty's 'definite change of state' predicates) (Section 5.1), which in turn is commonly used with some refinements in event semantics (starting with Bach 1981, 1986 and Parsons 1990) (Section 5.2). In sum, while Aristotelian aspectual classes are now established as generalizations over classes of predicates in the grammar of natural languages, their exact number and kind is not, and certainly Vendler's classification, despite its prominence, cannot be taken for granted. Hence, the two most basic questions still remain to be answered: What is the classification schema of aspectual classes and Aktionsart(en) that best fits the natural language data? What constitutes valid empirical evidence (like linguistic tests) for such a classification schema? (cf. article 12 [Semantics: Foundations, History and Methods] (Krifka) *Varieties of semantic evidence.*)

3 Tense logic

Aristotelian categories proved to be indispensable for the analyses of the contrast between simple and progressive sentences (cf. article 10 [this volume] (Portner) *Perfect and progressive*) and stimulated analyses of verb meanings within a formal (model-theoretic) semantics (cf. article 7 [Semantics: Theories] (Zimmermann) *Model-theoretic semantics*). The point of departure is Montague's characterization of the progressive in English (see Montague 1973): a progressive sentence is true at a given time *t* if and only if the corresponding non-progressive sentence is true at every moment throughout some open interval around *t* (see also Montague 1968; Scott 1970). This, however, fails to give us the right results for Kenny's (1963) entailment test (Section 2.1): namely, it wrongly predicts that *Jones is walking to Rome* entails *Jones has walked to Rome*, and from *Jones is walking* we can conclude *Jones has walked* just in case additional temporal and pragmatic assumptions about evaluation times are made. These problems stem from the Priorian tense logic presupposed by *PTQ*, in which sentences (under a given interpretation) are true at a moment of time. While this treatment is suitable for sentences with state predicates (*John has long arms, John is drunk*) or with punctual predicates (*The rock hit the window*), it fails for sentences like *John builds a house*, because, among others, it makes no sense to speak of their truth or falsity at a single moment of time.

Such observations led Bennett & Partee (1972) to revise tense logic by taking the notion of a true sentence at an interval of time as basic, which marks the inception of INTERVAL SEMANTICS as a new branch of tense logic (cf. article

13 [this volume] (Ogihara) *Tense*). In order to improve on *PTQ*'s analysis of the progressive, they propose an INTERVAL-WITHIN-A-SUPERINTERVAL characterization: A progressive sentence is true at an interval *I* if and only if *I* is a moment of time, and there exists an interval *I'* which contains *I*, and *I* is not an endpoint for *I'*, and the non-progressive form of the sentence is true at *I'*. The semantic difference between VPs like *walk to Rome* and *walk*, which gives rise to different entailments when they are used in the progressive, is characterized in terms of part-whole relations that structure intervals at which they are evaluated. (This idea foreshadows mereologically-based analyses of Aristotelian aspectual classes in event semantics in the 1980s.) *Walk to Rome* belongs to the class of NONSUBINTERVAL VPs: "If it took an hour to walk to Rome, one did not walk to Rome within the first thirty minutes of the hour" (Bennett & Partee 1972/2004:72). *Walk* falls under SUBINTERVAL VPs that "have the property that if they are the main verb phrase of a sentence which is true at some interval of time *I*, then the sentence is true at every subinterval of *I* including every moment of time in *I*" (Bennett & Partee 1972/2004:72). Now, given that *walk to Rome* is nonsubinterval, and given that the progressive sentence does not require for its truth at *I* that there be any complete (past) interval at which the non-progressive sentence is true (in contrast to *PTQ*), it follows that *Jones is walking to Rome* does *not* entail *Jones has walked to Rome*. While this is the right result, the interval-within-a-superinterval analysis also requires that the conditions for the truth of *Jones is walking to Rome* state that Jones must reach Rome at some time in the future. This requirement is too strong, because *Jones is walking to Rome* is true and can be felicitously uttered, even if Jones only covers a part of the path leading to Rome and never reaches Rome. This problem became known as the 'imperfective paradox' (see Dowty 1977) or the 'partitive puzzle' (see Bach 1986), and its solution still eludes linguists and philosophers alike (see Parsons 1990; Landman 1992; Portner 1998; Higginbotham 2004, among others) (cf. article 10 [this volume] (Portner) *Perfect and progressive*). When it comes to subinterval VPs in the progressive like *walk* in *Jones is walking*, the interval-within-a-superinterval analysis faces the following problem, observed by Taylor (1977: 218) and Bach (1981: 71): namely, it requires that the property of walking hold for the referent of *Jones* at all the single moments within some larger interval of walking, including its very first moment. This requirement is too strong, because what intuitively qualifies as walking takes up a subinterval larger than a single moment of time, i.e., a non-progressive sentence like *John has walked* is only true at certain sufficiently large proper subintervals of *Jones is walking*, and what they are requires appeal to pragmatics (see also Taylor 1977: 218). But this means that the inference of *John has walked* from *Jones is walking* has the status of a pragmatic inference, rather than of a semantically (logically) valid entailment.

Throughout the 1970s and the 1980s, analyses within interval semantics led to significant advances in the study of aspectual classes and their interaction with tense, grammatical aspect and adverbial phrases (van Benthem 1983; Dowty 1979, 1982; Heny 1982; Moens & Steedman 1988; Richards 1982; Rohrer 1980). This work sharpened our understanding of the explanatory depth of the analyses of verb meanings based on properties of intervals and moments of time, and it also uncovered the limits of such analyses. The problems related to a purely tense-logical characterization of Aristotelian classes led Taylor (1977) to proposing a new research program for their study grounded in space-time analogies. Taylor (1977) presupposes an interval-based semantics, just like Bennett & Partee (1972), but cites Dowty (1977) as the relevant previous work. His main goal is to provide an analysis of Aristotelian classes, namely, *state, energeia* and *kinêsis*, which he characterizes in terms of temporal meaning postulates (see Dowty 1979: 166ff for a summary), and their differential interactions with the progressive. Its main function, according to Taylor (1977: 206), is to distinguish a particular time, typically a moment, within a larger interval in which the corresponding non-progressive sentence would be true. This distinction is irrelevant for sentences that contain state predicates like *be hirsute* or *know French*, because they hold for their arguments at *any single* moment within larger intervals at which they are true. Consequently, combined with the progressive they are odd or ungrammatical, because the progressive contributes a meaning component that is not informative. Making it possible for a sentence to hold true at single moments of time is the key temporal property of state predicates setting them apart from all non-states. The latter entail a change of state and hence must be evaluated at intervals *larger than a single moment of time*. Intuitively, a change is a transition from one state of affairs to another, and therefore, in order to judge whether a change of state predicate is true of an individual, we need information about the physical state of the world at two distinct moments at least, i.e., at an interval (see e.g., Dowty 1979: 168; Kamp 1980). Since non-state predicates must be evaluated at intervals larger than a moment of time, the progressive contributes a meaning component that is informative and hence their combination is felicitous. Non-state predicates are divided into *energeia* like *walk* (Bennett & Partee's subinterval VPs) and *kinêsis* like *walk to Rome* (Bennett & Partee's nonsubinterval VPs). A purely temporally based delimitation of these two main classes is complicated by their behavior with respect to the subinterval property. While all *kinêsis* verbs are false at all the subintervals of main intervals at which they are true, *energeia* verbs fail to exhibit a uniform behavior with respect to the subinterval property. Some like *fall* or *blush* are true at all the subintervals larger than a moment, but others like *walk* are true at subintervals that are not only larger than a moment but sufficiently large (see also above). In order to clarify this temporal distinction, Taylor (1977) draws analogies to the spatial properties of objects in the denotation of nouns. *Energeia* verbs like *fall* or *blush* have denotations that pattern with HOMOGENEOUS mass nouns like *gold* in so far as their proper parts are alike. In contrast, the denotations of *energeia* verbs like *walk* pattern with HETEROGENEOUS mass nouns like *fruitcake* in so far as what they describe is divisible only down to certain MINIMAL PROPER PARTS whose size depends on pragmatic factors. To complete the space-time analogy, sentences with *kinêsis* (nonsubinterval) predicates like *walk to Rome* have denotations that are indivisible just like those of sortal nouns like *cat*. In sum then, substances (described by sortal nouns like *cat*) are to stuff (described by mass nouns like *gold*) like the temporal properties of *kinêsis* (nonsubinterval) predicates (*walk to Rome*) are to (subinterval and homogeneous) *energeia* predicates (*blush*).

Taylor's (1977) space-time analogy has wide-reaching theoretical consequences, since it implies that principles of individuation that apply to the denotations of nouns can be used as the basis for a theory of events, and aspectually relevant properties of verbs can be understood in terms of structural analogies to the meanings of count and mass nouns (cf. article 3 [Semantics: Typology, Diachrony and Processing] (Doetjes) *Count/mass distinctions*). Taylor's (1977) programmatic proposal was also instrumental in a shift from purely temporally-based theories of aspectual classes to mereologically-based ones developed in event semantics starting in the early 1980s (Section 5.1–5.3). At the same time, Taylor's (1977) work is instructive in so far as it brings to the fore the pervasive and subtle difficulties that we encounter when we try to characterize aspectual classes by means of properties that are based on our intuitions how entities are related to their proper parts. For instance, Taylor (1977) uses *stab* as a paradigm example for his *kinêsis* (nonsubinterval) predicates and *table* for sortal count nouns, but both have divisible denotations that may have proper parts describable by *stab* and *table*. (Mourelatos 1978 uses *clock* instead of Taylor's 1977 *table*, which is no less problematic, since there are clocks consisting of smaller clocks.) Such examples are also problematic for subsequent mereologically-based characterizations of count (sortal) nouns and telic predicates based on their intuitive indivisibility: namely, the property of ANTISUBDIVISIBILITY proposed by Bach (1981) (Section 5.2) and QUANTIZATION by Krifka (1986) (Section 5.3 and Section 6).

4 Dowty's aspect calculus

Dowty (1979) defines a new framework for a decompositional analysis (cf. article 7 [Semantics: Foundations, History and Methods] (Engelberg) *Lexical decomposition*, article 2 [Semantics: Lexical Structures and Adjectives] (Engelberg)

Frameworks of decomposition) of aspectual classes and a new program for the integration of lexical semantics with a model-theoretic semantics (cf. article 7 [Semantics: Theories] (Zimmermann) *Model-theoretic semantics*). Dowty's main thesis is that the temporal properties associated with aspectual classes, as captured in Taylor's (1977) temporal meaning postulates, are grounded in the change of state entailments and their absence in the different classes (Dowty 1979: 167), and in our expectations about the way changes happen over time (Dowty 1979: 185). The implementation of this thesis requires the background of an interval-based semantics and motivates three main aspectual classes, given in Tab. 9.1. namely, states, activities and definite (single/complex) changes of state.

Tab. 9.1: Aspectual classes: Dowty (1979, Chapter 3.8.3 *A Revised Verb Classification*)

momentary	interval			
no change	no change	change		
		indefinite change	definite change	
Non-Agentive: be empty; know	Non-Agentive: sit, stand, lie	Non-Agentive: make noise, roll, rain	Non-Agentive: notice, realize, ignite	Non-Agentive: flow from x to y, dissolve
Agentive: (possibly) be a hero	Agentive: sit, stand, lie	Agentive: move, laugh, dance	Agentive: reach, kill, point out (something to someone)	Agentive: build (a house), walk from x to y, walk a mile
habituals in all classes				
STATES		ACTIVITIES	SINGLE CHANGE OF STATE	COMPLEX CHANGE OF STATE

Aspectual classes are defined by means of formulas of aspect calculus, which provide tools for a decompositional analysis of predicates in general and allow us to represent systematic relations among classes of verbs as well as their shared selectional restrictions and entailments. In formulas of aspect calculus, state predicates are basic elements from which non-state predicates are formed by means of the vocabulary of standard first-order logic and three main abstract predicates: namely, DO (agentivity), BECOME (definite change of state) and CAUSE (causation) (Dowty 1979: 71, 122). Although state predicates are taken to be 'aspectually simple and unproblematic' (Dowty 1979: 71), Dowty's difficulties with fitting them into appropriate aspectual classes reveal that their semantic and ontological status is significantly more puzzling than that of most non-state predicates, and their relation to temporal notions is often unclear (see also Bach 1981; Carlson 1977; Chierchia 1995; Comrie 1976; Fernald 2000, for example). Following suggestions in Taylor (1977) and Carlson (1977), Dowty (1979: 184) settles on the main distinction between *momentary states* vs. *interval states*, using the compatibility with the progressive construction as the main diagnostic test. *Momentary state* predicates are incompatible with the progressive, because they are true at single moments of time (see Taylor 1977 in Section 3). *Interval state* predicates, which correspond to Carlson's (1977) STAGE-LEVEL state predicates (cf. article 8 [this volume] (Carlson) *Genericity*), freely occur in the progressive, because they have truth conditions involving intervals (Dowty 1979: 176, also Section 3 above), which in turn follows from the fact that they describe temporary (i.e., changeable) properties of individuals (Dowty 1979: 177ff).

Non-state predicates fall into two main classes, depending on the type of change they entail. One class comprises predicates that entail an INDEFINITE CHANGE of state (see Dowty 1979: 169ff) like *move*, for instance, since *any* change of location it describes qualifies as a situation of moving. Among other examples are *push a cart, raise the thermostat, dim the lights* (Dowty 1991: 568). The other class comprises predicates that entail a DEFINITE CHANGE of state. A paradigm example is *reach*; only a change with respect to a definite location, specified by its object, will qualify as a situation described by *reach*. The entailment of a 'definite change of state' is represented by means of a one-place predicate BECOMEϕ which is true at a (minimal) time interval t at whose initial bound $\neg\phi$ holds and at whose final bound ϕ holds (Dowty 1979: 140ff), where ϕ is a state (outcome, result) or an activity sentence (Dowty 1979: 124–125). The semantics of BECOME is inspired by von Wright's (1963, 1968) notion of a 'change of state' (Dowty 1979: 74ff) and Kenny's (1963) performances (Dowty 1979: 77–78), which entail the bringing about of a state or an activity (Section 2.1). Definite change of state predicates are divided into SINGLE DEFINITE CHANGES OF STATE (inchoatives, Dowty's achievements) and COMPLEX DEFINITE CHANGES OF STATE (causatives, Dowty's accomplishments) (Dowty 1979: 184). These two subclasses are derivationally related building on the analysis of the inchoative/causative alternation in Generative Semantics (Lakoff 1965; Gruber 1967): namely, single definite change of state predicates (3b) are derived from basic state predicates (3a) by means of BECOME, and these in turn serve as arguments of the CAUSE predicate (3c) in the derivation of complex definite change of state predicates.

(3) a. The room was empty.   **empty'**(room)
    b. The room emptied by 11pm.   BECOME **empty'**(room)
    c. John emptied the room.   [John does something] CAUSE
                                        [BECOME **empty'**(room)]

CAUSE is treated as a bisentential operator, [ϕ CAUSE Ψ], following Vendler (1967), Geis (1970), McCawley (1971), among others (Dowty 1972, 1979: 71, 91, 122). DO (Ross 1972) is intended to represent agentivity, but many agentive ACTIVITY verbs are represented by means of primitive non-logical predicate constants, which has the drawback that they are representationally indistinguishable from basic states in Dowty's aspect calculus. This inconsistency in the application of DO is somewhat attenuated by the fact that each aspectual class is split into an agentive and a non-agentive subclass, as Tab. 9.1 shows, with the net effect that agentivity is dissociated from aspectual classes. In the 1970's the idea that agentivity has a different status from the properties that cross-classify aspectual classes became established in other aspect classifications (see e.g., Comrie 1976; Mourelatos 1978; also Section 5.1 below) and today it is accepted across a wide range of theoretical frameworks.

Given that agentivity, represented by DO, is orthogonal to aspectual classes, BECOME and CAUSE are the key components in Dowty's aspect calculus. They stimulated some of the most fruitful debates regarding Dowty's decompositional analysis with respect to aspectual classes and also other parts of the grammar of natural languages (cf. article 2 [Semantics: Lexical Structures and Adjectives] (Engelberg) *Frameworks of decomposition*). They tend to revolve around three main issues. First, what is controversial is the logical status of BECOME and CAUSE as sentential operators and the kinds of arguments they take. Dowty (1979) defines CAUSE as a bisentential operator, but the majority of subsequent proposals (Chierchia 2004; Levin & Rappaport Hovav 1998; Parsons 1990; von Stechow 1995, to name just a few) assume a bievent structure of causatives (already proposed by Davidson 1967; Miller & Johnson-Laird 1976; Schank 1973). As Parsons (1990: 108–109) observes, it is counterintuitive to analyze what is caused as a proposition instead of an event; moreover, there is little evidence for CAUSE to function as an operator taking scope over sentences, because it does not interact with other scope bearing operators, such as quantifiers, nor does it create opacity. Similar objections can be raised against Dowty's treatment of BECOME. Second, what is not well understood and agreed upon is the relation of BECOME and CAUSE to each other and how they combine with other meaning components in the logical representation of predicates to yield aspectual classes and also finer-grained semantically coherent lexical classes of verbs. In current aspect studies, the notion of a 'definite change of state' represented by BECOME is identified with the core of telicity, namely with its inchoativity or transition component (see e.g., Pustejovsky 1991; Tenny & Pustejovsky 2000). Hence, the mutual independence of BECOME and CAUSE in the aspect calculus can be taken as implying a strong claim about the separation of telicity from causation in the organization of lexical semantic information, and at the level of sentential semantics. However, Dowty (1979) does not take this implication to its logical conclusion, because he uniformly analyzes accomplishments as causatives (Dowty 1979: 124–125, Chapter 3.8.3, and elsewhere), which is unjustified (see below). Third, there is no unanimity concerning the empirical domain of application of BECOME, which is shared by accomplishments and achievements, and no agreement on what constitutes empirical evidence for treating a predicate as causative, cross-linguistically and in a particular language (Alexiadou, Anagnostopoulou & Everaert 2004). It is, therefore, unsurprising that the nature of accomplishments and achievements as well as that of their superordinate category of telicity have been subjected to different interpretations and revisions since Dowty's (1979) original proposal, with the result that the boundary of telic predicates and the line between accomplishments and achievements have been in a constant flux. It is worth mentioning that Dowty (1991) appears to extend the causative analysis to certain achievement verbs, which are not causative in his 1979 work, when he characterizes verbs like *emerge, submerge, deflate, bloom, vaporize* and *decompose* as "achievement verbs which entail a complex rather than simple change of state" (Dowty 1991: 571, n.15). They constitute a subclass of unaccusatives (Rosen 1984), which as a whole class are taken to be causative, according to Chierchia (2004) and Pustejovsky (1995), among others. Reanalyses of classes of verbs as causatives, as we see in Dowty's (1979, 1991) work, are not uncommon, and the adequacy of existing proposals is best judged in connection with the insights gained in the research on causation in closely related fields of cognitive science, most importantly in philosophy and psycholinguistics.

Within the three main areas outlined above, two particular issues bear closer examination: namely, Dowty's uniform treatment of accomplishments as causatives and the notion of a 'definite change of state' represented by BECOMEϕ. In treating accomplishments as causatives, Dowty (1979: 183) follows Vendler (1957), but in departure from Vendler Dowty (1979) takes causation to be the single most important meaning component separating accomplishments from achievements, while agentivity and temporal extent are irrelevant (Dowty 1979: 183). Vendler's accomplishments are restricted to agent initiated actions that are temporally extended, and achievements largely correspond to non-agentive punctual occurrences. Dowty's accomplishments are temporally extended (*build a house*) or punctual (*shoot someone dead, break the window*), agentive or non-agentive (e.g, *the collision mashed the fender flat*). Dowty's achievements cut across the agentivity/non-agentivity line (e.g., *notice, kill*, see Dowty 1979: 184), and can be either punctual or nonpunctual (e.g, *melt, freeze*, see van Valin 1990: 223, n.2). Also contrary to Vendler, Dowty (1979: 183) observes that the lack of temporal extent is not necessarily correlated with the lack of agentivity. His examples are *reach the finish line, arrive in Boston*. Notice that both *reach* and *arrive* can freely occur with intentional subject-oriented modifiers: *Susan intentionally arrived in Seoul a few days in advance of the conference, We deliberately reached his doorstep an hour later than the time printed on the gilded invitation.* A uniform treatment of accomplishments as causatives has attained a considerable prominence in contemporary aspect studies (Croft 1991; Erteschik-Shir & Rapoport 2004; Foley & van Valin 1984; Jackendoff 1990: 75, 128, and references therein). We also commonly find decompositional analyses with events as primitive elements, in which directed motion predicates are decomposed into a causing motion event and a caused resultant state of reaching some goal (Croft 1991; Jackendoff 1990: 75, 128; see already Talmy 1972).

However, a uniform causative analysis of accomplishments is fraught with numerous problems, and in what follows, two will be briefly summarized. First, causation is neither a necessary nor a sufficient property of accomplishments. It is not a sufficient property, because there are causatives that are not accomplishments: *The clowns walked the elephants around in a circle for five minutes/#in five minutes.* Neither is causation a necessary property of accomplishments, because there are accomplishments that are not causatives. A case in point is given by directed motion predicates like *John drove a car from Boston to Detroit,* which are analyzed as causatives in Dowty (1972, 1979: 207–213, 216), but which lack the properties of causatives, according to van Valin & LaPolla (1997), Levin & Rappaport Hovav (1999), among others. Second, a uniform causative treatment of accomplishments has undesirable consequences for the analysis of complex predicates like those resulting from aspectual composition (Section 5.3), for instance: *John ate two apples* (accomplishment) vs. *John ate popcorn* (activity). Here, the accomplishment or activity interpretation depends on the quantificational properties of the Incremental Theme argument. From Dowty's (1979) analysis it would seem to follow that only accomplishment, but not activity, complex predicates of this type and possibly also their head verbs should be analyzed as causatives. But this means that it is the properties of the Incremental Theme argument that drive the decision whether a given complex predicate and possibly also its head verb are to be analyzed as causative. This is clearly unsatisfying, as Levin (2000) observes, also in the light of the fact that lexical causative verbs like *kill* or *break* are causative in all of their occurrences, and regardless of the quantificational properties of their objects. A causative analysis of verbs of consumption like *eat* is rejected by Higginbotham (2000), Levin (2000), van Valin & LaPolla (1997), to name just a few. These two problems suffice to illustrate that a uniform treatment of accomplishments as causatives is unjustified, and hence causation cannot be viewed as a meaning component that distinguishes between accomplishments and achievements. The idea that causation is dissociated from aspectual classes finds support in early approaches to aspect (see e.g., Bennett & Partee 1972; Garey 1957; Verkuyl 1972; McCawley 1976: 117) that cross-classify aspectual classes without any recourse to causation, and the same holds true of mereologically-based theories (see

Sections 5.2–5.3), which emphasize space-time analogies (Section 3 and 5.1) as the basis for a theory of aspectual classes.

Having seen that agentivity (represented by DO) is orthogonal to aspectual classes, as Dowty (1979) proposes, but causation (represented by CAUSE), as well, contrary to Dowty (1979), we are left with BECOME as the only aspectually relevant predicate in Dowty's aspect calculus. As has been observed, the notion of a 'definite change of state' represented by BECOME is now commonly taken to correspond to the inchoativity or transition core of telicity (see e.g., Pustejovsky 1991; Tenny & Pustejovsky 2000). The question then arises whether it is adequate for the representation of all telicity phenomena in natural languages. It turns out that it is too narrow, since in BECOMEϕ, ϕ stands for an outcome of a result state or an activity, which excludes a number of telic predicates that cannot be plausibly claimed to entail any such outcome. Among salient examples are paradigmatic telic predicates consisting of durational adverbials and activity verbs (Bach 1981: 74) like *smile for an hour*. The telicity of such predicates is straightforwardly accounted for in approaches to aspect that base their understanding of telic predicates on space-time analogies, assimilating them to sortal predicates, as in Taylor (1977) (Section 3), and emphasize the criterial properties of indivisibility (following Taylor 1977, Section 3) or countability (following Mourelatos 1978, Section 5.1). These properties are formalized in mereological approaches to aspect by Bach (1981, 1986) and Krifka (1986, 1992) (Section 5.2–5.3), but they can also be found under a different elaboration in cognitive theories like those of Jackendoff (1983, 1990, 1991, 1996) and Talmy (1985), for example. The disparity between the view of telicity based on space-time analogies and the view of telic predicates based on the notion of a definite change of state represented by Dowty's (1979) BECOME can be highlighted by their differential treatment of semelfactives (from Latin *semel* 'once', 'a single time' and *factive* related to *factum* 'event', 'occurrence'). Mourelatos (1978) uses the semelfactive verb *hit* as a paradigm example of a telic (his EVENT) predicate (Section 5.1). It belongs to the class of 'full-cycle resettable' verbs along with *knock, kick, slap, tap, blink, flash*, all of which describe situations that end with the return to the initial state (Talmy 1985). Hence, although it arguably entails a kind of definite change of state, it cannot be analyzed by means of BECOMEϕ, since it entails no resultant state or activity. It may also be mentioned that there is another proposal advocated by Smith (1991: 28) who argues that semelfactives neither fit Dowty's four aspectual classes nor are they telic, but instead ought to be treated as an atelic aspectual class *sui generis*. In sum, although the notion of telicity analyzed in terms of Dowty's (1979) BECOME is widespread, it represents just one among other valid intuitions about the nature of telicity.

The independence of BECOME in the aspect calculus also raises the question whether there is an independent level of logical (or lexical conceptual) representation based on the notion of a 'change of state' captured by BECOME, i.e., whether it is clearly distinct from other kinds of representation, and if so, what its properties are and how exactly they interact with properties of other types of representation of natural languages. (cf. article 4 [Semantics: Lexical Structures and Adjectives] (Levin & Rappaport Hovav) *Lexical Conceptual Structure*, article 4 [Semantics: Theories] (Jackendoff) *Conceptual Semantics*). Crucial empirical evidence for distinguishing among different proposals for logical-conceptual decompositions (cf. article 2 [Semantics: Lexical Structures and Adjectives] (Engelberg) *Frameworks of decomposition*) bearing on this issue and for evaluating their empirical predictions is to be sought in the cross-linguistic comparison of lexicalization patterns (cf. article 4 [Semantics: Lexical Structures and Adjectives] (Levin & Rappaport Hovav) *Lexical Conceptual Structure*, article 1 [Semantics: Theories] (Talmy) *Cognitive Semantics*).

5 Event semantics

5.1 Events in linguistics and philosophy

Event semantics rose to prominence in the late 1970s and the early 1980s when Davidson's (1967) analysis of action sentences led to adding of events, used as discourse referents, into the analysis of temporal structure at the discourse level within the Discourse Representation Theory (Kamp 1979; Kamp & Rohrer 1983) (cf. article 11 [Semantics: Theories] (Kamp & Reyle) *Discourse Representation Theory*). This stimulated a revived interest in Reichenbach's (1947) theory of tense and temporal anaphora (Partee 1984), with new connections to aspectual classes (Hinrichs 1986) as well as to dynamic semantic theories starting in the early 1990's (Kamp & Reyle 1993; ter Meulen 1995) (cf. article 12 [Semantics: Theories] (Dekker) *Dynamic semantics*).

On Davidson's account, action sentences involve implicit reference to and quantification over events (see also Ramsey 1927: 37). Any n-place action verb (e.g., *butter* in (4a)) is represented by a $(n+1)$-place predicate (4b), where the extra argument e is a singular term for an *event*, treated as a first-order variable of existential quantification. This implies that action sentences are indefinite descriptions of events. Davidsonian events constitute a basic ontological category along with ordinary objects, and are understood as particulars (particular datable occurrences that occur at a specific place and time), rather than universals (entities that can recur at different places and times), as in Montague (1974).

(4) a. *Jones buttered the toast with a knife.*
 b. ∃e[BUTTER(Jones,toast,e) ∧ WITH(knife,e)]
 c. ∃e[BUTTER(e) ∧ AGENT(Jones,e) ∧ THEME(toast,e) ∧ WITH(knife,e)]

In event-based analyses of linguistic phenomena (cf. article 8 [Semantics: Theories] (Maienborn) *Event semantics*), Davidson's (1967) original proposal underwent substantial modifications and extensions. (See Partee 2000 for differences in the understanding of events in linguistics and philosophy.) Within the Neo-Davidsonian theory (a term coined by Dowty 1989; see Dowty 1991: 553, n.7), and following Castañeda (1967), Parsons (1980) and Higginbotham (1983) propose to treat arguments in the same way as Davidson's (1967) adjuncts, i.e., as separate two-place predicates added conjunctively to the verb (4c). On this view, verbs are one-place predicates of events and their arguments two-place relations between participants and events, which are characterized as thematic relations in Parsons (1980).

A widening of ontological commitments beyond Davidson's view of events as changes in objects induced by agents raised questions whether an event argument is to be associated with every verbal predicate, including state predicates. Kratzer (1988/1995) argues that only stage-level predicates (in the sense of Carlson 1977) have an event argument (her situation argument). On another prominent view due to Higginbotham (1985, 2000), every predicate head of *V, N, A*, and *P* category in the *X*-bar system has an event argument, and introduces an explicit reference to the event argument as part of its meaning. Davidson's analysis of action sentences is extended to all sentences in Bach (1981, 1986), and Parsons (1990) follows suit. Similarly as Mourelatos (1978), Bach uses the aspectual classification into STATES, PROCESSES and EVENTS (originally used in Comrie 1976: 13, 48–51; see Mourelatos 1978, n. 23) for which Bach (1981: 69) coins the cover term 'eventualities', and reserves the term EVENT for telic predicates only.

(5) STATES: *The air smells of jasmine.* (Mourelatos 1978: 201)
 PROCESSES: *It's snowing.*
 EVENTS: (i) Developments: *The sun went down.*
  (ii) Punctual Occurrences: *The pebble hit the water.*

In an explicit departure from Vendler (1957) and Kenny (1963) (Section 2.1), Mourelatos (1978) separates aspectual classes from agentivity, and implicitly from causation, in contrast to Dowty (1979) (Section 4). Following Taylor's (1977) proposal (Section 3), among others, Mourelatos (1978) motivates the properties of aspectual classes mainly with recourse to the analogy 'mass : count = process/state : event'.

Telic predicates (his EVENT predicates) describe situations that "fall under SORTS that provide a PRINCIPLE of count" (Mourelatos 1978: 209) and "can be directly or intrinsically counted" (Mourelatos 1978: 209). This semantic and ontological claim is supported by linguistic tests. Only telic predicates are straightforwardly compatible with cardinal count adverbials, as in *fall asleep three times*. They are also realized in count-quantified existential constructions: *Vesuvius erupted three times* → *There were three eruptions of Vesuvius*. Atelic predicates cannot be combined with cardinal count adverbials, unless they first shift to telic interpretations, as in *run (*)three times*, and they are realized in mass-quantified existential constructions: *Onlookers shoved and screamed* → *There was shoving and screaming*. Apart from its interaction with quantification in natural language (cf. article 4 [this volume] (Keenan) *Quantifiers*), the direct structural analogy between individuals and event(ualitie)s is manifested in other linguistic phenomena, for instance in the domain of syntax and semantics of anaphora and reference, which can be taken to support Davidson's idea that events, similarly as individuals do, may serve as referents of linguistic expressions in a semantic model (but see ter Meulen 2000 for differences between events and individuals in this regard).

5.2 Mereology and event semantics with lattice structures

In event semantics, the analogy 'mass : count = process : event', whose origins are in Taylor (1977) (Section 3) and Mourelatos (1978) (Section 5.1), is formalized by means of the algebraic device of a complete join semilattice, and this idea inspired much of the subsequent research that takes events as basic entities in the domain of discourse. Bach (1981) lays the mereological foundation for this program, while Bach (1986) extends Link's (1983) lattice-theoretic semantics of plurals and mass terms to the domain of eventualities (cf. article 7 [this volume] (Lasersohn) *Mass nouns and plurals*). The mereological approach assumes the basic binary relation *part-of* '≤' defined from the *sum* '⊕' operation for forming 'sum individuals' or 'plural individuals' (Link 1983; Sharvy 1980). In Link (1983), the denotation of count nouns, their singular (*boy*) and plural forms (*boys*), contains subdomains structured by join semilattices. In a domain with three boys, John, Bill and Tom, the singular form *boy* has as its denotation the set consisting of these three atomic individuals. The denotation of the plural form *boys* are the four non-atomic elements (on a 'strict plural' interpretation), including, for instance, the plural/sum individual *John⊕Bill*, i.e., John and Bill taken together. (There are also uses of plural nouns that have the entire semilattice as denotation, including its atomic elements.) The denotation of mass nouns (*coffee*) has the form of a non-atomic join semilattice. In the domain of eventualities, as Bach (1986) proposes, the denotation of EVENT (telic) verbs like *arrive* has the structure of an atomic join semilattice, while the denotation of PROCESS (atelic) verbs like *swim* has the form of a non-atomic join semilattice. Mass nouns and process predicates also share the property of ADDITIVITY. For instance, if x is some quantity of water, and y also, then their mereological sum $x \oplus y$ is describable by *water*; if e falls under *run* and e' also, then $e \oplus e'$ is their sum describable by *run*. Count (sortal) nouns like *cat* and EVENT predicates like *build a cabin* have the property of ANTISUBDIVISIBILITY, because what they describe has no proper parts that are describable by *cat* and *build a cabin*.

Bach's event semantics with lattice structures straightforwardly motivates the cross-categorial constraints on the occurrence of quantifiers, observed by Mourelatos (1978) (Section 5.1): namely, some (e.g., *much*) have interpretations that restrict their application to the non-atomic domain of mass/process predicates: *much wine, he did not sleep much*. Others (e.g., *many, three*) operate over the domain of count/event predicates that is necessarily atomic: *many/three books; he arrived many/three times*. In subsequent research, such parallels in cross-categorial quantificational constraints are discussed in connection with the hypothesis that natural languages have two main types of quantificational ontology (Bach et al. 1995): quantification over individuals paradigmatically expressed by determiners like *three* (D-quantification) and quantification over events often expressed by adverbials like *three times* (A-quantification).

Second, event semantics with lattice structures allows us to motivate a parallel between the 'imperfective paradox' (Dowty 1977, 1979) and the 'partitive puzzle' posed by the nominal *part of* construction (Bach 1986). For example, *This is part of Mozart's Requiem* can be true and felicitously uttered, even if the requiem never existed or will exist in its entirety. Similarly, *Mozart was composing the Requiem when he died* is true, even if its non-progressive counterpart *Mozart composed the Requiem* is false. The unifying requirement is that there be a (whole) P to which some x or e stands in a *part-of* relation (Bach 1986: 12), which Krifka (1992: 47) formalizes as follows: PART = $\lambda P \lambda x' \exists x [P(x) \wedge x' \leq x]$ and PROG = $\lambda P \lambda e' \exists e [P(e) \wedge e' \leq e]$.

Third, cross-categorial parallels in shifting operations are generalized in terms of a many-to-one function (homomorphism) from count to non-count, and also EVENT to PROCESS meaning shifts. This suggests an intriguing asymmetry in shifting operations, which has remained largely unexplored. Count to non-count shifts and the parallel EVENT (telic) to PROCESS (atelic) shifts, as in *Much missionary was eaten at the festival* (by "Universal Grinder", see Pelletier 1975, following Lewis' suggestion) and *John ate the sandwich bit by bit for an hour, but still didn't finish it*, are predictable, nearly unrestricted, since they can be understood as removing the criterion of individuation inherent in count and EVENT (telic) predicates. In contrast, the opposite shifts, non-count to count and PROCESS to EVENT, are much less systematic and require a considerable effort on an interpreter's part. Such shifts are common with nouns denoting foodstuff bundled via "Universal Packager" (Bach 1986) into (conventional) PORTIONS, as in *After two beers he began to feel better*, or into KINDS, as in *He prefers Tuscan wines*. Almost any PROCESS (atelic) predicate can shift into an EVENT (telic) interpretation, as in *John ran* [e.g., a certain distance] *in an hour*, but this shift presupposes what is often a rather complex process identification of the requisite criterion of individuation for EVENT-hood in dependence on the linguistic and extra-linguistic context (cf. article 10 [Semantics: Lexical Structures and Adjectives] (de Swart) *Mismatches and coercion*).

5.3 The mereological approach to aspectual composition

There are two main observations that any adequate theory of aspectual composition must explain. First, the count/mass distinction (cf. article 3 [Semantics: Typology, Diachrony and Processing] (Doetjes) *Count/mass distinctions*) and quantificational properties (cf. article 4 [this volume] (Keenan) *Quantifiers*) of nominal arguments systematically influence the (a)telicity of complex predicates. For example, as Garey (1957) observes, *he played a Beethoven sonata* is telic, i.e., it "designates something that has a structure with a temporal ending to it" (Garey 1957: 107), because its direct object is a count term. In contrast, *he played a little Beethoven* with a mass object is atelic. Second, such systematic effects of nominal arguments on the (a)telicity of complex predicates depend on how the participants associated with them function in described eventualities, and hence ultimately on our knowledge that is lexical and pragmatic in nature. Implicitly, this idea is already present in Jacobsohn's (1933: 297) proposal that verbs like 'build' with *accusativus effectivus* (6a), i.e, 'accusative of creation', occur in telic (his 'perfective') predicates, while verbs like 'beat' with *accusative affectivus* (6b) in atelic (his 'imperfective') predicates. Although both (6a) and (6b) contain a singular count direct object in the accusative case, only (6a) is telic, but (6b) is atelic. Intuitively, this difference stems from the observation that an extent of an object of creation delimits the (temporal) extent of an event during which it comes into existence. In contrast, the extent of an object whose surface is affected merely by contact with another object, but does not necessarily change as a result of it, does not delimit an event of surface contact.

(6) a. Die Maurer   bauten das   Haus.   German
       the bricklayers built   the. ACC house. ACC
       'The bricklayers built the house.'

b. Der Mann schlug den Hund.
   the man beat the. ACC dog. ACC
   'The man beat the dog.'

The second observation clearly points to the meaning of verbs as the key motivating factor of aspectual composition, and it drives Krifka's (1986, 1992, 1998), and subsequently also Dowty's (1987, 1989, 1991), mereologically based theories of aspectual composition. They propose that it depends on a particular thematic property, namely, an Incremental Theme (cf. article 3 [Semantics: Lexical Structures and Adjectives] (Davis) *Thematic roles*), which is an entailment of certain episodic verbs and defined in terms of a homomorphism between the lattice structure (part structure) associated with the Incremental Theme argument and the lattice structure associated with the event argument. (The term 'Incremental Theme' was coined by Dowty (1987) and replaced Krifka's (1986, 1992) 'gradual Patient' or 'successive Patient'.) The most robust aspectual composition effects are triggered by verbs that are *strictly incremental* (Krifka 1998). The paradigm examples are verbs of creation (*build, write*), consumption (*eat, drink*) and destruction (*destroy, burn*). Intuitively, their Theme argument refers to an object that undergoes a permanent change of state in its physical extent/volume, as it gradually comes into existence or disappears during the course of an event.

Traditionally, the phenomena falling under the aspectual composition are understood as manifestations of what is essentially some kind of a 'semantic concord' (Leech 1969: 137) with respect to the [±countable] feature of nominal and verbal predicates (Mourelatos 1978: 204; Verkuyl 1972; Platzack 1979) (cf. article 1 [Semantics: Lexical Structures and Adjectives] (Bierwisch) *Semantic features and primes*). In order to capture this insight, Krifka (1986 and elsewhere) defines two cross-categorial mereological properties over the atomic and non-atomic lattice structures for objects and eventualities (see Link 1983, 1987; Bach 1986, Section 5.2). One is cumulativity, defined for objects in (7a), which formalizes Quine's (1960: 91) cumulative reference and Bach's (1981) additivity (Section 5.2). The other is quantization, which corresponds to Bach's (1981) antisubdivisibility (Section 5.2) and is defined for objects in (7b): A predicate P is quantized if and only if no entity that is P can be a subpart of another entity that is P.

(7) a. $CM(P) \leftrightarrow \forall x,y[P(x) \land P(y) \to P(x \oplus y)] \land \exists x,y[P(x) \land P(y) \land \neg x = y]$
       soup, apples
    b. $QUA(P) \leftrightarrow \forall x,y[P(x) \land P(y) \to \neg y < x]$
       an apple, two apples, a bowl of soup/apples

Quantized predicates are atomic like *apple* or apply to entities that consist of atoms like *three apples* (Krifka 1998). Quantized predicates also apply to measured quantities expressed by measure phrases like *a bowl of soup/apples, a liter of wine*. They are derived from cumulative predicates (e.g., *soup, wine, apples*) by means of extensive measure functions expressed by words for standard measures like *liter* or words for non-standard measures derived from containers like *bowl*. All quantized verbal predicates are telic, but not vice versa (Krifka 1998).

With this apparatus in place, the homomorphism entailment straightforwardly motivates the aspectual composition: namely, an incremental verb composed with a quantized Incremental Theme argument yields a quantized verbal predicate, and with a cumulative Incremental Theme argument a cumulative predicate, provided the resultant combination is understood as referring to a singular eventuality. The homomorphism entailment motivates not only which verb-argument combinations must obey aspectual composition, but also which are exempt from it like *beat the dog* (6b) or *push a cart*, for instance. Since *beat* and *push* do not lexically specify an incremental relation, their Theme argument *on its own* has no effect on the (a)telicity of its predication. For instance, even if it is count like *the dog* or *a cart*, it does not enforce the telicity of its predication.

The distinct advantage of Krifka's (1986 and elsewhere) proposal is that the aspectual composition directly follows from the standard semantic composition of a sentence. Moreover, the homomorphism entailment also motivates the cross-linguistic variation in the encoding of telicity. In Krifka's theory, its counterpart in the grammar of natural languages guarantees the 'transfer' of the quantization and cumulativity properties between the semilattices of objects and eventualities, and since a homomorphism generally preserves the inverse map, the 'transfer' works in both directions between the semilattices. Hypothesizing that the two semantic properties of quantization and cumulativity are universally available, Krifka proposes that the encoding of telicity is a function of their overt expression either by a nominal predicate operator on the Incremental Theme argument (e.g., Germanic languages) whose denotational domain are objects, or by a verbal predicate operator applied to the incremental verb (e.g., Slavic languages, Hindi, Chinese) whose domain are eventualities. Incremental Theme operators are determiner quantifiers, measure expressions, case inflection, prepositions or morphological exponents of the grammatical category of number, which interact with the lexical count vs. mass distinction. Common verbal predicate operators are affixes and particles. Natural languages can be divided into two main classes depending on which of the two main strategies they employ as their dominant encoding strategy.

6 Current trends

Semantic and pragmatic theories of aspectual classes and Aktionsart share two main theoretical assumptions. First, the meaning of verbs is the key motivating factor for a variety of (a)telicity phenomena. Second, events in the denotation of telic (accomplishment) predicates are delimited with respect to (measured) objects related to them, which presupposes that there is a systematic relation between events and the relevant (measured) objects. (See also Davidson's 1969 independent idea that events are often described and identified in terms of the objects to which they are 'in one way or another' related.) Consequently, telicity is generally viewed as yet another phenomenon in the grammar of natural languages that exploits systematic parallels between the ontological structure of event(ualitie)s and objects.

Three main types of object dimensions are distinguished with respect to which events can be delimited (see e.g., Tenny 1987, 1994; Ramchand 1997; Rappaport Hovav 2008, and references therein): (i) the extent/volume of an object (e.g., *John ate an apple*), (ii) the length of a path in physical space (e.g., *John drove from Boston to Chicago*), (iii) some other property of an object that can be measured on a scale (e.g., temperature, as in *The soup cooled*).

We may distinguish recent aspect theories according to which of these three object dimensions they emphasize in their theory formation. In (Neo-)Davidsonian event semantics (Section 5.1), it is largely driven by the phenomenon of aspectual composition, which ontologically presupposes that events are delimited with respect to the extent/volume of objects (Section 5.3). The path is the basic concept unifying a variety of telicity phenomena in the theories that are, to various degrees and often only implicitly, aligned with the tradition of Localism (Gruber 1965; Jackendoff 1972, 1983, 1990, 1996, and references therein). A paradigmatic example is the Conceptual Semantics approach to telicity by Jackendoff (1996) (cf. article 4 [Semantics: Theories] (Jackendoff) *Conceptual Semantics*). Assuming that our intuitions about the delimitation of events are the clearest for sentences with motion verbs (Jackendoff 1996: 315), their telic interpretations are derived when the path has an explicit endpoint (e.g., *Bill floated into the cave *for hours*) and atelic interpretations when it lacks such an endpoint (e.g., *Bill floated down the river for hours*). The elements of conceptual structure that represent changes of Themes in their physical location and coming to be in/at a location on a path serve to model all other changes of state of Themes/Patients, including those that are measured by degrees on a property scale. For instance, in telic property resultatives, as in *Willy watered/made/got the plants flat*, the Theme/Patient argument (here *the plants*) comes to be in the final state expressed by the resultative phrase (here *flat*). 'Path-based' approaches to telicity predominate in conceptual and cognitive frameworks (cf. article 1 [Semantics: Theories] (Talmy) *Cognitive Semantics*, article 4 [Semantics: Theories] (Jackendoff) *Conceptual Semantics*) and they generally assume some metaphoric or analogical extension mechanism(s) from the spatial domain to other domains (cf. article 11 [Semantics: Lexical Structures and Adjectives] (Tyler & Takahashi) *Metaphors and metonymies*), which have received empirical support from psycholinguistic studies on analogical reasoning strategies (cf. article 13 [Semantics: Typology, Diachrony and Processing] (Landau) *Space in semantics and cognition*). The notion of a generalized path for modeling changes in a variety of event dimensions is also used in formal and model-theoretic approaches to aspect, as in Krifka (1998), Gawron (2005), Zwarts (2008), among others. The notion of a scale as the main explanatory mechanism for (a)telicity phenomena has been gaining prominence since Hay, Kennedy & Levin (1999) (see e.g., Beavers 2008; Filip 2008; Kearns 2007; Kennedy & Levin 2008; Rappaport Hovav 2008, and references therein). Scalar approaches to telicity are best developed for 'degree achievements' (in the sense of Dowty 1979). They are derived from gradable adjectives like *cool* or *darken* that lexicalize a scale measuring a property predicated of the referent of their Theme argument. Sentences headed by degree achievements (DAs) alternate between telic and atelic interpretations, depending on the nature of the scale properties lexicalized by their adjectival base and context of use. Telic interpretations are enforced by overt expressions of the difference value (Kennedy & Levin 2008) in the relevant property change, as in *The soup cooled (by) 17 degrees in 30 minutes/*for 30 minutes*, where it is expressed by the measure phrase *17 degrees*. If the difference value is not expressed, the main challenge is to specify the semantic conditions and pragmatic factors (especially related to scalar implicatures) (cf. article 10 [Semantics: Interfaces] (Chierchia, Fox & Spector) *Grammatical view of scalar implicatures*) leading to telic (accomplishment) interpretations, given that they are favored by DAs lexicalizing closed scales like *darken*, as in *The sky darkened (in/for an hour)*, but resisted by certain DAs that lexicalize open scales like *widen*, as in *The gap widened (in/for ten minutes)*, which may only have an achievement interpretation with *in NP* temporal adverbials (Section 2.1) and are odd with endpoint-oriented modifications like *completely*, as in *#The gap widened completely in 90 seconds* (Kearns 2007).

While different theoretical approaches to aspect vary with respect to what constitutes the relevant 'measuring rod' for events (borrowing Kratzer's 2004 term), they all agree that it must be systematically related to events it delimits. There have been a variety of such object-event mapping relations proposed, including a homomorphism (Krifka 1986, 1992), also referred to as 'incremental relations' or 'incrementality' (Krifka 1998), the 'ADD TO' relation (Verkuyl 1972, 1989, 1993), the 'measuring out' relation captured by the telic MEASURE aspectual role (Tenny 1987, 1994), and 'structure-preserving binding relations' (Jackendoff 1996), to name just the most cited ones. Disagreements concern two main issues:

(i) the relation of such mapping relations to telicity, and (ii) their source, namely, in particular the extent to which they are determined by the lexical properties of verbs, or their context of use or by pragmatic factors, and if they are a lexical property of verbs, or what effects, if any, they have on argument selection.

As far as the first issue is concerned, in most semantic and pragmatic theories, telicity and the relevant mapping relations are fully independent of each other, as is suggested in the original proposal in mereologically based theories (Section 5.3, Dowty 1991; Filip 1989, 1993, inter alia). Incrementality is not necessary for telicity, because there are telic verbs that are not incremental like *hit* (Section 5.1), neither is it sufficient for telicity, because there are incremental predicates that are atelic like *eat apples/soup*. Consequently, incremental verbs like *eat*, which can head either telic (accomplishment) or atelic (activity) predications, are unspecified for telicity (Filip 1993/99). In contrast, in syntactically-based theories of aspect, incrementality and telicity are conflated in a single representational device, as in the telic MEASURE aspectual role in Tenny (1987, 1994) or the denotation of the inflectional head feature *[telic]* in Kratzer (2004).

Regarding the second main issue, the idea that verbs are lexically specified for object-event mapping relations was defended early on in the syntactic theories like Verkuyl's (1972 and also his later work). Subsequently, this idea enters the formulation of the *Aspectual Interface Hypothesis* by Tenny (1987, 1994), on which certain episodic verbs are specified for the telic MEASURE aspectual role, which generalizes over Themes of changes of state and Themes of changes of location in the lexical conceptual structure. The telic MEASURE aspectual role is uniformly linked to the (internal) direct object in the deep structure, which motivates the claim that argument selection is both lexically and aspectually driven. The systematic telicity-direct object link is also the cornerstone of current syntactic theories of aspect. It motivates not only the licensing of telicity by a dedicated functional projection above the VP, but also the independence of telicity from verb meaning (e.g., see Borer 2005; Kratzer 2004; Travis 1991; Verkuyl, de Swart & van Hout 2005, and references therein), in departure from Tenny's Hypothesis. Aspectual phenomena, such as aspectual composition, are motivated by the syntactic telicity-direct object link, rather than lexical meaning of verbs, which in turn is exploited to determine argument selection. Both aspect/telicity and argument selection are severed from the lexical semantics of verbs.

Current semantic and pragmatic theories of aspect are unified by the agreement that neither incrementality nor telicity are systematically linked to the direct object or due to a specific syntactic projection (see e.g., Ackerman & Moore 2001; Filip 1993, Jackendoff 1996; Rappaport Hovav & Levin 2005, and references therein). The main disagreements amongst them concern the claim that incremental relations are a lexical property of verbs, proposed by Krifka (1986, 1992) and integrated into Dowty's (1987, 1991) theory of thematic proto-roles and argument selection. On Dowty's view, they define the Incremental Theme property, one among other verbal entailments in the cluster concept of Proto-Patient, which may be lexicalized as the direct object or the subject of transitives, as in *At the turtle race, the winning turtle crossed the finish line in 42 seconds* (Dowty 1991; see also Filip 1990 and related examples in Declerck 1979). Both Krifka and Dowty also observe that incremental relations have a variety of verb-external sources, both semantic and pragmatic. For instance, *Mary saw seven zebras (for three minutes/ in three minutes)* (Krifka 1986) may have a telic (accomplishment) interpretation involving successive events of seeing of zebras, despite the fact that *see* on its own is non-incremental, which is facilitated by the quantificational properties of the direct object *seven zebras* and our general knowledge about visual perception. Incremental relations may also hold between an event argument and a semantic argument that is not syntactically realized, as in *John drove from Pittsburgh to Washington*, where it is a covert path implied by the source and goal PPs, or in *John was becoming an architect but was interrupted before he could finish his degree* (see Dowty 1991: 569), where the 'path' consists of the implied training stages.

Virtually any non-incremental episodic verb can be used as a basic building block of a telic sentence, provided we can establish incremental relations between its event argument and some suitable path or scale that has an explicit upper bound and with respect to which events described by that telic sentence can be delimited. What constitutes the 'suitable' path or scale is determined by the verb's meaning, other lexical material in a sentence and their interaction with pragmatic factors and cognitive principles of interpretation. This clearly indicates that incremental relations and the derivation of telic interpretations cannot be just confined to semantics. However, neither can they be entirely delegated to pragmatics. If the latter were true, then the telicity of a given predicate ought to be generally cancelable in a suitable linguistic or extra-linguistic context, but this prediction is not borne out for all the relevant cases. For instance, there are telic predicates resisting a shift into an atelic interpretation by means of the durative *for NP* adverbial, as in *John proved the theorem *for an hour* (Zucchi 1999: 351), and also disallowing continuations that negate the final stage of events in their denotation, as in *John proved the theorem, *but died before he could finish proving it*. This behavior strongly suggests that telicity is an *entailment* of such predicates, and since it is systematically linked to predicates headed by strictly incremental verbs, at least this class of verbs may be taken to be lexically specified for an Incremental Theme.

Based on such observations, Filip (1993) proposes that incremental relations generalize over a variety of telicity sources, and at least some verbs are lexically specified for Incremental Theme with all the relevant argument selection consequences, as in Krifka's and Dowty's theories, but incremental relations can also be a property of certain grammatical constructions, with the requisite homomorphism generalized to a structure-preserving mapping between parts of eventualities and parts of *scales* that measure incremental changes in a variety of dimensions. Among other representative views regarding the status of Incremental Theme and incremental relations in the grammar of natural languages, we may mention Rappaport Hovav & Levin (2002, 2005: 284–285) who conclude that incremental relations are a lexical property of verbs motivating a range of telicity phenomena, but play no role in lexically constrained argument selection. Jackendoff (1996: 315) argues that Incremental Theme is not a lexical property of verbs and pragmatic factors inducing incrementality in interaction with the lexical structures of the verb have no effect on argument structure.

Starting in the early 1990s path-based and scalar approaches to aspect have stimulated a broadening of the empirical focus from data covered by aspectual composition (Section 5.3) to telicity data that are of non-compositional nature, and whose analyses require pragmatic and cognitive principles of interpretation. In this larger empirical domain, the phenomenon of aspectual composition, which dominated the formation of early contemporary theories of aspect, now constitutes a special, rather than a central, case. The widening of the empirical domain also raised new questions about a unified analysis for the whole range of the relevant (a)telicity data, and about how much of the explanation should rest on pragmatics (see e.g., Depraetere 2007; Jackendoff 1996; Rappaport Hovav 2008). One of the main challenges for future research is to provide a representational system that integrates insights from semantic theories of event structure and pragmatic theories. The notion of a scale and scalar (quantity) implicature (cf. article 10 [Semantics: Interfaces] (Chierchia, Fox & Spector) *Grammatical view of scalar implicatures*) have recently been added to the key elements in articulating this integration (see e.g., Beavers 2008; Filip 2008; Filip & Rothstein 2005; Hay, Kennedy & Levin 1999; Kearns 2007; Kennedy & Levin 2008; Kratzer 2004; Krifka 1998; Rappaport Hovav 2008; Rothstein 2004, 2008; Wechsler 2005, and references therein). The notion of a scale, conceived of as an ordered set of units of measurements, establishes a link to Krifka's (1986, 1990 and elsewhere) mereological event semantics (Section 5.3), where the notion of measure function, imported from the measurement research that focuses on the relation between measures and mereological part-whole relations, serves to derive quantized predicates. While the notion of quantization is not unproblematic (see e.g., Filip 2000, 2005; Zucchi & White 2001, and references therein), when it comes to the characterization of telicity, the notion of measure function and other tools from the grammar of measurement like a scale have proven to be important meaning components in the analysis of aspectual classes (Filip 2000, 2005; Kennedy & Levin 2008, and references therein). The grammar of measurement in natural languages may also provide some answers to the perennially thorny issues in the domain of aspectual classes like the motivation for the prohibition against more than one delimitation being expressed within a single predication (see e.g., Bach 1981; Goldberg 1992; Tenny 1987, 1994), as illustrated by *run a mile for two hours, *wash the clothes clean white.

7 References

Ackerman, Farrell & John Moore 2001. *Proto-properties and Argument Encoding: A Correspondence Theory of Argument Selection.* Stanford, CA: CSLI Publications.
Agrell, Sigurd 1908. Aspektänderung und Aktionsartbildung beim polnischen Zeitworte: Ein Beitrag zum Studium der indogermanischen Präverbia und ihrer Bedeutungsfunktionen. *Lunds Universitets Arsskrift* (New series) I, iv.2. Lund: Håkan Ohlssons Buchdruckerei.
Alexiadou, Artemis, Elena Anagnostopoulou & Martin Everaert (eds.) 2004. *The Unaccusativity Puzzle. Explorations at the Syntax-Lexicon Interface.* Oxford: Oxford University Press.
Anderson, Stephen R. 1982. Where's morphology? *Linguistic Inquiry* 13, 571–612.
Bach, Emmon 1981. On time, tense, and aspect: An essay in English metaphysics. In: P. Cole (ed.). *Radical Pragmatics.* New York: Academic Press, 63–81.
Bach, Emmon 1986. The algebra of events. *Linguistics & Philosophy* 9, 5–16.
Bach, Emmon et al. (eds.) 1995. *Quantification in Natural Languages.* Dordrecht: Kluwer.
Beavers, John 2008. Scalar complexity and the structure of events. In: J. Dölling, T. Heyde-Zybatow & M. Schäfer (eds.). *Event Structures in Linguistic Form and Interpretation.* Berlin: de Gruyter, 245–267.
Bennett, Michael & Barbara H. Partee 1972. *Toward the logic of tense and aspect in English.* Santa Monica, CA: System Development Corporation. Reprinted with an Afterword: Bloomington, IN: Indiana University Linguistics Club, 1978. Reprinted in: B. H. Partee. *Compositionality in Formal Semantics: Selected Papers by Barbara H. Partee.* Oxford: Blackwell, 2004, 59–109.
van Benthem, Johan 1983. *Modal Logic and Classical Logic.* Napoli: Bibliopolis.
Binnick, Robert I. 1991. *Time and the Verb: A Guide to Tense and Aspect.* Oxford: Oxford University Press.
Borer, Hagit 2005. *In Name Only. Structuring Sense, vol. I. The Normal Course of Events. Structuring Sense, vol. II.* Oxford: Oxford University Press.
Castañeda, Hector-Neri 1967. Comments on Donald Davidson's 'The logical form of action sentences'. In: N. Rescher (ed.). *The Logic of Decision and Action.* Pittsburgh PA: University of Pittsburgh Press, 104–112.
Carlson, Gregory N. 1977. A unified analysis of the English bare plural. *Linguistics & Philosophy* 1, 413–458.
Carlson, Lauri 1981. Aspect and quantification. In: P. Tedeschi & A. Zaenen (eds.). *Syntax and Semantics 14: Tense and Aspect.* New York: Academic Press, 31–64.
Chierchia, Gennaro 1995. Individual-level predicates as inherent generics. In: G. N. Carlson & F. J. Pelletier (eds.). *The Generic Book.* Chicago, IL: The University of Chicago Press, 176–223.
Chierchia, Gennaro 2004. A semantics for unaccusatives and its syntactic consequences. In: A. Alexiadou, E. Anagnostopoulou & M. Everaert (eds.). *The Unaccusativity Puzzle. Explorations at the Syntax-Lexicon Interface.* Oxford: Oxford University Press, 22–59.

Cole, Peter (ed.) 1981. *Radical Pragmatics*. New York: Academic Press.
Comrie, Bernard 1976. *Aspect. An Introduction to the Study of Verbal Aspect and Related Problems*. Cambridge: Cambridge University Press.
Croft, William 1991. *Syntactic Categories and Grammatical Relations: The Cognitive Organization of Information*. Chicago, IL: The University of Chicago Press.
Dahl, Östen 1985. *Tense and Aspect Systems*. London: Blackwell.
Davidson, Donald 1967. The logical form of action sentences. In: N. Rescher (ed.). *The Logic of Decision and Action*. Pittsburgh, PA: University of Pittsburgh Press, 81-95. Reprinted in: D. Davidson. *Essays on Actions and Events*. Oxford: Clarendon Press, 1980, 105–122.
Davidson, Donald 1969. The individuation of events. In: N. Rescher (ed.). *Essays in Honor of C. G. Hempel*. Dordrecht: Reidel, 216–234.
Declerck, Renaat 1979. Aspect and the bounded/unbounded (telic/atelic) distinction. *Linguistics* 17, 761–794.
Depraetere, Ilse 1995. On the necessity of distinguishing between (un)boundedness and (a)telicity. *Linguistics & Philosophy* 18, 1–19.
Depraetere, Ilse 2007. (A)telicity and intentionality. *Linguistics* 45, 243–269.
Dowty, David R. 1972. *Studies in the Logic of Verb Aspect and Time Reference in English*. Ph.D. dissertation. University of Texas, Austin, TX.
Dowty, David R. 1977. Toward a semantic analysis of verb aspect and the English 'imperfective' progressive. *Linguistics & Philosophy* 1, 45–79.
Dowty, David R. 1979. *Word Meaning and Montague Grammar. The Semantics of Verbs and Times in Generative Semantics and in Montague's PTQ*. Dordrecht: Reidel.
Dowty, David R. 1982. Tense, time adverbs and compositional semantic theory. *Linguistics & Philosophy* 5, 23–59.
Dowty, David R. 1987. Aktionsarten, NP semantics, and the structure of events. Paper presented at *The Joint Association for Symbolic Logic/Linguistic Society of America Conference on Logic and Natural Language*. Stanford University, Stanford, CA, July 9-10.
Dowty, David R. 1989. On the semantic content of the notion 'thematic role'. In: B. H. Partee, G. Chierchia & R. Turner (eds.). *Properties, Types, and Meanings*, vol. II. Dordrecht: Kluwer, 69-130.
Dowty, David R. 1991. Thematic proto-roles and argument selection. *Language* 67, 547–619.
Erteschik-Shir, Nomi & Tova Rapoport 2004. Aspectual focus: Bare aspect. In: J. Guéron & J. Lecarme (eds.). *The Syntax of Time*. Cambridge, MA: The MIT Press, 217–234.
Fernald, Theodore B. 2000. *Predicates and Temporal Arguments*. Oxford: Oxford University Press.
Filip, Hana 1989. Aspectual properties of the AN-construction in German. In: W. Abraham & T. Janssen (eds.). *Tempus-Aspekt-Modus. Die lexikalischen und grammatischen Formen in den germanischen Sprachen*. Tübingen: Niemeyer, 259–292.
Filip, Hana 1993. *Aspect, Situation Types and Noun Phrase Semantics*. Ph.D. dissertation. University of California, Berkeley, CA. Published as *Aspect, Eventuality Types, and Noun Phrase Semantics*. New York: Routledge, 1999.
Filip, Hana 2000. The quantization puzzle. In: J. Pustejovsky & C. Tenny (eds.). *Events as Grammatical Objects, from the Combined Perspectives of Lexical Semantics, Logical Semantics and Syntax*. Stanford, CA: CSLI Publications, 3–60.
Filip, Hana 2005. Measures and indefinites. In: G. N. Carlson & F. J. Pelletier (eds.). *Reference and Quantification: The Partee Effect. Festschrift for Barbara H. Partee*. Stanford, CA: CSLI Publications, 229–288.

Filip, Hana 2008. Events and maximalization. In: S. Rothstein (ed.). *Theoretical and Crosslinguistic Approaches to the Semantics of Aspect*. Amsterdam: Benjamins, 217–256.
Filip, Hana & Susan Rothstein 2005. Telicity as a semantic parameter. In: J. Lavine et al. (eds.). *Formal Approaches to Slavic Linguistics (=FASL) XIV: The Princeton Meeting*. Ann Arbor, MI: University of Michigan Slavic Publications, 139–156.
Foley, William A. & Robert D. van Valin, Jr. 1984. *Functional Syntax and Universal Grammar*. Cambridge: Cambridge University Press.
Forsyth, J. 1970. *A Grammar of Aspect. Usage and Meaning in the Russian Verb*. Cambridge: Cambridge University Press.
Garey, Howard B. 1957. Verbal aspects in French. *Language* 33, 91–110.
Gawron, Jean Mark 2005. Generalized paths. In: E. Georgala & J. Howell (eds.) *Proceedings of Semantics and Linguistic Theory (=SALT) XV*. Ithaca, NY: Cornell University. http://www.rohan.sdsu/~gawron/salt_paper.pdf, August 9, 2011.
Geis, Jonnie 1970. *Some Aspects of Verb Phrase Adverbials in English*. Ph.D. dissertation. University of Illinois, Urbana, IL.
Gill, Kathleen 1993. On the metaphysical distinction between processes and events. *Canadian Journal of Philosophy* 23, 365–384.
Goldberg, Adele E. 1992. *Argument Structure Constructions*. Ph.D. dissertation. University of California, Berkeley, CA. Reprinted: Chicago, IL: The University of Chicago Press, 1995.
Groenendijk, Jeroen, Dick de Jongh & Martin Stokhof (eds.) 1987. *Studies in Discourse Representation Theory and the Theory of Generalized Quantifiers*. Dordrecht: Foris.
Gruber, Jeffrey S. 1965. *Studies in Lexical Relations*. Ph.D. dissertation. MIT, Cambridge, MA.
Gruber, Jeffrey S. 1967. Look and see. *Language* 43, 937–947.
Hay, Jennifer, Christopher Kennedy & Beth Levin 1999. Scale Structure underlies telicity in 'degree achievements'. In: T. Matthews & D. Strolovitch (eds.). *Proceedings of Semantics and Linguistic Theory (=SALT) IX*. Ithaca, NY: Cornell University, 127–144.
Heny, Frank 1982. Tense, aspect and time adverbials, Part II. *Linguistics & Philosophy* 5, 109–154.
Higginbotham, James 1983. The logic of perceptual reports: An extensional alternative to situation semantics. *Journal of Philosophy* 80, 100–127.
Higginbotham, James 1985. On semantics. *Linguistic Inquiry* 16, 547–593.
Higginbotham, James 2000. On events in linguistic semantics. In: J. Higginbotham, F. Pianesi & A. C. Varzi (eds.). *Speaking of Events*. Oxford: Oxford University Press, 49–79.
Higginbotham, James 2004. The English progressive. In: J. Guéron & J. Lecarme (eds.). *The Syntax of Time*. Cambridge, MA: The MIT Press, 329–358.
Hinrichs, Erhard 1985. *A Compositional Semantics for Aktionsarten and NP Reference in English*. Ph.D. dissertation. Ohio State University, Columbus, OH.
Hinrichs, Erhard 1986. Temporal anaphora in discourses of English. *Linguistics & Philosophy* 9, 63–82.
Isačenko, Aleksandr V. 1962. *Die russische Sprache der Gegenwart, Bd. I: Formenlehre*. Halle/Saale: Niemeyer.
Jackendoff, Ray S. 1972. *Semantic Interpretation in Generative Grammar*. Cambridge, MA: The MIT Press.
Jackendoff, Ray S. 1983. *Semantics and Cognition*. Cambridge, MA: The MIT Press.
Jackendoff, Ray S. 1990. *Semantic Structures*. Cambridge, MA: The MIT Press.
Jackendoff, Ray S. 1991. Parts and boundaries. *Cognition* 41, 9–45.

Jackendoff, Ray S. 1996. The proper treatment of measuring out, telicity, and perhaps even quantification in English. *Natural Language and Linguistic Theory* 14, 305–354.
Jacobsohn, Hermann 1933. Aspektfragen. *Indogermanische Forschungen* 51, 292–318.
Jakobson, Roman 1936. Beitrag zur allgemeinen Kasuslehre: Gesamtbedeutung der russischen Kasus. *Travaux du Cercle Linguistique de Prague* 6, 240–288. Reprinted in: R. Jakobson. *Selected Writings, vol. II: Word and Language*. The Hague: Mouton, 1971, 23–71.
Kamp, Hans 1980. Some remarks on the logic of change. In: Ch. Rohrer (ed.). *Time, Tense, and Quantifiers*. Tübingen: Niemeyer, 103–114.
Kamp, Hans 1979. Events, instants and temporal reference. In: R. Bäuerle, U. Egli & A. von Stechow (eds.). *Semantics from Different Points of View*. Berlin: Springer, 376–417.
Kamp, Hans & Christian Rohrer 1983. Tense in texts. In: R. Bäuerle, Ch. Schwarze & A. von Stechow (eds.). *Meaning, Use and Interpretation of Language*. Berlin: de Gruyter, 250–269.
Kamp, Hans & Uwe Reyle 1993. *From Discourse to Logic*. Dordrecht: Kluwer.
Kearns, Kate 2007. Telic senses of deadjectival verbs. *Lingua* 117, 26–66.
Kennedy, Christopher & Beth Levin 2008. Measure of change: The adjectival core of degree achievements. In: L. McNally & C. Kennedy (eds.). *Adjectives and Adverbs: Syntax, Semantics and Discourse*. Oxford: Oxford University Press, 156–182.
Kenny, Anthony 1963. *Action, Emotion and Will*. London: Routledge and Kegan Paul.
Klein, Wolfgang 1994. *Time in Language*. London: Routledge.
Kratzer, Angelika 1988. Stage-level and individual-level predicates. In: M. Krifka (ed.). *Genericity in Natural Language. Proceedings of the 1988 Tübingen Conference* (SNS-Bericht 88-42), 247–284. Reprinted in: G. N. Carlson & F. J. Pelletier (eds.). *The Generic Book*. Chicago, IL: The University of Chicago Press, 1995, 125–175.
Kratzer, Angelika 2004. Telicity and the meaning of objective case. In: J. Guéron & J. Lecarme (eds.). *The Syntax of Time*. Cambridge, MA: The MIT Press, 389–424.
Krifka, Manfred 1986. *Nominalreferenz und Zeitkonstitution. Zur Semantik von Massentermen, Individualtermen, Aspektklassen*. Doctoral dissertation. Ludwig-Maximilians-Universität München. Reprinted: München: Fink, 1989.
Krifka, Manfred 1992. Thematic relations as links between nominal reference and temporal constitution. In: I. Sag & A. Szabolsci (eds.). *Lexical Matters*. Stanford, CA: CSLI Publications, 29–53.
Krifka, Manfred 1998. The origins of telicity. In: S. Rothstein (ed.). *Events and Grammar*. Dordrecht: Kluwer, 197–235.
Lakoff, George 1965. *On the Nature of Syntactic Irregularity*. Ph.D. dissertation. Indiana University, Bloomington, IN. Published as *Irregularity in Syntax*. New York: Holt, Rinehart & Winston, 1970.
Landman, Fred 1992. The progressive. *Natural Language Semantics* 1, 1–32.
Langacker, Ronald W. 1990. *Concept, Image, and Symbol: The Cognitive Basis of Grammar*. Berlin: de Gruyter.
Levin, Beth 2000. Aspect, lexical semantic representation, and argument expression. In: A. Yu et al. (eds.). *Proceedings of the Annual Meeting of the Berkeley Linguistics Society (=BLS) 26*. Berkeley, CA: Berkeley Linguistics Society, 413–429.
Levin, Beth & Malka Rappaport Hovav 1998. Building verb meanings. In: M. Butt & W. Geuder (eds.). *The Projection of Arguments: Lexical and Compositional Factors*. Stanford, CA: CSLI Publications, 97–134.
Levin, Beth & Malka Rappaport Hovav 1999. Two structures for compositionally derived events. In: T. Matthews & D. Strolovich (eds.). *Proceedings of Semantics and Linguistic Theory (=SALT) IX*. Ithaca, NY: Cornell University, 199–223.

Levin, Beth & Malka Rappaport Hovav 2005. *Argument Realization*. Cambridge: Cambridge University Press.
Lepore, Ernest & Brian McLaughlin (eds.) 1985. *Actions and Events: Perspectives on the Philosophy of Donald Davidson*. Oxford: Blackwell.
Link, Godehard 1983. The logical analysis of plurals and mass terms. In: R. Bäuerle, Ch. Schwarze & A. von Stechow (eds.). *Meaning, Use, and Interpretation of Language*. Berlin: de Gruyter, 302–323.
Link, Godehard 1987. Algebraic semantics of event structures. In: J. Groenendijk, M. Stokhof & F. Veltman (eds.). *Proceedings of the Sixth Amsterdam Colloquium*. Amsterdam: ILLC, 243–272.
ter Meulen, Alice G. B. 1995. *Representing Time in Natural Language. The Dynamic Interpretation of Tense and Aspect*. Cambridge, MA: The MIT Press.
ter Meulen, Alice G. B. 2000. How to tell events apart. In: C. Tenny & J. Pustejovsky (eds.). *Events as Grammatical Objects, from the Combined Perspectives of Lexical Semantics, Logical Semantics and Syntax*. Stanford, CA: CSLI Publications, 377–392.
McCawley, James D. 1971. Tense and time reference in English. In: C. J. Fillmore & T. Langendoen (eds.). *Studies in Linguistic Semantics*. New York: Holt, Rinehart & Winston, 97–113.
McCawley, James D. 1976. Remarks on what can cause what. In: M. Shibatani (ed.). *Syntax and Semantics 6: The Grammar of Causative Constructions*. New York: Academic Press, 117–129.
von Miklosich, Franz 1868-1874. *Vergleichende Grammatik der slavischen Sprachen*. Wien: Wilhelm Braumüller.
Miller, George A. & Phillip N. Johnson-Laird 1976. *Language and Perception*. Cambridge, MA: Harvard University Press.
Moens, Marc & Mark Steedmann 1988. Temporal ontology and temporal reference. *Computational Linguistics* 14, 15–28.
Montague, Richard 1968. Pragmatics. In: R. Klibanski (ed.). *Contemporary Philosophy*. Firenze: La Nuova Italia Editrice, 102–121. Reprinted in: R. Thomason (ed.). *Formal Philosophy. Selected Papers of Richard Montague*. New Haven, CT: Yale University Press, 1974, 95–11.
Montague, Richard 1973. The proper treatment of quantification in ordinary English. In: J. Hintikka, J. M. Moravcsik & P. Suppes (eds.). *Approaches to Natural Language*. Dordrecht: Reidel, 221–242. Reprinted in: R. Thomason (ed.). *Formal Philosophy. Selected Papers of Richard Montague*. New Haven, CT: Yale University Press, 1974, 247–270.
Montague, Richard 1974. *Formal Philosophy. Selected Papers of Richard Montague*. Edited and with an introduction by Richmond H. Thomason. New Haven, CT: Yale University Press.
Mourelatos, Alexander P. D. 1978. Events, processes and states. *Linguistics & Philosophy* 2, 415–434. Reprinted in: P. Tedeschi & A. Zaenen (eds.). *Syntax and Semantics 14: Tense and Aspect*. New York: Academic Press, 1981, 191–212.
Parsons, Terence 1980. Modifiers and quantifiers in natural language. *Canadian Journal of Philosophy* (Supplement) 6, 29–60.
Parsons, Terence 1989. The progressive in English: Events, states and processes. *Linguistics & Philosophy* 12, 213–241.
Parsons, Terence 1990. *Events in the Semantics of English: A Study in Subatomic Semantics*. Cambridge, MA: The MIT Press.
Partee, Barbara H. 1984. Nominal and temporal anaphora. *Linguistics & Philosophy* 7, 243–286.
Partee, Barbara H. 1999. Nominal and temporal semantic structure: Aspect and quantification. In: E. Hajičová et al. (eds.). *Prague Linguistic Circle Papers* 3, 91–108.

Partee, Barbara H. 2000. Some remarks on linguistic uses of the notion of 'event'. In: C. Tenny & J. Pustejovsky (eds.). *Events as Grammatical Objects, from the Combined Perspectives of Lexical Semantics, Logical Semantics and Syntax.* Stanford, CA: CSLI Publications, 483–495.
Partee, Barbara H. 2004. *Compositionality in Formal Semantics: Selected Papers by Barbara H. Partee.* Oxford: Blackwell.
Pelletier, Francis J. 1975. Non-singular reference. *Philosophia* 5. Reprinted in: F. J. Pelletier (ed.). *Mass Terms: Some Philosophical Problems.* Dordrecht: Reidel, 1979, 1–14.
Platzack, Christer 1979. *The Semantic Interpretation of Aspect and Aktionsarten: A Study of Internal Time Reference in Swedish.* Dordrecht: Foris.
Portner, Paul 1998. The progressive in modal semantics. *Language* 74, 760–787.
Prior, Arthur N. 1957. *Time and Modality.* Oxford: Oxford University Press.
Prior, Arthur N. 1967. *Past, Present and Future.* Oxford: Oxford University Press.
Pustejovsky, James 1991. The syntax of event structure. *Cognition* 41, 47–81.
Pustejovsky, James 1995. *The Generative Lexicon.* Cambridge, MA: The MIT Press.
Quine, Willard van Orman 1960. *Word and Object.* Cambridge, MA: The MIT Press.
Ramchand, Gillian 1997. *Aspect and Predication. The Semantics of Argument Structure.* Oxford: Clarendon Press.
Ramsey, Frank 1927. Facts and propositions. *Aristotelian Society Supplementary Volume* 7, 153–170.
Rappaport Hovav, Malka 2008. Lexicalized meaning and the internal temporal structure of events. In: S. Rothstein (ed.). *Theoretical and Crosslinguistic Approaches to the Semantics of Aspect.* Amsterdam: Benjamins, 13–42.
Rappaport Hovav, Malka & Beth Levin 2002. Change of state verbs: Implications for theories of argument projection. In: J. Larson & M. Paster (eds.). *Proceedings of the Annual Meeting of the Berkeley Linguistics Society (=BLS) 28.* Berkeley, CA: Berkeley Linguistics Society, 269–280. Revised version in: N. Erteschik-Shir & T. Rapoport (eds.). *The Syntax of Aspect.* Oxford: Oxford University Press, 2005, 274–286.
Reichenbach, Hans 1947. *Elements of Symbolic Logic.* New York: Macmillan.
Richards, Barry 1982. Tense, Aspect, and Time Adverbials. Part I. *Linguistics & Philosophy* 5, 59–107.
Rohrer, Christian (ed.) 1980. *Time, Tense, and Quantifiers.* Tübingen: Niemeyer.
Rosen, Carol 1984. The interface between semantic roles and initial grammatical relations. In: D. Perlmutter & C. Rosen (eds.). *Studies in Relational Grammar 2.* Chicago, IL: The University of Chicago Press, 38–80.
Ross, John R. 1972. Act. In: D. Davidson & G. Harman (eds.). *Semantics of Natural Language.* Dordrecht: Reidel, 70–126.
Rothstein, Susan (ed.) 1998. *Events and Grammar.* Dordrecht: Kluwer.
Rothstein, Susan 2004. *Structuring Events.* Oxford: Blackwell.
Rothstein, Susan 2008. Telicity, atomicity and the Vendler classification of verbs. In: S. Rothstein (ed.). *Theoretical and Crosslinguistic Approaches to the Semantics of Aspect.* Amsterdam: Benjamins, 43–77.
Ryle, Gilbert 1949. *The Concept of Mind.* London: Barnes and Noble.
Sasse, Hans-Jürgen 2002. Recent activity in the theory of aspect: Accomplishments, achievements, or just non-progressive state? *Linguistic Typology* 6, 199–271.
Schank, Roger 1973. Identification of conceptualizations underlying natural language. In: R. Schank & K. Colby (eds.). *Computer Models of Thought and Language.* San Francisco, CA: W. H. Freeman Co, 187–247.
Scott, Dana 1970. Advice in modal logic. In: K. Lambert (ed.). *Philosophical Problems in Logic.* Dordrecht: Reidel, 143–173.

Sharvy, Richard 1980. A more general theory of definite descriptions. *Philosophical Review* 89, 607–624.
Smith, Carlota S. 1991. *The Parameter of Aspect*. Dordrecht: Kluwer.
Smotritsky, Meletiy 1619. *Grammar of Church Slavonic*. Kiev.
von Stechow, Arnim 1995. Lexical decomposition in syntax. In: U. Egli et al. (eds.). *Lexical Knowledge in the Organization of Language*. Amsterdam: Benjamins, 81–117.
de Swart, Henriëtte 1998. Aspect shift and coercion. *Natural Language and Linguistic Theory* 16, 347–385.
Talmy, Leonard 1972. *Semantic Structures in English and Atsugewi*. Ph.D. dissertation. University of California, Berkeley, CA.
Talmy, Leonard 1985. Lexicalization patterns: Semantic structure in lexical forms. In: T. Shopen (ed.). *Language Typology and Syntactic Description, vol. III: Grammatical Categories and the Lexicon*. Cambridge: Cambridge University Press, 130–176.
Taylor, Barry 1977. Tense and continuity. *Linguistics & Philosophy* 1, 199–220.
Tenny, Carol L. 1987. *Grammaticalizing Aspect and Affectedness*. Ph.D. dissertation. MIT, Cambridge, MA.
Tenny, Carol L. 1994. *Aspectual Roles and the Syntax-Semantics Interface*. Dordrecht: Kluwer.
Tenny Carol L. & James Pustejovsky 2000. A history of events in linguistic theory. In: C. L. Tenny & J. Pustejovsky (eds.). *Events as Grammatical Objects, from the Combined Perspectives of Lexical Semantics, Logical Semantics and Syntax*. Stanford, CA: CSLI Publications, 3–37.
Travis, Lisa 1991. Inner aspect and the structure of VP. *Cahiers de Linguistique de l'UQAM* 1, 132–146.
van Valin, Robert D., Jr. 1990. Semantic parameters of split intransitivity. *Language* 22, 221–260.
van Valin, Robert D., Jr. & Randy J. LaPolla 1997. *Structure, Meaning and Function*. Cambridge: Cambridge University Press.
Vendler, Zeno 1957. Verbs and times. *Philosophical Review* 56, 143-160. Reprinted in: Z. Vendler. *Linguistics in Philosophy*. Ithaca, NY: Cornell University, 1967, 97–121.
Verkuyl, Henk J. 1971. *On the Compositional Nature of the Aspects*. Doctoral dissertation. Utrecht University. Reprinted: Dordrecht: Reidel, 1972.
Verkuyl, Henk J. 1989. Aspectual classes and aspectual composition. *Linguistics & Philosophy* 12, 39–94.
Verkuyl, Henk J. 1993. *A Theory of Aspectuality: The Interaction between Temporal and Atemporal Structure*. Cambridge: Cambridge University Press.
Verkuyl, Henk, Henriëtte de Swart & Angeliek van Hout (eds.) 2005. *Perspectives on Aspect*. Dordrecht: Springer.
Wechsler, Stephen 2005. Resultatives under the event-argument homomorphism model of telicity. In: N. Erteschik-Shir & T. Rapoport (eds.). *The Syntax of Aspect*. Oxford: Oxford University Press, 255–273.
von Wright, Georg H. 1963. *Norm and Action. A logical enquiry*. London: Routledge and Kegan Paul.
von Wright, Georg H. 1968. An essay on deontic logic and the general theory of action. *Acta Philosophica Fennica* 21, 1–110.
Zucchi, Sandro 1999. Incomplete events, intensionality and imperfective aspect. *Natural Language Semantics* 7, 179–215.
Zucchi, Sandro & Michael White 2001. Twigs, sequences and the temporal constitution of predicates. *Linguistics & Philosophy* 24, 223–270.
Zwarts, Joost 2008. Aspects of a typology of direction. In: S. Rothstein (ed.). *Theoretical and Crosslinguistic Approaches to the Semantics of Aspect*. Amsterdam: Benjamins, 79–106.

Paul Portner
10 Perfect and progressive

1 Introduction —— 313
2 The perfect —— 313
3 The progressive —— 342
4 References —— 364

Abstract: This article surveys the major approaches to the semantics of the perfect and progressive. While it may not seem difficult to describe the meaning of these constructions informally, both present empirical puzzles, within and across languages, which show that initial descriptions do not do justice to their meanings. As a result, a range of analyses of the perfect and progressive have been developed. These analyses are important not only in their roles as attempts to formalize the meaning of the construction in question, but also because they have developed tools which have proven fruitful in other areas of linguistic theory.

1 Introduction

This article discusses two aspectual constructions which are prominent in English and many other languages, and which have received a great deal of attention within semantic theory. They are worth studying because they are of linguistic interest in their own right (as are the prominent constructions of any language) and more importantly because of the in-depth research they have triggered. We have learned a great deal about the temporal semantics, event semantics, modal semantics, and various other issues, from the progressive and the perfect.

2 The perfect

The perfect is a grammatical construction which is built from a participial verb phrase and an auxiliary, and which indicates temporal anteriority (roughly, pastness) as part of its meaning.

Paul Portner, Washington, DC, USA

https://doi.org/10.1515/9783110589443-010

(1) Ben has fallen asleep.

The most basic goal of theories of the perfect is an analysis of the type of anteriority it indicates. It is not simply the kind of past meaning expressed by the past tense, as we can see in English from the contrast in (2):

(2) a. *Ben has fallen asleep yesterday afternoon.
    b. Ben fell asleep yesterday afternoon.

It is generally assumed that this construction is identifiable across languages (at least, western Indo-European ones):

(3) Jean est   arrivé hier. (French, Schaden 2009)
    Jean be.pres arrived yesterday
    'Jean arrived yesterday.'

(4) Mario era   partito giovedì. (Italian, Giorgi & Pianesi 1997)
    Mario be.imperf departed Thursday
    'Mario had left Wednesday.'

(5) Eva hat   seit drei Stunden geschlafen. (German, Musan 2003)
    Eva have.pres since three hours   slept
    'Eva has slept for three hours.'

(6) Sigurd har   kommit. (Swedish, Rothstein 2008)
    Sigurd have.pres come
    'Sigurd has come.'

There are a number of important differences among the perfects of various languages, most famously in the acceptability of sentences like (2a), and their analysis is one of the main topics which has motivated contemporary studies.

When the tense of the sentence, represented on the auxiliary, is the present tense, as in (1), the construction is known as the present perfect. Likewise, we have the past perfect, future perfect, and tenseless perfects:

(7) a. Ben had fallen asleep.
    b. Ben will have fallen asleep.
    c. Having fallen asleep, Ben was carried to his bed.

Given that the perfect is a complex construction built out of multiple morphosyntactic pieces, a compositional analysis of the perfect must determine an appropriate syntactic analysis, figure out what components of the overall construction's meaning are associated with each piece, and understand the nature of the processes which combine these components together. It is also possible that some aspects of the perfect's meaning are not derived compositionally, but rather associated with the construction as a whole.

Almost all recent research on the perfect assumes a crucial role for pragmatics in explaining the meaning and use of the perfect, though there is not agreement on which component of pragmatic theory is relevant. An important role for pragmatics is motivated from two directions: first, some key data (e.g., that in (2a)) turns out to resist analysis in terms of compositional semantics, and thus some authors have turned to a pragmatic account. (Others turn to syntax, as we will see below.) And second, the intuitive function of the perfect seems to vary among various discourse contexts, giving rise to the tradition of identifying a number of "readings" of the perfect. Portner (2003) gives the following examples:

(8) Resultative perfect: Mary has read *Middlemarch*.

(9) Existential perfect: The earth has been hit by giant asteroids before (and probably will be again).

(10) Continuative perfect: Mary has lived in London for five years.

(11) Hot news perfect: The Orioles have won!

It is generally assumed that much of this variation is pragmatic in nature, though there remains controversy over whether the continuative perfect, i.e. examples in which the eventuality (in (10), of Mary living in London) continues up to the time indicated by the main tense (here the present), is semantically different from the others, or just pragmatically different.

In the discussion which follows, I make a distinction between primary theories of the perfect, and secondary theories. Primary theories, described in Section 2.2, are those designed to capture the most basic facts, such as anteriority. Moreover, it is often assumed that, if we can get the details right, the correct primary theory of the perfect will suffice to account for all of the relevant phenomena. In contrast to this view, other scholars have developed a number of secondary ideas about the perfect's meaning; these theoretical ideas, discussed in Section 2.3, are intended to be combined with one or the other primary theory, accounting for some body of facts which cannot be attributed to the core, or primary semantics.

In this overview, I will begin in section 2.1 by outlining the key data which forms the empirical base for contemporary research on the perfect. Then in section 2.2 I will outline the three primary theories which are important in the recent literature. In section 2.3, I will examine five secondary theories. In Section 2.4, I will discuss how the primary and second theories have been put together in the recent literature.

2.1 Outline of key data

In this section, I will list a number of linguistic phenomena which have been important in the development of semantic theories of the perfect. There is of course much more data which could be extracted from the large literature on the topic, and so in the interests of space and accessibility, it cannot be helped that I select a portion, with the goal of identifying the facts which are crucial to understanding the various theories and debates which we will turn to in later sections.

2.1.1 Continuative vs. non-continuative readings

Sometimes in a perfect sentence, the eventuality described by the verb phrase is still ongoing at the time indicated by the tense, and sometimes it must have been completed before that time. The former case, (12), is known as a continuative or universal perfect, while the latter, (13), is known as a non-continuative or existential perfect:

(12) a. John has been sick for several days.
 b. I have understood.
 c. Mary has been swimming since noon.

(13) a. John has slept.
 b. I have already eaten lunch.
 c. Mary has been swimming before.

Continuative readings are only possible with perfects built out of stative VPs, where in English the relevant notion of stativity includes individual level-predicates, copular sentences, and progressives, but not non-dynamic stage-level verbs (see Dowty 1979; Mittwoch 1988; Vlach 1993; Portner 2003; see Iatridou et al. 2003 for relevant crosslinguistic data). Thus (13a), which is stage level, does not have a continuative interpretation. Stative predicates also allow existential readings, as seen in (13c), while non-statives only allow existential readings. The particular combination of aspectual factors which allows for the continuative reading differs across languages. For example, in German a non-progressive activity predicate allows a continuative reading (presumably because the base verb covers the meanings which are expressed by both the progressive and non-progressive forms in English):

(14) Maria hat seit langem auf Hans gewartet. (Musan 2002: 143)
 Maria has since long on Hans waited
 'Maria has been waiting for Hans for a long time.'

There has been debate over whether the continuative/existential difference is grammatical or pragmatic in nature. The simplest form of pragmatic view says that the existential reading is basic, and that the continuative interpretation is really just a special case. The idea is that, in general, the present perfect entails the existence of some interval of time at which the core clause is true, and which begins before the speech time; if this interval happens to include the speech time, we have a continuative perfect. Against this hypothesis, Mittwoch (1988) points out that the continuative reading of (15) entails that Sam was in Boston on Tuesday, while its existential reading is false if he was there only on Tuesday.

(15) Sam has been in Boston since Tuesday.

Mittwoch's example shows that the continuative reading is not simply a subcase of the non-continuative reading.

A second fact which tends to favor a grammatical analysis is that it is very difficult to find a continuative interpretation in the absence of a temporal adverbial, as pointed out by Iatridou et al. (2003) and Portner (2003). The following contrast is from Portner:

(16) a. Mary has lived in London for five years.
 b. Mary has lived in London.

(Other relevant adverbials include *always* and the much-discussed *seit* in German, cf. e.g., von Stechow 2002; Musan 2002; Löbner 2002; Rathert 2004.) However, Nishiyama & Koenig (2004) dispute the claim that an adverbial is necessary for a continuative reading on the basis of the data in (17), reporting that their informants judge this sentence as having the continuative interpretation:

(17) John has been sick.

It would be helpful to know what exactly Nishiyama & Koenig's informants judged, since what's essential is not whether (17) can be true if John is still sick at the speech time, but rather whether it has a reading entailing that he is. And this will be a difficult point to judge, given that it is not in dispute that the sentence has an existential reading, which does not entail he is still sick.

Even though it is possible that (17) does have a continuative reading, this does not necessarily undermine the argument that the continuative/existential contrast has a grammatical basis. It is not essential to that argument that an adverbial be involved in every continuative sentence. Indeed, Vlach (1993) has already pointed out that perfects formed from a progressive have a continuative reading in the absence of an adverbial, and this did not deter Portner (2003) from making the argument. If Nishiyama & Koenig are right about (17), this shows that certain perfect copular sentences are like perfect progressives. Despite all of this, the lack of a continuative reading of (16b) remains a clear fact, and may still constitute an argument in favor of a grammatical analysis of the continuative/non-continuative contrast. What's essential, but not yet known, is whether the difference between the cases where the adverbial is a prerequisite for the continuative reading, and those where it is not, should be defined in pragmatic terms (e.g., the presence of the adverbial makes the continuative reading more plausible), or grammatical ones (e.g., a certain lexical class of verbs requires the adverbial). At first glance, it seems difficult to account for the sharp contrast seen in (18) in pragmatic terms:

(18) Child: Can John come out and play?
John's mother:
a. No, sorry, he's been sick. (Nishiyama & Koenig's example)
b. No, sorry, he has been living in London. (perfect progressive)
c. No, sorry, he has lived in London for several weeks now. (non-progressive perfect with an adverbial)
d. *No, sorry, he has lived in London. (non-progressive perfect with no adverbial)

Even this context which seems to support continuative readings for (18a–c) does not allow one for (18d). (Of course (18d) is fine if the mother means that people who have ever lived in London are unfit to play with the children, but it can't mean that he's unavailable to play because he is currently in London, in contrast to (18b–c).)

A third set of facts involving adverbials has also been used to argue that the continuative/non-continuative contrast is grammatical in nature. Dowty (1979) points out that preposing a *for* adverbial seems to force the continuative reading, as in (19a), and in contrast to (19b), which can be either continuative or non-continuative:

(19) a. For a week, Mary has lived in London.
   b. Mary has lived in London for a week.

Dowty's claim is supported by Mittwoch (1988) and Portner (2003), among others, but disputed by Abusch & Rooth (1990), Rathert (2003, 2004), and Nishiyama & Koenig (2004). While Abusch & Rooth and Nishiyama & Koenig give isolated examples about which judgments may differ, Rathert (2003) seeks to provide stronger evidence in the form of naturally occurring data. She cites the following passage (Rathert 2003: 378):

> To say I am frustrated with the problem of school lunches is just not going to cut it. I am positively erupting... and ash and lava are everywhere. My son started high school this year. I had heard someone say that this school had some healthy choices. NOT!!! *For two weeks he has eaten tacos without cheese, chicken nuggets and fries.* His other choices were popcorn shrimp and onion rings and sodas. This not only costs too much ($4) but is death food. A couple of years ago I called the man who oversees the buying and planning of all the school lunches. He claims that fast food is what kids get at home, and if kids are going to buy the school lunches, he needs to supply them with food they know and will buy. He claims that if he served them healthier food that the food service couldn't sustain itself because not enough kids would buy lunch. I suggested he might offer baked potatoes, rice, choices without cheese, and grilled meats and vegetables. And for about a month I saw changes on the menu. Then, back to the worst.

Rathert (2003: 378) says:

> The two weeks of unhealthy food cannot abut speech time because after these weeks the mother contacted "the man who oversees the buying and planning of all the school lunches". And even after this, "for about a month I saw changes on the menu. Then, back to the worst..."

However, this interpretation of the passage is not correct. The son started high school "this year", but the mother contacted the man in charge "a couple of years ago." Thus, clearly, she had contacted him before her son was in high school, and the temporary changes to the menu also happened before the son entered high school. In other words, the events which Rathert interprets as having followed the stretch during which had ate tacos, nuggets, and fries, actually represent a flashback to an earlier episode. The key sentence itself is indeed a continuative perfect.

Rathert (2004) gives a number of other naturally occurring examples, but none are without difficulties, and all must be assessed with the level of care given to those above. Rothstein (2008) also expresses skepticism of Rathert's conclusions on the basis of the fact that it is often not clear whether data found on the web were produced by native speakers. (From my reading of her examples, only one seems to show clear signs of having been produced by a non-native speaker.) In considering all of this, it is important to note that there are plenty of examples of continuative perfects with preposed *for* phrases, and plenty of non-continuative perfects with non-preposed *for* phrases. We do not expect ungrammatical forms to have zero occurrence in the web, only very low frequency, relative to similar forms. Overall, then, given that there are no, or at least extremely few, examples of non-continuative perfects with preposed *for* phrases, it seems likely that Dowty is correct, and that preposing really does disambiguate in favor of a continuative reading (though of course further corpus research may require us to rethink this matter once again). This in turn supports the hypothesis that the continuative/non-continuative contrast is grammatical in nature.

2.1.2 Interactions with adverbials

Across languages, the perfect shows varied interactions with temporal adverbials. While the data are complex, the most important facts concern whether the present perfect is compatible with an adverbial referring to a definite time in the past, present, or future. In German, all three are possible (data from Musan 2001: 361).

(20) a. Hans hat gestern den Brief geschrieben.   (Past adverbial)
   Hans has yesterday the letter written
   'Has wrote the letter yesterday.'
 b. Hans hat jetzt den Brief geschrieben.   (Present adverbial)
   Hans has now the letter written
   'Has has now written the letter.'
 c. Hans hat morgen den Brief geschrieben.   (Future adverbial)
   Hans has tomorrow the letter written
   'Hans will have written the letter tomorrow.'

In English, only a present adverbial is possible. In Italian, either a past or present adverbial is possible, but not a future adverbial. In Swedish, either a present or future adverbial is possible, but not a past adverbial (so long as we set aside a separate inferential use of the Swedish perfect form, see Rothstein 2008).

It is generally assumed that the possibility of having a future adverbial with the present perfect in a given language is dependent on the semantics of the present tense in that language. Thus, German fairly easily allows future time reference with the present tense, as seen in (21a), and Musan argues that this fact immediately accounts for (20c). In English, future time reference with the present tense is more restricted; example (21b) is only possible if there is a definite plan or schedule for John to leave:

(21) a. Im   Juni hat Maria Ferien. (Musan 2001: 372)
     in-the June has Maria vacation
     'Maria will have vacation in June.'
   b. John leaves tomorrow.
   c. *John has left tomorrow.

From Musan's perspective, one would probably say that (21c) is ungrammatical because the "planning" interpretation of the present tense is not compatible with the perfect, but as far as I know, it has never been carefully explained why this should be so.

Past temporal adverbials are incompatible with the present perfect in English and other languages, as in (22a), a fact which has been important in the development of theories of the perfect. This incompatibility is known as **the present perfect puzzle**, and its puzzling nature is made clear by two facts. First, note that (22b), lacking the adverbial, can be true if Mary arrived yesterday; this shows that the problem with (22a) is not with the temporal relations described, but with how they are described.

(22) a. *Mary has arrived yesterday.
   b. Mary has arrived.
   c. In the event my Lord, erm, that er your Lordship felt that further guidance was required, there are the two routes that I've *indicated* to your Lordship briefly *yesterday*, [...]
   d. *I have enjoyed yesterday's party.
   e. *Mary has arrived on yesterday's flight.
   f. #Mary has enjoyed that party.
   g. Mary has seen yesterday's visitor.

Schaden (2009) argues that combinations like (22a) are in fact possible, as in (22c) (his (13c)), but the attested examples which he provides are all representative of very formal contexts. A correct account will need allow for such sentences in a particular dialect or register, but also to explain their ungrammaticality elsewhere. I don't think it's been noticed before that the same phenomenon sometimes occurs when past time reference is implied by an argument, as in (22d), and non-temporal adverbials, as in (22e), when they entail the same kind of time restriction as a temporal adverbial would. Example (22f) is also unacceptable in a context where *that party* refers to the particular party which is known to have taken place yesterday, but is acceptable if it refers to a recurring weekly event. (22g) shows that the restriction in (22e) is not syntactic; it is acceptable because *yesterday's visitor* does not restrict the time at which Mary saw the person, unlike *yesterday's party* in (22d), where the enjoyment had to be yesterday if the party was.

Second, sentences parallel to (22a) in the past perfect or tenseless perfects are acceptable, as pointed out by McCawley (1971):

(23) a. Mary had arrived the day before.
     b. Having arrived yesterday, Mary is well-rested for the race.

The contrast between the present perfect, on the one hand, and past/tenseless perfects on the other, leads several linguists to conclude that the present perfect puzzle crucially involves the analysis of the present tense (e.g., Giorgi & Pianesi 1997; Portner 2003; Pancheva & von Stechow 2004; Rothstein 2008; but Schaden 2009 agues against this conclusion); thus, according to this view, the difference between a language like German, with no present perfect puzzle, and a language like English, concerns the syntax and/or semantics of the present tense. We'll return to the analysis of the present perfect puzzle in Section 2.2.

Another interaction between the perfect and adverbials is noted by Spejewski (1997):

(24) a.   Has Kay paid her bills this month.
     b. ??Has Kay paid her bills this week/today?

Assuming that bills typically must be paid on a monthly basis, *this week* is strange. This pattern contrasts with the simple past:

(25) Did Kay pay her bills this month/this week/today?

The version of (25) with *this month* can have an interpretation very close to (24), indicating that the speaker wants to know if Kay is up to date with her bills. What's important is that, in contrast to the case with the perfect, the other adverbials are also perfectly acceptable, and simply indicate that the speaker is asking the question for another reason. For example, *Did Kay pay her bills today?* could be asked because the speaker wants to know whether Kay has finally gotten around to paying her bills, or wishes to know whether she has received the loan she needed to get through some hard financial times. The key point shown by (24b) is that such an interpretation is not readily available with the perfect.

2.1.3 Variability of nature of current relevance

It is generally assumed that a present perfect sentence says something both about the past, and about the present. On this view, the meaning of (22b) involves both Mary's arrival, which is past, and something about the present, connected to Mary's arrival. The problem is that it is difficult to pin down the nature of this "current relevance" in a way which is both explicit and able to account for the full range of data. This difficulty has led some (e.g., von Stechow 2002) to argue explicitly for a high level of ambiguity in the perfect construction. However, others continue to pursue a unified analysis. One of the reasons it is so difficult to decide whether the perfect is ambiguous or not is that the current relevance of this form is quite difficult to pin down; there is no simple data illustrating relevance on a par with the temporal data given above in Sections 2.1.1–2.1.2. Since most of the data concerning relevance has arisen by way of providing motivation for one or the other of the theories of the perfect, it will prove useful to introduce the primary and some of the secondary analyses of the perfect in this section.

One way to think about current relevance is to insist that the time indicated by the sentence's tense plays a distinguished pragmatic role in the interpretation of the sentence. We can label this analysis the **indefinite past** view of the perfect, the idea being that the sentence describes an event in the past, but without giving any particular importance to the time at which this past event occurred. Rather, what's important is the time marked by the tense. For example, in the case of (22b), we describe Mary's arrival, but do not portray the moment of arrival as especially important; rather, by virtue of using the present tense, we treat the moment of speech as important. Section 2.2.1 will discuss the indefinite past approach.

Example (22b) also offers motivation for another way of understanding current relevance. It would be natural to use this sentence if we want to say not only that Mary arrived, but also that she is still here. We can integrate this way of viewing matters into the semantics by saying that the perfect introduces a **perfect state**, holding at the time indicated by the sentence's tense, linked in some way to the past event. Thus in (22b), the perfect state might be the state of Mary being here. Various approaches to the link between past event and perfect state will be discussed in Section 2.2.2. What is relevant to observe now is that, while it is easy to focus on the state of Mary's being here in example (22b), in other examples it is more difficult to identify the current relevance of the perfect with a particular state.

(26) a. The ghost has ceased to exist.
　　b. I have climbed all three of those mountains.
　　c. The Earth has been hit by giant asteroids before (and it probably will be again). (Portner 2003: 459)

Example (26a) does not report any current state of the ghost, since the ghost does not exist. If it reports any kind of state at all, presumably it is a state of the world as a whole, that of not containing the ghost in question. In order for (26b) to be appropriate, I do not have to be on top of all three mountains; nor do I have to be lacking toes due to frostbite or basking in fame. (26c) is similar to (26a); the asteroids need no longer exist, and the earth need show no signs of the impacts.

Data such as these have led other scholars to propose that current relevance is to be explained in terms of temporal relations. The basic idea of such **extended now** theories, and their descendents, is that the past event must have taken place not too long ago, where what counts as not too long ago is variable and pragmatically determined. The data in (26) is obviously relevant to evaluating this approach as well, since these sentence involve a wide variety of temporal relations between past event and speech time: in (26a), just a few moments, in (26b), perhaps 50 years, and in (26c), at least millions of years. According to the extended now approach, these differences would have to be attributable to pragmatic factors.

A classic argument in favor of the extended now approach is example (27), from McCoard (1978):

(27)   ??Gutenberg has discovered the art of printing.

The idea is that in any conversation in which we can easily imagine (27) being used, Gutenberg's discovery is too long ago to satisfy the temporal requirement of the perfect. The difference between (26) and (27) must be derived from the pragmatic underpinnings of the notion of extended now. As further evidence for the pragmatically-determined nature of the extended now, Portner (2003) points out that (27) can be made acceptable in the right context (i.e., a demon who has directed the development of information technology says *Now that Gutenberg has discovered printing and Berners-Lee has invented the world wide web, it's time to lead these humans to the next thing* ...) We will discuss extended now theories in Section 2.2.3.

Several other types of data are relevant to out understanding of the nature of current relevance. First, we have the pattern noted in (24). This is intuitively a relevance effect, since the problem with (24b) seems to be that the extra information provided by *this week*, as opposed to *this month*, is not relevant to the assumed point of the utterance, that Mary is up to date with her bills. These examples seem to show that the currently relevance of the perfect cannot be explained strictly in terms of events and states, since an event of Mary paying her bills last week, leading to her being currently up to date with her bills, could be truthfully described by the acceptable (24a). In other words, the information provided by the adverb, not just the identification of an event consistent with the adverb, is crucial.

Another type of data relevant to understanding relevance is the contrast in (28), observed by Chomsky (1970):

(28) a. ?Einstein has visited Princeton.
b. Princeton has been visited by Einstein.

This contrast, known as the **lifetime effect**, shows that it is often strange to use a sentence in the present perfect when the subject is no longer alive. Several authors have drawn a link between the lifetime effect and current relevance (Inoue 1979; Smith 1992; Portner 2003). It has been noted many times that lifetime effects are heavily dependent on intonation and context (Inoue, Portner), and that they do not arise to the same extent across languages (Musan 2002).

Portner (2003) cites the sequence in (29) as demonstrating the importance of current relevance in the interpretation of the perfect:

(29) (i) Mary has lived in London for five years. (ii) ??She has become ill.

The second sentence here is quite odd, and the reason seems to be that the event of her becoming ill is presented not as particularly connected to the present, but rather as part of a narration about the past. The example becomes acceptable if it is understood in a context where (29ii) can be seem as relevant, for example if it has been found out that certain toxins were released in London during the past five years, and we wish to give special medicine to anyone who became ill there during that time.

This diversity of data which is intuitively connected to a current relevance requirement of the perfect has led some scholars to the claim that it cannot be entirely accounted for in terms of any of the primary theories mentioned above. As a result, secondary analyses have been developed with the goal of accounting for some or all of the relevance facts. The first such analysis is the **informational relevance** approach to current relevance. Informational relevance theories aim to understand the perfect's current relevance in terms of the flow of information in conversation, relying in particular on the notion of discourse topic. According to this way of thinking, for example, (26b) might be used as a response to a suggestion that we climb Mt. A, Mt. B, or Mt. C. (The intended message might be "let's pick another mountain.") Section 2.3.2 will discuss informational relevance.

The other secondary analysis of relevance argues that the perfect conveys **repeatability**. Example (26c) would, on this perspective, provide a prime example of the use of the perfect: the past event of asteroids falling is relevant in the clear sense that a similar event might happen again. The unacceptability of (27) would be easy to explain on this analysis as well, though the contexts in which it is acceptable would then pose a problem. Example (28) shows that, if repeatability is correct, exactly what must be repeatable is dependent on the structure or intonation of the sentence. We will discuss repeatability in Section 2.3.3.

2.2 Primary theories of the perfect

There are three major primary theories of the perfect, approaches which aim to explain the core temporal semantics of the form (some kind of pastness, or temporal anteriority), as well as some or all of the other semantic properties outlined in Section 2.1. This section will provide an outline of each such primary theory.

2.2.1 Indefinite past theories

Indefinite past theories are based on the idea that the specific details of the event or state which the sentence describes are in some respect not especially important. Consider (1), repeated here.

(1) Ben has fallen asleep.

It might be that the specific time at which Ben fell asleep is not very important, or what happened before or after is not very important. Rather, in perfect sentences, something about the time indicated by the sentence's tense is more important. In (1), we're relatively more interested in something which is true at the speech time. Versions of this approach have been developed by Reichenbach (1947), Montague (1973), Inoue (1979), Klein (1992, 1994, 2000), Giorgi & Pianesi (1997), and Katz (2003). (We might classify the ideas of Stump 1985 as an indefinite past theory or as an extended now theory. See below.)

There are various ways one can go about making precise this intuition that the event or state described by the main clause is relatively unimportant. For example, we might refer directly to the time indicated by the sentence's tense, but existentially bind a variable tied to the underlying event or state:

(30) $\exists e[e<t \ \& \ t=now \ \& \ \text{Ben falls asleep at } e]$

The idea here would be similar to the observation that *He saw a cat* and *A cat saw him* are more likely to be "about" him than the cat. This way of thinking may be the motivation for Montague's rather programmatic analysis. In this simple form, however, it seems not to provide a basis for explaining the key facts outlined in Section 2.1.

From Reichenbach's early work, the literature has inherited some useful terms: speech time (S, the time at which a sentence counts as being produced, for semantic purposes), event time (E, the time of the event or state described by the core clause under the scope of tense, aspect, and modality operators), and reference time (R, the time described by the sentence's tense, when tense is present) Within this framework, Reichenbach proposes the following relations:

Present tense	Past tense	Future tense
R coincides with S	R precedes S	R follows S
(abbreviated S,R or S=R)	(R_S or R<S)	(S_R or S<R)

Perfect aspect	No perfect aspect
E precedes R	E coincides with R
(E_R or E<R)	(E,R or E=R)

Given these relations, a present perfect sentence has E_R,S (i.e., E<R and R=S). Klein replaces S, R, and E with TU ("time of utterance"), TT ("topic time"), and TSit ("time of situation"), respectively. While TU and TSit are just new labels, using TT adds an important ingredient to the indefinite past theory: As suggested by the word "topic", TT is described as the time about which a claim is being made; in the perfect, TSit is distinct from TT, and thus TSit is not the time about which a claim is being made. In contrast, in the simple past, where TSit and TT coincide, a claim is being made about TSit, or at least the part of TSit which is simultaneous with TT.

Based on the core ideas of the indefinite past theory, Klein proposes an explanation for the fact that the present perfect cannot occur with definite past adverbials (see (22a)). Following the intuition that TSit (i.e., E) is indefinite and less important than TT (i.e., R) in the perfect, he proposes a constraint to the effect that both TT and TSit cannot receive a definite temporal specification in a given perfect sentence. In the present perfect, TT coincides with TU, and so is definite, and thus TSit cannot be. This implies that it cannot be constrained by a definite temporal adverbial like *yesterday*. In order to explain the contrast with past perfects, where (23a) is acceptable, he would have to assume that the past tense is not definite; such an assumption is difficult to maintain, given the pronoun-like nature of the past tense (Partee 1984; see article 13 [this volume] (Ogihara) *Tense*).

Indefinite past theories have difficulties explaining the continuative/non-continuative contrast. Since they treat the continuative (universal) reading as a special case of the non-continuative (existential) one, they run into Mittwoch's problem discussed above. Moreover, they are unable to explain the link between continuative readings and aspectual class, namely the fact that (in some languages at least) the continuative reading is only possible when the clause under the scope of the perfect is stative. And finally, those versions of the approach which follow closely Reichenbach's system in linking the perfect to an E<R relation (such as Klein's and Giorgi & Pianesi's) seem unable to express the continuative meaning with certain adverbials. The following data is from Portner (2003):

(31) a. Mary has lived in London for five years.
b. Mary has lived in London since 1966.

Klein argues that E in (31a) is not Mary's entire time in London, but rather just the five-year-long subevent of it described by *Mary lived in London for five years*. This subevent is entirely past, and so the E<R (TSit<TT) relation is maintained; if it happens to be pragmatically suggested that the entire event (not the subevent) extends up to the speech time, we have the continuative reading. As pointed out by Kuhn & Portner (2002), however, such an analysis is not possible for (31b).

In its simple form, unaided by secondary components of meaning, the indefinite past theory seems unable to explain much of the other data outlined in Section 2.1. In particular, it does not address the adverbial data (except for Klein's proposal, discussed above) or the data which seem to reflect a requirement of current relevance. Because of this weakness of the core indefinite past theory, its proponents have been motivated to explore secondary components of meaning which might explain the facts. Indeed, several of the most important discussions of secondary components took place in the context of the indefinite past theory: Giorgi & Pianesi (1997) argue that the morphosyntax and semantics of the present tense is crucial to explaining some of the adverbial data (Sect. 2.3.1). Inoue (1979) gives the first account of informational relevance (see Sect. 2.3.2). Stump (1985) proposes that a markedness relation exists between the perfect and the simple past (see Sect. 2.3.4). And Katz (2003) proposes that the event type must be repeatable in a particular sense (Sect. 2.3.3). We will discuss the work which these proposals are designed to do below.

2.2.2 Perfect state theories

According to the perfect state approach, the meaning of the perfect is to be represented in terms of a state which holds at the time indicated by the sentence's tense. For example, on this view (22b) might indicate that Mary is currently still "here", i.e., at the location where she arrived. In this case, the state in question can be described as a result of the past event of Mary's arrival. As we have seen Section

2.1.3, however, not all perfects can easily be described in terms of a state which is literally the result of a past event described by the sentence, and so a more general concept is in order: the perfect state. This view is supported by many scholars (e.g., Moens & Steedman 1988; Parsons 1990; Kamp & Reyle 1993; ter Meulen 1995; Spejewski 1997; Smith 1992; de Swart 1998; Musan 2001; Nishiyama & Koenig 2004; Schaden 2009), and has many variants, sketched below in S1-S4, depending on the nature of the link proposed between the past event and the current state:

S1. The perfect state is a result of, or contingent upon, the past eventuality (Moens & Steedman 1988; Smith 1992; Spejewski 1997). We can describe this version of the perfect state approach as the Result State analysis.
S2. The relation between the past event and the current state is temporal, with the state beginning during the event or as it ends (Kamp & Reyle 1993; de Swart 1998).
S3. The perfect state is a special kind of "resultant state" (Parsons 1990; ter Meulen 1995; Musan 2001). The resultant state is to be distinguished from a result state. A resultant state is not an ordinary state which has been caused by the past event described by the sentence, but rather a kind of abstract state of the event's "having occurred".
S4. There are no semantic constraints on the identity of the perfect state (Nishiyama & Koenig 2004; Nishiyama 2006; Schaden 2009).

Many of these theories also assume that pragmatics is essential to identifying the perfect state, in particular those falling under S1 and S4. S1 requires such a pragmatic addendum because there will be typically many current results of any past event. Thus, if the only constraint on the use of the present perfect were that it have some current result, the perfect would virtually always be true whenever the past event described did in fact occur; in other words, it would be virtually equivalent to the past. Without a pragmatic addendum, S4 will also be equivalent to the statement that the event described by the sentence occurred. Of course, this is not a correct consequence; the data in Section 2.1 show that the perfect is not interchangeable with the past. Thus some pragmatic constraint is required. Though most of the theories under discussion have not included a detailed account of the pragmatic constraint, Nishiyama (2006) makes a specific proposal, namely that the identity of the result state is inferred by Gricean pragmatic mechanisms, in particular Levinson's (2000) I-Principle.

Perfect state theories have difficulty with relevance phenomena, such as the Gutenberg example (27). Gutenberg's discovery of printing has current results (and so a fortiori it has a resultant state) which are readily inferable. Nishiyama & Koenig (2004) argue that in it will never make sense to mention both the past event and the current result of this sentence in a particular context, but this does not seem to be so. (*"What contributions have Germans made which are still important to the German economy today?"—"Gutenberg discovered printing, which is the basis of our world-renowned academic handbook industry."*) More to the point, inferability using Gricean principles is supposed to be the pragmatic constraint in Nishiyama & Koenig's analysis, and so appealing to another constraint just means that the main proposal is either incomplete or incorrect. In fact, when we look at Nishiyama & Koenig's suggestion in detail, we actually find them appealing to the notion of discourse topic, i.e. informational relevance. Schaden (2009) takes another approach, suggesting an explanation for this type of relevance phenomena based on competition; see Section 2.3.4 below.

Similar points can be made concerning the other relevance phenomena mentioned in Section 2.1.3. For example, lifetime effects do not follow from the proposal that the perfect indicate the existence of a current state, so some additional pragmatic constraint is necessary. It is fair to conclude that the core Perfect State theory cannot explain the current relevance of the perfect, and some secondary analysis will be necessary.

Perfect State theories typically consider the continuative perfect to be a pragmatically determined subcase of the non-continuative perfect. Thus they run into Mittwoch's problem, described above. They also have difficulties explaining the grammatical restrictions on continuative readings, such as the relevance of adverbial position and aspectual class (Section 2.1.1). Musan (2001) offers an explanation for the role of aspectual class; in particular, she argues that achievement and accomplishment predicates do not allow continuative perfects because the perfect requires a "truth interval" to hold before the reference time. That is, in (32a) requires that there be a past interval in which "Noah be sick" is true; this is compatible with him still being sick. However, turning to (32b), if there is a past interval at which "Noah builds a plane" is true, he can't still be building it. Musan's explanation does not extend to (non-progressive) activity predicates like that in (32c), though as noted in Section 2.1.1, this is not a difficulty for German, where the simple past of activity predicates can cover the meaning expressed by the progressive in English.

(32) a. Noah has been sick. (continuative reading ok)
     b. Noah has built a plane. (no continuative reading)
     c. Noah has run. (no continuative reading)

Finally let us turn to how Perfect State theories explain some of the adverbial data given in 2.1.2. As pointed out by Portner (2003), examples like (24b) are problematical: an event of Mary paying her bills this week would result in an (inferable) state of her being up-to-date with her bills, so the sentence should be an acceptable way to find out if she's up-to-date. One might imagine Nishiyama and Koenig objecting that the speaker is asking for more information than is necessary, since simply asserting that she paid her bills within the last month would be sufficient to imply this current state, but Gricean principles do not seem to be sufficient to explain the unacceptability of (24b). Recall that the simple past sentence (25) is acceptable, and can be used to find out about other current states, such as whether she's well enough to pay bills. A Gricean theory like Nishiyama & Koenig's predicts that (24b) should be acceptable and have such a function.

The present perfect puzzle is also difficult for the Perfect State theory. One might be tempted to propose that temporal adverbials always restrict E (i.e., TSit), not R (TT), but this is not correct, as we see with past perfects (data from Portner 2003):

(33) a. On Tuesday I learned that Mary had arrived two days before.
b. Mary has arrived only recently.

In (33a) *two days before* describes the event time, not the reference time. In order to deal with the incompatibility of the present perfect with past adverbials in certain languages like English, the Perfect State theories will have to appeal to secondary features of meaning. In this vein, Schaden makes a proposal based on competition between the present perfect and simple past forms. See Section 2.3.4 for discussion of his theory. As noted above, he cites data like (22c) in support of this view that the combination of present perfect and past adverbial is not in general ruled out in English, but rather is possible only when the choice of the perfect form is pragmatically justified. He does not explain why such combinations are restricted to a particular register or variety of English. According to the competition view, we would expect them to be generally available when the pragmatic conditions are met, e.g., for (22a) to be acceptable when it's relevant both that Mary's arrival was yesterday and that she's still here today. This is not correct; the sentence is unacceptable in such contexts:

(34) A: We'd like a first-hand report of the incident which took place on yesterday's flight. Are any of the people who came on that flight still around?
B: *Yes, Mary has arrived yesterday.

2.2.3 Extended now theories

The central idea of extended now theories is that the perfect indicates that the event described by the clause under the scope of the perfect occurred within a restricted interval of time. According to classical version of this view, such as that of McCoard (1978), this interval ends with the speech time (more generally, the time indicated by the sentence's tense) but extends it into the past. Thus, (1) would say that Ben's falling asleep occurred within an interval of time which ends with the speech time. The initial point of the extended now can be determined by adverbials, implied by context, or left vague.

More recently, the literature has suggested other ideas about the relationship between the extended now and the speech time. One perspective is that it does not include the speech time, but rather abuts it (Spejewski 1997 Rathert 2003); another is that it may properly precede, abut, or include the speech time—i.e., just that no part of the extended now follows the speech time (Stump 1985; Pancheva & von Stechow 2004; Rothstein 2008). Because it is not always assumed that the interval in question actually contains the speech time, many scholars speak of the **perfect time span** rather than the extended now. In order to determine when the perfect time span ends, we can look at the compatibility of the present perfect with certain adverbials. For example, the behavior of German *immer* ('always') is revealing. Rothstein (2008) notes that in (35) the time during which the speaker lived in Berlin must properly precede the speech time:

(35) Ich habe immer in Berlin gewohnt, bis   ich nach Tübingen gezogen bin.
     I   have always in Berlin lived   until I to   Tübingen moved   am
     'I always lived in Berlin, until I moved to Tübingen.'

Assuming that *immer* entails that the situation described by the predicate occupies the entire extended now, these data show that the extended now can entirely precede the speech time. As pointed out by Rothstein, the pattern in (35) is impossible in English (*I have always lived in Washington, but then I moved to Boston*), a fact which suggests that the precise characterization of the perfect time span must differ from language to language.

Scholars working with the extended now tradition have done important work on the continuative/non-continuative distinction. Building on the work of Dowty (1979) and Mittwoch (1988); von Stechow (2002); Iatridou et al. (2003) and Pancheva & von Stechow (2004) propose that those adverbials which can license the continuative reading are ambiguous. On one interpretation, they introduce a universal quantifier over times, and this leads to the continuative reading; on the other they introduce an existential quantifier, producing the non-continuative reading. For example, in (12a), repeated below, John is sick at all times during the several-days-long extended now. By contrast, in (13a), he is asleep at some time during the (unspecified) extended now.

(12) a. John has been sick for several days.
(13) a. John has slept.

Iatridou et al. connect this difference to the fact that continuative readings are only possible with stative predicates (though they argue that stativity is not precisely the right concept). It is of course not ideal to propose a lexical ambiguity to account for the continuative/non-continuative contrast. More importantly, I do not know of a compositional proposal which works these ideas out in detail (though see Dowty's, Mittwoch's, and von Stechow's work for partial analyses).

Rathert (2003) rejects the ambiguity approach to the contintuative/non continuative contrast. To some extent, it appears that her analysis is based on scope, but this analysis is only applied to adverbials like *until* which themselves indicate the end of an interval. For example, the continuative reading of her example (36) amounts to the existential reading "there is an interval i during the perfect time span, and there is an interval j during i, which ends yesterday, and he runs at j". (On the existential reading, *bis gestern* would modify i, rather than j.)

(36) Er ist bis gestern gerannt.
     He is until yesterday run
     'He ran until yesterday.'

Assuming that the perfect time span ends yesterday (rather than at the speech time, as it would have to in English), this amounts to a continuative reading; but in a way, this reading is a pure accident, derived only because the adverbial happens to refer to the time which is also the end of the perfect time span. If the perfect time span extended until today, the adverbial in (36) would be interpreted in the same way, but we would not call it a continuative reading. Note that this analysis cannot apply to adverbials which do not indicate the end of an interval, since such adverbials cannot be used to say that the core event reaches the end of the perfect time span. In such cases, she appears to treat the continuative reading as a special case of the existential one. Thus, Rathert runs into Mittwoch's problem and cannot explain why continuative readings are affected by adverb position and aspectual class. Of course, this is partially to be expected, since as pointed out in Sect. 2.1.1, she argues that adverb position is irrelevant.

The extended now theory has little to say about the present perfect puzzle. While in its classic form, the theory predicts that past adverbials are unable to modify the extended now (since the extended now includes the speech time), past adverbials should be acceptable when the modify the event time, as we know they can from (33). As a result, scholars have turned to various secondary components of meaning to explain the present perfect puzzle: Rothstein invokes a syntactic relation between the tense and adverbials Sect. 2.3.1), Iatridou et al. (2003) suggests that repeatability is responsible (Sect. 2.3.3), and Pancheva & von Stechow (2004) explain the puzzle using a competition approach (Sect. 2.3.4).

The extended now approach aims to explain relevance phenomena in terms of the pragmatic significance of the extended now. The idea is that by indicating that an event is in the extended now, the speaker signals that the time at which it occurred is relevantly like the speech time. Thus, (26a) implies that the ghost is gone because the time when it vanished is not relevantly different from now, (26c) implies that asteroids could strike earth again, and (27) is odd because it's hard to think of a context in which time of Gutenberg's discovery would be considered one with the speech time. Example (29) is a problem, however, since (29i) seems to indicate that the extended now is five years long, and since the event in (29ii) falls within this time span, it should be acceptable. In other words, (29) suggests that relevance cannot be understood solely in temporal terms, though the temporal approach may be one part of a broader conception.

2.3 Secondary components of meaning

2.3.1 The role of the present tense

Given that the present perfect puzzle only occurs (in languages where it occurs at all) in the present perfect, and not in past, future, or tenseless perfects, one natural suggestion is that the grammar of the present tense is crucially involved in its explanation. We find several analyses along these lines: Portner (2003) proposes that the present tense carries a presupposition that the main event described by the sentence occurs within the extended now (and thus this theory is similar to extended now approaches to the perfect, except that the extended now is associated with the present tense). Pancheva & von Stechow (2004) propose that the present tense in English requires that the event time coincide with the speech time, while the present tense in German allows the event time to partially or completely follow the speech time; this distinction feeds into a competition-based analysis of the present perfect puzzle (see Sect. 2.3.4 below). Giorgi & Pianesi (1997) and Rothstein (2008) propose a syntactic accounts whereby the English perfect auxiliary places a restriction on the kinds of adverbials which may occur in the sentence. The two differ slightly in how they explain the lack of present perfect puzzle in Italian and German: Giorgi & Pianesi claim that such languages lack the present tense altogether (so that so-called present tense sentences are actually tenseless), while Rothstein argues that in German the auxiliary is too low to place a restriction on the kinds of adverbials which may occur. Schaden (2009) points out that it is difficult to extend Rothstein's assumption about the position of the auxiliary to Romance languages. Moreover, the syntactic account will have difficulties explaining why the present perfect puzzle also occurs with other varieties of adverbials and with arguments, as in (22d-e), and especially in the case where there is no explicit temporal expression, as in (22f).

Rothstein, and following him Schaden (2009), argues against analyses of the present perfect puzzle based on the semantics or pragmatics of the present tense on the grounds that we would expect the meanings of present tense sentences to be alike in languages which show the puzzle, and different from languages which do not. In this context, he points out that the Swedish present tense is like that in German in readily allowing reference to future events and to ongoing present events. In all of these respects, Swedish differs from English:

(37) a. I morgon reser jag till London. (Swedish)
        tomorrow go   I   to London
     b. Morgen   reise ich nach London. (German)
        tomorrow go   I   to   London
     c. #Tomorrow I go to London. (plan interpretation only)
     d. Han sover. (Swedish)
        he sleeps
     e. Er schläft. (German)
        he sleeps
     f. #He sleeps. (habitual interpretation only)

(The (37a, 37b, 37d, 37e) examples are from Rothstein 2008.) Despite the similarity between the present tenses of Swedish and German, the former shows the present perfect puzzle, while the latter does not.

While the data in (37) is problematical for Pancheva & von Stechow's version of the idea that the present tense is responsible for the present perfect puzzle, it is not relevant to Giorgi & Pianesi's proposal (or to Portner's, since he follows Giorgi & Pianesi in this respect). According to Giorgi & Pianesi, the facts in (37) are not due to the semantics of the present tense, but rather to the aspectual semantics of the verbs. In particular, they propose that verbs in English are obligatorily perfective, and in combination with the semantics of the present tense, this rules out the relevant interpretations of (37c) and (37f); in Swedish, German, and Italian, the verb is not obligatorily perfective, and so the uses in (37) are possible.

2.3.2 Informational relevance

Inoue (1979) and Portner (2003) argue the relevance meaning of the perfect is to indicate that the proposition expressed plays a particular role in the discourse. More precisely, both argue that the sentence must be closely related to the discourse topic. For example, Inoue brings out the problem of explaining the current relevance of *Einstein has visited Princeton* in (38):

(38) A: Which Nobel Laureates have visited Princeton?
B: Let's see, Einstein has (visited Princeton), Friedman has, ...

This example poses an interesting problem, in that it illustrates an exception to the lifetime effect, and thus a problem for any analysis of relevance which is based on the subject having a certain property at the reference time. Rather, according to Inoue, A's utterance sets up a topic, and the sentence *Einstein has visited Princeton* is relevant to this topic.

While Inoue's way of working the concepts of topic and relevance to a topic do not work (see Portner 2003 for discussion), Portner reformulates it in more precise and modern terms. Following the hypothesis that a discourse topic can be represented as an open question (e.g., von Fintel 1994; Roberts 1996; Büring 1997; McNally 1998), we can say that in (38) the topic is given explicitly by A's question. In this context, *Einstein has visited Princeton* is relevant because it helps to answer the question. We can call this secondary component of meaning "informational relevance" in the sense that the perfect is required to provide information which is strongly relevant to the discourse topic.

Two points remain to be clarified about the nature of discourse relevance. First, we need to better understand the nature of the relevance requirement. Portner considers it to be a presupposition, but Nishiyama & Koenig (2004) dispute this characterization. And second (and closely related to the first) we need to be more clear about how the relevance requirement of the perfect distinguishes it from the simple past. Portner (2003) makes the point that the simple past can easily be used as part of a narrative, and that each sentence of a narrative does not need to be individually relevant in the strong sense of answering the discourse topic (rather, it's felicitous for the narrative as a whole to answer the discourse topic); in contrast, the perfect cannot be used in this way. These considerations point to the need to develop the idea of informational relevance in tandem with research on topics, and on discourse semantics more generally.

2.3.3 Repeatability

The present perfect puzzle has also been explained in terms of the idea that the kind of event described by the sentence must be repeatable. That is, (1) would require that it be possible for Ben to fall asleep again, and (22a) would be unacceptable because it is impossible for Mary to arrive yesterday again. Iatridou et al. (2003) connects repeatability to the intriguing idea that the perfect creates a kind of existential sentence having to do with events, drawing a parallel between (39a–b):

(39) a. There are there dogs outside.
    b. Mary has smiled three times this week.
       (≈ "There are three smiling events by Mary so far this week.")

On this view, the present perfect puzzle is parallel to the definiteness effect of (40a), since the adverbial (e.g., in (40b)) causes the sentence to describe a definite event:

(40) a. *There is the dog outside.
    b. *Mary has smiled yesterday.

Iatridou's perspective also suggests a way of thinking of an exception to the present perfect puzzle noted by McCoard (1978), namely that past adverbial are possible in a list (data from Pancheva & von Stechow 2004). Lists also allow exceptions to the definiteness effect with *there* sentences:

(41) a. Do we have pets? There's Shelby, Fluffy, and the bird.
    b. John has played golf on Tuesday and ridden horseback on Wednesday.

Despite these advantages, Iatridou does not discuss obvious problems for repeatability. First, no explanation is provided for the absence of adverbial restrictions outside of the present perfect; and second, she does not discuss non-repeatable predicates like (42):

(42) The dog has died.

Obviously, an individual's death is unique, and so (42) should pattern with (40).
    Katz (2003) develops a more refined version of repeatability which is designed to handle examples like (42). According to him, the perfect presupposes that an event might occur in the future. Thus, (42) is acceptable, because we didn't know that the dog would die today; it might have died tomorrow. Katz also explains the lifetime effect seen in (28a) by noting that it is not considered possible that Einstein visits Princeton in the future. Where lifetime effects do not occur, as in (28b) and Inoue's (38), he appeals to the effects of focus structure on the presupposition. He argues that, because *Einstein* is focused, the presupposition of the perfect in this case does not involve Einstein; rather, it presupposes

that some relevant individual (i.e., some Nobel Laureate) might visit Princeton in the future. While he does not explain how the presupposition is calculated, it should be possible to achieve the desired results in terms of focus semantics.

The lack of phenomena parallel to the present perfect puzzle in the non-present perfects is problematical for Katz, though he avoid the problem by taking the present perfect to be a single unit, in effect unrelated to the past perfect and other perfect forms. Another problem is that his analysis seems to predict that perfects like (43) are impossible:

(43) It has been wonderful getting to know you this morning.

Apart from focus, the presupposition here should be that it might be wonderful getting to know you again in the future; this case is not like (42), in that at the time it's used, no one is presupposing that the speaker might get to know the addressee in the future. Focus on *getting to know you this morning* might solve the problem (leading to a presupposition that it might be wonderful in the future doing something relevant), but evidence would have to be provided that there really is focus in the relevant position. Moreover, some restrictions must be placed on the application of focus to the perfect's presupposition, since otherwise we'd expect to be able to rescue (22a) by focusing the adverbial or VP. More to the point, if focus can rescue (43), we'd expect it to be able to rescue (44) as well:

(44) *It has been wonderful getting to know you yesterday.

2.3.4 Competition

Several scholars have proposed an analysis of the present perfect puzzle in English (and other languages which display the puzzle) which is based on the idea that there is a competition between the present perfect and the simple past (preterit) tense. The present perfect is argued to be a more marked construction than the simple past, and assuming this is so, we expect that the past should be used unless there is a reason to prefer the perfect. In this context, Stump (1985) provides an indefinite past semantics for the present perfect, and he shows that when this indefinite past meaning is combined with a temporal adverbial referring to a definite time in the past, the sentence is always equivalent to what would be expressed by a past tense sentence with the same adverbial. Hence, Stump argues, the present perfect cannot be used with such adverbials. For example the present perfect in (45a) would lead to a meaning equivalent to the corresponding sentence with the simple past, (45b):

(45) a. *Mary has arrived yesterday.
    b. Mary arrived yesterday.

Since (45a–b) convey the same meaning, according to Stump, there can be no justification for using the perfect. Pancheva & von Stechow (2004) build a similar analysis based on the extended now theory, and Schaden (2009) does likewise based on the perfect state approach.

These competition-based analyses of the present perfect puzzle explain the lack of similar phenomena in tenseless perfects and the past perfect (as seen in (23)) by the fact that there is no alternative form which could be in a competition relation with these perfects. That is, there is no past tense in tenseless clauses, and there are no clauses containing two past tenses. Moreover, both Pancheva & von Stechow and Schaden propose that the present perfect puzzle is lacking in languages like German because the perfect and the past are not in the right kind of competition relation.

The various competition-based analyses differ in where they see the source of the competition between present perfect and past. Both Stump and Pancheva & von Stechow are tempted by pragmatic explanations which seem to be based on Gricean implicature. Stump points out that the perfect is morphologically more complex than the past, and so is more marked in these (Gricean "manner") terms. In addition, according to the semantic analyses provided both by Stump and by Pancheva & von Stechow, the present perfect in English is semantically less specific than (i.e., is entailed by) the past; hence, they claim, the past should be used unless there is a reason not to use it. More precisely, they suggest that, in English, the present perfect can only be used if the use of the past would lead to a false sentence. From this point, they make the same argument as Stump did: According to their semantic assumptions, the present perfect and the past are equivalent when combined with a definite past adverbial, and given this equivalence, the condition of use of the present perfect, namely that the use of the past is ruled out because it would lead to falsity, can never be met.

Neither Stump nor Pancheva & von Stechow are committed to a fully pragmatic account of the present perfect puzzle. Stump acknowledges that the markedness relation between the present perfect and past may have grammaticalized, and Pancheva & von Stechow think that something more than pure Gricean implicature must be involved (though they are open to the possibility that an appropriately grammatical analysis of scalar implicature may work: see article 10 [Semantics: Interfaces] (Chierchia, Fox & Spector) *Grammatical view of scalar implicatures*). Schaden explicitly denies that the markedness relation between the present perfect and past can be derived from anything. Rather he argues that the fact that the present perfect is more marked in English is a primitive fact. This point is crucial to him because he makes the unique claim that in languages which do not display the present perfect puzzle, the markedness relation is reversed. That is, in languages like German, the past is more marked than the present perfect. (This is in contrast to Pancheva and von Stechow, who simply claim that there is no markedness relation between the two forms in German.) Schaden further argues that a number of other differences between the pasts and perfects in the two classes of languages follow from this difference in the markedness relation.

2.3.5 General principles of temporal interpretation

Portner (2003) argues that some features of the perfect's meaning should not be attributed to any element in the sentence, but rather to general principles of interpretation. In particular, he argues that the perfect itself does not have any temporal meaning—it does not indicate indefinite past, result state, or extended now—but rather only introduces a relevance requirement in the form indicated in Sect. 2.3.2. Any temporal meaning comes either from the sentence's tense (recall his hypothesis that there is an extended now requirement associated with the present tense), or from general principles.

In support of the idea that principles not specific to the perfect construction are involved, Portner points out the similarities between the continuative/non-continuative contrast and the interpretation of tenses in embedded clauses and in discourse. Just as continuative perfects are only possible with statives, as seen in (12)–(13), we find different interpretative possibilities for statives and non-statives in subordinate clauses:

(46) a. Mary believed that John was sick/knew French.
     b. Mary believed that John died/ran a race.

Let us call the time at which Mary held these beliefs t_b. In (46a), Mary may have believed that John was sick at t_b, or that he was sick before t_b. The former is the "simultaneous" reading, and the latter the "shifted" reading. Example (46b) only has the shifted reading. See Abusch (1988, 1997), Ogihara (1989, 1995, article 13 [this volume] (Ogihara) *Tense*) for discussion. A similar difference occurs in discourse, where non-statives move the time of narration forward, while statives typically do not (e.g., with some differences, Hinrichs 1982; Partee 1984; Kamp & Reyle 1993). Portner argues that the simultaneity observed in (46a) and with statives in narration is the same as that we see with continuative readings of the perfect, and attempts to characterize a general principle which can account for both.

It is certainly a rather surprising hypothesis that the perfect lacks a temporal semantics, and that this absence of temporal meaning explains the choice between continuative and non-continuative readings. Nevertheless, the parallels between the perfect and the interpretation of tense in embedded clauses and in narration do need to be explained somehow, even if a non-construction-specific principle of the kind he develops is ultimately not the right way. As far as I know, no specific arguments against Portner's approach to the continuative/non-continuative contrast have been offered in the literature.

2.4 Putting the perfect back together

Above I've emphasized the main components which have been used to assemble analyses of the perfect. Most analyses assume that the meaning of the perfect is to be explained in terms of one primary theory in combination with one or more secondary theories. Of course each such combination embodies a hypothesis about how the phenomena are to divided up. Obviously analyses which make use of fewer independent meaning components are to be preferred, other things being equal. Thus an analysis which made use of just a primary theory would be ideal, if it could explain all of the facts (but unfortunately, it is probably impossible for such a theory to do so). Moreover, certain combinations of ideas should be seen as potentially redundant, and so to be dispreferred. For example, repeatability and informational relevance aim to explain similar groups of facts, and so it is unlikely that both will find a place in the correct analysis of the perfect in any single language. Assembling an account of the perfect out of these various pieces (and in some cases other pieces not mentioned here) is a delicate task.

Tab. 10.1 indicates how a number of important analyses of the perfect combine primary and secondary components. A name may occur in more than once cell, since a given theory may combine several secondary components.

Though I hope that it will prove useful, one must be cautious about using a table like this for direct comparison of theories. First of all, I have had to make judgment calls about how to describe certain theories; for example, Musan discusses the role of the present tense in certain facts observed with the German present perfect, but since these facts are not typically seen as having to do with the perfect itself, I do not represent this aspect of her discussion in the table. More importantly, not all analyses are equally comprehensive in their attempts to explain the important phenomena; nor are they all equally detailed and precise. Thus, to take an instance, Nishiyama & Koenig's (2004) paper is very brief, and it is not much more than suggestive on certain crucial issues; as a result, it is difficult to know such things as whether they mean to appeal to informational relevance in

Tab. 10.1: Classification of analyses of the perfect

		Primary Theories		
		Indefinite Past	Perfect State	Extended Now
Secondary Components	Present Tense	Giorgi/Pianesi		Portner, Pancheva/von Stechow, Rothstein
	Informational Relevance	Inoue		Portner
	Repeatability	Katz		Iatridou
	Competition		Schaden	Stump, Pancheva/von Stechow
	General principles			Portner
	None of the above; may appeal to ambiguity or pragmatic processes.	Klein	Parsons, Kamp/Reyle, Smith, de Swart, Musan, Nishiyama and Koenig	Mittwoch, Iatridou et al., von Stechow, Rathert

invoking the notion of discourse topic. Because of limitations such as these, any summary (including this table, as well as this article as a whole) can best be used as a guide as one aims to develop a deeper understanding of each component idea, and as one attempts to understand and evaluate individual proposals.

3 The progressive

The progressive is a periphrastic grammatical form used to say that some event is in progress, or ongoing, at the time indicated by the sentence's tense. For example, (47) indicates that Mary's action of walking was ongoing at some point in the past.

(47) Mary was walking.

Because it is used in this way, the English *be+VERB-ing* form can be referred to as "the English progressive". Other languages have similar periphrastic forms, though they have seldom been the specific subject of formal analysis.

In other instances, the term "progressive" is used to indicate a particular meaning or use of a grammatical form; for example, the Spanish imperfective (imperfecto) has among its many uses the ability to describe ongoing events (data from Cipria & Roberts 2000, (2b)):

(48) Ibamos   a la playa cuando nos   encontramos   con Miguel.
     go-1plu.IMPF to the beach when RECPR meet-1plu.PRET with Miguel
     'We were going to the beach when we ran into Miguel.'

The imperfecto can also express such other meanings as habituality and intention, and because of the variety of situations which may be described using the imperfecto, it would be confusing to call it, without qualification, "the Spanish progressive". Rather, we talk of a "progressive use" or "progressive meaning" of the imperfecto. In fact, a similar issue applies to the English progressive, given that it can be used to talk about a predicted future event.

(49) Mary is leaving town tomorrow.

For these reasons, there is some lack of clarity in what is meant by providing an analysis of the progressive. We may be talking about a progressive form, with all of its meanings and uses, or the progressive meaning (approximately: the event is ongoing) of a form which is not limited to this meaning. In many instances, semanticists are implicitly striving for an ideal balance between these two perspectives, trying to identify a class of meanings which should be given the same theoretical analysis as the ongoing-event meaning, while excluding as altogether distinct other meanings which are often expressed by the same form. Here we will mainly focus on the analysis of cases like (47) which have been taken to exemplify a core progressive meaning, although we will discuss briefly in Section 3.3 the prospects for providing a unified analysis of many or all of the uses of more wide-ranging forms like the Spanish imperfecto.

3.1 Outline of key data

As with the perfect, the literature on the progressive has identified a large amount of data relevant to its semantic analysis. In this section, I outline the key phenomena which must be attended to, but of course much has been left out as well (see Vlach 1981 in particular). This key data can be divided into two types: that having to do with the aspectual properties of sentences containing the progressive, and that which shows entailment patters relating progressive sentences to their non-progressive counterparts.

3.1.1 Aspectual facts

In the literature on aspectual classes, it is often noted that stative sentences do not occur in the progressive (e.g., Vendler 1967; Taylor 1977; Dowty 1979, among others; see also article 9 [this volume] (Filip) *Aspectual class and Aktionsart*):

(50) a. *She was knowing the answer.
  b. *She was being tall.

Let us call this the **no-statives property**. Our description of this property must be qualified by two points. First, it only applies to statives which describe a more or less permanent situation, Carlson's (1977) individual-level predicates; thus, sentences like (50c), based on *John sit over there*, which is stative by some criteria, do allow the progressive:

(50) c. John is sitting over there.

(See article 8 [Semantics: Theories] (Maienborn) *Event semantics* for relevant discussion.) And second, sometimes even individual level statives allow the progressive (cf. Partee 1977; Dowty 1979):

(51) Finally, I'm understanding how to solve this problem.

Such examples are often seen as resulting from coercion, that is a meaning shift which allows the preconditions for compositional interpretation to be met. In the case of (51), coercion would give a different, non-stative sense to the ordinarily individual-level stative clause *I understand how to solve this problem*. On coercion, see, for example, Moens & Steedman (1988), de Swart (1998), article 10 [Semantics: Lexical Structures and Adjectives] (de Swart) *Mismatches and coercion*, and article 9 [this volume] (Filip) *Aspectual class and Aktionsart* for further discussion.

A more subtle aspectual property of the progressive has been identified and discussed by Vlach (1981), Mittwoch (1988), Lascarides (1991), Hallman (2009), among others. Whatever the basic aspectual properties of the clause under the scope of the progressive, the progressive sentence itself entails that some process was ongoing at the time described by the sentence. Let us call this the **process property**. For example, in (52), the process in question is the one described by the activity sentence itself:

(52) Mary was running for an hour.

This example entails that the activity of Mary's running was ongoing for the entire hour. Moreover, because processes are internally homogenous, for virtually any long-enough interval of time during that hour, a process of Mary running was ongoing at that interval as well. With some accomplishment sentences, like (53a), from Landman (1992), the process in question is lexically determined; with other accomplishments and achievements, the nature of the process is more varied, as illustrated in (53b–c):

(53) a. Mary was building a house.
   b. Mary was realizing the answer.
   c. We are now arriving at our destination.

In (53a), the verb *build* indicates lexically the nature of the process which is described by the progressive sentence; it is a building process. As for (53b), while it normally takes but a moment to realize something, in this case it seems to take longer, long enough to count as a process. And while arriving somewhere is in principle an instantaneous change, in (53c) we focus on what is going on before the moment of arrival, and this yields an appropriate process which may be ongoing.

3.1.2 Completion and non-completion entailments

In certain cases, the present progressive form of a sentence entails its present perfect counterpart, while in other cases it does not (cf. Bennett & Partee 1978; Taylor 1977, among many others):

(54) a. John is smiling. *entails* John has smiled.
   b. John is deciding what to do. *does not entail* John has decided what to do.

Over the years, the field has identified a number of such entailments patterns, typically with the goal of showing a counterexample to one theory or another. In this section, I will outline some of this data, but without describing the theoretical discussion it was part of.

The distinction in (54) has been described in terms of the subinterval property (Bennett & Partee 1978). An expression has the subinterval property iff, whenever it is true at an interval of time i, it is true of all (or more accurately, all long-enough) subintervals of i. (One can define related properties for semantic systems making use of events or situations, rather than temporal intervals.) For example, the untensed clause *John smile* has the subinterval property, since any subinterval of an interval in which he smiles is also one in which he smiles. In terms of the most well-known aspectual classes of sentences, activity/process and state sentences have the subinterval property, while accomplishment and achievement sentences lack it.

The examples in (54) illustrate that a past progressive sentence entails its perfect counterpart only if it is based on a clause with the subinterval property. Let us describe this entailment by saying that such perfect sentences have the **completion property.** Progressive sentences not based on clauses with the subinterval property lack the completion property. Similarly, they fail to entail their future tense (and future perfect) correlates, as seen in (55a), and their simple past tense and future perfect correlates, as in (55b):

(55) a. John is deciding what to do. *does not entail* John will decide what to do/ John will (eventually) have decided what to do.
  b. John was deciding what to do. *does not entail* John decided what to do/ John will (eventually) have decided what to do.)

It is easy to confuse the observation concerning the process property discussed in Section 3.1.1 with the subinterval property. The subinterval property has to do with expressions, specifically the expression which is put into the progressive form. In (54a) we see the progressive of an expression which has the subinterval property (*John smile*), while in (54b), we see the progressive of an expression which lacks the subinterval property (*John be deciding what to do*); this difference correlates with the difference in entailment patterns observed in (54). In contrast, the process property has to do with the entailments of the progressive sentence itself; specifically, it states that every progressive sentence entails that some process was ongoing. There may or may not be any constituent in the syntax or abstract logical form of progressive sentences which describes this process—this is a matter on which different theories of the progressive may disagree—and hence there may or may not be any constituent with the subinterval property. Thus the process property and the relevance of the subinterval property are distinct observations about the progressive. Nevertheless, they are intuitively related, and they would ideally receive related explanations.

There has been much investigation of the precise nature of those examples, like (54b) and (55), where the present progressive fails to entail its past and future tense counterparts. In fact, the nature of these examples has been so central to theorizing about the meaning of the progressive that the lack of entailment has been given a name: the **imperfective paradox** (Dowty 1977). (This label is a bit misleading, as there is no paradox in the usual sense; rather, the imperfective paradox is an empirical problem with which semantic theory must come to terms.) The remainder of this subsection will be devoted to examples which are important to understanding the imperfective paradox. These data all involve clauses for which the paradox arises, that is, progressives based on clauses which lack the subinterval property.

First, we have what can be called the **interruption principle**. Though a past tense progressive sentence does not in general entail its non-progressive counterpart, it does entail the existence of a process which, if not interrupted, would lead to the truth of the non-progressive counterpart. Consider Dowty's example (56):

(56) John was crossing the street.

This sentence could be true even if John is hit by a truck when halfway across the street, and so it does not entail its simple past correlate, i.e. that he crossed the street. However, (56), in combination with the assumption that the process which it describes was not interrupted, does entail that he crossed the street. We find principles of this kind discussed especially clearly in the work of Dowty (1977) and Landman (1992). Note the implicit but crucial use of the process principle here: the relevance of interruptions is stated in terms of the process whose existence is entailed by (56).

Second, a range of data closely related to the imperfective paradox concerns the object arguments of verbs of creation. With such verbs, a progressive sentence does not entail the ultimate existence of an individual of the kind described by the object. For example, (53a) does not entail the existence of a house; we will refer to this property as the **failure of existence entailments**. The progressive contrasts with the simple past (57):

(57) Mary built a house.

Parsons (1990) raises an objection to the claim that (53a) fails to entail the existence of a house; he points out that, even though the sentence does not entail the existence of a complete house, it does entail that something got built which we might call an "incomplete house". Moreover, there are situations in which we are willing to describe an incomplete house as a house (he describes visiting the house which Jack London was building when he died). While objection is correct as far as it goes, it does not ultimately undermine the claim that the progressive forms of verbs of creation do not entail the existence of a thing describable by the object. As Landman (1992) points out, example (58) (his (9)) can be true even if the creation process brings the unicorn into existence not bit by bit, but rather all of a sudden, at the end of a series of incantations:

(58) God was creating a unicorn, when He changed His mind.

That is, (58) can be true even though nothing came to exist which could, by any stretch, be called a unicorn. Szabó (2004) makes some comments which might be seen as attempting to counter Landman's argument against Parsons. He observes that (59) (his (22b)) can be true even though there is no moment at which one could observe a circle in the water:

(59) Mary drew a circle in the water.

The relevance of this example for analyses of the progressive is that, if this non-progressive sentence fails to entail the existence of a individual of the kind described by the object, one might say that there is really no difference in existence entailments between progressive an non-progressive forms; thus, theories of the progressive would not have to explain any such difference. However, while (59) is interesting, at most it shows that the difference must be explained more carefully. As Szabó himself notes, (59) entails that all of the points of a circle were drawn in the water, even though they did not all exist simultaneously. The progressive counterpart of (59) does not entail even this. Of course we still must come to understand the semantics of (59). It is likely that *draw* is ambiguous, and has a meaning on which is not in fact a verb of creation. Even the quintessential creation verb *make* allows such a use when its object can be construed as shape or path ("hawks makin' lazy circles in the sky", from the musical *Oklahoma*), but not otherwise ("planes makin' loud noise in the sky"). What's different about *draw* is that pretty much any object of *draw* can be construed as a shape, in which case it means something like "make (shape) by means of drawing". In any case, however we come to understand the data with *draw*, Szabó's objection does not appear to touch Landman's central argument based on (58).

The third type of data relevant to the nature of the imperfective paradox concerns the status of altogether implausible outcomes. Landman observes that (60) (his (20)) is clearly false in a circumstance in which Mary was involved in a process of single-handledly attacking the Roman army.

(60) Mary was wiping out the Roman army.

Data like (60) indicate that a progressive sentence PROG+ϕ entails (or at least, in some sense implies) a modal sentence of the sort "it was not too farfetched a possibility that ϕ". For example, (60) entails *It was not too farfetched a possibility that Mary would wipe out the Roman army*, and since the latter is false, the former must be as well. Let us call this the **reasonableness principle**. Of course, the notion of reasonableness here demands further explanation.

The fourth point to be made relating to completion entailments and the imperfective paradox is really just a worry about the reasonableness property. Notice that we would consider (60) true (of some appropriate past time) if Mary did in fact succeed in wiping out the Roman army, even though this outcome is not reasonable in the ordinary sense. Thus, we must define "reasonable" for present purposes in such a way that what actually occurs automatically counts as reasonable. Let us call this the **actuality principle**.

The final issue to be mentioned in this section was discussed in various ways by ter Meulen (1985), Asher (1992), Bonomi (1997a), and Portner (1998). In many instances, there is a certain amount of indeterminacy concerning which of several seemingly incompatible progressive sentences is true. Landman discusses a clear example brought up by Roger Schwarzschild: suppose Roger takes a flight scheduled to go to Boston, and it is hijacked to Bismark, North Dakota. Speaking of a single time before the hijacking, either of the following might be considered true (though their conjunction is certainly false):

(61) a. Roger was flying to Boston (when his plane was hijacked).
    b. Roger was flying to Bismark (though he didn't know it).

This type of indeterminacy, which we may refer to as the **indeterminacy property** of progressives, has been discussed as if it only comes about with those sentences which display the imperfective paradox. In other words, the scholars mentioned above seem to assume that any indeterminacy in examples like (54a) (= *John is smiling*) must be of a different sort. Certainly (54a) can be indeterminate in some sense. For example, John might make an expression which is somehow in between a clear smile and a clear grimace; in that case, we may be uncertain as to whether *John is smiling* or *John is grimacing* is true. (We would likewise be uncertain whether *John smiled* or *John grimaced* is true.) As far as I know, we lack any explicit discussion of whether this indeterminacy is fundamentally different from that displayed in (61).

3.2 Theories of the progressive

There are two main theoretical approaches to the semantics of the progressive, what we may call the **event structure theory** and the **modal theory**. The former's main tools are the ontology of events (or similar notions, such as situations) and the relations, especially mereological relations, among these events and between events and ordinary objects. The latter's are the components of the theory of modality, in particular quantification over possible worlds, typically combined with some crucial ideas from the semantics of tense. Many versions of the modal theory also make essential use of events, but this not surprising, given that events are frequently a component of theories of tense and modality. In Sections 3.2.1–3.2.2 we will outline the main ideas of each approach.

In seeking to understand the range of analyses of the progressive, there is a fundamental distinction in direction of analysis which one should observe: some analysis aim to analyze progressive sentences (or VPs) in terms of their non-progressive counterparts, whereas others take the opposite approach. The significance of this distinction is clear when we consider sentences exemplifying the imperfective paradox. On the former (progressive from non-progressive) approach, the progressive form introduces some meaning which removes the entailment of completion; for example, in (53a), the progressive would take a meaning which entails that Mary finished building a house, and derive one which does not entail this (Dowty 1977; Landman 1992; Portner 1998, among others). On the latter (non-progressive from progressive) approach, the non-progressive sentence would be seen as adding a completion entailment to a meaning which otherwise lacks it (see, for example, Parsons 1990; Szabó 2004; Hallman 2009). In general, the modal theory follows the first direction of analysis, while research which follow the event structure theory might take either. See also Kuhn & Portner (2002) for general discussion.

3.2.1 The event structure theory

The most basic version of the event structure theory is outlined by Vlach (1981). His approach takes the process property as the fundamental fact to be explained, and analyzes the progressive schematically as follows:

(62) Prog[ϕ] is defined as Stat[Proc[ϕ] goes on]

Here Prog[ϕ] is the progressive form of a basic sentence ϕ, Proc[ϕ] is the process associated with ϕ, and Stat turns a process into a state. Thus, the meaning of (47), *Mary was walking*, works out as follows: ϕ is the sentence *Mary walk*; since this is a process sentence, Proc[ϕ] is simply the process described by ϕ, i.e. the process of Mary walking, and the whole thing describes the state of this process going on. Note that Vlach's analysis derives the meaning of the progressive from its non-progressive counterpart; thus, he counts on Proc explain the imperfective paradox by removing ϕ's completion entailments.

A number of points are unclear in Vlach's proposal (a point which he himself emphasizes), including: (i) how does Proc map a sentence to a process in general? (It's easy when that sentence already describes a process, but what about other aspectual classes?) (ii) What is it for a process to go on? And (iii), how is an ongoing process related to a state? Only point (i) receives significant discussion. Vlach states that when ϕ is a process sentence, Proc[ϕ] = ϕ, whereas when ϕ is an accomplishment or achievement sentence, Proc[ϕ] is a process which "leads to the truth of" ϕ (Vlach 1981: 228). Obviously the crucial next step for an approach such as Vlach's is to define when it is for a process to lead to the truth of a sentence, and one could attempt to give such a definition in various ways. In particular, one might do so in terms of event structure or in terms of modal semantics. Vlach's own comments on the topic suggest that he is thinking in terms of event structures, but he does not go beyond making comments on particular verbs and the puzzles associated with them. However this definition would ultimately be worked out, it must begin with a sentence (i.e., φ), or a full sentential meaning like a proposition, since the definition of Proc[φ] makes reference to the truth of φ. In this way, it is similar to the modal theories, discussed in Section 3.2.2. Most later versions of the event structure theory define the semantics of the progressive not in terms of truth-bearing meanings like that assumed for φ, but rather based on the properties of particular events or situations. (A pair of proposals within situation semantics have an intermediate status; Hinrichs 1983 and Cooper 1985 make use of constructs which are intended to be more abstract than events, but more concrete than propositions, namely event types and facts, respectively.)

Parsons (1990) represents the pure event-based approach in its most basic form. He proposes that the only difference between the semantics of a non-progressive sentence and its progressive counterpart is that the former asserts that an event culminates, while the latter asserts that a state holds (based on Parsons 1990: 234):

(63) a. *Mary arrived* = for some event e: e is an arrival and e's subject is Mary and e culminates before now.
b. *Mary was arriving* = for some event e: e is an arrival and e's subject is Mary, and e's in-progress state holds before now.

For Parsons, the relation between an event (which culminates) and its in-progress state (which holds) is a primitive fact, not one which can be defined in either direction. The theory can handle the imperfective paradox simply by making sure that no principles suggest an entailment relation between an in-progress state and its corresponding culminating event. However, for the same reason it fails to explain the completion entailment, the fact that (64a) entails (64b).

(64) a. John is smiling.
b. John has smiled.

He does present an analysis of this entailment, but the problem is that it is given in terms of a version of the theory presented earlier in the book (Chapter 9), rather than the final version (Chapter 12). In the former version, the meaning of a progressive is not given in terms of an in-progress state, but rather in terms of an event (a telic event or a process) which "holds". In these terms (63b) says that there was an event of Mary arriving which held before the speech time, and (63a) says that such an event culminated; likewise, (64a) asserts that there is an event of John smiling which holds at the speech time. Parsons proposes that what distinguishes a process verb like *smile* from a telic verb like *arrive* is that, whenever the former is true of an event which holds, it is true of culminating subevents of this event. Intuitively, processes culminate whenever they hold. Given this, (64a) entails (64b), since the latter asserts the existence of a culminating event. While this explanation of (64) is appealing, it cannot be extended directly to the later theory involving states. Rather, he will need to say something like "whenever the in-progress state of a process holds, there exist sub-events of this process which culminate".

At a more basic level, something else is unclear about Parsons' analysis. In (63b), what is the status of event e? The formula states that it is an arrival and has Mary as its subject, but it is not located in time; rather, only its in-progress state is located in time. Does the arrival event exist in its fully culminated form outside of our world's time line (perhaps in another possible world), with only its in-progress state being realized? Or does it exist in time but not in a way which is fully culminated? Later scholars working within the event structure approach suggest answers to questions such as these.

A tradition of research including ter Meulen (1985), Bach (1986), Link (1987), and Krifka (1992) further develops the event structure theory. The central idea of this work is that a progressive sentence describes a part of an event, in the same way that an common noun phrase of the form *part of X* describes a part of the individual referred to by X (example from Bach 1986):

(65)   We found part of a Roman aqueduct.

For example, (64a) would be true iff there exists a part of an event of John smiling. This intuition about the semantics of the progressive suggests an appealing account of the imperfective paradox. As Bach points out, (65) could be true even though the Romans never completed the aqueduct in question. Likewise, (53a) could be true even if there was never a complete event of Mary building a house; all that is required is that a part of such an event exist. This approach to the semantics of the progressive can be referred to as the **partitive analysis**. If the partitive analysis is to really provide a solution to the imperfective paradox, it must be able to explain what it is for there to be a part of an event of building a house, absent a complete building of a house. Both ter Meulen and Bach indirectly approach this question by discussing the analogous one in the nominal domain. Therefore, in order to understand Bach's and ter Meulen's analyses of the progressive, we must begin with their background assumptions about nominal semantics.

The crucial ideas for the partitive analysis originate in Link's (1983) theory of plurals and mass terms. Link proposes that nominal semantics be cast in terms of a highly structured domain consisting of at least two sub-domains, the count domain and the mass domain. Each realizes a rich mereological (part-of) structure, with the difference between the two being that the count domain is atomic (minimal units are "atoms", others are pluralities), whereas the mass domain is not (in principle, bits of stuff are indefinitely divisible). The mass domain is a subset of the atoms (and hence is a subset of the count domain), reflecting the idea that bits of stuff are themselves objects which can be counted. And finally, the domains are related by a homomorphism h from count to mass, such that for any object o in the count domain, $h(o)$ is the stuff of which o is made. See Fig. 10.1:

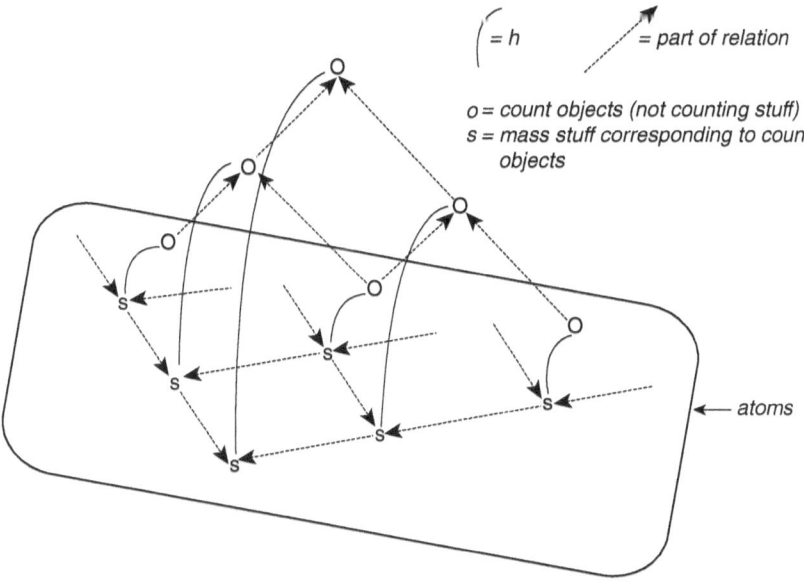

Fig. 10.1: The Partitive Analysis

The denotation of a count noun is a subset of the count domain (objects labeled either o or s), while that of a mass noun is a subset of the mass domain (objects labeled s). Typical count nouns describe objects not in the mass domain (objects labeled on o), but since the mass domain is a subset of the count domain (specifically, a subset of the set of atoms), a count partitive like *part of a Roman aqueduct* can describe a element of the mass domain.

If we insist (as might be thought natural) that something can be a part of an aqueduct only if there is an aqueduct it is part of, the relations might work as follows: the top o in Fig. 10.1 is the whole aqueduct; the s which corresponds to o, i.e., $h(o)$, is the stuff of which it is made; each part o' of o is a part of the aqueduct; and for any such o', $h(o')$ is the stuff that part is made of. But Bach wants us to think of things somewhat differently, since he wants for there to be a way to have a part of an aqueduct which is not part of any complete aqueduct.

He suggests that we have a concept of aqueduct stuff, from which we may define the set of parts of an aqueduct directly, without reference to complete aqueducts. For example, the maximal *s* (the *s* lowest in the diagram) might be all of the stone which makes of the structure under discussion in (65). Given its appearance, we classify it as aqueduct-stuff. In light of this, each *o* in the diagram, mapping onto aqueduct-stuff by *h*, is a part of an aqueduct. Yet there is no complete aqueduct.

Bach (1986) and ter Meulen (1985) would like for us to imagine the solution to the imperfective paradox on analogy to Fig. 10.1. The model should be extended to include events and processes, with the former corresponding to the count domain and the latter to the mass domain. Hence, the progressive sentence (64a) is true iff some John-smiling process *s* went on, and the non-progressive (64b) is true iff some John-smiling event *o* took place. Likewise, a sentence exemplifying the imperfective paradox, for example (53a), is true iff there is some Mary-building-a-house process *s*. As with the aqueduct, this does not entail that a complete event of building a house took place, though it does entail that part of such an event did.

As can be seen, this analysis understands a process of building a house as not being defined in terms of complete events of building a house. Nothing said so far explains what it is for an object to be complete (a complete aqueduct or house-building event), and early proponents of the partitive analysis like Back do not discuss the issue. Crucially, however the notion of completeness is analyzed, this is where the difference between sentences with the subinterval property and those lacking it will be explained. For example, we must ensure that, if (64a) is true (i.e., if there is some John-smiling process), some complete smiling event exists. In contrast, if (53a) is true (i.e., if there was some Mary-building-a-house process), this does not ensure that there was any corresponding complete event.

The above sketch is based essentially on Bach's work, and we find very similar ideas of ter Meulen, Link, and Krifka. None of these papers gives a full-fledged defense of the partitive analysis (and in some cases, much less detail than the above). More recently, Hallman (2009) attempts to work out the analysis in more detail, aiming both to provide empirical support in its favor and to determine precisely what assumptions need to be made if it is to explain the imperfective paradox.

Hallman's novel argument in favor of the partitive analysis has to do with the entailments of progressive sentences containing proportional quantifiers. Consider (66a) (his (5a)):

(66) a. The machine was rejecting exactly one third of the transistors.
 b. The machine rejected exactly one third of the transistors.

Hallman points out that (66a) entails a fairly even distribution of rejection events among all of the events where the machine either accepts or rejects a transistor.

Crucially, it is not true of the initial minute of a three minute interval in which the machine rejects no transistors for the first two minutes, and all of them during the final minute. By way of comparison, note that the non-progressive (66b) (his (4a)) would be true of the three minute interval. Thus, one cannot simply say that the progressive sentence (66a) is true of any part of an event in which (66b) is true. Rather, we must have an understanding of the process of rejecting exactly one third of the transistors which implies that the rejections are fairly evenly distributed.

Hallman's basic analysis of the progressive operator is as follows:

(67) PROG(ϕ) is true of a situation s iff ϕ is true of all relevant subsituations of s.

The analysis in (67) treats the process property as the core of the progressive's meaning. Given an appropriate analysis of quantifiers (see the paper for details), it explains the entailment of even distribution seen in (66a), since every relevant subpart of the situation described must be one in which the machine rejects exactly one third of the transistors. Moreover, according to Hallman, the progressive presupposes that ϕ is **cumulative,** in the sense of Krifka (1998): if ϕ is true of any pair of situation s_1 and s_2, it is true of their sum, s_1+s_2. This cumulativity requirement explains the infelicity of (68) (his (26b)), since *reject exactly six transistors* is not culumative:

(68) #The machine was rejecting exactly six transistors.

In order to extend this analysis to sentences in which the progressive does not seem to apply to a cumulative sentence, like (53a), Hallman argues that all predicates are basically cumulative. In other words, like Parsons (1990), Szabó (2004), and others, he proposes that the scope of the progressive in (53a) is a phrase which does not entail that a complete house is ever built. The completion entailments of the non-progressive *Mary built a house* (that the event culminated with a production of a complete house), must come from elsewhere.

Hallman goes farther than the advocates of the partitive analysis mentioned above in making a precise proposal concerning the source of completion entailments, building on the work of Kratzer (2004). Kratzer proposes that telicity is the result of a telic operator *[telic]* which applies to verb stems, adding the requirement that every part of the theme argument participates in the event. Assuming that V takes an event and a theme argument, Kratzer's definition of the telic form of V amounts to the following:

[telic](V) = $\lambda x \lambda e[V(e,x) \land \forall x'[x'\leq x \rightarrow \exists e'[e'\leq e \land V(e',x')]]]$

According to Hallman, the atelic form of *build* entails that for some part of its theme, the subject built that part. Applying *[telic]* to this, we gain the entailment that every part of the theme has a part which is built by the subject. In the case of Mary building the house, this implies that every part of the house was built.

A crucial difference between Hallman's version of the partitive analysis and that advocated by Bach, ter Meulen, and Parsons is that Hallman assumes that the theme argument itself (e.g., *the house*) is not interpreted partitively. That is, *house* must describe a complete, actual house, since otherwise, the adding *[telic]* to the verb would only entail that Mary built whatever part of a house is described by *house*. Hence, unlike the other advocates of the partitive analysis, Hallman does not analyze nominal partitives and progressives in parallel, but rather seeks to base a partitive analysis of the progressive on a non-partitive analysis of the theme argument.

Because it does not treat the object of a progressive verb partitively, Hallman's analysis cannot explain the failure of existence entailments in the same way as other partitive theories. In particular, applying (67) to (53a) entails that a complete house existed (and that at least part of it was built by Mary). In order to deal with this, he proposes to add a modal component to the progressive's meaning. In particular, he modifies (67) with the goal of allowing that the house exist in its complete form not in the actual world, but in some other possible world:

(69) PROG(ϕ) is true of a situation s iff ϕ is true of all relevant substituations of s and *[telic]*ϕ is true in some possible situation s'.

(There are a few unresolved technical problems here, including that Kratzer's *[telic]* operator applies to verbs stems, not to predicates or whole sentences, but we set them aside to focus on more conceptual issues.) Applied to (53a), the idea is that Mary built a complete house in some possible world (the world of s'), and that in the actual world (the world of s) she built a part of it. The thing which she built in the actual world is classified as a part of a house on the grounds that it is part of a complete house in another possible world. It is never made clear, however, exactly what assumptions are being made about the denotation of the common noun *house*. If it is meant to apply to parts of houses, it seems that the non-progressive sentence will fail to have the correct completion entailments, as discussed above: *[telic]* will only add the entailment that every part of the possibly incomplete house was built. Yet if it is meant to apply only to complete houses, adding the modal component to (69) will not fix the problem it is designed to fix, since the first conjunct of (69) is identical to (67), and hence by itself entails the existence of a complete house.

3.2.2 The modal theory

The first and purest version of the modal theory was proposed by Dowty (1977, 1979). Dowty's modal theory is pure in that it treats the progressive as an operator with a semantics very similar to that typically assigned to modal auxiliaries within formal semantics: the progressive combines a temporal reference with quantification over possible worlds (based on Dowty 1979: 149):

(70) PROG(φ) is true at an interval I and world w iff there is an interval I' such that I is a non-final subinterval of I', and for all $w' \in$ INR(<I,w>), φ is true at I' and w'.

INR is an accessibility relation as in modal semantics; INR(<I,w>) picks out the set of worlds (known as **inertia worlds**) which are like w up through I, and in which what is going on in w up through I continues "in ways most compatible with the past course of events" (Dowty 1979: 148). For example, (53a) is true at <I,w> iff in all worlds w' which are like w up through I, and in which matters develop in ways most compatible with what was going on in w before and during I, I develops into an interval I' in which Mary builds a house. More intuitively, Mary was doing something during I which, in worlds which unfold "normally" from that point on, she builds a house. (One might object that it is not accurate to call this a "pure" modal meaning, given that it involves a crucial reference to temporal relations; however, the meanings of classical modals like the modal auxiliaries also involve temporal notions (see Portner 2009 for discussion), so Dowty's analysis of the progressive is close to as purely modal as could be found in natural language. It is, of course, not pure when compared to the operators of modal logic.)

As a modal theory, Dowty's analysis easily solves the problem of the failure of existence entailments. The house in (53a) need not exist in the actual world, only in the accessible worlds w'. Dowty also discusses the no-statives property, endorsing an explanation that combines ideas outlined by Taylor (1977) and Carlson (1977). The idea is that stage-level predicates (including stage-level statives) are true or false at definite intervals, and so the meaning in (70) makes sense for them. In contrast, individual-level predicates indicate dispositions which are present at any moment within an interval as much as at any other; for this reason, it makes sense that we would not use a device like PROG in (70) for indicating a subinterval of a larger interval in which the non-progressive φ is true. This explanation is weak in that it does not predict that stage-level statives like *sit in the chair*, which are also true at any moment of an interval in which they are true, are different from individual-level statives, but Dowty sees such weakness as acceptable, arguing that we can only provide a plausible reason why individual-level statives are not possible, not a formal derivation of their ungrammaticality. Note that Carlson rules out progressives of individual-level predicates syntactically, an approach which is compatible with Dowty's analysis, though not one he chooses to follow.

Dowty's analysis also has important consequences for understanding the process property, though these are somewhat hidden in his broader discussion. His ideas on the progressive are embedded in a larger decompositional analysis of aspectual classes within interval semantics in a way which goes far towards explaining the process property (provided we set aside the specific problem for Dowty's analysis discussed below). The key to this explanation is the fact that (70) refers to a non-final subinterval of an interval in which the non-progressive ϕ is true: because it's an interval, an event which is otherwise seen as instantaneous must be construed as having duration, and because it's non-final, it must have to do with the process which goes on before a culminating event culminates.

Dowty also argues that the futurate progressive illustrated in (49) can be analyzed in the same terms as the regular "imperfective" progressive. He argues that such examples are simply the combination of the imperfective progressive with the tenseless future (e.g., *Mary leaves town tomorrow*). As discussed by many scholars (see Dowty's work for references), the tenseless future conveys a sense of planning or predetermination which is shared by the futurate progressive; thus (49) suggests that Mary has made plans to depart tomorrow. However, compared to the tenseless future, the futurate progressive implies less certainty. The contrast is illustrated in (71), Dowty's (1979) example (41):

(71)   a. The sun sets tomorrow at 6:57 PM.
       b. *The sun is setting tomorrow at 6:57 PM.

According to Dowty, (71a) means roughly that, at some point at or before the speech time, the facts determined that the sun sets at 6:57 tomorrow. If we combine this meaning with the semantics for the progressive in (70), we have the following: for some interval of time I containing the speech time, the facts before I determined that, for all futures during which what was going on during I continues normally, the sun sets at 6:57. Crucially, the set of futures in which the sun sets at 6:57 according to (71b) may be a subset of those in which it sets according to (71a). In particular, certain futures (relative to the speech time) may not contain I, and moreover some of the futures which contain I may not be involve inertia worlds. Thus, the analysis predicts that (71b) is weaker than (71a).

Despite its many advantages, Dowty's theory suffers from a problem which has led other authors to either modify or abandon the modal theory. Vlach (1981) points out that Dowty's definition of the set of inertia worlds does not work in many examples displaying the imperfective paradox. Consider (72):

(72) Max was crossing the street.

This sentence can be true (at an interval *I*) even if shortly after *I* a bus runs over Max. According to the analysis, it would be true if, in every world in which what is going on during *I* continues in ways most compatible with past events, Max crosses the street. But the bus was traveling down the street towards Max during *I*, and surely the expected way for events to unfold includes Max being hit. The problem here is that Dowty's definition of ineria worlds looks at what's going on throughout the entire world before and during interval *I*, and (72) can be true even in a world where Max being run over is all but inevitable.

Next we turn to the ways in which later modal theories have attempted to solve the problem posed by (72). Here we will consider four such theories: Asher (1992), Landman (1992), Bonomi (1997a), and Portner (1998). In the most general terms, they all agree on what must be done: something must be added to Dowty's analysis which will allow one to ignore the trajectory of the bus in evaluating (72). In other words, the core idea is that, if we ignore (for the time being) the oncoming bus, Max would have crossed the street. The question is how to ignore the bus. We see the following two main ideas:
1. **Events** or situations play an essential role in the semantics of the progressive. Events are useful because they are smaller than worlds in both temporal and spatial extent, and so the bus might be outside of the event(s) we pay attention to.
2. Progressives are evaluated with respect to a **perspective**. A perspective is something which selects a subset of the information available in a situation, and so can allow us to ignore information about the bus.

All of the modal analyses discussed below make use of events, and most also make use of the concept of perspective (though not always under that name). Moreover, particular analyses employ other interesting concepts, such as default semantics (Asher) or a closeness relation among worlds (Landman).

Each of the post-Dowty modal theories begins with the idea that a progressive sentence describes an event if and only if that event is part of an event of the kind described by the phrase under the scope of the progressive in relevant possible world or worlds. For example, (53a) is true of an event of Mary pouring concrete into a hole in the ground if this event is part of an event of building a house in the relevant possible world(s). Such an approach promises to maintain all of the advantages of Dowty's theory, if it can solve the problems with sentences displaying the imperfective paradox. Where the various modal theories differ is in how the relevant possible worlds are identified.

Portner (1998) takes the approach closest to Dowty's, aiming to treat the progressive as very similar to an ordinary modal operator. Portner works with a more sophisticated theory of modality than Dowty's, building on Kratzer's work (Kratzer 1977, 1982; for a description of Kratzer's theory, see article 14 [this volume] (Hacquard) *Modality*). In this context, he proposes that the progressive is a modal operator with (i) a circumstantial modal base, indicating that only worlds in which certain contextually specified facts hold, and (ii) a "non-interruption" ordering source, indicating that worlds in which the event is interrupted are to be ranked as less relevant than those in which it is not. For example, in the case of (53a), the modal base would include propositions like "Mary has purchased such-and-such supplies", "Mary intends to build a house", "Mary follows proper architectural plans for a house", the ordering source would contain propositions like "Mary is not injured" and "Mary does not run out of money". Given this background, the sentence would be true iff there was an event which, in all worlds compatible with this modal base, and in which as many of the ordering source propositions as possible are true, she builds a house. This basically means "Given the relevant facts, if she was not interrupted, Mary built a house".

Bonomi (1997a) has a very similar analysis, though one that is couched in terms which are not as closely tied to ideas familiar from the theory of modality. Bonomi's theory uses two contextually given parameters as well, a **Context of facts** and a **Stereotypical frame**. The former is very similar to the modal base: it is a set of events, and the meaning of the progressive only depends on courses of events in which all of these events occur; and the latter is very similar to the ordering source: we select from the relevant courses of events those in which the event in question develops normally. Hence, example (53a) is true iff, for some past event *e*, there is a set of relevant events (i.e., a context of facts) including *e*, and there is a stereotypical frame which says that in all courses of events in which the relevant events occur, and in which in which *e* develops normally, *e* is an event of Mary building a house.

Asher's (1992) system uses techniques even farther removed from the usual theories of modality, but the core idea remains the same. His analysis is based on a default, nomonotonic conditional operator >. The statement A>B can be read as "If A, infer B, unless there are specific reasons not to", or even "If A, then as a default B". Given this, Asher aims to treat progressives as an indication that some event occurred which would as a default lead one to infer that an event of the kind described by the phrase under the scope of the progressive occurred. Hence, (53a) means that some event occurred, the occurrence of which would as a default lead one to infer that Mary built a house.

The final post-Dowty modal theory we will consider is that of Landman (1992). His analysis develops the modal theory using ideas which are quite unique to the progressive, and not based on ideas found in the literature on modality. (Despite, it is still properly called a "modal theory", since the truth of a progressive sentence may depend on what happens in possible worlds other than the actual one.) For Landman, the key concept on which the rest of the analysis is built is that of one event being a **stage** of another. Stage-of is a sub-relation of part-of, so if an event is a stage of another, it is also part of it, but stage-of is more specific: "An event is a stage of another event if the second can be regarded as a more developed version of the first" (Landman 1992: 23). The idea of Landman's analysis, then, is that (53a) is true iff an event was going on which is a stage of (an event of) Mary building a house in the closest possible world in which all of its stages are realized (provided this world is "reasonable"). His precise analysis is developed in terms of a recursive definition of the **continuation branch** of an event; the continuation branch is designed to identify the closest possible world in which all of the event's stages are realized. For reasons of space, we will not examine the Landman's definition of continuation branch here.

As they are stated above, Portner's, Bonomi's, Asher's, and Landman's analyses all suffer from a failure to come to terms with the indeterminacy property discussed above. Consider (72). These theories all say, roughly, that this sentence is true iff an event was going on which would, if it developed normally, become an event of Max crossing the street. But couldn't we also look at this very same event, and describe it as in (73) (supposing that he did in fact walk into the path of a bus)?

(73) Max was walking into the path of an oncoming bus.

It seems that there are at least two incompatible ways that one and the same event could develop normally. This seems to show that the definition of "normal" must depend on more than just the facts about the event.

One way to respond to this problem would be to deny that (72) and (73) concern the same event. That is, prior to the arrival of the bus, Max was actually participating in two events: a street-crossing event (which was never completed) and a bus-intersecting event (which was). While formally this would solve the difficulty, is presents us with the challenge of explaining how these two events differ, and while it may be possible to meet this challenge, modal theories of the progressive have not taken this approach. Rather, they have dealt with the problem by assuming that a single event is relevant, but that this event can be seen in different ways. A "perspective" is intuitively a way of seeing an event or situation. One perspective makes us see what Max did as part of crossing the street, while another perspective makes us see it as part of an accident involving the bus. These two perspectives are relevant to the two ways of describing the event in (72)–(73).

Each theory develops the concept of perspective differently. For Portner, the property expressed by the predicate under the scope of the progressive contributes the perspective, and it is an argument of the modal base. Thus, it helps determine the set of relevant worlds by determining which facts about the world are to be considered; for example, in (73), we consider facts about the bus, while in (72), we do not. For Bonomi (who has an extensive discussion about perspective), both the Context of facts and Stereotypical frame are contextually determined, and are responsible for representing the perspective (or "point of view", as he terms it when describing his own analysis). For Asher, a perspective is a way of describing the event, and it feeds into the semantics as the antecedent of the default operator; hence, Asher hypothesizes that you can describe Max's walking event in different ways, one of which leads to the default conclusion that he crosses the street, the other to the default conclusion that he is hit by the bus. Landman notes the importance of perspective, but does not formalize it within his theory. Given that these scholars each develop the concept in a way designed to fit into the mechanics of the particular overall analysis, it is difficult to compare them directly. None of them relate the concept to a discussion of broader issues within semantic theory in a way which would allow us to bring to bear other knowledge in determining which analysis is superior to the others.

3.3 Progressive and imperfective

As pointed out above, many languages describe situations which would be described in English with the progressive by using a more general-purpose verb form, and this phenomenon has received significant attention within semantic theory in connection with the analysis of the imperfective in Romance languages. An example is the Spanish (48) above, from Cipria & Roberts (2000): this sentence naturally receives a reading very similar to the English past progressive, but the same verb form can express other meanings, including habituality, intention, and the simple past occurrence of an atelic event. French and Italian show a similar (but not identical) range of meaning. (Note that the imperfective always conveys past tense, a component of its meaning we ignore here.) In the semantics literature, we see three approaches to understanding the semantics of imperfectives:

1. Underspecification and coercion: de Swart (1998) argues that the imperfective places a purely aspectual restriction on the clause it combines with (specifically, it must describe a process or state). If the compositional semantics of this clause meets the condition, this by itself determines the meaning. Otherwise, a process of coercion shifts the meaning into one which meets the aspectual restriction.
2. Unified meaning within modal semantics: Cipria & Roberts (2000) provide an analysis of the Spanish imperfective which aims to provide a unified semantic value covering all of its various intuitive meanings. This unification has a temporal component, reflecting the fact that the imperfective in Spanish always concerns the past, and a modal component; the distinctions among intuitive meanings are based on the choice of modal accessibility relation. Within this framework, the modal analysis of the progressive (specifically, the version developed by Dowty) is a special case. Ferreira (2004) and Deo (2009) have developed similar ideas; Bonomi (1997b) also aims for a unified semantic analysis, but in rather different terms.
3. Syntactic explanation: Hacquard (2006) argues that the various meanings of the imperfective are introduced by distinct, phonologically null operators. In the case of the progressive, she assumes a PROG operator as defined by Portner (1998). The imperfective is used when one of the relevant class of operators is present immediately under the scope of tense. Conversely, the perfective form is used when a perfective operator occurs in that position.

While all three approaches are intuitively appealing, there has been little direct comparison of one to another. It is likely that we will not make real progress in understanding the relation of the imperfective to the progressive, and in understanding the semantics of the imperfective more generally, until clear arguments are given for preferring one approach to the others.

3.4 Final discussion of the progressive

As we have seen, semantic analyses of the progressive fall into two major groups: event-structure theories and modal theories. There is some overlap between the two (for example, Hallman's theory is basically an event-structure theory, but has a modal component), and there is a great deal of diversity within each group. Many analyses, even influential ones like Bach's, are given briefly, and as a result fail to address the full range of data relevant to the analysis of the progressive. In light of this situation, it may be useful to summarize whether each approach attempts an explanation of the major properties of the progressive outlined in

Section 3.1. Tab. 10.2 provides such a summary. Of course Tab. 10.2 should not be taken as an evaluation of theories, since each has important advantages and problems, including many discussed above.

Tab. 10.2: Theories of the Progressive

	No statives	Process	Completion property	Imperfective paradox	Failure of existence	Reasonableness	Actuality	Indeterminacy
Vlach	Y	Y	Y	Y	N	N	N	N
Parsons	N	N (Y)	N (Y)	Y	N	N	Y	N
Bach	N	Y	N	Y	Y	N	N	N
Hallman	N	Y	Y	Y	Y	Y	N	N
Dowty	Y	Y	Y	N	Y	N	N	N
Portner	N	N	Y	Y	Y	Y	Y	Y
Bonomi	N	N	N	Y	Y	Y	Y	Y
Asher	N	N	N	Y	Y	Y	Y	Y
Landman	N	Y	Y	Y	Y	Y	Y	N

Note that a "Y" only means that an explanation is offered—not that it must be evaluated as successful. In most cases I list "N" when a given author does not explicitly discuss a particular problem, even though one could imagine him or her adopting the explanation presented as part of another analysis; occasionally I list "Y" when a paper can be construed as implying an explanation for a given phenomenon, even though the point is not made clearly. For Parsons theory, "N (Y)" indicates that an explanation is offered in terms of the version of the analysis given in Chapter 9, but not in the version given in Chapter 12.

4 References

Abusch, Dorit 1988. Sequence of tense, intensionality, and scope. In: H. Borer (ed.). *Proceedings of the West Coast Conference on Formal Linguistics (= WCCFL) 7*. Stanford, CA: CSLI Publications, 1–14.
Abusch, Dorit 1997. Sequence of tense and temporal de re. *Linguistics & Philosophy* 20, 1–50.
Abusch, Dorit & Mats Rooth 1990. Temporal adverbs and the English perfect. In: J. Carter et al. (eds.). *Proceedings of the Annual Meeting of the North Eastern Linguistic Society (= NELS) 20*. Amherst, MA: GLSA, 1–15.

Asher, Nicholas 1992. A default, truth conditional semantics for the progressive. *Linguistics & Philosophy* 15, 463–508.
Bach, Emmon 1986. Natural language metaphysics. In: R. Barcan-Marcus, G. J. W. Dorn & P. Weingartner (eds.). *Logic, Methodology, and Philosophy of Science VII: Proceedings of the Seventh International Congress of Logic, Methodology, and Philosophy of Science*, Salzburg, Austria 1983. Amsterdam: Elsevier, 573–595.
Bennett, Michael & Barbara H. Partee 1978. *Toward the Logic of Tense and Aspect in English*. Bloomington, IN: Indiana University Linguistics Club. Reprinted in: B. H. Partee. *Compositionality in Formal Semantics: Selected Papers by Barbara H. Partee*. Oxford: Blackwell, 2004, 59–109.
Bonomi, Andrea 1997a. The progressive and the structure of events. *Journal of Semantics* 14, 173–205.
Bonomi, Andrea 1997b. Aspect, quantification, and *when* clauses in Italian. *Linguistics & Philosophy* 20, 469–514.
Büring, Daniel 1997. The great scope inversion conspiracy. *Linguistics & Philosophy* 29, 175–194.
Carlson, Greg N. 1977. *Reference to Kinds in English*. Ph.D. dissertation. University of Massachusetts, Amherst, MA.
Chomsky, Noam 1970. Deep structure, surface structure, and semantic interpretation. In: R. Jakobson & S. Kawamoto (eds.). *Studies in General and Oriental Linguistics Presented to Shiro Hattori on the Occasion of His Sixtieth Birthday*. Tokyo: TEC Corporation, 52–91.
Cipria, Alicia & Craige Roberts 2000. Spanish imperfecto and preterito: Truth conditions and aktionsart effects in a situation semantics. *Natural Language Semantics* 8, 297–347.
Cooper, Robin 1985. *Aspectual Classes in Situation Semantics*. Technical Report CSLI-84-14C. Stanford, CA, Stanford University.
Deo, Ashwini 2009. Unifying the imperfective and the progressive: Partitions as quantificational domains. *Linguistics & Philosophy* 32, 475–521.
Dowty, David 1977. Towards a semantic analysis of verb aspect and the English 'imperfective' progressive. *Linguistics & Philosophy* 1, 45–77.
Dowty, David 1979. *Word Meaning and Montague Grammar*. Dordrecht: Reidel.
Ferreira, Marcelo 2004. Imperfectives and plurality. In: R. B. Young (ed.). *Proceedings of Semantics and Linguistic Theory (=SALT) XIV*, Ithaca, NY: Cornell University, 1–18.
von Fintel, Kai 1994. *Restrictions on Quantifier Domains*. Ph.D. dissertation. University of Massachusetts, Amherst, MA.
Giorgi, Alessandra & Fabio Pianesi 1997. *Tense and Aspect: From Semantics to Morphosyntax*. Oxford: Oxford University Press.
Hacquard, Valentine 2006. *Aspects of Modality*. Ph.D. dissertation. MIT, Cambridge, MA.
Hallman, Peter 2009. Proportions in time: Interactions of quantification and aspect. *Natural Language Semantics* 17, 29–61.
Hinrichs, Erhard 1982. Temporal anaphora in discourses of English. Paper presented at the *Ohio State University Conference on the Semantics of Tense and Aspect in Discourse*, May 16–17, 1982. Columbus, OH: Ohio State University.
Hinrichs, Erhard 1983. The semantics of the English progressive. In: A. Chukerman, M. Marks, J. Richardson (eds.). *Papers from the Regional Meeting of the Chicago Linguistic Society (= CLS) 19*. Chicago, IL: Chicago Linguistic Society, 172–182.
Iatridou, Sabine, Elena Anagnostopoulou & Roumyana Pancheva 2003. Observations about the form and meaning of the perfect. In: A. Alexiadou, M. Rathert & A. von Stechow (eds.). *Perfect Explorations*. Berlin: de Gruyter, 153–204.

Inoue, Kyoko 1979. An analysis of the English present perfect. *Linguistics* 17, 561–589.
Kamp, Hans & Uwe Reyle 1993. *From Discourse to Logic*. Dordrecht: Kluwer.
Katz, Graham. 2003. On the stativity of the English perfect. In: A. Alexiadou, M. Rathert & A. von Stechow (eds.). *Perfect Explorations*. Berlin: de Gruyter, 205–234.
Klein, Wolfgang 1992. The present perfect puzzle. *Language* 68, 525–552.
Klein, Wolfgang 1994. *Time in Language*. London: Routledge.
Klein, Wolfgang 2000. An analysis of the German perfect. *Language* 76, 358–382.
Kratzer, Angelika 1977. What "must" and "can" must and can mean. *Linguistics & Philosophy* 1, 337–55.
Kratzer, Angelika 1981. The notional category of modality. In: H.-J. Eikmeyer & H. Rieser (eds.). *Words, Worlds, and Contexts*. Berlin: Mouton de Gruyter, 38–74.
Kratzer, Angelika 2004. Telicity and the meaning of objective case. In: J. Guéron & J. Lecarme (eds.). *The Syntax of Time*. Cambridge, MA: The MIT Press, 389–423.
Krifka, Manfred 1992. Thematic relations as links between nominal reference and temporal constitution. In: I. Sag & A. Szabolcsi (eds.). *Lexical Matters*. Stanford, CA: CSLI Publications, 29–53.
Krifka, Manfed 1998. The origins of telicity. In: S. Rothstein (ed.). *Events and Grammar*. Dordrecht: Kluwer, 197–235.
Kuhn, Steven & Paul Portner 2002. Tense and time. In: D. Gabbay & F. Guenthner (eds.). *Handbook of Philosophical Logic, vol. 6*. Dordrecht: Reidel, 277–346.
Landman, Fred 1992. The progressive. *Natural Language Semantics* 1, 1–32.
Lascarides, Alex 1991. The progressive and the imperfective paradox. *Synthese* 87, 401–447.
Levinson, Stephen C. 2000. *Presumptive Meanings: The Theory of Generalized Conversational Implicature*. Cambridge, MA: The MIT Press.
Link, Godehard 1983. The logical analysis of plurals and mass terms: A lattice-theoretical approach. In: R. Bäuerle, Ch. Schwarze & A. von Stechow (eds.). *Meaning, Use and Interpretation in Language*. Berlin: de Gruyter, 302–323.
Link, Godehard 1987. Algebraic semantics of event structures. In: J. Groenendijk, J. M. Stokhof & F. Veltman (eds.). *Proceedings of the Sixth Amsterdam Colloquium*. Amsterdam: ILLC, 243–262.
Löbner, Sebastian 2002. Is the German perfect a perfect perfect? In: G. Katz, S. Reinhard & P. Reuter (eds.). *Proceedings of Sinn und Bedeutung (=Sub) 6* (Publications of the Institute of Cognitive Science, vol. 1/2002). Osnabrück: University of Osnabrück, 255–273.
McCawley, James 1971. Tense and time reference in English. In: C. J. Fillmore & D. T. Langendoen (eds.). *Studies in Linguistic Semantics*. New York: Holt, Rinehart & Winston, 96–113.
McCoard, Robert 1978. *The English Perfect: Tense-Choice and Pragmatic Inferences*. Amsterdam: North-Holland.
McNally, Louise 1998. On recent formal analyses of topic. In: J. Ginzburg et al. (eds.). *The Tbilisi Symposium on Logic, Language and Computation: Selected Papers*. Stanford, CA: CSLI Publications, 149–162.
ter Meulen, Alice 1985. Progressives without possible worlds. In: W. H. Eilfort, P. D. Kroeber & K. L. Peterson (eds.). *Papers from the Regional Meeting of the Chicago Linguistic Society (= CLS) 21*. Chicago, IL: Chicago Linguistic Society, 408–423.
ter Meulen, Alice 1995. *Representing Time in Natural Language: The Dynamic Interpretation of Tense and Aspect*. Cambridge, MA: The MIT Press.
Mittwoch, Anita 1988. Aspects of English aspect: On the interaction of perfect, progressive and durational phrases. *Linguistics & Philosophy* 11, 203–254.

Moens, Marc & Mark Steedman 1988. Temporal ontology and temporal reference. *Computational Linguistics* 14, 15–28.
Montague, Richard 1973. The proper treatment of quantification in ordinary English. In: J. Hintikka, J. Moravcsik & P. Suppes (eds.). *Approaches to Natural Language*. Dordrecht: Reidel, 221–242.
Musan, Renate 2001. The present perfect in German: Outline of its semantic composition. *Natural Language and Linguistic Theory* 19, 355–401.
Musan, Renate 2002. *The German Perfect. Its Semantic Composition and its Interaction with Temporal Adverbials*. Dordrecht: Kluwer.
Musan, Renate 2003. *Seit*-adverbials in perfect constructions. In: A. Alexiadou, M. Rathert & A. von Stechow (eds.). *Perfect Explorations*. Berlin: de Gruyter, 253–276.
Nishiyama, Atsuko 2006 *The Semantics and Pragmatics of the Perfect in English and Japanese*. Ph.D. dissertation. University at Buffalo, Buffalo, NY.
Nishiyama, Atsuko & Jean-Pierre Koenig 2004. What is a perfect state? In: B. Schmeiser et al. (eds.). *Proceedings of the West Coast Conference on Formal Linguistics (= WCCFL) 23*. Somerville, MA: Cascadilla Press, 101–113.
Ogihara, Toshiyuki 1989. *Temporal Reference in English and Japanese*. Ph.D. dissertation. University of Texas, Austin, TX.
Ogihara, Toshiyuki 1995. Double access sentences and references to states. *Natural Language Semantics* 3, 177–210.
Pancheva, Roumyana & Arnim von Stechow 2004. On the present perfect puzzle. In: K. Moulton & M. Wolf (eds.). *Proceedings of the Annual Meeting of the North Eastern Linguistic Society (= NELS) 34*. Amherst, MA: GLSA, 469–483.
Parsons, Terry 1990. *Events in the Semantics of English: A Study in Subatomic Semantics*. Cambridge, MA: The MIT Press.
Partee, Barbara H. 1977. John is easy to please. In: A. Zampolli (ed.). *Linguistic Structures Processing*. Amsterdam: North-Holland, 281–312.
Partee, Barbara H. 1984. Nominal and temporal anaphora. *Linguistics & Philosophy* 7, 243–286.
Portner, Paul 1998. The progressive in modal semantics. *Language* 74, 760–787.
Portner, Paul 2003. The temporal semantics and modal pragmatics of the perfect. *Linguistics & Philosophy* 26, 459–510.
Portner, Paul 2009. *Modality*. Oxford: Oxford University Press.
Rathert, Monika 2003. Universal-existential puzzles. In: A. Alexiadou, M. Rathert & A. von Stechow (eds.). *Perfect Explorations*. Berlin: de Gruyter, 363–380.
Rathert, Monika 2004. *Textures of Time*. Berlin: Akademie Verlag.
Reichenbach, Hans 1947. *Elements of Symbolic Logic*. New York: Macmillan.
Roberts, Craige 1996. Information structure in discourse: Towards an integrated formal theory of pragmatics. In: J.-H. Toon & A. Kathol (eds.). *Papers in Semantics* (OSU Working Papers in Linguistics 49). Columbus, OH: Ohio State University, 91–136.
Rothstein, Björn 2008. *The Perfect Time Span: On the Present Perfect in German, Swedish, and English*. Amsterdam: Benjamins.
Sag, Ivan A. & Anna Szabolcsi (eds.) 2002. *Lexical Matters*. Stanford, CA: CSLI Publications.
Schaden, Gerhard 2009. Present perfects compete. *Linguistics & Philosophy* 32, 115–141.
Smith, Carlota S. 1992. *The Parameter of Aspect*. Dordrecht: Kluwer.
Spejewski, Beverly 1997. *The Perfect as Temporal Subordination*. Ms. Philadelphia, PA, University of Pennsylvania.

von Stechow, Arnim 2002. German *seit* 'since' and the ambiguity of the German perfect. In: B. Stiebels & I. Kaufmann (eds.). *More than Words: A Festschrift for Dieter Wunderlich*. Berlin: Akademie Verlag, 393–432.
Stump, Gregory T. 1985. *The Semantic Variability of Absolute Constructions*. Dordrecht: Kluwer.
de Swart, Henriëtte 1998. Aspect shift and coercion. *Natural Language and Linguistic Theory* 16, 347–385.
Szabó, Zoltán G. 2004. On the progressive and the perfective. *Noûs* 38, 29–59.
Taylor, Barry 1977. Tense and continuity. *Linguistics & Philosophy* 1, 199–220.
Tedeschi, Philip & Annie Zaenen (eds.) 1981. *Syntax and Semantics 14: Tense and Aspect*. New York: Academic Press.
Vendler, Zeno 1967. Verbs and times. In: Z. Vendler. *Linguistics in Philosophy*. Ithaka, NY: Cornell University Press, 97–121.
Vlach, Frank 1981. The semantics of the progressive. In: P. Tedeschi & A. Zaenen (eds.). *Syntax and Semantics 14: Tense and Aspect*. New York: Academic Press, 271–292.
Vlach, Frank. 1993. Temporal adverbials, tenses, and the perfect. *Linguistics & Philosophy* 16, 231–283.

Paul Portner
11 Verbal mood

1   Mood in broad perspective —— 369
2   Verbal mood in complement clauses —— 373
3   Verbal mood in other contexts —— 396
4   Conclusions —— 401
5   References —— 401

Abstract: Within semantic theory, verbal mood has been analyzed in terms of several theoretical approaches, most notably using the concepts of the possible worlds semantics for modality, but also based on ideas from temporal and nominal semantics. Most semantically-oriented research has focused on the indicative and subjunctive clauses which are selected by a higher predicate, and this paper gives an introduction to several theories developed on these grounds. The paper also briefly surveys work on verbal mood in other contexts, including relative clauses and adjunct clauses.

1 Mood in broad perspective

The term "mood" has been used to discuss a wide range of phenomena in natural language, and it is the purpose of this article to focus on one of them, what we call VERBAL MOOD. One way to define verbal mood is by example: it is the difference between clauses which is marked by indicative or subjunctive verb forms in languages which are traditionally described as having an opposition between such forms (e.g., German and Italian), as well as forms taken to be in the same paradigm as indicative and subjunctive (e.g., optative), and the same or very similar differences in other languages. According to this definition, verbal mood might not be marked on the verb (for example, in Romanian it is marked by a particle), and it might be unclear whether a particular verb form should be seen as marking verbal mood in the intended sense. As we will see below, much research on verbal mood has proceeded based on this kind of definition by example.

We might also define verbal mood on the basis of semantic theory: Verbal mood is a distinction in form among clauses based on the presence, absence, or type of

Paul Portner, Washington, DC, USA

https://doi.org/10.1515/9783110589443-011

modality in the grammatical context in which they occur. According to much semantic research on the indicative and subjunctive (and as we will see in detail below), these forms mark verbal mood in this sense. An advantage of this type of theoretical definition is that it allows us to automatically relate our thinking about verbal mood to other theoretical issues. Obviously, it draws a link to the analysis of modality (article 14 [this volume] (Hacquard) *Modality*), a well-developed and central part of semantic theory. But more importantly, it allows us to connect the study of verbal mood to a more general concept of mood, one which extends beyond verbal mood to encompass other phenomena which are sometimes described with the same label.

Though it is the purpose of this article to describe the state of research on verbal mood, as defined above, it is obvious that the concept of mood has been used by linguists to talk about a much wider range of phenomena. It may be useful to describe the broader context briefly. A general definition of "mood", under which verbal mood would fall as a subtype, might go as follows: Mood is a distinction (in form, meaning, or use) among clauses based on modal features of meaning in the context (either grammatical or conversational) in which they occur. Besides verbal mood, we can cite at least the following phenomena which seem to fall under the broad definition:

1. Notional mood   Philosophers and linguists sometimes speak of categories of meaning which bear some intuitive connection to the meanings associated with verbal mood, for example propositions which are taken to be necessary, possible, desired, and so forth. These can be described as "notional moods" (Jespersen 1924: 819–821). Categories divorced from any association with form are unlikely to be an appropriate topic of linguistic study, as Jespersen points out. However, sometimes we find elements or constructions, other than verbal moods, which seem to express the meanings of the same general type as are expressed by verbal moods. For example, dependent modals and infinitives have been treated this way (Palmer 1990, Portner 1997). In a context where the simple term "mood" is used to refer specifically to the indicative-subjunctive contrast, the term "notional mood" is useful to describe a wider range of grammatical forms which are associated with (verbal) mood-like meanings.
2. Sentence mood   Sentence mood (sometimes referred to as SENTENTIAL FORCE, Chierchia & McConnel-Ginet 1990, Zanuttini & Portner 2003) is the semantic side of the opposition among clause types. Thus we have declarative mood, interrogative mood, and imperative mood, among others. This concept of mood has roots in philosophy of language (Stenius 1967, Searle 1969), and many linguists who use the term "mood" in this way (e.g., Wilson & Sperber 1988, Lohnstein 2000, Zaefferer 2006) develop the perspective of speech act theory. In some theories, sentence mood is closely linked with verbal mood (Lohnstein 2000, Lohnstein

& Bredel 2004); the distinction is easily elided in discussions of the imperative, where a verbal mood and sentence mood frequently coincide. Within Native American linguistics, the sentence moods and other notional mood forms are sometimes grouped into a single category (e.g., Moshinsky 1974, Melnar 2004; see point 4 below). The concept of sentence mood seems especially prominent in the German syntax/semantics tradition; see, in addition to the works cited above, Hausser (1980, 1983), Meibauer (1990), and Reis (1999 2003), for example. It has also been studied in cognitive linguistics (Narrog 2005).
3. Many scholars, especially in the philosophy of language tradition, speak of a semantic distinction between SUBJUNCTIVE CONDITIONALS and INDICATIVE CONDITIONALS. In certain languages, the *if* clause of a conditional can be in the subjunctive mood, and this conveys a sense that the proposition expressed by that clause is less likely to be true, less congruent with assumed facts, or something of the sort. We will briefly discuss the role of verbal mood in conditionals in Section 3.3.
4. Mood in descriptive and typological linguistics Descriptive and typological studies use the term "mood", as well as "mode" and "modality", for a variety of elements whose meanings relate to the modal domain, to sentence mood, and to varieties of subordination. Palmer (2001) mentions several examples, in particular Donaldson (1980). Of the many important works in this area, I mention only a sampling: Axelrod (1993), Bugenhagen (1993), Bhat (1999), Bloomfield (1956), Boas (1911/2002), Bybee (1998), Chafe (1995), de Reuse (1994), Ekdahl & Grimes (1964), Elliot (2000), Fortescue (1984), Foster (1986), Melnar (2004), McGregor & Wagner (2006), Lichtenberk (1983), Parks (1976), Roberts (1990), Swift (2004), Woodbury (1981), and Zwicky (1985).

Note that terminology is not always used in the same way, and Mithun (1999) describes the situation as follows:

> The grammatical distinctions included under the heading *modality* in descriptions of individual languages vary, chiefly because the modal systems themselves have developed differently. Terminology varies as well. In some traditions, inflectional markers of modality are defined as *mood*, in others as *mode*. Further complicating matters is the fact that these terms, particularly *mode*, have sometimes been used for other kinds of distinctions as well, often aspectual. This is due in part to the fact that modal distinctions are often carried by tense or aspect markers.
>
> (Mithun 1999: 171).

The moods/modes discussed in these works have a variety of names descriptive of their meaning or function, for example "desiderative", "purposive", and "interrogative" (among many others). We often find the terms "realis" and irrealis" either as labels of particular moods/modes, or as classifications of moods/modes with more specific names. While it is likely that many of these forms could profitably be analyzed within the frameworks used to analyze the indicative and subjunctive, except for Baker & Travis (1997) and Matthewson (2010), discussed below, I am not aware of any formal analyses of specific elements labeled as mood/mode markers in this tradition.

It is not yet clear what range of phenomena, falling under these wide-ranging concepts, constitute a natural class for semantic analysis. As mentioned, this article will focus on the narrower domain of verbal mood.

Given the perspective that verbal mood reflects some modal feature of meaning in the context, it is inevitable that the study of mood would be intertwined with that of the relevant contexts. And indeed, that is what we find. The analysis of mood has proceeded hand in hand with the analysis of grammatical and pragmatic contexts which cause a particular form, like the indicative or subjunctive, to be selected.

In the case of verbal mood, most of the detailed, theoretically precise research has focused on complement clauses, presumably because we have good (which is not to say perfect) theories of the semantics of many of the types of predicates which select indicative or subjunctive clauses. For example, Hintikka (1961) developed the possible worlds analysis of the semantics of belief statements which is now standard in formal semantics, namely the idea that x *believes* p is true in a world w iff p is true in all of x's belief worlds in w. (See Section 2 for further discussion; x's belief worlds in w are the ones in which all of x's beliefs in w are true.) Theories of verb mood have tried to explain, in terms of this analysis, the mood selection of the verb which expresses belief in a particular language, for example why the complement of *believe* is subjunctive in Italian, (1), or why it is indicative in Spanish, (2).

(1) Gianni crede che Maria sia partita.
    Gianni believe.indic that Maria be.subj left
    'Gianni believes that Maria left.'

(2) Juan cree que María se fue.
    Juan believe.indic that María cl go.indic
    'Juan believes that María left.'

(Note that I will generally only gloss the root and mood of verb forms, since mood is what we're focusing on.) In this paper, we will focus mainly on theories of verbal mood in complement clauses, since this is where the relevant empirical and theoretical issues have been articulated most clearly (Section 2). In Section 3, we will examine ideas about verbal mood in other contexts, in particular root clauses (Section 3.1), relative clauses (Section 3.2), and adjunct clauses (Section 3.3). Finally, Section 4 provides brief conclusions.

2 Verbal mood in complement clauses

We begin this section by outlining some aspects of the distribution of subjunctive and indicative mood in complement clauses. (There are many other details which could be enumerated, but we focus on some of the most important patterns here.) Across languages, clauses selected by desiderative, directive, and modal predicates have a strong tendency to appear in the subjunctive:

(3) Spero   che   sia   felice. (Italian, Portner 1999)
    hope.indic that be.subj   happy
    'I hope that he is happy.'

(4) Il a   ordonné que je parte. (French, Farkas 1992)
    he have.indic ordered that I   depart.subj
    'He ordered me to leave.'

(5) E   posibil   să   fi   venit Ana. (Romanian, Farkas 1992)
    be.indic possible subj past come   Ana
    'It is possible Ana came.'

These tendencies are not without exception, though; for example, in French one desiderative (*espérer*, 'hope') selects the indicative:

(6) Jean espère   toujours que   Marie va   venir.
    Jean hope.indic   always   that Marie go.indic   come-inf
                                                 (French, Schlenker 2003)
    'Jean always hopes that Marie will come.'

There is greater variation in mood selection in other complement clauses. The verb of mental judgment 'believe' selects the subjunctive in Italian, but indicative in many other languages, including Romanian:

(7) Gianni crede   che   Maria sia   partita. (Italian, Portner 1999)
    Gianni believe.indic that Maria be.subj depart
    'Gianni believes that Maria will leave.'

(8) Maria crede   că   Ion i-a   scris.
    Maria believe.indic that Ion cl-have.indic written
                                                 (Romanian, Farkas 2003)

Emotive factives favor subjunctive in some languages (e.g., French) and indicative in others (e.g., Romanian):

(9) Marie   regrette   que   Paul   soit   parti. (French, Farkas 1992)
    Marie   regret.indic   that   Paul   be.subj   left
    'Marie regrets that Paul left.'

(10) Ion   e   trist   că   Maria   e   bolnavă.
     Ion   be.indic   sad   that   Maria   is.indic   sick
                                                       (Romanian, Farkas 2003)
     'Ion is sad that Maria is sick.'

Other types of predicates, including fiction verbs (e.g., 'dream'), assertion verbs (e.g., 'say'), factives (other than emotive factives, e.g. 'know'), and commissives (e.g., 'promise'), generally favor the indicative across languages:

(11) L'Anna   ha   somiat   que   els   pengüins   volaven.
     the-Anna   have.indic   dreamt   that   the   penguins   fly.indic
                                                                (Catalan, Quer 2001)
     'Anna dreamt that penguins fly.'

(12) L'Anna   diu   que   els   pengüins   volaven.
     the-Anna   say.indic   that   the   penguins   fly.indic
                                                     (Catalan, Quer 2001)
     'Anna says that penguins fly.'

(13) Maria   ştie   că   Ion   i-a   scris.
     Maria   know.indic   that   Ion   cl-has.indic   written
                                                      (Romanian, Farkas 2003)
     'Maria knows that Ion has written.'

(14) Il   promet   qu'il   partira. (French, Farkas 1992)
     he   promise.indic   that-he   leave.indic(fut)
     'He promises that he will leave.'

Some languages, for example German, may use a subjunctive form in a complement clause when the clause reports someone else's speech. This use occurs readily with assertion verbs, but is not limited to them (data from Fabricius-Hansen & Saebø 2004: 213).

(15) Er   behauptete, dass jemand   das Auto angefahren habe.
      he   claim.indic that somebody   the car   on-driven   have.subj
      'He claimed that somebody had driven into the car,...'

Clauses which serve as the complement of a predicate which typically selects the indicative may switch to the subjunctive under certain circumstances, for example when the matrix clause is negated or questioned, or when the complement clause is portrayed as being less certain (in some sense which remains to be better understood) than one would normally infer. See Farkas (1985, 1992) and Portner (1997, 1999) for discussion.

A traditional view of the semantics of verbal mood is expressed concisely and clearly by Jespersen (1924: 813): "It is much more correct to say that they express certain attitudes of the mind of the speaker towards the contents of the sentence, though in some cases the choice of a mood is determined not by the attitude of the actual speaker, but by the character of the clause itself and its relation to the main nexus on which it is dependent." Farkas (1985, 1992) discusses a number of earlier approaches to mood selection, including the analyses of Bolinger (1968), Hooper (1975), and James (1986). Her overview of this work shows the need for a precise, rigorous analysis within a linguistically oriented semantic theory. Subsequently, mainstream work on verbal mood within semantics has been based on the idea that mood selection is to be understood in terms of the same ideas as are used to analyze modal expressions, such as modal verbs and auxiliaries. I will label this line of research the MODAL APPROACH.

The modal approach hypothesizes that mood serves as an indication that the clause is in a particular kind of modal environment. The simplest version of this idea would be that one mood (it would be the subjunctive) occurs when the clause is in the local scope of a modal operator of any kind. It would be fairly accurate to say that such a mood (if it existed) serves to mark a clause as being irrealis, that is as being a clause whose truth or falsity is relevant at a world which need not be the actual world. (The idea that the subjunctive marks irrealis in this broad sense is not correct, as shown by the data in (6)–(14), but it serves to illustrate the modal perspective.) The modal approach obviously has a direct connection to the definition of mood given in Section 1.

While the bulk of semantic research on mood selection has followed the modal approach, certain other ideas have been discussed as well. The most important of these is the claim that verbal mood is to be understood in terms of ideas drawn from nominal semantics, what I will label the INDEFINITE APPROACH. The indefinite approach aims to explain mood distinctions in terms drawn from the theory of noun phrase semantics. This view claims that subjunctives are analogous to indefinite noun phrases, in particular to special indefinites such as *any N* in English. Given that *any* occurs in both negative polarity and free choice contexts (article 3 [Semantics: Sentence and Information Structure] (Giannakidou) *Polarity items*), the indefinite approach will claim that the distribution of the subjunctive is to be explained in the same terms as explains the distribution of negative polarity or free choice *any*. Of course, we have defined verbal mood in a way which links it to the presence of modal meaning in the context, and so the indefinite approach will take the stance that the distribution of both the relevant indefinites and mood is somehow related to modality. Besides the modal and indefinite approaches, some scholars have aimed to explain certain properties of verbal mood in terms of the temporal properties of indicative and subjunctive clauses. I will refer to this line of research as the TEMPORAL APPROACH.

In what follows, we'll discuss all three of these approaches. The modal approach will be covered in two subsections: In 2.1, we'll focus on the most well-known analyses on these lines, the one initially given by Farkas (1985) and later developments of it by her and others. Then, in Section 2.2, we'll consider other modal approaches. In 2.3, we will briefly cover the indefinite and temporal approaches.

Before moving onto these major semantic analyses of mood, it may be helpful to mention other significant work which does not fit readily into the groups mentioned above. Most closely related to the above, we have other work in formal semantics, some of which focuses on particular uses of mood. In this category is the research on the reportative subjunctive (Fabricius-Hansen & Saebø 2004), ideas about mood in centering theory (Bittner 2009), the connection between mood and control (Roussou 2009), and work which links verbal mood to sentence type (Han 1998, Lohnstein & Bredel 2004). There also is a rich history of research on verbal mood in descriptive and functional linguistics (e.g., Halliday 1970, Terrell & Hooper 1974, Lyons 1977, Palmer 1990, 2001, Lunn 1995), and some work in cognitive linguistics (e.g., Travis 2003). Of course there is much other research which discusses mood, but these focus primarily on one of the senses other than verbal mood mentioned in Section 1. For anyone who aims to be an expert in the semantics of mood, it is important to study all of these sources.

2.1 The modal approach of Farkas and colleagues

In order to understand the modal approach to verbal mood, it is necessary to have some background knowledge of two topics: the semantics of modality and the theory of pragmatic presupposition and assertion. I will begin this section by making a few remarks about these two, although readers who would like more detailed discussion should look elsewhere (article 14 [this volume] (Hacquard) *Modality*, article 14 [Semantics: Interfaces] (Beaver & Geurts) *Presupposition*). Modal theories of mood assume an approach to modality based on possible worlds. Modal operators are treated as quantifiers over possible worlds, and in the most basic such theories based on modal logic, there are two types of quantifiers: a universal modal quantifier □ and an existential modal quantifier ◇.

(16) a. For any world w, $[[□S]]^w = 1$ iff $[[S]]^{w'}=1$, for every possible world w' accessible from w.
b. For any world w, $[[◇S]]^w = 1$ iff $[[S]]^{w'}=1$, for some possible world w' accessible from w.

The □ can represent any strong modal in natural language (e.g., *necessary, must, ought*), with the differences among them having to do with which worlds are accessible. For example, if all logically possible worlds are accessible from w, the modal is interpreted as expressing logical necessity, whereas if the accessible worlds are those in which all the laws of w are upheld, the modal is interpreted as expressing a particular type of deontic necessity. This distinction can be made explicit using an ACCESSIBILITY RELATION.

(17) For any world w, $[[□S]]^w = 1$ iff $[[S]]^{w'}=1$, for every possible world w' such that R(w,w').

If R encodes a relation based on knowledge (it is an epistemic accessibility relation), we end up with an epistemic modal, while if it has to do with rules (it is a deontic accessibility relation), we end up with a deontic modal. Similar distinctions can be made among weak modals like *possible, might,* and *can*, modeled in terms of ◇. See Portner (2009) and Hacquard (article 14 [this volume] (Hacquard) *Modality*) for further details. In more sophisticated theories of modality, provision is made for a wider range of types of modals, not just □ and ◇; such theories will be introduced where they become relevant to the analysis of mood (Section 2.2 below).

The semantics of sentence-embedding verbs can, in many cases at least, be understood in terms of this theory of modality. For example, *believe* and *hope* can be understood like this (Hintikka 1961):

(18) a. $[[$ a believes that S $]]^w = 1$ iff $[[S]]^{w'}=1$, for every world w' in which everything that $[[$ a $]]$ believes in w is true.
b. $[[$ a hopes that S $]]^w = 1$ iff $[[S]]^{w'}=1$, for every world w' in which everything that $[[$ a $]]$ hopes for in w is true.

Comparing (18a) to (17), we note that *a believes that* can be seen as a kind of □, where accessibility is defined in terms of the subjects beliefs. That is, (18a) can fit into the mold of (17), if we allow for R to be the relation which holds between two worlds w and w' iff everything which the referent of the subject believes in w is true in w'. In this case we call R a doxastic accessibility relation, and might write it as DOX_a. Similar remarks hold for (18b), where the relevant accessibility relation would be called bouletic (perhaps represented BUL_a).

Modal theories of mood frequently also assume an understanding of the nature of discourse based on Stalnaker's analysis of assertion and presupposition (Stalnaker 1974, 1978). This analysis is also based on possible worlds, with the key constructs being the COMMON GROUND, a set of propositions mutually presupposed by the participants in a conversation, and the CONTEXT SET, the intersection of the common ground, representing the worlds which could be actual, as far as this mutually presupposed information goes. According to this model, assertion can be understood as a speaker's proposing of a new proposition for inclusion in the common ground, and an assertion is successful if it actually is added to the common ground. We represent successful assertion via the "+" operator, as follows:

(19) a. For any common ground CG, CG+S = CG∪{[[S]]}.
      b. For any context set C, C+S=C∩[[S]].

(In (16) we used truth conditions relative to a possible world, but in (19) we require a proposition. The proposition expressed by a sentence, [[S]], can be defined for present purposes as {w : [[S]]^w=1}.) Since the context set is the intersection of the common ground, (19b) is merely a corollary of (19a), not a separate principle.

The key idea of the approach to mood developed by Farkas (1992, 2003), Giannakidou (1997, 1999, 2009), and Quer (1998, 2001) is that there is an analogy between those verbs which embed indicatives, on the one hand, and the root-level function of assertion, on the other. The various proposals within this tradition attempt to make the analogy between indicative-selecting verbs and assertion precise in different ways. Farkas (1992) claims that indicative-embedding predicates introduce a single world in which their complement is true, while subjunctives introduce a set of worlds (or futures of a world). This perspective intuitively connects indicative embedding verbs to root-level assertion, since when we assert something, we are interested in its truth in a single world, the real world. However, the approach of Farkas (1992) cannot work for the simple reason that we cannot reduce indicative-embedding verbs to introducing a single world; one's beliefs can never identify a single world, but rather can only pick out a set of worlds, a fact accurately represented in the modal semantics (18).

Giannakidou develops Farkas's ideas using the concept of an INDIVIDUAL MODEL, essentially an accessibility relation. For example, one individual model is $M_{DOX}(a)$, the set of worlds accessible from the actual world via DOX_a. Another individual model M_E(speaker), which picks out the set of worlds compatible with the speaker's actual knowledge. A special class of individual models are the epistemic models; these are the belief models, knowledge models, dream models (the set of worlds in which a's dreams come true), and models of a reported conversation. Giannakidou then classifies grammatical contexts in which a clause can appear, such as the complement of a sentence-embedding verb, in terms of the property of VERIDICALITY: A context is veridical if it entails the truth of a clause in that position in some epistemic model. For example, the complement clause in (20a) is veridical, because the sentence entails that the truth of *it's raining* throughout M_{DOX}(Mary). In contrast, (20b) does not entail the truth of *it's raining* throughout M_{DOX}(Mary).

(20) a. Mary believes that it's raining.
 b. Mary hopes that it's raining.

Mood selection is explained in terms of veridicality: veridical contexts select indicative, and non-veridical ones, subjunctive.

Giannakidou's proposal suffers from a number of technical problems. For example, individual models are defined as always being a subset of the context set, but this is clearly impossible for many sentence-embedding verbs (e.g., what you believe, dream, or want is not presupposed to be true). There is also a nagging empirical problem, namely the fact that Greek subjunctive clauses are used under perception, aspectual, and implicative verbs; she suggests that these are not truly subjunctive clauses, despite their outward appearance as such. A more fundamental issue is the fact that it is not made explicit how veridicality is assessed in particular cases. Nothing explains why the only epistemic models are belief models, knowledge models, dream models, and reported conversation models. Moreover, nothing explains why $M_{DOX}(a)$ is the relevant individual model when assessing the veridicality of *believe* and *hope*, or how to determine which individual model we should consider with other sentence-embedding predicates.

Although Giannakidou does not predict in an explicit way the relevance of particular individual models to the determination of veridicality with particular predicates, she does provide reasons for her choices. With *believe*, the individual model is simply the accessibility relation used in the semantics of the verb, and a similar reason is appealed to with *dream* and *say*. With regard to desire verbs, however, the individual model should not be simply a buletic accessibility relation, since if it were, the complement clause would indeed be true throughout that model, and only the stipulation that buletic models don't count for veridicality would save the analysis from wrongly predicting the indicative. Giannakidou motivates the choice of a doxastic model as relevant for desire verbs by citing the work of Stalnaker (1974), Asher (1987), and Heim (1992). All of these authors have pursued the idea desire verbs are essentially COMPARATIVE: the semantics of *want* and *hope* involve an ability to compare worlds, making a judgment that some are preferable to others. More precisely, on Heim's analysis, (20b) is true iff, among the worlds in M_{DOX}(Mary), Mary prefers worlds in which it's raining to otherwise similar worlds in which it's not. In terms of Giannakidou's theory, this way of thinking about *hope* suggests that the right individual model to consider when judging veridicality is M_{DOX}(a), and hence motivates the decision to classify it as nonveridical. As we will see, many other scholars agree with the essence of this diagnosis of why subjunctive mood is selected by desire verbs. What's missing in Giannakidou's analysis, however, is a systematic way of linking the lexical semantics of a predicate to the determination of veridicality.

Quer (2001) develops the ideas of Farkas and Giannakidou in a slightly different direction. His key idea is that the subjunctive is triggered by a MODEL SHIFT. According to his view, the default, initial individual model is M_E(speaker), the model used for interpreting a root assertion. If we embed a sentence under *believe*, it uses the model M_{DOX}(a), for example in (20a) the individual model representing Mary's beliefs. (He actually says that a sentence embedded under *believe* uses M_E(a), but this would imply that belief entails knowledge.) The two models M_E(speaker) and M_{DOX}(a) are alike, in some respect, and the "shift" from one to the other does not trigger the subjunctive. In contrast, with (20b) the shift is from M_E(speaker) to a buletic model M_{BUL}(a). These latter two models are different enough that the subjunctive is triggered.

Under Quer's approach, models should be classified into similarity groups, so that shifts from one group to another can trigger mood choice. Just looking at the data, one concludes that one such group must include the individual models of epistemic, doxastic, fiction, and assertion elements, while the other must include those of desiderative, directive, and modal elements. The question is whether we can say precisely in what way the members of these groups are similar. (Actually, we just need to find a way to say that the members of one group are similar, since we might define the other group as the complement of the similarity group.) Quer suggests that the members of the desiderative-directive-modal group are similar because they have to do with comparison among worlds, as discussed above. Applied to *hope* in (20b), this amounts to "worlds where it's raining are preferable, according to Mary, to otherwise similar worlds in which it is not." Unfortunately, this idea about the semantics of desire predicates is not integrated into Quer's analysis, and indeed it cannot be so long as the analysis relies on the notion of an individual model to represent the semantic properties relevant to mood selection. The problem with individual models is that they are just sets of worlds (or perhaps accessibility relations); as such, they do not have enough structure to represent comparative information about the worlds they pick out. In Section 2.2, we will examine other modal approaches which more fully integrate the comparativity idea into the semantics of mood.

Farkas (2003) further develops the idea that there is something similar about the complement of an indicative-embedding verb and a root assertion. Whereas Giannakidou and Quer represent this in terms of a connection between M_E (speaker) and the individual model introduced by a verb like *believe*, Farkas fully utilizes Stalnaker's theory of assertion. Simplifying Farkas's definitions somewhat, let us assume that a discourse context c may have, as one part, a context set, W(c). According to Stalnaker's view outlined above, then, assertion of S in c involves a proposal to change W(c) to W(c)∩[[S]]. We define a context change as assertive in the following way:

(21) A context change is ASSERTIVE in c iff c+p = c', where c' is just like c except that W(c') = W(c)∩[[S]].

Clearly, assertion is assertive in a discourse context. The idea of Farkas's analysis is that sentence-embedding verbs are associated with contexts as well, what we may call DERIVED CONTEXTS (Stalnaker 1988, Heim 1992), and indicative is selected for a subordinate clause when that clause is related to a derived context in a way which is similar, in relevant respects, to how a root assertion is related to the discourse context. Thus, contexts play the role of individual models in the theories discussed above.

The way in which Farkas explains the workings of derived contexts is a bit complicated, but we can simplify it in a way which expresses the key ideas. The derived context for *believe* is very similar to the individual model $M_{DOX}(a)$, the only difference being that it is indexed to a world, so that the derived context is the set of worlds compatible with the subject's beliefs in a given world w. We may write this $M_{DOX}(a,w)$. The meaning of (20a) involves the assertive update $M_{DOX}(a,w)$+ [[it is raining]]. Things become more complex as we attempt to give the precise meaning for (20a) in a way which treats the whole sentence as asserting in the discourse context. Something like (22) is what's wanted; see Heim (1991) and Farkas (2003) for discussion.

(22) c+(20a) = c', where c' is just like c except that W(c') = W(c)∩{w : $M_{DOX}(a,w)$+ [[it is raining]] = $M_{DOX}(a,w)$}.

Assuming that the context change indicated by "+" in (22) is assertive, the condition $M_{DOX}(a,w)+[[$ it is raining $]] = M_{DOX}(a,w)$ will only hold if $M_{DOX}(a,w) \subseteq$ [[it is raining]], so that (22) implements the semantics of *believe* given in (18a). However, by stating it in terms of an assertive context change, Farkas is able to explain in what way the role of *it is raining* in (20a) is similar to a root assertion.

With *hope*, Farkas claims that the complement clause does not relate to its derived context via an assertive update. Instead, it is comparative, or to use Farkas's terminology, evaluative. Unfortunately, Farkas does not define the semantics of this type of predicate in a way which makes precise how comparativity/evaluativity is to work. However, she cites Heim (1992) in a way which suggests that she thinks Heim's semantics for desire predicates would serve the needs of her analysis. This expectation is questionable, however, as Heim's analysis does not make use of a non-assertive update, but rather embeds an assertive update within a more complex statement comparing sets of worlds. We will return to the question of how one might incorporate comparativity into the semantics of the subjunctive in Section 2.2.

One nice feature of Farkas's analysis is that it helps explain why emotive factives select subjunctive in some languages, and indicatives in another. For example, (23) is comparative, in that worlds in which it is raining are ranked as worse than ones in which it is not. Farkas describes this by saying that *be sad* is non-assertive, like *hope*; this explains why a language might choose subjunctive for the complement clause.

(23) Mary is sad that it is raining.

On the other hand, because *be sad* is factive, it shares something with *believe*. Farkas describes this by saying that the complement is DECIDED in its output context. It is not clear to me whether being decided has to do with the complement's status in the discourse context (i.e., presupposed) or in a derived context. If the definition can be worked out, the idea is that *be sad* can select the indicative in some languages because its complement is decided.

To summarize the findings of this section, the approach to mood which began with Farkas's seminal work has developed a set of core ideas in more and more refined ways over the years. It still faces challenges in explaining how the semantics of desire predicates (and that of others like them, such as directives) affects mood choice, but the key idea that they are somehow about evaluating or comparing alternative possible futures is highly appealing. This approach has had important offshoots in the literature, for example Beghelli's (1998) work on the relationship between mood and the interpretation of indefinites. In Section 2.2, we turn to a number of proposals which have much in common with the approach discussed above, but which use somewhat different tools to analyze the semantic basis of mood choice.

2.2 Other modal approaches

A number of semanticists working broadly within the modal approach to mood selection have developed analyses based on different ideas about the semantics of subjunctive-selecting verbs from the one assumed by the approach of Section 2.1: (i) Portner (1997) attempts to explain what is distinct about these predicates using situation semantics; (ii) Giorgi & Piansi (1997) build on the ordering semantics for modals developed by Kratzer (1977, 1981); (iii) Villalta (2008) similarly employs ordering, but mixes it with ideas from the theory of focus; and finally (iv) von Stechow (2004) and Schlenker (2003, 2005) sketch some ideas about mood based on the theory of logophoricity and indexicality (see article 17 [this volume] (Schlenker) *Indexicality and de se*). In what follows, I will briefly examine each of these approaches.

Portner (1997) discusses notional mood in English and the subjunctive-indicative contrast in Italian. The analysis of Italian is simpler and more relevant, so we will focus on it. (Recently, Matthewson 2010 develops Portner's approach in an interesting analysis of mood in St'át'imcets.) The essential idea is that there are semantic mechanisms in place which allow a mood morpheme to identify the modal accessibility relation and modal force with respect to which its clause is interpreted, and to place restrictions on them. In this respect, it instantiates the core idea of the modal approach more directly than the theories discussed in Section 2.1. For example, (24a) is analyzed as follows (based on Portner 1997, (68)):

(24) a. Riteneva   che in quella zona fosse   facile ritrovare qualche
       thought.indic that in this   area be.subj easy to-find a
       rivoltella.
       revolver
       'He thought that in this area it was easy to find a revolver.'
   b. {s: Ritenere$_{He}$(s) ⊆ [[subj(in quella zona essere facile ritrovare qualche rivoltella)]]^{s,NEC,RitenereHe}}

The semantic analysis in (24b) instantiates the modal approach to attitude verbs presented above: it essentially says that (24a) is true (in s) iff, in every world accessible via the doxastic accessibility relation Ritenere$_{He}$, it was easy to find a revolver. However, note that the accessibility relation has the status of a parameter of interpretation for the embedded clause (i.e., the semantic value function

[[ ]] depends on it). Portner calls it a MODAL CONTEXT. The presence of the modal context as a parameter allows the subjunctive morpheme to "check" whether that accessibility relation has the right properties for a subjunctive clause.

According to Portner (1997), the Italian subjunctive is the default mood, chosen whenever the indicative is not licensed. The indicative is licensed whenever the modal context (accessibility relation) is PROTOTYPICALLY FACTIVE:

(25) A modal context R is prototypically factive iff, for typical situations in the domain of R, $w_s \in R(s)$.

The modal context for *know* is prototypically factive, since it is strictly factive: if s is a situation in which I know a proposition, that proposition is true in the world of s. In contrast, the modal context introduced by *think* (i.e., *ritenere* in (24)) is not treated as prototypically factive, since we frequently think things that are not true. A verb of assertion like *say* is, however, treated as prototypically factive; in typical situations, we take what people say to be true (although in many situations, we do not).

This way of explaining each verb class reveals another important aspect of Portner's analysis: he does not attempt to provide semantic criteria which apply directly to every case of mood selection. Rather, he proposes that the semantic system provides guidelines for each category, and allows for some arbitrariness in how particular mood-selecting predicates are aligned with them. Thus, on this view, the fact that the Romanian correlate of *believe* selects indicative while the Italian version selects subjunctive reveals not a difference in the semantics per se, but rather only a difference in whether the strictly non-factive predicate is classified as prototypically factive or not - either choice makes sense. Portner makes an analogy to semantically based gender (noun class) systems, the idea being that certain such systems have a semantic basis, but this basis only underlies an actual pattern which contains a fair amount of arbitrariness and idiosyncrasy.

The analysis in terms of (stereotypical) factivity has obvious difficulties with emotive factives: since these are literally factive, they should always take indicative. Portner's proposal about the subjunctive arguments of emotive factives is that they are not actually interpreted as propositional arguments at all. Rather, they pick out events (modeled as a variety of situation); as a result, there is no modal context, and the indicative would not be licensed.

Portner's theory also allows for an explanation of the mood switch under negation. Recall that the complement of a verb which typically embeds the indicative will often be subjunctive when the matrix is negated. According to the analysis, this is because the negation combines with the modal operator in the matrix.

In (24), we see that a non-negated matrix verb has a modal force of necessity (that is, it is a universal quantifier); however, when such a verb is negated, as in (26) (Portner's (72)), the negation and necessity combine as in (25a), to yield a force of non-necessity, Neg-NEC, corresponding to absence of a subset relation. The resulting meaning is (26b):

(26) a. Non   sapevo   nemmeno   che   si   fosse   sposata.
       not   knew.indic   not even that   refl   was.subj   married
       'I didn't even know that she was married.'
   b. {s: Know$_i$(s) $\not\subseteq$ [[subj(si essere sposata)]]$^{s,\text{Neg-NEC,KnowI}}$}

In order to explain mood selection, the proposal is that the indicative presupposes not just a stereotypically factive modal context, but also a modal force of necessity. The force Neg-NEC therefore triggers subjunctive.

Portner (1997) also makes an attempt to explain the interpretation of mood in root contexts. The ordinary mood of root declaratives clauses is indicative, but as we will see in more detail in Section 3.1, subjunctive is sometimes possible, and gives rise to non-assertive meanings. To explain the fact that assertive clauses use indicative, Portner proposes that such clauses contain an assertion operator with the right properties to trigger indicative. He also discusses the use of indicative in contexts like the following (his (95); such data were originally pointed out by Farkas):

(27) I had a dream last night. My friend came to visit me.

The second sentence of (27) is indicative, even though it does not produce a root level assertion. Portner explains this fact by proposing that the modal context introduced by *dream* can persist in the discourse, and can be used in place of the assertion operator to interpret subsequent sentences. In this way, the modal context introduced by *dream* is like the root-level context of assertion, and triggers indicative. Though the paper does not discuss root subjunctives in Italian in any detail, the status of relevant examples in English is discussed. The idea is that root non-indicatives occur when a modal context of the kind which triggers non-indicative (e.g., one which is not stereotypically factive) is present in the context.

Giorgi & Pinesi (1997) develop a modal account of mood selection which makes an important contribution to our understanding of comparativity. Their analysis is based on Kratzer's (1977, 1981) theory of modality. Kratzer's work differs from simpler possible worlds theories of modality, based on modal logic, in that it makes use of two parameters of interpretation, the MODAL BASE and ORDERING

SOURCE. While one should look elsewhere for detailed discussion of Kratzer's theory (article 14 [this volume] (Hacquard) *Modality*, Portner 2009), some points are essential to understanding Giorgi & Pianesi's analysis. The modal base and ordering source together do the job of which, in simpler theories, is done by the accessibility relation. The modal base can be thought of as identifying the set of worlds relevant to the interpretation of a modal, while the ordering source ranks the relevant worlds as to how well they fit with some criterion. With a deontic modal like (28), for example, the modal base is circumstantial (a set of relevant facts), and the ordering source deontic (a set of relevant rules).

(28) That dog must stay outside.

Simplifying somewhat, the modal operator *must* says that in all of the worlds relevant (according to the modal base) which are best-ranked (according to the ordering), the dog stays outside. For example, the modal base might contain the information that the dog is large, and the ordering source the rule that large dogs do not come inside. In such a context, the best-ranked relevant worlds are all ones in which the dog stays out.

Giorgi & Pianesi's theory connects to comparativity because it is the role of the ordering source to compare worlds. For example, the deontic ordering source compares worlds in terms of how acceptable they are, according to the rules. Thus, when they say subjunctive-selecting predicates in French and Romanian make use of a non-null ordering source, they are in essence saying that comparativity is the reason these predicates trigger subjunctive. Though they do not give a detailed analysis, one can surmise that they hold the following hypotheses: (i) *believe* has a doxastic modal base and a null ordering source; (ii) *say* has an "assertive" modal base and a null ordering source; and (iii) *want* has a doxastic modal base and a buletic ordering source. Note that, if their assumptions about the modal character of each predicate hold, it is predicted that French and Romanian use subjunctive with *want*, and not with *believe* or *say*. This analysis seems not to be consistent with what they say about emotive factives, however. Emotive factives are assumed to have a non-null ordering source (giving the "emotive" meaning), and are correctly predicted to select the subjunctive in French. However, they take the indicative in Romanian. Giorgi & Pianesi appeal to factivity to explain this difference, but it is not clear how the factivity criterion interacts with the ordering source criterion.

In order to account for Italian (as well as several other languages, investigated in less depth), Giorgi & Pianesi propose that another factor, besides whether the ordering source is null, can be relevant. Specifically, they refer to the relationship between the modal base and the common ground. The doxastic modal base associated with *believe* might, according to Giorgi & Pianesi, have a null intersection with the common ground. In other words, one's beliefs might all be false. In this respect, the doxastic modal base is different from the common ground, and this fact results in Italian 'believe' choosing the subjunctive. As pointed out by Portner (1999), however, this fact is difficult to reconcile with the choice of indicative under verbs of assertion, since it seems easier to never say anything true than to never believe anything true. Giogi & Piansi also have an interesting discussion of imagination verbs like *dream*. Such verbs have a null ordering source, and moreover the modal base may persist in discourse, as observed above. Thus, it is like the common ground and triggers indicative.

Overall, Giorgi & Pianesi's theory brings up a range of semantic and pragmatic factors which are plausibly related to mood selection. However, each factor is appealed to only when needed, and it is not clear in the end what form the analysis is meant to take. It could be that the selection properties of each sentence-embedding predicate (or class of predicates) is decided independently, based on any one of the potentially relevant factors; or it could be that a single analysis is meant to apply across a given language to all predicates. However, if the latter is the case, it is not clear how the effects of the various relevant factors are to be assembled into a mood-selection prediction for each predicate.

Villalta (2000, 2006, 2008) also focuses on comparativity as a crucial factor in mood selection. Her analysis makes use of a mechanism like the ordering source to rank worlds, but rather than simply applying the ordering source mechanism of Kratzer (as Giorgi & Pianesi do), she proposes an analysis of subjunctive-selecting predicates in Spanish based on focus semantics.

Consider the following example (from Villalta 2008, (52)):

(29)   Marcela wants to go to the picnic.

On the kind of account suggested by Giorgi & Pianesi, this sentence is true if, in every world compatible with Marcela beliefs which is "best" from the point of view of her desires, she goes to the picnic. Villalta points out that this analysis has a problematical consequence in a context where Marcela believes that she can only go to the picnic if she works extra hours. In such a context, (29) should entail (30):

(30)   Marcela wants to work extra hours.

However, intuitively (29) may be in such a context, but (30) false.

According to Villalta, the solution to this problem is to give a semantics for *want* which is sensitive to contextual alternatives. Suppose that Marcela's alternative to going to the picnic is going to church. In that case, (29) says roughly that for every world in which she goes to church, there is a more desirable world in which she goes to the picnic, and not vice versa. (It also presupposes that both going to the picnic and going to church are compatible with her beliefs.) Likewise, suppose that the alternative to working extra hours is only working the required number of hours; in that case, (30) says that for every world in which she works the required number of hours, there is a more desirable world in which she works extra hours (and not vice versa). Assuming that the very best worlds are ones in which she works only the required number of hours and yet goes to the picnic, (29) will be true and (30) false.

Given this semantic analysis, it is essential to limit what can be a contextual alternative, since otherwise almost every plausible sentence with *want* would come out false, due to the availability of a better alternative. For example, the picnic may be nice, but an all-expense-paid weekend stay at the best hotel in Paris would be better. Villalta attempts to limit what can count as a contextual alternatives relevant to *want* in one way, by requiring that each alternative be compatible with the subjects beliefs, but this won't be enough; we'd still be able to consider an alternative like "Marcela gets an expense paid weekend in Paris or has smelts for lunch", which is compatible with her beliefs (smelts are on the menu), but still contains worlds better than any picnic. Rather, the real reason this is not a relevant alternative must be that it simply not the kind of alternative which the context makes available.

Villalta motivates the use of contextual alternatives in the semantics of sentence-embedding verbs by linking them to other elements which depend on alternatives. Focus sensitive operators like *only* depend on a set of alternatives for their meaning, and these alternatives are constrained by focus (see article 10 [Semantics: Sentence and Information Structure] (Hinterwimmer) *Information structure* and Rooth 1992):

(31) Marcela only went [$_F$ to the picnic].

Example (31) says that the only thing Marcela did, out of the relevant alternatives, is go to the picnic. All of the relevant alternatives involve her going someplace, as a result of focus on the PP. Likewise, Villalta claims, *want* is focus sensitive. Indeed, she proposes that all subjunctive-selecting predicates in Spanish are focus sensitive, though one should consider the arguments carefully. For example, she proposes that the following example shows *demand* to be focus sensitive (her (81)–(82)):

(32) His father demanded that Ted MARRY Alice.

(33) His father demanded that Ted marry ALICE.

Consider a context (based on Dretske 1972) in which Ted's father's has stipulated that Ted will only receive his inheritance if he's married (but it doesn't matter who he marries). Villata's claim is that, in such a situation, (32) is true, but (33) false. However, it seems to me that both are false (though perhaps (32) is less misleading). Villalta also makes the intriguing proposal that the subjunctive is chosen when an indicative-selecting predicate is negated, because negation is also focus sensitive. However, this wrongly predicts that subjunctive is licensed even under root negation, or (as she notes) in embedded clauses under any focus sensitive operator.

One way of seeing the significance of this discussion of contextual alternatives is to notice that, in Villalta's analysis, the contextual alternatives do much of the work which is done by the modal base (or accessibility relation) in other modal analyses. That is, the alternatives do the work of carving out the space of possible worlds which are relevant. For example, with (30), one of the contextual alternatives is "work only the required number of hours". There are worlds in which she works only the required number of hours and goes to the picnic (although these worlds are not compatible with Marcela beliefs), and hence (30) is false.

Having observed this connection between the role of contextual alternatives and that of the modal base, a strategy for solving the problem posed by (29)–(30) for Giorgi & Pianesi's analysis comes into view: Villalta's argument against such an account arose from the fact that the doxastic modal base delimited the range of relevant worlds. Therefore, (29) means that the best doxastically accessible worlds are ones in which she goes to the picnic, and since these are ones in which she works extra hours, (30) is entailed. But if a wider set were relevant (specifically worlds where she goes to the picnic but doesn't work extra hours), (30) would not follow from (29). The reason contextual alternatives solve the problem in Villalta's account is that they make relevant such worlds. But alternatively, it should be possible to make such worlds relevant in the competitor theory, simply by choosing a different modal base.

Schlenker (2003, 2005) and von Stechow (2004) outline a theory of mood based on the idea that mood has a meaning similar to that of grammatical person. This work, which builds primarily on data from German, French, and English, is based on the idea that logical forms contain variables referring to possible worlds, and that mood features place restrictions on the interpretation of these variables. It should be clear how this approach makes mood analogous to person: we can think of a pronoun as simply a variable, with the first person feature, for example, restricting the reference of that variable to the speaker.

The broader research agenda of which these authors' work on mood forms a part primarily focuses on indexicals. Schlenker has done important work on expanding our understanding of the semantics of indexicals from the rather simple system of English to a wider range of languages, in particular languages with logophoric and shiftable indexicals. For example, a shiftable person marking is one whose interpretation can be tied not to the actual context of utterance (as is familiar from English, where *I* always refers to the speaker of the sentence), but rather to an individual which plays a role analogous to the speaker in an embedded clauses. Schlenker (2002) gives the following Amharic example:

(34) *ĵon   ĵəgna   nə-ññ   yɨl-all*
     John   hero   be.PF-1sO   3M.say-AUX.3M
     'John says that he is a hero.'

Note that the first person marking on the embedded verb *be* indicates reference to the referent of the matrix subject (John), not the speaker. (For arguments that this agreement is really a kind of first person, see Schlenker's work.) Schlenker's analysis of this data is that the matrix verb *say* creates a derived context with respect to which the embedded clause is interpreted, and John counts as the speaker of that context. Amharic's first person elements may refer to the speaker of the derived context, unlike those in English, which always relate to the root, i.e. utterance, context.

Given the intuition that a shiftable indexical like that in Amharic relates to a derived context in a way parallel to how an English-type indexical relates to the root context, it is clear why an extension to mood is attractive. We have seen repeatedly within the tradition of the modal approach the idea that indicative indicates that a local operator creates a context which is somehow similar to a root-level utterance context, or that that subjunctive indicates that a local operator creates a context which is somehow different from a root-level utterance context. Treating mood as placing a person-like restriction on a world variable raises the hope of making these intuitions precise within the context of a broader theory.

The version of this approach proposed by von Stechow treats the subjunctive in German as feature which requires that the world variable of an embedded clause be bound by the embedding verb. This restriction explains the meanings available to the following (his (122)):

(35) a. Ich   dachte, Ihre   Yacht sei/wäre   länger   als   sie   ist.
        I   thought your   yacht be.subj   longer   than it   be.indic.
        'I thought your yacht was longer than it is.'

     b. #Ich dachte, Ihre   Yacht sei/wäre   länger   als   sie   sei/wäre.
        I   thought your   yacht be.subj   longer   than it   be.subj.
        'I thought your yacht was longer than it is.'

These examples differ in the mood choice of the verb in the comparative clause. The English translation, 'I thought that your yacht was longer than it is', is ambiguous. The first reading, rendered with the indicative in German by (33a), means that the speaker thought that the yacht was a certain length, and that length is greater than its actual length; the second, rendered with subjunctive in (33b), means that the speaker thought something impossible of the yacht, that its length (whatever that may be) is greater than its length. According to von Stechow's analysis, the interpretation in (35b) follows because the world argument in both the complement clause and the *than* clause is bound by *thought*, so that they refer to the same world. Hence the semantics comes out as "in all worlds w' compatible with the speaker's beliefs in w, the yacht's length in w' is greater than its length in w'." In contrast, in (35a) the world variable in the *than* clause can be bound by a root level operator, and so refers to the actual world. As a result, the sentence means "in all worlds w' compatible with the speaker's beliefs in w, the yacht's length in w' is greater than its length in w." While von Stechow's analysis nicely accounts for the contrast in (35), he does not attempt to extend it to a general analysis of mood in German.

Schlenker's analysis is somewhat more ambitious. He considers a wider range of constructions in several languages, with a focus on French, though he does not develop as complete and methodical an analysis as some of the theories discussed above. Like Portner, Schlenker considers the subjunctive to be the default mood, and identifies a particular licensing condition for the indicative which reflects the intuition that it is used when the clause's semantic context is relevantly like that of a root assertion.

According to Schlenker, the indicative introduces a presupposition that the reference of a world variable is in the context set of the discourse or in the set of worlds which plays an analogous role in a derived context. He locates context sets with respect to events, via a function CS. Thus, if e* is an event of someone speaking in a conversation, CS(e*) is the context set of that conversation. Derived contexts work similarly: if e is a propositional attitude event (for example, an event of someone believing), CS(e) is the set of worlds compatible with that attitude (e.g., compatible with that person's beliefs). The function CS can apply to any relevant event, including events of saying, lamenting, and wanting. Given such a function, the presupposition of the indicative, written w{CS(e)}, indicates that world w (the world with respect to which the clause is evaluated) is in the context set associated with event e. As for the choice of event, e is not grammatically determined, but rather identified with some event available in the grammatical context.

In a simple root clause, e is identified with the speech event e* (as it's the only event around which has a context set) and w with the actual world w*. In the case of (36), this leads to the presupposition that the actual world is in the context set. The subjunctive cannot be used, because a principle of Maximize Presupposition says that presuppositions must be marked if they are met. (Examples are from Schlenker 2005.)

(36) Il pleut.
 it rains.indic
 'It's raining.'

(37) Jean pense   qu'il   pleut.
 Jean thinks   that-it rains.indic
 'Jean thinks that it's raining.'

(38) Jean espère qu'il   pleut.
 Jean hope   that-it rains.indic
 'Jean hopes that it is raining.'

If the indicative is present in the complement of *think*, as in (37), e is identified with the thinking event and w quantified over by the matrix verb; as a result, the presupposition is that every world compatible with what Jean thinks is compatible with Jean's beliefs. Finally, Schlenker considers *espérer* 'hope', which selects the indicative in French, as seen in (36). (*Vouloir* 'want' selects the subjunctive.) Here the event of the indicative presupposition is the hoping event, so the sentence presupposes that every world compatible with what Jean hopes is compatible with what he believes—in effect, that one can only hope for what one believes possible. *Hope* does have presupposition roughly of this kind, a fact also discussed by Portner (1992).

While Schlenker's theory provides an interesting way of looking at facts like those in (36)–(38), it fails to truly explain mood selection in these cases because nothing in the theory determines which event is used to generate the indicative presupposition. Note that in (37) and (38), the matrix verb's event was chosen. But in other subordinate clauses (for example, with *nier* 'deny'), the indicative presupposition can be based on the utterance event e*. If e* were chosen in (37), we'd end up with a presupposition that everything John thinks is compatible with the discourse context set, and in (38), the resulting presupposition would be that everything Jean hopes is compatible with the discourse context set. Schlenker tries to rule out the latter, saying that "In general, there need be no relation between what Jean hopes and what the speaker or addressee take for granted" (Schlenker 2005: 26), but this is the fact to be explained. Since this reading is not contradictory, the analysis predicts that it should be available when the subjunctive is present. Even more to the point, the analysis seems to predict that, if e* is chosen and the resulting presupposition is not met, subjunctive would not be ruled out by Maximize Presupposition. (It would not be out-competed by the indicative, because the indicative is not licensed on the logical form under consideration, the one based on CS(e*)). Hence, the subjunctive should be possible.

2.3 Other theories: the indefinite approach and the temporal approach

The central idea of the indefinite approach to verbal mood is that mood marks an opposition parallel to one of those marked by definiteness in the nominal domain. For example, Giannakidou (1997, 1999) argues that the subjunctive mood in Greek is licensed by the same semantic property, nonveridicality, as a large class of polarity items. Given that the special indefinite *any*, and its correlate in other languages, is a canonical polarity item (and the one which figures most prominently in her discussion), this theory draws a close connection between mood and indefiniteness.

Baker & Travis (1997) argue for an even more direct link between mood and definiteness. They consider a three-way opposition among verbal forms in Mohawk, proposing that these indicate definiteness (*wa'-*, 'factual'), indefiniteness (*v-*, 'future'), and negative polarity (*a-*, 'optative') in the description of an event. The factual morpheme, which is argued to mark definiteness, is used to give a past interpretation to root clauses, and may be used in the complements of verbs like *think* and *know*. The future morpheme, argued to indicate indefiniteness, gives future meaning in root clauses, is used in generic conditional sentences, and is found in the complement of *wish* and *promise*, and can also be used with *think* and *know*. The opatative morpheme is seen as a negative polarity version of the future.

The intuition behind Baker & Travis's analysis can be most easily seen by looking at generic conditionals (their (8), with glosses simplified):

(39) Toka v-kenvsko' akaret, v-yukhrewahte' ake-nistvha.
    if   fut-steal   cooke   fut-punish   my-mother
    'If I steal/stole a cookie, my mother will punish/punishes/would punish me.'

According to the theory, the *v-* morpheme makes each clause into an indefinite description of an event. An implicit generic operator binds an event variable, giving rise to the meaning represented in (40):

(40) $GEN_{e,x}$ [cookie(x) & steal(me, x, e)] [∃e'[M(e)=e' & punish(my-mother, me, e')]]

The function M "matches" each event e (of stealing) with another (punishing) event e'.

In simple root clauses, *v*- indicates the event occurs in the future, while *wa'*- indicates that it occurs in the past. This distinction is linked to definiteness by the idea that, from the perspective of any point in time, there is a single past but multiple futures (The Branching Time model: Dowty 1979, Kamp & Reyle 1993). As a result of this asymmetry, one can talk about the past by referring (using the indefinite *wa'*-) to a past event, but in order to talk about the future, one must quantify over the various futures, and this quantification requires the indefinite *v*-. However, despite the intuitive link between past and definiteness, and between future and indefiniteness, the theory does not motivate as strong a link between these concepts as we find in the grammar of Mohawk. On the one hand, it is not clear why *v*- cannot be used to create an indefinite description of past events. On the other, the reasoning which is meant to rule out definite reference to future events involves some unclear assumptions about the relationship between possible worlds and past or future events. In any case, one can refer to future events (*I look forward to the publication of this volume!*), so if the analysis is to be maintained, something very specific must be said about Mohawk.

In order to compare Baker & Travis's analysis to other theories of mood, we should consider how it explains the distribution of mood morphemes in complement clauses. Baker & Travis hypothesize that the definiteness or indefiniteness of a complement clause must match the semantics of the selecting predicate. The complement of *want*, for example, is claimed to require an indefinite description of an event. A definite description of an event (that is, a complement clause marked by *wa'*-) would indicate that what is wanted is a definite past event, and this is incompatible with the future-oriented lexical semantics of *want*. In contrast, *think* is compatible with either an indefinite or definite description of the complement clause's event, since one can think about past or future events. This discussion indicates that the distribution of *wa'*- and *v*- in complement clauses is explained by their temporal entailments, and as such, their proposal has a close affinity with the temporal approach to mood selection more generally. We turn to the temporal approach next.

The temporal approach has been pursued mainly in the syntax literature (Picallo 1984, 1985, Progovac 1993), but has also had some influence in semantic studies (von Stechow 1995, Giannakidou 2009). These analyses aim to explain the fact that subjunctive clauses often have a more restricted temporal interpretation than indicative clauses. For example, the complement of *want* must be interpreted as present or future relative to the time of wanting, while the complement of *know* can be past, present, or future relative to the time of knowing:

(39) a. Mary wants for it to be raining/to rain.
 b. Mary knows that it was raining/is raining/will rain.

The central idea of all of these analyses is that the subjunctive is, or is associated with, a tense morpheme which is dependent on a higher temporal operator in the sentence. For Picallo, the relationship is one of anaphora: the subjunctive clause's tense is anaphoric to a higher tense. For Progovac and von Stechow, the relationship follows from the need for the subjunctive clause's tense to delete under identity with a higher tense. For Giannakidou, the subjunctive marker introduces a time variable which must be bound by a lambda operator in the complementizer position; in the case of a complement clause, the lambda abstraction results in a property of times which serves as the argument of the higher predicate. While Giannakidou does not discuss the temporal interpretation of indicative complements in detail, they would presumably not be temporal properties, since they need to be somehow different from subjunctives; however, such a proposal would run contrary to work on the semantics of tense in such contexts (Ogihara 1996, 2007, Abusch 1997). One problem which faces all of these versions of the temporal theory is that the temporal properties which motivate the idea of a dependent tense only hold with selected subjunctives, not with those triggered by negation or in adjunct clauses, for example, a fact pointed out by Raposo (1986), Suñer & Padilla-Rivera (1987), Suñer (1986), and Quer (1998). The temporal interpretation of non-selected subjunctives is still rather poorly understood.

While the temporal approach furthers our understanding of the temporal interpretation of subjunctive clauses, it does not provide an explanation of the distribution of subjunctive and indicative forms. The reason for this is that it does not explain why the special dependent tense would be especially associated with subjunctive contexts. For example, as far as our current understanding goes, there's no reason why one cannot know a fact with the temporal properties which would result from subjunctive marking; this would be to know something which is necessarily present or future with respect to the time of the knowing. Nor is there a reason why one cannot want something with the temporal properties which would result from indicative marking; indeed, since indicative is compatible with future meaning, it should be possible to express meanings equivalent to what we get with the subjunctive. Nevertheless, though the temporal theory probably does not fare well as an independent theory of verbal mood, the works in question make an important contribution to our understanding of the temporal semantics of complement clauses. In other words, we will eventually need to combine our analysis of the contribution of indicative and subjunctive themselves with an analysis of the temporal semantics of indicative and subjunctive clauses which are selected by a higher predicate, and the works cited above provide an essential foundation for this project.

3 Verbal mood in other contexts

3.1 Root clauses

Verbal mood shows a correlation with sentence type: Both declarative and interrogative clauses are expressed using the indicative, while imperative clauses show variation. Many languages have a distinct imperative form, often classified as a mood, and we also find indicative, subjunctive, and infinitive clauses in this clause type, even in languages which have a dedicated imperative form. For example, the Italian imperative employs a distinct imperative form in ordinary second person singular imperatives, (40a), a form of the indicative in the second person plural, (40b), subjunctive in the (formally third person) polite imperative (40c), and infinitive in the negative imperative (40d) (data from Zanuttini 1997: 106–108).

(40) a. Telefona!
      call.imp.2sg
      'Call [her]!'

   b. Telefonatele   tutti   i   giorni!
      call.indic.2pl-her every   the   days
      'Call her every day!'

   c. Lo   dica   pure!
      it   say.subj.3sg   indeed
      'Go ahead and say it!'

   d. Non   telefonarele!   / Non   le   telefonare!
      neg   call-inf-her   / neg   her   call-inf
      'Don't call her!'

Forms of the imperative clause type drawn from a distinct verbal paradigm are sometimes called "true imperatives", while those identical to indicatives, subjunctives, or infinitives are called "suppletive imperatives".

Languages differ in which verbal mood is used for various kinds of suppletive imperatives. For example, Spanish uses subjunctive in the second person plural, as seen in (41) (data from Rivero 1994):

(41) a. Den-me   el   libro!
       give.subj.2pl-me the   book
       'Give me the book!'

    b. Que me   den   el   libro!
       that me   give.subj.2pl   the book
       'Give me the book!'

The data above illustrate the fact that suppletive imperatives often show special syntactic properties. For example, the indicative in (40b) has the clitic *le* following the verb, rather than preceding it as would be the case in a declarative, and the infinitive in (40d) allows either verb-clitic or clitic-verb order, although only the former is possible in other contexts. Example (41b) illustrates the possibility of using an overt complementizer with a suppletive imperative. It is likely that certain suppletive imperatives contain non-overt structure which is relevant to the semantics; for example, Kayne (1992) argues that the infinitive form illustrated in (40d) is embedded under a null element, and that the clitic-verb order, when it occurs, is the result of clitic-climbing onto the null element. See Rivero (1994), Zanuttini (1997) and Han (1998) for discussion.

This is not the place to explore the syntax and semantics of imperatives in any detail (for discussion, see article 6 [Semantics: Sentence and Information Structure] (Han) *Imperatives*). However, there is an issue for the semantics of mood which should be addressed. The widespread use of subjunctives and infinitives for imperative (or at least imperative-like) meaning has led many researchers to assume that subjunctives have a special affinity for directive interpretations. For this reason, they have sought to connect the directive semantics of imperatives to the analysis of the semantics of subjunctives in the theory of verbal mood; see, for example, Portner (1997), Han (1998), and Schlenker (2005). The general idea is that the directive meaning of imperatives is a subcase of the range of meaning compatible with subjunctives generally, so that it is natural for subjunctive form to be recruited for imperatives. However, while this way of looking at the situation leads us to expect that a root subjunctive can be used with an imperative-like communicative meaning, it does not capture the intuition that suppletive imperatives really are imperatives. And although other uses of root subjunctive are possible, for example to express supposition and astonishment, as in (42), it does not explain why these are less common (Italian data from Moretti & Orvieto 1981, cited in Portner 1997):

(42) a. L'avesse   anche   detto lui. (de Lampedusa, *Il gattopardo*)
        it-have.subj   also   said   he
        'Suppose he had said it too.'

b. Che   sia   nel   bagno? (Cassola, *Una relazione*)
   that   be.subj   in-the   bath
   'She's in the bath?!'

From a broader perspective, the main puzzle posed by root contexts for the theory of verbal mood is why root indicatives (especially declaratives) are very flexible in their discourse function, while imperatives and root subjunctives are more restricted. Truckenbrodt (2006) has pointed out that root declaratives can be easily used to assert, to ask a question, and to impose a requirement, thus covering the range of functions associated with interrogatives and imperatives (data from Truckenbrodt 2006: 259).

(43) a. It is raining.
     b. Is it raining?
     c. You will go home now.

In contrast, root imperatives cannot have such a range of meaning, and can only achieve the perlocutionary effects of assertion and asking by very indirect means, as seen in (42).

(44) a. Believe me when I say that it is raining.
     b. Please tell me whether it is raining (because I want to know).

The same may be said for root subjunctives—as illustrated in this section, their range of functions in root clauses is quite restricted. In order to explain the interpretation of verbal moods in root clauses, the theory of mood must be linked with the theory of sentence types within an analysis of discourse semantics. As mentioned in Section 1, there is quite a bit of research work on sentence types; see Lohnstein (2000), Ginzburg & Sag (2001), Zanuttini & Portner (2003), Portner (2004), Schwager (2005), Truckenbrodt (2006), Zaefferer (2006) for recent discussion and pointers into the broader literature.

3.2 Relative clauses

Quine pointed out the semantic interest of alternations between indicative and subjunctive in relative clauses (Quine 1956: 177):

(45) a. Procuro   un   perro   que   habla.
        seek   a   dog   that   talk.indic
        'I am looking for a dog that talks.'

b. Procuro un perro que hable.
   seek   a   dog   that talk.subj
   'I am looking for a dog that talks.'

Quine describes the example in (45a) as having the "relational sense", and provides the logical form (46a), and (45b) as having the "notional sense", (46b):

(46) a. ∃x[x is a dog & x talks & I seek x]
     b. I strive that ∃x[x is a dog & x talks & I find x]

Roughly speaking, (45a) entails the existence of a talking dog, while (45b) does not. Quine did not suggest any analysis of the subjunctive, of course, but only used the example to begin discussion of the problem of scope interactions between quantifiers and propositional attitudes.

More recently, linguists have focused more on the contribution of the subjunctive itself in this type of contrast. The essential idea is that the subjunctive in a relative clause is licensed when the noun phrase containing the clause is dependent on an operator which would trigger the subjunctive in a complement clause. For example, Beghelli (1998) provides the following example from Italian:

(47) a. Gianni voleva un dottore che era   comprensivo.
        Gianni wanted a doctor that was.indic understanding.
        'Gianni wanted a doctor who was understanding.'

     b. Gianni voleva un dottore che fosse   comprensivo.
        Gianni wanted a doctor that was.subj understanding.
        'Gianni wanted a doctor who would be understanding.'

If we think of the relevant kind of dependency as scope, we can say that the indicative is used in (47a) because the complement is interpreted outside the scope of the verb *voleva*, while the subjunctive is triggered in (47b) because it is inside the verb's scope. The exact treatment of this contrast depends both on the analysis of subjunctive licensing, and on the treatment of the dependency relation. See Farkas (1985, 1992), Kampers-Manhe (1991), Quer (1998, 2001), Giannakidou (1999), and Panzeri (2006) for discussion.

3.3 Adjunct clauses

Finally we turn to the distribution of verbal mood in adjunct clauses. Among adjunct clauses, verbal mood has been studied most extensively, by far, in *if* clauses. There is a tradition in philosophy and logic of distinguishing two types of conditional sentences, INDICATIVE CONDITIONALS and SUBJUNCTIVE CONDITIONALS. The reason for this terminology can be seen in a language like Catalan or Spanish, where we find *if* clauses containing either mood (Catalan data from Quer 1998: 235):

(48) a. Si   arriben   a   l'hora,   aconseguiran   entrades.
         if   arrive.indic.pres   at   the-time   get.fut   tickets
         'If they arrive on time, they will get tickets.'

   b. Si   arribessin   a   l'hora,   aconseguirien entrades.
         if   arrive.subj.past   at   the-time   get.cond   tickets
         'If they arrived on time, they would get tickets.'

   c. Si   haguessin   arribat   a   l'hora,   haurien   aconseguit
         if   have.subj.past   arrived   at   the-time   have.cond   gotten
         entrades.
         tickets
         'If they had arrived on time, they would have gotten tickets.'

The sentence with an indicative *if* clause, (48a), implies that they might very well arrive on time, while the version which uses subjunctive, (48b), suggests that it is unlikely they will arrive on time. Further changing the *if* clause to contain a subjunctive past perfect, as in (48c), creates a sentence about a hypothetical past event of arriving on time, and implies that such an event did not occur. Examples like (48c) are often referred to as COUNTERFACTUAL CONDITIONALS, though as pointed out as early as Anderson (1951), they do not entail counterfactuality. We can group the two kinds of conditionals expressed with subjunctive antecedents in Catalan under the label UNREAL CONDITIONALS (cf. Palmer 2001), and oppose them to the REAL CONDITIONAL (48a).

Despite the link which we observe between subjunctive and unreal conditionals in (48), Iatridou (2000) argues that the unreal meaning is conveyed not by the subjunctive, but rather by the past tense/aspect morphology. She shows that, across languages, tense/aspect forms are used to convey unreal meaning. (We see this connection clearly in English, cf. the translations in (48)). Subjunctive only occurs in unreal conditionals in combination with a past form. A language like French, which has a present form of the subjunctive but not a past one, uses a past form of the indicative to express meanings like (48b–c). Thus, it appears that the subjunctive in (48b–c) is licensed by some feature of the sentence associated with unreal or counterfactual meaning, but does not contribute such meaning to the sentence. As far as I know, there has been no work attempting to link the licensing conditions for the subjunctive in (48b–c), in languages which have it, with the broader theory of mood selection. There has, of course, been a great deal of work on the semantic distinction between real and unreal conditionals (see article 15 [this volume] (von Fintel) *Conditionals* for references), but in light of preceding discussion, this research should probably be seen as really concerning the contribution of tense/aspect forms, not verbal mood.

Apart from *if* clauses, there has been very little work on the semantics of verbal mood forms in adjunct clauses. A fairly extensive discussion of Catalan is provided by Quer (1998), focusing on concessive clauses. However, while this work establishes a foundation for further study, he does not provide a semantic analysis or even specific hypotheses about the role of mood in these constructions.

4 Conclusions

Research on the semantics of verbal mood has largely reached a conclusion on two key intuitions about the indicative-subjunctive contrast: First, it is to be explained in terms of modal properties of the context in which a clause occurs. Second, the indicative is licensed on contexts which are somehow similar to root assertion, and the subjunctive in contexts which are somehow different. The literature shows us a range of ideas for how to best understand what is common to those contexts which license each mood. Work on the semantic contribution of mood in root contexts, relative clauses, and adjunct clauses is at a much more primitive state of development, and is ripe for future study. In the long run, semanticists will need to understand the connections between verbal mood and mood in the various other senses described in Section 1.

5 References

Abusch, Dorit 1997. Sequence of tense and temporal de re. *Linguistics & Philosophy* 20, 1–50.
Anderson, Alan Ross 19951. A note on subjunctive and counterfactual conditionals. *Analysis* 11, 35–38.
Asher, Nicholas 1987. A typology for attitude verbs and their anaphoric properties. *Linguistics & Philosophy* 10, 125–197.
Axelrod, Melissa 1993. *The Semantics of Time. Aspectual Categorization in Koyukon Athabaskan*. Lincoln, NE: University of Nebraska Press.

Baker, Mark & Lisa Travis 1997. Mood as verbal definiteness in a tenseless language. *Natural Language Semantics* 5, 213–269.

Beghelli, Filippo 1998. Mood and the interpretation of indefinites. *The Linguistic Review* 15, 277–300.

Bugenhagen, Robert 1993. The semantics of irrealis in the Austronesian languages of Papua New Guinea. A cross-linguistic study. In: Ger P. Reesink (ed.). *Topics in Descriptive Austronesian Linguistics*. Leiden: Vakgroep Talen en Culturen van Zuidoost-Azie en Oceanie, University of Leiden, 1–39.

Bhat, D. N. Shankara 1999. *The Prominence of Tense, Aspect and Mood*. Amsterdam: Benjamins.

Bittner, Maria. 2009. Tense, Mood, and Centering. Ms. New Brunswick, NJ, Rutgers University. http://www.rci.rutgers.edu/~mbittner/pdf%20files%20for%20web/bittner09_tmc.pdf. December 29, 2010.

Bloomfield, Leonard 1956. *Eastern Ojibwa, Grammatical Sketch, Texts and Word List*. Ann Arbor, MI: The University of Michigan Press.

Boas, Franz 1911/2002. Introduction. In: Franz Boas. *Handbook of American Indian Languages. Part 1*. Washington: Smithsonian Institution, Bureau of American Ethnology, 1–83 Reprinted: Thoemmes Press, 2002. Bristol, UK.

Bolinger, Dwight 1968. *Aspects of Language*. New York: Harcourt, Brace & World.

Bybee, Joan 1998. 'Irrealis' as a grammatical category. *Anthropological Linguistics* 40, 257-271.

Chafe, Wallace 1995. The realis-irrealis distinction in Caddo, the northern Iroquoian languages, and English. In: J. Bybee & S. Fleischman (eds.). *Modality in Grammar and Discourse*. Amsterdam: Benjamins, 349–365.

Chierchia, Gennaro & Sally McConnell-Ginet 1990. *Meaning and Grammar: An Introduction to Semantics*. Cambridge, MA: The MIT Press.

de Reuse, Willem Joseph 1994. *Siberian Yupik Eskimo. The Language and its Contact with Chukchi*. Salt Lake City, UT: University of Utah Press.

Donaldson, Tamsin 1980. *Ngiyambaa: The Language of the Wangaaybuwan*. Cambridge: Cambridge University Press.

Dowty, David 1979. *Word Meaning and Montague Grammar*. Dordrecht: Reidel.

Dretske, Fred I. 1972. Contrastive statements. *Philosophical Review* 81, 411-437.

Ekdahl, Muriel & Joseph E. Grimes 1964. Terena verb inflection. *International Journal of American Linguistics* 30, 261-268.

Elliot, Jennifer 2000. Realis and irrealis: Forms and concepts of the grammaticalisation of reality. *Linguistic Typology* 4, 55-90.

Fabricius-Hansen, Cathrine & Kjell Johan Saebø 2004. In a mediative mood: The semantics of the German reportative subjunctive. *Natural Language Semantics* 12, 213–257.

Farkas, Donka 1985. *Intensional Descriptions and the Romance Subjunctive Mood*. New York: Garland.

Farkas, Donka 1992. On the semantics of subjunctive complements. In: P. Hirschbühler & K. Koerner (eds.). *Romance Languages and Modern Linguistic Theory*. Amsterdam: Benjamins, 69–104.

Farkas, Donka 2003. Assertion, belief, and mood choice. Paper presented at the *Workshop on Conditional and Unconditional Modality*, Vienna, Austria.

Fortescue, Michael K. 1984. *West Greenlandic*. London: Croom Helm.

Foster, Michael K. 1986. Updating the terminology of tense, mood, and aspect in northern Iroquoian descriptions. *International Journal of American Linguistics* 52, 65–72.

Giannakidou, Anastasia 1997. *The Landscape of Polarity Items*. Doctoral dissertation. University of Groningen.

Giannakidou, Anastasia 1999. Affective dependencies. *Linguistics & Philosophy* 22, 367–421.
Giannakidou, Anastasia 2009. The dependency of the subjunctive revisited: Temporal semantics and polarity. *Lingua* 119, 1883–1908.
Ginzburg, Jonathan & Ivan A. Sag 2001. *Interrogative Investigations: The Form, Meaning, and Use of English Interrogatives*. Chicago, IL: The University of Chicago Press.
Giorgi, Alessandra & Fabio Pianesi 1997. *Tense and Aspect: From Semantics to Morphosyntax*. Oxford: Oxford University Press.
Halliday, Michael 1970. Functional diversity in language as seen from a consideration of modality and mood in English. *Foundations of Language* 6, 322–361.
Han, Chung-hye 1998. *The Structure and Interpretation of Imperatives: Mood and Force in Universal Grammar*. Ph.D. dissertation. University of Pennsylvania, Philadelphia, PA.
Hausser, Roland R. 1980. Surface compositionality and the semantics of mood. In: J. Searle, F. Kiefer, & M. Bierwisch (eds.). *Speech Act Theory and Pragmatics*. Dordrecht: Reidel, 71-95.
Hausser, Roland R. 1983. The syntax and semantics of English mood. In: F. Kiefer (ed.). *Questions and Answers*. Dordrecht: Reidel.
Heim, Irene 1992. Presupposition projection and the semantics of attitude verbs. *Journal of Semantics* 9, 183–221.
Hintikka, Jaakko 1961. Modality and quantification. *Theoria* 27, 110–128.
Hooper, Joan B. 1975. On assertive predicates. In: J. Kimball (ed.). *Syntax and Semantics* 4. New York: Academic Press, 91-124.
Iatridou, Sabine 2000. The grammatical ingredients of counterfactuality. *Linguistic Inquiry* 31, 231–270.
James, Francis 1986. *Semantics of the English Subjunctive*. Vancouver, BC: University of British Columbia Press.
Jespersen, Otto 1924/1992. *The Philosophy of Grammar*. London: Allen & Unwin. Reprinted (With a new Introduction and Index by James D. McCawley): Chicago, IL: The University of Chicago Press, 1992.
Kamp, Hans & Uwe Reyle 1993. *From Discourse to Logic*. Dordrecht: Kluwer.
Kampers-Manhe, Brigitte 1991. *L'Opposition Subjonctif/Indicatif dans les Relatives*. Doctoral dissertation. University of Groningen.
Kayne, Richard S. 1992. Italian negative infinitival imperatives and clitic climbing. In: L. Tasmowsky & A. Zribi-Hertz (eds.). *De la Musique à la Linguistique. Hommages à Nicolas Ruwet*. Ghent: Communication and Cognition, 300–312.
Kratzer, Angelika 1977. What "must" and "can" must and can mean. *Linguistics & Philosophy* 1, 337–55.
Kratzer, Angelika 1981. The notional category of modality. In: H.-J. Eikmeyer & H. Rieser (eds.). *Words, Worlds, and Contexts*. Berlin: de Gruyter, 38–74.
Lichtenberk, Frantisek 1983. *A grammar of Manam*. Honolulu: University of Hawaii Press.
Lohnstein, Horst 2000. *Satzmodus – kompositionell. Zur Parametrisierung der Modusphrase im Deutschen*. Berlin: Akademie Verlag.
Lohnstein, Horst & Ursula Bredel 2004. Inflectional morphology and sentence mood in German. In: H. Lohnstein & S. Trissler (eds.). *The Syntax and Semantics of the Left Periphery*. Berlin: Mouton de Gruyter, 235–264.
Lunn, Patricia V. 1995. The evaluative function of the Spanish subjunctive. In: J. Bybee & S. Fleischman (eds.). *Modality in Grammar and Discourse*. Amsterdam: Benjamins, 429–449.
Lyons, John 1977. *Semantics*. Cambridge: Cambridge University Press.

Matthewson, Lisa 2010. Cross-linguistic variation in modality systems: The role of mood. *Semantics and Pragmatics* 3, 1–74.
McGregor, William B. & Tamsin Wagner 2006. The semantics and pragmatics of irrealis mood in Nyulnyulan languages. *Oceanic Linguistics* 45, 339–379.
Meibauer, Jörg 1990. Sentence mood, lexical category filling, and non-propositional *nicht* in German. *Linguistische Berichte* 130, 441–465.
Melnar, Lynette R. 2004. *Caddo Verb Morphology*. Lincoln, NE: University of Nebraska Press.
Mithun, Marianne 1999. *The Languages of Native North America*. Cambridge: Cambridge University Press.
Moretti, Giovanni & Giorgio Orvieto 1981. *Grammatica Italiana*. Perugia: Editrice Benucci.
Moshinsky, Julius 1974. *A Grammar of Southeastern Pomo*. Berkeley, CA: University of California Press.
Narrog, Heiko 2005. Modality, mood, and change of modal meanings: A new perspective. *Cognitive Linguistics* 16, 677–731.
Ogihara, Toshiyuki 1996. *Tense, Attitudes, and Scope*. Dordrecht: Reidel.
Ogihara, Toshiyuki 2007. Attitudes without monsters: A Japanese perspective. In: C. Tancredi et al. (eds.). *Proceedings of Semantics and Linguistic Theory (= SALT) XVI*. Ithaca, NY: Cornell University. http://research.nii.ac.jp/salt16/proceedings.html. December 29, 2010.
Palmer, Frank 1990. *Modality and the English Modals*. New York: Longman.
Palmer, Frank 2001. *Mood and Modality*. 2nd edn. Cambridge: Cambridge University Press.
Panzeri, Francesca 2006. Subjunctive relative clauses. In: P. Denis et al. (eds.). *Proceedings of the 2004 Texas Linguistics Society Conference*. Somerville, MA: Cascadilla Press, 60–68.
Parks, Douglas R. 1976. *A Grammar of Pawnee*. New York: Garland.
Picallo, M. Carme 1984. The Infl node and the null subject parameter. *Linguistic Inquiry* 15, 75–101.
Picallo, M. Carme 1985. *Opaque Domains*. Ph.D. dissertation. City University of New York, New York.
Portner, Paul 1997. The semantics of mood, complementation, and conversational force. *Natural Language Semantics* 5, 167–212.
Portner, Paul 1999. The semantics of mood. *Glot International* 4, 3–9.
Portner, Paul 2004. The semantics of imperatives within a theory of clause types. In: K. Watanabe & R. B. Young (eds.). *Proceedings of Semantics and Linguistic Theory (= SALT) XIV*. Ithaca, NY: Cornell University, 235–252.
Portner, Paul 2009. *Modality*. Oxford: Oxford University Press.
Progovac, Ljiljana 1993. The (mis)behavior of anaphora and negative polarity. *The Linguistic Review* 10, 37–59,
Quer, Josep 1998. *Mood at the Interface*. The Hague: Holland Academic Graphics.
Quer, Josep 2001. Interpreting mood. *Probus* 13, 81–111.
Quine, Willard van Orman 1956. Quantifiers and propositional attitudes. *Journal of Philosophical Logic* 53, 177–187.
Raposo, Eduardo 1986. Some asymmetries in the binding theory in Romance. *The Linguistic Review* 5, 75–110.
Reis, Marga 1999. On sentence types in German. An enquiry into the relationship between grammar and pragmatics. *Interdisciplinary Journal for Germanic Linguistics and Semiotic Analysis* 4, 195–236.
Reis, Marga 2003. On the form and interpretation of German wh-infinitives. *Journal of Germanic Linguistics* 15, 155–201.

Rivero, Maria-Luisa 1994. Negation, imperatives and Wackernagel effects. *Rivista di Linguistica* 6, 39–66.
Roberts, John R. 1990. Modality in Amele and other Papuan languages. *Journal of Linguistics* 26, 363-401.
Roussou, Anna 2009. In the mood for control. *Lingua* 119, 1811-1836.
Schlenker, Philippe 2002. Indexicality, logophoricity, and plural pronouns. Handout, November 2002, UCLA and Institut Jean-Nicod.
Schlenker, Philippe 2003. A plea for monsters. *Linguistics & Philosophy* 26, 29–120.
Schlenker, Philippe 2005. The lazy frenchman's approach to the subjunctive (speculations on reference to worlds and semantic defaults in the analysis of mood). In: T. Geerts, I. van Ginneken & H. Jacobs (eds.). *Romance Languages and Linguistic Theory 2003: Selected papers from "Going Romance"*. Amsterdam: Benjamins, 269–310.
Schwager, Magdalena 2005. *Interpreting Imperatives*. Doctoral dissertation. University of Frankfurt.
Searle, John 1969. *Speech Acts*. Cambridge: Cambridge University Press.
Stalnaker, Robert 1974. Pragmatic presupposition. In: M. Munitz & P. Unger (eds.). *Semantics and Philosophy*. New York: New York University Press, 197–213.
Stalnaker, Robert 1978. Assertion. In: P. Cole (ed.). *Syntax and Semantics 9: Pragmatics*. New York: Academic Press, 315–332.
Stalnaker, Robert 1987. *Inquiry*. Cambridge, MA: The MIT Press.
Stalnaker, Robert 1988. On the representation of context. *Journal of Logic, Language and Information* 7, 3–19.
von Stechow, Arnim 1995. Lexical decomposition in syntax. In: U. Egli et al. (eds.). *Lexical Knowledge in the Organization of Language*. Amsterdam: Benjamins, 81–177.
von Stechow, Arnim 2004. Binding by verbs: Tense, person and mood under attitudes. In: H. Lohnstein & S. Trissler (eds.). *The Syntax and Semantics of the Left Periphery*. Berlin: Mouton de Gruyter, 431–488.
Stenius, Erik 1967. Mood and language game. *Synthese* 17, 254–274.
Suñer, Margarita 1986. On the referential properties of embedded finite clause subjects. In: I. Bordelois, H. Contreras & K. Zagona (eds.). *Generative Studies in Spanish Syntax*. Dordrecht: Foris, 183–203.
Suñer, Margarita & José Padilla-Rivera 1987. Sequence of tenses and the subjunctive, again. *Hispania* 70, 634–642.
Swift, Mary D. 2004. *Time in Child Inuktitut. A Developmental Study of an Eskimo-Aleut Language*. Berlin: Mouton de Gruyter.
Terrell, Tracy & Joan Hooper 1974. A semantically based analysis of mood in Spanish. *Hispania* 57, 486–494.
Travis, Catherine 2003. The semantics of the Spanish subjunctive: Its use in the natural semantic metalanguage. *Cognitive Linguistics* 14, 47–69.
Truckenbrodt, Hubert 2006. On the semantic motivation of syntactic verb movement to C in German. *Theoretical Linguistics* 32, 257–306.
Villalta, Elisabeth 2000. Spanish subjunctive clauses require ordered alternatives. In: B. Jackson & T. Matthews (eds.). *Proceedings of Semantics and Linguistic Theory (= SALT) X*. Ithaca, NY: Cornell University, 239–256.
Villalta, Elisabeth 2006. *Context Dependence in the Interpretation of Questions and Subjunctives*. Doctoral dissertation. University of Tübingen.
Villalta, Elisabeth 2008. Mood and gradability: An investigation of the subjunctive mood in Spanish. *Linguistics & Philosophy* 31, 467–522.

Wilson, Deirdre & Dan Sperber 1988. Mood and the analysis of non-declarative sentences. In: J. Dancy, J. Moravcsik & C. Taylor (eds.). *Human Agency: Language, Duty and Value*. Stanford, CA: Stanford University Press, 77–101.

Woodbury, Anthony 1981. *Study of the Chevak Dialect of Central Yup'ik Eskimo*. Ph.D. dissertation. University of California, Berkeley, CA.

Zaefferer, Dietmar 2006. Deskewing the Searlean picture: A new speech act ontology for linguistics. In: *Proceedings of the Annual Meeting of the Berkeley Linguistics Society* 32(1), 453–464.

Zanuttini, Rafaella 1997. *Negation and Clausal Structure. A Comparative Study of Romance Languages*. Oxford: Oxford University Press.

Zanuttini, Rafaella & Paul Portner 2003. Exclamative clauses: At the syntax-semantics interface. *Language* 79, 39–81.

Zwicky, Arnold M. 1985. The Hidatsa mood markers. *International Journal of American Linguistics* 51, 629–630.

Jane Grimshaw
12 Deverbal nominalization

1. Introduction —— 407
2. The background —— 408
3. Deverbal nominals denoting ordinary individuals —— 410
4. Event and fact nominals —— 417
5. Arguments, modifiers and adjuncts —— 424
6. Some nominalization puzzles —— 428
7. Summary —— 432
8. References —— 433

Abstract: Deverbal nominals have a wide range of meanings. They can be synonymous with underived nouns. They can denote an argument of the predicate they are based on, or have a result interpretation. They can denote facts and events. Unlike embedded clauses, deverbal nominals do not denote propositions. They participate in the structural relations that other nouns allow: they take prepositional complements and are modified by adjectives and possessives. In their complex event and fact meanings, however, they differ from other nouns in their argument-taking abilities, which resemble those of verbs. English deverbal nominals are formed with a number of different suffixes, and properties of the nominals can vary as a function of the suffix. The aspectual characteristics of each verb also affect whether a deverbal counterpart exists, and what its properties can be. While research on the topic has explicated many of the observed regularities, there remain numerous gaps in the system, nominals which are predicted to exist but do not, or which do not have the expected properties. Current research seeks to discover the principles governing the interaction of lexical meaning, aspect and morphology, which will explain the attested patterns.

1 Introduction

The linguistic representation of predicates and their ability to combine with arguments is justifiably at the center of linguistic research, and deverbal nominals offer a unique window on the topic. Deverbal nominalization is special in ways which make

Jane Grimshaw, New Brunswick, NJ, USA

https://doi.org/10.1515/9783110589443-012

it both extraordinarily complex and extraordinarily revealing. Deverbal nominals (henceforth "d-nominals") such as *assignment* and *continuation* are remarkable for the variety of meanings that they exhibit. They have been said to denote, *inter alia*, results, manners, actions, processes, events, states, ordinary objects, facts and propositions. It appears that they can have any meaning that an underived nominal can have, and others which are unique to them, made possible by their verbal qualities. They are special syntactically since they are nominal expressions related to verbs. They are morphologically intricate, involving many different morphemes associated with different semantic and grammatical characteristics. Nominalization is highly sensitive to aspect, and restrictions on nominalization provide a key source of information concerning the representation of events in language. The argument-taking properties of d-nominals are related to those of verbs and to those of other nouns, in complex ways which we are beginning to understand. All in all, a successful theory of deverbal nominalization promises unique insights into the complex interplay of principles governing meaning, syntax, and morphology.

2 The background

The ground-breaking work on this topic was carried out in the 1960s by Lees (1960) and Vendler (1967), who were the first to systematically study d-nominals within formal linguistic theory. They distinguished nouns which denote concrete objects, actions, and facts/propositions. These classic examples are from Lees (1960: 64):

(1) His drawing fascinated me …
    a. because he always did it lefthanded.
    b. because I didn't know he could be persuaded so easily.
    c. because it was so large.

In (1a) *drawing* refers to an action, as *did it* in the continuation makes clear, in (1b) it refers to the fact that he did some drawing and in (1c) it refers to a physical object, which has spatial dimensions. Evidence concerning the meanings of *drawing* stems from the relationship between the d-nominal and what Vendler called "containers"—the predicates that the nominals combine with. "It is events, processes and actions, and not facts or results, that occur, take place, begin, last and end. The former, and not the latter, can be watched, heard, followed, and observed…" (Vendler 1967: 141) In contrast, facts or results can be held to be probable. Vendler's analytical technique remains a crucial component of current research. The following, modified from Zucchi's (1993) presentation of Vendler's results, compares a nominal with the *–ing* morphology of (2) with a d-nominal in *–ance* combined with the event-taking predicate *was slow*.

(2) a. The performance of the song was slow. (Event)
b. The performing of the song was slow. (Event)
c. *His performing the song was slow. (Fact)
d. *That he performed the song was slow. (Fact)

The paradigm in (2) is explained if the d-nominal in (2c) and clausal subject in (2d) denote a fact (or perhaps a proposition, but see section 4.3), while the first two nominals denote events.

Nominalization is not found in every language. Koptjevskaja-Tamm (1988: 81–83) suggests that languages which do not have d-nominals have other ways to express the same meanings in the form of a non-clausal argument, comparable to English "acc–*ing*" structures, infinitives and finite complement clauses, which are sometimes treated as nominalized in the literature (e.g. Chierchia 1984) because they occur as arguments. However, their internal structure is essentially that of main clauses: they have non-possessive subjects and bare nominals as objects, for example. Since they have none of the internal grammatical characteristics of nominalized phrases, and are not subject to the kinds of semantic constraints to be discussed here, I exclude them from consideration.

Subsequent research has built on the basic mode of analysis illustrated by (2), and established a continuum of deverbalization (see Portner 1992), with forms at one end having mostly verbal properties, while at the other end lie d-nominals having principally (or entirely) nominal properties. Two extremes are illustrated in (3) and (4).

(3) a. She dropped *the examination*.
b. *The assignment* was hard to read.

(4) a. *Their examining the document* surprised us.
b. I didn't approve of their assigning that problem.

Here, *examination* and *assignment*, d-nominals corresponding to *examine* and *assign*, seem hardly verbal at all, having meanings very much like the nouns *book* or *problem*, which have no matching verb. They fall at the nominal end of the continuum. In contrast, *examining* and *assigning* in (4) seem hardly nominal: they even take direct nominal complements (*the document*, *that problem*) rather than prepositional phrases, which "true" nouns never do.

The variety of nominals which can correspond to a single verb can be illustrated by the verb *examine*. These include *examination* referring to an ordinary object, as in (3a), and to an event as in *the examination lasted three hours*. A fact reading is plausible for *The doctor deplored the careless examination of the patient*. Other d-nominal forms are *examining* as in (4a) and in expressions like *the examining of the substance*. Finally, there are *examiner* and *examinee*. The range of forms and meanings based on *examine* is particularly rich, but many other examples can be found below.

The structural representation of d-nominals has been explored intensively. It is generally agreed that they are DPs with some verbal structure within; the amount of verbal structure varying depending on the nominal and on the proposed analysis (an issue taken up briefly in section 4.4). In (3a) *the examination* may have no verbal syntax at all, being represented approximately as in (5), just like *the exam* or *the dog*.

(5) [$_{DP}$ the [$_{NP}$ examination]]

While the title of this article implies that the nouns discussed here are derived from verbs in some sense, a current school of thought originating in Picallo (1991) holds that all complex words are derived from category-less lexical heads, and given their category by the functional structure that encases them. (See Harley & Noyer 1999, Alexiadou 2001 and Borer 2005.) Thus *examination* is not derived from the verb *examine*. Instead, both are constructed from the same root, composing with one or more functional heads related to the *v* introduced in Kratzer (1996). Despite the interest of this perspective, since most of the semantically focused research reported on here assumes deverbalization, the present article largely, but never crucially, adopts that perspective.

The verbal-nominal continuum of d-nominal meanings provides an organizing structure to the domain, which I will exploit. Section 3 of the article describes research on d-nominals which refer to individuals, and section 4 discusses the most verb-like nominals, those which refer to events and facts. Section 5 highlights similarities and differences between the formal structures of modification for underived nouns and d-nominals. Current puzzles and research focusing on them are the topic of section 6. Section 7 summarizes the main points of the article.

3 Deverbal nominals denoting ordinary individuals

At the least verbal end of the continuum are nouns which refer to ordinary individuals. They fall into three groups. The first I will refer to as "participant nominals". They correspond to a *participant* in the event described by the verb they are related to. The second is often termed a "result" nominal, and names the outcome of an event. The third is a residual category. Research on these d-nominals aims to explain observed restrictions on the nominalization based on the verbs concerned, and thus contributes to the theory of natural language predicates.

3.1 Participant nominals

Examples include *employer* or *writer*, which denote ordinary individuals, and can have counterparts which are very similar in nature but do not correspond to a verb, as illustrated in Tab. 12.1.

Tab. 12.1: Participant nominals with and without verbal bases

Affix		
actor –*er*	singer ~ surgeon	lover ~ fan
actor –*er*	teacher ~ cook	employer ~ boss
-*ant*	defendant ~ criminal	
-*ee*	employee ~ maid	
instrumental –*er*	shredder ~ knife	heater ~ furnace

Nominals formed with -*er*, and –*ee* have been intensively investigated. (Lieber 2004 offers a recent review.) Nominals of this type correspond to an argument of the base verb: if *employ* is a relation between an agent and a patient, then *employer* is the name of the agent argument, and *employee* the name of the patient argument.

Two principal results have emerged from current research. First, although the d-nominals might look just like their simple counterparts, they seem to preserve some properties of the verbal base, such as argument structure or complement-taking abilities, and/or an event component in their interpretation. Second, the relationship between these nominals and the verbs they correspond to reflects the nature of the arguments of the verbs.

Levin & Rappaport (1988) and Rappaport Hovav & Levin (1992) propose that some –*er* d-nominals have an event-related interpretation. They argue, for example, that *the destroyer of the city* refers only to a person who has participated in an event of destruction, while the kind of ship called *a destroyer* qualifies even if it never leaves the dock. It is not uncontroversial that this property is connected to deverbal status. Barker & Dowty (1993: 60) note the same property for some nouns with no verbal base. A *criminal* must have participated in a crime, and a *victim* must have been harmed in some way. However, there is another apparent reflex of the verbal nature of these nouns: the complement structure of –er derived nominals. Rappaport Hovav & Levin (1992) argue that –er nominals can maintain the complement structure of the base verb, but only when they have an event-related reading. They cite cases such as (6), their (12c), building on the analysis of *frequent* as an event modifier used in Grimshaw (1990) to detect aspectual structure in event nominals (see section 4).

(6) A frequent buyer of lottery tickets

They contrast *waxer* in (7a) and (7b), (their 15a,b).

(7) a. I know that Dan is a frequent waxer of parquet floors.
     b. *I know that this mop is a frequent floor waxer.

Their proposal is that (7a) contains the eventive *waxer* with the complement of the verb *wax*, and it allows modification by *frequent*. In contrast, (7b) involves a non-eventive noun and does not allow the modification. If correct, this research shows that even d-nominals which refer to individuals retain some event properties, and it implicates the linguistic theory of events (cf. article 8 [Semantics: Theories] (Maienborn) *Event semantics* and article 9 [this volume] (Filip) *Aspectual class and Aktionsart*) in the theory of their representation.

Thus, as stated at the beginning of this section, deverbal nominalization corresponding to an argument of the verb provides a very important tool for investigating the nature of the representation of predicates in general. There are two broadly different hypotheses about the nature of arguments of lexical predicates. One is that they have purely semantic representations, whether in terms of thematic roles or some other semantic analysis of their arguments (see Barker & Dowty 1993). The other is that they also have a more syntactic representation, often referred to as "argument structure", which provides a narrow range of information about arguments, such as whether they are "internal" or "external", cross-cutting major semantic differences, in thematic role for instance. This view has been championed in particular by Beth Levin and Malka Rappaport (see their work cited here, also cf. article 3 [Semantics: Lexical Structures and Adjectives] (Davis) *Thematic roles* and article 4 [Semantics: Lexical Structures and Adjectives] (Levin & Rappaport Hovav) *Lexical Conceptual Structure*. Argument nominalization can be used to test what arguments are distinguished by the linguistic representation system. Two important studies of the matter have reached opposite conclusions. Levin & Rappaport (1988) and Rappaport Hovav & Levin (1992) conclude that thematic role labels are *not* present in the representation which is the input to –er suffixation. Barker (1998) concludes that they *are* present in the representation which is the input to –ee suffixation.

The argument concerning *-er* nominals is based on several related observations. First, such nominals can be based on unergative verbs (*opener, user*) but not on unaccusatives. This is why examples like **appearer* and **waner* are impossible. Second, transitive-intransitive pairs show a revealing pattern. A verb which has a transitive causative meaning (e.g. "x opens y") and a corresponding intransitive change of state meaning (e.g. "y opens"), has a derived nominal with only the interpretation associated with the transitive verb. An *opener* opens things, it does not itself open. Third, even non-agentive predicates can participate in the eventive nominalization pattern, where they take complements just like agentive predicates do. This is illustrated in (8), which is based on their examples.

(8) a. If you are the holder of a Visa or MasterCard...
 b. Jobs are the best indicator of a sound economy.

The researchers conclude that *-er* nominals with preserved complement structure correspond to the external argument of the base verb. Therefore they can be derived only from verbs which have external arguments, explaining why unaccusatives don't participate. There is no way, the researchers claim, that this generalization can be maintained by reference to semantic roles alone, since there is no single semantic role which encompasses all cases. The verb *murder* has an Agent as its subject, *hold* an Experiencer, perhaps, and *indicator* perhaps a Source. Whatever the correct labels might be they are not identical. This argument aims to establish the formal representation of "argument structure", separate from a representation in terms of thematic roles. Rappaport Hovav & Levin (1992: 129) conclude more generally that "productive deverbal morphological processes do not make reference to θ-role labels."

Barker (1998) reaches the opposite conclusion for nouns in *–ee*: namely that they are formed not on the basis of the syntactic argument structure of the stem verb, but in accordance with three purely semantic constraints. Barker argues that the referent of an *-ee* noun must be sentient; and it must lack full "volitional control". Further it must be "episodically linked": "the referent of a noun phrase headed by an *-ee* noun must have participated in an event of the type corresponding to the stem verb." Working from a database of 1500 naturally-occurring examples, Barker (1998: 750) argues that there is no single characterization of the base verb which makes the denotation of the *-ee* form a natural class *syntactically*. Subjects of verbs can undergo *-ee* affixation, as can objects and indirect objects and the objects of governed prepositions. The phenomenon is, he suggests, syntactically "blind". It is tempting to think that the right generalization concerns the notion of an "internal" argument, which would rather neatly match the Levin & Rappaport analysis of *–er*, and seem to provide further support for the reality of argument structure. This is challenged by the existence of *-ee* nominals corresponding to the subjects of transitives and (unergative) intransitives. As representative examples, Barker (1998: 705) cites (9) and (10).

(9) Subjects of intransitive verbs: The retiree retired.

> Escapee, standee, resignee, dinee, enlistee, returnee, advancee, arrivee, ascendee, deferee, embarkee, relaxee, sittee

(10) Subjects of transitive verbs: The attendee attended the concert.

> deferree, forgettee, offendee "convicted criminal", pledgee "person who pledges funds to a charity", representee "a (parliamentary) representative", signee "one who has signed a contract or register", withstandee

The grammaticality of some of these examples seems questionable, although they are attested in the data Barker is studying and they are comprehensible with effort. A look at the 385 million word Corpus of Contemporary American English (Davies 2008), reveals that of the transitives in (10), *pledgee* occurs once (in connection with fraternities), *offendee* has 2 exemplars, where it means "person offended" and thus corresponds to the object of *offend*. Two cases of the noun *signee* clearly refer to signatories, but in the remaining 121 examples it refers to a player with a contract. It is therefore not clear whether it corresponds to the subject of *sign*, or the object of *sign* as in *Someone signed this player (to a contract)*. Similar remarks hold for the intransitives. The data is complex and not easy to interpret.

Barker concludes that *-ee* suffixation is properly understood in terms of a thematic role instantiating the three semantic constraints, and not in terms of argument structure. Placing this conclusion next to that drawn by Rappaport Hovav & Levin highlights the on-going debate concerning the mapping between the semantics of arguments and their syntactic expression. Does lexical semantics directly and singly determine whether a particular verb can combine with a particular affix, or is there a further representation, such as an argument structure, which may reflect meaning but is not itself semantic, which determines how verbal arguments are affected by morphology and how they are realized? The question remains open.

3.2 Result nominals

Also individual denoting, and hence minimally verb-like, are "result" nominals. Many of these have an event-denoting interpretation in addition to their result reading. Their behavior under event readings will be discussed in section 4. Here I continue to focus on d-nominals which do not refer to events.

True result interpretations are related to the aspectual analysis of the base verbs (Vendler 1967, Dowty 1979, cf. article 9 [this volume] (Filip) *Aspectual class and Aktionsart*). Aspect characterizes the structure of an event described by a verb and its complements. The verbs labeled "accomplishments" or "complex changes of state" in the literature have an event structure which breaks down into two parts: an activity phase, and a culmination. Within accomplishments, the "creation" verbs form a relatively uniform group of predicates for which the existence of the entity referred to by the direct object is a result of the first sub-event. In *they built a house*, a house which didn't exist before exists at the end of the building event. The object changes state (here comes into existence) as the event unfolds. The result nominal *building* is the argument of a predicate of existence in the resulting state component of the event structure. The d-nominal of *build* thus refers to what comes into existence, so characterizing it as a "result" is accurate. Like *–er* and *–ee* nominals, these result nominals correspond to an argument of their base. The noun *invention* is another example: an event in which they invented a new recipe has as its result an entity which is both a recipe and an invention. Similarly, *a collection* refers to the result of event(s) of collecting. While these nominals are related to verbs, they can match simple nominals semantically as *–er* and *–ee* nominals do (see Tab. 12.1); *building* is like *cabin* and *apartment*, and *collection* resembles *anthology*.

Bisetto & Melloni (2007) analyze a second kind of nominal, also accurately characterized as "result". These are derived from the *transcribe* subclass of "image creation" verbs of Levin (1993: 171–172), also discussed in Dowty (1991). They are distinct from other result nouns in that the "result" that they refer to does not correspond to an argument of the verbal predicate. Consider the d-nominal *transcription*. If a text is transcribed the result is a transcription of the text, which was not previously in existence. However it is not the transcription that was transcribed but the text. What came into existence is something other than the referent of the verb's direct object, so at the end of the event there are two entities, a text and its transcription, where previously there was just a text. Similarly if a verb is nominalized, what comes into existence is a nominalization, not the verb.

Both kinds of result nominal correspond to predicates, which have a complex event structure, involving an activity and a change of state.

3.3 Residual individual nominals

The remaining nouns cannot legitimately be characterized as "results", since the nominal is not the subject of a culminating state predicate, although the term is occasionally extended to them. (11) illustrates some of the range of meanings that we find within these nominals.

(11) transport~transportation, propose~proposal, refer~referral, confer~conference, manage~management, agree~agreement, mix~mixture, store~storage, cover~coverage, cut~cut

The management can refer to "those who manage" and what is assigned is an *assignment*. In these cases the same suffix *–ment* nominalizes the subject of *manage* and the object of *assign*. For some verbs the d-nominal corresponds to a direct object: what is contributed is a *contribution*. In contrast, what is examined is not an *examination*, what is solved is not a *solution* (but a problem), what is transported is not *transportation*, and what is covered (e.g. *the newspapers covered the election*) is not *coverage*. Perhaps *transportation* is the means of transporting or corresponds to the subject of *transport*?

It is characteristic of these nouns that they can undergo considerable semantic drift, and have meanings which are quite distant from those of their bases. Consider the noun *conference* for example. People can *confer* on a street corner or by e-mail, but neither of these is "a conference" and people participating in a conference are not "conferring". Among them we can discern an unwieldy mass of metonymic relations, which clearly demands some systematic analysis. The complexity and apparent idiosyncracy of this domain is daunting and it is noteworthy that the literature is largely based on a small number and unsystematic selection of examples. It seems likely that no single analysis holds of all instances.

It is not yet known, then, how much systematicity is hidden from our current analytical insight.

What is clear is that when the meaning of the d-nominal is predictable, it is controlled by the nominalizing morpheme together with the verbal base. In their cross-linguistic investigation, Comrie & Thompson (1985) identify and exemplify affixes which create d-nominals referring to "agents", "instruments", "manners", "locations", "results/objects" and "reasons". Koptjevskaja-Tamm (1988) reports "way" and "manner" readings. Comrie & Thompson (1985: 357) cite Sundanese examples including the following:

(12) a. dataŋ   "to arrive"
     b. paŋdataŋ   "reason for arrival"
     c. daek   "to be willing"
     d. paŋdaek   "reason for being willing"

Such nominals exemplify a further type of nominalization, involving neither results nor arguments of the verb.

All of the English d-nominals discussed in this section have denotations like nouns which are not deverbal at all. *A building* has the same grammatical properties as *a cabin,* which is not deverbal and *two nominalizations* has the same properties as *two nouns*. All of the nouns pluralize, can be indefinite, can be counted and so forth. The ways in which these d-nominals are more verb-like than underived nouns are both subtle and controversial, as was evident in the discussion of *-er* and *-ee*. They constitute the most nominal and least verbal deverbal nominals, and contrast with the more verb-like nominals in the system.

4 Event and fact nominals

There is a fundamental distinction within event d-nominals between those which are essentially like underived nouns, and those which are much more closely related to verbs. The nouns *exam* and *examination* offer a clear instance of the distinction. They can refer to a physical object, as in (13a). Alternatively, they can refer to events, when they are arguments of event-selecting predicates, as in (13b, c). However *examination* also combines with phrases corresponding to arguments of *examine*, as in (13d, e). In contrast *exam* cannot occur with these complements as (13f) shows.

(13) a. They tore up their examinations/exams
 b. The examination/exam took place at 6 pm.
 c. We witnessed the examination/exam.
 d. They examined the patient carefully.
 e. The careful examination of the patient revealed that he was healthy.
 f. *The careful exam of the patient revealed that he was healthy.

It is widely agreed that this phenomenon can be explained if *examination* is verb-like in allowing arguments, but *exam* is not. Thus, there must be two kinds of event nominals, those which, like *exam* and *event*, are not argument-takers, and those which like *examination* are (sometimes) argument–takers. This follows Grimshaw (1990), where it is argued that event nominals which are not argument-taking are not associated with decomposition into aspectual structure and participants. Grimshaw labels nouns that refer to events, but have no aspect or arguments "simple" event nominals. The nouns *event* and *exam* are instances. D-nominals which are associated with arguments and aspect, in contrast, are "complex" event nominals. In (13e), *examination* is a complex event nominal.

Detailed studies have been carried out on event nominals and related phenomena in several languages. The studies include Hazout (1990), Picallo (1991), Crisma (1993), Rozwadowska (1997), Siloni (1997a, 1997b), Schoorlemmer (1998), Alexiadou (2001) and several papers in Giannakidou & Rathert (2009). See also Rozwadowska (2005) and Alexiadou, Haegeman & Stavrou (2007) for recent surveys.

This section focuses on event nominalization, starting in 4.1 with nominals built from latinate morphemes *–ion* etc. and moving in 4.2 to *–ing* forms. In 4.3, I examine fact interpretations, and finally I show that both fact and event nominals in both *–ion* etc. and *-ing* are possible for all non-stative aspectual classes (section 4.4). The goal is to explicate general, shared properties of the fact and event nominals. I postpone the discussion of stative meanings until section 6, as they pose numerous challenges for current theories.

4.1 Properties of complex event nominals

D-nominals like *meeting/procedure/argument/rehearsal* and underived nominals like *event/ surgery/party/game* can all be subjects of event-selecting predicates like *take place* and *happen*. Such nouns are often labeled "event", "process" or "action", although the terms are not reliably used in exactly the same way.

Two important properties distinguish complex event nominals from other event denoters: They take true arguments, which can be obligatory if the verbal base has an obligatory argument. They license aspectual modifiers—adjectives related to the internal analysis of the event referred to by the nominal, and temporal/durational PPs which are sensitive to telicity (cf. article 9 [this volume] (Filip) *Aspectual class and Aktionsart*). These two properties coincide, according to a line of reasoning drawn from Grimshaw (1990).

Event-modifying adverbs like *constantly*, *frequently* and *habitually* are grammatical in (14a) and their adjectival counterparts in (14b). Since *examine patients* can be telic or atelic, both *in* and *for* PPs are possible in both examples.

(14) a. They frequently/constantly examine patients in/for an afternoon.
　　 b. The frequent/constant examination of patients in/for an afternoon leads to better diagnoses.

The verb *examine* takes an obligatory internal argument, and this property is maintained in the complex event nominal: omission of the argument makes both (15a) and (15b) ungrammatical.

(15) a. *They frequently/constantly examine in/for an afternoon.
　　 b. *The frequent/constant examination in/for an afternoon leads to more accurate diagnoses.

Grimshaw (1990) proposes that aspectual structure licenses the modifiers, and allows preservation of the argument structure of the verb. Hence obligatory arguments and aspectual modifiers are possible in the same environments.

When *examination* has a simple event reading, or an individual reading, it behaves like *exam*: the aspectually licensed PPs and *frequent/constant* adjectives are impossible (for a singular noun). In fact, *examination* behaves in these cases just like the underived *party*.

(16) *The frequent exam/examination/party was a mistake/happened in the fall.

This pattern is found for other d-nominals with different morphology. The nouns *appointment*, *seizure*, and *storage* are ambiguous, but aspectually licensed modifiers of the singular are possible only when they are argument-takers, and their objects must be expressed.

(17) a. The frequent appointment of unqualified workers for extended periods of time damaged the company.
 b. *The frequent appointment (for extended periods of time) damaged the company.

(18) a. The habitual seizure of illegal substances at the Canadian border is alarming.
 b. *The habitual seizure (at the Canadian border) is alarming.

(19) a. The government doesn't recommend the frequent storage of perishable food for many days without refrigeration.
 b. *The government doesn't recommend the frequent storage for many days without refrigeration.

There are other ways to induce the complex event reading. According to the proposal in Grimshaw (1990), the agentive interpretation of a possessive is consistent only with the complex event reading of a d-nominal. The noun has an argument structure to license the agent, and this again makes its object obligatory. Because of variability in the well-formedness of possessive subjects in d-nominals, I illustrate this only for one (clear) case.

(20) *The company's appointment damages business.

(20) is grammmatical if the *of* PP from (17a) is added. The inclusion of a *by* PP corresponding to the subject of the base also forces the presence of an object if the d-nominal is based on a transitive verb. The logic is the same as for possessives.

(21) a. *The collection by the students was frowned on.
 b. The collection of butterflies by the students was frowned on.

If the internal argument is expressed in some other way, as a possessive, for example, the argument structure of a complex event noun should be satisfied. This may be the case in (22) but the issue is controversial. (See Anderson 1978 on "affectedness", Snyder 1998, Grimshaw 1990, and Schoorlemmer 1998.)

(22) a. The patient's examination
b. The director's appointment

In sum d-nominals with complex event interpretations can have obligatory arguments, just like verbs.

4.2 Event nominals in –ing

The meanings and meaning distinctions within -ing nominals broadly parallel those of the d-nominals in –ion etc. Building on the earlier research (see section 2) we see that they refer to individual objects in (23), or to simple events in (24). The count examples in (23) (*mending* is non-count) can be pluralized, combine with indefinite determiners, and otherwise behave just like other individual denoting nominals.

(23) His mending was in a big pile; The dentist replaced a filling; The binding of the book was broken.

The simple event nouns, like *exam* in (16), cannot combine with aspectual modifiers: it is ungrammatical to include *for several hours* in (24), for example even though *fight*, *sing* and *read* are activities.

(24) The fighting/singing/reading takes place after the bars close; The killings were reported in the papers.

D-nominals in –ing can also denote complex events as (25) exemplifies:

(25) a. The (cook's) careful simmering of the chicken made good broth.
b. The careful simmering of the chicken for the whole afternoon made good broth.

These d-nominals, often called "nominal" gerunds, have the same basic properties as the d-nominals of section 4.1, but see sections 5 and 6 for some important differences. Their internal argument is obligatory: omitting *of the chicken* in (25b) leads to ungrammaticality. Their head nouns can take prepositional, but not bare nominal complements. They combine with determiners and they can have a possessive "subject", or one introduced by *of*. It has been said that either a determiner or a possessive must be present in an *-ing* nominal, see Lees (1960: 65) and Wasow & Roeper (1972). This does not seem to be true under a non-episodic interpretation: *careful simmering of a chicken always yields good broth*. The external distribution of *–ing* nominals is that of DPs. All of these properties are shared with d-nominals formed with *–ion* etc. Another construction headed by *–ing* often known as a "verbal gerund" also has the external distribution of a DP, but has almost entirely the internal structure of a clause (see Jackendoff 1977 and Abney 1987). Its lexical head is a verb, not a noun, and it takes bare nominal complements.

(26) We appreciated the cook's having carefully simmered a chicken.

Despite their morphological resemblance, verbal gerunds are not subject to the restrictions governing *–ing* nominals presented in section 6.

4.3 Fact readings

Many works (see Lees 1960, Vendler 1967, Zucchi 1993 and Peterson 1997) agree that *-ing* nominals can denote a "fact" in examples like (27a). As Zucchi (1993) points out, if they can also have "proposition" interpretations, *inform* can be held to combine with a proposition in both (27a) and (27b), allowing for a uniform analysis.

(27) a. The cook was informed of the collapsing/melting of the icing.
     b. The cook was informed that the icing collapsed/melted.

This argument seems problematic, however. It is a remarkable fact that no event d-nominals, or embedded clauses other than *that* clauses, combine with the predicates *true* or *false*, as the ungrammaticality of (28a,b) illustrates. Only *that* clauses combine with these predicates, as in (28c).

(28) a. *The/their shooting (of) the hunters is true.
     b. *The/their assassination of the hunters is true.
     c. That they shot/assassinated the hunters is true.

(See section 6 for the case of d-nominals with sentential complements, also Zucchi 1993: 63 on the problem posed by *believe*.) The evidence, I conclude, supports the view that propositional interpretations are impossible for d-nominals, and that what we see in (27a) is a fact interpretation.

Nominals formed with –*ion* etc., discussed in 4.1, also have fact readings. The following examples have prominent fact interpretations, although it is difficult to completely eliminate event interpretations.

(29) a. The government was appalled by the company's appointment of unqualified workers.
b. The seizure of so many illegal substances at the Canadian border is a credit to the customs officers.
c. The storage of perishable food without refrigeration led to prosecution.
d. The collection of butterflies by the students shocked the conservation organization.

Like event d-nominals, those with fact interpretations can have obligatory "object" arguments; the *of* PPs are obligatory in (29) as in (17–19) and (21). Snyder (1998) questions the existence of aspectual modifiers like *constant/frequent* in event nominals, arguing that they are found only with fact interpretations. While it is certainly true that fact d-nominals can contain these adjectives, the examples in (30) seem to be unambiguously event nominals, since replacing *the frequent examination* with *the fact that the patient was examined frequently* leads to ill-formedness. This suggests that the context is compatible with an event interpretation but not with a fact meaning, yet the aspectual modifiers are grammatical.

(30) a. The frequent examination of the patient revealed that she was suffering from malaria.
b. The frequent examination of the patient is essential during the first trimester of a pregnancy.

While English does not show any formal correlate of the event versus fact/proposition semantic contrast, at least none that have been identified to date, other systems do. In Russian, for example, pronominal subjects of action nominals are pre-nominal possessive pronouns when the nominal has an event reading, and instrumental post-nominal pronouns when the nominal has a fact reading, as reported in Koptjevskaja-Tamm (1988: 167–168).

4.4 Nominalization across aspectual classes

In gross, there are d-nominals corresponding to verbs across all aspectual classes. To demonstrate this I provide examples of d-nominals based on activities, accomplishments and achievements. (See section 6 for state predicates.) It should be noted that some examples are awkward enough to merit further investigation.

The d-nominals in (31) are based on activity predicates. They exemplify *-ing* and *-ion* forms, and both d-nominals have complex event and fact interpretations. (Throughout this section examples with fact interpretations tend to allow an event interpretation in addition.)

(31) a. Careful simmering of the chicken for a whole day yields clear broth. (Event)
 b. Careful simmering of the chicken for a whole day made it delicious. (Fact)
 c. The investigation of the robbery for several weeks resulted in an arrest. (Event)
 d. The investigation of the robbery for several weeks was reported in the paper. (Fact)

Those in (32) are based on accomplishments. Again they include an *-ing* nominal and a nominal in *-ion*, and again both nominals are shown with complex event and fact interpretations. I provide an additional *-ing* example based on *write*, which is more clearly acceptable than the sentences based on *prepare*.

(32) a. The cookbook doesn't recommend the preparing of the dish in three minutes. (Event)
 b. The chef was amazed by the preparing of the meal in three minutes. (Fact)
 c. The cookbook doesn't recommend the preparation of the meal in three minutes. (Event)
 d. The chef was amazed by the preparation of the meal in three minutes. (Fact)

(33) a. I've never witnessed the writing of a paper in only three days. (Event)
 b. The writing of the paper in only three days did not improve its quality. (Fact)

It is widely reported in the literature (see, for example, the references in Alexiadou, Haegeman & Stavrou (2007: 531) that *-ing of* nominalizations must be atelic. The existence of examples like (32) and (33) shows that this is not the case. Similarly, a change of state predicate can have a telic d-nominal:

(34) The melting of the winter ice in three days caused heavy flooding.

The d-nominals of achievements (instantaneous events) in (35) are based on the verb *appoint* used above:

(35) a. The appointing of unqualified workers for extended periods of time is common in large companies. (Event)
b. The government was appalled by the company's continued appointing of unqualified workers. (Fact)
c. The appointment of unqualified workers for extended periods of time is common in large companies. (Event)
d. The government was appalled by the company's continued appointment of unqualified workers. (Fact)

The forgoing summarizes properties of complex event and fact nominals. It has emphasized similarities within the set of *-ing* and *-ion* complex event and fact nominals, but some very significant variation exists within them, and is currently being investigated. This is part of the focus of section 6.

5 Arguments, modifiers and adjuncts

Are satellites of nouns just like arguments of verbs, never like arguments of verbs, or sometimes like arguments of verbs? Are they instead similar to phrases associated with inherently relational nouns, which are not deverbal, such as *father, similarity, hostage*? Does the theory of thematic roles, and related proposals govern nouns as well as verbs? This is a much-studied issue (article 3 [Semantics: Lexical Structures and Adjectives] (Davis) *Thematic roles*, article 6 [this volume] (Barker) *Possessives and relational nouns* and Barker & Dowty 1993, Rappaport 1983, Dowty 1989, Grimshaw 1990, Kratzer 1996).

The answer, which is compatible with most of the evidence, is that the *structure* of d-nominals is basically determined by the syntax of DP, as outlined in 5.1. However the considerations presented in 5.2 suggest that the nature of the *relationship* between the modifying or complementing expressions and the noun is similar to that for verbs when the d-nominal has an event or fact interpretation.

5.1 Structural properties of d-nominals

With respect to form, d-nominals are like other nouns. Koptjevskaja-Tamm (1988: 227) observes that d-nominals cross-linguistically recruit their morphology and syntax from the nominal system, and this is decidedly so for English. Like all other nouns, d-nominals never take bare nominals as complements. In transitivity, then, they differ strikingly from verbs. In (14a), for example, the verb has a bare nominal as its complement, while *of* introduces the complement of the d-nominal in (14b). This pattern is fully general for nouns of all meanings: *a lot of the books, on top of the books, boxes of apples, a picture of Fred* are all ungrammatical if *of* is omitted. In Government-Binding Theory (Chomsky 1981), this difference is attributed to case assignment, with nouns unable to assign case to their complements. In much current work it is attributed to properties of the functional heads within the nominal system. See Alexiadou, Haegeman & Stavrou (2007) for references.

Possessives and prepositional complements, including *of* and *by* phrases, occur with all nominals, including those which are not event-denoting and not deverbal.

(36) a. the company's employees, the students' suggestion
 b. his definition of the issue, a mixture of coffee and tea, the denotation of this expression
 c. a performance by the Royal Shakespeare Company, all recommendations by untenured faculty

(37) a. The gang's thefts took place around 1pm.
 b. The theft of the document occurred during the night.
 c. Thefts by teenagers are on the rise.

(38) a. The gang's victim was badly injured.
 b. The victim of the crime was badly injured.

It has been suggested, however, that the structure of d-nominals, at least those which denote events or facts, is partly verbal, containing a VP in Hazout (1995) for Hebrew and Arabic (challenged in Siloni 1997a, 1997b); T, Asp and Voice-Event in van Hout & Roeper (1998); two Aspect projections above a VP in Fu, Roeper & Borer (2001); Num, Asp and v in Alexiadou (2001). These proposals resemble in some ways the Lees (1960) analysis, in which d-nominals have clausal structure. The NP in (39) exemplifies the analysis of van Hout & Roeper (1998).

(39) [$_{NP}$ -*ing*/-*tion*/-*er* [$_{TP}$ T [$_{AspP}$ Asp [$_{EventP}$ Event [$_{VP}$ V]]]]]

A rather direct piece of evidence supporting verbal syntactic structure within event nominals is their (rather marginal) ability to host adverbials. Comrie & Thompson (1985: 389–391) report that (40) is considered quasi-acceptable by some speakers.

(40) ?The enemy's destruction of the city rapidly

D-nominals in -*ing* also marginally admit modification by adverbs. (41) is from Jespersen (1946: 109).

(41)   The shutting of the gates regularly at ten o'clock had rendered our residence very irksome to me.

Such examples pose a challenge. If complex event nominals contain verbal structure, why are the examples with adverbs not perfect? If they do not contain verbal structure, why are they not simply ungrammatical?

5.2 Relational properties of d-nominals

Most early work on nouns and what they combine with held that all nouns lack the argument-taking properties of verbs. This was based partly on the assumption, contradicted by some of the examples in section 4, that arguments of nouns are always optional (e.g. Higginbotham 1983 and Bierwisch 1989). Dowty (1989: 88–91) took optionality as a fundamental property to be explained, proposing that neo-Davidsonian event modification governs satellites in nominals, while an "ordered argument system" governs the argument-taking capacity of verbs. In sharp contrast, Giorgi & Longobardi (1991) propose that arguments of nouns and verbs are the same in kind and that their thematic structure is the same, although both are subject to cross-linguistic variation. Stiebels (1999) claims, based on a study of Nahuatl, that argument realization is essentially identical in nouns and verbs, and that even non-event nominals inherit argument structure from verbs. (Although she does note that whether internal arguments of nouns must be realized depends on the interpretation of the nominal.)

Other theories distinguish among nouns based on meaning. Barker & Dowty (1993: 60–61) posit a verbal proto-role system and a nominal system and propose that "... where the noun denotes a true event, the verbal proto-roles are relevant..." concluding "... the traditional conception of verbal thematic roles is not adequate for describing the behavior of ultra-nominal nouns..." Grimshaw (1990) proposes that *of* PPs are arguments in true event d-nominals and not elsewhere, while *by* phrases (like possessives) are adjuncts, which are associated with suppressed argument positions. Zucchi (1993) argues that *by* phrases and *of* phrases are arguments when they occur with d-nominals. While in English complements there is no evidence from form to distinguish fact/event nominals from others,

Zubizarreta (1987) established that result nominals in Italian, French and Spanish express an agent-like modifier with a genitive, while event nominals use the equivalent of *by*: this is exemplified for Spanish by (42):

(42) a. La descripción del paisaje de Pedro (Result)
    b. La descripción del paisaje por Pedro (Event)
        "The description of the landscape of/by Pedro"

Such evidence supports the conclusion that the relational properties of fact and complex event nominals do indeed differ from those of individual nominals. See Rozwadowska (2005) and Alexiadou, Haegeman & Stavrou (2007) for further references.

There is yet more to be said, though, since even in complex event and fact nominals, the most verb-like d-nominals, the role of *by* and *of* phrases is more limited than in clauses, see Chomsky (1970), Rappaport (1983), Dowty (1989). The verb *present*, for example, allows its Goal to be realized as a direct object, but the corresponding d-nominal admits only a prepositional Goal.

(43) a. They presented gifts to the staff. They presented the staff with gifts.
    b. The presentation of gifts to the staff.... *The presentation of the staff with gifts....

A similar observation has been made for *by*. D-nominals of stative predicates such as *fear* allow their Experiencer argument to be expressed by a possessive as in (44b), but not a *by* PP as in (44c), which seems to introduce only agents in nominals, but is unrestricted with (passive) verbs, as in (44d).

(44) a. Some people fear flying.
    b. Some people's fear of flying is extreme.
    c. *(The) fear of flying by some people is extreme.
    d. Flying is feared by some people.

Another striking difference is that nouns do not require "subjects", even when they have an internal argument.

(45) a. The (doctor's) examination of the patients was a mistake/happened in the fall.
    b. The collection of butterflies (by the students) was frowned on.

For d-nominals, subjects are optional, and can be realized in a number of different ways. Apart from possessives and *by* phrases, they can be realized as adjectives: in *the Spanish decision to reduce the tariffs* the adjective *Spanish* encodes information about the decider (Chomsky 1970). According to proposals made by Grimshaw (1990), Zucchi (1993), Dowty (1989) the external argument of a d-nominal is like that of a passive: it is "suppressed", "existentially bound" or perhaps realized by a null element. The possessive and *by* phrase are related to this argument, but they are not required for satisfaction of the argument structure, and hence are optional. The argument structure of the active verb in (46) thus has two open positions, while that of the passive verb and the nominalization has just one. ("Ø" stands for the unrealized or silent argument.)

(46) *examine* (x, y); *examined* (Ø, y); *examination* (Ø, y)

In sum, it seems that the structure of d-nominals is basically determined by the syntax of DP, but the nature of the relationship between the modifying or complementing expressions and the noun are partly, but only partly, verb-like when the d-nominal has an event or fact interpretation. The search for a deeper understanding of these properties of nouns and verbs is prominent on the agenda for the future, and the solution seems likely to shed light on the fundamental notions of "predicate" and "argument".

6 Some nominalization puzzles

In general here I have emphasized the systematic and shared properties of d-nominals. It must be said, however, that their properties remain challenging to understand, and this section describes some of the puzzles they currently pose to researchers.

One nominalization puzzle that has already been encountered concerns a missing interpretation: if it is true, as suggested in section 4.3, that propositional readings are impossible for d-nominals, what is the explanation? In fact, the only d-nominals that function productively as an argument of *true* and *false* are those which correspond to predicates which take sentential complements. Yet these d-nominals introduce yet another puzzle: even though they combine with *true* and *false* this is not because they denote propositions. While (47) is grammatical, it does not mean "the proposition that Mary claimed/stated that the earth is flat is false". Rather the propositions for which truth is being assessed are those that form the content of the statement or claim, just as for nouns with no verbal base like *idea* or *story*.

(47) Mary's claim/statement that the earth is flat is false.

This is why (47) and (48) are not contradictory

(48) That Mary stated/claims that the earth is flat is true.

Two other facts add to the problem. First, these d-nominals lack fact or event inter-pretations altogether (see Stowell 1981 and references there), and second, sentential complements to nouns, but not to verbs, are always optional (Grimshaw 1990).

(49) a. Mary claims/stated *(that it was raining).
    b. Mary's claim/statement is true.

Presumably the interpretation of the d-nominal lies behind the optionality of the complement, but there is no current explanation for either. Moreover we cannot yet explain why the d-nominals do not have fact, event or propositional interpretations.

When we extend the Bisetto & Melloni (2007) analysis of result nominals, reviewed in section 3, to *-ing* d-nominals, we find an unpredicted but apparently systematic gap. An *-ing* result nominal, which corresponds to the object of an ordinary creation verb can exist with a result reading: what is built is a *building*, what is written is *writing*, what is painted is a *painting*. However, an *-ing* version of the *transcription* variety of result d-nominal seems to be impossible: *describing*, *modifying*, *transcribing*, and *nominalizing* do not exist at all as result nouns. Why not?

Other puzzles for the theory promise insight into the theory of event representation, which is of foundational importance in understanding deverbal nominalization. One such case is causative verbs, generally analyzed as corresponding to events which have internal subparts. They show revealing nominalization patterns, which have puzzled researchers for 40 years, and led to a variety of (not always consistent) empirical and theoretical proposals. Chomsky (1970) states that causatives do not form "transitive" d-nominals (e.g.*the farmer's growth of the corn*). Smith (1972) proposes that those which nominalize with latinate morphology do have such d-nominals (e.g. *the submersion of the car by the thieves*) and Pesetsky (1995) argues that causative verbs which lack inchoative variants have transitive nominalizations. Harley & Noyer (2000) argue that alternating verbs (i.e. those which do have inchoatives) can have transitive d-nominals provided that the external argument can be construed as what Levin & Rappaport (1995) call an "external cause", as in *the army's explosion of the bridge*. Sichel (2010) proposes that the external argument of a causative and a d-nominal of the *-ion* kind must be a direct participant in the event it refers to, eliminating both #*The sun's postponement of the hike* and #*The sun postponed the hike*. She derives this requirement from a general constraint on the complexity of events that single roots and d-nominals other than those in *-ing* can refer to, providing a convincing demonstration of the role of events in the theory of nominals. This extended sequence of investigations has shed light on causativization, the nature of agents and cause arguments, and the role of event structure in the properties of predicates; cf. article 4 [Semantics: Lexical Structures and Adjectives] (Levin & Rappaport Hovav) *Lexical Conceptual Structure* for extensive discussion and relevant references.

Aspect is again at issue in the behaviour of intransitives. Zwicky (1971) and Levin (1993: 205) note that intransitive activity predicates, like *shout, groan* (belonging to the "manner-of-speaking" group), have d-nominals with no extra morphology. They do not seem to satisfy the criteria for being complex event nominals. The paradigm in (50) illustrates the point.

(50) a. The boys' shout(s) (cf. The boys shouted.)
     b. *The boys' shout of the score/for 5 minutes (cf. The boys shouted the score for 5 minutes.)
     c. *The boy's constant shout (cf. The boys shouted constantly.)

This seems to be true for unergative predicates in many systems. (See Alexiadou 2001 and Rozwadowska 2005 for further discussion of intransitive verbs and nominalization.) Picallo (1991), for example, showed that unergative intransitives in Catalan nominalize only to results, explaining why they do not allow the equivalent of *by* phrases, which are licensed only in complex event nominals. (See the discussion of (42).) Like the English (unergative) *shout* verbs, the Catalan verbs don't participate in the morphological system which supports event nominalization. In contrast, both unergative verbs and unaccusatives form complex event nominals in Polish and Russian (Rowzwadowska 1997, Schoorlemmer 1998). In Hebrew verbs of emission and contact have corresponding event nominals (Sichel 2010). Clearly aspect and morphology are both playing a role here but the exact nature of their interaction is not clear.

Yet another aspectual puzzle concerns nominalization of stative predicates and nominalizations with stative meanings. Stative verbs never have nominalizations in *-ing* as Lees (1960: 66) pointed out. (51) illustrates the generalization using several different stative verb types:

(51) a. *The (students') believing/knowing of the story ...
     b. *The (students') loving/resenting of their families ...

c. *The (children's) resembling of their parents...
d. * The (bucket's) containing of poison was frightening.
e. *The (children's) possessing of bicycles ...
f. *The (theory's) entailing of the right results ...

In contrast, verbal gerunds can be formed from state predicates. Removing *of* from the examples in (51) yields grammatical verbal gerunds. This is presumably due to the fact that verbal gerunds are simply forms of the verbs themselves. What explains the restriction? It seems likely that the gap should be attributed to *–ing* itself. Zucchi (1993: 83–84) posits a rule, which constructs the meanings of *–ing* nominals from the base verbs, which simply stipulates that the verb must be [-stative]. Borer (2005: 244) proposes that *–ing* is a "modifier of originator", hence requires an event, not a state, as its complement.

D-nominals with a state interpretation do exist, for example those based on the psychological predicates for which the experiencer is the direct object: *the weather annoyed me, his behavior embarrassed his friends*. The nominals name the state resulting from the event described by the verb and its arguments. (See Rappaport 1983, Grimshaw 1990, Pesetsky 1995.)

(52) annoyance, embarrassment, bewilderment, astonishment, humiliation, perturbation, surprise

The de-adjectival noun *happiness* and de-verbal noun *embarrassment* have the same kind of meaning in this view. The predicates they combine with in (53) do not combine with facts or with events—neither an event nor a fact can fade within an hour, or be intense.

(53) a. Her friend's behavior embarrassed Susan. Her embarrassment faded in an hour.
b. Her friend's behavior made Susan happy. Her happiness was intense.

As expected if they denote states, the cause of the change of state cannot be realized by an agentive form, such as a *by* phrase (Dowty 1989):

(54) *Her intense embarrassment by the waiter (cf. She was embarrassed by the waiter)

Why do these d-nominals lack event/fact meanings? Adding to the situation, when we return to *-ing* we find that it forms neither state nor event/fact nominals with the predicates just discussed: *annoying, embarrassing, bewildering, astonishing*, etc. do not exist at all as nouns.

(55) Her friend's behavior embarrassed Susan. *Her/the embarrassing occurred in the evening/was intense.

Why not?

7 Summary

Deverbal nominalization has attracted a major research effort for the past 40 years and more. The insights of the works reviewed here remain at the core of current research, which aims to answer a cluster of questions: what is the relationship between the meaning of a verb and the meaning of a nominal derived from that verb? What does the morphology contribute? What properties do d-nominals have, and how are they related to nouns, on the one hand, and verbs on the other? What is predictable, and what is arbitrary?

Although deverbal nominals are enormously complex, they are not unsystematic. There is a coherent relationship between the meaning of a d-nominal and its formal properties: nominals referring to individuals are less like verbs than nominals, which refer to complex events or facts.

Some deverbal nominals appear to have all of the meanings that nominals not derived from verbs have, patterning exactly like non-deverbal nouns grammatically and semantically. However, some deverbal nominals denoting events or facts preserve some verbal properties which are not retained in nominals with other meanings. Proposals attempting to explicate the systematic characteristics of these more verb-like nominalizations draw on three principal theoretical resources. Deverbal nominals are held to preserve (some of) the syntactic structure of verbs; to preserve the thematic/argument structure of verbs; and to preserve the event structure/aspect of verbs.

The ultimate theory of nominalization will explain, to the extent that explanation is possible, how the properties of a nominal follow from the properties of nouns in general, the nature of the affixation involved, and the properties of the noun's verbal core. The argument structure and aspectual characteristics of the verb, the thematic relations of its arguments and the properties of the deverbalizing affix are all known to make systematic contributions to the nature of a d-nominal.

Acknowledgements: I thank Daniel Altshuler, Adrian Brasoveanu, Veneeta Dayal, Paul Portner, Alan Prince and Roger Schwarzschild for many valuable discussions of the material in this article.

8 References

Abney, Steven 1987. *The English Noun Phrase in its Sentential Aspect*. Ph.D. dissertation. MIT, Cambridge, MA.
Alexiadou, Artemis 2001. *Functional Structure in Nominals: Nominalization and Ergativity*. Amsterdam: Benjamins.
Alexiadou, Artemis, Liliane Haegeman & Melita Stavrou 2007. *Noun Phrase in the Generative Perspective*. Berlin: de Gruyter.
Anderson, Mona 1978. Prenominal genitive NPs. *The Linguistic Review* 3, 1–24.
Barker, Chris 1998. Episodic -*ee* in English: A thematic role constraint on new word formation. *Language* 74, 695–727.
Barker, Chris & David Dowty 1993. Non-verbal thematic proto-roles. In: A. Schafer (ed.). *Proceedings of the Annual Meeting of the North Eastern Linguistic Society (= NELS) 23*. Amherst, MA: GSLA, 49–62.
Bierwisch, Manfred 1989. Event nominalization: Proposals and problems. *Linguistische Studien* 194, 1–73.
Bisetto, Antonietta & Chiara Melloni 2007. Result nominals: A lexical-semantic investigation. In: G. Booij et al. (eds.). *On-line Proceedings of the Fifth Mediterranean Morphology Meeting (= MMM5)*, 393–412. http://mmm.lingue.unibo.it/proc-mmm5.php. August 15, 2009.
Borer, Hagit 2005. *The Normal Course of Events*. Oxford: Oxford University Press.
Chierchia, Gennaro 1984. *Topics in the Syntax and Semantics of Infinitives and Gerunds*. Ph.D. dissertation. University of Massachusetts, Amherst, MA.
Chomsky, Noam 1970. Remarks on nominalization. In: R. A. Jacobs & P. S. Rosenbaum (eds.). *Readings in English Transformational Grammar*. Waltham, MA: Ginn & Co., 184–221.
Chomsky, Noam 1981. *Lectures on Government and Binding*. Dordrecht: Foris.
Comrie, Bernard & Sandra Thompson 1985. Lexical nominalization. In: T. Shopen (ed.). *Language Typology and Syntactic Description*, vol. III: *Grammatical Categories and the Lexicon*. Cambridge: Cambridge University Press, 349–398.
Crisma, Paola 1993. On adjective placement in Romance and Germanic event nominals. *Rivista di Grammatica Generativa* 18, 61–100.
Davies, Mark 2008. *The Corpus of Contemporary American English (COCA)*: 385 Million Words, 1990-present. http://www.americancorpus.org. August 17, 2009.
Dowty, David 1979. *Word Meaning and Montague Grammar. The Semantics of Verbs and Times in Generative Semantics and in Montague's PTQ*. Dordrecht: Reidel.
Dowty, David 1989. On the semantic content of the notion of "thematic role". In: G. Chierchia, B. Partee & R. Turner (eds.). *Properties, Types and Meaning*. Dordrecht: Kluwer, 69–129.
Dowty, David 1991. Thematic proto-roles and argument selection. *Language* 67, 547–619.
Fu, Jingqi, Thomas Roeper & Hagit Borer 2001. The VP within process nominals: Evidence from adverbs and the VP anaphor *do so*. *Natural Language and Linguistic Theory* 19, 549–582.

Giannakidou, Anastasia & Monika Rathert (eds.) *2009. Quantification, Definiteness and Nominalization*. Oxford: Oxford University Press.

Giorgi, Alessandra & Giuseppe Longobardi 1991. *The Syntax of Noun Phrases: Configuration, Parameters, and Empty Categories*. Cambridge: Cambridge University Press.

Grimshaw, Jane 1990. *Argument Structure*. Cambridge, MA: The MIT Press.

Harley, Heidi & Rolf Noyer 1999. Distributed Morphology. *Glot International* 4, 3–9.

Harley, Heidi & Rolf Noyer 2000. Formal vs. encyclopedic knowledge: Evidence from nominalization. In: B. Peters (ed.). *The Lexicon–Encyclopedia Interface*. Amsterdam: Elsevier, 349–374.

Hazout, Ilan 1990. *Verbal Nouns: Theta Theoretic Studies in Hebrew and Arabic*. Ph.D. dissertation. University of Massachusetts, Amherst, MA.

Hazout, Ilan 1995. Action nominalizations and the lexicalist hypothesis. *Natural Language and Linguistic Theory* 13, 355–404.

Higginbotham, James 1983. Logical form, binding and nominals. *Linguistic Inquiry* 14, 395–420.

van Hout, Angeliek & Thomas Roeper 1998. Events and aspectual structure in derivational morphology. In: H. Harley (ed.). *Papers from the UPenn/MIT Roundtable on Argument Structure and Aspect* (MIT Working Papers in Linguistics 32). Cambridge, MA: MIT, 175–220.

Jackendoff, Ray 1977. *X-bar Syntax: A Study of Phrase Structure*. Cambridge, MA: The MIT Press.

Jespersen, Otto 1946. *A Modern English Grammar on Historical Principles. Part V: Syntax, Fourth Volume*. London: Allen and Unwin. Reprinted: Northhampton: John Dickens & Co., 1961, 1965, 1970.

Koptjevskaja-Tamm, Maria 1988. *A Typology of Action Nominal Constructions*. Doctoral dissertation. University of Stockholm.

Kratzer, Angelika 1996. Severing the external argument from its verb. In: J. Rooryck & L. Zaring (eds.). *Phrase Structure and the Lexicon*. Dordrecht: Kluwer, 109–137.

Lees, Robert 1960. The grammar of English nominalizations. *International Journal of American Linguistics* 26, 1–205.

Levin, Beth 1993. *English Verb Classes and Alternations: A Preliminary Investigation*. Chicago, IL: The University of Chicago Press.

Levin, Beth & Malka Rappaport 1988. Nonevent -*er* nominals: A probe into argument structure. *Linguistics* 26, 1067–1083.

Levin, Beth & Malka Rappaport Hovav 1995. *Unaccusativity*. Cambridge, MA: The MIT Press.

Lieber, Rochelle 2004. *Morphology and Lexical Semantics*. Cambridge: Cambridge University Press.

Pesetsky, David 1995. *Zero Syntax: Experiencers and Cascades*. Cambridge, MA: The MIT Press.

Peterson, Philip 1997. *Fact Proposition Event*. Dordrecht: Kluwer.

Picallo, Carme 1991. Nominals and nominalizations in Catalan. *Probus* 3, 271–316.

Portner, Paul 1992. *Situation Theory and the Semantics of Propositional Expressions*. Ph.D. dissertation. University of Massachusetts, Amherst, MA.

Rappaport, Malka 1983. On the nature of derived nominals. In: L. Levin, M. Rappaport & A. Zaenen (eds.). *Papers in Lexical-Functional Grammar*. Bloomington, IN: Indiana University Linguistics Club, 113–142.

Rappaport Hovav, Malka & Beth Levin 1992. -*er* nominals: Implications for a theory of argument structure. In: T. Stowell & E. Wehrli (eds.). *Syntax and Semantics 26: Syntax and the Lexicon*. New York: Academic Press, 127–153.

Rozwadowska, Bożena 1997. *Towards a Unified Theory of Nominalizations. External and Internal Eventualities*. Wroclaw: Wydawnictwo Uniwersytetu Wroclawskiego.

Rozwadowska, Bożena 2005. Derived nominals. In: M. Everaert & H. van Riemsdijk (eds.). *The Blackwell Companion to Syntax, vol. II*. Malden, MA: Blackwell, 24–55.

Schoorlemmer, Maaike 1998. Complex event nominals in Russian: Properties and meanings. *Journal of Slavic Linguistics* 6, 205–254.

Sichel, Ivy 2010. Event-structure constraints on nominalization. In: A. Alexiadou & M. Rathert (eds.). *The Syntax of Nominalizations across Languages and Frameworks*. Berlin: Mouton de Gruyter, 159–198.

Siloni, Tal 1997a. Event nominals and the construct state. In: L. Haegeman (ed.) *The New Comparative Syntax*. New York: Longman, 165–188.

Siloni, Tal 1997b. Noun Phrases and Nominalizations: *The syntax of DPs*. Dordrecht: Kluwer.

Toshiyuki Ogihara
13 Tense

1   Introduction —— 436
2   Theories of tense —— 438
3   Tense morphemes, adverbials, and quantification —— 443
4   Tense in embedded contexts —— 448
5   Tense and modality —— 458
6   References —— 461

Abstract: Tense is an extremely important ingredient of natural language in that a tense morpheme or some other expression carrying temporal information is virtually a required element in matrix sentences. It is clear that the temporal information conveyed by an entire sentence involves both an existential quantifier and contextual restriction to a salient past interval. However, it is not easy to provide a precise semantic contribution made by tense morphemes themselves because they interact with various types of temporal adverbials and quantificational expressions. The previous research suggests that overt or covert temporal adverbials (e.g., *once, every Sunday, in the past*) are carriers of temporal information and not tense morphemes themselves. Turning to embedded clauses, this chapter argues for the position that a verb complement clause denotes a property, i.e., a set of individual-time-world triples. The last section briefly discusses the interaction of tense and modality. Although tense and modality are largely independent of each other, there are some circumstances in which their interaction is undeniable. As an instance, the case of *be going to* is presented as a hybrid form involving both temporal and modal ingredients.

1 Introduction

Tense is an important ingredient of natural language, and it normally takes the form of a verbal affix. For example, English has a tense morpheme *-ed* that indicates temporal anteriority. It is referred to as a past tense morpheme. In general, one uses this morpheme to describe an event or state that took place in the past, although using present perfect is also a possibility. For example, in order to describe

---

Toshiyuki Ogihara, Seattle, WA (USA)

https://doi.org/10.1515/9783110589443-013

a completed event of closing the door by John, one uses (1a) or (1b). Using sentences like (1c) or (1d) would not be able to describe the said situation.

(1)   a. John closed the door.
      b. John has closed the door.
      c. (#)John closes the door.
      d. (#)John will close the door.

There are some important differences between (1a) and (1b). But they are both capable of indicating situations that are located wholly in the past, and (1a) and (1b) are both acceptable in the situation under discussion. On the other hand, the simple present tense in (1c) and the future tense in (1d) are incapable of indicating a past event as in the described situation. For the purpose of this chapter, I will concentrate on the past tense morpheme, ignoring the perfect. The perfect is normally considered to be a construction that conveys some aspectual information. For example, (1b) not only indicates a past event of John's closing the door but also suggests the existence of a current state that results from the event (i.e., the state of the door's being closed or, in some cases, John's experience that resulted from closing the door). Although it is not an easy task to characterize the English present perfect in precise terms (see article 10 [this volume] (Portner) *Perfect and progressive*) it seems safe to assume that its main semantic role is not to locate an event or state described by the verb at a particular past time.

The fact that each matrix clause is tensed in many natural languages, including English and Japanese, indicates the importance of tense. This in turn suggests the importance of temporal information in natural language since tense is associated with it. In this sense, tense is different from locative expressions (e.g., *in Seattle*) and manner adverbials (e.g., *quickly*, *slowly*). They are never obligatory in the sense that their presence is not required to make the sentence in question grammatical. This is true even when the event in question obtains at a particular location and in a particular manner. For example, (2) shows that even if John ate a bag of popcorn quickly in the movie theater, the information about the manner (*quickly*) or the location (*in the movie theater*) does not have to be mentioned in the sentence. Nevertheless, a tense morpheme is obligatorily included in the sentence.

(2)   John ate a bag of popcorn.

In this chapter, I shall discuss how tense interacts with other important expressions within the sentence such as events, temporal adverbials and modality. I shall discuss the behavior of tense in embedded clauses as well.

2 Theories of tense

Having stressed the importance of tense for natural language semantics, let us turn to some possible means of formalizing the semantic effects of tense. In the tradition of tense logic (Prior 1957, 1967), tense is understood to correspond to an existential quantifier over a set of times. Prior (1957, 1967) introduces operators **P** ("it has been the case that α") and **F** ("it will be the case that α"). This approach is adopted in Montague's work (1973) as well, though Montague employs **H** for the present perfect, and **W** for the future modal *will*. The operators **H** and **W** receive existential quantifier interpretations in that they mean "there is a past time at which..." and "there is a future time at which...", respectively. Despite the fact that Prior and Montague deal with the English present perfect in their systems, it is generally assumed that **P** (or **H**) corresponds to the past tense morpheme (i.e., *-ed*). Partee (1973), Enç (1987) and Kamp & Reyle (1993) (among others) show that the English simple past cannot be described in terms of the semantics associated with **P** or **H**. If we assume that **P** means *-ed*, then (3a) receives the interpretation given informally in (3b).

(3) a. John saw Mary.
    b. ∃t [t is earlier than now ∧ John sees Mary at t]

This purely existential analysis of the past tense morpheme *-ed* is inadequate for many reasons. But I shall postpone this discussion and move on to an analysis of tensed sentences that is substantially different from that of tense logic.

Davidson's (1967) analysis of declarative sentences gives us another way of looking at tensed sentences. Davidson claims that a declarative sentence involves an existential assertion about an event. In this system, events are primitive entities. Davidson himself was not concerned so much about how tense-related information is formalized within his system. However, it is relatively straightforward to extend his system to incorporate the information associated with tense. For example, (4a) can be symbolized as in (4b). "Time" in (4b) indicates that function that maps an event to its "temporal trace" (temporal trace function), which is the time that the event occupies.

(4) a. Jones buttered the toast.
    b. ∃e[Time(e) < now & butter(Jones, the toast, e)]

Davidson's approach can be used to account for the behavior of adverbs, among others. Prior's approach (as interpreted by some linguists) and this particular extension of Davidson's approach (which includes an analysis of tense in terms a temporal trace function) share the view that tensed sentences involve an existential assertion. They both amount to the claim that a sentence in the past tense is used to assert that there is a past time at which a relevant situation obtains.

This straightforward application of tense logic to the English past tense morpheme has problems. The same criticism applies to Davidson's approach as long as its semantics is given in terms of simple existential quantification over past times. Partee (1973) points out that a sentence in the past tense is used to talk about a particular past time under discussion, not to claim the existence of a past time that satisfies some descriptive content. Partee's example involves negation as shown in (5a). The scenario is that the speaker utters it while driving on the freeway after leaving home. The point of (5a) is that it cannot receive the interpretation in (5b) or the one in (5c). What (5a) really means is that the speaker failed to turn off the stove before leaving home. Partee claims that the correct interpretation is represented as in (5d), where the free variable t receives an appropriate value from the context. The free variable t is presupposed to denote a past time. Just as a free pronoun is used to indicate a particular individual supplied in the context of use with an added presupposition about the gender of the individual, tense is claimed to involve the existence of a free variable with an added presupposition.

(5) a. I didn't turn off the stove.
   b. There is a past time t such that I do not turn off the stove at t.
   c. It is not the case that there is a past time at which I turn off the stove.
   d. It is not the case that I turn off the stove at t. (where the value of t is provided by the context and t is presupposed to be a past time)

The important point in (5d) is that it does not involve existential quantification over (past) times. The upshot of Partee's discussion is that (5a) shows that past tense does not make an existential claim about times. Past tense is like a free time variable with a presupposition that its value must be a past time. The value of the free variable is supplied by the context. Partee's contention makes a valid point, and it clearly shows that simple (i.e., unrestricted) quantification over past times does not accurately represent the meaning of past tense.

It is important for me to discuss Reichenbach's (1947) analysis of tense here in connection with Partee's proposal about tense. Reichenbach proposes that a correct account of tense in natural language involves three temporal concepts: speech point (S), event point (E), and reference point (R). Intuitively, R represents the time salient at a particular point in discourse. Recall that in Partee's (1973) account the denotation of the free temporal variable is determined by the context, and this interval is considered to be one that is salient in the context. It is natural to construe Reichenbach's reference point as the denotation of the free variable in Partee's account. Reichenbach persuasively argued for the idea that the crucial difference between the simple past (e.g., (6a)) and the past perfect (e.g., (6b)) is the relationship between R and E. As the diagrams in (6) indicate, (6a) requires that R and E be co-temporal, whereas (6b) requires that E precede R.

(6) a. John left Seattle.   R,E ___ S
     b. John had left Seattle.   E ___ R ___ S

Reichenbach's analysis is incorporated in Kamp & Reyle's (1993) Discourse Representation Theory analysis of tense. This will be discussed below.

The discussion so far establishes that the interpretation of tense cannot be accounted for in terms of simple existential quantification over past times and is context sensitive. But this is hardly the whole story. Partee (1984) concedes that a simple free variable analysis of tense has its own problems. Free pronouns are used to denote individuals that are salient in the context. For example, (7) shows that under its most natural interpretation the pronoun *he* that occurs in the second sentence refers back to John. In other words, the pronoun *he* denotes the same individual that *John* refers to. On the other hand, the time of John's sitting down is understood to be shortly *after* the time of his entering the room. So the case of temporal anaphora is not completely parallel to that of nominal anaphora. This point will be elaborated below when we discuss Discourse Representation Theory.

(7) John entered the room. He sat down.

Another problem with the free variable analysis of past tense is that an event sentence often requires existential quantification over times and contextual restriction upon the quantificational force. Consider the example in (8).

(8) A: Did you know that Mary was in Seattle last year as a visiting scholar? Mary told me that she and you met in London ten years ago and that she wanted to see you again. Did you see her?
    B: Yes, I did. As a matter of fact, we did a research project together.

Given that A knows that B first met Mary ten years ago, A's question *Did you see her?* cannot be taken to involve simple existential quantification over past times. It must be about a specific time interval, the last academic year. However, A's question clearly does not talk about a specific moment within the year in question either. B's answer *Yes I did* is truthful only if there was an event of B's seeing

Mary within the time frame in question. This means that B's positive answer is taken to have the interpretation symbolized as in (9), in which the time of seeing is restricted to the appropriate time frame. Here, the verb *see* is analyzed as a three-place predicate involving two individuals and a time interval. The intuitive truth condition of **see(B, Mary, t)** is that B sees Mary at t. The notation used here is that of Ogihara (1996), which slightly differs from Dowty (1979) in that a predicate like *see* contains an extra argument place for a time. Dowty, by contrast, used an **At** operator to introduce a temporal variable into the logical language. The subset symbol is used in (9) to indicate a "subpart" relation between two intervals. This notation is based upon the assumption that an interval is defined as a set of instants with "no gaps". The reader is referred to Dowty (1979) and Ogihara (1996) for technical details.

(9) $\exists t[t \subseteq$ last-academic-year $\wedge$ see(B, Mary, t)]
Paraphrase: there is a time t such that t is within the last academic year and B sees Mary at t.

The same is true of Partee's example (5a). In this case, the contextually specified time is shorter than the case of the above scenario. Nevertheless, there would be some interval any part of which is suitable for turning off the stove in this situation as well. Although it is important to turn off the stove soon after cooking, there is no particular moment when this has to happen. As long as the stove is turned off soon enough, everything is fine. So (5a) should receive the interpretation symbolized in (10). This in turn shows that (5a) too requires both existential quantification and contextual restriction.

(10) $\neg\exists t[t \subseteq i \wedge$ turn-off(the speaker, the stove, t)]
where i indicates the interval that starts when the cooking is finished and lasts for a minute (say).

Having established that an accurate account of the tense must involve both existential quantification and contextual restriction, I now move on to a survey of the analysis of tense within Discourse Representation Theory (abbreviated as DRT). Kamp & Reyle (1993) present a proposal within DRT which employs Reichenbach's (1947) concept of Reference point. The role of Reference time (which roughly corresponds to the value of the free time variable in Partee's (1973) analysis) is conceptualized in a dynamic way in DRT in that each sentence in a discourse updates it for the next sentence. This mechanism partly depends upon the aspectual nature of the sentence in question. When the sentence in question is an event sentence, the event it describes is understood to be located after the current Reference point, and the time of the event becomes the new Reference point to be used by the following sentence. On the other hand, when the sentence in question is a state sentence, the state being described contains the current Reference time, and the current Reference time is used again for the next sentence in the discourse. (11) shows the difference between events and states in a narrative discourse.

(11) a. E1: John arrived at the airport. S1: <u>Mary was (already) at the ticket counter.</u> E2: He apologized for being late.
 b. E1: John arrived at the airport. E2: <u>He immediately went to the ticket counter.</u> E3: The airline agent greeted him.

E indicates an event, S a state. (11a) is a discourse that consists of an event sentence, a state sentence, and another event sentence. Note that S1 overlaps E1. This is because the new Reference point that is introduced by the first sentence for the second sentence (which equals E1) is contained within the time of S1. Thus, S1 is understood to overlap E1. E2, which the third sentence describes, is then understood to follow E1. This is shown graphically in (12a). On the other hand, (11b) produces a different semantic effect. (11b) consists of three event sentences, and each of them moves the narrative time forward. Thus, E1 is followed by E2, which is in turn followed by E3.

(12) a. _____E1___E2_____
          S1
 b. _____E1_E2_E3_____

The above discussion shows that a situation described by the sentence in question is not usually simultaneous with the current Reference point. In the case of an event, the event in question is placed slightly after the current Reference point; in the case of a state, it (generally) includes the Reference point. This suggests that DRT's use of Reference point deviates slightly from the way Reichenbach employs it. But DRT's account is a refinement of Reichenbach's and preserves the basic intuitions behind it.

Let me make one side remark here about the status of events and times in semantic theory. Kamp & Reyle (1993) follow Davidson in presuming that events are primitive entities and then define an instant as a maximal set of pairwise overlapping events. This means that instants are derived from events. The idea here is that positing events as primitive entities is better than deriving intervals or events from durationless instants. Kamp & Reyle's position is that it is not plausible that we recognize durationless instants in the same way that we recognize regular individuals such as humans and objects. Although this is definitely a viable position, it is not easy to settle the question of the relationship between times and events empirically one way or the other. For example, if we assume that events are primitives, we must ask some difficult questions such as the following: (i) Can the same event be described in many different ways? (ii) Is the same event found across different worlds? Thus, it is arguable that events may be derived from intervals, if not from instants. These are extremely interesting but difficult issues. Accordingly, I shall not take a stand on this controversy. I believe that we can discuss the semantic issues of tense without taking a stand on the ontological questions about times and events.

3 Tense morphemes, adverbials, and quantification

In Section 2, I discussed some problems with the view that tense involves simple existential quantification over times. After discussing Partee (1973, 1984), Davidson (1977), etc., I tentatively concluded that both reference to a particular interval (contributed by an overt or covert adverbial) and existential quantification are needed. In this section, I shall discuss sentences in which overt temporal adverbials occur. Let me start with a relatively straightforward case which involves an adverbial making reference to a specific interval, such as *in 1985*. One could write a predicate logic formula (containing a variable for times) of the form given in (13b) to represent the meaning of (13a).

(13) a. John left the U.S. in 1985.
b. $\exists t[t < now \land leaves(John, the\ U.S., t) \land t \subseteq 1985]$

Assuming that *1985* denotes (the interval that corresponds to) the year 1985, and that the preposition *in* indicates a sub-part relation between the time of John's leaving and the interval denoted by 1985, one can represent as in (13b) the meaning attributed to (13a). A similar representation is possible with an event variable and a temporal trace function. (13b) shows that both existential quantification and contextual restriction are needed to account for the semantics conveyed by (13a), which involves both past tense and a temporal adverbial.

We need to discuss how the reading represented in (13b) is obtained in a compositional way. We also need to discuss sentences containing multiple adverbials or some special frequency adverbials like *exactly twice*. Let me discuss them in turn.

First, if we assume that a VP that contains past tense is interpreted as in (14a), then there is no way that an adverbial could be added in a compositional way because (14a) can only be combined with the meaning of a name (like *John*), and an adverbial would have to be left unprocessed. This means that (14b) cannot be processed compositionally if we assume that (14a) indicates the denotation of *left*.

(14) a. $\lambda x \exists t\, [t < now\, \&\, leaves(x, t)]$
  b. John left yesterday.

To correct this problem, Dowty (1979) introduces a proposal that works as follows: (i) any tensed sentence obligatorily contains a (covert or overt) temporal adverbial; (ii) the adverbial has as part of its meaning an existential quantifier; (iii) each adverbial is classified into three types (past, present and future), and combines with a tenseless sentence to yield a tensed sentence containing a desired tense morpheme. For example, *yesterday* is a past tense adverbial, and it combines with a tenseless sentence like *John take a walk* to yield a past tense sentence *John took a walk yesterday*. For example, (15) is analyzed semantically as in (16). (16) is in the spirit of Dowty's (1979) analysis except that times are introduced as arguments of verbs as in Ogihara (1996). P_t and Q_t indicate variables ranging over sets of times.

(15) John left yesterday.

(16) 1. John leaves $\Rightarrow \lambda t[leaves(j, t)]$
  2. yesterday $\Rightarrow \lambda P_t\, \exists t[P_t(t) \wedge t \subseteq yesterday]$
  3. John left yesterday $\Rightarrow \lambda P_t\, \exists t[P_t(t) \wedge t \subseteq yesterday](\lambda Q_t\, \lambda t''[t'' < now \wedge Q_t(t'')])$ $(\lambda t'[leaves(j, t')])$
  4. $\lambda P_t\, \exists t[P_t(t) \wedge t \subseteq yesterday](\lambda t''[t'' < now \wedge leaves(j, t'')])$
  5. $\exists t[t < now \wedge leaves(j, t) \wedge t \subseteq yesterday]$

According to this approach, some temporal adverbials such as *today* belong to multiple types because they are compatible with more than one tense morpheme.

According to Dowty's system, each English sentence contains exactly one temporal adverbial that introduces an existential quantifier and a restriction on the domain of quantification. Thus, Dowty needs a special provision for sentences which do not contain temporal adverbs. That is, his system has a rule which introduces an existential quantifier in the semantics when there is no overt temporal adverbial in the sentence. Put informally, this is like positing a covert adverb *at least once*. Dowty's proposal does not account for cases in which multiple adverbials occur in single sentences as exemplified by (17).

(17) John left in August in 2008.

This problem is solved in Stump's (1985) proposal in which an existential quantifier is introduced as part of a truth definition. In this proposal, even after a tense morpheme is introduced, the resulting expression is a function from times into truth values. Until the matrix-clause-level existential quantifier is introduced by the truth definition, the "sentence" is semantically a temporal abstract (a function from times into truth values). This allows it to be combined with any number of temporal adverbials, which are "temporal abstract modifiers" (functions of type <<i,t>,<i,t>>). Thus, Stump can explain the fact that multiple adverbials can occur in the same sentence. At the matrix level, the truth definition says this: the sentence is true iff there is a time t such that F(t) = 1, where F indicates the temporal abstract denoted by the entire sentence. In this way, Stump does not need to posit a covert adverbial *at least once* because this semantic role is satisfied by the truth definition. (18) shows how Stump's proposal deals with (17).

(18) 1. John left ⇒ λt [t < now ∧ leaves(j, t)]
    2. in August ⇒ λP_t λt_2 ∃t_3[P_t(t_2) & t_2 ⊆ t_3 ∧ August(t_3)]
    3. in 2008 ⇒ λP_t λt_2 [P_t(t_2) ∧ t_2⊆ 2008]
    4. John left in August ⇒
       λt ∃t_1[t < now ∧ leaves(j, t) & t⊆ t_1 ∧ August(t_1)]
    5. John left in August in 2008 ⇒
       λt [∃t_1[t < now ∧ leaves(j, t) ∧ t ⊆ t_1 ∧ August(t_1)] ∧ t⊆ 2008]
    6. The sentence is true iff there is a time t_3 such that
       ⟦λt[∃t_1[t < now ∧ leaves(j, t) ∧ t⊆ t_1 ∧ August(t_1)] ∧ t⊆ 2008]⟧ (t_3) = true

Stump's account is not without problems. Bäuerle (1978) shows that special frequency adverbials like *exactly three times* are not compatible with a separately introduced existential quantifier. In other words, if an existential quantifier must be introduced in addition to overt frequency adverbials like *exactly three times*, we cannot account for the semantics of sentences like (19a). This is shown in (20a, b). Note here that ∃$_3$! is defined as a special existential quantifier that indicates the existence of exactly three objects. (20a), which Stump's theory predicts, gives us the wrong truth condition because even when (19a) is true, one can choose an interval t within yesterday such that t contains exactly two events of John's sneezing. In other words, we would incorrectly predict that (19a) entails (19b) because (20a) entails (20b). On the other hand, (20c) is never true because when there is at least one event of John's sneezing yesterday, there are infinitely many times t within yesterday such that an event of John's sneezing occurs within t.

(19) a. John sneezed exactly three times yesterday.
b. John sneezed exactly twice yesterday.

(20) a. $\exists t[\exists_3!t'[t < now \wedge t' \subseteq t \wedge sneeze(j, t') \wedge t \subseteq yesterday]$
b. $\exists t[\exists_2!t'[t < now \wedge t' \subseteq t \wedge sneeze(j, t') \wedge t \subseteq yesterday]$
c. $\exists_3!t'[\exists t[t < now \wedge t \subseteq t' \wedge sneeze(j, t) \wedge t' \subseteq yesterday]$

In order to account for its semantics correctly, one needs to suppress the existential closure operation. Ogihara's (1996) solution is to "nullify" the existential quantifier force of the external existential quantifier in (20a) by equating **t'** and **t** as shown in (21).

(21) $\exists_3!t'[\exists t[t < now \wedge t=t' \wedge sneeze(j, t) \wedge t' \subseteq yesterday]$

This works, but it is admittedly ad hoc. In addition, this account is untenable under Stump's theory because an existential quantifier is introduced as part of the truth definition and is required to be the outermost quantifier.

Ogihara (1994) notes another potential problem that involves adverbials, which is that NPs (or PPs) that quantify over temporal intervals do not have scope over tense morphemes (assuming that tense introduces an existential quantifier over past times). The relevant examples are given in (22).

(22) a. John dated Mary every Sunday.
b. John got up at 6 a.m. every morning.

The problem is that (22a) cannot mean that every Sunday t is such that t is within the contextually salient past time T and John dates Mary at t. This is simply because not every Sunday is located in the past of the utterance time. In order to provide a good truth condition, one must assume that the adverbial *every Sunday* denotes a set of Sundays that are located in the past. One possible explanation of this fact is to adopt the view that any DP denotation is restricted by the contextual information. This is the view expressed by von Fintel (1994), Stanley & Szabó (2000) and others. The DP *every student* in (23) does not involve all students in the world on its most natural reading. Similarly, *every Sunday* in (22a) should be interpreted in such a way that it involves a relevant set of past Sundays. The idea is that in order for (22a) to be true, the relevant Sundays have to be located in the past. This is the only way to make sense of the claim made by (22a).

(23) Every student passed the test.

Ogihara (2006) notes, however, that even in examples like (24), the relevant meetings have to be restricted to past ones and that this fact cannot be accounted for in terms of pragmatics alone. For example, assume that the context restricts the relevant meetings to a set of some future meetings. Assume further that there is a past event of Mary's kissing John. If so, it is true that for each relevant meeting, there is an event of Mary's kissing John prior to it and (24) is predicted to be true on this scenario. However, this is not consistent with our intuitions. This indicates that a temporal adverbial in a sentence in the past tense is somehow required to describe past times even if this is not absolutely necessary to make the sentence true. But, then, the question is how we ensure that this happens in a principled manner.

(24) Mary kissed John before every meeting.

Ogihara's (2006) solution is to provide a covert adverbial *in the past* as the anchor of a cascade of temporal adverbials. For example, (22a) is assumed to have an underlying sentence of the form in (25). In reality, the relevant Sundays must be more restricted in that they are presumably a proper subset of the set of Sundays in the past. But the point is that a covert or overt adverbial that restricts the denotation of *Sunday* must be one that indicates a past interval.

(25) John dated Mary every Sunday (in the past).

This proposal stems from the fact that overt adverbials like *in the past* do occur in English sentences in the past tense as in (26). (26) is found on the web (http://www.nineplanets.org/mars.html). The bold-facing is due to the present author.

(26) However, data from Mars Global Surveyor indicates that Mars very likely did have tectonic activity sometime **in the past**.

Assuming that *in the past* means what it literally means, we wonder what the past tense morpheme itself means. If past tense also meant 'in the past', then we would have two expressions that have the same (or almost the same) interpretation in sentences like (26). Depending upon how the two sources of anteriority interact, it is possible that this redundancy could result in the wrong truth conditions. Thus, Ogihara (2006) concludes that the past tense morpheme itself does not introduce past time information. The way anteriority information is introduced is that there is an overt or covert adverbial *in the past*. In (22a) the temporal PP *every Sunday* is followed by a covert adverbial *in the past*, which would correct the problem mentioned above. As for the role of tense morphemes, they require the presence of relevant temporal adverbials. For example, we can entertain the hypothesis that a past tense morpheme has no semantic contribution to make and, instead, requires the presence of a past-oriented temporal adverbial. This is presumably accomplished by a syntactic feature. For example, one could require that a past tense morpheme have a [+past] feature that must agree with a temporal adverbial that bears the same feature. This is similar in sprit to Bäuerle's discussion of adverbials like *exactly once*. It is also arguable that Dowty's (1979) strategy of introducing a tense syncategorematically (see above) formalizes the same idea that I am proposing here.

4 Tense in embedded contexts

Tense morphemes in embedded contexts behave in different ways in different languages. Among the many different types of embedded clauses, verb complements and relative clauses have been dealt with extensively in the literature. In this section, I shall concentrate upon verb complements. Regarding the behavior of tense morphemes in other types of embedded clauses, the reader is referred to such works as Abusch (1997) and Ogihara (1996).

Enç (1987) argues with Partee (1973) that the time a verb complement clause talks about is a particular time in the same sense that a referential pronoun denotes a particular individual. For example, (27a) is analyzed as in (27b) in the syntax. The important point here is that the matrix clause tense and the verb complement tense are occurrences of the same tense (i.e., past) and are coindexed. As a result, the coindexed tenses denote the same time.

(27) a. John said that Mary was pregnant.
    b. John said$_1$ that Mary was$_1$ pregnant.

According to Enç, the embedded past tense *was* (or its index 1) denotes a contextually salient time located earlier than the utterance time. Enç argues for the view that a past tense morpheme in English is either indexical (i.e., denoting a past time in relation to the utterance time) or anaphoric (i.e., refers to the same time as a "local" tense). The term indexical is used to describe an expression whose denotation depends upon the context of use. This hypothesis makes the right prediction with examples like (27a, b). Since the matrix clause tense with index 1 obtains its denotation in relation to the utterance time, the embedded past tense with the same index 1 also denotes a time prior to the utterance time. This reading is intuitively acceptable and is referred to as a **simultaneous reading**. On the other hand, examples like (28), which contain multiple embeddings with a future auxiliary *would* in the intermediate clause, defy an indexical analysis of English tenses. The example is due to Abusch (1988) and is inspired by a similar example in French discussed by Kamp & Rohrer (1984).

(28) Mary decided a week ago that she would say to her mother in ten days at breakfast that they were having their last meal together.

On the most natural interpretation of (28), the time of their having their last meal together is cotemporaneous with the time of her saying to her mother. Given the adverbials in the sentence, this time is located later than the utterance time. Nevertheless, a past tense occurs in the lowest clause, which describes the time of their last meal. Thus, the lowest past tense (i.e., *were*) is not an indexical past tense. If the *would* in the intermediate clause is the past tense form of the future auxiliary, which we assume it is, the past tense is presumably coindexed with the matrix clause tense. This analysis is reasonable assuming that the tense on *would* indicates the time from which the future meaning of the auxiliary computes its meaning. That is, we predict that the time of her saying to her mother is located later than the deciding time. But the lowest past tense morpheme in (28) cannot possibly be indexical or anaphoric because it does not denote a time prior to the utterance time and cannot denote the same time as the time of deciding. Thus, the natural interpretation of (28) is not accounted for by Enç's proposal.

Before we discuss a solution to the problem, we shall turn to some relevant Japanese data. Unlike English, Japanese verb complement clauses have present tense (or perhaps no tense) for simultaneous readings even when the matrix clause is in the past tense. This is shown in (29a). In (29a) the complement clause is in the present tense, and the entire sentence receives a simultaneous interpretation. This is surprising from the viewpoint of English because a past tense is used in the same circumstance in English for the same meaning. But the verb complement clause in (29a) is not a quotation. Note that the embedded clause contains a reflexive pronoun *zibun* 'self' which can (and must) refer back to the matrix subject *Taro* in this instance, and yet, it cannot be used in a direct quote to indicate the speaker as shown in (29b). The correct direct discourse form is given in (29c). Thus, we should assume that the complement clause is an indirect discourse form on a par with an English sentence like (27a).

(29) a. Taroo-wa zibun-ga byooki-da to it-ta.
    Taro-TOP self-NOM be-sick-PRES that say-PAST
    'Taro said that he (himself) was sick.' (simultaneous)

b. #Zibun-ga byooki-desu.
   self-NOM be-sick-PRES
   Intended: 'I am sick.'

c. Watasi-wa byooki-desu.
   I-TOP   be-sick-PRES
   'I am sick.'

It should be clear to the reader by comparing Japanese and English verb complement clauses that a present tense occurs in Japanese where a past tense is required in English. Traditionally, the fact that past tenses occur "in sequence" in examples like (27a) and (28) is referred to as a sequence-of-tense phenomenon. From the descriptive point of view, the basic issue is how to account for the discrepancy in tense forms between direct discourse and indirect discourse in English when the matrix clause is in the past tense. For example, (27a) expresses the same temporal relations as the direct discourse variant in (30). Note that in (30) the complement clause is in the present tense rather than in the past tense.

(30) John said, "Mary is pregnant."

Traditional grammarians explain the above facts in terms of an implicit conversion process that changes a present tense in the direct discourse variant to a past tense in the indirect discourse variant. This enables us to obtain indirect discourse forms from direct discourse forms. This also gives us a hint as to how to deal with the semantics correctly. We can (and in fact should) assume that direct discourse forms are primary and suited for semantic interpretation, and indirect discourse forms are derived forms which are required for non-semantic (perhaps syntactic) reasons. This is indeed the view that Ogihara (1996) espouses in his treatment of English and Japanese tense phenomena. This view is in agreement with Abusch's (1988, 1997) proposal about the semantics of attitude verbs such as *believe* and *think* (though there are some differences in detail). The basic idea is that the tense forms of verbs in verb complement clauses in English are not directly subject to semantic interpretation. Technically, the discrepancy between English and Japanese regarding tense forms in verb complements is dealt with by a sequence-of-tense rule in English, which deletes in the syntax a tense morpheme under identity with the immediately higher tense. This can be shown in (31), which indicates how the sequence-of-tense rule applies to (28). In (31), the future auxiliary is indicated by the form *woll*, which is assumed to be the underlying form shared by *will* and *would*.

(31) 1. Mary decided a week ago that she would say to her mother in ten days at breakfast that they were having their last meal together.
2. Mary PAST decide a week ago that she PAST woll say to her mother in ten days at breakfast that they PAST be having their last meal together.
3. Mary PAST decide a week ago that she ~~PAST~~ woll say to her mother in ten days at breakfast that they ~~PAST~~ be having their last meal together.

The two PASTs that are struck through are assumed deleted. The deleted tenses are understood to be "null tenses" and are interpreted as such. How exactly this is done is shown in the rest of this section. The reader is also referred to Higginbotham (1995, 2002), who also deals with the sequence-of-tense phenomena and presents a view that slightly diverges from the position discussed above.

Let us now turn to the various accounts of the semantics of attitude reports. The semantic study of attitude verbs has played an important role in the development of formal semantics. It is clear that an attitude verb creates an intensional context in that the verb's denotation cannot be a relation between individuals and truth values. Otherwise, we would not be able to account for the fact that given two true statements, one and the same individual can have different attitudes toward them. For example, it is possible for (32a) and (32b) to have different truth values.

(32) a. John believes that Washington, D.C. is the capital of the U.S.
b. John believes that Austin is the capital of the State of Texas.

So it was proposed that we need the proposition associated with the complement clause (i.e., its intension) as the object of the attitude (Frege 1892). A proposition could be formalized either as a set of worlds or a set of world-time pairs in more recent work in formal semantics. If the time specified by the past tense in the complement clause is assumed to be a referential expression and denotes a particular time as in Enç's (1987) proposal, then it would be sufficient for the object of attitude to be a set of worlds. Let us repeat the example (27) as (33) here and discuss its semantics. Assuming that (33a) is indexed as in (33b), Enç's proposal leads to an analysis of (33b) in which John stands in the saying relation to the proposition given in (33c) at $g_c(1)$ (where g_c is the assignment function provided by the context) in the actual world. The assumption is that $g_c(1)$ is a past time that is salient in the context.

(33) a. John said that Mary was pregnant.
b. John said$_1$ that Mary was$_1$ pregnant.
c. {w | Mary is pregnant at $g_c(1)$ in w}

It is now important to specify truth conditions for sentences like (33b). Hintikka (1969) proposes that the attitude holder (i.e., the subject) at any world-time pair has access to a specific set of worlds. For example, in the case of the verb *believe*, the attitude holder has access to a set of possible worlds that are intuitively those that are consistent with what s/he believes in the actual world. Since the verb used in (33a) is *say*, this must be adjusted in the following way: the attitude holder has access to a set of possible worlds that are intuitively those that are consistent with what s/he says in the actual world. This type of semantic adjustment must be made for each complement-taking verb being used, e.g., *think, doubt, hear*, etc. According to this analysis, the content of what the subject said in the actual world at t_1 can be paraphrased as follows: Mary is pregnant at t_1 in all worlds that are consistent with what John says at t_1. Supposing that the content of what John said at t_1 in the actual world is indeed consistent with what is actually the case at t_1, we can conclude that Mary is pregnant in the actual world at t_1. Although this result appears satisfactory at first glance, it could be problematic when it is tested against some complex examples, such as the following (Ogihara 1996):

(34) When John woke up at 3 a.m., he thought that it was 6 a.m.

According to the account presented above, the pronoun *it* refers to 3 a.m., and the content of John's thinking at 3 a.m. should be presented as follows: 3 a.m. = 6 a.m at 3 a.m in all worlds consistent with what John thought at 3 a.m. Since this is a contradiction, John could not possibly think the world was that way, and so we must find a better way of analyzing the semantics of attitude verbs.

A more recent account of propositional attitude verbs that builds on Hintikka's semantics relies on Lewis' (1979) idea about attitudes. Lewis contends that expressing an attitude means self-ascribing a property. This clearly departs from the traditional idea that verbs like *believe* express "propositional attitudes" because according to Lewis, such verbs express relations between individuals and properties. Lewis himself was concerned with examples that involve properties of individuals such as (35).

(35) Heimson believes that he is Hume.

(35) describes a belief of a madman named Heimson, who thinks that he himself is Hume, which he is not. If we regard the pronoun *he* in the complement clause as a referential pronoun denoting Heimson, then the embedded proposition is a contradiction: Heimson = Hume. If the object of belief is indeed a contradiction (i.e., necessarily false proposition), then we must conclude that Heimson believes all other contradictions as well. This is clearly an undesirable conclusion and is

parallel to the problem found above with (34). To correct this problem, Lewis (1979) proposes that the object of an attitude is a property and that having an attitude should be described in terms of the subject's self-ascribing a property. This type of attitude is referred to as *de se* attitude. Ignoring times, one can define a property as a set of world-individual pairs. (35) could be accounted for if we assume that Heimson stands in the belief relation to the following property: {<w,x> | x is Hume in w}. This enables us to say that Heimson stands in the belief relation to this property but not to some other property like {<w,x> | x is Aristotle in w}.

Ogihara (1996) extends Lewis' view to attitudes involving times. The account starts with the assumption (as mentioned above) that the tense morphemes found in Japanese verb complement clauses provide the "right forms" for semantic interpretation. First, let us look at the Japanese example (36). It is analyzed as in (37).

(36) Taroo-wa Hanako-ga byooki-da to it-ta.
Taro-TOP Hanako-NOM be-sick-PRES that say-PAST
'Taro said that Hanako was sick' (simultaneous reading only)

(37) At some relevant past time t_1 in the actual world, Taro stands in the saying relation to the following set of world-time pairs (or "property of times"): {<w,t> | Hanako is sick at t in w}

(37) shows that the complement clause denotes a proposition which is not about a particular time. The intuition that the time of Hanako's being sick is simultaneous with the time of Taro's saying is not captured directly. Instead, we adopt Lewis' idea about *de se* attitudes, and think of a set of world-time pairs as a "property of times". (37) is then reanalyzed in terms of Taro's self-ascribing the property in question. If Taro self-ascribes the property of being located at a world-time pair *<w,t> such that Hanako is sick at t* in w, and if we assume furthermore that Taro spoke the truth, then Hanako would indeed be sick at the time Taro spoke. To do this more technically, we should assume that in the actual world at the time of his saying, Taro has access to {<w,t> | <w, t> is compatible with what Taro says in the actual world at the time of his saying}. For Taro to self-ascribe the property of being located at a world-time pair in {<w,t> | Hanako is sick at t in w} means that this set must completely contain the set of world-time pairs to which Taro has access. If Taro spoke the truth at the time of his saying, this means that {<w,t> | <w, t> is compatible with what Taro says in the actual world at the time of his saying} contains the pair consisting of the actual world and the time of Taro's saying. On this assumption, we can conclude that Hanako would indeed be sick in the actual world at the time of Taro's saying. This accounts for the reading of (36).

We now turn to the English case, which is exactly the same except that we posit a sequence-of-tense rule that deletes past tense morphemes under identity with closest c-commanding tenses. That is, (27a) (repeated here as (38)) is analyzed as in (39). Since each lower past tense has been deleted by the time the structure is semantically interpreted, the semantic component can deal with the complement clause in (39) in the same way as the corresponding Japanese example in (36). That is, the embedded clause is a tenseless clause in (39) and is understood to denote the set of world-time pairs indicated there. If at the time of his saying John indeed has the property that he self-ascribes, then Mary is pregnant at the time of John's saying in the actual world. This is the desired simultaneous interpretation.

(38) John said that Mary was pregnant.

(39) LF: John PAST say that Mary ~~PAST~~ be pregnant
Interpretation: At a particular past time in the actual world, John talks as if he self-ascribes the property of being located at {<w,t> | Mary is pregnant at t in w}

There are cases in which a property (i.e., a set of world-time-individual triples) is needed as the denotation of the embedded clause. The case in point is (40), which presents a situation in which the agent is doubly confused in that he self-ascribes a property he does not have and that he also locates himself at the wrong time (Ogihara 1996). Suppose that Mark Chapman came to believe that if he killed John Lennon he would become John Lennon. Chapman tried to kill John Lennon by means of a time bomb and set it so that it would go off at 10 p.m. in Lennon's apartment. At 9 p.m., Chapman somehow thought that it was 10 p.m. and thought "I am now John Lennon". (40) is a report of this attitude. The property, which is the object of Chapman's thought, is given in (41). This analysis provides the right semantics for (40).

(40) At 9 p.m., Mark Chapman thought with great satisfaction that he was (finally) John Lennon now that it was 10 p.m.

(41) {<w,t,x> | x is John Lennon at t in w and t = 10 p.m.}

Let us lastly turn to a substantially different view on propositional attitude reports. Schlenker (1999, cf. article 17 [this volume] (Schlenker) *Indexicality and de se)* and Anand & Nevins (2004), among others, discuss various issues involving propositional attitudes referring to languages like Zazaki, Slave and Amharic. In these languages, some nominal indexicals such as first and second person pronouns could occur in verb complements to refer to the speaker and the hearer of the event described by the complement clause, rather than those of the utterance event depicted by the entire sentence. That is, the first and second person pronouns that occur in a verb complement clause are reinterpreted in the attitude event context as if the "speech act context" is shifted to the one in the past. This is attested in (42). In (42a) the first person pronoun is interpreted as the agent in the context of John's saying, namely John. In (42b) the first and second person pronouns are interpreted in the (fictitious) context of the window's saying to the speaker of the entire sentence. So the first person is the window and the second person is the agent of the speech act associated with the entire sentence.

(42) a. john Jägna näNN yt-lall
John hero I-am says-3 sg.m
'John says that he is a hero.'

b. mäskotu alƏkkäffätƏllƏNN alä
window I-won't-open-for-you said
'The window wouldn't open for me.'

According to Schlenker (1999), Japanese is like Amharic with regard to tense morphemes in that the present and past tenses are interpreted in relation to the attitude event being reported. This is reasonable assuming that present and past tense morphemes in Japanese are (shiftable) indexical expressions. That is, Japanese present and past are indexicals (sensitive to the utterance context), and when they appear to measure their denotations from the time of the higher predicate, they are in fact interpreted in relation to the attitude context. However, a question remains as to why first or second person pronouns (*watasi* 'I', *anata* 'you', etc.) in Japanese are not shiftable.

Schlenker's proposal is based upon the idea that a so-called propositional attitude verb is a relation between individuals and contexts, though other formulations of the analysis of shiftable indexicals and logophors such as von Stechow (2002) are more similar to my proposal. According to Schlenker's proposal, *John said that φ* is true iff at the salient past time all contexts that are compatible with what John said are contexts in which φ is true. This semantic proposal for "propositional attitude verbs" manipulates contexts and verbs are "monsters" in Kaplan's terms (1977). But then this account faces a challenge from the familiar phenomena in English and other European languages, namely sequence-of-tense and "sequence-of-person" phenomena. That is, instead of the tense morpheme and indexical pronouns that are interpreted in relation to the embedded context,

English employs tense morphemes and pronouns that appear to be "anaphoric" to higher tenses and nominals, and this fact cannot be dealt with by Schlenker's proposal. It is arguable that von Stechow's proposal, which deletes presuppositions associated with indexicals, accounts for the data more naturally.

Although the monster-based approach has some intuitive appeal, it has problems, too. Ogihara (2006) discusses some of them. First, if attitude verbs are true manipulators of contexts, then we expect all relative indexicals to behave in the same way. However, even in Amharic many occurrences of indexicals are ambiguous between absolute and relative uses. For example, (43) is ambiguous between the two readings because the Amharic first person pronoun 'I' is interpretable either as the speaker of the embedded context or the speaker of the entire utterance.

(43) Situation: John said 'I like X', but Mary (she) didn't hear what the X was.
mǝn ǝwädalläx^w ǝndaläalsämac ǝm
what I-like that-he-said she-didn't-hear
'She didn't hear what he$_i$ said he$_i$ liked' or
'She didn't hear what he$_i$ said I liked'

This seems to weaken Schlenker's argument because this shows that only some occurrences of indexicals are shiftable. If the semantics of attitude verbs truly involves quantification over contexts, this restriction seems to be an artificial property which requires explication. This also means that even when two indexical expressions occur in the same minimal clause, it is possible for only one of them to be shifted. I made a similar point above regarding Japanese when I said that Japanese tense morphemes are arguably shiftable indexicals but first and second person pronouns are not.

Anand & Nevins (2004) propose two interesting restrictions upon "monsterous" operations in some languages:

(44) a. *Shift-Together*: The indexicals in Zazaki and Slave show shifting under certain modal verbs, but cannot shift independently.
b. Within-language variation in indexical shifting: In Slave, the same indexical shifts obligatorily, optionally, or not at all, depending on the modal verb it is under.

(44a) requires that a shifting of the context behaves like an operator in that all indexicals in structurally lower positions are affected by it. This means that a configuration given as (45) is disallowed. This point is also summarized in article 17 [this volume] (Schlenker) *Indexicality and de se*.

(45) *[... attitude verb δ [... shifted indexical attitude verb ... [non-shifted indexical]]]

Although this proposal makes an interesting prediction about the behavior of nominal indexicals, it is not clear what prediction this proposal makes for tense morphemes. For example, the Japanese tenses are "shifted" in attitude contexts. For Anand & Nevins, this presumably means that the Japanese present receives a "shifted context time" reading under attitude verbs. On the other hand, the English present is assumed to refer to the utterance time even in such contexts. This appears to mean that in English tenses are not shiftable. Prima facie, this makes (44a) untestable regarding tense. In addition, the interpretation of a non-shifted tense morpheme embedded under a tensed attitude verb is not straightforward and produces what is often referred to as "double-access" interpretations, as discussed by Ogihara (1995, 1996) and Abusch (1988, 1991, 1997). An example is given in (46). The verb *is*, the present tense form of *be*, occurs in the verb complement clause in (46). It does not receive a purely simultaneous reading, unlike (36). But this does not mean that the present tense verb *is* is just an unshifted indexical; the reading in question does not concern Taro's claim about Hanako's sickness obtaining at the utterance time. The reading in question, a "double-access" reading, concerns both the time of Taro's saying and the utterance time of (46). This reading requires a complex analysis, and a monster-based proposal does not seem to contribute a new perspective to this topic.

(46) Taro said that Hanako is sick.

The above discussion shows that a more traditional system in which attitude verbs quantify over a relevant set of tuples (involving such entities as worlds, times and individuals) is at least empirically adequate and is possibly superior to a monster-based approach.

Lastly, if only attitude verbs allow (some) indexicals to be interpreted in relation to shifted contexts, then it would be hard to explain the behavior of Japanese tense morphemes in relative clauses as shown in (47). The preferred reading of (47) is that the time of the man's crying is simultaneous with the time of Taro's seeing him.

(47) Taroo-wa nait-e iru otoko-o mi-ta.
Taro-TOP cry-PROG-PRES man-ACC see-PAST
'Taro saw a man who was crying.'

Since a relative clause is not embedded under an attitude verb, there is no reason that the alleged "present tense morpheme" in Japanese could be interpreted in relation to the time of Taro's seeing. As shown above, the proposal presented by Ogihara (1996) is different from Schlenker's in that Japanese present tense always means "relative present". By interpreting tenseless sentences in relation to immediately higher tenses, one can account for the "relative reading" of the relative clause tense. In sum, the recent proposals about the semantics of attitude verbs, which involve quantification over contexts, are very interesting but have some non-trivial problems.

5 Tense and modality

The interaction of tense and modality is undoubtedly an interesting area of research. The reader is also referred to article 14 [this volume] (Hacquard) *Modality*. In straightforward cases, the question of possibility/probability/likelihood (modality-related issues) is independent of the question of temporal location (tense-related issues). So one could say this of any of the three in (48).

(48) a. It is possible that Mary was in the room.
 b. It is possible that Mary is in the room.
 c. It is possible that Mary will be in the room.

The periphrastic form *be possible* is used in (48) for an epistemic modal meaning. The speaker could be ignorant about the past, present, or future. But could she be confident or ignorant about them in the same way? Some say yes. Others are not so sure. So this is where people's opinions differ. For example, Enç (1987) assumes that *will* is a modal auxiliary and not a tense morpheme. In terms of distribution, it patterns with other modal auxiliary verbs such as *can*, *must*, etc. But more importantly, the issue here is whether natural language deals with the future in the same way as the past. Enç's (1997) position is that natural language treats the future in a way different from the past. Essentially, the future auxiliary (*will/ would*) is understood as a mixed modal-temporal operator. According to this viewpoint, it is possible that people know about the past and the present because the facts have been established, but people cannot be sure about the future because it is not knowable. Thus, one cannot assert that something definitely happens at a future time. This is a view influenced by pragmatic considerations and is controversial. Truthconditionally, it is arguable that the future is no different from the past. That is, a future tense sentence is true iff the state of affairs described by the sentence takes place in the future (either at a particular time or at some future time). Montague (1973) straightforwardly encodes this view.

As far as the interaction of full-fledged modal auxiliary verbs (e.g., *may, must, can*) and past tense is concerned, their interaction depends on various factors including the type of modal meaning involved and the idiosyncratic properties of each modal verb. It appears that as far as epistemic interpretations are concerned, tense forms of modal verbs do not affect the Reference time, i.e., the time under discussion. For example, *may* has what may be referred to as its past tense form, i.e., *might*; but using *might* instead of *may* does not shift the temporal location of the contextually salient time to the past. For example, (49a) and (49b) both concern the epistemic possibility that concerns the utterance time. The only difference is that (49b) makes a weaker claim than (49a). In order to talk about a past time, one must indicate the pastness in terms of the perfect as in (49c). In the case of *must*, there is no past tense form in the first place. Thus, just as in *may*, *must* requires the perfect in order to indicate a past time. (49e) concerns a salient time in the past. Turning to *can*, we also find the same pattern as shown in (49f, g, h).

(49) a. John may be around.
 b. John might be around.
 c. John may/might have been around.
 d. John must be around.
 e. John must have been around.
 f. John can be around.
 g. John could be around.
 h. John could have been around.

On the other hand, deontic readings of modals produce different results. (50a) is impossible if it is to receive a deontic interpretation. (50b) is equally anomalous. Instead, we must use a sentence like (50c) or (50d).

(50) a. #John might smoke here. (Intended: John was allowed to smoke here.)
 b. #John may/might have smoked here. (Intended: John was allowed to smoke here.)
 c. John was allowed/permitted to smoke here.
 d. John could smoke here.

But some future-oriented constructions lead us to suspect that tense and modality are not as independent as one hopes. I present a couple of examples that show that the way natural language encodes future information is intertwined with the way it encodes possibility and probability. First, the progressive aspect is arguably a temporal-modal operator as argued for by Dowty (1979). See also article 10 [this volume] (Portner) *Perfect and progressive* about the progressive and the perfect.

Dowty claims that progressive sentences like (51a, b) involve probability assessment in that a progressive sentence is true at t iff in all worlds that are exactly like the actual one up to t and develop in expected ways (called "inertia worlds") there is a time "surrounding" t at which a corresponding sentence without the progressive is true. When the speaker sees John, who is walking on a crosswalk and moving toward the other side of the street, she can say (51a) truthfully, according to our intuitions. However, even when (51a) is true, it does not guarantee that John eventually reaches the other side of the street. As shown in (51b), John's attempt to cross the street may be interrupted by an external force. Since John was hit by the bus, he presumably did not get to the other side of the street.

(51) a. John is crossing the street.
b. John was crossing the street when he was hit by the bus.

Given the data like (51a, b), Dowty presents a theory of the progressive which is influential to this day. More recent accounts of the progressive such as Landman (1992) incorporate the temporal-modal ingredients of Dowty's proposal though some new ideas have also been incorporated.

One could say that the progressive is an aspectual operator and aspects should be distinguished from tenses. However, the special progressive form *be going to* is used to indicate a future situation as in the first sentence in (52a), which is very close in meaning to (52b). It is arguable that *be going to* is a "future tense" that offers an alternative way of talking about the future. But when the whole situation shifts to the past, a clear difference between *would* and *was going to* emerges as shown in (52c, d).

(52) a. John is going to attend the meeting.
b. John will attend the meeting.
c. John was going to attend the meeting, but the weather prevented him from doing so.
d. ??John would attend the meeting, but the weather prevented him from doing so.

(52c) is perfectly acceptable and conveys that John intended and planned to attend the meeting. But the first sentence in (52d) conveys something more definitive. Given a contextually salient past time *t*, there is a time later than *t* at which John attends the meeting. In fact, this time must be earlier than the utterance time. For instance, for (53) to be true, the child's becoming King must be earlier than the utterance time. This shows that the interaction between modality and future-oriented thoughts is extremely complicated to say the least.

(53) A child was born who would be King.

It seems that the behavior of *would* in (52d) and (53) is consistent with the view that future tense is a tense and not a modal expression. By contrast, (52c) seems to show that *be going to* is a temporal-modal expression just like regular *be V-ing* expressions used for the progressive interpretation. This supports Dowty's (1979) view on the progressive. For a detailed analysis of *be going to*, the reader is referred to Wulf (2000).

This chapter is indebted to the following survey articles that have a similar purpose in mind: Enç (1996), Kuhn, Steve and Paul Portner, (2002). I also thank Paul Portner for his comments on an earlier version and Laurel Preston for her help with proofreading and editing.

6 References

Abusch, Dorit 1988. Sequence of tense, intensionality and scope. In: H. Borer (ed.). *Proceedings of the Seventh West Coast Conference on Formal Linguistics (= WCCFL)* 7. Stanford, CA: CSLI Publications, 1–14.
Abusch, Dorit 1991. The present under past as *de re* interpretation. In: D. Bates (ed.). *Proceedings of the Tenth West Coast Conference on Formal Linguistics (= WCCFL)* 10. Stanford, CA: CSLI Publications, 1–12.
Abusch, Dorit 1997. Sequence of tense and temporal *de re*. *Linguistics & Philosophy* 20, 1–50.
Anand, Pranav & Andrew Nevins 2004. Shifty operators in changing context. In: K. Watanabe & R. B. Young (eds.). *Proceedings of Semantics and Linguistic Theory (= SALT) XIV*. Ithaca, NY: CLC Publications, 20–37.
Bäuerle, Rainer 1978. *Temporale Deixis, temporale Frage*. Tübingen: Narr.
Davidson, Donald 1967. The logical form of action sentences. In: N. Rescher (ed.). *The Logic of Decision and Action*. Pittsburgh, PA: University of Pittsburgh Press, 81–95.
Davidson, Donald 1977. The method of truth in metaphysics. In: P. A. French, T. E. Uehling Jr. & H. K. Wettstein (eds.). *Midwest Studies in Philosophy 2: Studies in the Philosophy of Language*. Morris, MN: University of Minnesota Press, 244–254. Reprinted in: D. Davidson. *Inquiries into Truth and Interpretation*. Oxford: Clarendon Press, 2001, 199–214.
Dowty, David 1979. *Word Meaning and Montague Grammar: The Semantics of Verbs and Times in Generative Semantics and in Montague's PTQ*. Dordrecht: Reidel.
Enç, Mürvet 1987. Anchoring conditions for tense. *Linguistic Inquiry* 18, 633–657.
Enç, Mürvet 1996. Tense and modality. In: S. Lappin (ed.). *The Handbook of Contemporary Semantic Theory*. Oxford: Blackwell, 345–358.
Fintel, Kai von 1994. *Restrictions on Quantifier Domains*. Ph.D. dissertation. University of Massachusetts, Amherst, MA.
Frege, Gottlob 1892. Über Sinn und Bedeutung. *Zeitschrift für Philosophie und philosophische Kritik* 100, 25–50.

Higginbotham, James 1995. Tensed thoughts. *Mind and Language* 10, 226–249.
Higginbotham, James 2002. Why is sequence of tense obligatory? In: G. Preyer & G. Peter (eds.). *Logical Form and Language*. Oxford: Clarendon Press, 207–227.
Hintikka, Jaako 1969. Semantics for propositional attitudes. In: J. Davis, D. J. Hockney & W. K. Wilson (eds.). *Philosophical Logic*. Dordrecht: Reidel, 21–45.
Kamp, Hans & Christian Rohrer 1984. *Indirect Discourse*. Ms. Austin, TX, University of Texas/Stuttgart, University of Stuttgart.
Kamp, Hans & Uwe Reyle 1993. *From Discourse to Logic*. Dordrecht: Kluwer.
Kaplan, David 1977. *Demonstratives: An essay on the semantics, logic, metaphysics, and epistemology of demonstratives and other indexicals*. Ms. Los Angeles, CA, UCLA. reprinted in: J. Almog, J. Perry & H. Wettstein (eds.). *Themes from Kaplan*. Oxford: Oxford University Press, 1989, 481–614.
Kuhn, Steve & Paul Portner 2002. Tense and time. In: D. Gabbay & F. Guenthner (eds.). *The Handbook of Philosophical Logic, Volume VI*. 2nd edn. Dordrecht: Reidel, 277–346.
Landman, Fred 1992. The progressive. *Natural Language Semantics* 1, 1–32.
Lewis, David 1979. Attitudes *de dicto* and *de se*. *The Philosophical Review* 88, 513–543.
Montague, Richard 1973. The proper treatment of quantification in ordinary English. In: J. Hintikka, J. M. E. Moravcsik & P. Suppes (eds.). *Approaches to Natural Language. Proceedings of the 1970 Stanford Workshop on Grammar and Semantics*. Dordrecht: Reidel, 221–242. Reprinted in: R. H. Thomason (ed.). *Formal Philosophy: Selected Papers of Richard Montague*. New Haven, CT: Yale University Press, 1974, 247–270.
Ogihara, Toshiyuki 1994. Adverbs of quantification and sequence-of-tense phenomena. In: L. Santelmann & M. Harvey (eds.). *Proceedings of Semantics and Linguistic Theory (= SALT) IV*. Ithaca, NY: Cornell University, 251–267.
Ogihara, Toshiyuki 1995. Double-access sentences and reference to states. *Natural Language Semantics* 3, 177–210.
Ogihara, Toshiyuki 1996. *Tense, Attitudes, and Scope*. Dordrecht: Kluwer.
Ogihara, Toshiyuki 2006. Tense, adverbials and quantification. In: R. Zanuttini et al. (eds.). *Crosslinguistic Research in Syntax and Semantics: Negation, Tense, and Clausal Architecture*. Washington, DC: Georgetown University Press, 231–247.
Partee, Barbara H. 1973. Some structural analogies between tenses and pronouns in English. *The Journal of Philosophy* 70, 601–609.
Partee, Barbara H. 1984. Nominal and temporal anaphora. *Linguistics & Philosophy* 7, 243–286.
Prior, Arthur N. 1957. *Time and Modality*. Oxford: Oxford University Press.
Prior, Arthur N. 1967. *Past, Present, and Future*. Oxford: Oxford University Press.
Reichenbach, Hans 1947. *Elements of Symbolic Logic*. New York: Macmillan.
Schlenker, Philippe 1999. *Propositional Attitudes and Indexicality: A Cross-Categorial Approach*. Ph.D. dissertation. MIT, Cambridge, MA.
Stanley, Jason & Zoltan Szabó 2000. On quantifier domain restriction. *Mind & Language* 15, 219–261.
Stechow, Arnim von 2002. *Binding by Verbs: Tense, Person and Mood under Attitudes*. Ms. Tübingen, University of Tübingen.
Stump, Gregory 1985. *The Semantic Variability of Absolute Constructions*. Dordrecht: Reidel.
Wulf, Douglas 2000. *The Imperfective Paradox in the English Progressive and Other Semantic Course Corrections*. Ph.D. dissertation. University of Washington, Seattle, WA.

Valentine Hacquard
14 Modality

1 Introduction —— 463
2 Properties of modals —— 464
3 Modal logic and the quantificational approach to modals —— 466
4 Kratzer's unifying account —— 469
5 The *epistemic vs. root* distinction —— 477
6 Questioning the modal semantics of modals —— 490
7 Modality and its kin —— 495
8 Conclusions —— 496
9 References —— 498

Abstract: Modality is the category of meaning used to talk about possibilities and necessities, essentially, states of affairs beyond the actual. This article reviews the approach to modals inherited from modal logic, in terms of quantification over possible worlds, with particular attention to the seminal work of Angelika Kratzer. In addition, it introduces more recent work on the interaction of modals with other elements, in particular with tense and subjects, which challenges classical approaches, and presents new directions.

1 Introduction

Modality is the category of meaning used to talk about possibilities and necessities, essentially, states of affairs beyond the actual. We can talk about what we *must* do, if we are to obey the law (we *must* pick up after our dogs), or what we *may* do to fulfill our desires (we *may* go on sabbatical), what *could* happen if global warming isn't abated (the world as we know it *could* disappear), or what *would* have been if Cleopatra's nose had been shorter (the face of the world *would* have been changed). All of these hypothetical states of affairs may never come to be, yet we are able to talk about them, by using modal words. Modality is expressed by many categories of lexical items: adverbs like *maybe*, nouns like *possibility*, adjectives like *possible*, or auxiliary verbs like *must*, *may*, *should* or *have to*. This article focuses on modal auxiliaries, since their

Valentine Hacquard, Maryland (USA)

https://doi.org/10.1515/9783110589443-014

relatively well-established properties serve as a good basis to present issues and theories of modality. We start by reviewing the approach to modals inherited from modal logic, in terms of quantification over possible worlds, with particular attention to the seminal work of Angelika Kratzer. We then turn to more recent work on the interaction of modals with other elements, in particular with tense and subjects, which challenges classical approaches, and present new directions.

2 Properties of modals

Natural language modals seem to vary along (at least) two dimensions: 'force' (whether they express possibility or necessity), and type of interpretation, or modal 'flavor'. In English, *possibility* modals include *may, might, can,* and *could*. *Necessity* modals include *should, must, would,* and *have to*. Rather than considering possibility or necessity with respect to *all* non-actual states, natural language modals often seem to be relative to a certain body of laws, desires, or information, giving rise to the various 'flavors' of modality. *Epistemic* modality (from Greek *episteme 'knowledge'*) expresses possibilities and necessities given what is known, based on what the available evidence is; *deontic* modality (from Greek *deon 'obligation'*), possibilities and necessities given a body of laws or rules, i.e., permissions and obligations; *abilitive* modality, possibilities given the subject's physical abilities; *teleological* and *bouletic* modality, possibilities and necessities given particular goals and desires (from Greek *telos 'goal'* and *boule 'wish'*). The following examples illustrate:

(1) a. Epistemic
(In view of the available evidence,) John *must/might/may* be the murderer.

b. *Deontic*
(In view of his parents' orders,) John *may* watch TV, but he *must* go to bed at 8 pm.

c. *Ability*
(In view of his physical abilities,) John *can* lift 200 lbs.

d. *Teleological*
(In view of his goal to get a PhD,) John *must* write a dissertation.

e. *Bouletic*
(In view of his desire to retire at age 50,) John *should* work hard now.

While certain modal auxiliaries are restricted in the kinds of interpretation they can receive (*might*, for instance, only has epistemic interpretations), many others can express various kinds of flavors: *may* and *must* have epistemic or deontic interpretations, *have to* epistemic, deontic, circumstantial, teleological, or bouletic ones, etc. This is not a peculiarity of English. Instead, this multiplicity of modal meanings is quite pervasive across languages (cf. Fleischman 1982, Traugott 1988, Bybee, Perkins & Pagliuca 1994, Palmer 2001, though see Nauze 2008 for statistical evidence that this multiplicity is not as frequent as originally thought). To cite just a few examples, French *pouvoir* (*can*) and *devoir* (*must*), or Italian *potere* (*can*) and *dovere* (*must*), can all express circumstantial, deontic, teleological, bouletic and epistemic modality. Similarly, Malay *mesti* (*must*) (Drubig 2001), Cairene Arabic *laazim* (*must*), and Tamil permission and debitive suffixes (Palmer 2001) receive both epistemic and deontic interpretations.

A standard classification separates epistemic modals from all others, subsumed under the label 'root' modals (Hoffmann 1966). As we will see, several semantic and syntactic factors correlate with this distinction: epistemics deal with possibilities that follow from the speaker's knowledge, whereas roots deal with possibilities that follow from the circumstances surrounding the main event and its participants; epistemics are taken to be *speaker*-oriented, roots *subject*-oriented (Bybee, Perkins & Pagliuca 1994); epistemics tend to take widest scope whereas root modals take narrowest scope with respect to each other, and to various scope bearing elements.

Under all types of interpretations, possibility and necessity modals enter into patterns of entailments and logical equivalences similar to those involving universal and existential quantifiers. *Must* and *may* are *duals* of each other, just as *some* and *every* (cf. Horn 1972):

(2) a. John *must* be home ⇒ John *may* be home
   b. John *may* be home ≡ It is *not* the case that it *must* be the case that John is *not* home
   c. John *must* be home ≡ It is *not* the case that it *may* be the case that John is *not* home

(3) a. *Every student* is home ⇒ *Some student* is home
   b. *Some student* is home ≡ It is *not* the case that *every student* is *not* home
   c. *Every student* is home ≡ It is *not* the case that *some student* is *not* home

Standard semantic approaches to modals stemming from philosophical modal logic derive these equivalences by giving them a quantificational analysis. Necessity modals are *universal*, while possibility modals are *existential*, quantifiers over *possible worlds*; this is what underlies the difference in *force*. And just as the set of students in *every student* needs to be restricted to a salient subset (we rarely talk about every single student in the universe), the set of worlds modals quantify over needs to be restricted to a particular subset. This subset is in turn what determines the particular *flavor* that the modal receives: if a modal quantifies over worlds compatible with what is known, the modal is interpreted epistemically, if it quantifies over worlds compatible with certain laws, it is interpreted deontically, etc.

In section 3, we review the quantificational approach to modality inherited from modal logic, and turn to Kratzer's theory in section 4. Section 5 and 6 delve into particulars of the two main classes of modals (epistemics and roots), and illustrate some of the challenges each poses for a Kratzerian approach in particular, and quantificational approaches in general, and discuss the new directions these challenges have opened up. Section 7 looks at the connection between modals and other categories of meaning.

3 Modal logic and the quantificational approach to modals

Though philosophers have been concerned with modality since Aristotle's modal syllogisms, an explicit model theory, in the modern sense, for a modal logic was only made possible in the 1960s with the advent of *possible worlds*, developed in the works of Carnap (1957), von Wright (1951), Prior (1957), Kanger (1957), Hintikka (1961), and Kripke (1963) (for a history of the development of possible worlds, see Copeland 2002). The notion of a possible world can be traced back at least to Leibniz, according to whom the 'universe' (the *actual world*) was one (in fact, the best one) among an infinite number of possible worlds living in God's mind. Possible worlds can be viewed as possible 'ways things could have been' (Lewis 1973). There are many, many ways things could have been: think about the world as it is, but where the Eiffel Tower was destroyed after the World Expo, or one where the Eiffel Tower was never in Paris, but in London, or one where it is one millimeter taller, one where it is two millimeters taller, etc. You will see that we can conceive of a potentially infinite number of different worlds. Note that any change, however small, from one world to the next may require differing chains of events leading to this change, and may further have unavoidable repercussions, so that it may not be possible to find two worlds differing *only* in where the Eiffel Tower is located (think about all the Eiffel Tower postcards grandparents around the world would be receiving from London). Yet, there are still countless ways the world could be, and each of these ways represents a different possible world. While the ontological status of possible worlds is a topic of serious debate in the philosophical literature, linguists usually do not worry about such metaphysical issues; they assume that we have the capacity to represent alternative states of affairs, and that it is this capacity that we are referring to when we talk about possible worlds.

There are many concerns of modal logic which we cannot go over here (for an introduction to modal logic, see Hughes & Cresswell 1996; for a detailed overview of modal logic's contribution to the semantics of modality, see GAMUT 1991, Kaufmann, Condoravdi & Harizanov 2007, Portner 2009; and for an overview of the model theoretic and possible worlds semantics assumed in this section, see article 7 [Semantics: Theories] (Zimmermann) *Model-theoretic semantics*. We will dive right in by assuming a propositional logic, composed of atomic sentences ($p, q, r...$) and sentential connectives ($\wedge, \vee, \rightarrow, \neg$), with the addition of the possibility ($\Diamond$ 'diamond') and necessity ($\Box$ 'box') operators, which combine with formulae to form new formulae ($\Diamond p, \Box p...$). The introduction of possible worlds was crucial in allowing the extension of the model-theoretic apparatus to modal logic, by having the valuation of a sentence not be *absolute* (either true or false), as in standard propositional logic, but *relative* to a possible world: a sentence is true or false *in a world w*, depending on the facts in w. It may be true in one world, and false in another. The truth of modalized formulae (e.g., $\Box p$) is likewise relative to a possible world, but in such a way that their valuation depends on the truth of p itself in *other* possible worlds—modals have a displacing effect. In a possible worlds framework, $\Diamond$ and $\Box$ can be viewed as an existential and a universal quantifier over possible worlds respectively. $\Diamond p$ is true if p is true in *some* world, and $\Box p$ is true if p is true in *all* worlds. This quantificational treatment explains the logical equivalences in (2) ($\Diamond p \Leftrightarrow \neg\Box\neg p$ and $\Box p \Leftrightarrow \neg\Diamond\neg p$). However, it doesn't yet capture the contingency of modal statements: just as a sentence p can be true or false in a world w, we want $\Diamond p$ and $\Box p$ to be relative to a world. Moreover, this kind of pure (unrestricted) modality, called *alethic* modality (from Greek *aletheia* 'truth'), is just one of many types of modalities, such as *deontic, epistemic,* or *temporal* modalities, which we want to model. Both the contingency and the relativization of modals to a particular type of modality are achieved by having the set of worlds the modal quantifies over be restricted to a particular subset, relative to a world of evaluation. This is done via an *accessibility relation*.

Accessibility relations are binary relations over a set of worlds W, which pick out for each world w of W, a set of accessible worlds w'. Various kinds of accessibility relations can be defined: an epistemic relation picks out for each world w a set of worlds w' in which all of the facts known in w are true, a deontic relation picks out for each world w a set of worlds w' in which all of the rules of w are obeyed, etc.

(4) $R_{epis}(w,w')$ = {w'| w' is a world in which all of the facts known in w hold}
$R_{deontic}(w,w')$ = {w'| w' is a world in which all of laws of w are obeyed}

Formally, the accessibility relation is taken to be a parameter of a *model* (sometimes called a *Kripke model*). A model M consists of a pair <F,V>, where F is a *frame*, consisting of a pair <W,R>, with W, a set of worlds, and R, an accessibility relation. V is a valuation function which assigns truth values (1 and 0) to every atomic sentence at each world in W. R determines for each world w of W a set of accessible worlds $w9$, in which the proposition p is evaluated. Modals quantify over the worlds determined by the accessibility relation: $\Diamond p/\Box p$ are true if p is true in some/all of the worlds picked out by the accessibility relation.

(5) a. $V_{M,w}(\Diamond p) = 1$ iff in some world w' in W, such that $R(w,w')$, $V_{M,w'}(p) = 1$
    b. $V_{M,w}(\Box p) = 1$ iff in every world w' in W, such that $R(w,w')$, $V_{M,w'}(p) = 1$

What patterns of inference are valid for various types of modal reasoning can be explained and captured in terms of the properties that the accessibility relation for the corresponding modal logic should have. For example, accessibility relations can be serial, reflexive, transitive, etc. Different modalities are differentiated via the different properties that their accessibility relations have:

(6) a. R is *serial* iff for every w in W there is a world w' in W such that $R(w,w')$
    b. R is *reflexive* iff for every w in W, $R(w,w)$
    c. R is *transitive* iff for every w,w',w'' in W, if $R(w,w')$ and $R(w',w'')$ then $R(w,w'')$

Seriality, for instance, corresponds to *consistency*: it implies that the set of worlds picked out by the accessibility relation is not empty. This is an important property to prevent modals from quantifying vacuously. *Reflexivity* corresponds to *realism*: with a reflexive accessibility relation, $\Box p$ implies p. Epistemic relations are reflexive, but deontic ones aren't. Reflexivity further differentiates epistemic (knowledge-based) from doxastic (belief-based) accessibility relations. With an epistemic relation the world of evaluation is accessible from itself, but not with a doxastic relation: the world of evaluation may not be compatible with what is *believed* to be true. We will see in section 4.2 that there is some controversy surrounding the 'realistic' status of natural language epistemic modals: if their accessibility relation is reflexive, a sentence such as *it must be raining* should entail *it is raining*; yet intuitively, the former is somehow 'weaker' than the latter.

Modal logic is concerned with patterns of inferences in various modalities, independently of each other, and certainly independently of any idiosyncrasies of the natural language words that correspond, perhaps imperfectly, to these notions. Yet, some of the insights there have been crucial to our understanding of natural language modals, and the formal apparatus of quantification over possible worlds and accessibility relations is central to current semantic accounts of modality.

4 Kratzer's unifying account

Moving back to the realm of natural language modals, recall from section 2 that, sometimes, the same modal auxiliaries can receive several interpretations. Take the ambiguous sentence *John may watch TV*: it either expresses a deontic possibility (*John is allowed to watch TV*), or an epistemic one (*for all we know, it is possible that John is a TV watcher*). Is this due to a lexical ambiguity of the modal? Do English speakers store two different *may*s in their lexicon (either as homonyms or polysemes)? Such an ambiguity is tacitly assumed in semantic analyses that focus on particular subtypes of modality (Groenendijk & Stokhof 1975 for epistemic *may*, Kamp 1975 for deontic *may*), and, perhaps, postulating ambiguity for certain modal words may not be too big of an issue, given that there are modal words which are never ambiguous (e.g., *might*). However, this multiplicity of modal meanings is common enough cross-linguistically, and in languages from different families, so as to make a lexical ambiguity account unlikely: it is highly improbable that the same lexical accident should be found in language after language. Rather, it seems that we should give a single meaning for those modals that show an ambiguity, and derive the variety of flavors via some contextual factors (providing lexical restrictions for unambiguous modals like *might*). This is exactly what Kratzer proposes, in a series of influential papers.

In section 3 it was shown that different kinds of modalities can be explained as different accessibility relations. But how are these accessibility relations associated with a particular modal word? One possibility is that they are hard-wired in the denotation of modals. Epistemic *may* would differ from deontic *may* by combining with an epistemic vs. a deontic accessibility relation *in the lexicon*. This is what is usually assumed, for instance, for attitude verbs, which are traditionally analyzed as universal quantifiers over a set of worlds determined by an accessibility relation hard-wired in the semantics of each verb (e.g., *believe* takes a doxastic accessibility relation; *want* a bouletic one; cf. Hintikka 1962). Could modals work the same way? One crucial difference between modals and attitude verbs is that, while a modal like *may* can be associated with at least two different accessibility relations, the accessibility relation of an attitude like *believe* seems fixed: *believe* never gets a bouletic interpretation. Thus, if we were to hard-wire the accessibility relation in a modal's lexical entry, we would end up with as many lexical entries as there are possible interpretations, which seems undesirable, especially since this ambiguity is found in language after language.

Kratzer was the first to point out the improbability of an ambiguity account for natural language modals, and to give them a linguistically realistic semantics. We turn to her account now, focusing on two main ideas: (i) that context partly determines the meaning of modals; (ii) that modals are 'doubly-relative', which avoids shortcomings of previous accounts.

4.1 The role of context

Kratzer (1977) shows the improbability of an ambiguity account for natural language modals as follows. Not only do modals come in various flavors, but each flavor itself seems to come in many subflavors. Take our deontic statement *John may watch TV*. It could be understood as a permission with respect to various rules: his father's, his mother's, a dorm or a prison. An ambiguity account becomes hopeless: not only would we need as many *may*s as there are possible flavors, but each of these *may*s would itself be ambiguous between various *may*s.

Now, a modal flavor can be specified unambiguously with an '*in view of*' phrase, as in the following examples:

(7) a. *In view of his vast knowledge of celebrity gossip*, John *may* watch TV.
 b. *In view of his father's orders*, John *may* watch TV.

This phrase doesn't seem redundant. This means, Kratzer argues, that the *may* it combines with cannot be specified for a particular interpretation, and must instead be a kind of 'neutral' *may*, which needs to be added to our growing list of homonyms.

What if, instead, we took neutral *may* to be the only *may*? The '*in view of*' phrase would itself provide the modal flavor. This would solve the hopeless homonymy problem. But what about cases in which such a phrase is missing? Kratzer proposes that its content is then supplied by the *context of utterance*, via what she calls a *conversational background*. Sentences are always uttered against a conversational background, which, Kratzer argues, can fill in information for modals that isn't explicit. Formally, a conversational background is represented as a function from worlds to sets of propositions. These propositions correspond to bodies of information, facts, rules, etc., responsible for determining the modal flavor. Take the sentence *Mary must be the culprit*. Imagine that this sentence is uttered in a context where we are discussing a recent crime. In the course of our conversation, we discuss facts related to the crime, such as the fact *that the crime was committed yesterday, that Mary has no alibi, that she has a good motive, that no one else has a motive*, etc. All these propositions together form the set of facts known in our world. This set of facts is contingent. Things could have been different: Mary could have had an alibi, Paul, a motive, etc. Thus, what is known in this world may be different from what is known in some other world. What a conversational background does, then, is assign a (different) set of propositions to each world of the domain. An *epistemic* conversational background is a function *fepis*, which assigns to each world w in W the following set of propositions:

(8) $f_{epis}(w)$ = {p| p is a proposition that expresses a piece of established knowledge in w for a group of people, a community...}

There is a tight connection between a conversational background and an accessibility relation. Recall section 2's epistemic relation:

(9) $R_{epis}(w,w')$ = {w'| w' is a world in which all of the facts known in w hold}

A proposition p corresponds to a set of worlds, namely, the set of worlds in which p is true. A set of propositions A corresponds to a set of sets of worlds, and its *intersection* to a set of worlds, namely, the worlds in which all of the propositions of A are true. Thus, from a conversational background f (which assigns to each world a set of propositions), we can derive the corresponding accessibility relation Rf by intersecting, for each world w, the set of propositions that f assigns to that world:

(10) $R_{epis}(w,w')$ = ∩f(w) = {w'| w' is a world in which all of the propositions p (such that p expresses a piece of established knowledge in w) hold}

Thus Kratzer's system is formally equivalent to previous quantificational accounts. The novelty is that the determination of the set of accessible worlds is not hard-wired in the lexical entry of the modal. Rather, it arises from a contextually-provided conversational background f, formally represented as a parameter of the interpretation function, as in the following lexical entries, adapted from Kratzer (1991):

(11) For any world w, conversational background f:
 a. $[\![must]\!]^{w,f} = \lambda q_{<st>}. \forall w' \in \cap f(w): q(w') = 1$ (*in set talk* $\cap f(w) \subseteq q$)
 b. $[\![can]\!]^{w,f} = \lambda q_{<st>}. \exists w' \in \cap f(w): q(w') = 1$ (*in set talk* $\cap f(w) \cap q \neq \emptyset$)

Modal statements of the form '*must p*' or '*can p*' are true relative to a conversational background f if and only if p is true in *all* or *some* of the worlds in which the propositions of the conversational background are true. Note that because the conversational background is treated as a parameter, iterated modals, as in

John might have to leave, should be evaluated against the same conversational background, and thus receive the same interpretation. Kratzer (1978) proposes a dynamic way to allow modals in the same sentence to be relative to different conversational backgrounds. Alternatively, one could represent the conversational background in the object language as a covert argument of the modal (we will see a case of this in section 5.5).

To sum up, Kratzer's introduction of conversational backgrounds preserves the main insights of traditional quantificational accounts of modals, and explains why modals can receive various kinds of interpretations without having to postulate massive lexical ambiguity.

4.2 The double relativity of modals

Consider the following sentence, uttered in a context where John murdered someone:

(12) John must go to jail.

(12) should say that in all of the worlds in which the law is obeyed, John goes to jail. But surely, in all of the worlds in which the law is obeyed, there is no murder! So here is our conundrum: how can we talk about worlds where the law is obeyed, when the law has been broken? The problem with the semantics outlined above for sentences like (12) is that it treats the cold fact that John committed murder and the content of the law on a par. We need to separate facts from (moral) ideals. If we cannot get around the fact that murder was committed, we can still talk about moral obligations, *given* the resulting morally imperfect state of affairs. What (12) should say, then, is that the best way to obey the law in the imperfect world in which John committed murder is to have John go to jail.

To capture this, Kratzer (1981, 1991) proposes that modals be relative not to just one but two conversational backgrounds. The first is what she calls a *modal base*. It is made up of a set of facts, which is always consistent. In our example (12), the modal base notably contains the fact that John committed a murder. The second conversational background, dubbed the *ordering source*, consists of a set of ideals, moral or other (which may or may not be consistent), which imposes an ordering on the worlds of the modal base. Modals end up quantifying over the *best* worlds of the modal base, given the ideal set by the ordering source.

Both types of conversational backgrounds are functions from worlds to sets of propositions. For the modal base f, these propositions are relevant facts (e.g., *that John murdered Bill*). For the ordering source g, these propositions are ideals (e.g., *that murderers go to jail*). From the set of propositions g(w), Kratzer proposes an ordering ≤$_{g(w)}$, which ranks worlds according to how close they come to satisfying the ideal given by g:

(13) The ordering ≤$_{g(w)}$:
For all u,z ∈W, for any g(w) ⊆ ℘(℘(W)):
u ≤$_{g(w)}$ z iff {p: p ∈ g(w) and z ∈ p} ⊆ {p: p ∈ g(w) and u ∈ p}

The ordering states that for any pair of worlds *u, z, u* is closer to the ideal set by *g(w)* if the set of propositions true in *z* is a subset of the set of propositions true in *u*. Imagine two worlds *u* and *z* in which John committed a murder, and where John goes to jail in *u*, but not in *z*. Take a deontic ordering source containing two propositions: *that murder is a crime* and *that murderers go to jail*. Both worlds violate the first law, but *u* is closer to the ideal set by the ordering source than *z*, since in *u*, the murderer John goes to jail, but not in *z*: the set of propositions of the ordering source true in *u* is a superset of the set of propositions true in *z*.

Our doubly-relative necessity modal looks as follows:

(14) For any world w, modal base f and ordering source g,
⟦**must p**⟧^{w,f,g} is true iff:
For all u ∈ ∩f(w), there is a v ∈ ∩f(w) such that v ≤$_{g(w)}$ u and
For all z ∈ ∩f(w): if z ≤$_{g(w)}$ v, then z ∈ p

A necessity modal requires that for all worlds *u* of the modal base, there is a world *v* that comes closer to the ideal imposed by the ordering source, and in all worlds *z* closer than *v* to the ideal, the proposition *p* expressed by its complement is true: *p* is true in all of the most ideal worlds of the modal base. We can simplify this definition by making the so-called 'limit assumption', i.e., by assuming that there always are accessible worlds that come closest to the ideal, call these worlds *Best*$_{g(w)}$(∩f(w)) (for arguments in favor of the limit assumption, see Stalnaker 1984; the 'Best' operator is from Portner 2009). We obtain the following lexical entries:

(15) For any world w, and conversational backgrounds f, g:
⟦**must**⟧^{w,f,g} = λq$_{<st>}$.∀w'∈ Best$_{g(w)}$ (∩f(w)): q(w') = 1.
⟦**can**⟧^{w,f,g} = λq$_{<st>}$. ∃w'∈ Best$_{g(w)}$ (∩f(w)): q(w') = 1.
where *Best*$_{g(w)}$(X) selects the most ideal worlds from X, given the ordering given by g(w)

This doubly-relative system allows Kratzer to solve a problem with previous accounts, namely the problem of 'inconsistencies'. Standard (singly-relative) quantificational accounts break down when the set of propositions that the modal is relative to is inconsistent, that is, when two of the propositions cannot both be true in a world. When a conversational background is inconsistent (i.e., when the corresponding accessibility relation is not serial), its intersection is empty, and the modal quantifies over an empty set. In this case, a sentence comes out as trivially true if the modal has universal force, and trivially false, when it has existential force. To see why, take the singly-relative lexical entries in (11). In set talk, a *necessity* modal requires that the worlds provided by the conversational background be a subset of the set of worlds that make up the propositional complement ($\cap f(w) \subseteq q$). Given that the empty set is a subset of any set, any necessity statement comes out as trivially true. A *possibility* modal requires the non emptiness of the intersection of the set of worlds provided by the conversational background and the set of worlds that make up the propositional complement ($\cap f(w) \cap q \neq \emptyset$). Since the intersection of the empty set with another set is always empty, any possibility statement comes out as trivially false.

This type of problem typically arises with deontic modality, in cases where laws conflict with one another, or bouletic modality, in cases of conflicting desires. Consider a toy example from Kratzer (1977, 1991), where the law consists of judgments handed down by various judges. One uncontested judgment states that murder is a crime. Two other judgments (from different judges), however, conflict: one states that goat owners are liable for the damage caused by their goats, while the other states that they aren't. The law thus consists of three propositions: *that murder is a crime, that goat owners are liable, that goat owners are not liable*. This set is inconsistent. Thus, the necessity statement in (16a) is wrongly predicted to be true, and the possibility statements in (16b) and (16c) wrongly predicted to be false:

(16) a. Murder must not be a crime.
 b. Goat owners may be liable for damage caused by their goats.
 c. Goat owners may not be liable for damage caused by their goats.

Let's see how the doubly-relative system avoids this problem. The law consisting of the three judgments, make up our deontic ordering source. Let's assume the modal base is empty (the ordering orders all worlds in W). We find four types of worlds: type 1 worlds, where murder is a crime and goat owners are liable; type 2 worlds, where murder is a crime and goat owners are *not* liable; type 3 worlds, where murder is *not* a crime and goat owners are liable; type 4 worlds, where murder is *not* a crime and goat owners are *not* liable. The worst worlds are those in which murder is not a crime (type 1 and 2 worlds are respectively more ideal than type 3 and 4, since one of the propositions of the ordering source hold in type 1 and 2 but not in type 3 or 4). Worlds of type 1 and 2 cannot be ordered with respect to each other, since the set of propositions true in each cannot stand in a subset relation, and both types make up the 'best' worlds, i.e., those that the modals quantify over. It is true that goat owners are liable in some of these worlds (type 1), not liable in some others (type 2), and that murder is a crime in all of them.

A further advantage of the doubly-relative system is that it provides an explanation for the problematic intuitions we get about epistemic modals, mentioned in section 2. Recall that we should expect sentences with epistemic necessity modals (17b) to entail their unmodalized counterparts (17a), given the reflexivity of their accessibility relation (i.e., the world of evaluation—here the actual world—should be one of the accessible worlds). Yet, intuitively, (17b) doesn't seem to entail (17a):

(17) a. It is raining.
b. It must be raining.

In Kratzer's doubly-relative system, it doesn't need to. Indeed, the modal could take an ('stereotypical') ordering source, which would force the modal to quantify only over the *most normal worlds* of the (epistemic) modal base. Thus, while the world of evaluation would be one of the worlds selected by the modal base, given that this modal base is realistic (i.e., it corresponds to a reflexive accessibility relation), it could well be atypical, and hence not be among the most *normal* of these worlds.

Before we turn to particularities of conversational backgrounds, let's mention a final benefit of the ordering source, discussed at length in Kratzer (1981, 1991), which is that it gives us a means of deriving graded notions of modality (e.g., *slight possibility*), by invoking more or less far-fetched possibilities. Graded modality is however a complex topic that may require technologies beyond the doubly-relative system. The interested reader should consult Yalcin (2007) and Portner (2009).

4.3 Modal bases and ordering sources

According to Kratzer, there are two kinds of modal bases. The *epistemic* modal base picks out worlds in which *what is known* in the base world holds. The *circumstantial* modal base picks out worlds in which *certain circumstances* of the base world hold. The difference may seem subtle, but it, in fact, involves reasoning from qualitatively different kinds of premises, and leads to truth conditional differences.

Circumstantial modality looks at the material conditions which cause or allow an event to happen; epistemic modality looks at the knowledge state of the speaker to see if an event is compatible with various sources of information available. The following example illustrates this contrast with *might* and *can*, each of which have idiosyncratic constraints that force *might* and disallow *can*, to select an epistemic modal base:

(18) a. Hydrangeas might be growing here.
    b. Hydrangeas can grow here.   Kratzer (1981)

The sentence in (a) is evaluated against an epistemic modal base: to the best of my knowledge, it is possible that hydrangeas are growing here. The sentence in (b) is evaluated against a circumstantial modal base, which includes circumstances such as the quality of the soil, the climate, etc. (a) and (b) differ truth conditionally: if I know for a fact that there are no hydrangeas in this part of the world, (a) is false; however, if the circumstances are still conducive to hydrangeas' growth, the sentence in (b) is true.

Epistemic modal bases combine with ordering sources related to information: what the normal course of events is like (stereotypical ordering source), reports, beliefs, rumors, etc. *Circumstantial* modal bases combine with various kinds of ideals, yielding the various root interpretations: deontic (laws), bouletic (wishes), or teleological (aims). Note that the ordering source may also be empty, as with the circumstantial modal in (18b).

To sum up, in a Kratzerian system, a modal is a quantifier over possible worlds, restricted by a **modal base** (*circumstantial* or *epistemic*), which returns a set of accessible worlds, which can then be ordered by an **ordering source**, to yield the most ideal worlds of the modal base. Both modal bases and ordering sources are contextually determined (when not overt). This allows for a single lexical entry for *must* and for *can*, and their counterparts in various languages, which differ only in **force** of quantification (universal vs. existential).

Kratzer (1981, 1991) treats modality as an autonomous system, mostly putting aside the way it interacts with other elements such as tense or negation. While this tack was very useful in isolating general properties of modality and providing a unified theory, we will see how the interaction of modality with various elements requires that this account now be expanded.

5 The *epistemic vs. root* distinction

We have seen that, cross-linguistically, the same modal words can express both epistemic and root modality, a fact which Kratzer's context-sensitive account successfully captures. We will now see the flipside of the coin: just as systematically, epistemics and roots *differ* from each other in ways, which cast doubt on a unifying account. In the typology literature, epistemics and roots are sometimes taken to differ in that the former express 'propositional modality' (i.e., the speaker's judgment about a *proposition*), and the latter, 'event modality' (i.e., the speaker's attitude towards a potential *event*) (Jespersen 1924, Palmer 2001). Even more frequently, epistemics are said to be *speaker*-oriented, and roots *subject*-oriented (cf. Bybee, Perkins & Pagliuca 1994). This difference is sometimes formally captured by having *root* (but not *epistemic*) modals enter into a thematic relation with the subject (Perlmutter 1971, Ross 1969, Jackendoff 1972). In Kratzer's system, the difference between roots and epistemics is a matter of modal base: epistemic interpretations arise from an epistemic modal base, root interpretations from a circumstantial one. Kratzer (1991) already suggests that the difference in modal bases could be correlated to Perlmutter and Ross's epistemic vs. root distinction in terms of argument structure. It is not entirely clear, however, how this correlation can be formalized without losing some of the unifying power of her system: how can we encode that epistemic and deontic *must*s differ not just in modal bases, but in argument structure as well, without postulating two different lexical entries? What's worse, epistemics further differ from roots in their temporal relativity: epistemic modals are evaluated at the speech time, root modals at the time provided by the main tense of the sentence. Take the ambiguous sentence *John had to be home*. When the modal receives a root (deontic) interpretation, it expresses a *past* obligation given John's circumstances *then* to be home *then*. When it receives an epistemic interpretation, it expresses a *present* necessity, given what is known *now*, that at some past time John was home.

We will explore the hypothesis that what underlies these systematic differences in time and individual relativity is a difference in height of interpretation: epistemics scope at the 'S-level', roots scope at the 'VP-level', following *Cinque's hierarchy*. Based on a careful cross-linguistic survey of the positioning of adverbs and various functional elements like tense and modals, Cinque (1999) proposes that functional heads are universally organized along a rigid universal hierarchy, in which epistemic modals appear higher than root modals, as shown below:

(19) Cinque's hierarchy (*irrelevant projections omitted*)

$\text{Mod}_{epis} > \text{Tense} > \text{Aspect} > \text{Mod}_{volitional} > \text{Mod}_{deontic\ necessity} > \text{Mod}_{ability/deontic\ possibility}$

We now turn to evidence that supports such a hierarchical split.

5.1 Interaction between modals

Recall that in English, modals *may* and *have to* are ambiguous between epistemic and deontic readings. Interestingly, however, when they are stacked together, the ambiguity disappears:

(20) John may have to watch TV.

This sentence can only mean that it is possible, given what is known, that John has an obligation to watch TV, not that it is allowable that it be epistemically necessary that John watches TV. This restriction in ordering follows easily if modals have dedicated slots, with the highest reserved for epistemics and the lowest for roots.

Alternatively, the unattested ordering could perhaps be ruled out on conceptual grounds: no matter how tyrannical the issuer of a command, he may not be able to demand that a state of affairs be epistemically necessary. Yet, consider the following example from von Fintel & Iatridou (2004), which argues against conceptual impossibility. Imagine a scenario in which "an insurance company will only pay for an expensive test if there is a possibility that the patient may have Alzheimher's". Such a state of affairs can be reported as follows, with a deontic modal taking scope over an epistemic adjective:

(21) For the test costs to be reimbursed, it has to (DEONTIC) be possible (EPISTEMIC) that the patient has Alzheimer's.

Interestingly, this embedding possibility does not seem available with modal auxiliaries, at least in English. (20) doesn't seem able to receive an interpretation where the first modal is read deontically and the second epistemically. German may be different. Kratzer (1976) argues that the following example can receive an interpretation where the embedded modal auxiliary *können* receives an epistemic interpretation while the modal *müssen* is interpreted deontically (though see Nauze 2008, for claims that the embedded modal is not interpreted epistemically).

(22) Und auch in Zukunft muss diese Schnecke [...] Saugfüsse haben können.
 And also in future must this snail suction.feet have might
 And even in the future, this snail must possibly have suction feet.
 [translation from Nauze (2008)]

Why should there be a difference between German and English? Why should there be a difference in English between adjectives like *possible* and modals like *may*? What these examples seem to show is that the ordering restriction in sentences like (20) cannot be solely based on conceptual grounds: it seems possible to embed a modal adjective with an epistemic interpretation (if we grant that '*possible*' indeed refers to an epistemic, and not just a circumstantial possibility). Adjectives and modal auxiliaries may have different properties that would allow the former to embed, but not the latter, so that Cinque's hierarchy may not be so much about types of modality, but rather types of modal auxiliaries. It is also possible, more generally, that counterexamples like (22) result from biclausal structures, in which the epistemic modal is part of an embedded clause, though further empirical support and cross-linguistic inquiry is needed (von Fintel & Iatridou 2004).

5.2 Interaction with the subject

As mentioned earlier, a traditional distinction between epistemics and roots is that the former are *speaker-oriented* and the latter *subject-oriented*. We now review some evidence for this distinction, based on the interaction of modals with the subject.

One type of evidence is the way quantificational subjects scope with respect to the modal. Brennan (1993) shows that while epistemics are able to take scope over a quantificational subject, roots, such as ability modals, cannot. Consider the following pair of examples:

(23) a. Every radio may get Chicago stations and no radio may get Chicago stations.
       b. #Every radio can get Chicago stations and no radio can get Chicago stations.

With epistemic *may* in (23a), no contradiction arises, suggesting that *every radio* is interpreted below the modal: *it may be that every radio gets Chicago stations and (it may also be that) no radio gets Chicago stations*. The contradictoriness of (23b) with root *can*, however, suggests that *every radio* has to be interpreted above the modal. Note that while certain speakers may find the conjunction in (23a) anomalous (presumably for pragmatic reasons), all agree that the two conjuncts are compatible in a way that the conjuncts in (23b) are not.

While (23) shows that a quantifier like *every* can scope below an epistemic modal, von Fintel & Iatridou (2003) argue that in fact, it must. This is their Epistemic Containment Principle (ECP), according to which a quantifier cannot bind its trace across an epistemic modal. The ECP is illustrated in the infelicitous example below:

(24) #Every student may be the oldest student.

The infelicity of (24) indicates that the only possible interpretation is one where the modal takes scope over the quantifier (#*it is possible that all of the students are the oldest*), while the felicitous surface scope is ruled out by the ECP (*For every student x, it is possible that x is the oldest*) (for discussion and refinements, see Tancredi 2007 and Huitink 2008).

The scopal facts, then, argue that epistemics can (and perhaps must) take scope over quantifier subjects, but that root modals cannot. Why should this be? One common explanation is that epistemics and roots differ in argument structure: roots are control predicates which enter into a thematic relation with the subject, while epistemics are raising predicates, with no particular relation to the subject. Supporting evidence comes from idioms and expletives (Brennan 1993). As idiom chunks lose their idiomatic meaning in control constructions (*e.g., #the shit wants to hit the fan*), the example in (25) suggests that root *can* takes an individual and a property as arguments, while epistemic *might* takes a proposition:

(25) The shit might/#can hit the fan.

However, while there does seem to be some connection between the subject and a root modal, Bhatt (1998), Hackl (1998) and Wurmbrand (1999) argue that this connection cannot be due to a control configuration. Focusing on deontic modals, Bhatt and Wurmbrand independently show that obligations do not necessarily fall on the subject. Consider the following examples:

(26) Jonny must brush his teeth. Bhatt (1998)

(27) The plants must be watered.

The obligation is likely to be on the addressee of (26) rather than on Jonny, if he is a small child (for instance, his babysitter), and on the implicit agent, rather than on the plants, in (27), suggesting that the purported thematic relation between the modal and the subject is not syntactic. In Wurmbrand's terminology, deontics do not involve 'syntactic control', but rather 'semantic control'. This is corroborated by the fact that deontics do not necessarily require an agentive subject, and allow expletive subjects:

(28) There have to be fifty chairs in this room. Bhatt (1998)

It should be noted, however, that while these examples show that some deontics are best analyzed as raising predicates, they do not necessarily show that *all* deontics, let alone all *roots* are raising. Brennan (1993), for instance, argues that deontics split into two categories: what she calls *ought to be* deontics and *ought to do* deontics, using Feldman's (1986) terminology. Brennan argues that the former are S-level modals, just like epistemics, and the latter VP-level modals, like other roots. If such a distinction really is grammaticized, *must* in (26) could be ambiguous between an *ought to be* (obligation on the addressee) and *ought to do* (obligation on the subject) interpretation, with two different argument structures underlying this ambiguity. Evidence that *all* modals are raising predicates come from examples involving the most root-like type of modality, namely, ability modals. Hackl (1998) shows that some ability modals allow expletive *it* subjects (29a). Moreover, they do not always force their *subject* to enter into a particular relation with them: *can* in (29b) seems to express a capacity of *the pool*, rather than that of *a lot of people*:

(29) a. It can rain hard here. Hackl (1998)
b. A lot of people can jump in this pool.

The supporting evidence for a control analysis of modals is thus controversial at best. If we need a raising analysis for some roots, then by Occam's razor, we should avoid postulating two different kinds of argument structures for the same modals. While obligees and permittees are usually identified with an overt argument of the verb, the above examples show that they do not always need to; the context may be able to provide salient individuals around which the modality is centered. A possible explanation for the lack of idiomatic meaning with roots, as in (25), is that root modality somehow needs to centered around *some* participant of the VP event, but not necessarily its subject (Hacquard 2006). In most cases, the main participant *is* the subject, and hence properties of the subject are highlighted. In other cases, however, the location or properties of other participants of the event are more relevant (*here* or *the pool*). The fact that modal statements involving idiom chunks seem to improve when a location is added corroborates the intuition that the relevant factor is not argument structure, but rather whether the modality can be anchored to one of the VP event's participants:

(30) The shit can really hit the fan in this part of the world. Hacquard (2006)

To sum up, the interaction of modals with subjects shows some differences between roots and epistemics, although the evidence doesn't seem to warrant a control vs. raising split. In principle, this could have been otherwise. There is nothing about modality *per se* that would prevent this. In fact, predicates like *able to* are modal and require a control analysis. The purported thematic relation between a root modal and the subject instead seems to highlight the fact that root modals are centered around the circumstances of the event described by the main predicate, and especially, but not necessarily, those of its agent, confirming Palmer's intuition that root modality is 'event' modality.

Recall that we started this section with the traditional speaker vs. subject orientation of epistemic and root modals. We have seen that root modals do not always center around the subject, but rather around some participant of the main event. I would like to close this section by showing that epistemics are not always tied to the speaker either. When an epistemic appears in the complement of an attitude verb, the epistemic state that the modal seems to report is that of the attitude holder, not of the speaker:

(31)   a. Every boy$_1$ thinks he$_1$ must$_1$ be stupid.   Stephenson (2007)
    b. Every contestant$_1$ thinks he$_1$ might$_1$ be the winner.   Speas (2004)

We can thus refine the traditional subject vs. speaker orientation split as follows: *roots* are anchored to a *participant of the main event*, *epistemics* to the local 'attitude' holder: the *speaker* when the modal is in a matrix (though cf. section 6.2), the *attitude holder* when the modal is in the complement of an attitude verb.

5.3 Interaction with negation

The interaction between modals and negation is also suggestive, though a clear pattern doesn't yet emerge. Cross-linguistically, epistemics tend to be interpreted above negation, and roots below it (Coates 1983, Drubig 2001). The Malay examples below illustrate:

(32)   a. Dia mesti tidak belajar. (epistemic)   Drubig (2001)
        he must not   study
    b. Dia tidak mesti belajar. (deontic)
        he not   must study

Mesti (*must*) is ambiguous between an epistemic and a deontic interpretation. However, when it appears structurally above negation (*tidak*), the modal only gets an epistemic interpretation, and when below, it only gets a deontic one. Parallel cases can be seen in English, though the modal and negation appear in a fixed order on the surface. The sentence in (33) is ambiguous between an epistemic and a deontic interpretation. However, when the modal takes scope over negation, it must be interpreted epistemically, while, if it takes scope below, it must receive a deontic interpretation:

(33) John may not watch TV...
    a. ... he never knows any celebrity gossip.   epistemic: may>not
    b. ... his dad is very strict.   deontic: not>may

There are, however, counterexamples (Cormack & Smith 2002, Palmer 2001). The following examples contain modals with epistemic interpretations, which seem to scope under negation:

(34) a. Jane doesn't have to be at home.
    b. Jane need not be home.
    c. Jane can't be home.

Several factors, beyond the epistemic/root distinction, seem to conspire to make the interaction of modals with negation a complex matter, such as the possibility/necessity distinction (Cormack & Smith 2002), the position of negation, which varies cross-linguistically, and idiosyncrasies of various modal auxiliaries (for a thorough typological overview, see de Haan 1997). At best, we find the following weak, but suggestive, generalization (R. Bhatt and A. Rubinstein, p.c.): when a modal is ambiguous between a root and an epistemic interpretation, it is never the case that the modal scopes above negation when it receives a deontic interpretation and below it when it receives an epistemic one, though, all other cases are attested (negation takes scope over the modal no matter the interpretation, negation takes scope in between the two, or below both).

5.4 Interaction with tense

Traditional accounts of modality in general (and Kratzer's specifically) usually ignore the relationship between modals and tense. However, it has been shown that modals cannot be relative just to a world, but to a time as well (cf. Thomason 1984, Ippolito 2002): circumstances or evidence change through time; what was a possibility in the past may not be one in the future, and vice versa. Importantly, what this time *is* seems to depend on the particular interpretation of the modal: with a root interpretation, the modal's time of evaluation has to be the time provided by tense. With an epistemic interpretation, it has to be the local 'now': the speech time in matrix contexts, the attitude internal 'now' when in the complement of attitude verbs (cf. Iatridou 1990, Picallo 1990, Abusch 1997, Stowell 2004).

Consider the following example, where *have to* gets a *root* (teleological) interpretation; the circumstances and goal of the subject are evaluated at the time provided by tense (past). (35) expresses a necessity, given Mary's circumstances *then*, to take the train *then*. It cannot express a necessity given her circumstances *now* to have taken the train *then*.

(35)   Mary had to take the train to go to Paris.

The evaluation time of an *epistemic* modal can never be future-shifted. The only interpretation for (36) is that it may **now** be the case that Marikos will be dead tomorrow, but not that **tomorrow**, it will be possible that Marikos is dead:

(36)   Marikos may be dead tomorrow.   Groenendijk & Stokhof (1975)

Nor can it be back-shifted. Consider the following example:

(37)   Mary had to be the murderer.   ✓mod$_{epis}$>past, *past>mod$_{epis}$

Imagine that the evidence gathered at the beginning of the investigation, a week ago, all pointed to Mary being the murderer: she had no alibi, but many a motive. Yesterday, however, Poirot established that the murder had been committed one hour earlier than originally thought. This fact immediately cleared Mary, who was seen by several eyewitnesses elsewhere at that time. In this scenario, (37) is judged false: it cannot describe the epistemic state that held at the time when the evidence pointed to Mary. In order for us to report such a past state, we need additionally an embedding attitude verb (as in (38a)), an indirect discourse past tense (as in (38b); Boogart 2007), or an *overt* conversational background (as in (38c)):

(38)   a. Two days ago, Poirot thought that Mary had to be the murderer.
       b. This didn't make sense, thought Poirot... Mary had to be the murderer.
       c. Given what we knew then, Mary had to be the murderer.

In all these cases, a past morpheme appears on the modal. However, it lacks the characteristic backshifting of a true semantic past tense. For instance in (a), the modal's time of evaluation must be Poirot's thinking time; it cannot precede it. The past morpheme on the modal reflects instead a 'sequence of tense' rule, where the embedded tense morphologically agrees with the higher past tense on 'think', cf. article 13 [this volume] (Ogihara) *Tense*. (Note that there are some situations in which some speakers find the past epistemic interpretation of (37) acceptable. However, these situations all seem to be narrative contexts, which also involve some kind of temporal subordination or free indirect discourse. Similar complications occur with the 'assessor' of epistemic claims, cf. section 6.2.)

One counterexample to this generalization is put forth by von Fintel & Gillies (2008a), who argue that, in the following exchange, B's utterance expresses a *past epistemic possibility*:

(39) A: Why did you look in the drawer?
      B: My keys might have been in there. (=It was possible that my keys were in there)

However, this reading seems to only arise in answers to a *why* question, where the temporal shifting of the epistemic could be due to a covert *because*, able to shift the evaluation parameters (Stephenson 2007).

Finally, the temporal interpretation of modals seems to further differentiate *epistemic* from '*metaphysical*' modality (the modality involved in counterfactuals). Consider the following examples from Condoravdi (2002), who argues that the following contrast results from different scope configurations between the modal *might* and the Perfect (cf. article 10 [this volume] (Portner) *Perfect and progressive*) along with a felicity condition on the selection of a modal base:

(40) a. They might (already) have won the game.
      b. They might (still) have won the game.

(a) gets an epistemic interpretation, facilitated by 'already': *it is possible, as far as we know right now, that at some past time they won the game*; (b) gets a metaphysical interpretation, facilitated by 'still': *there was a possibility at some past time, that they would win the game* (with the further inference that they in fact didn't). Here again, with an epistemic interpretation, the modal's time of evaluation seems unable to get backshifted, even in the presence of a potential backshifter (perfect).

The lack of forward or backshifting of epistemics' time of evaluation is often captured formally by not allowing epistemics to be in the scope of tense (cf. Iatridou 1990, Abusch 1997, Picallo 1990, Abraham 2001, Stowell 2004), either by encoding in the lexical entry of epistemics that they be evaluated at the local time of evaluation or by hard-wiring their position above the tense projection, in line, again, with Cinque's hierarchy.

5.5 Reconciling Kratzer and Cinque

We see that modals interact differently with tense, negation, and quantifiers depending on their interpretation: modals with epistemic interpretations scope high, modals with root interpretations scope low, as in Cinque's hierarchy, where epistemics and roots occupy different fixed positions. This pattern challenges Kratzer's unifying account, according to which epistemics and roots are two contextual variants of the same modal words. Indeed, if modals must appear in predetermined positions, based on their interpretation, then something beyond a contextual parameter must be specified in each of their lexical entries to derive their structural properties. The behavior of epistemic and root modals leads us to two conflicting cross-linguistic generalizations. On the one hand, the same words seem to systematically be used to express both root and epistemic modality, in line with a Kratzerian account. On the other, epistemics and roots seem to systematically differ, notably in the positions in which they appear.

5.5.1 Diachronic and structural approaches

There are several lines one can take to give our syntax and semantics enough freedom to handle idiosyncrasies of roots and epistemics, and still explain why the same words are used cross-linguistically to express root and epistemic modality. One type of explanation for why modals share the same form while having a semantic life of their own is to appeal to a diachronic (or metaphoric) process. Epistemic interpretations tend to develop cross-linguistically from root ones, and interestingly, this historic trend is matched by children's acquisition of modals, with root modals being acquired first (Sweetser 1990, Papafragou 1998). Thus, one could argue that modals are polysemous, but not accidentally so: their various senses are related. For Sweetser (1990), modals encode 'force dynamics' of potential barriers and driving forces. These forces operate in the concrete, external world for root modals, but can be metaphorically extended to the realm of the mental or the abstract, to yield epistemic modality. However, while such diachronic accounts seem to be empirically rooted, they cannot be the full story. It is unclear why each of these senses should inherit the set of scopal (and other) properties it does.

A common way to derive these scopal properties is to assume two different positions (VP-level vs. S-level) for roots and epistemics, by essentially giving them separate lexical entries (cf. Jackendoff 1972, Picallo 1990, Butler 2003, a.o.). This postulation of different lexical entries for roots and epistemics unfortunately leaves unexplained why both types of modality are expressed by the same lexical items cross-linguistically. Brennan (1993) presents an interesting variant, in which modals come in different types, VP-level and S-level modals, but where the root/epistemic distinction is not directly encoded in these two types. The reason most roots correspond to VP-modals and epistemics to S-modals is not a grammatical fact, but the result of certain ontological commitments made and reinforced by the community of language users, which could have been different. This allows Brennan to successfully derive two positions for roots and epistemics without encoding the flavor distinction in the modals' lexical entries (hence resolving the tension between the two conflicting cross-linguistic generalizations). Yet, the arbitrariness of the correlation between modal type (VP vs. S) and modal flavor is questionable, given that this correlation does not hold only in a single language, or language family, but across languages of different pedigrees. Why should different communities of speakers converge on the same ontological commitments?

5.5.2 Event-relativity approach

Let's review the time and individual restrictions that seem to constrain the interpretation of modals. We saw that modals are generally relative to a time. For epistemics in main clauses, this time is the speech time; for epistemics in complements of attitude verbs, it is the attitude 'now'; and for roots, it is the time provided by tense. Modals are also generally relative to an individual. For epistemics in main clauses, the individual is the speaker, for epistemics in attitude contexts, it is the attitude holder, and for roots, it is often the subject, and sometimes, another participant of the VP event. Putting aside the flavor difference for a moment, one way to recast these generalizations is to say that modals are relative to time/individual pairs, and that crucially, not all time/individual combinations are attested. A modal is either anchored to the speaker at the speech time (*may* in (41a) describes an epistemic possibility for the *speaker* at the *speech time*), the attitude holder at the attitude time (*may* in (41b) describes an epistemic possibility for Mary at her *thinking time*), or a participant of the VP event at the time of the VP event, provided by tense (*have to* in (41c) describes a circumstantial necessity for *John* at the *fleeing time*):

(41) a. John may have seen the murderer.
 b. Mary thought that John may have seen the murderer.
 c. John had to flee the scene.

What we do not find are modals anchored to the speaker at the time provided by tense, or to the subject at the speech time (unless, of course, these two times coincide, i.e., with present tense). Why does the interaction of modals with tense and with individuals to go hand in hand, rather than being independent of each other?

One way to derive these time/individual constraints is to make a modal relative to an *event* rather than a world of evaluation (Hacquard 2006, 2010). Doing so will restrict the modal's interpretation by anchoring it to particular time/individual pairs, namely the running time and participants of the event it is relative to. Under this view, the meaning of a modal is not only constrained by the context and the idiosyncrasies of its lexical entry, but by its grammatical environment as well.

We have already seen intuitions that modals are centered around an event: the main event for root modals, and the speech event for epistemics (cf. Jespersen 1924, Palmer 2001, Zagona 2007). In Hacquard (2006, 2010), I propose to cash out this event-relativity by using a Kratzerian semantics, except that modals (and in particular modal bases) are relative to an *event* of evaluation, rather than a *world* of evaluation. There are three kinds of events that modals can be anchored to: speech events, VP-events and attitude events. I argue that by relativizing modals to an event rather than a world of evaluation, one gets all and only the attested time-individual pairs: the running time and participants of the events of evaluation. Modals are thus either relative to the VP event (and hence its participants— e.g., the subject— and its running time—determined by tense), the speech event (and hence the speaker and the speech time), or an attitude event (and hence its attitude holder and attitude time).

Here is a formal sketch: modals keep their standard lexical entries, but their modal bases take an event pronoun *e*, which needs to be bound locally. Assuming that in a standard world-relative system, modal bases and worlds are represented in the *object language,* and not as parameters, the only difference between a world-relative and an event-relative system is that the argument of the modal base *f* for the latter is an event rather than a world pronoun:

(42) a. *world-relative modal*

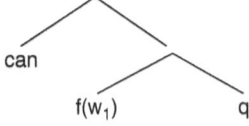

b. *event-relative modal*

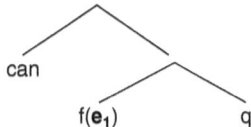

In the Davidsonian tradition, verbs (including attitude verbs) are predicates of events, whose event argument is quantified over by Aspect (article 9 [this volume] (Filip) *Aspectual class and Aktionsart*). There are two types of event binders: Aspect, and a default speech event e_0, which I assume is represented in the object language. The event-relativity of the modals in (41) is derived as follows; modals can appear (for type reasons) in either one of two positions within a clause, roughly corresponding to Brennan's S-level vs. VP-level modals: above tense or above the VP. In a main clause, a modal located above tense is bound by the speech event e_0 (41)/(43a); in a complement clause, a modal located above the embedded tense is bound by the aspect that quantifies over the embedding attitude event e_2 ((41)/(43b); a modal located below tense and aspect is bound by the aspect that quantifies over the VP event e_1 (41)/(43c):

(43) a. John may have seen the murderer.

　　　[$_{CP}$ **e_0** λe_0　　Mod f(e_0) [$_{TP}$ T　　Asp$_1$ λe_1[$_{VP}$ V e_1]]]

　　　　　　　　　　may　　　　　*past*　*pfv*　　*J. see murderer*

b. M. thought that J. may have seen the murderer.

　　[$_{CP}$ e_0 λe_0 T **Asp$_2$** λe_2 Att **e_2** [$_{CP}$ Mod f(e_2) [TP T Asp$_1$ λe_1[VP V e_1]]]]

　　　　　　　　　　　　thought　*may*　　　　　　　　*J. see murderer*

c. John had to flee the scene.

　　[$_{CP}$ e_0 λe_0 [$_{TP}$ T　**Asp$_1$** λe_1 Mod f(e_1) [$_{VP}$ V **e_1**]]]

　　　　　　　　past pfv　　　　*have to*　　*J. flee*

This derives the right time and individual constraints. The connection between the type of events modals are relative to and the root and epistemic distinction is indirect. I propose that, usually, only modals relative to speech and attitude events can combine with an epistemic modal base because only those events have associated 'propositional content' (i.e., the propositions that make up the attitude, such as a set of beliefs), which provides an information state required by an epistemic modal base. VP-event-relative modals, on the other hand, get a default circumstantial modal base:

(44) a. $f_{epis}(e) = \lambda w'. w'$ is compatible with the 'content' of e
　　　b. $f_{circ}(e) = \lambda w'. w'$ is compatible with the circumstances of e

Many complications arise, which we cannot discuss here. The main advantage of an event relative system, is that it allows for a single (flavor independent) entry for modals à la Kratzer, but whose meaning is partly constrained by its grammatical environment (i.e., it depends on what the closest event binder is), making sense of the fact that low modals in Cinque's hierarchy (i.e., those that scope *below* aspect) receive a root interpretation, while high modals (i.e., those that scope *above* tense) receive an epistemic interpretation.

6 Questioning the modal semantics of modals

In section 5, we saw how epistemics and roots differ in their interactions with tense, negation and subjects. These interactions showed us that modality cannot be a completely hermetic system, as its interpretation is affected, and perhaps partly determined, by neighboring grammatical elements. The tension there was to reconcile a unifying account with an account that could derive these scope interactions. We now turn to two different and independent challenges to any 'modal' account of modals more generally: in section 6.1 we discuss a puzzle involving *root* modals and their interaction with aspect, where modals seem to lose their modal dimension and force their complement clause to be actualized. In section 6.2 we discuss claims that *epistemics* are not part of the proposition expressed by the sentence they appear in: they do not involve quantification over possible worlds, but merely make an extra-truth conditional contribution.

6.1 Root modals as implicative predicates?

This section discusses the interaction of root modals and aspect. Consider the following Greek example from Bhatt (1999), which shows that ability modals do not always merely express a possibility, but sometimes force the proposition expressed by their complement to occur in the actual world. Such '*actuality entailments*' (using Bhatt's terminology) happen when modals combine with *perfective*, but not with *imperfective* aspect:

(45) a. Borusa   na sikoso   afto to trapezi
    can-**impf**.1s NA lift.nonpast.pfv.1s this the table,
    ala δen to sikosa.   Bhatt (1999)
    but NEG it lift-impf
    '(In those days) I could lift this table, but I didn't lift it.'

b. Boresa   na tu miliso   (#ala δen tu milisa).
can-pst.**pfv** NA him talk.nonpast.pfv.1s #but neg him talk.past-pfv
'I was able to talk to him (#but I didn't talk to him).'

This is not an idiosyncrasy of the Greek ability modal. Bhatt shows that the effect happens in languages, which, unlike English, have an overt morphological distinction between perfective and imperfective aspect, such as Hindi, French, Italian, Bulgarian, etc. Furthermore, this effect further extends to *all* root interpretations (Hacquard 2006).

Actuality entailments pose a serious challenge for any modal account, by seemingly eradicating the very property of displacement that defines modals. They further show the dangers of focusing on languages like English or German, which sometimes have idiosyncratic properties that can obscure the bigger picture (such as not distinguishing aspect morphologically). Should we give up standard accounts? Are root modals not modals after all? Bhatt (1999) in fact proposes an account of the ability modal, which denies altogether that it is a modal, and treats it instead as an *implicative* predicate. Following Karttunen's (1971) analysis of the implicative *manage*, Bhatt argues that with an ability statement, what is asserted is the complement clause, and a further meaning component, that the complement requires some effort, is added as a conventional implicature. The lack of actuality entailment with imperfective arises from an additional layer of modality associated with the imperfective itself.

Hacquard (2006, 2009) proposes a way to derive actuality entailments and keep a relatively standard modal semantics for root modals. Root modals are regular quantifiers over possible worlds, and actuality entailments arise from the configuration of aspect and the modal: while epistemics scope above tense and aspect and are thereby immune to actuality entailments, root modals scope below aspect, and are thus susceptible to them. Given that aspect is what quantifies over the VP event, it locates that event in time and in a *world*. By having (perfective) aspect scope over the modal, that world has to be the actual world (imperfective brings in an additional layer of modality as in Bhatt 1999). Under this account, actuality entailments are ultimately of the same nature as the scope interactions of root and epistemic modals with tense and subjects, and the problem reduces to explaining why epistemics and roots scope in different positions.

6.2 Do epistemics contribute to truth conditional content?

It is often assumed in the descriptive literature that epistemics do not contribute to the truth conditional content of the sentence they appear in, but rather express a speaker's comment about, or commitment to, the proposition expressed by their complement (cf. Halliday 1970, Palmer 2001). This intuition has been formalized recently in various ways, from treating epistemics as *evidentials* (Westmoreland 1998, Drubig 2001), to having them modify or perform a different speech act, such as a kind of 'doxastic advice' (Swanson 2006). There is, for instance, a tight connection between evidentials and epistemics, as both deal, to a certain extent, with speakers' *evidence* (cf. Aikhenvald 2004). Evidentials are often said *not* to contribute to the truth conditional content of the sentence they combine with, but rather indicate the speaker's grounds for expressing that sentence (cf. Faller 2002); likewise, accounts of epistemics as evidentials take them to lack truth conditional content. The precise nature of the connection between the two categories is under active debate: some argue that epistemics are a kind of evidentials, and thus lack truth conditional content (Drubig 2001), others that *evidentials* are a kind of epistemic modals, and thus make a truth conditional contribution in terms of quantification of possible worlds (McCready & Ogata 2007, Matthewson, Rullman & Davis 2007). There is at least some evidence that epistemic modals have an evidential component, as argued by von Fintel & Gillies (2007), with examples like (46):

(46) It must be raining.

A speaker can utter (46) felicitously in a windowless room after seeing a few people coming in with wet umbrellas, but not when standing outside in pouring rain. This indicates that an epistemic modal's felicity conditions require that the evidence the modal claim is based on be indirect, or involve an inference.

The main supporting evidence for all non-truth-conditional accounts of epistemics is the fact that epistemics are notoriously hard to embed. As we saw, they tend to scope over tense, negation, and quantifiers. It has further been claimed that they cannot occur in questions, in antecedents of conditionals, or in complements of attitude verbs (cf. Jackendoff 1972, Drubig 2001). There are, however, counterexamples to these unembedability claims. We saw, for instance, that some epistemics scope under negation. Furthermore, the ability of epistemics to embed seems to depend on Lyons' (1977) *subjective/objective* distinction. Subjective epistemics are taken to rely on the speaker's personal and subjective evidence, while objective epistemics rely on more objective grounds, which the speaker shares with a relevant community. A modal in a sentence such as '*it might rain*' is in principle ambiguous between a subjective reading (say, if I utter this sentence not having read any weather report, based solely on the dubious fact that my arthritis is acting up), and an objective one (say, if it is uttered by a meteorologist after consulting various radar maps). Lyons claims that only *subjective* epistemics lack truth conditional content, while *objective* epistemics get an ordinary modal semantics, a claim supported by the fact that while subjective epistemics resist embedding, objective ones embed more freely—they can appear in questions (Papafragou 2006), and in the scope of quantifiers, obviating the 'ECP' (Tancredi 2007).

A subjective/objective split, however, raises a by-now familiar dilemma: if objective and subjective epistemics are truly separate modals, which differ in whether they make a truth conditional contribution, why should they share a lexical entry? A perhaps more promising way to derive a subjective/objective distinction while maintaining a unified account is to have the modal be relativized either to the speaker's information state for the former, or that of the speaker and his community for the latter (cf. Papafragou 2006, Portner 2009; von Fintel & Gillies 2008b propose an interesting pragmatic way of deriving this distinction, which may avoid having to lexicalize this information).

But why should such a distinction correlate with epistemics' ability to embed? Perhaps, subjective epistemics can embed to the same extent than objective ones, but some embeddings are unattested for felicity reasons. Papafragou (2006), for instance, argues that subjective epistemics do not appear in questions, since it would be odd for a speaker to ask his addressee about his own epistemic state. As a matter of fact, we do actually find subjective epistemics in some attitude contexts (Portner 2009); *might* in (47) seems to express a *subjective* epistemic possibility based on John's *subjective* beliefs:

(47) John believes that it might be raining.

The question of whether epistemics can embed—and if not, what in their semantics prevents them to do so—requires further empirical investigation. What is clear at this point is that, while we do find cases of embedded epistemics, their distribution is still limited: as we saw, epistemics cannot scope under tense, apparently regardless of the subjective/objective distinction. Furthermore, while there does seem to be something to the subjective/objective distinction, both the data supposed to tease them apart and the nature of the distinction are still somewhat controversial.

Another challenge to traditional accounts is the claim that any *assessor* of an epistemic modal statement can disagree with its content (even if she is not part of the conversation, but merely eavesdropping), and thus that the truth of an epistemic statement is relative not merely to the speaker, but to the perspective of the sentence's *assessor* (MacFarlane 2011, Egan, Hawthorne & Weatherson 2004, Stephenson 2007, a.o.). While the kind of data used in support of assessor-relativity suggests that the question of whose information state epistemics are relative to is quite complex, there seem to be ways to account for it without invoking the 'assessor' machinery. Recall from our discussion of the subjectivity of epistemics that they seem to sometimes not be relative solely to the knowledge of the speaker, but to that of the speaker and her community. It could be that, sometimes, a sentence's assessor is really part of the speaker's community, whose knowledge state needs to be factored in (cf. von Fintel & Gillies 2007).

The precise nature of epistemic modality is thus still a matter of debate. There are, however, good reasons for wanting to maintain a truth conditional account in terms of quantification over possible worlds. First, epistemics can embed and contribute to truth conditional content, as the following contrast shows (von Fintel & Gillies 2007):

(48) a. If there *might* have been a mistake, the editor will have to reread the manuscript.
 b. If there is a mistake, the editor will have to reread the manuscript.

Second, epistemic modals *are* expressed by the same words as other kinds of modals cross-linguistically. How, then, can we derive their idiosyncrasies? With respect to the embedability facts, we saw several solutions that give epistemics widest scope, and thereby derive their difficulty to embed under certain categories. What about other peculiarities? One way to capture idiosyncrasies of modals, while maintaining a standard semantics in terms of quantification over worlds, is to encode them in a separate dimension of meaning. For instance, to handle the evidential nature of epistemics, von Fintel & Gillies (2007) suggest that epistemic modals needn't be evidentials *per se*: they could contribute an extra speech act of 'proffering' beyond their standard truth conditional contribution as quantifiers over possible worlds. Portner (2009) takes such a line further by proposing that other modals also contribute an extra speech act: for deontics, a command, for roots, an assertion responsible for actuality entailments. However, while encoding such a dimension is a step forward in being able to account for peculiarities of various modalities while maintaining a unified truth conditional semantics, it ultimately faces our original dilemma of explaining why these various modalities are expressed by the same modal words cross-linguistically: even if encoded in a separate dimension, modality-specific information still needs to be lexically specified in separate entries. That is, unless, one could find a (non lexical) way to have the type of performativity somehow fall out from the type of modality.

7 Modality and its kin

Several systems share many similarities with modals, and one may question the extent to which these similarities are due to the limited set of resources these systems can appeal to, or whether they reflect deeper dependencies. To understand the connection between modals and these various systems, it has proven fruitful to look at the way they interact. One such system is *mood*. Mood and modality are often discussed together, as they seem intimately connected, in that both signal the non actual; certain languages do not have modal auxiliaries but a rich mood system, others, like English, have an impoverished mood system, but a rich modal auxiliary system (Palmer 2001). Are the two separate systems, or alternatives to one another? How do they interact in languages that have both systems (e.g., Romance languages)? There, modals seem to systematically select for subjective mood (when they do not combine with an infinitival complement), suggesting that mood may be more of a morphological reflex, rather than a semantically contentful category. For more on mood, see Farkas (1985), Giannakidou (1997), Portner (1997), and article 11 [this volume] (Portner) *Verbal mood*.

Another system to consider is *evidentiality*. We saw that epistemic modals share similarities with evidentials. Is it that epistemic modals are really evidentials? Or that evidentials are really modals? Alternatively, could there be two separate systems, standing in some kind of dependency? One possibility is that evidentials impose restrictions on a modal's conversational background, say, by determining the ordering source of epistemic modals, as suggested by Portner (2007). This could explain why epistemic modals seem to have an evidential component, without forcing them to *be* evidentials. Further research on the interaction of the two systems in languages that have both rich evidential and modal systems will shed more light on the connection between the two.

Another case at hand is *imperatives* (article 6 [Semantics: Sentence and Information Structure] (Han) *Imperatives*). Imperatives share many similarities with modals, and are sometimes argued to employ, in part, the Kratzerian machinery, cf. Han (1999). Portner (2007) shows that imperatives can receive the same flavors of interpretation as root modals (deontic, bouletic, teleological). A sentence such as *Have an apple!*, for instance, could be taken as an order or an invitation, depending on context. Yet, imperatives and modals differ in important ways: while it is fairly uncontroversial that root modals make a truth conditional contribution, this is not so for imperatives. So, whence the similarities? Portner argues that imperatives and root modals are intimately connected, in part because of the way the discourse evolves and affects context-sensitive modals. Just like declaratives are added to the common ground and affect the interpretation of subsequent modals (which is why the following sequence is infelicitous:

It isn't raining. #It might be raining), imperatives affect the interpretation of subsequent root modals by helping determine their ordering source. So here again, we find a potential dependency that goes beyond the appeal to the same resources.

Finally, consider attitude verbs. We mentioned that attitude verbs share many similarities with modals: they can have epistemic/doxastic-type interpretations (*know, believe*) or root-like interpretations (bouletics 'want', 'wish', commands 'order'...). Are these two systems analogous but independent, or is there a deeper connection? The connection might simply be that both involve quantification over possible worlds (Hintikka 1962). However, evidence for a deeper connection comes from the fact that epistemic modals cannot appear in the complements of all attitude verbs. Anand & Hacquard (2009) argue that epistemics cannot appear in complements of root-like attitudes (49b), but only in that of what Stalnaker (1984) calls 'attitudes of acceptance' (49a), and propose that epistemic modals are in fact anaphoric to the *content* of an embedding attitude verb of the right type:

(49)   a. John {believes, argues, assumed} that the Earth might be flat.
       b. *John {hopes, wishes, commanded} that the Earth might be flat.

Comparing modals and various systems such as mood, evidentials, or attitude verbs, and looking at the way they interact, it appears that their similarities may not be completely accidental, but may reflect instead the appeal to the same resources, and sometimes even deeper, perhaps anaphoric, dependencies.

8 Conclusions

We began with the cross-linguistic generalization that the same words express various flavors of modality, a fact supported by Kratzer's unifying account, which captures modals' context-dependency. We saw that this pan-modal generalization was counterposed by several flavor-specific idiosyncrasies, which cast doubt on unification (and more generally, challenge analyses in terms of quantification over possible worlds). Thus, while context undeniably plays an important role in determining the flavor of modals, it cannot by itself disallow say, an epistemic modal to be evaluated in the past or the future, or to scope below a quantifier or negation; and yet, this is what we find cross-linguistically. We considered new accounts, which reconciled these two generalizations either by making the semantics of modals partly dependent on their grammatical environment, or by exploring additional dimensions of meaning.

For reasons of space, this survey article had to be limited in scope both theoretically and empirically. In the remaining paragraphs, I will mention some of the areas we skipped, and provide references for the interested reader. We focused on modals and their interactions at the sentence level. But modals, being context sensitive, are clearly affected by the way discourse evolves, as we briefly mentioned in section 7. This is illustrated in cases of so-called *modal subordination*, where modals appear in anaphoric relations cross-sententially (cf. Roberts 1989, Geurts 1995, Frank 1997, and article 14 [Semantics: Sentence and Information Structure] (Geurts) *Accessibility and anaphora*). Theory-wise, we focused on static approaches; however, theoretical alternatives are found in dynamic frameworks (cf. Groenendijk, Stokhof & Veltman 1996 and references therein). Beyond framework differences, the way discourse affects a modal's interpretation, or the issues surrounding subjective and objective epistemic modality (in particular, the way they affect and are affected by the knowledge state of discourse participants), both seem like good areas to better understand the division of labor between semantics and pragmatics, and the representation of meaning in static or dynamic terms (cf. von Fintel & Gillies 2007, Yalcin 2007). Empirically, our discussion was limited to modal auxiliaries, ignoring nouns, adjectives, and adverbs. But adverbs like *possibly* or *necessarily* express the same kinds of possibilities and necessities that modal auxiliaries do, and are traditionally given the same semantics. One interesting research question is how modal auxiliaries and modal adverbs interact, and in particular, the puzzling non-additive, but rather 'agreeing' effect that results from so-called *modal concord* (cf. Geurts & Huitink 2006, Zeijlstra 2008). We have also ignored the modal component involved in some non-lexical categories of meaning as well, such as tense, aspect, or mood (for discussion, see articles 9 [this volume] (Filip) *Aspectual class and Aktionsart*, 11 [this volume] (Portner) *Verbal mood*, and 13 [this volume] (Ogihara) *Tense*), or the covert modality present in infinitivals (Bhatt 1999), as well as the modality involved in conditionals, which played a major role in shaping Kratzer's theory (article 15 [this volume] (von Fintel) *Conditionals*). While we focused on the interaction of modals with *viewpoint* aspect, we ignored the interaction of modals with the *lexical* aspect of the verb phrase they combine with, and in particular the fact that stative verbs tend to force epistemic interpretations of the modals they combine with (e.g., *John must love Mary*), while eventives tend to force root interpretations (e.g., *John must go to Paris*).

An important lesson we learned from looking at the interactions of modals with elements like tense or aspect is that these elements seem to constrain the interpretation of modals. While earlier work either de-emphasized these constraints or derived them by appeal to syntactic design, we may now be in a position to start explaining these puzzles without recourse to cartographic appeal. For example, as we saw, epistemic interpretations are restricted by whether a modal scopes above tense. Perhaps only high scoping modals get epistemic interpretations because modals obey local dependencies, and epistemic interpretations depend on a 'high' element (such as a speech or attitude event). Perhaps, more generally, the interpretation of modals is constrained by various elements because these elements participate in determining that interpretation. The moral of the past decade is this: now that we have robust accounts of modality, which can handle both the logical properties of modals and their context-dependency, we no longer need to study modality as a hermetic system. The next chapter, it seems, will be to explain exactly how modals affect and are affected by their surrounding environment, both at the sentence level and the discourse level.

For helpful comments and discussion, many thanks to Pranav Anand, Kai von Fintel, Nathan Klinedinst, Dave Kush, Terje Londhal, Paul Pietroski, Paul Portner, Alexis Wellwood, and especially Rajesh Bhatt.

9 References

Abraham, Werner 2001. Modals. Toward explaining the 'epistemic non-finiteness gap'. In: R. Müller & M. Reis (eds.). *Modalität und Modalverben im Deutschen*. Hamburg: Helmut Buske Verlag, 7–36.
Abusch, Dorit 1997. Sequence of tense and temporal de re. *Linguistics & Philosophy* 20, 1–50.
Aikhenvald, Alessandra 2004. *Evidentiality*. Oxford: Oxford University Press.
Anand, Pranav & Valentine Hacquard 2009. Epistemics with attitudes. In: T. friedman & S. Ito (eds.). *Proceedings of Semantics and Linguistics Theory (SALT) XVIII*. Ithaca, NY: CLC Publications. http://hdl.handle.net/1813/13025, December 28, 2010.
Bhatt, Rajesh 1998. Obligation and possession. In: H. Harley (ed.). *Papers from the UPenn/MIT Roundtable on Argument Structure and Aspect, MITWPL* 32. Cambridge, MA: MIT, 21–40.
Bhatt, Rajesh 1999. *Covert Modality in Non-Finite Contexts*. Ph.D. dissertation. University of Pennsylvania, Philadelphia, PA.
Boogart, Rony 2007. The past and perfect of epistemic modals. In: L. de Saussure, J. Moescher & G. Puskas (eds.). *Recent Advances in the Syntax and Semantics of Tense, Aspect and Modality*. Berlin: Mouton de Gruyter, 47–69.
Brennan, Virginia. 1993. *Root and Epistemic Modal Auxiliary Verbs*. Ph.D. dissertation. University of Massachusetts, Amherst, MA.
Butler, Jonny 2003. A minimalist treatment of modality. *Lingua* 113, 967–996.
Bybee, Joan, Revere Perkins & William Pagliuca 1994. *The Evolution of Grammar: Tense, Aspect and Modality in the Languages of the World*. Chicago, IL: The University of Chicago Press.
Carnap, Rudolph 1957. *Meaning and Necessity*. Chicago, IL: The University of Chicago Press.
Cinque, Guglielmo 1999. *Adverbs and Functional Heads: A Cross-Linguistic Perspective*. Oxford: Oxford University Press.

Coates, Jennifer 1983. *The Semantics of the Modal Auxiliaries*. London: Croom Helm.
Condoravdi, Cleo 2002. Temporal interpretations of modals. In: D. Beaver, S. Kaufman, & B. Clark (eds.). *Stanford Papers in Semantics*. Palo Alto, CA: CSLI Publications, 59–88.
Copeland, Jack 2002. The genesis of possible worlds. *Journal of Philosophical Logic* 31, 99–137.
Cormack, Annabel & Neil Smith 2002. Modals and negation in English. In: S. Barbiers, F. Beukema & W. van der Wurff (eds.). *Modality and its Interaction with the Verbal System*. Amsterdam: Benjamins, 133–163.
Drubig, Hans B. 2001. *On the Syntactic Form of Epistemic Modality*; Ms. Tübingen, University of Tübingen.
Egan, Andy, John Hawthorne & Brian Weatherson 2004. Epistemic modals in context. In: G. Preyer & G. Peter (eds.). *Contextualism in Philosophy*. Oxford: Oxford University Press, 131–169.
Faller, Martina 2002. *Semantics and Pragmatics of Evidentials in Cuzco Quecha*. Ph.D. dissertation. Stanford University, Stanford, CA.
Farkas, Donka 1985. *Intensional Descriptions and the Romance Subjunctive Mood*. New York: Garland.
Feldman, Fred 1986. *Doing the Best We Can*. Dordrecht: Reidel.
von Fintel, Kai 2006. Modality and Language. In: D. Borchert (ed.). *Encyclopedia of Philosophy*. New York: Macmillan, 20–27.
von Fintel, Kai & Anthony Gillies 2007. An opinionated guide to epistemic modality. In: T. Gendler & J. Hawthorne (eds.). *Oxford Studies in Epistemology, Vol. 2*. Oxford: Oxford University Press, 32–62.
von Fintel, Kai & Anthony Gillies 2008a. CIA Leaks. *Philosophical Review* 117, 77–98.
von Fintel, Kai & Anthony Gillies 2008b. *Might* made right. In: A. Egan & B. Weatherson (eds.). *Epistemic Modality*. Oxford: Oxford University Press.
von Fintel, Kai & Sabine Iatridou 2003. Epistemic Containment. *Linguistic Inquiry* 34, 173–198.
von Fintel, Kai & Sabine Iatridou 2004. Seminar Notes. Ms. MIT, Cambridge, MA.
Fleischman, Suzanne 1982. *The Future in Thought and Language: Diachronic Evidence from Romance*. Cambridge: Cambridge University Press.
Frank, Anette 1997. *Context Dependence in Modal Constructions*. Doctoral Dissertation, University of Stuttgart.
Gamut, L.T.F. 1991. *Logic, Language, and Meaning. Vol. 1: Introduction to Logic; Vol. 2: Intensional Logic and Logical Grammar*. Chicago, IL: The University of Chicago Press.
Geurts, Bart 1995. *Presupposing*. Doctoral dissertation. University of Stuttgart.
Geurts, Bart & Janneke Huitink 2006. Modal concord. In: P. Dekker & H. Zeijlstra (eds.). *Proceedings of the ESSLLI Workshop Concord Phenomena at the Syntax-Semantics Interface, Malaga*. Malaga: University of Malaga, 15–20.
Giannakidou, Anastasia 1997. *The Landscape of Polarity Items*. Ph.D. dissertation. University of Groningen.
Groenendijk, Jeroen & Martin Stokhof 1975. Modality and conversational information. *Theoretical Linguistics* 2, 61–112.
Groenendijk, Jeroen, Martin Stokhof & Frank Veltman 1996. Coreference and modality. In: S. Lappin (ed.). *The Handbook of Contemporary Semantic Theory*. Oxford: Blackwell, 179–213.
de Haan, Ferdinand 1997. *The Interaction of Modality and Negation*. New York: Garland.
Hackl, Martin 1998. On the Semantics of '*Ability* Ascriptions'. Ms. MIT, Cambridge, MA.
Hacquard, Valentine 2006. *Aspects of Modality*. Ph.D. dissertation. MIT, Cambridge, MA.

Hacquard, Valentine 2009. On the interaction of aspect and modal auxiliaries. *Linguistics & Philosophy* 32, 279–315.
Hacquard, Valentine 2010. On the event relativity of modal auxiliaries. *Natural Language Semantics* 18, 79–114.
Halliday, Michael 1970. Functional diversity in language as seen from a consideration of modality and mood in English. *Foundations of Language* 6, 322–361.
Han, Chung-hey 1999. Deontic modality, lexical aspect and the semantics of imperatives. In: *Linguistics in the Morning Calm 4*. Seoul: Hanshir Publications, 479–495.
Hintikka, Jakko 1961. Modality and quantification. *Theoria* 27, 119–128.
Hintikka, Jakko 1962. *Knowledge and Belief*. Ithaca, NY: Cornell University Press.
Hoffmann, T. Ronald 1966. Past tense replacement and the modal system. In: A. Oettinger (ed.). *Mathematical Linguistics and Automatic Translation*. Harvard Computational Laboratory. Report NSF-17. Cambridge, MA: Harvard University.
Horn, Laurence. 1972. *On the Semantic Properties of the Logical Operators in English*. Bloomington, IN: Indiana University Linguistics Club.
Hughes, George & Max Cresswell 1996. *A New Introduction to Modal Logic*. London: Routledge.
Huitink, Janneke 2008. Scoping over epistemics in English and Dutch'. In: *Current Issues in University and Diversity of Languages. Collection of Papers Selected from CIL 18*. Seoul: Linguistic Society of Korea, 2077–2089.
Iatridou, Sabine 1990. The past, the possible and the evident. *Linguistic Inquiry* 21, 123–129.
Ippolito, Michela 2002. *The Time of Possibilities*. Ph.D. dissertation. MIT, Cambridge, MA.
Jackendoff, Ray 1972. *Semantic Interpretation in Generative Grammar*. Cambridge, MA: The MIT Press.
Jespersen, Otto 1924. *A Modern English Grammar*. Copenhagen: Einar Munksgaard.
John MacFarlane, 2011. Epistemic modals are assessment-sensitive. In B. Weatherson & A. Egan (eds.), *Epistemic Modality*. Oxford: Oxford University Press, 144–178.
Kamp, Hans 1975. Reference and quantification in tense and model logic. In: S. Schmidt (ed.). *Pragmatics II*. München: Fink, 150–197.
Kanger, Stig 1957. The Morning Star paradox. *Theoria* 23, 1–11.
Karttunen, Lauri 1971. Implicatives. *Language* 47, 340–358.
Kaufmann, Stephan, Cleo Condoravdi & Valentina Harizanov 2007. Formal approaches to modality. In: W. Frawley (ed.). *The Expression of Modality*. Berlin: Mouton de Gruyter, 72–106.
Kratzer, Angelika 1976. Was *können* und *müssen* bedeuten können müssen. *Linguistische Berichte* 42, 128–160.
Kratzer, Angelika 1977. What *must* and *can* must and can mean. *Linguistics and Philosophy* 1, 337–355.
Kratzer, Angelika 1978. *Semantik der Rede: Kontexttheorie, Modalwörter, Konditionalsätze*. Königstein: Scriptor.
Kratzer, Angelika 1981. The notional category of modality. In: H.-J. Eikmeyer & H. Rieser (eds.). *Words, Worlds, and Contexts. New Approaches in Word Semantics*. Berlin: Mouton de Gruyter, 38–74.
Kratzer, Angelika 1991. Modality. In: A. von Stechow & D. Wunderlich (eds.). *Semantik: Ein internationales Handbuch zeitgenössischer Forschung*. Berlin: Mouton de Gruyter, 639–650.
Kripke, Saul 1963. Semantical analysis of Modal Logic I, Normal Propositional Calculi. *Zeitschrift für mathematische Logik und Grundlagen der Mathematik* 9, 67–96.

Lewis, David 1973. *Counterfactuals*. Cambridge, MA: Harvard University Press.
Lyons, John 1977. *Semantics*. Cambridge: Cambridge University Press.
MacFarlane John, 2011. Epistemic modals are assessment-sensitive. In B. Weatherson & A. Egan (eds.), Epistemic Modality. Oxford: Oxford University Press, 144-178.
Matthewson, Lisa, Hotze Rullman & Henry Davis 2007. Evidentials as epistemic modals: Evidence from St'at'imcets. In: J. van Craenenbroeck (ed.). *The Linguistics Variation Yearbook* 7. Amsterdam: Benjamins, 201–254.
McCready, Eric & Norry Ogata 2007. Evidentiality, modality and probability. *Linguistics & Philosophy* 30, 147–206.
Nauze, Fabrice 2008. *Modality in Typological Perspective*. Ph.D. dissertation. Amsterdam University.
Palmer, Frank R. 2001. *Mood and Modality*. 2nd edn. Cambridge: Cambridge University Press.
Papafragou, Anna 1998. The acquisition of modality: implications for theories of semantic representations. *Mind & Language* 13, 370–399.
Papafragou, Anna 2006. Epistemic modality and truth conditions. *Lingua* 116, 1688–1702.
Perlmutter, David 1971. *Deep and Surface Structure Constraints in Syntax*. New York: Holt, Rinehart & Winston.
Picallo, Carme 1990. Modal verbs in Catalan. *Natural Language and Linguistic Theory* 8, 285–312.
Portner, Paul 1997. The semantics of mood, complementation, and conversational force. *Natural Language Semantics* 5, 167–212.
Portner, Paul 2007. Imperatives and modals. *Natural Language Semantics* 15, 351–383.
Portner, Paul 2009. *Modality*. Oxford: Oxford University Press.
Prior, Arthur 1957. *Time and Modality*. Oxford: Oxford University Press.
Roberts, Craige 1989. Modal subordination and pronominal anaphora in discourse. *Linguistics & Philosophy* 12, 683–721.
Ross, John R. 1969. Auxiliaries as main verbs. In: W. Todd (ed.). *Studies in Philosophical Linguistics (Series 1)*. Evanston, IL: Great Expectations Press, 77–102.
Speas, Peggy 2004. Person (and mood and tense) and indexicality. Paper presented at the *Harvard Workshop on Indexicals, Speech Acts, and Logophors*, November 20, 2004.
Stalnaker, Robert 1984. *Inquiry*. Cambridge, MA: The MIT Press.
Stephenson, Tamina 2007. *Toward a Theory of Subjective Meaning*. Ph.D. dissertation. MIT, Cambridge, MA.
Stowell, Tim 2004. Tense and modals. In: J. Guéron & J. Lecarme (eds.). *The Syntax of Time*. Cambridge, MA: The MIT Press.
Swanson, Eric 2006. *Interaction with Context*. Ph.D. dissertation. MIT, Cambridge, MA.
Sweetser, Eve 1990. *From Etymology to Pragmatics: Metaphorical and Cultural Aspects of Semantic Structure*. Cambridge: Cambridge University Press.
Tancredi, Chris 2007. A Multi-Modal Theory of I-Semantics. Ms. Tokyo, University of Tokyo.
Thomason, Richard 1984. Combinations of tense and modality. In: D. Gabbay & F. Guenthner (eds.). *Handbook of Philosophical Logic, Vol. 2*. Dordrecht: Reidel, 135–165.
Traugott, Elizabeth 1988. Pragmatic strengthening and grammaticalization. In: S. Axmaker, A. Jaisser & H. Singmaster (eds.). *Proceedings of the 14th Annual Meeting of the Berkeley Linguistics Society*. Berkeley, CA: Berkeley Linguistics Society, 406–416.
Westmoreland, Robert 1998. *Information and Intonation in Natural Language Modality*. Ph.D. dissertation. Indiana University, Bloomington, IN.
von Wright, Georg 1951. *An Essay on Modal Logic*. Amsterdam: North-Holland.
Wurmbrand, Susi 1999. Modal verbs must be raising verbs. In: S. Bird et al. (eds.). *Proceedings of the West Coast Conference on Formal Linguistics* 18. Somerville, MA: Cascadilla Press, 599–612.

Yalcin, Seth 2007. Epistemic modals. *Mind* 116, 983–1026.
Zagona, Karen 2007. On the syntactic features of epistemic and root modals. In: L. Eguren & O. Fernandez Soriano (eds.). *Coreference, Modality & Focus: Studies on the Syntax/ Semantics Interface*. Amsterdam: Benjamins, 221–236.
Zeijlstra, Hedde 2008. Modal concord is syntactic agreement. In: M. Gibson & T. Freidman (eds.). *Proceedings of Semantics and Linguistics Theory XVII*. Ithaca, NY: CLC Publications, 317–332.

Kai von Fintel
15 Conditionals

1 Conditional meanings and ways of expressing them —— 503
2 Types of conditionals —— 505
3 The classic accounts and beyond —— 507
4 The restrictor analysis —— 515
5 Recent alternatives to the restrictor analysis —— 517
6 Interactions —— 519
7 Further reading —— 526
8 References —— 526

Abstract: This article introduces the classic accounts of the meaning of conditionals (material implication, strict implication, variably strict conditional) and discusses the difference between indicative and subjunctive/counterfactual conditionals. Then, the restrictor analysis of Lewis/Kratzer/Heim is introduced as a theory of how conditional meanings come about compositionally: if has no meaning other than serving to mark the restriction to an operator elsewhere in the conditional construction. Some recent alternatives to the restrictor analysis are sketched. Lastly, the interactions of conditionals (i) with modality and (ii) with tense and aspect are discussed. Throughout the advanced research literature is referenced while the discussion stays largely non-technical.

1 Conditional meanings and ways of expressing them

Conditionals are sentences that talk about a possible scenario that may or may not be actual and describe what (else) is the case in that scenario; or, considered from "the other end", conditionals state in what kind of possible scenarios a given proposition is true. The canonical form of a conditional is a two-part sentence consisting of an "antecedent" (also: "premise", "protasis") marked with *if* and a "consequent" ("apodosis") sometimes marked with *then* (the syntax and

---

Kai von Fintel, MIT, Cambridge, MA (USA)

https://doi.org/10.1515/9783110589443-015

semantics of *then* is an interesting subject, which we won't cover here, see e.g. Iatridou 1993):

(1) If Grijpstra played his drums, (then) de Gier played his flute.

Conditional meanings can be conveyed with other means as well, each of which merits its own study:

(2) Had he admitted his guilt, he would have gotten off easier.

(3) Take another step and I'll knock you down.

(4) He was pushed or he wouldn't have fallen down the cliff.

(5) Without you, I would be lost.

(6) *I* would have beaten Kasparov.

Some languages are reported to have no conditional construction of the *if ... then*-type and use paratactic means only (see e.g. Levinson 2000: 125 on Guugu Yimithirr):

(7) Nyundu budhu dhadaa, nyundu minha maanaa bira.
 You   maybe go   you   meat get   for sure
 'Maybe you will go, (then) you will certainly get meat.'
 = 'If you go, you'll get meat.'

The cross-linguistic study of conditionals and the various means by which conditional meanings can be expressed is only in its infancy. Here, we will focus on the canonical *if ...(then)* construction of English as our object of investigation.

The semantics of conditionals is an exceptionally rich topic at the intersections of semantics, pragmatics, philosophy of language, and the cognitive science of reasoning. The concept of conditionality is in many ways central to human thought and action. One might note that conditionals are a primary exhibit for one of the "design features" of human language: displacement (Hockett & Altmann 1968).

Exactly what conditionals mean and how they come to mean what they mean is one of the oldest problems in natural language semantics. According to Sextus Empiricus, the Alexandrian poet Callimachus reported that the Greek philosophers' debate about the semantics of the little word *if* had gotten out of hand:

"Even the crows on the roof-tops are cawing about which conditionals are true". It finally became too much for Cicero, who famously complained in his *Academica*:

> In this very thing, which the dialecticians teach among the elements of their art, how one ought to judge whether an argument be true or false which is connected in this manner, 'If it is day, it shines', how great a contest there is;—Diodorus has one opinion, Philo another, Chrysippus a third. *Need I say more?*

It is unclear whether we are any closer to solving Cicero's Problem.

2 Types of conditionals

There are four types of conditionals that have been distinguished in the literature. Starting with a type that often gets short shrift (as it will here; see though DeRose & Grandy 1999, Siegel 2006, and Predelli 2009, among others), there are conditionals variously called speech act conditionals, biscuit conditionals, relevance conditionals:

(8) There are biscuits on the sideboard if you want them. (Austin 1956)

(9) I paid you back yesterday, if you remember. (P.T. Geach p.c. to Austin 1956)

These conditionals do not state in any sense conditions under which the consequent is true, rather they seem to somehow operate on a higher speech act level.

Another not all that well-studied kind of conditional is what Iatridou called "factual" conditionals (called "premise conditionals" in Haegeman 2003), conditionals that often echo someone else's introduction of the antecedent:

(10) If you're so clever, why don't you do this problem on your own?

(11) If it is indeed that late, we should leave.

The two main kinds of conditionals that semantic research has been concerned with are usually called indicative and subjunctive/counterfactual conditionals:

(12) a. If Grijpstra played his drums, de Gier played his flute. (indicative)
 b. If Grijpstra had played his drums, de Gier would have played his flute.

(subjunctive/counterfactual)

The terminology is of course linguistically inept (as we'll discuss in section 6.2, the morphological marking is one of tense and aspect, not of indicative vs. subjunctive mood), but it is so deeply entrenched that it would be foolish not to use it. Superficially, the striking difference between the two kinds of conditionals is that indicative conditionals somehow convey that the truth of the antecedent is an open issue, while subjunctive conditionals seem to convey that the antecedent is false. (Are there conditionals that convey that the antecedent is true? Perhaps, if one considers locutions like *since* or *given that* to be conditional connectives.) Upon closer investigation, it is not possible to maintain that subjunctive conditionals are invariably counterfactual in this sense, as shown dramatically by an example due to Anderson (1951):

(13) If Jones had taken arsenic, he would have shown just exactly those symptoms which he does in fact show.

A doctor who utters (13) might be prepared to use it as part of an argument that the antecedent is in fact true, so the subjunctive conditional could not be conveying counterfactuality as part of its meaning. There are some subjunctive conditionals that arguably are automatically counterfactual, for example the ones that Ippolito (2003) calls "mismatched past counterfactuals" and the verb-first counterfactuals studied by Iatridou & Embick (1993):

(14) If Charlie had married Sally tomorrow, he would have had his bachelor party tonight. #So, let's see whether the party is tonight.

(15) Had Charlie married Sally yesterday, they would have left on their honeymoon by now. #So, let's see whether they're gone.

Even abstracting away from the issue of counterfactuality, there are strong reasons to conclude that the two kinds of conditionals are quite different in their meaning. This is best shown by minimal pairs, the most famous one of which is due to Adams (1970):

(16) a. If Oswald didn't kill Kennedy, someone else did.
b. If Oswald hadn't killed Kennedy, someone else would have.

While most people would accept (16a) as true (since they know that Kennedy was assassinated), only the most conspiracy-minded would accept (16b).

The meaning of the indicative conditional seems to correspond fairly accurately to the "Ramsey Test" (Ramsey 1931):

If two people are arguing "If p will q?" and are both in doubt as to p, they are adding p hypothetically to their stock of knowledge and arguing on that basis about q.

Knowing that Kennedy was assassinated and having maybe only the slightest doubt that the assassin may not have been Oswald, our stock of knowledge incremented hypothetically with *Oswald didn't kill Kennedy* would support *somebody else killed Kennedy*, and thus we accept (16a) as true.

Informally, (16b) is evaluated quite differently. We are invited to go back to the time around Kennedy's assassination and project how things would have turned out if Oswald hadn't killed Kennedy. And many of us have only the haziest ideas of what would have happened, certainly no conviction that some assassination was inevitable. So, we reject (16b).

The questions for the semanticist are two-fold: (i) what is the formal analysis of the different meanings that conditionals convey, and (ii) how are these meanings compositionally derived? A quick look at the examples suggests that there are significant differences in meaning deriving from the tense/aspect/mood morphology on the verbs in the two clauses. So, in the end, we'd like a compositional analysis that explains the semantic effects of these morphological choices. First, though, we will focus on the prior question here: what do conditionals mean?

Before we turn to the main theories of conditional meaning, we should note that semantic analyses of conditionals are also responsible for explaining a host of facts concerning the combination of conditionals with other constructions. These include: the role of *then* in the consequent, complex conditionals like *only if*, *even if*, *unless*, modals in the consequent, disjunctions in the antecedent, negative polarity items in the antecedent (cf. article 3 [Semantics: Sentence and Information Structure] (Giannakidou) *Polarity items*), embedding of conditionals under quantifiers (cf. article 4 [this volume] (Keenan) *Quantifiers*), conditional questions (cf. article 5 [Semantics: Sentence and Information Structure] (Krifka) *Questions*), conditional imperatives (cf. article 6 [Semantics: Sentence and Information Structure] (Han) *Imperatives*). Only some of these will be touched on in this article. The field is wide open for a lot of exciting future research.

3 The classic accounts and beyond

The classic analyses of conditionals, some of whom were already discussed by the crows of Alexandria, are (i) *if ...(then) ...* as a truth-functional connective, material implication, (ii) the strict conditional analysis, (iii) the non-monotonic possible worlds analyses of Stalnaker and Lewis.

3.1 Material implication

If conditionals correspond to a two-valued truth-functional connective, it has to be the one dubbed "material implication", which yields falsity if and only if the antecedent is true but the consequent is false. Suber (1997) presents a good example motivating this distribution of truth-values. A professor who declares that *If I am healthy, I will come to class* can only be said to have broken her promise if she is healthy but doesn't come to class. Clearly, if she is healthy and comes to class, she'll have spoken the truth. And if she is sick, it is immaterial whether she comes to class (going beyond the call of duty and beyond what she promised) or doesn't—neither case constitutes a breaking of the promise.

One of the "paradoxes of material implication" (not paradoxes in the sense of a formal system that is internally incoherent, but shortcomings in the match between the formal analysis and the natural language data it might be thought to cover) is that disbelief in the antecedent p should result in a proportionate willingness to believe *if p, q*, no matter what the consequent q might be, because as soon as the antecedent is false, material implication makes the conditional true no matter what the consequent is. Clearly, this does not correspond to the actual behavior of language users. Just because I find it unlikely in the extreme that the sun will explode in a minute from now, I do not find it likely at all that if the sun explodes in a minute from now, a Vogon Constructor spaceship will come and rescue all of Earth's inhabitants.

There are several heroic efforts (cf. in particular Jackson 1979, 1987) to maintain that material implication is an adequate semantics for natural language conditionals—in particular, indicative conditionals. The general idea is to supplement a material implication *semantics* with a sophisticated pragmatics of *assertibility*, whether derivable via standard Gricean conversational implicature or stipulated as a construction-specific conventional implicature. Jackson argues that indicative conditionals trigger a conventional implicature that the assertion as a whole is robust with respect to the antecedent; that is, that a speaker who utters an indicative conditional is not just claiming that the material conditional is true but is also signalling that should the antecedent turn out to be true they would still claim that the material conditional is true. In the exploding sun example, above, Jackson would say that while I do (almost) believe that the indicative conditional is true, strictly speaking, because I believe that the antecedent is very likely to be false, I do not believe in the robustness of the conditional relative to its antecedent. If it turned out to be true that the sun will explode in a minute from now, I would then not believe the material conditional anymore. So, I'm not in a position to assert the conditional because I would be sending the wrong signal (that my belief in it was robust with respect to the antecedent). Edgington (2007: 135–138) raises an important objection to the implicature-based accounts: the non-equivalence between indicative conditionals and material implication doesn't just arise at the level of assertibility. The problem with the exploding sun example isn't just that I can't assert it properly, rather: I don't even believe the conditional to the extent I should. Bennett (2003: Chapters 2 and 3) gives other strong arguments against Grice/Jackson-style theories; at the same time, the perhaps quixotic goal of defending material implication with non-truth-conditional enhancements continues to be pursued, see for example Rieger (2006).

In linguistic work, the material implication account (pragmatically enriched or not) is usually dismissed because of the unsurmountable problems it faces when one looks at embedded conditionals. One such case is the embedding of indicative conditionals under nominal quantifiers:

(17) a. Every student will succeed if he works hard.
  b. No student will succeed if he goofs off.

As first discussed by Higginbotham (1986), the material implication analysis may be adequate for (17a) but it is clearly wrong for (17b), which would be predicted to mean that every student goofs off and doesn't succeed.

3.2 Possible worlds semantics for conditionals

C.I. Lewis (1918) proposed his "strict implication" as a better approximation of ordinary conditionals. According to this analysis, *if p, q* is true iff the material implication is *necessarily* true. This would for example deal quite well with the fact that the exploding sun conditional is not one that one should believe just because the antecedent is very likely to be false. Whether or not it is even possible that a Vogon Constructor fleet would rescue Earth's inhabitants it is certainly possible that the sun explodes and we are not rescued, and thus the material implication is not necessarily true, and thus the strict implication account predicts that the conditional is false, which is a good reason not to believe it.

If one assumes a possible worlds semantics for notions like necessity, the strict implication analysis amounts to the claim that *if p, q* is true iff q is true in all worlds in which p is true. By far the most influential semantics for conditionals, in particular counterfactual conditionals, developed independently by

Stalnaker (1968) and Lewis (1973), departs from the strict implication analysis in that it doesn't quantify over *all p*-worlds but just about a distinguished subset thereof. This move is motivated in part by problems with conditional inferences, as we will soon see.

To a first approximation, the Stalnaker/Lewis analysis assumes an *ordering* of the set of worlds according to how similar they are to the world of evaluation (the one for which the truth of the conditional is being evaluated). Rather than saying that *if p, q* is true iff *q* is true in *all* worlds in which *p* is true, the Stalnaker/Lewis account selects from the worlds in which *p* is true those that are most similar to the evaluation world and claims just about those most similar *p*-worlds that they are *q*-worlds. This has significant effects on what kind of inferences will be valid with conditionals.

Under the strict implication analysis, the pattern known as Strengthening the Antecedent, for example, is predicted to be valid:

(18) Strengthening the Antecedent
if p, q
∴ *if p & r, q*

If all (contextually relevant) *p*-worlds are *q*-worlds, then *a fortiori* all *p&r*-worlds, a subset of the *p*-worlds, have to be *q*-worlds.

This pattern becomes invalid in the Stalnaker/Lewis analyses. If the *p*-worlds that are most similar to the evaluation world are all *q*-worlds, that does necessitate that the most similar *p&r*-worlds are also all *q*-worlds. Lewis (1973) gives a humorous example:

(19) a. If kangaroos had no tails, they would topple over.
 b. ⇏ If kangaroos had no tails but used crutches, they would topple over.

(19a) intuitively does not license the inference to (19b). The similarity-based analyses explain why: the worlds where kangaroos have no tails but that are otherwise as similar as possible to the evaluation world are not worlds where kangaroos use crutches, so the first conditional does not connect logically to the second conditional. The Stalnaker/Lewis analyses thus differ from the strict implication analysis in being *non-monotonic* or as Lewis put it "variably strict".

Other patterns that are expected to be valid under the strict implication analysis but arguably aren't are Hypothetical Syllogism and Contraposition:

(20) *Failure of the Hypothetical Syllogism (Transitivity)*
If Hoover had been a Communist, he would have been a traitor.

If Hoover had been born in Russia, he would have been a Communist.
⇛ If Hoover had been born in Russia, he would have been a traitor.

[Example due to Stalnaker 1968]

(21) *Failure of Contraposition*
(Even) if Goethe hadn't died in 1832, he would still be dead now.
⇛ If Goethe were alive now, he would have died in 1832.

[Example due to Kratzer 1979]

The non-monotonic analyses predict correctly that Hypothetical Syllogism (Transitivity) fails because even if all the closest (most similar to the evaluation world) p-worlds are q-worlds and all the closest q-worlds are r-worlds, we are not necessarily speaking about the same q-worlds (the q-worlds that p takes us to may be rather remote ones). So in the Hoover-example, we get the following picture: The closest p-worlds in which Hoover was born in Russia (but where he retains his level of civic involvement), are all q-worlds in which he becomes a Communist. On the other hand, the closest q-worlds in which he is a Communist (but retaining his having been born in the United States and being a high level administrator) are all r-worlds in which he is a traitor. The closest p-worlds do not include the closest q-worlds, so the Transitive inference does not go through.

Again, the non-monotonic analyses correctly predict that Contraposition fails because the assumption that the closest p-worlds are q-worlds does not preclude a situation where the closest non-q-worlds are also p-worlds. The selected p-worlds in which Goethe didn't die in 1832 are all q-worlds where he dies nevertheless (well) before the present. But of course, the closest (in fact, all) non-q-worlds (where he is alive today) are also p-worlds where he didn't die in 1832.

Lewis and Stalnaker differ in their assumptions about the similarity ordering. Stalnaker assumes that for any (non-contradictory) antecedent and any evaluation world, there will be a unique most similar antecedent world. Lewis neither makes this Uniqueness Assumption nor the weaker Limit Assumption (that for any antecedent and evaluation world, there is a set of most similar antecedent worlds). For discussion of this difference, see Lewis (1973: 19–21) and Stalnaker (1984: Chapter 7, esp. pp. 140–142); Pollock (1976), Herzberger (1979), and Warmbrod (1982) argue for the Limit Assumption as well. Informally, here, we have been using the Limit Assumption but not the Uniqueness Assumption when we talk about the most similar or closest antecedent worlds. The issues discussed under this heading are relevant for the attempt we'll mention later to treat conditionals as definite (plural?) descriptions of possible worlds; see section 5.1.

A variant of the ordering based semantics is given by "premise semantics", inspired by Goodman (1947) and Rescher (1964) and developed in rival forms by Kratzer (1977, 1979, 1981) and Veltman (1976). Lewis (1981) showed that technically the two approaches are intertranslateable. More recent work in the premise semantic tradition includes Kratzer (1989), Djordjevic (2005), Veltman (2005), Kanazawa, Kaufmann & Peters (2005), Kratzer (2005).

3.3 The indicative/subjunctive distinction

We have now surveyed the three classic theories of conditional meaning, and we will soon look at more recent variants and alternatives. At this point, though, let us discuss how one could approach the indicative/subjunctive distinction in terms of the classic approaches.

While the Oswald/Kennedy pair shows that indicatives and subjunctives have distinct truth-conditions, it is not obvious *how* distinct they should be seen as. Do they have distinctly different kinds of meanings? Or is the difference more subtle?

Among philosophers and logicians, it is very commonly held that quite different approaches are appropriate. David Lewis, for example, thought that his variably strict semantics was not applicable to indicatives (he favored material implication plus Jackson's pragmatic enrichment for those). Others adopt even more radically different analyses for indicatives, such as the conditional assertion view or the "No Truth-Value" (NTV) view, both of which we'll briefly discuss below.

Some indication that the semantics for the two kinds of conditionals shouldn't be all that different comes from the fact that they seem to show the same kind of inference patterns (or invalidity patterns). For example, Strengthening the Antecedent fails with indicatives just as it did with subjunctives:

(22) a. If John left before noon, he arrived in time for the meeting.
  b. $\not\Rightarrow$ If John left before noon but got in a car accident, he arrived in time for the meeting.

For a linguistically realistic semantics, it would also be relevant that both kinds of conditionals employ the connective *if* (although we'll soon see that that might not actually mean that much) and that the only overt distinction between the two kinds lies in tense and aspect morphology, which might suggest that there shouldn't be a deep semantic division.

Stalnaker (1975) argues that his version of the non-monotonic semantics for conditionals is applicable to both indicatives and subjunctives and that the only difference is that indicatives come with the default assumption that the selected antecedent world is within the context set (the set of worlds that are compatible with the current assumptions of the conservation). In other words, the subjunctive conditional is chosen when for some reason, the speaker does not want the assumption in place that the selected antecedent world is compatible with what is taken for granted. As explored in von Fintel (1998), this approach predicts not only that subjunctives are chosen when the antecedent is known to be counterfactual but also in Anderson-type cases, as repeated here:

(13) If Jones had taken arsenic, he would have shown just exactly those symptoms which he does in fact show.

Within the context set, all the worlds are trivially worlds where Jones shows the symptoms he shows. So, for the conditional to be non-trivial the world that the antecedent is taking us to needs to be outside the context set, even though the speaker in the end intends the hearer to infer that Jones did take arsenic. Since the conditional needs to reach outside the context set, we need to use subjunctive marking.

3.4 Dynamic strict analyses

Let us return to the argument from the apparent failure of Strengthening the Antecedent. When Lewis discussed this, he tried to forestall the idea that what is treated as semantic non-monotonicity in his account could actually be explained in a strict implication account by saying that the contextually relevant set of worlds that the conditional quantifies over is easily shifted in a sequence of sentences. He argued that this move would not be able to explain the well-formedness of what became known as Sobel Sequences:

(23) If the USA threw its weapons into the sea tomorrow, there would be war; but if all the nuclear powers threw their weapons into the sea tomorrow, there would be peace.

Lewis deliberately put this example "in the form of a single run-on sentence, with the counterfactuals of different stages conjoined by semicolons and *but*", suggesting that it would be a "defeatist" move to say that in such a tight sequence the context could shift in response to the introduction of a new antecedent clause.

Defeatist or not, based on an observation by Heim (MIT class handout), von Fintel (2001b) develops such an account. Heim had noted that Lewis' Sobel Sequence cannot be reversed:

(24) ??If all the nuclear powers threw their weapons into the sea tomorrow, there would be peace; but if the USA threw its weapons into the sea tomorrow, there would be war.

This is unexpected from the point of view of a semantically non-monotonic analysis. In von Fintel's paper, a dynamic strict analysis is developed in which the antecedent has the potential to expand the "modal horizon", the set of contextually relevant possible worlds which the conditional then ranges over. It is shown that if the expansion of the modal horizon is governed by the same similarity ordering used in the Stalnaker/Lewis systems, the analysis replicates the truth-conditions of those systems for isolated or discourse-initial conditionals. The context shifts become only relevant in sequences of conditionals and then create the appearance of semantic non-monotonicity. One crucial argument von Fintel gives for his account is that negative polarity items are licensed in the antecedent of conditionals and that therefore we would prefer a monotonic analysis. It turns out, however, that only a very special notion of monotonicity (dubbed Strawson Downward Entailingness) holds for von Fintel's conditionals: these conditionals are downward monotone in their antecedent only under the assumption that the initial context is such that the modal horizon is already large enough to be unaffected by any of the conditionals in the sequence. This idea is explored for other puzzles for NPI-licensing in von Fintel (1999); cf. also article 3 [Semantics: Sentence and Information Structure] (Giannakidou) *Polarity items*. The dynamic strict analysis is developed further by Gillies (2007) and critically compared to a pragmatically supplemented non-monotonic analysis by Moss (2007).

3.5 Conditional assertion

For at least some types of conditionals, it may make sense to think of the *if*-clause as operating at a speech act level. That is, perhaps, the *if*-clause does not actually change the truth-conditions of the consequent clause it is attached to, but it marks that the content of the consequent clause is only to be considered as asserted if the antecedent is true. This "conditional assertion" account might be most appropriate for "biscuit-conditionals" (mentioned earlier), see DeRose & Grandy (1999), for example. Lycan (2006) argues that conditional assertion accounts are not to be taken seriously as analyses of indicative conditionals in general.

3.6 NTV

An even more radical approach says that conditionals have no truth-conditions at all. This "NTV" (for "no truth-value", a name given by Lycan 2001) account argues that conditionals do not make truth-evaluable claims but "express" that the speaker has a high subjective probability for the consequent, given the antecedent. The account is prominently championed by Adams (1965), Gibbard (1981), and Edgington (1986), among others. Lycan (2001) gives quite a few reasons to think the account cannot be maintained; see also Bennett (2003) for discussion. As far as I know, the NTV account has had no impact at all in linguistic work on natural language semantics (but see Kaufmann 2005a and Cohen 2009).

4 The restrictor analysis

The dominant approach to the semantics of conditionals in linguistics is not so much an alternative to the accounts we have discussed so far, and in particular not to the Stalnaker/Lewis analysis, but a radical rethinking of the compositional structure of conditional sentences. It began with Lewis' (1975) paper on adverbial quantification, which dealt with sentences like

(25) If it is sunny, we always/usually/mostly/rarely/sometimes/never play soccer.

Lewis argued that there was no plausible semantics for the conditional connective that would interact compositionally with the adverbs of quantification to give correct truth-conditions for these sentences. Instead, he argued that the *if*-clause added no conditional meaning of its own to the construction. The idea is that the only "conditional" operator in the structure is the adverb and that *if* merely serves to introduce a restriction to that operator. In other words, where naively one would have thought that (25) involved the combination of an adverbial quantificational operator with the conditional expressed by *if*, Lewis argued that there was just one operator and that *if* didn't express any kind of conditional operator of its own.

Lewis himself did not generalize this idea; nowhere else in his writings does he give any indication that *if*'s found elsewhere are to be treated on a par with the *if* in adverbially quantified sentences. (It should be noted that in the adverbial quantification paper, Lewis does suggest that the *if* found in construction with probability operators is also not a conditional operator of its own, although he doesn't say whether it is to be seen as a restrictor in those cases.

It is a shame that Lewis did not connect his insights in the adverbial quantification paper to the problems surrounding conditional probability, as discussed for example in Lewis (1976); cf. also Hájek (1993). Kratzer (1986) does make the connection; for some recent discussion see Rothschild 2010 and Egré & Cozic 2011.)

Kratzer took the logical step and argued that Lewis' idea should be applied to all conditional constructions. She put the point very concisely in Kratzer (1986): "The history of the conditional is the story of a syntactic mistake. There is no two-place *if ...then* connective in the logical forms for natural languages. *If*-clauses are devices for restricting the domains of various operators. Whenever there is no explicit operator, we have to posit one."

It should be noted that this proposal is not really a proposal meant to overturn any prior conceptions about the meaning of various conditional constructions. Rather, it is a proposal for how the meaning of those constructions comes about compositionally. The central idea is that *if* itself does not carry any distinctive conditional meaning, rather it is, so to speak, a helper expression that modifies various quantificational/modal operators (cf. article 14 [this volume] (Hacquard) *Modality*). As indicated in the quote from Kratzer, this doesn't just apply to when an overt operator combines with an *if*-clause but also when an *if*-clause occurs on its own with no overt operator in sight. In that case, Kratzer suggests, there must be a covert, or at least not obviously visible, operator. What one might call bare indicative conditionals either contain a covert epistemic necessity modal or a covert generic frequency operator (≈ *usually/always*):

(26) a. If he left at noon, he's home by now. [epistemic necessity]
 b. If he leaves work on time, he has dinner with his family. [generic frequency]

In bare counterfactual conditionals, one should consider the possibility that the modal form *would* is the operator restricted by the *if*-clause, an idea bolstered by the fact that there are *if*-less *would*-sentences such as (6), repeated here:

(6) I would have beaten Kasparov.

Following Partee (1991), the restrictor theory of *if*-clauses is sometimes called the "Lewis/Kratzer/Heim" analysis (henceforth restrictor), because after the initial idea of Lewis and the generalization by Kratzer, the application of the story to the analysis of donkey anaphora by Heim (1982) played a large role in the triumph of the theory in linguistic circles.

It should be pointed out that while we earlier stressed the desire to have a uniform(ish) analysis of indicative and subjunctive conditionals, partially because both are *if...then* constructions, the restrictor analysis opens up a potentially large gap between them. The uniform presence of *if* would be almost entirely beside the point: how big the difference between the two kinds is depends on what, if any, difference there is between the modal operators present in them.

5 Recent alternatives to the restrictor analysis

5.1 Conditionals as definites

Some work has recently explored an alternative to the restrictor analysis that does give *if* a more substantial role to play. The idea explored by Schein (2003), Schlenker (2004), and Bhatt & Pancheva (2006) is that *if*-clauses are definite plural descriptions of possible worlds. These works point out a series of syntactic and semantic ways in which *if*-clauses behave much alike to definite descriptions (in particular, free relatives). An interesting subplot in that exploration is whether the semantics (for both *if*-clauses and for definite descriptions) should be non-monotonic, as argued by Lewis, or monotonic (supplemented with discourse dynamics). Schlenker (2004) leaves this as an open question.

5.2 Three-valued conditionals

Lewis (1975: n. 4) mentioned an alternative to the restrictor analysis of *if*:

> What is the price of forcing the restriction-marking if to be a sentential connective after all? Exorbitant: it can be done if (1) we use a third truth value, (2) we adopt a far-fetched interpretation of the connective if, and (3) we impose an additional permanent restriction on the admissible cases.

The idea would be to give *if p, q* a three-valued semantics where it is true if p and q are true, false if p is true but q is not, and has the third truth-value if p is false. Then, operators can be defined so as to quantify only over cases where the truth-value of the embedded conditional is not the third truth-value, which is equivalent to them quantifying over p-cases only. This idea goes back to Belnap (1970, 1973) and despite Lewis' denunciation of it as carrying an exorbitant price tag, it has been revived recently by Geurts (2004b), von Fintel (2007), and Huitink (2008, 2009a,b, 2010). (Note that McDermott 1996 had argued that such a three-valued semantics was in fact adequate for at least certain simple conditionals.)

One argument in favor of paying the price and adopting this analysis comes from the behavior of conditionals in discourse. As pointed out by von Fintel (2007), examples like the following present a severe challenge to the restrictor analysis (the problem was first identified in von Fintel 2003):

(27) A: If he didn't tell Harry, he told Tom.
B: Probably so.
B': That's very unlikely.

In such dialogues, a propositional anaphor (*so*, *that*) appears to refer back to the conditional in A's utterance. In the restrictor analysis, the only conditional proposition made available by A's utterance is an epistemically modalized conditional. But the utterance by B and B9 are not interpreted as involving that epistemic conditional embedded under *probably* or *unlikely*. Rather, *probably so* is interpreted as a simple probability conditional. So, it appears that the best account would be one where A's and B's utterances share a "bland" conditional meaning that then a local operator could be applied to (covert epistemic modal in A's utterance and probability operator in B's utterance). Adopting the Belnap meaning for conditionals, we can analyze the dialogue in as follows:

(28) A: If he didn't tell Harry, he told Tom.
must (if he didn't tell Harry, he told Tom) in all worlds compatible with the evidence where the embedded conditional has a truth-value (i.e. where he didn't tell Harry), he told Tom

B: Probably so.
probably (if he didn't tell Harry, he told Tom) in most worlds compatible with the evidence where the embedded conditional has a truth-value (i.e. where he didn't tell Harry), he told Tom

There are obvious questions and worries about the Belnap-style approach. One is whether the Belnap conditional can stand on its own (as argued by McDermott 1996) or whether it always requires an operator to embed it (if so, the account would mimic the restrictor analysis very closely). Another topic that would need to be sorted out is that using three-valued semantics for the mechanics of this account precludes using three-valued semantics for modelling presupposition (as is often done) at the same time, since clearly the antecedents of conditionals are not presupposed to be true.

5.3 Another non-restrictor analysis of *if*

Gillies (2009a,b) has been developing an account that also tries to restore a conditional meaning for *if*-clauses and achieve the restricting effect in a more indirect way than done in the restrictor approach. In his analysis, *if* expresses a contextually restricted strict implication operator, which means that there is no need for the covert operators needed in the restrictor account. To model the interactions with other overt operators correctly, the semantics for *if* has a second component which has it restrict the domain for any operators that might be in its scope. An interesting difference between the revived three-valued analysis and Gillies' analyis is that in the former operators that end up being restricted by an *if*-clause take the conditional in their scope, while in the latter they appear in the consequent of the conditional in the scope of the *if*-clause. One expects that this will be of crucial importance in deciding between the accounts.

Note that Gillies' account will face the same problems with the behavior of conditionals across speakers as the restrictor analysis and thus appears at a disadvantage to the Belnap-style approach.

6 Interactions

A crucial topic in conditional semantics is how conditionals interact with other expressions. This has already been a thread in the preceding sections. Here, we will look a bit more at the interaction of conditionals with modality and with tense/aspect. Space precludes a discussion of complex conditionals like *even if*, *only if*, and *unless* conditionals; for some work on complex conditionals see Bennett (1992), von Fintel (1994: Chapters 4 and 5), and Lycan (2001).

6.1 Conditionals and modals

The restrictor analysis predicts that *if*-clauses should be able to restrict any kind of modal operator, epistemic operators and deontic operators:

(29) *if*-clause restricting epistemic modals:
   a. If Grijpstra played his drums, (then) de Gier must have played his flute.
   b. If Grijpstra played his drums, (then) de Gier might have played his flute.
   c. If Grijpstra played his drums, (then) de Gier played his flute.[= covert epistemic necessity]

(30) *if*-clause restricting deontic modals:
   a. If you broke the vase, you ought to apologize.
   b. If you're over 21, you are allowed to buy beer in this store.

6.1.1 Kratzer's version of the Samaritan Paradox

Kratzer (1991) argues that the restrictor approach to deontic conditionals is the crucial ingredient in the solution of a conditional version of the Samaritan Paradox. The first step in that story, though, is to consider the original non-conditional version of the paradox as introduced by Prior (1958). Imagine that someone has been robbed and John is walking by. It is easy to conceive of a code of ethics that would make the following sentence true:

(31) John must help the person who was robbed.

If modal semantics only involved quantification over a set of accessible worlds, one would have said that (31) says that in all of the deontically accessible worlds (those compatible with the code of ethics) John helps the person who was robbed. Prior's point was that under such a semantics, something rather unfortunate holds. Notice that in all of the worlds where John helps the person who was robbed, someone was robbed in the first place. Therefore, it will be true that in all of the deontically accessible worlds, someone was robbed. Thus, (31) will entail:

(32) It must be that someone was robbed.

It clearly would be good not make such a prediction, since we might very well want (31) to be true and (32) to be false.

A doubly-relative analysis of modality, as proposed by Kratzer (1991) and surveyed in article 14 [this volume] (Hacquard) *Modality*, can successfully avoid this unfortunate prediction. Such an analysis assumes that an ordering is imposed on the set of accessible worlds, with different "ordering sources" being associated with different flavors of modality (this can be seen as a generalization of the similarity-based ordering in the Stalnaker/Lewis analysis of conditionals). We can then conceive of (31) as being uttered with respect to a circumstantial modal base that includes the fact that someone was robbed. Among those already somewhat ethically deficient worlds, the relatively best ones are all worlds where John helps the victim.

Note we still have the problematic fact that among the worlds in the modal base, all are worlds where someone was robbed, and we would thus appear to still make the unfortunate prediction that (32) should be true. But this can now be fixed. For example, we could say that *must p* is semantically defective if *p* is true throughout the worlds in the modal base. This could be a presupposition or some other ingredient of meaning. So, with respect to a modal base which predetermines that someone was robbed, one couldn't felicitously say (32).

Consequently, saying (32) would only be felicitous if a different modal base is intended, one that contains both *p* and non-*p* worlds. And given a choice between worlds where someone was robbed and worlds where nobody was robbed, most deontic ordering sources would presumably choose the no-robbery worlds, which would make (32) false, as desired.

The paradox as presented by Kratzer (1991) has a conditional form:

(33) If a murder occurs, the jurors must convene.

Kratzer points out that if one tried to analyze (33) as a material implication embedded under deontic necessity, then one quickly runs into a problem. Surely, one wants the following to be a true statement about the law:

(34) There must be no murder.

But this means that in the deontically accessible worlds, all of them have no murders occuring. Now, this means that in all of the deontically accessible worlds, any material implication of the form "if a murder occurs, *q*" will be true no matter what the consequent is since the antecedent will be false. Since that is an absurd prediction, (33) cannot be analyzed as material implication under deontic necessity. The combination of the restrictor approach to *if*-clauses and the doubly-relative theory of modals can rescue us from this problem. (33) is analyzed as the deontic necessity modal being restricted by the *if*-clause. The set of accessible worlds is narrowed down by the *if*-clause to only include worlds in which a murder occurs. The deontic ordering then identifies the best among those worlds and those are plausibly all worlds where the jurors convene.

6.1.2 An expected ambiguity

As pointed out at various times (as far as I know, independently in unpublished work by Craige Roberts and by Geurts 2004a), the existence of covert operators in Kratzer's analysis may predict that sentence with an overt operator and an *if*-clause are in fact ambiguous: one reading where the *if*-clause restricts the overt operator and another reading where the *if*-clause restricts a covert operator that somehow combines with the overt operator. An example from Sarah Moss (term paper for a 2005 MIT class) shows the reality of that prediction:

(35) If Caspar vacuums on Saturday, then Chris has to cook dinner on Sunday.

There is a straightforward "one operator" reading of (35) where it expresses a rule of the group sharing the apartment: every acceptable scenario in which Caspar vacuums on Saturday is one where Chris cooks dinner on Sunday; this reading is obtained by having the *if*-clause restrict the deontic modal *have to*. But there is also a "two operator" reading where one says that if it were a given observation that Caspar vacuums on Saturday then one would be able to conclude from that that Chris has the obligation to cook dinner on Sunday. This two operator reading can be obtained if one assumes that the *if*-clause restricts a covert epistemic necessity modal, which then in turn embeds the deontic necessity modal *have to*. In this reading, (35) would be essentially equivalent to a sentence with two nested overt modals:

(36) If Caspar vacuums on Saturday, then Chris must have to cook dinner on Sunday.

(There are discussions of "iffy oughts"—that is, sentences combining *if*-clauses with deontic modals — which might profit from considering the possibility of such an ambiguity. See for example, in the linguistic literature: Frank 1996 and Zvolensky 2002. In philosophy as well, deontic conditionals are of increasing interest, see for example Kolodny & MacFarlane 2010.)

6.1.3 More on epistemic conditionals

At various points, we have assumed that a reasonable analysis of conditionals like (37) treats them as implicitly modalized with an epistemic necessity operator:

(37) If Grijpstra played his drums, (then) de Gier played his flute.

Kratzer (1986, 2010) argues that this assumption can help solve a famous puzzle due to Gibbard (1981: 231). Consider this scenario:

> Sly Pete and Mr. Stone are playing poker on a Mississippi riverboat. It is now up to Pete to call or fold. My henchman Zack sees Stone's hand, which is quite good, and signals its content to Pete. My henchman Jack sees both hands, and sees that Pete's hand is rather low, so that Stone's is the winning hand. At this point, the room is cleared. A few minutes later, Zack slips me a note which says "If Pete called, he won", and Jack slips me a note which says "If Pete called, he lost".

The problem Gibbard saw with this example is that (i) both observers are entirely justified in saying what they're saying, neither is mistaken about anything, but (ii) the two sentences they utter are intuitively contradictory: it can't be that it is true that if Pete called, he won at the same time as it is true that if Pete called, he lost. An obvious move to capture (i) is to say that the conditionals are epistemic conditionals and that each of them is about the respective speaker's epistemic state. But then it is hard to understand intuition (ii). Gibbard despaired of giving any account where conditionals express propositions and so took his puzzle as an argument for an NTV approach.

In recent work, much progress has been made on understanding the context-dependency of epistemic modals in the debate between relativist and contextualist accounts; see for example Egan, Hawthorne & Weatherson (2005), MacFarlane (2011), Stephenson (2007b), and von Fintel & Gillies (2008, 2011). One would then expect that integrating these insights into the analysis of epistemic conditionals might help understand the Sly Pete puzzle. This is indeed what Stephenson (2007a) and Weatherson (2009) do within a relativist analysis of epistemic modality and what Kratzer (2010) does within a contextualist analysis based on von Fintel & Gillies (2011). This is not the place to adjudicate between these two approaches, but one can expect fireworks to continue in this domain.

6.2 Conditionals and tense & aspect

We will not be able to discuss the syntax of conditionals in this article (cf. Bhatt & Pancheva 2006) but we should take a look at the morphological fine structure of conditionals. It is quite apparent that in English at least, the indicative/subjunctive classification of conditionals is marked by tense and aspect morphology:

(38) a. If Grijpstra played his drums, de Gier played his flute.
b. If Grijpstra had played his drums, de Gier would have played his flute.

The earliest works taking the role of tense and aspect in the semantics of conditionals seriously came from Dudman (1983, 1984, 1988, 1989). Work on the interaction of tense and conditionals in philosophical logic includes Nute (1982, 1991); Thomason & Gupta (1980); Thomason (1985). A more recent seminal contribution is Iatridou (2000). Since then there has been a proliferation of work on this topic; see Arregui (2005, 2007, 2009); Copley (2006); Ippolito (2007); Kaufmann (2005b); Schulz (2008); von Stechow (2007). Here, we can only introduce some basic facts and generalizations.

The central observation is that what is commonly called subjunctive in "subjunctive conditionals" is an additional layer (or two) of past tense morphology, no matter whether the referred to state of affairs is temporally located in the past, present, or future:

(39) a. If Roman comes to the party tomorrow, it will be a grand success.
b. If Roman came to the party tomorrow, it would be a grand success.
c. If Roman had come to the party tomorrow, it would have been a grand success.

(40) a. If Roman is at the post office now, he is missing the meeting.
b. If Roman were at the post office now, he would be missing the meeting.
c. If Roman had been at the post office now, he would have been missing the meeting.

(41) a. If Roman left before noon, he arrived in time.
b. If Roman had left before noon, he would have arrived in time.

Iatridou (2000) discusses this basic pattern (although she doesn't discuss the two layer pasts in future or present conditionals) and proposes that the additional past does not serve a temporal function. Instead, she argues that the past tense has a schematic semantics that can be applied both temporally and modally: past is an "exclusion feature", it marks that the topic set excludes the speaker set (the analysis is related to earlier ideas that the modal use of past relies on it being a marker of "remoteness", see for example Steele 1975,

James 1982, and Fleischman 1989). When past is used temporally it marks the times talked about as distinct from the now of the speaker (an additional wrinkle is needed to explain why past means past rather than non-present = past or future). When past is used modally it marks the worlds talked about as distinct from the actual world of the speaker (this does not mean that modally used past is a counterfactuality marker; rather, the intent is to derive something very much like the Stalnaker-analysis of the import of subjunctive marking, see the discussion in section 3.3 above).

The alternative to Iatridou's account is to try to maintain that the additional pasts in subjunctive conditionals do after all retain their usual temporal meaning. This idea goes back to Dudman (1983, 1984, 1988, 1989) and has been pursued by Ippolito (2003, 2007) and Arregui (2005, 2009), among others. We do not have the space to survey the details of these accounts. Let's rather look at a simplified sketch. Suppose that the extra layer of past tense marks that what the conditional quantifies over is a set of worlds that *were* accessible from the evaluation world at a past tense but may not be anymore. This is typically embedded in a branching futures version of possible worlds semantics. As the time index progresses, more and more open futures are precluded. Imagine that at some point in time, it was an open possibility that Roman would leave before noon, but by the present time it is settled that he did not. Then, assuming that the conditional employs a "historical necessity"-type of accessibility relation, the time index needs to be moved to the past to make sure that the domain of accessible worlds includes at least some worlds where he did leave before noon. Hence, the need for past tense marking on the modal (*would = will + PAST*) in *If Roman had left before noon, he would have arrived on time*; the past tense in the antecedent may be a mere agreement phenomenon.

What then about the indicative conditional in (41a)? Clearly, if we assume a historical necessity modal, at the time of utterance it is already settled whether Roman did or did not leave before noon. So, if there need to be at least some antecedent worlds in the domain of the modal, the covert modal in (41a) cannot be a historical necessity modal. Thus, it is not mysterious why (41a) is naturally analyzed as involving a (covert) epistemic necessity modal.

In this story, then, the difference between indicative and subjunctive is two-fold: (i) type of accessibility relation/type of modal (epistemic vs. historical), (ii) time index on the modal (present vs. past). An obvious question is whether these differences cross-cut: are there past epistemic conditionals? Are there present historic necessity conditionals? The answer to the second question is possibly yes: *If Roman comes to the party tomorrow, it will be a grand success* might arguably be a non-epistemic conditional. The answer to the first question might be expected to be no, since it is well-known that epistemic modals resist embedding under past tense (cf. article 14 [this volume] (Hacquard) *Modality*).

One possibly problematic fact for the view just sketched comes from hindsight counterfactuals (Barker 1998; Edgington 2003):

(42) [A randomly tossed coin comes up heads.]
    a. If you had bet on heads, you would have won.
    b. If you bet on heads, you will win.

While (42a) seems acceptable and true after the coin has come up heads, there is no time in the past at which (42b) would have been rational to assert. While that doesn't mean that there wasn't a time at which the indicative conditional was true, it does throw some doubt on the simple idea that the only difference between (42a) and (42b) is the temporal perspective.

7 Further reading

Many references were given throughout this article. Here are some highlighted readings. Indispensable classics are Stalnaker (1968) and Lewis (1973). Good overviews: Edgington (2007) and Bennett (2003). On disjunctive antecedents and related problems: van Rooij (2006) and Alonso-Ovalle (2009). On the syntax of conditionals: Iatridou (1991) and Bhatt & Pancheva (2006). On the contribution of *then*: Iatridou (2003). On the phenomenon of conditional strengthening: van der Auwera (1997a,b), Horn (2000), and von Fintel (2001a). On the psychology of conditionals: Oaksford & Chater (2003), Over & Evans (2003), and Evans & Over (2004).

I would like to thank my teacher Angelika Kratzer and my colleagues Irene Heim and Bob Stalnaker: without them I wouldn't understand a thing about conditionals. Thanks also to my frequent collaborators Sabine Iatridou and Thony Gillies: without them I wouldn't have anything to say about conditionals. Finally, thanks to Andy Fugard, Thony Gillies, Janneke Huitink, and Rich Thomason for comments on a draft of this article.

8 References

Adams, Ernest W. 1965. A logic of conditionals. *Inquiry* 8, 166–197.
Adams, Ernest W. 1970. Subjunctive and indicative conditionals. *Foundations of Language* 6, 89–94.
Alonso-Ovalle, Luis 2009. Counterfactuals, correlatives, and disjunctions. *Linguistics & Philosophy* 32, 207–244.

Anderson, Alan Ross 1951. A note on subjunctive and counterfactual conditionals. *Analysis* 12, 35–38.
Arregui, Ana 2005. *On the Accessibility of Possible Worlds: The Role of Tense and Aspect*. Ph.D. dissertation. University of Massachusetts, Amherst, MA.
Arregui, Ana 2007. When aspect matters: The case of would-conditionals. *Natural Language Semantics* 15, 221–264.
Arregui, Ana 2009. On similarity in counterfactuals. *Linguistics & Philosophy* 32, 245–278.
Austin, J. L. 1956. Ifs and cans. *Proceedings of the British Academy* 42, 107–132.
van der Auwera, Johan 1997a. Conditional perfection. In: A. Athanasiadou & R. Dirven (eds.). *On Conditionals Again*. Amsterdam: Benjamins, 169–190.
van der Auwera, Johan 1997b. Pragmatics in the last quarter century: The case of conditional perfection. *Journal of Pragmatics* 27, 261–274.
Barker, Stephen J. 1998. Predetermination and tense probabilism. *Analysis* 58, 290–296.
Belnap, Nuel D., Jr. 1970. Conditional assertion and restricted quantification. *Noûs* 4, 1–12.
Belnap, Nuel D., Jr. 1973. Restricted quantification and conditional assertion. In: H. Leblanc (ed.). *Truth, Syntax and Modality: Proceedings of the Temple University Conference on Alternative Semantics, vol. 68*. Amsterdam: North-Holland, 48–75.
Bennett, Jonathan 1982. Even if. *Linguistics & Philosophy* 5, 403–418.
Bennett, Jonathan 2003. *A Philosophical Guide to Conditionals*. Oxford: Oxford University Press.
Bhatt, Rajesh & Roumyana Pancheva 2006. Conditionals. In: M. Everaert (ed.). *The Blackwell Companion to Syntax, vol. 1*. Oxford: Blackwell, 638–687.
Cohen, Ariel 2009. Probability in semantics. *Language and Linguistics Compass* 3, 265–281.
Copley, Bridget 2006. *Temporal Orientation in Conditionals (or, How I Learned to Stop Worrying and Love UFOs)*. Ms. Paris, CNRS/University of Paris 8.
DeRose, Keith & Richard E. Grandy 1999. Conditional assertions and "biscuit" conditionals. *Noûs* 33, 405–420.
Djordjevic, Vladan 2005. *Counterfactuals*. Ph.D. dissertation. University of Alberta, Edmonton, AB.
Dudman, V. H. 1983. Tense and time in English verb clusters of the primary pattern. *Australian Journal of Linguistics* 3, 25–44.
Dudman, V. H. 1984. Conditional interpretations of if-sentences. *Australian Journal of Linguistics* 4, 143–204.
Dudman, V. H. 1988. Indicative and subjunctive. *Analysis* 48, 113–122.
Dudman, V. H. 1989. Vive la révolution! *Mind* 93, 591–603.
Edgington, Dorothy 1986. Do conditionals have truth-conditions? *Critica* 18, 3–30.
Edgington, Dorothy 2003. Counterfactuals and the benefit of hindsight. In: P. Dowe & P. Noordhof (eds.). *Cause and Chance: Causation in an Indeterministic World*. London: Routledge, 12–27.
Edgington, Dorothy 2007. On conditionals. In: D. M. Gabbay & F. Guenthner (eds.). *Handbook of Philosophical Logic, vol. 14*. Dordrecht: Springer, 127–221.
Egan, Andy, John Hawthorne & Brian Weatherson 2005. Epistemic modals in context. In: G. Preyer & G. Peter (eds.). *Contextualism in Philosophy: Knowledge, Meaning, and Truth*. Oxford: Oxford University Press, 131–170.
Egré, Paul & Mikaël Cozic 2011. If-clauses and probability operators. *Topoi* 30, 17–29.
Evans, Jonathan & David Over 2004. *If*. Oxford: Oxford University Press.
von Fintel, Kai 1994. *Restrictions on Quantifier Domains*. Ph.D. dissertation. University of Massachusetts, Amherst, MA.

von Fintel, Kai 1998. The presupposition of subjunctive conditionals. In: U. Sauerland & O. Percus (eds.). *The Interpretive Tract* (MIT Working Papers in Linguistics 25). Cambridge, MA: MIT, 29–44.

von Fintel, Kai 1999. NPI licensing, Strawson entailment, and context dependency. *Journal of Semantics* 16, 97–148.

von Fintel, Kai 2001a. *Conditional Strengthening: A Case Study in Implicature*. Ms. Cambridge, MA, MIT. http://web.mit.edu/fintel/fintel-2001-condstrength.pdf. December 18, 2010.

von Fintel, Kai 2001b. Counterfactuals in a dynamic context. In: M. Kenstowicz (ed.). *Ken Hale: A Life in Language*. Cambridge, MA: The MIT Press, 132–152.

von Fintel, Kai 2003. *Epistemic Modals and Conditionals Revisited*. Handout, Colloquium at the University of Massachusetts, Amherst, MA.

von Fintel, Kai 2007. *If: The Biggest Little Word*. Paper (plenary address) presented at the *Georgetown University Roundtable*, March 8, 2007. http://mit.edu/fintel/gurt-slides.pdf. December 18, 2010.

von Fintel, Kai & Anthony S. Gillies 2011. 'Might' made right. In: A. Egan & B. Weatherson (eds.). *Epistemic Modality*. Oxford: Oxford University Press, 108–130.

von Fintel, Kai & Anthony S. Gillies 2008. CIA leaks. *The Philosophical Review* 117, 77–98.

Fleischman, Suzanne 1989. Temporal distance: A basic linguistic metaphor. *Studies in Language* 13, 1–50.

Frank, Anette 1996. *Context Dependence in Modal Constructions*. Doctoral dissertation. University of Stuttgart.

Geurts, Bart 2004a. *On an Ambiguity in Quantified Conditionals*. Ms. Nijmegen, University of Nijmegen.

Geurts, Bart 2004b. *Unary Quantification Revisited*. Ms. Nijmegen, University of Nijmegen.

Gibbard, Alan 1981. Two recent theories of conditionals. In: W. Harper, R. Stalnaker & G. Pearce (eds.). *Ifs: Conditionals, Belief, Decision, Chance, and Time*. Dordrecht: Reidel, 211–247.

Gillies, Anthony S. 2007. Counterfactual scorekeeping. *Linguistics & Philosophy* 30, 329–260.

Gillies, Anthony S. 2009a. Iffiness. *Semantics and Pragmatics* 3, 1–42.

Gillies, Anthony S. 2009b. On truth-conditions for if (but not quite only if). *The Philosophical Review* 118, 325–349.

Goodman, Nelson 1947. The problem of counterfactual conditionals. *Journal of Philosophy* 44, 113–128.

Haegeman, Liliane 2003. Conditional clauses: External and internal syntax. *Mind & Language* 18, 317–339.

Hájek, Alan 1993. *Conditional Probability*. Ph.D. dissertation. Princeton University.

Heim, Irene 1982. *The Semantics of Definite and Indefinite Noun Phrases*. Ph.D. dissertation. University of Massachusetts, Amherst, MA. Reprinted: Ann Arbor, MI: University Microfilms.

Herzberger, Hans 1979. Counterfactuals and consistency. *Journal of Philosophy* 76, 83–88.

Higginbotham, James 1986. Linguistic theory and Davidsons program in semantics. In: E. LePore (ed.). *Truth and Interpretation: Perspectives on the Philosophy of Donald Davidson*. Oxford: Blackwell, 29–48.

Hockett, Charles F. & Stuart A. Altmann 1968. A note on design features. In: T. A. Sebeok (ed.). *Animal Communication: Techniques of Study and Results of Research*. Bloomington, IN: Indiana University Press, 61–72.

Horn, Laurence 2000. From if to iff: Conditional perfection as pragmatic strengthening. *Journal of Pragmatics* 32, 289–326.

Huitink, Janneke 2008. *Modals, Conditionals and Compositionality*. Ph.D. dissertation. Radboud University of Nijmegen.

Huitink, Janneke 2009a. *Domain Restriction by Conditional Connectives*. Ms. Frankfurt, University of Frankfurt.

Huitink, Janneke 2009b. Partial semantics for iterated if-clauses. In: A. Riester & T. Solstad (eds.). *Proceedings of Sinn und Bedeutung 13*. Stuttgart: University of Stuttgart, 203–216.

Huitink, Janneke 2010. Quantified conditionals and compositionality. *Language and Linguistics Compass* 4, 42–53.

Iatridou, Sabine 1991. *Topics in Conditionals*. Ph.D. dissertation. MIT, Cambridge, MA.

Iatridou, Sabine 1993. On the contribution of conditional then. *Natural Language Semantics* 2, 171–199.

Iatridou, Sabine 2000. The grammatical ingredients of counterfactuality. *Linguistic Inquiry* 31, 231–270.

Iatridou, Sabine & David Embick 1993. Conditional inversion. In: M. Gonzalez (ed.). *Proceedings of the North Eastern Linguistic Society 24*. Amherst, MA: GLSA, University of Massachusetts, 189–203.

Ippolito, Michela 2003. Presuppositions and implicatures in counterfactuals. *Natural Language Semantics* 11, 145–186.

Ippolito, Michela 2007. Semantic composition and presupposition projection in subjunctive conditionals. *Linguistics & Philosophy* 29, 631–672.

Jackson, Frank 1979. On assertion and indicative conditionals. *The Philosophical Review* 88, 565–589.

Jackson, Frank 1987. *Conditionals*. Oxford: Blackwell.

James, Deborah 1982. Past tense and the hypothetical: A cross-linguistic study. *Studies in Language* 6, 375–403.

John MacFarlane, 2011. Epistemic modals are assessment-sensitive. In B. Weatherson & A. Egan (eds.), *Epistemic Modality*. Oxford: Oxford University Press, 144–178.

Kanazawa, Makoto, Stefan Kaufmann & Stanley Peters 2005. On the lumping semantics of counterfactuals. *Journal of Semantics* 22, 129–151.

Kaufmann, Stefan 2005a. Conditional predictions: A probabilistic account. *Linguistics & Philosophy* 28, 181–231.

Kaufmann, Stefan 2005b. Conditional truth and future reference. *Journal of Semantics* 22, 231–280.

Kolodny, Niko & John MacFarlane 2010. Ifs and oughts. *The Journal of Philosophy* 108, 115–143.

Kratzer, Angelika 1977. What "must" and "can" must and can mean. *Linguistics & Philosophy* 1, 337–355.

Kratzer, Angelika 1979. Conditional necessity and possibility. In: R. B®auerle, U. Egli & A. von Stechow (eds.). *Semantics from Different Points of View*. Berlin: Springer, 117–147.

Kratzer, Angelika 1981. Partition and revision: The semantics of counterfactuals. *Journal of Philosophical Logic* 10, 201–216.

Kratzer, Angelika 1986. Conditionals. In: A. M. Farley, P. Farley & K.-E. McCullough (eds.). *Proceedings from the Regional Meeting of the Chicago Linguistic Society 22. Papers from the Parasession on Pragmatics and Grammatical Theory*. Chicago, IL: Chicago Linguistic Society, 1–15.

Kratzer, Angelika 1989. An investigation of the lumps of thought. *Linguistics & Philosophy* 12, 607–653.

Kratzer, Angelika 1991. Modality. In: A. von Stechow & D. Wunderlich (eds.). *Semantik—Semantics. Ein internationales Handbuch zeitgenössischer Forschung—An International Handbook of Contemporary Research* (HSK 6). Berlin: de Gruyter, 639–650.

Kratzer, Angelika 2005. Constraining premise sets for counterfactuals. *Journal of Semantics* 22, 153–158.

Kratzer, Angelika 2010. Conditionals. In: A. Kratzer. *Modals and Conditionals Again*. To be published by Oxford University Press. http://semanticsarchive.net/Archive/TkzNmRlM/modals-conditionals.pdf. December 21, 2010.

Levinson, Stephen 2000. *Presumptive Meanings: The Theory of Generalized Implicature*. Cambridge, MA: The MIT Press.

Lewis, Clarence I. 1918. *A Survey of Symbolic Logic*. Berkeley, CA: University of California Press.

Lewis, David 1973. *Counterfactuals*. Oxford: Blackwell.

Lewis, David 1975. Adverbs of quantification. In: E. Keenan (ed.). *Formal Semantics of Natural Language*. Cambridge: Cambridge University Press, 3–15.

Lewis, David 1976. Probabilities of conditionals and conditional probabilities. *The Philosophical Review* 85, 297–315.

Lewis, David 1981. Ordering semantics and premise semantics for counterfactuals. *Journal of Philosophical Logic* 10, 217–234. Reprinted in: D. Lewis. *Papers in Philosophical Logic*. Cambridge: Cambridge University Press, 1998, 77–96.

Lycan, William G. 2001. *Real Conditionals*. Oxford: Clarendon Press.

Lycan, William G. 2006. Conditional-assertion theories of conditionals. In: J. Thomson & A. Byrne (eds.). *Content and Modality: Themes from the Philosophy of Robert Stalnaker*. Oxford: Oxford University Press, 148–163.

MacFarlane John, 2011. Epistemic modals are assessment-sensitive. In B. Weatherson & A. Egan (eds.), Epistemic Modality. Oxford: Oxford University Press, 144-178.

McDermott, Michael 1996. On the truth conditions of certain if-sentences. *The Philosophical Review* 105, 1–37.

Moss, Sarah 2007. *On the Pragmatics of Counterfactuals*. Ms. Cambridge, MA, MIT.

Nute, Donald 1982. *Tense and Conditionals*. Technical Report IMS/University of Stuttgart. Revised version: Research Report AI-1991-02, Artificial Intelligence Programs, University of Georgia, Athens, GA, 1991. http://www.ai.uga.edu/ftplib/ai-reports/ai199102.ps. December 18, 2010.

Nute, Donald 1991. Historical necessity and conditonals. *Noûs* 25, 161–175.

Oaksford, Mike & Nick Chater 2003. Conditional probability and the cognitive science of conditional reasoning. *Mind & Language* 18, 359–379.

Over, David E. & Jonathan St. B. T. Evans 2003. The probability of conditionals: The psychological evidence. *Mind & Language* 18, 340–358.

Partee, Barbara H. 1991. Topic, focus and quantification. In: S. Moore & A. Z. Wyner (eds.). *Proceedings of Semantics and Linguistic Theory 1*. Ithaca, NY: Cornell University, 159–188.

Pollock, John 1976. *Subjunctive Reasoning*. Dordrecht: Reidel.

Predelli, Stefano 2009. Towards a semantics for biscuit conditionals. *Philosophical Studies* 142, 293–305.

Prior, Arthur N. 1958. Escapism: The logical basis of ethics. In: A. I. Melden (ed.). *Essays in Moral Philosophy*. Seattle, WA: University of Washington Press, 135–146.

Ramsey, Frank P. 1931. General propositions and causality. In: R. B. Braithwaite (ed.). *The Foundations of Mathematics and Other Logical Essays*. London: Kegan Paul, Trench, & Truber, 237–255.

Rescher, Nicholas 1964. *Hypothetical Reasoning*. Amsterdam: North-Holland.
Rieger, Adam 2006. A simple theory of conditionals. *Analysis* 66, 233–240.
van Rooij, Robert 2006. Free choice counterfactual donkeys. *Journal of Semantics* 23, 383–402.
Rothschild, Daniel 2010. Do indicative conditionals express propositions? Forthcoming in *Noûs* 47.1, 49–68.
Schein, Barry 2003. Adverbial, descriptive reciprocals. *Philosophical Perspectives* 17, 333–367.
Schlenker, Philippe 2004. Conditionals as definite descriptions (A referential analysis). *Research on Language and Computation* 2, 417–462.
Schulz, Katrin 2008. Non-deictic tenses in conditionals. In: T. Friedman & S. Ito (eds.). *Proceedings of Semantics and Linguistic Theory 18*. Ithaca, NY: Cornell University, 694–710.
Siegel, Muffy E.A. 2006. Biscuit conditionals: Quantification over potential literal acts. *Linguistics & Philosophy* 29, 167–203.
Slote, Michael A. 1978. Time in counterfactuals. *The Philosophical Review* 87, 3–27.
Stalnaker, Robert 1968. A theory of conditionals. In: N. Rescher (ed.). *Studies in Logical Theory*. Oxford: Blackwell, 98–112.
Stalnaker, Robert 1975. Indicative conditionals. *Philosophia* 5, 269–286.
Stalnaker, Robert 1984. *Inquiry*. Cambridge, MA: The MIT Press.
von Stechow, Arnim 2007. Tense and presuppositions in counterfactuals. Paper presented at the University of Oslo, October 10, 2007. http://www2.sfs.nphil.uni-tuebingen. de/~arnim10/Handouts/TensPresCF.pdf. December 18, 2010.
Steele, Susan 1975. Past and irrealis: Just what does it all mean? *International Journal of American Linguistics* 41, 200–217.
Stephenson, Tamina 2007a. Indicative conditionals have relative truth conditions. In: M. Elliott et al. (eds.). *Proceedings from the Regional Meeting of the Chicago Linguistic Society 43*. Chicago: Chicago Linguistic Society, 231–242.
Stephenson, Tamina 2007b. Judge dependence, epistemic modals, and predicates of personal taste. *Linguistics & Philosophy* 30, 487–525.
Suber, Peter 1997. *Paradoxes of Material Implication*. Lecture notes for the course "Symbolic Logic". Earlham College, Richmond, IN. http://www.earlham.edu/~peters/courses/log/ mat-imp.htm. December 18, 2010.
Thomason, Richmond H. & Anil Gupta 1980. A theory of conditionals in the context of branching time. *The Philosophical Review* 89, 65–90.
Thomason, Richmond H. 1985. Note on tense and subjunctive conditionals. *Philosophy of Science* 52, 151–153.
Veltman, Frank 1976. Prejudices, presuppositions and the theory of conditionals. In: J. Groenendijk & M. Stokhof (eds.). *Amsterdam Papers in Formal Grammar, vol. 1*. Amsterdam: Department of Philosophy, University of Amsterdam, 248–281.
Veltman, Frank 2005. Making counterfactual assumptions. *Journal of Semantics* 22, 159–180.
Warmbrod, Ken 1982. A defense of the limit assumption. *Philosophical Studies* 42, 53–66.
Weatherson, Brian 2009. Conditionals and indexical relativism. *Synthese* 166, 333–357.
Zvolenszky, Zsófia 2002. Is a possible-worlds semantics of modality possible? A problem for Kratzers semantics. In: B. Jackson (ed.). *Proceedings of Semantics and Linguistic Theory 12*. Ithaca, NY: Cornell University, 339–358.

Eric Swanson
16 Propositional attitudes

1 Attitude ascriptions —— 533
2 The variety of attitudes —— 533
3 Selected coreference puzzles, and the analysis of 'believes' —— 537
4 Some treatments of coreference puzzles —— 539
5 Modeling doxastic states —— 543
6 'Local' presupposition satisfaction: Another puzzle of attitude ascription —— 549
7 Conclusion —— 558
8 References —— 558

Abstract: Verbs like 'believes,' 'knows,' 'suspects,' 'hopes,' and 'worries'—verbs that, at the level of logical form, can take clauses as their complements—are generally taken to denote intentional attitudes borne to a proposition. For this reason they are known as propositional attitude verbs. It is difficult to construct a semantics and pragmatics adequate to the features of these verbs. Any successful theory must explain why, within the scope of an attitude ascription, substitution of coreferring terms sometimes seems to change the truth value of the ascription. This feature of attitude ascriptions seems to entail that coreferring terms can have different semantic values; other compelling arguments seem to show that coreferring terms must have the same semantic value. After surveying other important features of propositional attitude verbs, and presenting several coreference puzzles, this article discusses conceptions of mental content intended to help resolve such puzzles. It then explores the importance of subjective uncertainty to attitude ascriptions and to formal semantics in general. It concludes by sketching an approach to the semantics of attitude ascriptions that coheres with the standard ways of representing subjective uncertainty. This approach also unifies the treatment of coreference puzzles and the treatment of presupposition carrying expressions in attitude ascriptions.

Eric Swanson, Ann Arbor, MI (USA)

https://doi.org/10.1515/9783110589443-016

1 Attitude ascriptions

Attitude ascriptions include sentences like

(1) Liem hopes that Santa is coming soon.
(2) He suspects that Santa will give him a rocket.
(3) Some children worry that if Santa gets lost, the reindeer won't know how to find their house.

These sentences have the form 'NP VPs that ø,' where 'VP' denotes some intentional attitude, and (bracketing the question of its denotation) 'that ø' is a finite clause headed by a complementizer. Attitude ascriptions come in many other forms, of course. But everyone agrees that (1)–(3) represent the sort of claim we are aiming to give a semantics for when we give a semantics for attitude ascriptions in general.

It is very common to think that any semantics for attitude ascriptions presupposes a theory of the relations that believers bear to propositions—abstract objects that represent or embody truth-evaluable intentional content. These relations are commonly called *propositional attitudes*. The nature of propositions and the nature of the relations we putatively bear to them is hotly debated. So it is helpful for certain purposes to explore the features of attitude ascriptions without making substantive presuppositions about propositions and propositional attitudes. Temporarily bracketing questions about the nature of content makes it easier to appreciate considerations from all the different fields that bear on attitude ascription: (at least) epistemology, philosophy of mind, philosophy of language, semantics, and pragmatics.

2 The variety of attitudes

The 'propositional' attitudes are a motley bunch: we can know, learn, regret, believe, imagine, fear, wish, want, pretend, suppose, surmise, suspect, predict, speculate, doubt, prove, disprove, infer, ..., that ø. Following Huddleston & Pullum (2002), I will say that a verb is *factive* just in case it carries the presupposition that its complement clause is true, and that a verb is *entailing* just in case in the positive declarative it entails the truth of its complement (1008–1009). (Throughout I have in mind pragmatic presupposition, in Stalnaker's sense (1974); cf. article 14 [Semantics: Interfaces] (Beaver & Geurts) *Presupposition*.) These categories cut across each other, although it's sometimes overlooked that verbs can be factive without being entailing, and vice versa.

Tab. 16.1: Categories of attitude verbs.

	Entailing	Non-Entailing
Factive	find out, know, remember	confess, regret, resent
Non-Factive	discover, establish, prove	believe, infer, suspect

Verbs like 'believe' are neither factive nor entailing; I leave the production of examples to the reader. For entailing verbs that differ primarily in their factivity—that is, in whether they carry the presupposition that their complements are true—contrast

(4) NASA just found out that there's life on the moon!

(5) NASA just discovered that there's life on the moon!

Utterances of (4) generally presuppose that there's life on the moon and utterances of (5) generally don't. But both sentences entail that there is life on the moon: you can neither find out nor discover that ø unless it's actually the case that ø. So 'find out' is factive and entailing, whereas 'discover' is not factive, but is entailing. And here are some examples that show that 'confess' and 'resent' generally presuppose the truth of their complements without entailing it:

(6) She confessed to taking the money, but later recanted. It turned out that she had been trying to cover up a friend's mistake.

(7) I resented him for leaving all the work to me, until I learned how much he had already done.

Finally, some verbs with an attitudinal component to their meaning, like 'disprove,' 'refute,' 'lie,' and 'fib,' entail the falsity of their clausal complements. These verbs more naturally take noun phrases, but in negative or contrastive environments they take clausal complements fairly easily: "It wasn't disproved that the earth was flat until …"; "His investigators claim UnitedHealth manipulated data and even lied that its reimbursement rates were based on national research" (Associated Press, "Cuomo to sue major health insurers," February 13, 2008).

A successful theory of attitude ascriptions must explain why, within the scope of an attitude ascription, substituting for one term another term that corefers with it sometimes seems to change the truth value of the ascription. I discuss this phenomenon at length in sections 3, 4, and 6. A successful theory must also explain how the facts that some attitude ascriptions seem to express entail that believers stand in intentional relations—relations of 'aboutness'—to nonexistent objects. As Brentano (1874: 50) seminally put it: "Every mental phenomenon is characterized by what the scholastics of the Middle Ages called the intentional ...inexistence (*Inexistenz*) of an object (*Gegenstand*), and what we could call ...the reference to a content, a direction upon an object (by which we are not to understand a reality in this case), or an immanent objectivity." These features of attitude ascriptions are more than a little mysterious, and motivate a vast amount of work (cf. article 3 [Semantics: Foundations, History an Methods] (Textor) *Sense and reference* and article 4 [Semantics: Foundations, History and Methods] (Abbott) *Reference*).

And they are distinctive enough that other expressions that exhibit these features are sometimes taken to be covert attitude ascriptions. For example, Quine (1956) analyzes 'NP1 is hunting NP2' as, roughly, 'NP1 strives to make it the case that NP1 finds NP2'. This lets him apply explanations of substitution failure and 'intentional inexistence' in the complements of clausal intentional verbs to intentional verbs with complements that are not overtly clausal. It also lets him distinguish between two readings of sentences like 'Ernest is hunting lions'—one that relates Ernest to a particular lion and another that leaves open the question whether there is a particular lion that he is hunting:

(8) $\exists x(x$ is a lion and Ernest strives that Ernest finds $x)$

(9) Ernest strives that $\exists x(x$ is a lion and Ernest finds $x)$

Considerable ingenuity has been applied to the project of analyzing all intentional attitude ascriptions as being, fundamentally, propositional attitude ascriptions. (See especially den Dikken, Larson & Ludlow 1996, 1997. McCawley 1974, Karttunen 1976, and Ross 1976 marshal syntactic considerations in favor of the view.) Such efforts have hefty burdens to discharge, since they are not successful unless every apparently non-clausal intentional verb can be plausibly paraphrased without using any such verbs. Whether or not 'I want x' is plausibly paraphrased as 'I desire that I have x,' it's hard to find clausal paraphrases of 'ignore,' 'love,' 'insult,' and many other non-clausal intentional verbs. (See Montague 2007 for discussion of potential clausal semantics for 'love'.)

Verbs used to ascribe desires, like 'want,' 'hope,' and 'wish,' raise problems that it will be instructive to linger on. On an extremely simple approach to attitude ascriptions, which I will call the *naïve possible worlds approach,* the complement of an attitude ascription denotes a set of possible worlds, or *possible worlds proposition.* (According to textbook intensional semantics, clauses denote possible worlds propositions, so this approach looks quite natural from that theoretical point of view.) On one version of this approach, 'Liem hopes that ø' is true just in case Liem's most preferred worlds are all worlds in which it is true that ø. Similarly, 'Liem believes that ø' is true just in case all of the possible worlds compatible with Liem's beliefs—that is, all of the possible worlds in which all Liem's beliefs in the world of evaluation are true—are worlds in which it is true that ø. This semantics for 'hopes' founders on the fact that our preferences are generally not closed under entailment. From the fact that

(10) John hopes that you leave later.

it does not follow, intuitively, that

(11) John hopes that you leave.

But all the worlds in which you leave later are worlds in which you leave. So on the naïve possible worlds semantics we are considering, (10) wrongly entails (11) (cf. Prior 1958, Forrester 1984).

It would be overhasty to conclude that we should not model the contents of our preferences using possible worlds propositions. Following Stalnaker (1984: 84–90), Heim (1992) details a theory according to which (11) means (roughly) "that John thinks that if you leave he will be in a more desirable world than if you don't leave" (Heim 1992: 193), and (10) means that Jones thinks that if you leave later he will be in a more desirable world than if you don't leave later. (Cf. Hansson 1969, van Fraassen 1972, 1973, Lewis 1973, article 14 [this volume] (Hacquard) *Modality*, and article 15 [this volume] (von Fintel) *Conditionals*.) More precisely, on Heim's semantics, (10) means that for any world *w* compatible with what John believes, John prefers every world in which you leave later that is maximally similar to *w* (among worlds in which you leave later) to any world in which you do not leave later that is maximally similar to *w* (among worlds in which you do not leave later). On this semantics, then, the truth of (10) does not entail that John has the preferences that would make (11) true. But as far as this particular problem is concerned, we may still model the contents of our preferences using possible worlds propositions, with the help of an ordering source (that itself may be modeled using possible worlds propositions: see Lewis 1981). As Heim (1992: 195–206) argues, this kind of approach also helps explain a host of other features of desire reports. The prima facie failure of a 'possible worlds approach' here spurred refinements resulting in a more explanatory overall theory than we might have come to otherwise. It is more complicated to refine our models of belief states enough to avoid the result that what is truly ascribed by 'believes,' in a context, is closed under entailment; I take up that project in section 5.

3 Selected coreference puzzles, and the analysis of 'believes'

'Believes' is one among many intentional verbs, as we have seen. But it is the uncontested central case in the literature on attitude ascriptions. By restricting our attention to it we can focus on some of the most challenging features of attitude ascriptions. It's quite plausible that a successful treatment of those features as they are exemplified by 'believes' could be applied to verbs that express relevantly similar attitudes.

In his ground-breaking "On Sense and Reference," Frege introduces a puzzle about belief—and so, to some extent, about 'believes'—that has to do with the cognitive significance of identity statements (cf. article 3 [Semantics: Foundations, History an Methods] (Textor) *Sense and reference*).

> If the sign 'a' is distinguished from the sign 'b' only as an object (here, by means of its shape), not as a sign (i.e. not by the manner in which it designates something), the cognitive value of $a = a$ becomes essentially equal to that of $a = b$, provided $a = b$ is true.
>
> (Frege 1892: 152)

But, as Frege observes, the two sentences differ in their cognitive significance, in the sense that

> $a = a$ holds *a priori* and, according to Kant, is to be labelled analytic, while statements of the form $a = b$ often contain very valuable extensions of our knowledge and cannot always be established *a priori*.
>
> (Frege 1892: 151)

The substitution of coreferring terms in attitude ascriptions elicits similar phenomena: it's easy to realize that $a = a$, but to discover that $a = b$ can be a hard-won achievement.

Frege puts the problem in terms of phonologically and orthographically distinct signs, but this isn't essential to coreference puzzles. Kripke (1979: 902) asks us to consider Pierre, who has very different 'London' and '*Londres*' beliefs, and Peter, who believes that there are two people named 'Paderewski'—one a famous pianist with considerable musical talent and the other a Polish nationalist leader with no musical talent. We can imagine contexts in which it's appropriate to say

(12) Peter believes that Paderewski had musical talent.

and we can also imagine contexts in which it's appropriate to say

(13) Peter believes that Paderewski had no musical talent.

even if we believe that Peter is not guilty of any logical errors. I think that we can even imagine contexts in which *either* (12) or (13) can be used appropriately to target beliefs of Peter's that correlate with his 'famous pianist' and 'Polish politician' beliefs. (This isn't to say, of course, that we could appropriately use one right after the other; using one changes the context to make uses of the other inappropriate.) This leads Kripke (1979: 906) to suggest that in this case, and in others like it, "our normal practices interpretation and attribution of belief are subjected to the greatest possible strain, perhapseven to the point of breakdown. So is the notion of the *content* of someone's assertion, the *proposition* it expresses."

It's not even essential to coreference puzzles that the coreferring terms be *names*. Adapting a case due to Mark Richard: Imagine that Al, talking to Betty on the telephone, sees a woman in a distant phone booth about to be hit by a runaway steamroller, and wishes he could warn her of the danger. But Al does not realize that Betty is the woman he sees in the phone booth. Then it seems Al could say truly to Betty

(14) I believe I can inform you of her danger over the telephone.

But Al could not say truly

(15) I believe I can inform her of her danger over the telephone. (Richard 1983: 439–440)

Examples like these suggest that the substitution of coreferring proper names, pronouns, and demonstratives can make a difference to the truth conditions of an attitude ascription. Given other plausible assumptions, these examples seem to show that coreferring proper names, pronouns, and demonstratives can have different semantic values (cf. article 4 [Semantics: Foundations, History and Methods (Abbott) *Reference*, article 1 [this volume] (Büring) *Pronouns*, and article 13 [Semantics: Interfaces] (Diessel) *Deixis and demonstratives*).

4 Some treatments of coreference puzzles

Indeed, semantic theories with this commitment were once extremely common. Many philosophers (including Frege, Russell, Carnap, and Searle) held that there could be differences between coreferential terms that made for semantic differences between attitude ascriptions of which they were a part. Some such semantic treatments, like Frege's, posit a systematic shift in meaning whereby proper names have a different semantic value in the context of an attitude ascription than they otherwise would. For Frege (1892: 160) the "customary" semantic value of a finite clause is a truth value, but when a clause is the complement of an attitude ascription its semantic value is instead a "thought." (I translate '*Bedeutung*' as 'semantic value'; this is a bit anachronistic, since it's now common to presuppose that semantic values are intensional, although *Bedeutungen* are not.) Frege attributes a wide range of features to sense, listed below:

1. "By employing a sign we express its sense and designate its *Bedeutung* [referent]" (Frege 1892: 156).
2. Senses are compositional: the sense of a sentence is determined by the senses of its parts, and their arrangement (Frege 1892: 156).
3. "Every grammatically well-formed expression figuring as a proper name always has a sense," whether or not it has a referent (Frege 1892: 153).
4. The thought expressed by "Odysseus was set ashore at Ithaca while sound asleep" "remains the same whether 'Odysseus' has a *Bedeutung* [referent] or not" (Frege 1892: 157).
5. The sense of a sign "contains" a "mode of presentation" of the object designated by the sign (Frege 1892: 152).
6. A sign's sense "may be the common property of many people, and so is not a part or a mode of the individual mind." This supposed to help explain how it is that "a common store of thoughts ...is transmitted from one generation to another" (Frege 1892: 154).
7. The sense of a proper name "is grasped by everybody who is sufficiently familiar with the language or totality of designations to which it belongs" (Frege 1892: 153).

It's not uncharitable, I think, to think of Frege as saying that the phenomena associated with attitude ascriptions make it plausible that *something* has these features, and that by 'sense' he means whatever it is that in fact *does* have these features (cf. article 3 [Semantics: Foundations, History an Methods] (Textor) *Sense and reference*).

Some of the features on their own are mysterious—if senses are not "a part or a mode of the individual mind" then what kind of thing *are* they, and how do we have access to them?—and there's considerable tension between items on the list, as well. For example, it's hard to see why linguistic competence ensures "grasp" of an object's modes of presentation. And it's hard to see how whether Odysseus existed could fail to make a difference to the modes of presentation associated with 'Odysseus.' Contemporary neo-Fregeans thus usually abandon or modify one or more of these desiderata. But Frege's enumeration of the features of sense helps make it clearer what an *ideal* theory of attitude ascriptions might aim for. And Frege's decision not to complicate the semantics of names that occur outside attitude ascriptions is also instructive. The puzzles of coreferring terms in attitude ascriptions, like so many in philosophy of language, are rooted in ignorance: what body or bodies of information make the difference between being ignorant of the fact that $a = b$ and knowing that $a = b$? So it's entirely unsurprising that the semantics of attitude ascriptions can be sensitive to what the ascribee does and doesn't know. But it's another matter altogether, as Frege must have seen, to think that facts about what is and isn't known have any bearing on the semantics of 'simple' sentences that do not make attitude ascriptions.

Russell (1919: 7), by contrast, treats ordinary proper names in a semantically uniform way: wherever they occur, they are disguised definite descriptions. On any plausible analysis, definite descriptions enter into scope relations with quantifiers and other operators, including the operators whereby we make attitude ascriptions. For example, uttered today

(16)   The president of the United States will always be male.

can be interpreted as making the uncontroversial claim that Barack Obama will always be male, or as making the very controversial claim that for all future times t, the president of the United States at t is male at t (Heim 1991: 7). Similarly, Russell (1905: 44–45) observes that when we say

(17)   George IV wondered whether Scott was the author of *Waverley*.

> ...we normally mean "George IV wished to know whether one and only one man wrote *Waverley* and Scott was that man"; but we *may* also mean: "One and only one man wrote *Waverly*, and George IV wished to know whether Scott was that man."... [which might also] be expressed by "George IV wished to know, concerning the man who in fact wrote *Waverly*, whether he was Scott."

Because coreferential but distinct proper names might well 'disguise' different definite descriptions, Russell has a straightforward answer to the question how "Al knows that $a = a$" and "Al knows that $a = b$" can come apart in truth value.

These attitude ascriptions are, on Russell's view, not essentially different from the attitude ascriptions

(18) Al knows that the *F* is the *F*.

and

(19) Al knows that the *F* is the *G*.

Even if the *F* is the *G*, (28) and (29) clearly can have different truth values. And Russell's analysis gives a lucid account how believers can apparently stand in intentional relations to nonexistent objects denoted by proper names: they simply falsely believe that there is something that satisfies the definite description associated with the proper name. As I mentioned earlier, on any plausible analysis of definite descriptions they can enter into scope relations. On Russell's own analysis, the scope facts are a result of the quantificational structure that definite descriptions contribute to logical form. But a sufficiently rich intensional semantics can also capture the scope facts, without treating definite descriptions as quantificational (Heim 1991: 19–22; cf. article 4 [Semantics: Foundations, History and Methods] (Abbott) *Reference*; article 2 [this volume] (Heim) *Definiteness and indefiniteness*; and article 4 [this volume] (Keenan) *Quantifiers*).

The development of modal logic in the middle of the twentieth century brought in its wake an assault on 'descriptivism'—broadly construed to include theories of proper names on which they were associated with either Fregean senses or Russellian descriptions—that found powerful and synoptic expression in Kripke's *Naming and Necessity* (1980). There Kripke forcefully argued that proper names were rigid designators, where a rigid designator is an expression that designates the same object in all possible worlds. (More precisely: an expression is rigid just in case its intension is constant.) One crucial datum was that "it's a contingent fact that Aristotle ever did *any* of the things commonly attributed to him today" (Kripke 1980: 75). This was inconsistent with many descriptivist views of the time. Searle (1958: 172), for example, claimed that "it is a necessary fact that Aristotle has the ...inclusive disjunction of properties commonly attributed to him: any individual not having at least some of these properties could not be Aristotle" (cf. article 14 [this volume] (Hacquard) *Modality*).

Until attention was focused on proper names' modal profile, it was common to presuppose that they had variable intensions in the sense that the world of evaluation—a semantic parameter shiftable by modal expressions—could make a difference to what a name contributed to the determination of the truth value of a sentence in which it occurred. This presupposition is arguably latent, for example, in the view that (1) the identity of Hesperus and Phosphorus is knowable only a posteriori and (2) all 'a posteriori truths' are contingent (Kripke 1980: 101–105). And broadly descriptivist semantics in effect exploited the putative variability of the intensions of proper names to explain coreference puzzles. But Kripke and others elicited intuitions about the modal profile of proper names that strongly suggested that their intensions are actually *constant* over (at least) the metaphysically possible worlds. These intuitions thus make obvious trouble for views that explain coreference puzzles by appeal to variable intensions. Many also take intuitions about rigidity to make trouble for views that model the content of attitude ascriptions purely intensionally, with a set of possible worlds: together with the fact that Hesperus is Phosphorus, the rigidity of proper names like 'Hesperus' and 'Phosphorus' entails that the possible worlds in which Hesperus is F are exactly the possible worlds in which Phosphorus is F. But then the possible worlds model of the content of the belief that Hesperus is F does not differ from the possible worlds model of the content of the belief that Phosphorus is F. As Soames influentially put it, "one can always find psychologically non-equivalent sentences which are true in the same circumstances, and, hence, [would be] assigned the same content" if belief were modeled using sets of possible worlds (Soames 1987: 231; cf. Scheffler 1955, 41–42).

Together these considerations encouraged the refinement of old treatments of attitude ascription, and the development of new ones. Some philosophers try to accommodate intuitions about rigidity with carefully tailored descriptivist semantics (see, e.g., the discussion in Stanley 1997). Salmon (1986), Soames (1987, 2002), and Thau (2002), among many others, explain coreference puzzles by appealing to implicatures or other pragmatic effects. In both these camps the apparent problems with characterizing mental content in terms of sets of possible worlds encourage many philosophers to defend conceptions of content on which it has more structure than a set of possible worlds. Some argue that content must be individuated so finely that its putative structure quite closely parallels the syntactic structure of sentences (Larson & Ludlow 1993, King 1996). King (2007: 57) goes so far as to hold that "the structure of a proposition will be identical to the syntactic structure of the sentence expressing it." One point adduced in favor of such views is that they allow us to "see how" it is possible to "believe a proposition while failing to believe another necessarily equivalent to it" (King 2007: 57): " '1 = 2' and '2 = 1' express different propositions in virtue of having their constituents differently combined" (97). Some take structured propositions to help solve this important aspect of the problem of logical omniscience; others think solving the problem requires a fuller characterization of the putative difference in the contents expressed by '1 = 2' and '2 = 1' (for more, see Stalnaker 1991, 1998).

For the most part approaches like these were motivated by features that noun phrases exhibit in attitude ascriptions. Another important line of thought, initially motivated by the behavior of noun phrases in discourse (Karttunen 1976, Kamp 1981, and Heim 1982), posited a different kind of structure in mental content. Discourse phenomena motivate, as Kamp (1988: 158) puts it, "a theory of meaning and context dependent interpretation of English ...that goes beyond what sets of possible worlds are able to reveal" as representers of context. "Contextual structure" (Kamp 1998: 165) cannot be represented with a set of possible worlds, according to Kamp; a (highly structured) Discourse Representation Structure or DRS can represent it. Kamp uses a famous minimal pair due to Barbara Partee to press his point:

(20) a. Exactly one of the ten balls is not in the bag.
 b. It is under the sofa.

(21) a. Exactly nine of the ten balls are in the bag.
 b. It is under the sofa.

The missing ball is readily available as the referent of 'it' in (20-b); it is relatively hard to read 'it' in (21-b) as referring to that ball. Kamp writes: "if propositions are sets of possible worlds, the two assertions [(20-a) and (21-a)] express the same proposition. ...So the resulting contexts [after those assertions] ...will be equal to each other. We must conclude that no difference can be predicted if contexts are identified with sets of possible worlds," according to Kamp (1988: 158). By contrast the DRSs associated with (20-a) and (21-a) differ: (20-a) introduces a discourse referent, where (21-a) does not, which "links *it* to the subject of the first sentence" (Kamp 1988: 162, cf. article 11 [Semantics: Theories] (Kamp & Reyle) *Discourse Representation Theory*). Nicholas Asher (1986: 134), among others, put such rich representations of context and context change potential to work in attitude ascriptions: "DRSs ...take on a new role as characterizations of the objects of mental states." This approach aspires to unify the representation of context and the representation of mental content. To the extent to which it successfully discharges this ambition it has a prima facie advantage over approaches that say nothing about discourse relations and the behavior of noun phrases in discourse.

5 Modeling doxastic states

There is much to be said in defense of modeling the contents of attitude ascriptions (and contexts) using sets of possible worlds (see especially Lewis 1981b and

Stalnaker 1984, 1991, 1996, 1998, 1999b). Rather than rehearsing that dialectic I want to explore a source of pressure against structured conceptions of content: the representation of credence (cf. Chalmers 2009).

Credence is not an 'on/off' attitude: it comes in degrees. For example, if I believe that rain is likelier than snow tonight, I lend more credence to the proposition that it will rain tonight than I do to the proposition that it will snow tonight. The language of attitude ascription reflects the degreed nature of credence. Consider (22):

(22) Al believes it will probably rain.

This sentence prima facie ascribes to Al moderate but not full credence in the proposition that it will rain, not full credence in the proposition that it will probably rain: we would not put "probable rain" on the list of things Al is sure about. And some attitude verbs pretty clearly ascribe less than full credence even with 'unhedged' complements:

(23) As the clouds grew darker, he slowly became more confident that it would rain.

(24) Betty surmised that it would rain.

(25) Clara suspects and Doug doubts that it will rain.

Modeling doxastic states with probability spaces makes it possible to give elegant semantic entries for such verbs. For example, it's trivial to give entries for 'suspects' and 'doubts' with the result that (25), for example, is true just in case Clara gives credence above some threshold to the proposition that it will rain, and Doug gives credence below some other threshold to *the very same* proposition—the proposition denoted in the context of utterance by 'it will rain'. To be sure, one could try to develop a view on which (25) ascribes full beliefs with distinct contents—a 'suspecting' full belief to Clara, and a 'doubting' full belief to Doug. But such a view would have the unenviable burden of explaining how it can be that, despite the difference in the contents of their putative full beliefs, Clara suspects what Doug doubts.

Probability spaces are especially attractive and popular tools for representing credence because of their expressive power and accessibility. By a *probability space* I mean a triple $\langle W, F, \mu \rangle$ such that:

1. F is a Boolean algebra over W (where a *Boolean algebra* over a set W is a set of subsets of W that includes W itself and is closed under complementation and union);

2. $\mu(\cdot)$ is a function from $F \rightarrow [0, 1]$;
3. $\mu(W) = 1$;
4. If M and N are disjoint elements of F, then $\mu(M \cup N) = \mu(M) + \mu(N)$.

For simplicity I assume that W is finite. W is generally a set of possible worlds, making F a set of sets of worlds—a set of possible worlds propositions. $\mu(\cdot)$ assigns values to the elements of F. F may be as spare as $\{\emptyset, W\}$, it may be as rich as the power set of W, and it also may be any Boolean algebra over W in between. I will occasionally refer to μ, for a given probability space, as its *probability measure* (Halpern 2003: 15–16).

Ordinary talk about subjective uncertainty is often overtly probabilistic: weather forecasters, bookies, and the passengers on the Clapham omnibus all hedge their predictions in ways that conform to the probability axioms. (If they disregarded the axioms, then it would be easy to imagine a forecast that said that frost and no frost were both 70% likely, and a bookie who gave two to one odds for all four horses in a race.) It's also routine to compare credences in ways that are well modeled by probability spaces. I may rightly and justifiedly tell you that it's twice as likely to rain as it is to snow, for example, although I do not have an opinion about the likelihood of precipitation. This can be modeled with a constraint on probability spaces that favors lending twice as much credence to rain as to snow. Moreover, belief in indicative conditionals can and arguably should be analyzed as a kind of comparison of probabilities which, thanks to Lewis' celebrated 'triviality results,' provably cannot be reduced to the probability of a proposition. (See especially Lewis 1976 and Gibbard 1981; cf. article 15 [this volume] (von Fintel) *Conditionals*.) The conditional probability of C given A, relative to a probability measure $\mu(\cdot)$, is $\frac{\mu(A \cap C)}{\mu(A)}$. So for the conditional probability of C given A to be high, it must be the case that $\mu(A \cap C) \approx \mu(A)$.

Epistemically hedged claims have distinctive effects on context and on conversational participants' belief states, and are subject to distinctive norms governing their use. It is difficult (if not impossible) to find propositions that give the meaning of epistemically hedged claims. One way to see this is to notice that it is difficult (if not impossible) to find propositions the use of which is governed by the same norms as those that govern epistemically hedged claims. (See MacFarlane 2003, Egan, Hawthorne & Weatherson 2005, Swanson 2006, 2008, 2010, and Yalcin 2007 for detailed work in this vein.) Another way to see this is to notice that if epistemically hedged claims *did* express propositions, then there would have to be a function from every way each proposition can be hedged and each proposition to propositions. Intuitively, this function would take a *partial belief*—a particular credence in [0,1] borne to a particular proposition—and yield a proposition that a believer fully believes just in case she has that *partial* belief. We shouldn't take the existence of a function with the appropriate features on faith, and to my knowledge no one has tried to argue that one exists. (Kratzer 1991 develops a treatment of a few 'graded modals,' but I do not see how to generalize her approach very far; cf. article 14 [this volume] (Hacquard) *Modality*.) Showing that there *is* such a function, incidentally, would be a discovery of first importance, since it would show that in representing doxastic uncertainty, at least, the probability space is a mere *façon de parler* that is reducible without loss of expressive power to a set of full beliefs.

The attractive features of probability spaces come with significant prima facie drawbacks, however. In particular, in modeling believers with probability spaces we impute to them a kind of logical omniscience. First, the necessary proposition—thought of in this setting as the proposition true in all the elements of W—is ruled a certainty for any believer. Second, the probability axioms constrain degrees of uncertainty in several substantive ways. For example:

- A believer's credence in the proposition that $\emptyset$ is a function of her credence in the proposition that $\neg \emptyset$ and vice versa: $\mu(A) = 1 - \mu(\bar{A})$;
- A believer's credence in the proposition that $\emptyset$ or ψ is a function of her credence in the propositions that $\emptyset$, that ψ, and that $\emptyset$ and ψ;
- A believer's credence in an entailment of some proposition must be at least as great as her credence in the entailer.

All this appears to have the problematic result that, if doxastic states are accurately modeled by probability spaces, believers believe all the entailments of the things they believe, are certain of the necessary proposition, cannot lend different credences to propositions true in exactly the same possible worlds, and so on. These are analogues of already mentioned problems with non-probabilistic representations of belief using possible worlds propositions (cf. Soames 1987). That is little succor—they are serious problems nevertheless. But I think we should try to solve (or at least mitigate) these problems rather than simply abandoning the probabilistic framework. By way of illustration I now sketch one example of a solution to a prima facie problem for probabilism. The problem can be seen as analogous to closure under entailment—discussed in section 2—but it is for belief instead of desire.

Because probability measures simply need to be defined over the elements of *some* Boolean algebra over W, we can use probability spaces to model doxastic states without assuming that believers are opinionated about every proposition. This feature of probability spaces allows us to use distinct but closely related probability spaces to model 'overlooked' and 'seen' possibilities, thereby affording a treatment of overlooked inferences. One probability space is defined over both those possibilities the believer overlooks and those she sees, measuring her credences with respect to all those possibilities. I call this her *fine credal space*. The other probability space is defined only over those possibilities she sees, representing (for any normal person) a proper subset of the credences represented by her fine credal space. This space characterizes all her credences *except* those borne to any possibilities she overlooks; I call this her *coarse credal space*. The domain of the coarse credal function is a subset of the domain of the fine credal function. Given a probability space P and any subalgebra S of the propositions measured by P, it's easy to show that a function that is defined on exactly the propositions in S and that agrees with P on their values must be a probability measure. So the probability measure of the coarse credal space will agree with the probability measure of the fine credal space with respect to the values assigned to any proposition that is measured by both spaces—the propositions in the algebra of the coarse credal space. A coarse credal space so defined accommodates a fine credal space just as a map accommodates an overlay: a fine credal space might add information about latent dispositions, for example, without conflicting with the 'seen credences' represented by the coarse space.

The assumption that the set of seen possibilities is an algebra makes that set closed under Boolean operations. This imposes constraints on the work that can be done by the formalism: it does not help represent a believer who sees the possibility that ϕ and sees the possibility that ψ but overlooks a possibility yielded by any Boolean operation on the proposition that ϕ and the proposition that ψ. For example, the formalism doesn't help us represent such a believer if she overlooks the possibility that $\neg\phi$, or overlooks the possibility that $\phi \vee \psi$, or overlooks the possibility that $\phi \wedge \psi$, or overlooks the possibility that $\phi \vee \neg\phi$, or .... But for many cases I do not think that this limitation of the framework is implausible or unwelcome. For example, although I crack eggs with one hand, it wasn't until I reflected on how I do it that I came to see the possibility that the right way to crack an egg is with the large end in your palm. (And this despite the fact that I always picked up eggs that way before I realized that I had such a disposition.) But once I saw *that* possibility, I ipso facto saw the possibility that the right way to crack an egg is *not* with the large end in your palm. It's helpful to think of the closure properties of the formalism in this way: each seen possibility imposes a boundary on W, in such a way that any proposition whose boundaries can be defined purely in terms of the boundaries laid down by seen possibilities is itself a seen possibility. To see a possibility, in this sense, is to see a way of distinguishing between possible worlds.

This framework lets us represent believers without imputing full logical omniscience to them, at least in that we can model believers who overlook (certain) entailments and entailers of possibilities they see. For example, suppose that T entails U, and that U entails V. Suppose also that our believer sees the possibilities represented by S, T, and V but overlooks the possibility represented by U. Then the coarse credal space will measure any subset of W that carves W solely along black lines in Fig. 60.1, but will omit those subsets that carve along any gray line. The fine credal space may measure every subset of W.

	T	~T	U	~U	V	~V
S						
~S						

Fig. 16.1: Coarse and fine credal spaces.

The coarse space thus can leave unseen certain entailers and entailments of seen possibilities. This is important because I may see the possibility that my partner castles, for example, while overlooking the possibility that she castles or moves *en passant*. This same formal device reconciles the folk conception of belief, and natural semantics for 'believes,' with closure under entailment: we can say that our fine-grained commitments are closed under entailment, although often we do not *see* all those commitments, and we can say that we *believe* that ø only if we see the possibility that ø. Beyond the closure properties already discussed, the framework puts no unusual constraints on the norms that govern the relationships between overall doxastic states and the possibilities a believer sees and overlooks. Moreover, it allows us to precisely characterize one doxastic change induced by 'might' statements, as I have argued elsewhere (Swanson 2006, 2010; cf. Yalcin 2011): they themselves are often used to 'raise' possibilities, making overlooked possibilities seen without committing the speaker to much else.

To be sure, this formal apparatus does not let us represent believers who 'overlook the necessary proposition,' if such there be. But the formal tools for the representation of credence will doubtless be refined over time. The prima facie problems with our current tools don't give us good reason, on their own, to think that 'probably ø' expresses a proposition, or that 'surmise' and 'doubt' express sui generis intentional attitudes. Of course, there may be other reasons to try to defend such hypotheses. But this section has provided some reasons not to depart too quickly from the 'coarse' individuation conditions for the contents of attitudes that make it possible to represent credence using the tools of probability theory. What of the considerations discussed in sections 3 and 4, which suggested that content must be individuated finely? The next section argues that other phenomena exemplified by attitude ascriptions motivate an approach that solves coreference puzzles compatibly with coarse individuation of content.

6 'Local' presupposition satisfaction: Another puzzle of attitude ascription

Suppose that Ken is blindfolded, and that he is trying to guess who is speaking. We can tell from Ken's guesses that he believes that Louise has spoken once. But we also know that Louise has not spoken—Ken mistakenly thought that someone who sounds like Louise was Louise. That person speaks again, and I say to you

(26) Ken believes that Louise has spoken again.

(26) plainly does not exhibit presupposition failure in this context. But it is not common ground between us that Louise has spoken, and it does not become common ground between us that Louise has spoken. Moreover, (26) *would* exhibit presupposition failure if it weren't common ground between us that Ken thinks Louise has already spoken once. This suggests that, even when embedded in the 'that' clause of a belief ascription, 'again' carries presuppositions—presuppositions that in the conversation as described are satisfied by what we take to be Ken's belief state. The example shows that these presuppositions need not be satisfied by the conversational participants' belief states or the conversational common ground (cf. article 14 [Semantics: Interfaces] (Beaver & Geurts) *Presupposition*).

I want to give a couple more examples to show that this phenomenon is not overly exotic. (See also Stalnaker 1988: 157–158.) Suppose we believe and presuppose that there are no spies at the party. But it's also common ground between us that Hob believes there are several. The people that Hob thinks are spies leave, and I say to you

(27) Hob believes that every spy has left.

(27) does not exhibit presupposition failure in this context. But we might expect that it would, because in simple sentences 'every spy' carries the presupposition that it has a non-empty domain, and it's common ground that it has an empty domain. Fortunately, in the conversation described, the presuppositions carried by 'every spy' are satisfied by what we take to be Hob's belief state.

Or suppose we believe and presuppose that Sue has never smoked, but it's also common ground between us that Tom is convinced that Sue does smoke. Then (28) will not exhibit presupposition failure, even though (29) would.

(28) Tom believes that Sue has quit smoking.

(29) Sue has quit smoking.

In (28), the presuppositions carried by 'quit' can be satisfied by what we take to be Tom's belief state; in (29) they would have to be satisfied by the conversational common ground.

It's easy to create more examples like these:

1. Take an expression 'α' that in simple sentences generally carries the presupposition that ψ.
2. Give an example of a conversation in which it is common ground that $\neg\psi$.
3. Consider a non-negated belief ascription that includes 'α' in its 'that' clause, as used in that conversation.
4. Notice that the belief ascription carries the presupposition that the ascribee believes that ψ.

(Karttunen 1973a, 1973b, 1974 influentially claims that 'A believes that $\emptyset$' always presupposes that A believes that ψ, for any presupposition 'ψ' normally carried by '$\emptyset$'; see Heim 1992 for a recent development of the view. Geurts 1998 offers a battery of arguments against Karttunen's generalization.)

To reiterate, in such examples we have a presupposition that cannot be satisfied by the conversational common ground. It *would* be satisfied by what the conversational participants take to be the ascribee's belief state, for purposes of conversation. And in fact, and very broadly speaking, there is a sense in which it *is* so satisfied. I follow Geurts (1998: 584–585) in classifying this phenomenon as a kind of local accommodation. To say that an expression is *locally accommodated* in this sense is just to say that some or all of its presuppositions are satisfied by something other than the 'basic' or 'global' conversational context (cf. Heim 1983: 254–255).

It is important to note that locally accommodated expressions need not be noun phrases, as we have seen with 'again' and 'quit'. (Karttunen 1968a, 1968b, 1976 are arguably the first serious discussions of local accommodation of noun phrases; the bulk of the literature since then has followed Karttunen in this focus.) My aim is to offer a theory that unifies the behavior of noun phrases and the behavior of other kinds of expressions in attitude ascriptions. Failure to do this, I fear, might tempt us to a theory that looks explanatorily adequate for noun phrases but that turns out, in the end, to be redundant. The guiding ideas of the approach I sketch here are (1) that proper names, demonstratives, and the like are presupposition-carrying expressions, (2) that they exhibit distinctive behavior as a result, and (3) that they thus warrant the treatment we would give to any other presupposition-carrying expression. On this way of approaching attitude ascriptions, the behavior of presupposition-carrying expressions in attitude ascriptions demands a treatment that brings an explanation of coreference puzzles in its wake. By focusing one or two levels higher in the taxonomy of linguistic phenomena than is common in work on attitude ascription—at the level of presupposition carriers rather than the level of proper names or of definite noun phrases—this kind of approach aspires to unify some otherwise seemingly disparate features of attitude ascriptions. (For a view that is in some respects similar to this one, see Stalnaker 1988. Our approaches diverge in several places, and my approach fills in many details where Stalnaker's is neutral, but I won't catalog the differences here.)

It's not immediately obvious how to treat local accommodation in attitude ascriptions. We could try saying that the complement of the attitude ascription is interpreted relative to a single context that is distinct from the conversational context. Or we could say that the complement is interpreted relative to multiple contexts, at least one of which is distinct from the conversational context. On the one-context approach, although the whole sentence (28) is interpreted relative to two contexts, the complement clause "that Sue has quit smoking" is interpreted relative to a *single* context:

(30) [Tom believes]^{c_1} [that Sue has quit smoking]^{c_2}

Heim (1992) takes this kind of approach. On the multiple-context approach, by contrast, the complement clauses of attitude ascriptions can be interpreted relative to, say, the "basic [global] context" and the "derived [local] context," which is the "set of all possible situations that might, for all the speaker presupposes, be compatible with [the addressee's] beliefs" (Stalnaker 1988: 157; see Geurts 1998 for another example of this approach). In principle *both* of these contexts are "available to be exploited" in interpreting the complement clause (Stalnaker 1988: 158).

Multiple-context approaches provide a straightforward treatment of sentences like (31), uttered when Tom is not present and it's common ground that the woman demonstrated has never smoked.

(31) Tom believes that that woman has quit smoking.

In particular, we can say that the global context satisfies the presuppositions of the demonstrative 'that woman,' while the local context satisfies the presuppositions of 'quit.' But one-context approaches can handle this sort of example, too, as long as they give an appropriate story about the content of c_2. Clearly such approaches cannot simply identify c_2 with Stalnaker's local context because c_2 does not satisfy the presuppositions of 'that woman.' But c_2 could be the actual conversational context tweaked just enough so that needed presupposition-satisfying content can come from what we presuppose to be Tom's beliefs: could be, as it were, a 'mix' of Stalnaker's basic (global) and derived (local) contexts. This is in effect just taking what Heim (1983: 254–255) says about local accommodation in general, and applying it to belief ascriptions.

How, then, can we decide between one-context and multiple-context approaches? If our aim were simply to explain how local accommodation in belief ascriptions affects *whether* presupposition failure occurs, then I suspect that there wouldn't be much basis for this decision. But there is good reason to think that local accommodation also can affect *how* an expression in the complement of an attitude ascription is interpreted, and I think that multiple-context approaches do better at accounting for certain cases of this kind.

The hypothesis that local accommodation can affect how expressions are interpreted—henceforth, the *local interpretation hypothesis*—may sound radical. It contravenes Kaplan (1977: 510–511), for example, who influentially insists that "no operator can control the character of the indexicals within its scope," that English does not contain "operators like 'In some contexts it is true that', which attempt to meddle with character" and even that "such operators *could not be added* to English." (He seems to think these claims follow from the hypothesis that "Indexicals, pure and demonstrative alike, are directly referential" (Kaplan 1977: 492).) But Kaplan (1977) himself cites Rich Thomason's "Never put off until tomorrow what you can do today," and Partee (1989: 270) offers many fascinating examples like "In all my travels, whenever I have called for a doctor, one has arrived within an hour." Whether or not these examples are best analyzed as cases of local accommodation, they lend plausibility to the idea that the context relevant to the interpretation of a given expression needn't be the global context. (Cf. article 4 [Semantics: Foundations, History and Methods] (Abbott) *Reference*, article 17 [this volume] (Schlenker) *Indexicality and de se*, and article 12 [Semantics: Interfaces] (Zimmermann) *Context dependency*.)

Moreover, it is theoretically costly to deny the local interpretation hypothesis. We would need strong reasons to resist it, once we countenance local accommodation as part of the explanation of the readings of (26)–(28) already discussed. It is hard to see what those reasons could be.

(26) Ken believes that Louise has spoken again.

(27) Hob believes that every spy has left.

(28) Tom believes that Sue has quit smoking.

On the treatment of these sentences that I sketched earlier, local contexts are sometimes available to satisfy presuppositions carried by expressions in 'that'-clauses. And it is widely accepted that context can affect the interpretation of many expressions. It would be invidious to insist that although a local context is available to a given context sensitive expression, the interpretation of that expression is blind to the local context, influenced only by the global one.

It is also fruitful to endorse the local interpretation hypothesis. Consider the following example. Conversational context plausibly makes a difference to the intension associated with 'best' with respect to at least the two dimensions of the class of contestants and the scale of comparison. In non-embedded environments these two dimensions are obviously both determined by the global conversational context. But embedded environments are more complicated. Suppose Steve evaluates cakes 1 through 5, ranking 1 best, 2 next best, and so on to 5, which he says is worst. Unbeknownst to him, a cake contest is going on, and we know that exactly cakes 3, 4, and 5 are the competitors. But of the cakes in the contest, Steve thinks that cake 3 is the best. Keeping all this in mind, I think there is a reading on which (32) is true:

(32) Steve thinks cake 3 is the best.

This suggests that the global conversational context here determines the class of competitors relevant to the intension of 'best.' Now suppose that it is common ground that Steve is evaluating the cakes on the basis of how light they are—1 is like gossamer, 5 is far too dense—and it's also common ground that flavor is the only relevant scale of comparison for purposes of the contest. If the global conversational context also determined the scale of comparison for 'best,' then (32) would have to attribute to Steve the belief that cake 3 is the best of cakes 3, 4, and 5 *in flavor*. But it has a reading, I think, on which it attributes the belief that cake 3 is the best of the relevant cakes by whatever *Steve's* scale of comparison is.

Phenomena like these threaten to crop up for any expression that is sensitive to context in multiple dimensions. We might analyze (32) in a purely intensional way—as, roughly, "In every world w compatible with Steve's beliefs, cake 3 is the best among the actual class of competitors according to the scale of comparison operative in w," but this treatment is committed to an surprising amount of syntactic complexity in an expression like 'best.' Moreover, I think it is quite odd to insist that although conversational context determines the scale of comparison when 'best' occurs in unembedded environments, it is determined by the binding of intensional variables in cases like (32). Finally, if it's common ground that Steve is evaluating on the basis of texture (although he is in fact evaluating on the basis of density) then I think there's a reading of (32) on which it attributes to him the belief that cake 3 is the best with respect to texture. But the intensional treatment cannot explain this reading, because the scale of comparison, if not determined by the conversational context, can be determined only by Steve's actual beliefs, and not by what we presuppose his beliefs to be.

We can avoid these problems by appealing to local accommodation. For example, on a one-context view we could say that 'cake 3 is the best' is interpreted relative to a single context according to which the class of competitors is cakes 3, 4, and 5, and the scale of comparison is lightness. Or, on one multiple-context view we might say that the class of competitors is determined by the global context, whereas the scale of comparison is determined by the local context. Or, because the local context is given not by Steve's beliefs simpliciter but rather by what the conversational participants *presuppose* to be Steve's beliefs, we might say that the local context determines both the class of competitors and the scale of comparison. On this line, we treat it as true for purposes of conversation that Steve knows something about the contest (by knowing which cakes are the competitors) without pretending that he knows everything we know about it (since 'best' can still be evaluated relative to his scale of comparison). The content of that pretense is the local context. Note that there's nothing remarkable about this local context: it's easy to imagine global conversational contexts in which it's presupposed that cakes 3, 4, and 5 are the competitors and the scale of competition is either left an open question or resolved to features that are not in play in the actual competition. With the flexibility it affords in our explanations of these phenomena, the local interpretation hypothesis looks quite fruitful.

We have not yet considered any cases that will help us decide between one-context and multiple-context approaches to local accommodation. The most compelling such cases are those in which it seems plausible that occurrences of the same expression in an embedded environment get different interpretations. As Stalnaker (1988: 159) notes in passing, his two-context approach can "account for Russell's notorious yacht":

(33) Speaking of Russell's yacht—Moore believes that it is longer than it is.

Very roughly, the idea is that the two occurrences of 'it' in (33) are interpreted relative to different contexts, and the differences between those contexts—the local and global contexts—are such that the two occurrences are interpreted differently. As a result the complement clause as a whole does not express a or the necessarily false proposition. But if, by contrast, the complement clause of (33) is always interpreted relative to a single context, then *whatever* recipe we give for 'mixing' the global and local contexts we will not be able to explain the belief ascription in (33), because both occurrences of 'it' will be interpreted relative to the same context. Similarly for

(34) Pierre doesn't realize that London is London.

By holding that the two occurrences of 'London' have different denotations because they are interpreted relative to relevantly different contexts, we have the beginnings of a story of how (34) can mean that Pierre doesn't realize that some contingent proposition is true. It is very hard to see how to tell such a story on a one-context approach.

In characterizing the effects that context can have on semantic interpretation, it's helpful to treat any given expression—'again,' 'every,' 'quit,' 'best,' 'it,' 'Paderewski,' 'London,' or what have you—as associated not only with an intension or intensions, but also with a *hyperintension*. As I will use the term, the hyperintension of an expression is a relation between contexts and intensions or semantic values. To a first approximation, a context bears the hyperintension of an expression to some intension or intensions just in case, in that context, the expression is best interpreted by those intensions. (Strictly speaking we should be careful not to assume that there are such 'best interpretations,' but the necessary workaround would lead us far afield.) Positing hyperintensions makes it easier to characterize the following hypotheses about the relationship between context, semantics, and linguistic competence:

1. Language users can get by perfectly well without knowing everything there is to know about the hyperintensions of their language's expressions.
2. Much of the knowledge that is relevant to knowing about the features of an expression's hyperintension is both a posteriori and, intuitively, non-linguistic. While one can't be linguistically competent without *some* knowledge of hyperintensions, linguistic competence itself needn't bring much knowledge of hyperintensions. (Cf. Chalmers 2006 and article 6 [Semantics: Theories] (Hobbs) *Word meaning and world knowledge*.)
3. Some contexts may not yield an intension for a given expression. So an expression's hyperintension need not be defined for every possible context.

4. A context may determine more than one intension for a given expression. For example, in a context that does not resolve whether we are talking about color or weight, I claim that 'light suit' has (at least) two semantic values. One is the semantic value that it would have in a context that did resolve that we were talking about color, and the other is the semantic value that it would have in a context that resolved that we were talking about weight. (Intensional functional application can still apply to combinations of *particular* images of contexts under hyperintensions, yielding a proposition for each combination. If context doesn't determine exactly one intension for an expression in a sentence, then in general it won't determine exactly one intension for the sentence, either.)

Kaplan (1977: 495), like many others, allows that directly referential expressions are associated with "semantical rules which determine the referent in each context of use." According to the view I am urging here, hyperintensions simply codify the rules whereby particular intensions come to be the semantic values of expressions in particular contexts. Despite the complexity of typical hyperintensions, the intensions associated with an expression that Kaplan would classify as "directly referential" will, in normal contexts, be simple constant functions. I am bracketing some hard questions about (among other things) which expressions are indexical, the nature of the hyperintensions associated with indexical expressions, and our knowledge of those hyperintensions (cf. article 6 [Semantics: Theories] (Hobbs) *Word meaning and world knowledge*). Those issues to the side, however, I agree with Kaplan (1977: 506, n. 31) that proper names are not associated with a "cognitive content" that fixes their reference in all contexts. More specifically, I agree that competent language users may be ignorant of many features of an expression's hyperintension (points 1 and 2 above) and that hyperintensions needn't fix terms referents in all contexts (points 3 and 4 above).

In dramatic cases of identity confusion, like that described in the background for (34), it's plausible that the contexts provided by local accommodation will determine more than one intension for the relevant locally accommodated expression. (I think that the hypothesis that even in global contexts they sometimes determine more than one intension helps explain anaphoric reference to nonexistent objects, but for present purposes I am not taking a stand on the question.) We also get a better characterization of the content of Pierre's beliefs if we drop the assumption that 'London' in (34) refers, in either of its occurrences, to actual objects: in effect we instead appeal to objects that *would* have been the referent of 'London,' if the world had been different in relevant ways, to characterize Pierre's belief state in an accurate and efficient way. As in the simpler cases considered earlier, we use counterfactual reasoning to determine the relevant features of these hyperintensions: we ask how we would interpret 'London' if the presuppositions we brought to bear on its interpretation were more like some of Pierre's 'London' beliefs. Thus a pair of hyperintensions both of which take the actual conversational context to a constant intension—thereby counting as coreferential and rigid—may take a context introduced by local accommodation to quite different intensions.

It is important to see that a proper name need not *always* be locally accommodated when we presuppose that the ascribee believes that the name has a different referent than we do. Even if it's common ground that Glenda knows Bob Dylan only as her childhood friend Robert Zimmerman, if she thinks he has a beautiful voice then in some contexts (35) seems true.

(35) Glenda believes that Bob Dylan has a beautiful voice. (Saul 1998: 366)

I suggest that in such contexts we see the globally accommodated reading of 'Bob Dylan,' because it is manifest that what the speaker is trying to convey with (35) is that Glenda believes that *a voice with the qualities of Dylan's* is beautiful.

This kind of treatment lets us give a simple, clean treatment of coreferential proper names, demonstratives, pronouns and the like. Names that are coreferential in a context of use have the same constant intension (and so the same referent) in *that* context, but in other contexts may have constant intensions picking out different referents. So while we learn much about the semantics of attitude ascription from coreference puzzles, such puzzles do not force us to complicate the semantics of simple sentences. Moreover, because this treatment of coreference puzzles does not involve Fregean senses or any other 'fine-graining' of content, it is compatible with the probabilistic representations of doxastic states that claims like (25) make attractive.

(25) Clara suspects and Doug doubts that it will rain.

Finally, this treatment unifies two important features of attitude ascription:

1. Names that are coreferential in the *global* context often seem to make different semantic contributions to attitude ascriptions.
2. Presupposition carrying expressions in attitude ascriptions are often interpreted from a point of view more like that of the ascribee that like that of the conversational participants.

I think this account is quite plausible once we think of proper names as just another kind of presupposition-carrying expression, thus warranting the treatment we would give to any other presupposition-carrying expression. The prospects for extending this kind of treatment to discourse anaphora are promising, I think, but extending the approach in that direction must be left for another time.

7 Conclusion

Work on attitude ascription within the philosophical literature has been dominated by the consideration of coreference puzzles. These puzzles are inarguably important: no serious theory of attitude ascription can afford to ignore them. Some aspects of logical omniscience are similarly serious and vexing. Nonetheless, probabilistic language finds a natural home in attitude ascription, as I argued at the beginning of section 5. We must either work within the constraints imposed by the probabilistic representation of doxastic states, or work to loosen those constraints by developing different ways to represent subjective uncertainty.

There is much, much more to say about attitude ascription. I hope to have made the case that sustained interaction between a broad range of researchers—those who most naturally self-identify as working in semantics, pragmatics, philosophy of language, philosophy of mind, and epistemology—will help make future research fruitful.

For helpful discussion thanks to Sarah Moss, Paul Portner, Mark Richard, Bob Stalnaker, and Steve Yablo.

8 References

Asher, Nicholas 1986. Belief in discourse representation theory. *Journal of Philosophical Logic* 15, 127–189.

Brentano, Franz 1874. The distinction between mental and physical phenomena. Translated by D. B. Terrell. In: R. M. Chisholm (ed.). *Realism and the Background of Phenomology*. Atascadero, CA: Ridgeview, 1981, 39–70.

Chalmers, David J. 2006. Two-dimensional semantics. In: E. Lepore & B. C. Smith (eds.). *The Oxford Handbook of Philosophy of Language*. Oxford: Oxford University Press, 574–606.

Chalmers, David J. 2009. *Frege's Puzzle and the Objects of Credence*. Ms. Canberra, Australian National University. http://www.consc.net/papers/credence.pdf, December 20, 2009.

den Dikken, Marcel, Richard Larson & Peter Ludlow 1996. Intensional 'transitive' verbs and concealed complement clauses. *Rivista di Linguistica* 8, 331–348.

den Dikken, Marcel, Richard Larson & Peter Ludlow 1997. *Intensional Transitive Verbs and Abstract Clausal Complementation*. Ms. New York, SUNY Stony Brook. http://semlab5.sbs.sunysb.edu/~rlarson/itv.pdf, September 7, 2009.

Egan, Andy, John Hawthorne & Brian Weatherson 2005. Epistemic modals in context. In: G. Preyer & G. Peter (eds.). *Contextualism in Philosophy: Knowledge, Meaning, and Truth*. Oxford: Oxford University Press, 131–168.
Egan, Andy & Brian Weatherson (eds.) 2009. *Epistemic Modality*. Oxford: Oxford University Press.
Forrester, James W. 1984. Gentle murder, or the adverbial samaritan. *Journal of Philosophy* 81, 193–197.
van Fraassen, Bas C. 1972. The logic of conditional obligation. *Journal of Philosophical Logic* 1, 417–438.
van Fraassen, Bas C. 1973. Values and the heart's command. *Journal of Philosophy* 70, 5–19.
Frege, Gottlob 1892. On *Sinn and Bedeutung*. Translated by M. Black. In: M. Beaney (ed.). *The Frege Reader*. Oxford: Blackwell, 1997, 151–171.
Geurts, Bart 1998. Presuppositions and anaphors in attitude contexts. *Linguistics & Philosophy* 21, 545–601.
Gibbard, Alan 1981. Two recent theories of conditionals. In: W. Harper, R. Stalnaker & G. Pearce (eds.). *Ifs: Conditionals, Belief, Decision, Chance, and Time*. Dordrecht: Reidel, 211–247.
Halpern, Joseph Y. 2003. *Reasoning About Uncertainty*. Cambridge, MA: The MIT Press.
Hansson, Bengt 1969. An analysis of some deontic logics. *Noûs* 3, 373–398.
Heim, Irene 1982. *The Semantics of Definite and Indefinite Noun Phrases*. Ph.D. dissertation. University of Massachusetts, Amherst, MA.
Heim, Irene 1983. On the projection problem for presuppositions. In: P. Portner & B. H. Partee (eds.). *Formal Semantics: The Essential Readings*. Oxford: Blackwell, 249–260.
Heim, Irene 1991. *Articles and Definiteness*. Ms. Cambridge, MA, MIT. Originally published in German as "Artikel und Definitheit" in: A. von Stechow & D. Wunderlich (eds.). *Semantik—Semantics. Ein internationales Handbuch zeitgenössischer Forschung—An International Handbook of Contemporary Research* (HSK 6). Berlin: de Gruyter, 1991, 487–535.
Heim, Irene 1992. Presupposition projection and the semantics of attitude verbs. *Journal of Semantics* 9, 183–221.
Huddleston, Rodney & Geoffrey K. Pullum (eds.) 2002. *The Cambridge Grammar of the English Language*. Cambridge: Cambridge University Press.
Kamp, Hans 1988. Comments on Stalnaker. In: R. H. Grimm & D. D. Merrill (eds.). *Contents of Thought*. Tucson, AZ: University of Arizona Press, 156–181.
Kaplan, David 1977. Demonstratives. In: J. Almog, J. Perry & H. Wettstein (eds.). *Themes from Kaplan*. Oxford: Oxford University Press, 481–563.
Karttunen, Lauri 1968a. *What Do Referential Indices Refer To?* (RAND Paper P-3854). Santa Monica, CA: RAND Corporation. http://www.rand.org/pubs/papers/P3854, September 20, 2009.
Karttunen, Lauri 1968b. *What Makes Definite Noun Phrases Definite?* (RAND Paper P-3871). Santa Monica, CA: RAND Corporation. http://www.rand.org/pubs/papers/P3871, September 20, 2009.
Karttunen, Lauri 1973a. *The Last Word*. Ms. Austin, TX, University of Texas.
Karttunen, Lauri 1973b. Presuppositions of compound sentences. *Linguistic Inquiry* 4, 167–193.
Karttunen, Lauri 1974. Presupposition and linguistic context. *Theoretical Linguistics* 1, 181–194.
Karttunen, Lauri 1976. Discourse referents. In: J. D. McCawley (ed.). *Syntax and Semantics 7: Notes from the Linguistic Underground*. New York: Academic Press, 363–385.
King, Jeffrey C. 1996. Structured propositions and sentence structure. Journal of *Philosophical Logic* 25, 496–521.
King, Jeffrey C. 2007. *The Nature and Structure of Content*. Oxford: Oxford University Press.

Kratzer, Angelika 1991. Modality. In: A. von Stechow & D. Wunderlich (eds.). *Semantik—Semantics. Ein internationales Handbuch zeitgenössischer Forschung—An International Handbook of Contemporary Research* (HSK 6). Berlin: de Gruyter, 639–650.
Kripke, Saul 1979. A puzzle about belief. In: P. Ludlow (ed.). *Readings in the Philosophy of Language.* Cambridge, MA: The MIT Press, 875–920.
Kripke, Saul 1980. *Naming and Necessity.* Cambridge, MA: Harvard University Press.
Larson, Richard K. & Peter Ludlow 1993. Interpreted logical forms. In: P. Ludlow (ed.). *Readings in the Philosophy of Language.* Cambridge, MA: The MIT Press, 993–1038.
Lewis, David K. 1973. *Counterfactuals.* Malden, MA: Blackwell.
Lewis, David K. 1976. Probabilities of conditionals and conditional probabilities. *The Philosophical Review* 85, 297–315.
Lewis, David K. 1981a. Ordering semantics and premise semantics for counterfactuals. *Journal of Philosophical Logic* 10, 217–234. Reprinted in: D. K. Lewis. *Papers in Philosophical Logic.* Cambridge: Cambridge University Press, 1998, 77–96.
Lewis, David K. 1981b. What puzzling Pierre does not believe. *The Australasian Journal of Philosophy* 59, 283-289. Reprinted in: D. K. Lewis. *Papers in Metaphysics and Epistemology.* Cambridge: Cambridge University Press, 1999, 408–417.
MacFarlane, John 2003. *Epistemic Modalities and Relative Truth.* Ms. Berkeley, CA, University of California. http://johnmacfarlane.net/epistemod-2003.pdf, September 20, 2009.
McCawley, James D. 1974. On identifying the remains of deceased clauses. *Language Research* 9, 73–85.
Montague, Michelle 2007. Against propositionalism. *Noûs* 41, 503–518.
Partee, Barbara H. 1989. Binding implicit variables in quantified contexts. In: C. Wiltshire, B. Music & R. Graczyk (eds.). *Papers from the Regional Meeting of the Chicago Linguistic Society 25.* Chicago, IL: Chicago Linguistic Society, 342–365. Reprinted in: B. H. Partee. *Compositionality in Formal Semantics.* Oxford: Blackwell, 2004, 259–281.
Portner, Paul & Barbara H. Partee (eds.) 2002. *Formal Semantics: The Essential Readings.* Oxford: Blackwell.
Prior, Arthur N. 1958. Escapism: The logical basis of ethics. In: A. I. Melden (ed.). *Essays in Moral Philosophy.* Seattle, WA: University of Washington Press, 135–146.
Quine, Willard van Orman 1956. Quantifiers and propositional attitudes. *Journal of Philosophy* 53, 177–187.
Richard, Mark 1983. Direct reference and ascriptions of belief. *Journal of Philosophical Logic* 12, 425–452.
Ross, John R. 1976. To have have and not to have have. In: M. Jazayery, E. Polomé & W. Winter (eds.). *Linguistic and Literary Studies in Honor of Archibald A. Hill.* Lisse: Peter de Ridder, 263–270.
Russell, Bertrand 1905. On denoting. *Mind* 14, 479–493. Reprinted in: G. Ostertag (ed.). *Definite Descriptions: A Reader.* Cambridge, MA: The MIT Press, 1998, 35–49.
Russell, Bertrand 1919. Descriptions. In: B. Russell. *Introduction to Mathematical Philosophy.* London: Allen and Unwin, 167–180. Reprinted in: P. Ludlow (ed.). *Readings in the Philosophy of Language.* Cambridge, MA: The MIT Press, 1997, 323–334.
Salmon, Nathan 1986. *Frege's Puzzle.* Cambridge, MA: The MIT Press.
Saul, Jennifer 1998. The pragmatics of attitude ascription. *Philosophical Studies* 92, 363–389.
Scheffler, Israel 1955. On synonymy and indirect discourse. *Philosophy of Science* 22, 39–44.
Searle, John 1958. Proper names. *Mind* 67, 166–173.

Soames, Scott 1987. Direct reference, propositional attitudes, and semantic content. In: N. Salmon & S. Soames (eds.). *Propositions and Attitudes*. Oxford: Oxford University Press, 197–239.

Soames, Scott 2002. *Beyond Rigidity: The Unfinished Semantic Agenda of Naming and Necessity*. Oxford: Oxford University Press.

Stalnaker, Robert C. 1974. Pragmatic presuppositions. In: M. Munitz & P. Unger (eds.). *Semantics and Philosophy*. New York: New York University Press, 197–213. Reprinted in: R. C. Stalnaker. *Context and Content*. Oxford: Oxford University Press, 1999, 47–62.

Stalnaker, Robert C. 1984. *Inquiry*. Cambridge, MA: The MIT Press.

Stalnaker, Robert C. 1988. Belief attribution and context. In: R. H. Grimm & D. D. Merrill (eds.). *Contents of Thought*. Tucson, AZ: University of Arizona Press, 140–156. Reprinted in: R. C. Stalnaker. *Context and Content*. Oxford: Oxford University Press, 1999, 150–166.

Stalnaker, Robert C. 1991. The problem of logical omniscience, I. *Synthese* 89, 425–440. Reprinted in: R. C. Stalnaker. *Context and Content*. Oxford: Oxford University Press, 1999, 241–254.

Stalnaker, Robert C. 1996. Impossibilities. *Philosophical Topics* 24, 193–204.

Stalnaker, Robert C. 1998. On the representation of context. *Journal of Logic, Language and Information* 7, 3–19. Reprinted in: R. C. Stalnaker. *Context and Content*. Oxford: Oxford University Press, 1999, 96–113.

Stalnaker, Robert C. 1999a. *Context and Content*. Oxford: Oxford University Press.

Stalnaker, Robert C. 1999b. The problem of logical omniscience, II. In: R. C. Stalnaker. *Context and Content*. Oxford: Oxford University Press, 255–273.

Stanley, Jason 1997. Names and rigid designation. In: B. Hale & C. Wright (eds.). *A Companion to the Philosophy of Language*. Oxford: Blackwell, 555–585.

Swanson, Eric 2006. *Interactions with Context*. Ph.D. dissertation. MIT, Cambridge, MA.

Swanson, Eric 2008. Modality in language. *Philosophy Compass* 3, 1193–1207.

Swanson, Eric 2010. How not to theorize about language of subjective uncertainty. In: A. Egan & B. Weatherson (eds.). *Epistemic Modality*. Oxford: Oxford University Press.

Thau, Michael 2002. *Consciousness and Cognition*. Oxford: Oxford University Press.

Yalcin, Seth 2007. Epistemic modals. *Mind* 116, 983–1026.

Yalcin, Seth 2011. Nonfactualism about epistemic modality. In B. Weatherson & A. Egan (eds.), *Epistemic Modality*. Oxford: Oxford University Press, 295–332.

Philippe Schlenker
17 Indexicality and *De Se* reports

1   Kaplan's theory of indexicality —— 562
2   *De Se* readings —— 577
3   Monsters and shifted indexicals —— 586
4   Logophoric pronouns —— 601
5   *De Se* readings and logophoric expressions in other domains —— 605
6   Bicontextualism —— 608
7   References —— 613

Abstract: Indexicals are context-dependent expressions such as I, you, here and now, whose semantic value is determined by the context in which they are uttered (e.g., I denotes John if uttered by John, and Mary if uttered by Mary). In English, these expressions typically depend on the actual context of speech, i.e. the context in which they are in fact uttered. In other languages, however, some indexicals may depend on the context of a reported speech act, so that what is literally John says that I am a hero may mean that John says that he, John, is a hero; in such cases, we say that the indexical is 'shifted' because it is evaluated with respect to a context that is different from the context of the actual utterance. In yet other languages, there are dedicated expressions for this reported use, with a pronoun he* that can only appear in indirect discourse; these 'logophoric expressions' can, at least as a first approximation, be analyzed as indexicals that are obligatorily shifted. This chapter provides an overview of the semantics of indexical and logophoric expressions, with special reference to recent theoretical and cross-linguistic analyses.

1 Kaplan's theory of indexicality

The modern theory of indexicality owes much to philosophers of language, who were interested in the foundations of semantics, and more specifically in the general form of the procedure by which sentences are interpreted. The standard theory, due to David Kaplan, has three main tenets (Kaplan 1977/1989, 1978).

Philippe Schlenker, Paris (France) and New York (USA)

https://doi.org/10.1515/9783110589443-017

(i) The interpretation function, henceforth written as $[\![\,.\,]\!]$, must be relativized to a context parameter *in addition* to the other parameters (e.g., time, world, assignment function) which are independently necessary for the analysis of non-indexical expressions.

(ii) Contexts are ontologically distinct from other parameters; in particular, they are strictly more fine-grained than individuals, times or possible worlds. In fact, it is often helpful to think of a context c as a triple of the form $<c_a, c_t, c_w>$, where c_a, c_t and c_w are respectively the agent (also called 'speaker' or 'author'), the time and the world of c (for some applications it is useful to add a hearer coordinate c_h or a location coordinate c_l).

(iii) Unlike other parameters, which can typically be 'manipulated' by various operators, the context parameter remains fixed throughout the evaluation of a sentence. Purported operators that violate this condition are called 'monsters', and are claimed by Kaplan not to exist in natural language (though they can easily be defined in a formal language).

(i) is generally accepted. But (ii) and (iii) need not be.

Let us first consider (ii). Some authors (e.g., Stalnaker 1981, 1999; von Stechow & Zimmermann 2005) have attempted to develop theories of indexicality in which contexts are ontologically on a par with some other parameter—in Stalnaker's case, the world parameter. A similar decision may also appear natural if one adopts an event- or situation-semantics, since the speech act is certainly an event or a situation of a particular sort. When such a move is made, any discussion of context dependency must provide an *independent* criterion for determining which parameter 'counts' as the context, on pain of causing endless terminological confusion.

This, in turn, has consequences for (iii): if there is no ontological difference between the context and other parameters, one may be tempted to *define* the context to be that parameter (if there is one) which cannot be manipulated by any operator. This move turns (iii) into a truth by definition (see for instance Lewis 1980 and Zimmermann 1991 for such a view). By contrast, Kaplan took (iii) to be a substantive empirical claim. Any definitional move is of course admissible, but only confusion will result if various definitions are mixed without proper warning. In the rest of this paper, we adopt (i) and (ii) (taking contexts to be ontologically distinct from times and worlds), and we submit (iii) to closer empirical and formal scrutiny.

Kaplan's "prohibition against monsters" was primarily motivated by a philosophical thesis, according to which *indexicals are directly referential*. This view should be understood by opposition to the Fregean view of meaning, which encompasses two claims: (a) all linguistic expressions—including indexicals—refer to objects *indirectly*, by virtue of a 'sense' (= *Sinn*), and (b) an expression found in indirect discourse does not refer to its standard denotation (= *Bedeutung*) but rather to its sense (= *Sinn*). If (b) held of all expressions, including indexicals, one would expect that in indirect discourse these may fail to have their usual denotation—so that *John said that I am stupid* might attribute to John a claim about John himself rather than about me, the speaker. In Kaplan's technical framework, this would mean that attitude verbs are 'monsters', which he denied on the basis of English data. He thus took his thesis of direct reference to have not just conceptual but also empirical motivation. As we will see, the latter can be challenged. We start by reconstructing Kaplan's formal analysis, leaving aside the philosophical issue of direct reference; we then subject it to closer empirical scrutiny (see Zimmermann 1991 for a more thorough survey of Kaplanian semantics).

1.1 Context vs. index

We begin with an informal characterization of a *context* as a speech situation, which should minimally specify who is talking, at what time and in what possible world; in many cases we will also need to specify who the addressee is. Contexts may be taken to be primitive, in which case one must define various functions that return the agent [= speaker], hearer [= addressee], location, time and world of a context c, henceforth written as c_a, c_h, c_l, c_t and c_w. Alternatively, contexts may be identified with tuples of the form <speaker, (addressee), time of utterance, world of utterance, etc>. The speaker, addressee, time and world of the context are sometimes called its 'coordinates'.

1.1.1 Contexts and other parameters

Why couldn't we treat indexical expressions as constants—which would endow them with the behavior of, say, proper names as standardly analyzed? First, the value of indexicals is far less stable than that of proper names: the speaker and addressee normally use a proper name to refer to the same individual, but this is certainly not the case of the expression *I*. Second, analyzing indexicals as constants would miss something important about the *cognitive* role they play. Kaplan was especially interested in two types of cases: sentences which are in some sense *a priori* true, although one would not want to say that they are necessarily true; and examples in which the cognitive significance of a statement does not just encompass information about the world, but also about where in the world the speaker is—or in other words, in which context the speaker is located.

Consider the sentences in (1):

(1) a. I am here now.
     b. I exist.

Without knowing anything about the world, we can determine that these sentences must be true; they are in that sense *a priori* true. Yet they do not have the form of logical tautologies; the presence of indexicals is crucial to obtain this kind of *a priori* truth, as can be seen if we replace *I*, *here* and *now* in (1) with *John*, *New York*, and *Wednesday, April 9, 2008* respectively (the resulting statement cannot be determined to be true unless one knows something about the world).

The opposite situation also occurs: one may know everything there is to know about the world, and yet fail to know the value of a sentence containing indexicals. This may happen if the speaker knows in which world he is, but not in which context he is—in other words, he does not know *where* in the world he is located (note that this situation is formally conceivable since contexts are strictly more fine-grained than possible worlds). An example is provided by John Perry and further elaborated by David Lewis:

> An amnesiac, Rudolf Lingens, is lost in the Stanford library. He reads a number of things in the library, including a biography of himself, and a detailed account of the library in which he is lost... He still won't know who he is, and where he is, no matter how much knowledge he piles up, until that moment when he is ready to say, "*This* place is aisle five, floor six, of Main Library, Stanford. *I* am Rudolf Lingens."
>
> (Perry 1993: 21)

Lewis comments:

> It seems that the Stanford library has plenty of books, but no helpful little maps with a dot marked "location of this map." Book learning will help Lingens locate himself in logical space. (...) But none of this, by itself, can guarantee that he knows where in the world he is. He needs to locate himself not only in logical space but also in ordinary space.
>
> (Lewis 1983: 138)

In Perry's scenario, Lingens is certainly in a position to say *Lingens is <at time t> in the Stanford Library*, but not *I am <at time t / now> in the Stanford Library*. The first person pronoun is in this case an 'essential indexical' because it cannot be replaced with any non-indexical expression if its cognitive content is to be preserved.

The first observation suggests that an adequate characterization of *a priori* knowledge should be given in terms of *truth in all conceivable contexts* (we come back to the term 'conceivable' below):

(2) A sentence S is a priori true if and only if for each conceivable context c, S is true in c.

The second observation suggests than an adequate characterization of belief (the psychological attitude, not the semantic relation denoted by the verb *believe*) should involve contexts as well. Taking a hint from the tradition of epistemic logic, we can say that an agent—say Lingens—believes a sentence S just in case for each context c *compatible with Lingens's belief*, S is true in c.

At this point, it may be tempting to try to do everything with a single parameter, the context parameter. This won't work, however. Following the tradition of modal logic, we may analyze the semantics of *necessarily* in terms of a modal parameter p:

(3) $[\![$necessarily F$]\!]^p$ = true if and only if for every p' [which stands in a predetermined relation to p], $[\![$F$]\!]^{p'}$ = true.

Now let us suppose that the parameter *p* is just the context parameter. We just saw that *I exist* is *a priori* true. This means that for every conceivable context c', $[\![$I exist$]\!]^{c'}$ = true. But then it follows that the sentence *I necessarily exist* is true as well! Similarly for: *I couldn't fail to exist*, and any number of more felicitous paraphrases of the philosopher's semi-technical jargon. Necessary existence is, at best, a property of God, but certainly not one that any ordinary speaker enjoys; the analysis has gone awry.

The error, Kaplan suggests, is to take modal operators such as *necessarily* to manipulate the context parameter. If we introduce a distinction between a world parameter and a (strictly more finely individuated) context parameter, we will be able to have our cake and eat it too on condition *I* is evaluated with respect to the context parameter, while *exist* is evaluated with respect to the world parameter:

(4) a. $[\![$I$]\!]^{c, w} = c_a$
    b. $[\![$exist$]\!]^{c, w}$(d) = true if and only if d exists in w.

Before we come to the derivation of the desired truth conditions, we must make two further assumptions.

Assumption 1. In accordance with the intuitive characterization we provided above, contexts should be *possible* speech situations (or for some applications:

possible speech *or thought* situations). As a result, the coordinates of a context must satisfy certain constraints of coherence, in particular those in (5):

(5) For any context c, the agent of c exists at the world of c; more generally, the agent of c is at the location of c at the time of c and in the world of c.

Assumption 2. When we evaluate a root sentence F pronounced in a context c, we assess its truth value by taking the context parameter to be c *and the world parameter to be the world of c*.

Our earlier observations can now be made compatible (we abbreviate 'if and only if' by 'iff').

(i) *I exist* is *a priori* true because in any context c, $[\![I\ exist]\!]^{c,\ c_w} = [\![exist]\!]^{c,\ c_w}([\![I]\!]^{c,\ c_w}) = [\![exist]\!]^{c,\ c_w}(c_a) =$ true iff c_a exists at c_w. But by (5), the latter condition is always satisfied.

(ii) Still, *I necessarily exist* need not be true: $[\![necessarily\ I\ exist]\!]^{c,\ c_w} =$ true, iff for every w' [which stands in a pre-determined relation to c_w], $[\![I\ exist]\!]^{c,\ w'} =$ true, iff for every w' [which stands in a pre-determined relation to c_w], $[\![exist]\!]^{c,\ w'}(c_a) =$ true, iff for every w' [which stands in a pre-determined relation to c_w], c_a exists in w'.

But of course w' need not be the world of c—and hence we correctly predict that the sentence need not be true.

Once this simplified framework is in place, we can add further parameters—in particular a time parameter t, and an assignment function s, which will provide a value for individual variables. We can then treat more complex examples by positing appropriate lexical rules; for instance, *now* can be analyzed as an indexical operator, which 'replaces' the time of evaluation t with the time coordinate of the context, c_t:

(6) $[\![now\ F]\!]^{c,\ t,\ w} = [\![F]\!]^{c,\ c_t,\ w}$

In the tradition of modal logic, past and future tenses can be treated as existential temporal operators, which quantify over moments that precede or follow the time of evaluation. One usually makes the further assumption that the present tense is either morphologically absent or that it remains uninterpreted, so that it leaves the time parameter unmodified.

(7) a. $[\![PAST\ F]\!]^{c,\ t,\ w} =$ true iff for some t' < t, $[\![F]\!]^{c,\ t',\ w} =$ true
    b. $[\![FUT\ F]\!]^{c,\ t,\ w} =$ true iff for some t' > t, $[\![F]\!]^{c,\ t',\ w} =$ true

(Further operators could be defined along similar lines—for instance *some day* or *everyday* could be treated as operators that quantify over days, following the model of (7).)

Normally, a tense operator shifts the time of evaluation of every expression that appears in its scope. However, thanks to the *now* operator, the time parameter may be shifted back to the time of the context of utterance. Thus in (8a), analyzed for simplicity as (8a′), the *now* operator makes it possible for the definite description to denote the person who is the president *at the time of utterance* (in the derivation of the truth conditions, we assume that at all times there is exactly one president):

(8) a. John will mourn the person who is now president.
    a′. FUT John mourn the now president
    b. $[\![(a')]\!]^{c, t, w}$ = true iff for some $t' > t$, $[\![$ John mourn the now president $]\!]^{c, t', w}$ = true,
iff for some $t' > t$, John mourns at t' in w $[\![$the now president$]\!]^{c, t', w}$,
iff for some $t' > t$, John mourns at t' in w the one and only person d such that $[\![$now president$]\!]^{c, t', w}(d)$ = true,
iff for some $t' > t$, John mourns at t' in w the one and only person d such that $[\![$president$]\!]^{c, c_t, w}(d)$ = true,
iff for some $t' > t$, John mourns at t' in w the one and only person d that is president *at c_t* in w.

In this case, the same reading could be obtained by moving the definite description out of the scope of the tense operator (with the Logical Form: *[the president] λx FUT John mourn x*). But in other cases, as in (9), this operation is syntactically implausible, or it does not suffice to yield the desired results, or both.

(9) Some day, it will be the case that every person now studying with John will be on the editorial board of *Linguistic Inquiry*.

It can be checked that *it will be the case that* is a scope island, and furthermore that the truth conditions of the sentence require that the quantifier *every person now studying with John* be in the scope of the existential time operator *some day*. Still, it is essential that *now studying* be evaluated with respect to the time of utterance. The semantics we have given for the *now* operator (similar to Kamp 1971) makes this easy to achieve.

Entirely parallel arguments can be made in the world domain with respect to an analogous 'actually' operator, whose semantics is defined as follows:

(10) 　⟦actually F⟧$^{c, t, w}$ = ⟦F⟧$^{c, t, c_w}$

All the readings available in the temporal case can be replicated in the modal case. There is one peculiarity, however: contrary to what is often assumed, the word *actually* does not display the behavior of a *bona fide* indexical—when embedded under other modal quantifiers it gives rise to many more ambiguities than a world indexical would (Cresswell 1990) (the apparent absence of world indexicals does not follow from the present framework).

Let us make two further remarks for future reference; they apply to temporal and modal talk alike, but for simplicity we restrict attention to the temporal case.

(i) When the word *now* is dropped from (9), we obtain an ambiguous sentence: *person who is studying with John* can be understood either as *person studying with John at the future time* under consideration, or *person studying with John at the present time*. The first reading is predicted by our modal analysis (since the present tense has no semantics), but the second is not. Here it appears that we have more readings than the modal analysis predicts; in fact, the present tense displays in this case the behavior of a variable, which may be bound (by *some day*) or left free—which gives rise to distinct readings.

(ii) When (9) is embedded under further operators, more complicated readings are obtained if *now* is replaced with *then*—or is just omitted. Thus in (11) *then* is dependent on *each year*, even though the quantifier *all of the students then studying with him* is in the scope of the time operator *some day*.

(11) Each year, it was clear to John that, some day, all of the students <then> studying with him would be on the Editorial Board of *Linguistic Inquiry*.

The *now* operator won't help us in this case, because *then* doesn't refer to the time of utterance, but rather displays the behavior of a variable bound by the time quantifier *each year*.

The difficulties in (i) and (ii) (as well as their counterparts in the world domain) have often been taken to suggest that temporal and modal talk might in the end involve resources that are as rich as object talk—and in particular that despite initial appearances there are temporal and modal pronouns, as well as quantifiers (see Cresswell 1990 for a detailed discussion of these problems). This point will matter in Section 3.2.1 when we discuss the precise nature of monsters (should they be 'modal' or 'quantificational'?).

1.1.2 *Character vs. content*

The interpretation function as we have analyzed it is characterized by the simultaneous presence of several parameters, which are manipulated by different expressions. In the literature, one often presents things as if the interpretation function took its context and its world arguments in a particular order. The idea is that an expression is first evaluated with respect to a context, which yields the *semantic content* of that expression. One then feeds a world of evaluation to this content to obtain the value of the expression. In this *façon de parler*, the meaning of an expression, called by Kaplan a 'character', is a function from contexts to contents; and a content is just a function from worlds (or world-time pairs) to objects (which may be truth values).

(12)   Character and Content

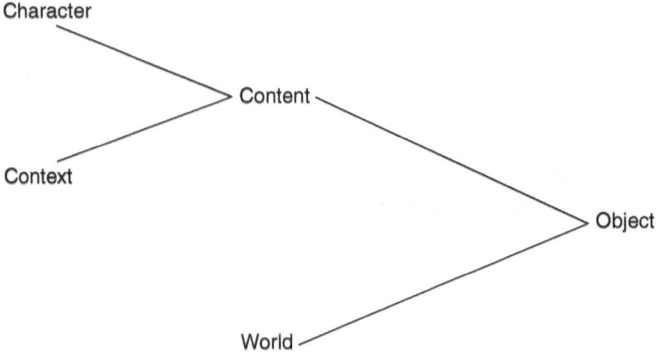

In this picture, what provides the cognitive significance of an expression is, as a first approximation, its *character*: it is because 'Lingens is at Stanford' and 'I am at Stanford' have different characters that Lingens can believe the former (because he has complete knowledge of the world he is in) without thereby believing the latter (because he does not know in which context he is located). By contrast, what provides the closest Kaplanian equivalent of Frege's notion of sense is the *content* of the sentence. The prohibition against monsters entails that modal operators may only be sensitive to the content of an expression, not to its full character (more precisely: any operator Op that is not monstrous guarantees that if F and F' have the same content but possibly different characters in a context c, $Op\ F$ and $Op\ F'$ have the same value when evaluated in c). To take an example, on the assumption that the proper name *Lingens* is rigid and thus denotes the same individual in all possible worlds, the character of the sentence S = *I am Lingens* can be characterized as follows (for simplicity, we leave out time dependency):

(13) Character(S) = λc λw [c_a = Lingens]

Similarly, the character of S' = *I am here* is the following:

(14) Character(S') = λc λw [c_a is at c_l in w]

On the assumption that c* is a context whose agent is Lingens and that he is at Stanford, the content of S and S' is:

(15) Content(S) = Character(S)(c*) = [λc λw c_a = Lingens](c*) = λw [Lingens = Lingens].

(16) Content(S') = Character(S')(c*) = [λc λw c_a is at c_l in w](c*) = λw [Lingens is at c^*_l in w].

In the tradition of epistemic logic, we take an individual to believe a proposition just in case *each of the worlds w' compatible with his beliefs is one that makes that proposition true*. Applying this strategy to the contents of S and S', we see that x believes the content of S just in case each of the worlds w' compatible with x's beliefs guarantees that [λw Lingens = Lingens](w') = true, which is of course always the case. So the content of S is one that anyone should believe. But things are different with S': x believes the content of S' just in case each of the worlds w' compatible with x's beliefs guarantees that [λw Lingens is at c^*_l in w](w') = true, or in other words that Lingens is at c^*_l in w'—which is by no means trivial. In other words: the content of S of trivial, but that of S' isn't (in Perry's example, it is only because Lingens has read all the books and has perfect non-indexical knowledge that he knows that Lingens is at Stanford).

When we turn to the characters of these sentences, however, the situation is reversed: the character of S is non-trivial, whereas the character of S' is. But before we can make this point clear, we must ask *what it means to believe a character* in the first place. A common assumption—though not one that Kaplan himself endorses—is that an individual i believes a character χ just in case *each of the contexts c compatible with what i believes guarantees that χ(c)(c_w) = true* (Haas-Spohn 1995); in other words, for each such context c, the character χ evaluated at that context *and at the world of that context* returns the value 'true'. This certainly makes intuitive sense: in essence, Lingens believes the character of S just in case each context compatible with his beliefs is one in which S is true in the sense of Assumption 2 of Section 1.1.1. This immediately derives the result that the character of S' is trivial while that of S isn't:

- Lingens believes the character of S (= *I am Lingens*) just in case every context c' compatible with his beliefs is one that guarantees that $[\lambda c\, \lambda w\, c_a = \text{Lingens}](c')(c'_w)$ = true, i.e. that c'_a = Lingens. But this is precisely the kind of knowledge that Lingens *lacks*, so the character of S is certainly not one that Lingens believes.
- Lingens believes the character of S' (= *I am here*) just in case every context c' compatible with his beliefs is one that guarantees that $[\lambda c\, \lambda w\, c_a \text{ is at } c_l \text{ in } w]$ $(c')(c'_w)$ = true, i.e. that c'_a is at c'_l in c'_w. But by definition of a context, this *is* trivial, and so everyone—including Lingens, despite his amnesia—believes the character of S'.

The same analysis carries over to a vivid example discussed by Kaplan. If David sees in the mirror someone that he doesn't recognize, but who happens to be David himself, there will be a considerable cognitive difference depending on whether he thinks *My pants are on fire* or *His pants are on fire*. Both sentences have the same content—they make the same claim about the world, namely that David's pants are on fire. But they have very different characters, which accounts for the cognitive difference between them.

Interestingly, in order to determine whether an individual does or does not believe a character χ, we need not have access to *all* of χ; rather, all that matters is what χ does to pairs of arguments of the form $<c, c_w>$ for any context c. In other words, all we need to have access to is the *diagonal* of the character χ, defined as follows:

(17) $\delta(\chi) = \lambda c\, \chi(c)(c_w)$

If χ is the character of a clause, the diagonal of χ can be identified with a set of contexts. And the analysis of belief as a relation between an individual and the diagonal of a character is *exactly* the traditional notion of belief inherited from epistemic logic, with the only difference that possible worlds are now replaced with a strictly more fine-grained type of entity, contexts.

1.1.3 Proper vs. improper contexts

Kaplan's analysis of *a priori* truth crucially depends on certain constraints on possible contexts; in particular, as was mentioned in (5), the agent of a context must by definition be at the location of the context at the time and in the world of the context (this is what guarantees that *I am here now* or *I exist* are *a priori* true). But this constraint might in some cases be too strong (Predelli 1998), for instance if (18) is heard on an answering machine:

(18) I am not here right now. Please leave a message after the tone.

Predelli suggests that one should countenance *improper contexts* to solve the problem—where a context is taken to be improper in case it violates Assumption 1 above (in Predelli's example, the speaker may *fail* to be at the location of the context in the world of the context). This certainly makes very good sense; but when one adopts this measure, one immediately loses Kaplan's result that *I am here now* should be *a priori* (and for him *logically*) true. In order to regain Kaplan's result, we must define a notion of *a priori* knowledge that does not make reference to *all* contexts, but only to *proper* ones.

1.2 The prohibition against monsters and indirect discourse

At this point there is nothing in our analysis to block the existence of operators that manipulate the context parameter—just like tense and modal operators manipulate the time and world parameters respectively. In fact, if the diagonal operator we defined above were made part of the *object* language, it would be precisely a Kaplanian monster. To define it in full generality within a semantics with time and world parameters, as well as individual variables, we posit the lexical rule in (19) (c is a context, s is an assignment function, t is a time parameter, and w is a world parameter):

(19) $[\![\delta\ F]\!]^{c,\,s,\,t,\,w} = \lambda c'\ [\![F]\!]^{c',\,s,\,t,\,c'_w}$

(If contents are analyzed as functions from world-time pairs (rather than worlds) to truth values, it is more natural to define the diagonal operator in such that a way that it also shifts the time parameter, i.e. as $[\![d\ F]\!]^{c,\,s,\,t,\,w} = \lambda c'\ [\![F]\!]^{c',\,s,\,c'_t,\,c'_w}$.)

It is immediate that any indexical that is caught in the scope of the object-language operator δ will be evaluated under a possibly non-actual context c', for various values of c'. In this case, our operator simultaneously shifts the context and the world parameters (and in the alternative definition also the time parameter); but only the context-shifting part is crucial to make it a Kaplanian monster.

Given that that δ is used so naturally in the meta-language to describe people's *attitudes*, one might expect that natural language makes use of something like this operator in the semantics of attitude *reports*. So why does Kaplan claim that such operators do not exist in natural language? Initially, there appears to be overwhelming empirical evidence for this conclusion: in English, it is difficult to find operators that can shift the context with respect to which indexicals are evaluated. This is most easily seen by contrasting the semantic behavior of *I* with that of the definite description *the person talking* which, unlike the former, depends on the time and world of evaluation rather than on the context of utterance:

(20) a. At some point, the person talking was tired.
 ⇒ need not be a claim about the speaker
 b. At some point, I was tired.
 ⇒ must be a claim about the speaker.

Now it could be argued that the operator or quantifier *at some point* is just not the right expression to shift the context parameter. But Kaplan argues that similar facts obtain with other operators, which suggests that such a shift simply cannot be effected:

(21) a. In some contexts / speech situations, the person talking was tired.
 ⇒ need not be a claim about the speaker
 b. In some contexts / speech situations, I was tired.
 ⇒ must be a claim about the speaker.

Taking a hint from our analysis of attitudes a few paragraphs back, we could hope that attitude verbs might be more successful context shifters; but initial evidence suggests the contrary:

(22) John believes / claims that I am tired.
 ⇒ must make a claim about the speaker, not about John.

Arguably there are cases in which *I* can be used with a shifted reading, in particular in newspaper articles:

(23) Mr Greenspan said he agreed with Labor Secretary R.B. Reich "on quite a lot of things". Their accord on this issue, he said, has proved "quite a surprise to both of us."

(Cappelen & Lepore 1997)

But such examples might be better analyzed as instances of partial quotation, whose use is justified by considerable pragmatic pressure: it is very important for a journalist to quote the person's precise words in order to be accurate, even if this is done at the expense of the grammar of natural language (see Anand 2006 for a more detailed discussion of partial quotation in this context).

We will see shortly that *some* attitude operators can be found which can shift the context parameter in much more ordinary contexts. Before we get there, however, we should say a word about the standard view of indirect discourse.

– The first observation is that *attitude reports appear to be strictly less fine-grained than attitudes are*. As we observed before, there is an important difference between thinking *My pants are on fire* or *His pants are on fire*, even in case both possessive pronouns refer to the same individual. Still, in indirect discourse both situations can be reported by saying: *John thinks that his pants are on fire* (where *his* refers to John):

(24) John thinks: 'My pants are on fire'

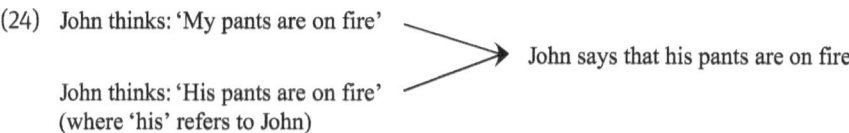

John says that his pants are on fire

John thinks: 'His pants are on fire'
(where 'his' refers to John)

– Kaplan accounts for this observation by positing a semantics in which *John thinks that his pants are on fire* is true just in case there is *some* character which John asserts, and whose content in the context of John's thought act is that John's pants are on fire (we disregard time dependency):

(25) *John says that his pants are on fire* (where *his* denotes John) is true in world w* iff there is a character χ such that:
  (i) the content of χ given the context of John's speech act (call it c) is that John's pants are on fire: $\chi(c) = \lambda w$ John's pants are on fire in w, and
  (ii) John asserts χ in w*.

There are two ways in which this analysis could be extended: first, it could presumably be applied to other attitude verbs, such as *believe*, rather than just to verbs of saying; second, one may wish to give a reductive analysis of what it means to 'assert' or to 'believe' a character, using the diagonal operator defined above. Applied to belief reports, this extension leads to the following analysis:

(26) *John believes that his pants are on fire* (where *his* denotes John) is true (at time t* in world w*) iff there is a character χ such that:
  (i) the content of χ given the context of John's thought act (call it c) is that John's pants are on fire: $\chi(c) = \lambda w$ John's pants are on fire in w, and
  (ii) for each context c' compatible with John's belief in w*, $[\delta(\chi)](c') = $ true, i.e. $\chi(c')(c'_w) = $ true.

As von Stechow & Zimmermann (2005) show (following Crimmins 1998), this semantics makes the unfortunate prediction that *John believes that his pants are on fire* should be true as soon as John's pants really are on fire. Consider (27), calling its character χ* (where *actually* has the semantics defined above):

(27) It is either not so that John's pants are actually on fire, or else John's pants are on fire.

The problem is that any rational individual can realize that (27) uttered in a context c and evaluated in the world c_w of c is true. This is because χ*(c)(c_w) is true just in case: John's pants are not on fire in c_w, or John's pants are on fire in c_w—which is a tautology. Thanks to the *actually* operator, however, the *content* of χ* in c is χ*(c) = λw [John's pants are not on fire in c_w or John's pants are on fire in w]. With the assumption that John's pants are in fact on fire in c_w, we get: χ*(c) = λw [John's pants are on fire in w]. So with the rule in (26) we predict that the sentence *John believes that his pants are on fire* should be true—no matter what John's beliefs really are! The analysis has gone wrong; we will soon explore an alternative.

Before we get to actual cases of context shift, it is important to be clear about one class of examples which it would be incorrect to analyze in this way. Heim (1991) noted that indexical pronouns can sometimes display the behavior of bound variables:

(28) Only I did my homework.
    a. Reading 1: [only I] λx x did x's homework
    b. Reading 2: [only I] λx x did my homework
    (note that on Reading 1 the variable must range over non-speakers)

On superficial inspection, it may seem that on the bound reading the possessive pronoun fails to denote the speaker, and thus that some form of context shift is taking place. A much better hypothesis, however, is that in this particular configuration the person features of the bound pronoun can remain uninterpreted. Why this is so is a complex matter, but it is clear that this phenomenon *is by no means restricted to indexical features:* the same generalization holds in (29) of the pronoun *her*, which on its bound reading may range over non-female individuals.

(29) Only Mary did her homework
    a. Reading 1: [only Mary] λx x did x's homework
    b. Reading 2: [only Mary] λx x did Mary's homework

We will henceforth leave these examples aside (but see for instance Heim 2007; Kratzer 2008 and Rullmann 2003, 2004, 2008 for recent discussions).

2 *De Se* readings

Kaplan's analysis of indirect discourse is challenged by two kinds of cases. In this section, we consider examples in which the *truth conditions* predicted by his analysis are incorrect. In Section 3 we will consider cases that involve not just truth conditions but also *indexical morphology* (see also Sauerland 2007 for an introduction to the semantics of indirect discourse).

2.1 The existence of *De Se* readings: PRO

As it turns out, there are English constructions that make it possible to *distinguish* in indirect discourse between thoughts or sentences that have different characters but the same content. Specifically, PRO, the unpronounced subject of an infinitive embedded under an attitude verb, is always understood to report a first-person (or second-person) thought (Morgan 1970; Chierchia 1987), as is illustrated in the following scenario.

(30) John is so drunk that he has forgotten that he is a candidate in the election. He watches someone on TV and finds that that person is a terrific candidate, who should definitely be elected. Unbeknownst to John, the candidate he is watching on TV is John himself.
   a. True: John hopes that he will be elected
   b. False/#: John hopes PRO to be elected
      (by contrast, b is ok in a scenario in which the thought was: 'I should be elected')

Arguably, similar facts hold in the second person:

(31) At a party, John is told that somebody named 'Mary' is being particularly obnoxious. He tells the person he is having a conversation with: 'Mary should leave'. But that person is none other than Mary herself.
   a. True: John told Mary that she should leave
   b. False/#: John told Mary PRO to leave
      (by contrast, b is ok if the discourse was: 'Leave!').

Interestingly, an artificial pronoun very much like PRO, called *he**, was posited by the philosopher Castañeda for purely conceptual reasons (Castañeda 1966, 1967, 1968). In effect, PRO embedded under an attitude verb is an English realization of Catañeda's *he** (in other environments, however, PRO has different uses; but we will see below that in languages that have logophoric pronouns *he** is unambiguously instantiated). It should be added that Szabolcsi (2009) argues suggests that *overt* instances of PRO in other languages must equally be read De Se (she further suggests that the semantics of the infinitive rather than the lexical semantics of *PRO* is responsible for the De Se effect).

Since Kaplan's analysis of indirect discourse was designed to *predict* that such distinctions cannot be made in indirect discourse, it is ill-suited to account for these contrasts. In the semantic literature, scholars have generally followed Chierchia (1987) in taking these data to show that the semantics of attitude reports is more fine-grained than was usually thought in possible worlds semantics. The idea is that the value of a clause embedded under an attitude verb may be as fine-grained as a set of triples of the form <individual, time, world>. It is immediate that such triples are homologous to contexts. Technically, however, no syntactic or morphological connection to indexicality was posited in Chierchia's treatment. Rather, it was assumed that a λ-operator could appear at the 'top' of the embedded clause to bind an individual variable. For simplicity, we represent this operator above an empty complementizer C, though this is just for notational convenience:

(32) John hopes λi C PRO_i to be elected

The crucial assumption is that, in attitude reports, PRO must always be bound by the closest λ-operator:

(33) Syntactic condition on PRO
When embedded under an attitude verb, PRO must be bound by the closest c-commanding λ-operator.

The syntactic condition has the effect of ruling out (34a–b) while allowing for (34c–d):

(34) a. *John λi hopes λk C PRO_i to be elected
b. *John hopes λk C PRO_i to be elected
c. John λi hopes λk C PRO_k to be elected
d. John hopes λk C PRO_k to be elected

To obtain interpretable structures, we must still say what the role of the complementizer is. We will assume that it simply returns a proposition when applied to a clause (in type-theoretic terms, it returns a function of type <i, <s, t>>, which takes a time argument (of type i) and a world argument (of type s) to yield a truth value).

(35) $[\![C\ F]\!]^{c,\,s,\,t,\,w} = [\![\text{that } F]\!]^{c,\,s,\,t,\,w} = \lambda t'_i\, \lambda w'_s\, [\![F]\!]^{c,\,s,\,t',\,w'}$

Combined with the Logical Form in (32), this semantics guarantees that the embedded clause denotes a function of type <e, <i, <s, t>>>, where e is the type of individuals; this function can be assimilated to a set of triples of the form <individual, time, world>; and as noted such triples are homologous to contexts:

(36) $[\![\lambda i\ C\ PRO_i \text{ to be elected}]\!]^{c,\,s,\,t,\,w} = \lambda x'_e\, \lambda t'_i\, \lambda w'_s\, [\![F]\!]^{c,\,s[i \rightarrow x'],\,t',\,w'}$

This makes it possible to apply to the object-language operators *believe*, *hope*, etc., the very same semantics we introduced to describe attitudes (rather than attitude reports) in Section 1.1.2: an individual x stands in the 'believe' relation to a set F of contexts just in case each *context* (rather than *world*) compatible with what x believes is in F. This is precisely the semantics we adopt in (37), with minor changes due to the fact that F is essentially characterized as a set of triples rather than as a set of contexts.

(37) a. $[\![\text{believes}^{De\ Se}]\!]^{c,\,s,\,t,\,w} (F_{<e,\,<i,\,st>>})(x) = \text{true}$
iff for each context c' compatible with what x believes at t in w, $F(c'_a)(c'_t)(c'_w) = \text{true}$
b. $[\![\text{hope}^{De\ Se}]\!]^{c,\,s,\,t,\,w} (F_{<e,\,<i,\,st>>})(x) = \text{true}$
iff for each context c' compatible with what x hopes at t in w, $F(c'_a)(c'_t)(c'_w) = \text{true}$

It follows that *John hopes to be elected* is true just in case John stands in the 'hope' relation to the *diagonal* of the sentence *I be-elected*. More precisely, we see in (38) that the conditions under which the first sentence is true are exactly those under which John stands in the 'hope' relation to this diagonal, which we call Δ.

(38) a. $[\![\text{John hopes}^{De\ Se}\ \lambda i\ C\ PRO_i \text{ to be elected}]\!]^{c,\,s,\,t,\,w}$
$= [\![\text{hopes}^{De\ Se}\ \lambda i\ C\ PRO_i \text{ to be elected}]\!]^{c,\,s,\,t,\,w} (j)$
$= [\![\text{hopes}^{De\ Se}]\!]^{c,\,s,\,t,\,w} (j)([\![\lambda i\ C\ PRO_i \text{ to be elected}]\!]^{c,\,s,\,t,\,w})$
$= [\![\text{hopes}^{De\ Se}]\!]^{c,\,s,\,t,\,w} (j)(\lambda x_e\ [\![C\ PRO_i \text{ to be elected}]\!]^{c,\,s[i \rightarrow x],\,t,\,w})$
$= [\![\text{hopes}^{De\ Se}]\!]^{c,\,s,\,t,\,w} (j)(\lambda x_e\, \lambda t'\, \lambda w'\ [\![PRO_i \text{ to be elected}]\!]^{c,\,s[i \rightarrow x],\,t',\,w'})$

$= [\![hopes^{De\ Se}]\!]^{c,\ s,\ t,\ w}(j)(\lambda x_e \lambda t' \lambda w'\ x\ is\ elected\ at\ t'\ in\ w')$
= true   iff   for each context c' compatible with what j hopes at t in w, $[\lambda x_e \lambda t' \lambda w'\ x\ is\ elected\ at\ t'\ in\ w'](c'_a)(c'_t)(c'_w)$ = true,
          iff   for each context c' compatible with what j hopes at t in w, c'_a is elected at c'_t in c'_w.

b. $\Delta = [\![\ \delta\ [I\ be\text{-}elected]\ ]\!]^{c,\ s,\ t,\ w}$ $= \lambda c'\ [\![I\ be\text{-}elected]\!]^{c',\ s,\ c'_t,\ c'_w}$
                                                                              $= \lambda c' c'_a$ is elected at c'_t in c'_w

John stands in the 'hope' relation to Δ   iff for each context c' compatible with what j hopes at t in w, $\Delta(c') = 1$,
iff for each context c' compatible with what j hopes at t in w, c'_a is elected at c'_t in c'_w.

To be complete, this analysis would have to be supplemented with an account of morphological agreement. In a nutshell, the difficulty is that even though PRO is bound by an operator in the embedded clause, it still inherits its morphological features from an argument of the matrix clause. The details are somewhat stipulative on every account, but there is some evidence that the features in question remain uninterpreted:

(39) a. John, a transsexual, PRO hopes to become a woman and to buy himself / *herself a car.
     b. All candidates think that they are going to win.

Although in (39a) the semantics should permit the feminine features of *herself* to be interpreted (because in each context compatible with what John hopes, he is a woman), we see that the masculine pronoun must in fact be employed; it is plausible that it inherits its features from PRO, which in turn has to receive them from *John*—despite the fact that the De Se analysis crucially posits that *PRO* is *not* bound by *John*. The same reasoning arguably applies to (39b): although each candidate has a singular De Se thought (*I will win*), the plural must still be employed in the embedded clause. The details of the agreement mechanism are complex and should in part be determined by considerations that go beyond the present article (see for instance Heim 1991, 2005, 2007; Kratzer 1998; von Stechow 2002, 2003; Schlenker 1999, 2003; Anand 2006 and Rullmann 2008 for discussion).

It has sometimes been suggested that similar agreement rules apply to the features of pronouns and to those of tense, which in some languages is known to remain uninterpreted under past tense attitude verbs:

(40) Yesterday John decided that tomorrow at lunch time he would tell his mother that they <u>were</u> having their last meal together. (after Kamp & Rohrer 1983)

The underlined past tense refers to an event that occurs *after* all the other events mentioned in the sentence, and thus the past tense features of this verb are presumably uninterpreted (see for instance Ogihara 1996; Abusch 1997; Kratzer 1998; Schlenker 1999; see article 13 [this volume] (Ogihara) *Tense*).

Importantly, the observations we just made about *PRO* need not entail anything about the nature of indexicality, because there is no reason to treat *PRO* as an indexical expression; rather, it appears to be a variable that imposes certain conditions on its binder. So to summarize the discussion at this point:

(i) The data we have considered are entirely compatible with Kaplan's prohibition against monsters.
(ii) However, Kaplan's analysis of indirect discourse is falsified by the existence of De Se readings.

As we will see below, it turns out that there *is* strong evidence that some attitude verbs can embed clauses that include the diagonal operator, or something similar to it.

2.2 De Se vs. De Re

Before we go any further, we should make the relation between De Se and De Re readings somewhat more precise.

2.2.1 *De Se vs. De Re and binding*

It is sometimes believed that the distinction between De Se and De Re readings can be reduced to that between binding and 'accidental coreference'. *This is incorrect:* the De Se/De Re distinction can be replicated when every pronoun is bound by a quantifier, as shown below:

(41) a. Every candidate hopes that he will be elected.
     b. Every candidate hopes to be elected.

(41b) requires that every candidate's hope be of the form: *I will be elected* (in the first person). No such requirement holds in (41a). This is expected under the present approach, since two Logical Forms can be generated, each of which involves bound variables:

(42) a. Bound Reading, De Re
[every candidate] λi t_i hope λk that he_i is elected.
b. Bound Reading, De Se
[every candidate] λi t_i hope λk C PRO_k to be elected.

2.2.2 A De Re reading is compatible with a De Se situation

What is the precise logical relation between a De Se and a De Re reading? The accepted answer in the literature is quite simple: *De Se readings are strictly stronger than De Re readings* because any situation compatible with the former is compatible with the latter, but not vice versa.

To see that a De Re attitude is compatible with a situation in which the agent has a De Se attitude, consider a mixed case, in which some candidates think: *I should be elected*, while others think (about themselves, though without realizing it): *He should be elected* (Zimmermann 1991). The sentence *Every candidate hopes that he is elected* would seem to be true in this situation. But the embedded *he* cannot be read De Se, or else the sentence would come out as false. Thus *he* is read De Re. This suggests that a De Re reading is compatible with a De Se situation. The near-consensus is that this holds true in all cases.

This result is not unexpected when one considers in greater detail the standard analysis of quantification across attitude reports. The basic problem, laid out in Quine (1956), is that in the following situation we might both want to say that Ralph believes, of Ortcutt, that he is a spy; and that Ralph believes, of Ortcutt, that he is not a spy:

> There is a certain man in a brown hat whom Ralph has glimpsed several times under questionable circumstances on which we need not enter here; suffice it to say that Ralph suspects he is a spy. Also there is a gray-haired man, vaguely known to Ralph as rather a pillar of the community, whom Ralph is not aware of having seen except once at the beach. Now Ralph does not know it, but the men are one and the same. Can we say of *this man* (Bernard J. Ortcutt, to give him a name) that Ralph believes him to be a spy?
>
> (Quine 1956: 179)

On the assumption that Ralph's beliefs are closed under conjunction, catastrophic results follow if we analyze *Ralph believes of Ortcutt that he is a spy* and *Ralph believes of Ortcutt that he is not a spy* truth-conditions as in (i) and (ii):

(i) every context c compatible with what Ralph believes (at the time of utterance in the actual world) satisfies: Ortcutt is a spy at c_t in c_w;
(ii) every context c compatible with what Ralph believes (at the time of utterance in the actual world) satisfies: Ortcutt is not a spy at c_t in c_w.

It follows from (i) and (ii) that no context whatsoever is compatible with Ralph's beliefs—a result that normally obtains with irrational individuals, who believe both a proposition and its negation. But this is not Ralph's case—his only failing is that he doesn't realize that the individuals he saw in different circumstances are one and the same.

Kaplan (1969) solved the problem by analyzing quantification across attitude reports in existential terms. In a nutshell, the sentence *Ralph believes, of Ortcutt, that he is a spy* was taken to be true just in case there is some description (or 'mode of presentation') D of Orctutt such that Ralph believes something of the form: *D is a spy* (in the final analysis, the existential quantification over D must be further restricted). The key to Kaplan's analysis is that the combination of the following statements does *not* entail that Ralph holds contradictory beliefs:

(43) a. For some description D of Ortcutt, Ralph believes: *D is a spy*.
b. For some description E of Ortcutt, Ralph believes: *E is not a spy*.

Let D* be a description that 'witnesses' the truth of (a), and let E* be a description that witnesses the truth of (b). If D* ≠ E*, we obtain no implication that Ralph should hold contradictory beliefs.

As Kaplan observes, the analysis must be constrained on pain of making incorrect predictions. Anybody would agree that *the shortest spy is a spy*, but we wouldn't therefore want to conclude that everybody believes of the shortest spy (say, Smith) that he is a spy. For this reason, Kaplan adds a condition to ensure that the existential quantification is over 'vivid' descriptions, where 'vivid' is a cover term for various constraints whose form is largely left unspecified. Still, no matter how one explicates the term, it would seem that one stands in a *very* vivid relation to oneself. If so, the description *the person identical to me* should always count as a 'vivid' description. But this goes to show that any De Re pronoun should in principle be compatible with a De Se situation, in which the agent holds a first person thought (e.g., *I should be elected*).

There is currently no particularly elegant way to implement Kaplan's analysis—all accounts need important stipulations. Here we go for a syntactic one, which is illustrated in (44c): De Re terms of type e in attitude reports are syntactically replaced with a variable of type <e ,<i, <s, e>>> (abbreviated as eise), which in effect denotes an 'acquaintance relation' that associates to every individual e, time i and world s the individual that stands in a certain relation to e, i, s (we call this the 'De Re' transformation).

(44) a. Ralph believes that Ortcutt is a spy, *analyzed as*:
b. Ralph believe λi that Ortcutt be-a-spy
c. [∃δ $_{eise}$: R(δ)(Ortcutt)(Ralph)] Ralph believe λi that δ(i) be-a-spy

Here R(δ)(Ortcutt)(Ralph)] indicates tha*t:*

a) *δ is* a description of Ortcutt when evaluated in the context of Ralph's thought act.
b) *δ* is 'vivid' in the context of Ralph's thought act.

In Quine's example, *δ* could for instance correspond to the description *the man I saw at the beach*, or *the man I saw wearing a brown hat*.

It should be noted that some authors take *δ* to be a free variable whose value must be provided by the discourse situation; under such an analysis, a simpler Logical Form is obtained:

(45) Ralph believe λi that δ(i) be-a-spy

Under this simpler analysis, it is left to the context to provide reasonable constraints on what the implicit description can be.

2.2.3 Does he a De Se reading?

It turns out to be difficult to determine whether a pronoun like *he*, which is known to have a De Re reading, *also* has a De Se reading (the situation was much simpler with PRO, which simply does not have a De Re reading). Most researchers believe that it does, but the argument is subtle. The problem is a standard one in semantics: *John thinks that he will win the election* uncontroversially has a De Re reading; and we wish to determine whether it also has a De Se reading, which is logically stronger than the De Re one. The difficulty is that any situation that verifies the De Se reading will equally verify the De Re reading. On the other hand, if a situation makes the De Se reading false but the De Re reading true, a charitable interpreter might well select the De Re reading to maximize the truth of the speaker's utterance, and thus even if the De Se reading exists, we will fail to 'see' it. Percus & Sauerland (2003a) solve the problem by using quantified examples (or rather an example with *only*, which has a quantificational semantics):

(46) A group of drunken election candidates watching campaign speeches on television do not recognize themselves in the broadcast. John, the only confident one, thinks "I'll win", but does not recognize himself in the broadcast. Bill and Sam, both depressive, think "I'll lose" but are impressed by the speeches that happen to be their own and are sure "*that* candidate" will win. Peter, also depressive, happens to be impressed not by his own speech but by John's.

Only John thinks that he will win.

Percus & Sauerland (2003a) give the sentence as true in the situation at hand, and they argue that this proves the existence of the De Se reading of *he*. To understand their argument, we must consider the various conceivable Logical Forms and argue that the judgment couldn't be accounted for if *he* only had a De Re reading.

(47) LF1: [Only John] $\lambda i\ t_i$ thinks λk that he_m will win, where m denotes John
(De Re, free)
LF1′: [Only John] $\lambda i\ [\exists \delta_{eise}: R(\delta)(m)(m)]\ t_i$ thinks λk that $\delta(k)$ will win
LF2: [Only John] $\lambda i\ t_i$ thinks λk that he_i will win (De Re, bound)
LF2′: [Only John] $\lambda i\ [\exists \delta_{eise}: R(\delta)(i)(i)]\ t_i$ thinks λk that $\delta(k)$ will win
LF3: [Only John] $\lambda i\ t_i$ thinks λk that he_k will win (De Se)

If only De Re readings were available, the sentence could only be analyzed as LF1 or LF2—and thus as LF1′ or LF2′ after the De Re transformation has been applied. But LF1′ is predicted to be false, because Peter does have a De Re belief that John is going to be elected. Similarly, LF2 is predicted to be false, because Bill and Sam each thinks about himself—De Re—that he is going to be elected. By contrast, if *he* can have a De Se reading, LF3 should be available too; and it is correctly predicted to be true, since only John has a De Se thought of the form: *I will be elected* (none of the other individuals has a De Se belief that he himself will be elected).

It should be noted that there have been attempts to take the De Re Logical Form as basic, and the De Se reading as derivative. Of course all such accounts must explain why *PRO* only has a De Se reading; there are several possible directions:

- Syntactically, one could decide to represent in the Logical Form both the De Re nature of the reading *and* the 'implicit description' under which it is obtained (see for instance Schlenker 2003).
- One could also give a pragmatic account of the distinction; this is attempted in particular in Maier (2006) (following an earlier suggestion by Reinhart 1990). But something still needs to be said to explain why PRO is unambiguously read *De Se*; in Maier's framework, certain pronominal entries specify constraints that must be satisfied by the acquaintance relation that gives them their denotation (Maier also applies this device to shifted indexicals).

2.2.4 Syntactic Constraints on De Se Readings

Since in the present analysis a De Se reading is obtained by binding a variable to a λ-abstractor introduced by an attitude operator, there could in principle be further syntactic constraints on the relation between a De Se pronoun and its antecedent. Percus & Sauerland (2003b) claim that such constraints exist in dream reports, as in (48):

(48)   a. John dreamed that he was marrying his granddaughter.
         b. John dreamed that his granddaughter was marrying him.

They argue on the basis of intricate scenarios that if *he* is read De Re in (48a), *his* must be read De Re as well; by contrast, even when *him* is read De Re in (48b), *his* can still be read De Se. They conclude that a De Re pronoun pro_1 that refers to an attitude holder x can block the De Se reading of the pronoun pro_2 in the configuration *[x dreams that ... pro_1 ... pro_2...]* if *pro1* c-commands pro_2 ('Oneiric Reference Constraint'). This constraint is further discussed by Hardt (2003) and Anand (2006), who suggests that it is an instance of a more general condition (the 'De Re Blocking Effect'), which has analogous effects on some logophoric pronouns, and ultimately derives from economy constraints on binding discussed in Fox (2000).

3 Monsters and shifted indexicals

In this section, we suggest that Kaplan's analysis was not just wrong about De Se readings, but also about monsters: there are languages in which (some) attitude operators behave like Kaplanian monsters (a conclusion consonant with Israel

& Perry 1996). But how can we establish the existence of such beasts? We will discuss examples that have the form of (49), where <I> and <here> are indexicals such as *I* and *here*:

(49) John says that   ... <I>   ...   <here> ...

The argument will have three steps, each of which is compulsory if the claim that a monster has been sighted is to have any substance.

(i) First, by inspecting the truth conditions, we argue that this hypothesis is *compatible* with the semantics of the sentence. Often one only checks that the shifted indexical has roughly the right meaning—for instance that in *John says that I am a hero* the embedded pronoun intuitively refers to John rather than the actual speaker. But within the present framework, a *bona fide* shifted indexical should obligatorily be read *De Se*; if possible, then, the De Re / De Se distinction should be considered when shifted indexicals are discussed (this is admittedly difficult when one cannot do detailed fieldwork on the relevant constructions).

(ii) Second, we will have to exclude the possibility that the embedded clause is quoted. On almost any theory, it is unsurprising that *John says: 'I am a hero'* attributes to John a (De Se) claim about John himself. This is because in cases of quotation, the verb *say* can be taken to establish a relation between an individual and a string of words, rather than between an individual and the *meaning* of the embedded clause (this explains why meaningless strings can be quoted in direct discourse but not used in indirect discourse; thus it makes sense to say: *John said: 'Glubibulga'*, but not: *John said that glubibulga*). In English, the presence of the complementizer *that* rules out such a quotative reading, but other languages could conceivably have quotative complementizers, and thus some care is needed to exclude the possibility that the embedded is simply quoted.

Fortunately, there are several ways to *force* a clause to be used rather than mentioned. The key observation is that quotations are generally 'opaque' to grammatical processes; as a result, grammatical dependencies cannot normally 'cross' quotation marks. Two examples are provided below; for illustrative purposes, we use the English sentence *John says I like cheese* as a test case. Without punctuation (or special intonation), the sentence is ambiguous: one reading is quotational: *John says: 'I like cheese'*. The other reading is non-quotational: *John says <that> I like cheese*. One could be tempted to posit that the first reading involves a Kaplanian monster, but this hypothesis would soon be refuted by the observation that *I* obligatorily refers to the actual speaker when a grammatical dependency crosses the boundaries of the embedded clause—forcing the latter to be used rather than quoted. This explains why in this simple example *I* is disambiguated when an interrogative element is extracted from the embedded clause, or when it includes a Negative Polarity Item licensed by a matrix negation:

(50) a. What did John say I ate?
  OkNon-shifted Reading: What did John say I (= the speaker) ate?
  *Shifted Reading: What did John say he (= John) ate?

  b. John didn't say I ate any cheese.
  OkNon-shifted Reading: John didn't say I (= the speaker) ate any cheese.
  *Shifted Reading: John didn't say he (= John) ate any cheese.

We will see that the same tests argue in other languages for the existence of *bona fide* shifted indexicals.

(iii) Finally, we will want to exclude the possibility that the purported indexicals are in fact anaphoric elements. This is no trivial matter: anaphoric expressions can often have, among others, a deictic reading, whereby they pick their denotation from the context. What distinguishes such anaphoric elements from *bona fide* indexicals is that the latter can never have unambiguously anaphoric readings. To make the point concrete, consider the behavior of the adverbial *later*:

(51) a. I'll go for a walk later.
  b. This morning, John promised that he would go for a walk later.
  c. I met John yesterday morning. Later he went for a walk.
  d. Whenever John makes a mistake, he later owns up to it.

In (51a), *later* is evaluated with respect to the time of utterance; this is compatible with two hypotheses: *later* could have an indexical component, which must be evaluated with respect to a context; or it could have an anaphoric element, which can pick out as its denotation any salient moment—including in some cases the time of speech. In (51b), *later* is evaluated with respect to the time of John's speech act; this is compatible with either hypothesis, *on condition* that we add to the first hypothesis that *later* is a shiftable indexical. But in (51c), we see that *later* has an anaphoric rather than an indexical behavior, since it can be evaluated with respect to a salient moment which is not the time coordinate of any context. *Later* behaves as if it had a concealed variable argument

(= *later than t*), whose value may be provided by the context or by a linguistic antecedent (in (51d), the antecedent is a time quantifier).

As was shown earlier, the De Se semantics we postulated for attitude verbs makes it conceivable that they (or operators they associate with) might be monsters. In the rest of this section we claim that this is indeed the case in some constructions. No claim is made to exhaustivity; there are for instance relevant data for Engenni in Thomas (1978); for Aghem in Hyman (1979); for Navajo in Hale & Platero (1998) and Speas (1999) ; for Ancient Greek in Bary & Maier (2003); for Ancient Egyptian in Kammerzell & Peust (2002); for American Sign Language in Lillo-Martin (2009) and Lee et al. (1997); for Catalan Sign Language in Quer (2005); for Italian Sign Language in Zucchi (2004). (Recanati 2004 discusses further possible cases of context shift.)

3.1 Pure monsters: Operators that manipulate the context parameter

Let us suppose, for the moment, that the lexical entry we posited for *say* remains fixed, but that a monstrous construction can be obtained by combining *say* with the diagonal operator δ which we hypothetically introduced in the object language in (38b). We also saw that such a Logical Form is easily interpreted by our existing rules:

(52) John say δ I be a hero.

What should be the behavior of such a construction?

(i) First, we should be able to find some expressions that (a) qualify as indexicals, and yet (b) receive a shifted interpretation precisely when they are embedded under *say*.
(ii) Second, whenever one indexical gets shifted in this way, we expect that all other indexicals that appear in the scope of the same attitude operator should be shifted as well. This is because shifting is only possible if the diagonal operator is present; but because the latter is a simple modal operator, it shifts the context of evaluation of *all* indexicals that are in its scope. This has two consequences: when two indexicals are in the same clause, they must 'shift together', as stated in (53).

(53) Shift Together (Anand & Nevins 2004)

If an indexical is shifted in the scope of a modal operator, all other indexicals in the same clause must be shifted as well.

... attitude verb ... δ [... shifted indexical₁ .... shifted indexical₂ ...]

(iii) Third, since δ is a simple *modal* operator, once it has shifted the value of the context parameter, the latter's original value is lost once and for all—and no expression found in the scope of δ may recover the initial context parameter. In other words, the pattern represented in (54) is predicted to be impossible:

(54) No Intervening Binder (Anand & Nevins 2004; Anand 2006)
*[... attitude verb δ [... shifted indexical ... attitude verb ... [... non-shifted indexical ...]]]

Anand & Nevins (2004) and Anand (2006) convincingly show that both properties are in fact satisfied by the verb *vano* ('say') in Zazaki, an Indo-Iranian language on which they did original fieldwork. There is just one complication: *vano* can but need not select the operator δ. For the rest, the data are as predicted. Anand (2006) presents an extensive survey, as well as detailed scenarios designed to test for the availability of the various readings. We only provide a brief summary of his conclusions.

(i) Zazaki indexicals can shift in constructions that rule out quotation, as indicated by extraction and NPI-licensing tests (it can be shown independently that *kes* is indeed a negative polarity item):

(55) Extraction in Zazaki
a. čeneke [ke Heseni va **mi** *t* paci kerda] rindeka
girl   that Hesen said I   *t* kiss did   pretty.be-PRES
'The girl that Hesen said {Hesen, I} kissed is pretty.' (Anand and Nevins, 2004)

b. Piyaa-o [ke Rojda va ke **mi** *t* paci kerd] Ali biyo
Person that Rojda said that I   *t* kiss did   Ali was
'Ali was the person that Rojda said {Rojda, I} kissed.' (Anand and Nevins, 2004)

(56) NPI licensing in Zazaki
a. Rojda ne va ke **mi** kes   paci kerd
Rojda not said that I   anyone kiss did
'Rojda didn't say that she kissed anyone.' (Anand and Nevins, 2004)

b. Tawa Alii   va   ke **mi** kes   paci kerd
   Q   Ali. OBL said that I   anyone kiss did
   'Did Ali say that I kissed anyone?' OR
   'Did Ali say that he kissed anyone?'

(ii) It can also be checked that in any given clause, either all indexicals are shifted, or none is, as shown in (57). In sentences with multiple clauses, if a shifted indexical appears under an attitude verb, indexicals that appear under lower attitude verbs must be shifted as well, as shown in (58).

(57) Zazaki obeys Shift Togeter
  vizeri   Rojda Bill-ra va kɛ   ɛz to-ra   miradiša   (Anand and Nevins, 2004)
  yesterday Rojda Bill-to said that I you-to angry be-PRES
  'Yesterday Rojda said to Bill, "I am angry at you."'
  'Yesterday Rojda said to Bill, "AUTH(c) is angry at ADDR(c)."'
  '*Yesterday Rojda said to Bill, "AUTH(c) am angry at you."'
  '*Yesterday Rojda said to Bill, "I am angry at ADDR(c)."'
  (AUTH(c) and ADDR(c) refer to the author and addressee of the actual context)

(58) Zazaki obeys No Intervening Binder
  (Andrew$_U$): Ali$_A$ mi$_U$.ra va   kɛ   Heseni$_H$ to$_U$-ra va ɛz$_{\{H,A,*U\}}$ braye Rojda-o
              Ali me-to said that Hesen you-to said I   brother Rojda-GEN
  'Ali said to Andrew that Hesen said to Andrew that {Hesen, Ali, *Andrew} is Rojda's brother.' (Anand and Nevins, 2004)
  (U refers to the Utterer—in this case Andrew; A refers to Ali, and H refers to Hesen)

These data fall out nicely from a monstrous analysis, but they are very difficult to explain for other accounts. Let us just mention two.

– One could try to explain away these Zazaki data in terms of partial quotation. The analysis would posit that for some reason Zazaki allows some words—in particular indexicals—to be quoted within a clause which is itself used rather than mentioned. On this view, then, (56) would be analyzed as *Rojda didn't say that "I" kissed anyone*, with partial quotation of *I*, under a semantics that would have to be determined. This would explain why the first person pronoun appears to refer to someone other than the actual speaker. But this would *fail* to account for *Shift Together* and *No Intervening Binder*. In addition, Anand (2006) notes that a partial quotation analysis predicts that the report is faithful to the *words* used by the agent of the

reported speech act, whereas the monstrous analysis does not impose such a condition—and correctly so, as Anand argues on the basis of a detailed empirical analysis.
- One could also try to explain the Zazaki data by postulating that indexicals are De Se pronouns with special conditions of use. But the generalization discussed by Anand & Nevins (2004) concerns all indexicals (including temporal and locative adverbials), not just pronouns. This makes it very unlikely that we are just dealing with cases of accidental homophony between De Se pronouns and indexicals.

For completeness, it should be mentioned that Anand & Nevins (2004) and Anand (2006) argue that some language have 'partial diagonalization operators' which are selected by certain verbs but not by others. Their suggestion is that some operators only manipulate 'part' of a context, leaving the other coordinates fixed; Anand's typology is shown in (59) (excluding his study of Chinese *zìjǐ*, which displays a more complex behavior). An alternative possibility to analyze these examples is to posit a more powerful system of quantification over contexts, with rich lexical entries which specify which indexical can depend on which context variables; as we will now see, there might be other reasons to posit such a powerful system.

(59) Typology of monstrous operators (Anand 2006)

Cross linguistic variation

	VERB	LEXICAL ENTRIES	CLASS DESCRIPTION
AMHARIC, AGHEM	SAY	[say (OP_{per})]	optionally shifts 1st/2nd-per indexicals
NAVAJO	SAY	[say (OP_{per})]	optionally shifts 1st/2nd-per indexicals
SLAVE	TELL	[tell (OP_{per})]	optionally shifts 1st/2nd-per indexicals
	WANT	[want (OP_{auth})]	optionally shifts 1st-per indexicals
	SAY	[say (OP_{auth})]	obligatorily shifts 1st-per indexicals
ZAZAKI	SAY	[say (OP_v)]	optionally shifts all indexicals
ENGLISH	ALL	[att-verb]	no indexical shift

3.2 Quantificational monsters: Quantifiers over contexts

3.2.1 *Motivations*

Some researchers have argued that natural language (also) has monstrous operators that are less directly Kaplanian, in that they are not *modal operators* that manipulate a context *parameters*, but rather *quantifiers* that bind a context *variable*. In fact, the quantificational analysis was discussed in the literature before Anand & Nevins (2004) discovered their remarkable data. There were several reasons for this alternative treatment context shifting.

(i) First, natural language does not generally appear to have temporal or modal operators, which manipulate a parameter and give rise to the kind of 'memory loss' we discussed above, but rather temporal and modal quantifiers, which *allow* expressions in their scope to depend on them but do not *force* them to do so. As was announced in Section 1.1.1, when the full range of data is considered, they suggest that a semantics which has the full power of explicit quantification over times and worlds as well as individuals is needed to deal with temporal and modal talk in natural language (see Cresswell 1990 for a thorough discussion). Early research on shifted indexicals thus started from the assumption that, *if* context shifting is at all allowed in natural language, it too should proceed by way of quantification of context variables. Anand & Nevins's data suggest that this assumption was incorrect for Zazaki, since their own monsters display a perfectly standard modal (rather than quantificational) behavior.

(ii) Still, it could be that *other* monsters are of the quantificational rather than of the modal variety. The debate is still rather open, but some examples are worth discussing.

– Preliminary data from Amharic were discussed in Schlenker (2003) (see also Anderson & Keenan 1985 for earlier data). First, it was observed that Amharic first and second person markers may denote a non-speaker or a non-hearer when embedded under an all-purpose attitude verb (whose original meaning is 'say'), but not in relative clauses. Second, extraction tests were applied to show that the appearance of shifting is not a consequence of quotation. Third, it was shown in Anand (2006) that a shifted first person pronoun in Amharic may only be read De Se, as is expected if it is a shiftable indexical. Fourth, it was observed in Schlenker (2003) that two occurrences of a first person feature that occur in the same embedded environment may be evaluated with respect to different contexts, which suggests that *Shift together* fails to hold.

(60) Amharic 1st person pronouns (apparently) fail to obey Shift Together (Anand 2006)
John lij-e   ay-ittazzəzəññ   alə
John son-my NEG.3s-obey.mkimperf-1sO say. PERF. 3sm
'John$_i$ said, "my son will not obey AUTH(c)." '
'John$_i$ said, "AUTH(c)'s son will not obey me." '

Anand (2006) confirms these data for about half of his Amharic informants, but he argues that they are best analyzed by positing an ambiguity: the Amharic first person marker may behave as an unshiftable indexical, or as a logophoric element, which according to Anand falls under a different generalization. Furthermore, he suggests that second person markers do *not* display this pattern and obey his 'Shift Together' constraint:

(61) Amharic 2nd person pronouns obey Shift Together (Anand 2006)
John Bill lij-ih   ay-ittazzəzə-ih   alə-w
John Bill son-your NEG.3s-obey.mkimperf-2smO-NEG say.PERF.3sm-3smO
'John$_i$ say to Bill$_j$, "your$_j$ son will not obey you$_j$." '
'John$_i$ said to Bill$_j$, "ADDR(c)'s son will not obey ADDR(c)." '
'*John$_i$ said to Bill$_j$, "ADDR(c)'s son will not obey you." '
'*John$_i$ said to Bill$_j$, "your son will not obey ADDR(c)." '

– The Russian present tense is sometimes claimed to be a shiftable indexical (Schlenker 2003; see Kondrashova 1998 for a different view). It does have some of the desired properties: it may denote a non-present moment in attitude reports, but in general it may not in relative clauses, or for that matter in other complement clauses that are not themselves in an intensional construction (on the other hand, like the English present tense it may denote a non-present moment when it is in the scope of a future operator, as in: *In 20 years, little Johnny will marry a woman who loves him*).

(62) The Russian present tense is monster-like
  a. Shifting is possible under attitude verbs
     petja$_i$ skazal, čto on$_i$ plačet.   [Russian]
     Pejta$_i$ said   that he is-crying
     'Petja said that he was crying [at the time of his utterance]'

  b. Shifting is not possible in relative clauses
     petja$_i$ vstretil čeloveka, kotoryj plačet.   [Russian]
     Pejta   met   person,   who   is crying

'Petja met a person who is crying/cries.'
NOT: 'Petja met a person who was crying [at the time of the meeting].'

c. Shifting is not possible under *it happened that* (cf. Janssen & van der Wurff 1996)
často slu čalos', čto Miša plakal / *plačet
*often happened that Misha cried / *is-crying*
'It often happened that Misha cried.' (not: 'cries')

Crucially, when a first person pronoun co-occurs with a shifted present tense, it is still taken to denote the actual speaker (rather than the agent of the report), which shows that Russian violates *Shift Together*. Furthermore, the present tense of a relative clause embedded under a clause whose tense is itself shifted may still be 'unshifted', and thus denote the time of utterance—as shown in (63); this suggests that Russian also violates *No Intervening Binder*.

(63) v 1980 godu Petja sprosil menja, rabotaet li na KGB
 in 1980 year Petja asked me works whether on KGB
 čelovek, kotoryj pravit stranoj.
 person who rules country
 'In 1980, Petja asked me whether the person who is <now> ruling the country works for the KGB.'

– Schlenker (2003) also mentions the behavior of French *dans deux jours (in two days)*, which he claims to display the characteristic behavior of a shiftable indexical. Importantly, *dans deux jours* contrasts with *après-demain*, which behaves like a well-behaved Kaplanian (unshiftable) indexical. Schlenker extends the analysis to English *two days ago* vs. *the day before yesterday*, but these data have been debated, and might be incorrect or subject to important cross-individual variation:

(64) My brother has informed me repeatedly over the years that my mother had asked the night before where I had been two days ago.

Assuming that *the night before* is evaluated with respect to my brother's speech act, it was claimed in Schlenker (2003) that there are two readings for 'two days ago': it may be evaluated with respect to the time either of my mother's or of my brother's speech act.

– Abusch (1997) discusses the case of *might* and *ought* in English, which closely mirror the behavior of Russian present tense verbs: their time of evaluation may be a non-actual context, but only in case they are in the scope of an attitude operator or of a present tense (the latter fact does not follow from a theory of indexicality).

(65) a. When he was 15, John was in love with a girl who ought to study more.
⇒ the girl John was in love with ought to study more now.
b. John thought that his girlfriend ought to study more / thought that his girlfriend was someone who ought to study more.
⇏ John's girlfriend ought to study more now.

It is clear that when other indexicals occur in the same clause as *might* or *ought*, the former fail to shift even when the latter do; here too *Shift Together* is violated. Furthermore, even when two occurrences of *ought* are embedded under the same attitude verb, they may be evaluated with respect to different contexts; thus in (68), *ought to be expelled* is shifted, but *ought to be prosecuted* can still be interpreted with respect to the time of utterance.

(66) In 1980, John asked whether the person who ought to be prosecuted for Politkovskaja's murder knew someone who ought to be expelled from the Central Committee.

- It should be added that Anand (2006) mentions examples from Slave (Rice 1986) and Catalan Sign Language (Quer 2005) which suggest that *Shift Together* might be too strong for these languages as well.
- Expressives—for instance ethnic slurs—indicate that a given agent has a (typically negative) attitude towards someone or something. Thus the term *honky* indicates that the agent has a negative attitude towards white people. Whether this is semantically an assertion, a presupposition, or a conventional implicature is a question we will not go into here (see Potts 2007 and commentaries for a survey of the debate). What matters for our purposes is that at least some expressives can be understood with a shifted reading, whereby it is the agent of a reported thought act who is supposed to hold the relevant attitude:

(67) a. #I am not prejudiced against Caucasians. But if I were, you would be the worst honky I know.
b. I am not prejudiced against Caucasians. But John, who is, thinks/claims that you are the worst honky he knows. (Schlenker 2003; Potts 2007)

Interestingly, *honky* and similar terms fail to obey Shift Together:

(68) I am not prejudiced against Caucasians. But Pierre, who is, has repeatedly made the claim that you are the worst honky that the frog's mother knows.

It appears to be possible to interpret *honky* from Pierre's standpoint but *frog* from the speaker's perspective, which suggests that expressives violate Shift Together (it can also be noted that the *that*-clause is embedded in a syntactic island—the complex Noun Phrase *[the claim that ...*—which makes it unlikely that any kind of covert movement of one of the expressives out of the scope of the attitude operator could be responsible for the mixed reading we observe). (See Harris & Potts 2009 for a different view on related data.)

3.2.2 Solution strategies

What should be done if some of these examples turn out not to involve an accidental ambiguity between indexicals and logophoric elements (as noted above, Anand 2006 posits such an ambiguity in Amharic)? The simplest solution is probably to take these sentences to involve an abstractor over contexts represented at the top of the embedded clause. For simplicity, we take the complementizer itself to be the λ-operator, though this is just for notational convenience. We henceforth work within a purely extensional system, with object-language variables over individuals, times, worlds, and contexts; an assignment function is thus supposed to provide a value of the right type for all three categories of variables (we have introduced a type c for *contexts*, hence the notation c_c, which indicates that the meta-linguistic variable c' has type c)

(69) $[\![\text{that}_{c_i} \, F \,]\!]^{c, s} = \lambda c'_c \, [\![\, F \,]\!]^{c, s \, [c_i \to c']}$

There may also be 'standard' complementizers, which only abstract over times and possible worlds; we analyze them with the following syntax and semantics (here t_i indicates that t is a meta-linguistic variable denoting times, of type i; while w_s indicates that w is a meta-linguistic variable denoting worlds, of type s):

(70) $[\![\text{that}_{t_k, w_l} \, F \,]\!]^{c, s} = \lambda t_i \, \lambda w_s \, [\![\, F \,]\!]^{c, s[t_k \to t, w_l \to w]}$

In fact, we can generalize this procedure to allow for simultaneous abstraction over individuals, time and worlds; this leads to a near-notational variant of (69):

(71) ⟦ that$_{x_i, t_k, w_l}$ F ⟧$^{c, s}$ = $\lambda x'_e \lambda t'_i \lambda w'_s$ ⟦ F ⟧$^{c, s[x_i \to x', t_k \to t', w_l \to w']}$

In principle we do not quite get the same model-theoretic objects with (71) and (69), even if we treat contexts as triples of an individual, a time and a world. This is because, as was noted at the outset, contexts are usually taken to satisfy some non-trivial semantic constraints: not just any tuple of the right type can be called a 'context'; but in the definition in (71) we obtain, in effect, a function that takes *any* triple of the right kind and outputs a truth value. By itself this need not be a crucial difference: the semantics of attitude verbs can be adapted to neutralize it (in the contexts-as-triples approach, just take attitude verbs to quantify over *those triples that are possible contexts*). The main difference between the two approaches is syntactic and morphological: the definition in (69) makes it clear that the dependency involves contexts; the definition in (71) doesn't. Proponents of the latter approach (e.g., Schlenker 1999 and von Stechow 2002, 2003) are thus forced to enrich this definition with diacritics on variables to indicate that they are not 'normal' variables—which is essential in order to derive the morphological idiosyncracies of variables which are dependent on attitude verbs; we come back to this point below.

Our 'old' lexical entries for attitude verbs can be retained in the extensional analysis. We must just ensure that the time and world arguments that appear in the embedded clause appear in the 'right' syntactic position to be compatible with the semantic type of the verb. Finally, in order to allow for expressions that depend on the actual context, we introduce a distinguished variable c^*, with the following assumption (to be slightly revised below):

(72) Assumption about context variables (preliminary version)
   a. c^* is a free variable that always denotes the context of the actual speech act.
   b. No other context variable can be free.

This analysis makes it possible to represent a variety of readings; for simplicity, I assume that *two days ago* does allow for these readings (the reader may replace mentally with the corresponding French sentence with *dans deux jours*).

(73) John said that Mary left two days ago.
   a. Reading 1 ('shifted' reading for *two days ago*)
   c^*_w t_k John say that$_{c_i}$ c_{iw} two-days-ago-c_i Mary leave
   In words: every context c_i compatible with what John says at time t_k in the world of c^* satisfies: Mary leave two days before the time of c_i in the world of c_i

b. Reading 2 ('non-shifted' reading for *two days ago*)
   $c^*_w\ t_k$ John say that$_{c_i}\ c_{iw}$ two-days-ago-c^* Mary leave
   In words: every context c_i compatible with what John says at time t_k in the world of c^* satisfies: Mary leave two days before the time of c^* in the world of c_i

To interpret these structures, we assume that c^*_w, c^*_t denote the world and time coordinates of c^*, and that *two-days-ago-c_i* denotes the time which is two days before the time of c_i:

(74) For any context-denoting expression c',
   a. ⟦ c'_a ⟧^{c,s} = the agent of ⟦ c' ⟧^{c,s}; ⟦ c'_t ⟧^{c,s} = the time of ⟦ c' ⟧^{c,s}; ⟦ c'_w ⟧^{c,s} = the world of ⟦ c' ⟧^{c,s}.
   b. ⟦two-days-ago-c'⟧^{c,s} = the time which is two days before the time of ⟦ c' ⟧^{c,s}

With these lexical rules, the reader can check that we obtain the desired readings.

But this analysis raises a question: how can we guarantee that *yesterday* cannot be shifted? In other words, how can the present framework draw a distinction between unshiftable and shiftable indexicals? A simple solution is to introduce a feature ±c^*: an indexical expression which carries the feature +c^* must take as argument the distinguished variable c^*, which denotes the context of utterance; an indexical expression which is unspecified for ±c^* can take as argument any context variable it desires. So *yesterday* is stipulated to carry the feature +c^*, whereas *two days ago* is left unspecified. In similar fashion, we can account for the difference between English *I* and Amharic *I*—call it I_{Amh}—by positing that the former is specified for +c^*, while the latter is unspecified, which allows it to be used with a shifted reading:

(75) John says that I be-a-hero
   $c^*_w\ t_k$ John say that$_{c_i}\ c_{iw}\ c_{it}\ I_{Amh}$-$c_i$ be-a-hero

It should be noted that this analysis can also account for the De Se reading of PRO *if* we stipulate by brute force that PRO spells out something like c_{ia} (with appropriate syntactic constraints to guarantee that c_i is bound locally).

An important argument for this typology is that in one and the same language some indexicals are shiftable while others are not. I refer the reader to the literature for some such examples (e.g., Schlenker 1999, 2003; Anand 2006). The difficulty, however, is that the standard version of this approach (in which c^* is always a free variable) approach fails to do justice to the generalizations uncovered by Anand & Nevins (2004), since it predicts that *Shift Together* and *No Intervening Binder* should always *fail* to hold. What we need is a more nuanced analysis, which allows for the possibility of both types of cases: some attitude verbs should behave, *à la* Anand & Nevins, like modal context-shifters, while others should probably be treated as quantifiers over contexts.

There is a solution, which was suggested by Ede Zimmermann (p.c.): one may simply postulate that the diagonal operator in Zazaki is in fact a lambda-operator that binds the distinguished variable c^*:

(76) $[\![\delta_{c^*} \; F \;]\!]^{c, s} = \lambda c'_c \; [\![\; F \;]\!]^{c, s \, [c^* \to c']}$

Zimmermann's suggestion requires a small modification of our assumption about context variables stated in (72): we must now allow the variable c^* to be bound, but only by the operator δ_{c^*}.

We can now derive Anand & Nevins's data if we assume that (a) all Zazaki indexicals are specified for the feature $+c^*$, and that (b) *vano* ('say') can optionally embed δ_{c^*}. In such cases, δ_{c^*} will by force shift the point of evaluation of all the indexicals that are in its scope; and since all indexicals must take c^* as their argument, whenever one indexical shifts in a given clause, all other indexicals must shift as well. In this analysis, then, Zazaki is just like English, except that *vano* ('say') can embed the special diagonal operator δ_{c^*}.

As things stand, then, it seems that we need the context abstractor *that*$_{c_i}$ in (69), which can bind any context variable c_i; for Zazaki, we must also postulate the existence of δ_{c^*} in (76), which will emulate within an extensional system the behavior of a modal context-shifter. And of course we will need *that*$_{t_k, w_l}$ in (70) for those intensional verbs which are not attitudinal. Can we stop here? If we did, we would predict that *every attitude verb that gives rise to De Se readings can in principle shift the context of evaluation of (some) indexicals*. However this claim might conceivably be too strong: in Amharic, it appears that only one all-purpose attitude verb can shift the context of evaluation of indexicals. It could be that all other attitude verbs fail to give rise to De Se readings. But if not, we might need a more nuanced approach, which *also* makes use of the complementizer *that*$_{x_i, t_k, w_l}$ in (71), which simultaneously binds three variables. Depending on whether an attitude verb selects *that*$_{x_i, t_k, w_l}$, *that*$_{c_i}$ or δ_{c^*}, different cases will arise.

- An attitude verb that selects *that*$_{x_i, t_k, w_l}$ will give rise to De Se readings (due to the simultaneous abstraction over individuals, times and worlds), but it will not shift the context of any indexical;

– $that_{c_i}$ will shift the context of evaluation of those indexicals that do not carry the feature +c* (since those can only take as argument the designated context variable c*, which cannot be bound by $that_{c_i}$);
– in Zazaki, *vano* ('say') can embed δ_{c^*} $that_{c^*}$, which obligatorily shifts the context of evaluation of all indexicals that have the feature +c*.

Yet another possibility would be to *only* posit some versions of the complementizer $that_{x_i, t_k, w_l}$, but to add to it a system of diacritics on the variables (together with an appropriate system of feature transmission) to constrain the interpretive possibilities of various indexicals, which could now be treated as bound variables of a particular kind (see Heim 2005, 2007 and Stechow 2002, 2003 for a system of this kind). The choice among these analytical possibilities is still open, but Anand (2006) provides an in-depth discussion of their empirical consequences.

4 Logophoric pronouns

We saw above that a feature ±c* is useful to distinguish between shiftable and unshiftable indexicals: the latter carry the feature +c*, while the former are unspecified for it. This leads one to expect that there should be −c* expressions as well; these would be obligatorily shifted indexicals, i.e. expressions with a distinguished morphology which can only be read De Se.

Such pronouns have been described in a variety of languages, notably Ewe, studied in Clements (1975), and Gokana, discussed in Hyman and Comrie (1981) (see also Hagège 1974, von Roncador 1988, and Oshima 2006). Summarizing cross-linguistic data, Clements characterized logophoric pronouns as elements that satisfy conditions (i)–(iii) (Clements 1975: 171):

(i) logophoric pronouns are restricted to *reportive contexts* transmitting the words or thought of an individual or individuals other than the speaker or narrator;
(ii) the antecedent does not occur in the same reportive context as the logophoric pronoun;
(iii) the antecedent designates the individual or individuals whose words or thoughts are transmitted in the reportive context in which the logophoric pronoun occurs.

It is interesting that this description was written before the De Se debate touched linguistics. Strikingly, this behavior corresponds exactly to what one would expect from expressions that are lexically specified to be De Se pronouns. But the history of the term 'logophoric' developed somewhat differently.

– Historically, logophoricity gained prominence in the linguistic (and especially syntactic) literature before the issue of De Se readings entered semantics. Specifically, Sells (1987) studied logophoricity in terms of three primitive notions: the *source*, which is the 'intentional agent of communication'; the *self*, whose mental state the proposition describes; and the *pivot*, which is the physical center of deixis. Sells wrote:

> I will propose that there is no unified notion of logophoricity and that instead there are three more primitive "roles" in discourse: the SOURCE, the SELF, and the PIVOT. The SOURCE is the one who makes the report (for example, the speaker). The SELF represents the one whose "mind" is being reported: the PIVOT represents the one from whose point of view the report is made." As will become clear, I understand PIVOT in a very physical sense as the "center of deixis" (...) if someone makes a report with Mary as the PIVOT, that person is understood as (literally) standing in Mary's shoes. These roles define different discourse environments, depending on the specification of each-namely, whether each role is predicated of a sentence-internal referent or of the external speaker. The basic idea of the analysis is that "logophoric" pronouns will link to some NP *in virtue of the fact that it is associated with a particular role;* such information about roles will be represented in the discourse structure.
>
> (Sells 1987: 455–456)

Each of these roles could in principle be predicated of the speaker, or of a sentence-internal referent. Different verbs behave differently with respect to these notions: for instance, in *x says that p*, *x* simultaneously carries the roles of source, self and pivot; in *x was distressed that p*, which does not involve a speech act verb, the source is the actual speaker, while the self and the pivot were taken to be *x*; and in *Max was reading when Maria came to visit him*, which is not an attitude report, *Max* might be the pivot of the sentence, while the actual speaker carries the roles of source and self. Thus Sells's typology is more fine-grained than the one that comes out of the De Se analysis; but it is also less worked out semantically, since it does not include any model-theoretic interpretation (though Sells does provide logical forms within Discourse Representation Theory). In essence, Sells went on to suggest that logophoric pronouns depend on the source, while other expressions may have different specifications. It is likely that future work will seek to combine this level of fine-grainedness with the more precise semantic analyses that were developed later.

- The term 'logophoricity' is sometimes extended to a variety of cases in which a pronoun—especially an emphatic or reflexive one—is used to refer to a person whose thoughts are particularly salient, even in the absence of an attitude verb (e.g., Reinhart & Reuland 1993). Some confusion can result if the same term is applied to phenomena that are rather different in nature; he we will stick to Clements's characterization.

    Several questions arise in the study of logophoric pronouns in the strict sense.

(i) First, are they obligatorily read De Se? The literature suggests that this is so, but in fairness the fine-grained semantic work needed to establish this has only been done by few (see Anand 2006 for data).
(ii) Second, are there only author-denoting logophoric pronouns, or also hearer-denoting logophoric pronouns? Mupun (Frayzingier 1985, 1993) appears to have some hearer-denoting logophoric pronouns, but the data are complex and would require closer analysis.
(iii) Third, are there locality and/or intervention effects on the licensing of logophoric pronouns? Here the answer appears to depend on the language. Clements (1975) as well as Hyman and Comrie (1981) imply that no such effects exist in Ewe and Gokana; on the other hand, Anand (2006), following Adesola (2005), claims that such effects exist in Yoruba, which he assimilates to the De Re blocking effect we saw at work in Section 2.2.4.
(iv) Fourth, do logophoric pronouns exist in all persons? In general, first person logophoric pronouns appear to be rare or non-existent; but there might be pragmatic constraints that explain this fact (see Schlenker 2003 and Anand 2006 for discussion). Gokana is in this respect of particular interest, because the logophoric marker does not appear on the pronoun but rather as a suffix on the verb, and it seems to be available in all persons—though it is obligatory in the third person, optional in the second person, and 'dispreferred' in the first person (interestingly, the logophoric marker appears on the verb when the subject, object or even a possessor is logophoric).
(v) What happens with plural logophoric pronouns? Clements (1975), Hyman & Comrie (1981), and Frajzyngier (1993) note that the logophoric markers of Ewe, Gokana and Mupun display an interesting pattern in which logophoric marking can or must be obtained as soon as a plural pronoun overlaps in

reference with the agent of the thought- or speech-act which is reported. The connection between indexicality and logophoricity makes this pattern relatively unsurprising: as is relatively uncontroversial, first person plural pronouns carry first person features even though they often denote a group that only overlaps in reference with the speaker (this pattern is particular clear in Mandarin, where wo^3men is morphologically composed of the first person pronoun and a plural marker).

(vi) Do non-logophoric forms give rise to disjoint reference effects when a logophoric form could be used with a co-referential interpretation? The traditional view is that disjoint reference effects are indeed obtained, as is illustrated in (77):

(77) a. kofi be yè-dzo (Ewe, Clements 1975)
   Kofi say LOG-leave
   'Kofi says that he (=Kofi) left.'

   b. kofi be e-dzo (Ewe, Clements 1975)
   Kofi say he/she-left
   'Kofi says that he (≠ Kofi) left.'

Most contemporary accounts, however, predict a more subtle pattern: disjoint reference effects should hold *only* on the De Se reading; the non-logophoric pronoun should thus be free to give rise to coreferential readings in non-De Se contexts (see Anand 2006 for discussion).

(vii) Is a special complementizer needed to license logophoric pronouns? Here the answer appears to depend on the language. In Ewe, Clements suggests that logophoric pronouns are only allowed when a special complementizer (*be*), which etymologically means *say*, is present. In Gokana, logophoric pronouns are always acceptable when a special complementizer, which also means 'say', is used; but sometimes logophoric pronouns are also acceptable in its absence, as in indirect questions.

(viii) Do logophoric pronouns have to be syntactically embedded under an overt attitude verb? Data discussed by Clements (1975) suggest that this is not so, and that long discourses can contain logophoric pronouns without any overt embedding; but in such cases, Clements's descriptions suggest that they are understood as instances of modal subordination, whereby a thought is presented as being reported despite the absence of an attitude operator:

The antecedent of the logophoric pronoun in Ewe need not occur in the same sentence, but may occur several sentences earlier. In such cases (...) the subsequent sentences of the discourse will continue to present the events described by the narrator from the point of view of the same individual or individuals.

(Clements 1975: 170)

5 *De Se* readings and logophoric expressions in other domains

5.1 World logophors?

Since Partee (1973) it has become common to treat tense in anaphoric terms; the same approach has sometimes extended to mood (Stone 1997). This might lead one to expect that there might exist logophoric tenses and moods. No clear case of logophoric tense appears to be known. But it has been argued that some moods are indeed logophoric. This in particular the case of the German "Konjunktiv I", a subjunctive which is basically restricted to attitude reports:

(78) Der Peter meint, a. es sei später, als   es tatsächlich ist.
     the Peter thinks   it be later   than it really   is

                       b. es ist später, als   es tatsächlich ist.
                          it is later   than it really   is

                       c. *es sei später, als es tatsächlich sei.
                          it be later   than it really   be

                       d. *es ist später, als es tatsächlich sei.
                          it is later   than it really   be

Although the German indicative (glossed as 'is') may be interpreted either inside or outside the scope of an attitude verb, the latter possibility is precluded for the 'Konjunktiv I' (glossed as 'be'). This directly accounts for the deviance of (78c-d) Sometimes the attitude operator need not be overt, as in (79):

(79) a. Er sagte, sie sei schön. Sie habe grüne Augen.   (Jäger 1971)
        He said she be pretty. She have green eyes.

b. Er sagte, sie sei schön. Sie hat grüne Augen. (Jäger 1971)
He said, she be pretty. She has green eyes

As Jäger (1971) observes, in (79a), which involves a Konjunktiv I form of *have*, the second sentence must be read from the standpoint of the attitude holder, so that it is interpreted as: 'He says/thinks that she has green eyes'. No such reading is forced in (79b). This effect is rather strikingly reminiscent of the one found in Ewe under similar circumstances, as was discussed in (viii) above.

There are interesting—and ill-understood—semantic constraints on logophoric pronouns and the Konjunktiv I. As mentioned, logophoric pronouns almost never occur in the first person; and the Konjunktiv I does not usually occur in the first person present. Schlenker (2003) gives a unified semantic/pragmatic explanation of these phenomena, but an alternative—and empirically deeper—analysis has been offered by Fabricius-Hansen & Saebø (2004) for the Konjunktiv I. These analyses should be compared to broader analyses of *evidentials*, which have sometimes been analyzed in terms of context shift; see Sauerland & Schenner (2007) for a very fine-grained discussion of Bulgarian evidentials from this broader perspective.

5.2 Event De Se?

So far we have entirely disregarded event semantics. But Higginbotham (2003) suggested that infinitives are not just De Se with respect to their individual argument (*PRO*), but also with respect to their event argument. Here are some of the contrasts he discussed (they are in the first person but would work just as well in the third person; Portner 1992 offers further facts and a different theoretical perspective):

(80) a. I remember walking to school in the 5th grade.
b. I remember that I walked to school in the 5th grade.

Most adults are in a position to utter (80b) truly, but very few have such a good memory that they could assert (80a), which requires that one actually remembers the event of walking rather than the general fact that one did walk in the past.

For present purposes, we can account for the distinction by replacing time arguments with event arguments—which are presumably more fine-grained: to every event there corresponds a time (the time of that event), but distinct events may occur at the same time. This move must of course be made consistently—the lexical semantics of expressions (e.g., verbs) must be revised to replace the time argument with an event argument. With this framework in place, the only thing to observe is that the infinitive is read De Se not just with respect to its individual argument, but also with respect to its event argument. By contrast, a full clause need not be read De Se with respect to either (though it may be multiply ambiguous; as in the case of *he*, the issue of the De Re / De Se ambiguity for elements that are already known to have a De Re reading is quite complex). To make things concrete, we give in (81) a revised semantics for the complementizer, treated as a simultaneous λ-abstractor over individuals, events and possible worlds (it is identical to our earlier 'De Se' complementizer, except that abstraction over times is replaced with abstraction over events):

(81) $[\![\text{that}_{x_i, e_k, w_l} \, F]\!]^{c,s} = \lambda x'_e \lambda e'_i \lambda w'_s [\![F]\!]^{c, s[x_i \to x', e_k \to e', w_l \to w']}$

We can now represent the Logical Forms of (80) by positing an unpronounced De Se complementizer in the first case:

(82) a. w* e* I remember ~~that~~$_{x_i, e_k, w_l}$ w_l e_k PRO$_i$ walking to school
     b. w* e* I remember that$_{x_i, e_k, w_l}$ [∃e_m: e_m ≈ e_k] w_l e_m I walking to school

Here e_m ≈ e_k indicates that the events e_m and e_k occured at the same time; and it is assumed for ease of comparison that the embedded occurrence of *I* in the tensed complement has a De Se interpretation. It is then clear that (82a) is read De Se with respect to its event argument, whereas (82b) isn't—despite the fact that both are read De Se with respect to their subject argument. Of course an analysis of the infinitive would have to explain why in attitude reports its event argument must be bound by the closest λ-abstractor; but this question already arose—and was left open—with respect to PRO.

Related contrasts can be found in French:

(83) a. J'ai   l'impression   de greloter.
        I have the impression to shiver.
     b. J'ai   l'impression   que je grelotte.
        I have the impression that I shiver.

In a situation in which I see myself in a mirror, realize that this is me, and get the impression that the person I see is shivering, it is possible to use the full complement, as in (83b), but it is far less natural to use the infinitive, as in (83a). No such contrast obtains if I have an internal feeling of shivering (if anything, the infinitive is more natural in this case). Importantly, the fact that *PRO* is read De Se is unlikely to explain this contrast: in both cases, I have full knowledge of the identity of the person under discussion. Rather, we appear to obtain a De Se / De Re contrast, not with respect to the individual argument of the verb, but with respect to its event argument.

6 Bicontextualism

In the foregoing discussion, we have assumed that there was a single notion of 'context'. In Kaplanian theories, the interpretation function literally takes just one context parameter as argument; this also holds of monstrous versions of Kaplan's modal semantics. In theories that countenance quantification over contexts, things are a bit more complex: a sentence may be evaluated with respect to an assignment function that assigns different denotations to different context variables. Still, these various contexts do not come with distinct roles; they are all contexts of speech or of thought. In recent research, however, it has been argued that even unembedded sentences must be evaluated with respect to two distinct types of context. Two separate phenomena have led researchers to this conclusion (within very different theoretical frameworks): Free Indirect Discourse on the one hand, and epistemic modals and predicates of taste on the other. Since nobody claims that these phenomena should be unified, if we accept the conclusions of each line of investigation we will have to conclude that every sentence is evaluated with respect to at least three different sorts of context. We won't take a position on this issue, but will briefly sketch each line of argument.

6.1 Free indirect discourse

Free Indirect Discourse is a type of reported speech, found primarily in literature, in which different indexicals are evaluated with respect to different contexts, *even in the absence of any (overt) attitude operator:*

(84) a. Tomorrow was Monday, Monday, the beginning of another school week! (Lawrence, *Women in Love*; cited in Banfield 1982)
 b. #He thought: 'Tomorrow was Monday, Monday, the beginning of another school week!'
 c. #He thought that tomorrow was Monday, Monday, the beginning of another school week!

(85) Where was he this morning, for instance? Some committee, she never asked what. (Woolf, *Mrs Dalloway*; cited in Banfield 1982)

The thought expressed in (84a) and (85) is attributed to the character whose attitude is described rather than to the narrator; it can optionally be followed by a post-posed parenthetical, such as ', he thought' or ', he said'. Descriptively, Free Indirect Discourse behaves as a mix of direct and of indirect discourse: tenses and pronouns take the form that they would have in an attitude report (e.g., *She wondered where <u>he was</u> that morning*), while everything else -including *here, now, today, yesterday* and the demonstratives (e.g., *this*)- behaves as in direct discourse. In other words, a passage in Free Indirect Discourse may be obtained by changing the person and tense markers of a quotation to those of an indirect discourse embedded under an attitude verb in the desired person and tense. Importantly, the indexicals that 'shift' in Free Indirect Discourse in English do not do so in standard indirect discourse (though it may well be that indexicals that shift in standard indirect discourse must do so in Free Indirect Discourse, as is discussed below). This fact alone shows that shifting in Free Indirect Discourse is not entirely reducible to the issues we discussed earlier.

There are two general lines of analysis of Free Indirect Discourse: it may be seen as a special form of direct discourse, with no attitude operator; or as a special form of indirect discourse, with a concealed and non-standard attitude operator. The puzzle, which is laid out in great detail in Sharvit (2008), is that *Free Indirect Discourse has properties of both direct and indirect discourse*.

Let us start with the properties that Free Indirect Discourse shares with direct discourse. First, as seen in (84)–(85), indexicals other than tense and person behave as in direct discourse. Second, clauses in Free Indirect Discourse behave syntactically as if they were (as they seem to be) *un*embedded. Banfield (1982) (Section 2.1) lists an impressive array of arguments for this conclusion. In particular, she observes that a passage in Free Indirect Discourse is never preceded by a complementizer (e.g.¹, **That he would marry Ann tomorrow, John thought a week ago*); second, she notes that all sorts of elements that can never occur in embedded clauses can still appear in Free Indirect Discourse (for instance *Oh, he was tired, John said* is a possible Free Indirect Discourse; by contrast, *John said that oh he was tired* is ungrammatical; similarly the repetition of *Monday* in (84) would be impossible in an indirect discourse). Third, direct questions are entirely natural in Free Indirect Discourse, but unacceptable in embedded clauses:

(86) a. Why was John so happy today? (Mary wondered)
 b. #Mary wondered why was John so happy today?

Fourth, a sentence in Free Indirect Discourse does not allow for any De Dicto/De Re ambiguity, unlike a clause embedded under an attitude operator, as illustrated in the following contrast due to Reinhart (1983):

(87) a. Oedipus believed that his mother wasn't his mother.
   b. #His mother was not his mother, Oedipus believed.

Fifth, Free Indirect Discourse is much more faithful to the *words* used in the thought which is reported than De Dicto indirect discourse is. *John thought that Peter or Sam would come* is equivalent to: *John thought that Sam or Peter would come*, with the order of the disjuncts reversed; and no speaker would have any difficulty accepting both sentences as true descriptions of one and the same event. But from: *Tomorrow Peter or Sam would come, Ann thought* it seems much harder to infer: *Tomorrow Sam or Peter would come, Ann thought.* Somehow one gets the sense that at most one of these sentences should be true of a given thought act, exactly as with quotations: if *Ann said: 'Tomorrow Sam or Peter will come'*, it can't also be true of the same event that *Ann said: 'Tomorrow Peter or Sam will come'* (of course one often doesn't care whether Ann said one or the other, but this is a different issue).

The properties that Free Indirect Discourse shares with standard indirect discourse concern the behavior of pronouns and tense. First, in simple cases tense and pronouns are evaluated 'from the perspective of the speaker' (rather than from the perspective of the agent of the thought, as would be the case in direct discourse). Second, Sharvit (2003) claims on the basis of Hebrew data that *those indexicals that shift in Standard Indirect Discourse also shift in Free Indirect Discourse* (her argument, which would need to be extended to other languages, is that the Hebrew present tense shifts in both environments). Further similarities between Free Indirect Discourse and Standard Indirect Discourse are discussed in Sharvit (2008).

Turning to the analyses, there are—unsurprisingly—two main lines: one emphasizes the similarities with direct discourse, and the other one with standard indirect discourse.

Several researchers have taken Free Indirect Discourse to be an instance of direct discourse which is evaluated with respect to two different contexts at the same time (Banfield 1982; Doron 1991; Schlenker 2004). One possible theory (Schlenker 2004) starts from a conceptual distinction between two notions of context. The *Context of Thought* is the point at which a thought originates; it includes a thinker, a time of thought and a world of thought (in some cases a thought might also have an intended addressee, especially if it corresponds to a speech act). The *Context of Utterance* is the point at which the thought is expressed; it includes a speaker, a hearer, a time of utterance and a world of utterance. Grammatically, (a) tenses and pronouns depend on the Context of Utterance (henceforth called υ), while (b) all other indexicals (including the demonstratives, as well as *here*, *now*, and *yesterday*) depend on the Context of Thought (henceforth called θ). For obvious reasons, the difference rarely matters in everyday life (usually, the point at which a thought is formed is not significantly different from that at which it is expressed). But in literature, a narrator may write *as if* the Context of Thought θ or the Context of Utterance υ (or both) may be taken to be distinct from the physical point at which the narrator's words are expressed. In particular, in Free Indirect Discourse the *Context of Utterance* is set to the actual context, but the Context of Thought is taken to be located somewhere else (thus c = υ and θ ≠ c). This creates the impression that, quite literally, another person's thoughts are articulated through the speaker's mouth, with interesting literary effects, as seen in (84) and (85). (It was also claimed in Schlenker 2004 that the opposite pattern, i.e. c = θ and υ ≠ c, is found in a different literary style, the 'Historical Present'. For simplicity we disregard this point in what follows).

This analysis might explain why Free Indirect Discourse shares some important properties with direct discourse. But it makes entirely incorrect predictions about cases in which a Hebrew present tense denotes a past moment in Free Indirect Discourse (as it may in Standard Indirect Discourse). This and related observations lead Sharvit (2008) to posit a special attitude operator in Free Indirect Discourse, one that shifts the world parameter, as well as (a) the context of evaluation of all indexicals, and (b) the denotation of apparently free pronouns (which are evaluated from the thinker's perspective, so to speak; technically, Sharvit's operator quantifies over assignment functions, which means that all pronouns end up being bound). Finally, (c) an agreement mechanism similar to that used for standard indirect discourse guarantees that De Se pronouns inherit the 'right' morphological features (see Sharvit 2004, 2008 for an implementation).

Although the empirical and conceptual issues raised by Free Indirect Discourse might be some of the most fascinating in all of indexicality theory, the relative paucity of work informed by recent semantic theory has left the debate rather open (though some of the excellent descriptive literature on this topic will hopefully be brought to bear on this issue in future research).

6.2 Semantic relativism

Semantic Relativism holds that the behavior of certain expressions—notably predicates of taste and epistemic modals—is best analyzed within a semantics that countenances both a context of use and a 'context of assessment' (see, among others, MacFarlane 2005, 2007, and Lasersohn 2005). The basic argument has three steps:

Step 1. The truth conditions of predicates of taste and epistemic modals suggest that they are context sensitive: *Roller-coasters are fun* is true just in case roller-coasters are fun *for the speaker*. *It might rain tomorrow* is true just in case there is some world compatible with what the speaker believes in which it rains tomorrow.

Step 2. The patterns of disagreement that are found with predicates of taste or epistemic modals are different from those that are obtained with standard indexicals:

(88) John says: My name is 'John'.
 Peter says: My name is not 'John'.
 => John and Peter do not disagree

(89) John says: Roller-coasters are fun.
 Peter says: Roller-coasters are not fun.
 => John and Peter disagree

(90) John says: It might rain tomorrow.
 Peter says: It's not the case that it might rain tomorrow
 => John and Peter disagree

Step 3. Predicates of taste and epistemic modals depend on a context parameter, but not on the *same* context parameter as standard indexicals. Rather, they depend on the *context of assessment*, i.e. the context which respect to which the truth of a sentence is assessed, rather than the context in which the sentence is uttered. When one assesses the truth of two claims, one has no choice but to evaluate them with respect to *one and the same context of assessment* (by definition of what a context of assessment is!). By contrast, in such situations one evaluates 'normal' indexicals with respect to the context of utterance in which they were originally pronounced, not with respect to the new context. This accounts for the contrast between (88) on the one hand and (89)–(90) on the other.

The debate about semantic relativism is a particularly lively one, and it should certainly be considered entirely open at this point. The arguments that bear on this discussion are both empirically subtle and conceptually complex. Without doing justice to the debate, let us note that the argument for bicontextualism is less direct in the case of Semantic Relativism than it is in the case of Free Indirect Discourse. In the latter case, the argument is a standard truth-conditional one: if *now* and the present tense were interpreted relative to the same context, one would expect certain sentences that are coherent to be contradictory (the same argument applies to other indexicals). In the case of Semantic Relativism, the argument for bicontextualism is based on a discrepancy between two kinds of intuitions: truth-conditional data on the one hand, and intuitions about agreement / disagreement on the other. The latter might be analyzed in semantic terms; but there might also be arguments in favor of a pragmatic analysis. One reason to believe this is that even when a statement is made explicitly indexical, we get strong intuitions that two individuals disagree even when their statements are truth-conditionally compatible:

(90) Ann says: I believe that President Bush is in Japan.
Bill says: And I believe that he isn't.

There is little doubt that Ann and Bill contradict each other. And yet the literal meanings of their utterances are compatible—in fact, trivially so if both are sincere (see also von Fintel & Gillies 2008 for discussion). In this case some additional semantic or pragmatics facts appear to be responsible for the impression that Bill has contradicted Ann. It is not entirely obvious how this intuition should be spelled out, nor whether the pragmatic strategy could be successfully applied to all cases that have been taken to argue for semantic relativism.

***

As will be clear, our understanding of indexicality has changed significantly since Kaplan's pioneering work. On a formal level, semantic studies of attitude reports have been forced to take seriously the possibility of shifting the context parameter and/or of quantifying over context-like entities. On an empirical level, a rich typology of attitude operators and indexical expressions has been uncovered across languages; the extent of language and/or lexical variation in this domain is only beginning to be understood. As a result, foundational studies of indexicality are now inextricably tied with detailed typological work.

Thanks to Pranav Anand for allowing me to copy-and-paste some examples from his dissertation, and to Ora Matushansky, Chris Potts and Anna Szabolcsi for discussion of some examples. Special thanks to Paul Portner for providing detailed comments on this article.

7 References

Abusch, Dorit 1997. Sequence of tense and temporal *de re*. *Linguistics & Philosophy* 20, 1–50.
Adesola, Oluseye 2005. *Pronouns and Null Operators—A-bar Dependencies and Relations in Yorùbá*. Ph. D. dissertation. Rutgers University, New Brunswick, NJ.

Anand, Pranav & Andrew Nevins 2004. Shifty operators in changing contexts. In: K. Watanabe & R. B. Young (eds.). *Proceedings of Semantics and Linguistic Theory (= SALT) XIV*. Ithaca, NY: CLC Publications, 20–37.

Anand, Pranav 2006. *De De Se*. Ph.D. dissertation. MIT, Cambridge, MA.

Anderson, Stephen R. & Edward L. Keenan 1985. Deixis. In: T. Shopen (ed.). *Language Typology and Syntactic Description, Vol. 3: Grammatical Categories in the Lexicon*. Cambridge: Cambridge University Press, 259–308.

Banfield, Ann 1982. *Unspeakable Sentences (Narration and Representation in the Language of Fiction)*. Boston, MA: Routledge & Kegan Paul.

Bary, Corien & Emar Maier 2003. Ancient Greek monsters. Talk given at the Workshop *Szklarka Poreba 4*, Poland.

Cappelen, Herman & Ernie Lepore 1997. Varieties of Quotation. *Mind* 106, 429–450.

Castañeda, Hector-Neri 1966. He: A study in the logic of self-consciousness. *Ratio* 8, 130–157.

Castañeda, Hector-Neri 1967. Indicators and quasi-indicators. *American Philosophical Quaterly*, 4, 85–100.

Castañeda, Hector-Neri 1968. On the logic of attributions of self-knowledge to others. *The Journal of Philosophy* 65, 439–456.

Chierchia, Gennaro 1987. Anaphora and attitudes *de se*. In: B. van Bartsch & E. van Boas (eds.). *Language in Context*. Dordrecht: Foris.

Clements, George N. 1975. The logophoric pronoun in Ewe: Its role in discourse. *Journal of West African Languages* 10, 141–77.

Cresswell, Maxwell 1990. *Entities and Indices*. Dordrecht: Kluwer.

Crimmins, Mark 1998. Hesperus and Phosphorus: Sense, pretense, and reference. *The Philosophical Review* 107, 1–47.

Doron, Edit 1991. Point of view as a factor of content. In: S. Moore & A. Wyner (eds.). *Proceedings of Semantics and Linguistic Theory (= SALT) I*, Ithaka, NY: CLC Publications, 51–64.

Fabricius-Hansen, Cathrine & Kjell J. Saebø 2004. In a mediative mood: The semantics of the German reportive subjunctive. *Natural Language Semantics* 12, 213–257.

von Fintel, Kai & Anthony S. Gillies 2008. CIA Leaks. *Philosophical Review* 117, 77–98.

Frajzyngier, Zygmunt 1985. Logophoric systems in Chadic. *Journal of African Languages and Linguistics* 7, 23–37.

Frajzyngier, Zygmunt 1993. *A Grammar of Mupun*. Berlin: Dietrich Reimer Verlag.

Haas-Spohn, Ulrike 1995. *Versteckte Indexikalität und subjektive Bedeutung*. Berlin; Akademie Verlag. English translation: http://www2.sfs.nphil.uni-tuebingen.de/Alumni/ Dissertationen/ullidiss/, February 4, 2010.

Hagège, Claude 1974. Les pronoms logophoriques. *Bulletin de la Société de Linguistique de Paris* 69, 287–310.

Hale, Kenneth & Paul Platero 1996. *Negative Polarity Expressions in Navajo*. Ms. Cambridge, MA, MIT.

Hardt, Daniel 2003. Sloppy identity, binding, and centering. In: R. B. Young & Y. Zhou (eds.). *Proceedings of Semantics and Linguistic Theory (= SALT) XIII*. Ithaca, NY: CLC Publications, 109–126.

Harris, Jesse A. & Christopher Potts 2009. Perspective-shifting with appositives and expressives. Ms. Amherst, MA University of Massachusetts Stanford, CA, Stanford University.

Heim, Irene 1991. Class hand-outs on 'Control' (Seminar taught by Heim & Higginbotham, Spring 1991): 'Interpretation of PRO' (Feb. 22), 'The first person' (March 8), and a hand-out on 'connectedness' (April 12).

Heim, Irene 2005. *Features on Bound Pronouns.* Ms. Cambridge, MA, MIT.

Heim, Irene 2007. *Person and Number on Bound and Partially Bound Pronouns.* Ms. Cambridge, MA, MIT.

Higginbotham, James 2003. Remembering, imagining, and the first person. In: A. Barber (ed.). *Epistemology of Language.* Oxford: Oxford University Press, 496–533.

Hyman, Larry M. (ed.) 1979. *Aghem Grammatical Structure* (Southern California Occasional Papers in Linguistics 7). Los Angeles, CA: University of Southern California.

Hyman, Larry M. & Bernard Comrie 1981. Logophoric reference in Gokana. *Journal of African Languages and Linguistics* 3, 19–37.

Israel, David & John Perry 1996. Where monsters dwell. In: J. Seligman & D. Westerståhl (eds.). *Logic, Language and Computation* 1. Stanford, CA: CSLI Publications, 1996, 303–316.

Jäger, Siegfried 1971. *Der Konjunktiv in der deutschen Sprache der Gegenwart*, München: Hueber.

Janssen, Theo & Wim van der Wurff (eds.) 1996. *Reported Speech.* Amsterdam: Benjamins.

Kammerzell, Franz & Carsten Peust 2002. Reported speech in Egyptian: Forms, types and history. In: T. Güldemann & M. von Roncador (eds). *Reported Speech as a Meeting Ground for Different Linguistic Domains.* Amsterdam: Benjamins, 289–322.

Kamp, Hans 1971. Formal properties of 'now'. *Theoria* 37, 227–273.

Kamp, Hans & Christian Rohrer 1983. Tense in texts. In: R. Bäuerle, C. Schwarze & A. von Stechow (eds.). *Meaning, Use and Interpretation of Language.* Berlin: de Gruyter, 250–269.

Kaplan, David 1969. Quantifying in. In: D. Davidson & J. Hintikka (eds.). *Words and Objections.* Dordrecht: Reidel, 221–243.

Kaplan, David 1977/1989. Demonstratives. An essay on the semantics, logic, metaphysics, and epistemology of demonstratives and other indexicals. Ms. Los Angeles, CA, University of California. Reprinted in: J. Almog, J. Perry & H. Wettstein (ed.). *Themes from Kaplan.* Oxford: Oxford University Press, 1989, 481–563.

Kaplan, David 1978. On the logic of demonstratives. *Journal of Philosophical Logic* 8, 81–98.

Kaplan, David 1989. Afterthoughts. In: J. Almog, J. Perry & H. Wettstein (ed.). *Themes from Kaplan.* Oxford: Oxford University Press, 481–563.

Kondrashova, Natalia 1998. *Embedded Tenses in English and Russian.* Ms. Ithaca, NY, Cornell University.

Kratzer, Angelika 1998. More structural analogies between pronouns and tenses. In: D. Strolovitch & A. Lawson (eds.). *Proceedings of Semantics and Linguistic Theory (= SALT) VIII*, Ithaca, NY: CLC Publications, 92–110.

Kratzer, Angelika 2009. Making a pronoun: Fake indexicals and windows into the properties of pronouns. *Linguistic Inquiry* 40, 187–237.

Lasersohn, Peter 2005. Context dependence, disagreement, and predicates of personal taste. *Linguistics & Philosophy* 28, 643–686.

Lee, Robert G., Carol Neidle, Dawn MacLaughlin, Ben Bahan & Judy Kegl 1997. Role shift in ASL: A syntactic look at direct speech. In: C. Neidle, D. MacLaughlin & R. G. Lee (eds.). *Syntactic Structure and Discourse Function: An Examination of Two Constructions in ASL.* (Technical Report 4). Boston, MA: Boston University, 24–45.

Lewis, David 1980. Index, context, and content. In: S. Kanger & S. Ohman (eds.). *Philosophy and Grammar*. Dordrecht: Reidel, 79–100. Reprinted in: D. Lewis. *Papers in Philosophical Logic*. Cambridge: Cambridge University Press, 1998, 21–44.

Lewis, David 1983. Attitudes de dicto and de se. In: D. Lewis (ed.). *Philosophical Papers—Vol. 1*. Oxford: Oxford University Press, 133–159.

Lewis, David 1998. *Papers in Philosophical Logic*. Cambridge: Cambridge University Press.

Lillo-Martin, Diane 2009. *Utterance Reports and Constructed Action in Sign and Spoken Languages*. Ms. Hartford, CT, University of Connecticut.

MacFarlane, John 2005. Making sense of relative truth. *Proceedings of the Aristotelian Society* 105, 321–339.

MacFarlane, John 2007. Relativism and disagreement. *Philosophical Studies* 132, 17–31.

Maier, Emar 2006. *Belief in Context: Towards a Unified Semantics of De Re and Se Attitude Reports*. Ph.D. dissertation. University of Nijmegen.

Morgan, Jerry 1970. On the criterion of identity for noun phrase deletion. In: *Papers from the Regional Meeting of the Chicago Linguistic Society (= CLS)* 6. Chicago, IL: Chicago Linguistic Society, 380–389.

Ogihara, Toshiyuki 1996. *Tense, Attitudes, and Scope*. Dordrecht: Kluwer.

Oshima, David Y. 2006. *Perspectives in Reported Discourse*. Ph.D. dissertation. Stanford, CA, Stanford University.

Partee, Barbara 1973. Some structural analogies between tenses and pronouns in English. *The Journal of Philosophy* 70, 601–609.

Percus, Orin & Uli Sauerland 2003a. On the LFs of attitude reports. In: M. Weisgerber (ed.). *Proceedings of Sinn und Bedeutung 7*. Konstanz: Universität Konstanz, 228–242.

Percus, Orin and Uli Sauerland 2003b. Pronoun binding in dream reports. In: M. Kadowaki & M. Kawahara (eds.). *Proceedings of the North East Linguistic Society (= NELS)* 33. Amherst, MA: GLSA, 265–283.

Perry, John 1979. The problem of the essential indexical. *Noûs* 13, 3–21. Reprinted in: J. Perry. *The Problem of the Essential Indexical and Other Essays*. Oxford: Oxford University Press, 1993, 3–49.

Perry, John. *The Problem of the Essential Indexical and Other Essays*. Oxford: Oxford University Press, 1993.

Portner, Paul 1992. *Situation Theory and the Semantics of Propositional Expressions*. Ph.D. dissertation. University of Massachusetts, Amherst, MA. http://scholarworks.umass.edu/dissertations/AAI9305882, February 7, 2010.

Potts, Christopher 2007. The expressive dimension. *Theoretical Linguistics* 33, 165–197.

Predelli, Stefano 1998. Utterance, interpretation and the logic of indexicals. *Mind & Language* 13, 400–414

Quer, Josep 2005. Context shift and indexical variables in sign languages. In: E. Georgala & J. Howell (eds.). *Proceedings of Semantic and Linguistic Theory (= SALT) XV*. Ithaca, NY: CLC Publications, 152–168.

Quine, Willard van Orman 1956. Quantifiers and propositional attitudes. *Journal of Philosophy* 53, 177–187.

Recanati, François 2004. *Indexicality and Context-Shift*. Ms. Paris, Institut Jean-Nicod.

Reinhart, Tanya 1983. Point of view in language: The use of parentheticals. In: G. Rauh (ed.). *Essays on Deixis*. Tübingen: Narr, 169–194.

Reinhart, Tanya 1990. Self-representation. Lecture delivered at the Princeton Conference on Anaphora, Princeton University, October 1990.

Reinhart, Tanya & Eric Reuland 1993. Reflexivity. *Linguistic Inquiry* 24, 657–720.
Rice, Karen 1986. Some remarks on direct and indirect speech in Slave (Northern Athapaskan). In: F. Coulmas (ed.). *Direct and Indirect Speech*. Berlin: de Gruyter, 47–76.
von Roncador, Manfred 1988. *Zwischen direkter und indirekter Rede*. Tübingen: Niemeyer.
Rullmann, Hotze 2003. Bound-variable pronouns and the semantics of number. In: B. Agbayani, P. Koskinen & V. Samiian (eds.). *Proceedings of the Western Conference on Linguistics (= WECOL)*. Fresno, CA: California State University, 243–254.
Rullmann, Hotze 2004. First and second person pronouns as bound variables. *Linguistic Inquiry* 35, 159–168.
Rullmann, Hotze 2008. Binding and person/number features: Prospects and challenges for a semantic approach. In: R. B. Young & Y. Zhou (eds.). *Proceedings of Semantics and Linguistic Theory (= SALT) XIII*. Ithaca, NY: CLC Publications, 258–275.
Sauerland, Uli 2007. Belief report basics. Lecture Notes for a course taught at the EGG Summer School, Brno, Czech Republic, August 2007.
Sauerland, Uli & Mathias Schenner 2007. Embedded evidentials in Bulgarian. In: E. Puig-Waldmüller (ed.). *Proceedings of Sinn und Bedeutung* 11. Barcelona: Universitat Pompeu Fabra, 495–509.
Schlenker, Philippe 1999. *Propositional Attitudes and Idexicality: A Cross-Categorial Approach*. Ph.D. dissertation. MIT, Cambridge, MA.
Schlenker, Philippe 2003. A plea for monsters. *Linguistics & Philosophy* 26, 29–120.
Schlenker, Philippe 2004. Context of thought and context of utterance (A note on free Indirect discourse and the historical present). *Mind &Language* 19, 279–304.
Sells, Peter 1987. Aspects of logophoricity. *Linguistic Inquiry* 18, 445–479.
Sharvit, Yael 2003. Embedded tense and Universal Grammar. *Linguistic Inquiry* 34, 669–681.
Sharvit, Yael 2004. Free indirect discourse and *de re* pronouns. In: R. Young (ed.). *Proceedings of Semantics and Linguistic Theory (= SALT) XIV*. Ithaca, NY: CLC Publications, 305–322.
Sharvit, Yael 2008. *The Puzzle of Free Indirect Discourse*. Ms. Hartford, CT, University of Connecticut.
Speas, Margaret 1999. Person and point of view in Navajo. In: *Papers for Ken Hale: Proceedings of the West Coast Conference on Formal Linguistics (= WCCFL)* 18. Stanford, CA: CSLI Publications.
Stalnaker, Robert 1981. Indexical belief. *Synthese* 49, 129–151.
Stalnaker, Robert 1999. *Context and Content*. Oxford: Oxford University Press.
von Stechow, Arnim 2002. *Binding by Verbs: Tense, Person and Mood Under Attitudes*. Ms. Tübingen, University of Tübingen.
von Stechow, Arnim 2003. Feature deletion under semantic binding: Tense, person, and mood under verbal quantifiers. In: M. Kadowaki & M. Kawahara (eds.). *Proceedings of the North East Linguistic Society (= NELS)* 33. Amherst, MA: GLSA, 397–403.
von Stechow, Arnim & Thomas Ede Zimmermann 2005. A problem for a compositional treatment of de re attitudes. In: G. Carlson & F. J. Pelletier (eds.). *Reference and Quantification: The Partee Effect*. Stanford, CA: CSLI Publications, 207–228.
Stone, Matthew 1997. *The Anaphoric Parallel between Modality and Tense*. Technical Report IRCS- 97-06. Philadelphia, PA, University of Pennsylvania.
Szabolcsi, Anna 2009. Overt nominative subjects in infinitival complements in Hungarian. In: M. den Dikken & R. Vago (eds.). *Approaches to Hungarian 11: Papers from the New York Conference*. Amsterdam: Benjamins, 251–276.

Thomas, Elaine 1978. *A grammatical description of the Engenni language. (Summer Institute of Linguistics Publication (= SIL)* 60). Arlington, TX: University of Texas.
Zimmermann, Thomas E. 1991. Kontextabhängigkeit. In: A. von Stechow & D. Wunderlich (eds.). *Semantik – Semantics. Ein internationales Handbuch der zeitgenössischen Forschung – An International Handbook of Contemporary Research* (HSK 6). Berlin: de Gruyter, 156–229.
Zucchi, Sandro 2004. *Monsters in the Visual Mode?* Ms., Milan, Università degli studi di Milano.

Index

adverbial 138, 279–282, 293–297, 302, 317–322, 327, 328, 331–335, 338, 425, 436, 437, 443–449, 592
Aktionsart 274–306, 343, 344, 412, 415, 418, 489, 497
argument 9, 15–21, 28–30, 41, 52–62, 81, 89, 92, 116, 119, 133–143, 150–162, 169–172, 179, 180, 195–199, 214–228, 240, 244, 255, 275, 281–305, 318, 324, 347, 354–356, 408–432, 444, 473–480, 509, 532, 550, 568–572, 598, 606–613
aspect 57, 74, 75, 91–96, 276–282, 286–293, 301–305, 327, 341, 371, 384, 400, 407–417, 425–432, 459, 477, 489–491, 497, 503–512, 519–524, 542
aspectual class 274–306, 328, 330, 333, 343–345, 350, 358, 412, 415, 418, 422, 489, 497
aspectual composition 292, 298–305
attitude ascriptions 532–544, 549–552, 557, 558
attitude reports 451, 454, 573, 575, 578, 579, 582–584, 594, 602, 605–609, 613
attitude 78, 375, 399, 451–454, 496, 532, 533, 537, 548, 573–575, 579

bare mass nouns 150, 162
bare NPs 149–154, 164–173, 215
bare possessives 178, 197
belief 78, 79, 97, 99, 372, 379, 380, 452, 453, 509, 536–538, 542–556, 566, 572, 575, 585
bicontextualism 608, 612
binding 1–5, 13–21, 27–30, 52–55, 66, 113–117, 133–141, 158, 177, 193, 194, 216, 221, 240, 262, 302, 420, 554, 581, 586
– theory 27–30, 43, 425
– vs. coreference 19–21, 28, 29
bound vs. free pronouns 16, 23, 44, 611

categorical judgments 238
character vs. content 570–572
choice function 3, 65, 66, 70, 71, 74, 86–92, 97, 100, 101, 129
collective and distributive readings 137, 224–228

completion and non-completion entailments 345–349
compositionality 120, 181, 182, 188, 193
conditional assertion 512, 514
conditionals 49, 50, 78, 83, 371, 393, 400, 401, 492, 497, 503–526, 536, 545
– and modals 519–523
– and tense & aspect 523–526
conservativity 121–123, 129
construct state 178, 186, 191, 192
context vs. index 564–573
continuative vs. non-continuative readings 316–320, 330, 333, 341
coreference 5, 19–21, 28, 29, 532, 537–539, 542, 549, 551, 557, 558, 581
– puzzles 537–543, 549, 551, 557
count nouns 35–37, 40, 47, 71, 113, 131–132, 143, 160–163, 170, 204–208, 212–214, 217, 220–223, 247, 255–259, 267, 287, 295–300, 345–354, 380, 388, 420, 583

decompositional analysis 283, 287–292, 358
definite descriptions 7, 11, 42–44, 49, 50, 56–59, 78, 95, 120, 168, 188–192, 222, 248–253, 294, 393, 394, 517, 540, 541, 568, 574
definiteness 13, 33, 36–42, 49, 67, 75, 95, 98, 129, 130, 149–153, 164–166, 177, 183, 188–192, 223, 259–267, 337, 393, 394, 541
de re readings 71–74, 78–82, 96, 581–586, 607
determiners 11, 35–44, 48–54, 58–62, 76, 77, 112–131, 134–143, 150–173, 183–191, 197, 198, 204–206, 209–223, 233, 240–244, 255–259, 263, 264, 297–300, 420, 421
determiners for mass nouns 36, 131, 132, 162
deverbal nominalization 407–432
discourse prominence 70, 71, 74, 105, 106
d-linking 74, 75, 101–103
d-nominal 408–432
domain restriction 33, 40–42, 64–67, 86–90, 97, 100, 101, 104
donkey sentences 3, 12, 13, 44, 140, 142
double genitives 178, 186, 197, 198
double relativity of modals 472–475
doxastic states 543–548, 557, 558

https://doi.org/10.1515/9783110589443-018

dynamic logic 141

epistemic specificity 70, 73, 74, 83, 93–97, 101, 102
epistemic vs. root distinction 477–490
event 142, 228, 232, 235, 236, 241, 277, 294–305, 323–329, 334, 337, 343, 349–362, 391–394, 408–432, 438, 442–445, 455, 460, 476, 481, 482, 487–490, 606, 607
– and fact nominals 408–410, 417–432
– semantics 275, 283–287, 294–301, 305, 313, 344, 412, 606
– structure theory 349–352, 363
exceptional scope behavior 73, 74, 83–93, 106
extended now theories 324, 326, 331, 333, 339

familiarity 71, 74, 75, 98, 102, 103, 166, 189–191
formal link problem 14
free indirect discourse 485, 608–612

generalized quantifiers 2, 35, 37, 112–116, 120, 122, 126, 127, 142, 218, 223, 224, 243, 249
generic 3, 46–49, 71, 137–139, 150–152, 155–159, 165, 168–171, 191, 204, 215, 216, 232–235, 238–265, 268, 393, 516
– operator 215, 216, 238–241, 261, 393
– quantification 46, 250, 255, 258, 259
– reference 168, 238, 247–256, 259–265
genericity 33, 34, 46, 49, 149, 150, 154, 217, 232–234, 238, 240, 244, 247, 255, 258–260, 263, 289

habitual 232–235, 238, 239, 242, 245, 248, 260, 278, 288, 335, 343, 362, 418, 419

if 114, 117, 139, 142, 503, 504, 507–510, 514–516, 519–522, 593, 599, 611
imperfective paradox 285, 297, 346–354, 359, 360, 364
indefiniteness 3, 13, 33, 36, 37, 40, 67, 75, 95, 98, 129, 153, 166, 188, 192, 223, 259, 260, 263, 264, 267, 393, 394, 541
indefinite past theories 323, 326–328, 342
indefinite singulars 239, 254, 255, 258, 259, 262–266
indexical definites 56–59
indexicality 23, 52–55, 62, 142, 383, 454, 456, 552, 562, 563, 578, 581, 596, 604, 611, 613

indexicals 57, 250, 389, 390, 455–457, 552, 562–565, 569, 573, 586–593, 596–601, 608–612
indicative 244, 369–401, 503–509, 512–517, 524–526, 545, 605
indicative/subjunctive distinction 371, 396, 401, 512–513
informational relevance 325, 328, 330, 335, 336, 341, 342
intensionality 245, 246, 267
intermediate scope readings 55, 63–65, 84–93, 100, 104
intersective determiners 124–127, 131, 134

kinds 47–49, 60, 149, 153, 157–168, 204, 215–217, 220, 250, 259, 260, 267–269, 298, 465, 512

lattice structure 296–299
lifetime effect 325, 330, 336, 337
local presupposition satisfaction 549–558
logical type of determiners 131–137
logophoric pronouns 23, 578, 586, 601–606

mass nouns 35–37, 131, 132, 137, 143, 158, 160–163, 170, 204–228, 255–259, 352–354
– denotation 204, 212–224, 287, 296
material implication 50, 503, 507–509, 512, 521
mereology 160, 287, 296–300, 349
modal approach 375, 376, 381, 383, 390
modal base 360, 362, 385–389, 472–477, 485, 488, 489, 521
modality 327, 349, 360, 369–371, 377, 385, 458–461, 463–498, 519, 520, 523
modal logic 283, 357, 377, 385, 463–468, 541, 566, 567
monsters 455, 563, 564, 569, 570, 573, 581, 586, 589, 593
– and shifted indexicals 586–601
– prohibition against 563, 570, 573–576
– quantificational 593–601
mood 369–401, 495–497, 506, 507, 605

natural classes of determiners 117–119
nominalization 178, 199, 268, 407–418, 422, 423, 428–432

– across aspectual classes 422–424
– puzzles 428–432 428
Nominal Mapping Parameter 158–163, 169
notional mood 370, 371, 383
nouns 11, 14, 24, 35–37, 40–53, 120, 129–137, 150–157, 160–167, 172, 177–200, 204–228, 257, 259, 275, 282, 287, 296–298, 353, 407–421, 424–429, 432, 463, 497
number neutrality 169–172

opaque contexts 71–74, 78–83, 106
ordering source 360, 385–387, 472–476, 495, 496, 520, 521, 536

parameterization
– semantic 157–164
– syntactic 154–157
participant nominals 195, 410, 411
partitivity 72–75, 102, 103, 130, 198
perfect 313–342, 437, 459, 485
perfective vs. imperfective 276, 277
perfect state theories 328–331, 339, 342
plural 1–4, 10–11, 22–26, 35–36, 48–62, 121–131, 137, 149–152, 155–173, 187, 198, 199, 204–219, 222–226, 234–243, 254–268, 274–275, 296, 396, 511, 517, 580, 603
– and dependent plurals 61, 198
– and mass expressions 205, 206, 256
– denotation 11, 24, 160–162, 172, 204, 209–213
– pronouns 1, 10, 22–24, 603, 604
possessive compounds 178, 192, 193
possessive weak definites 187, 190–192
possessives 114, 115, 129, 177, 178, 181–200, 407, 419, 424–427
possible worlds 349–361, 369–372, 377–385, 389–394, 452, 463–468, 476, 490–496, 508–514, 517, 525, 535–536, 541–547, 563–565, 570–578, 597, 607
– semantics for conditionals 509–512, 517
pragmatic strengthening 44–46
predicative uses 39, 40, 187, 188, 190
present perfect puzzle 321, 322, 331–340
present tense 278, 282, 314, 320–323, 327–335, 340–342, 437, 449, 450, 457, 458, 487, 567, 569, 594–596, 610–612
presuppositionality 33, 37, 38, 72–75, 102, 103

progressive 277–279, 282–286, 289, 297, 313, 316–318, 330, 342–364, 437, 459–461, 485
– and imperfective 277, 285, 346–352, 358, 362, 363
pronominal content 22–26
pronouns 1–30, 42–44, 64, 72–81, 85, 96, 113, 140, 178, 189, 197, 208, 238, 422, 440, 455, 456, 538, 557, 569, 575–581, 586, 592–594, 601–606, 609–611
– as descriptions 1, 10–16, 42–44
– definite 1–6, 15, 23, 72, 76, 77
– demonstrative 1–5, 42
– indefinite 2, 3, 72, 76, 77
properties of modals 267, 459, 464–466, 468, 476, 498
propositional attitudes 78, 391, 399, 452–455, 532–558

qualia type-shifters 185, 186
quantificational
– approach to modals 464–468
– monsters 593–601
– narrowing 193–195
quantifier 2, 13, 40, 59, 62, 66, 81–89, 93, 100, 112–143, 194, 199, 204, 208, 214–221, 243, 244, 332, 377, 438, 444–446, 465, 479, 480, 507, 569, 593, 620
– adverbial 137–142

Ramsey Test 506
reciprocal pronouns 2, 24–27
referential anchoring 70, 74, 98–102, 105, 106
referential-attributive distinction 56–59, 72
relational nouns 177–200, 424
relative clauses 2, 49, 76, 197, 369, 372, 398–401, 448, 457, 458, 593–595
restrictor analysis 46, 515–519
result nominals 414, 415, 427, 429
root clauses 372, 391–398

salience 15
saliency 7, 8
Samaritan Paradox 520
scope 17, 18, 50–67, 72, 75, 80–93, 97, 100, 105, 113, 133, 151, 153, 172, 193, 240, 399, 465, 479–483, 490, 491, 519, 541, 568
– islands 55, 60, 66, 73, 83–87, 568

semantic relativism 611–613
sentence mood 370, 371
shifted indexicals 457, 586–593, 601
simultaneous reading 448, 449, 453, 457
specificity 34, 70–83, 86, 90–98, 101–107, 129, 153, 166
– effects 104
stage- or individual-level predicates 38, 137, 215, 216, 239, 241, 295, 344, 357, 358
subjunctive 369–401, 503–506, 512, 513, 517, 524, 525, 605
subordination 237, 238, 371, 485, 497, 604

telic vs. atelic 117, 275, 296–298, 302–304
temporal approach 334, 376, 393–395
tense 284–287, 314, 322, 323, 327, 334, 335, 339, 340, 346, 395, 436–461, 484–489, 524, 525, 581, 595, 609, 610
– and modality 349, 436, 458–461
– in embedded contexts 448–458
– logic 275, 283, 284, 438, 439
– morphemes 395, 436–439, 443–450, 453–458
– theories of 349, 438–443
three-valued conditionals 50, 517–519
topicality 72–75, 104, 105, 241, 264, 265
two place (polyadic) determiners 134–136
type-shifter 182–187
type-shifting 39, 40, 79–82, 91, 155–158, 177, 181–184, 187, 194, 224, 242, 263, 269
types of conditionals 400, 505–507, 514

uniqueness 12, 13, 33–46, 49, 98, 160, 166, 170, 187–192, 197, 198, 511

verbal mood in complement clauses 372–396

weak definites 46–49, 187, 190–192
wide scope indefinites 62–67, 75, 81–88
world logophors 605

www.ingramcontent.com/pod-product-compliance
Lightning Source LLC
Chambersburg PA
CBHW031538300426
44111CB00006BA/97